ABSTRACTS

OF

KARL RAHNER'S

UNSERIALIZED ESSAYS

ABSTRACTS

OF

KARL RAHNER'S

UNSERIALIZED ESSAYS

BY

DANIEL T. PEKARSKE, SDS

MARQUETTE STUDIES IN THEOLOGY

NO. 60

ANDREW TALLON, SERIES EDITOR

LIBRARY OF CONGRESS CATALOGING-IN-PUBLICATION DATA

Pekarske, Daniel T.
Abstracts of Karl Rahner's unserialized essays /
by Daniel T. Pekarske.
p. cm. — (Marquette studies in theology ; No. 60)
Includes bibliographical references and index.
ISBN-13: 978-0-87462-737-4 (pbk. : alk. paper)
ISBN-10: 0-87462-737-0 (pbk. : alk. paper)
1. Rahner, Karl, 1904-1984—Abstracts. 2. Catholic Church—Doctrines—Abstracts. 3. Theology, Doctrinal—Abstracts. I. Title.
BX4705.R287A2 2009
230'.2—dc22
2009006396

© 2009 Marquette University Press
Milwaukee, Wisconsin 53201-3141
All rights reserved.
www.marquette.edu/mupress/

FOUNDED 1916

COVER DESIGNER & ILLUSTRATOR COCO CONNOLLY

♾The paper used in this publication meets the minimum requirements of the American National Standard for Information Sciences—
Permanence of Paper for Printed Library Materials, ANSI Z39.48-1992.

MARQUETTE UNIVERSITY PRESS
MILWAUKEE

The Association of Jesuit University Presses

INTRODUCTION

Everyone familiar with Karl Rahner knows that his genre of choice is the theological essay. Over three hundred such essays were brought together in his massive 23-volume series, *Theological Investigations*. Everyone familiar with Karl Rahner also knows there are many more essays scattered here and there across the theological landscape. Some of these essays stand alone, such as *On the Theology of Death* or *Hominisation*. Others are contributions to periodicals, to collections, or to jointly-authored works. But most can be found in relatively slim volumes that focus on particular topics such as *Mary, Mother of the Lord*, *Nature and Grace*, *Biblical Homilies*, etc.

This volume contains abstracts of what I call, for lack of a better term, Rahner's "unserialized essays" which have appeared in English over the years. That is to say, these abstracts do *not* include his three complete books (*Spirit in the World*, *Hearer of the Word*, *Foundations of Christian Faith*), his many dictionary and encyclopedia articles, or any of the essays that appear in *Theological Investigations*. Nor does the current book include interviews or jointly-authored material where Rahner's contribution is not clearly identifiable (e.g., *Unity of the Churches* co-authored with Fries). Lastly, no attempt has been made to review all the material that has appeared in periodicals or in the Rahner anthologies that have proliferated since his death, most of which material had been published elsewhere.

With all that material set aside is there much left? Actually yes, quite a lot. There are almost forty-five individual titles published in English, along with a number of individual articles that appeared over the years as contributions to books edited by others. I have included here as many of these as I could find in the time allotted for this project, without making any claim the current collection is exhaustive.

As for the quality and importance of these essays, it would be a mistake to think that all of Rahner's really serious theological work had already been collected in his *Theological Investigations*, so that these essays must simply be popularizations or spiritual *ferverinos*. Quite the contrary! One finds here very serious theological reflections and very profound spiritual meditations. They are for the most part first class theological essays.

The abstracts are presented alphabetically by the English title of the book in which they appeared. Individual articles that were single contributions to Festschrifts or to other edited books are gathered into one section called "Articles in Books" (abbreviated AB). The substantial number of articles that appeared in the journal *Concilium* are listed among the books under the heading *Concilium* (C).

Each abstract provides bibliographical information including where possible the essay's original German title along with references to any other English language editions. This is followed by a brief **Abstract**, a listing of the major **Topics** covered in the article, a list of **Subsidiary Discussions** with the relevant page numbers, and finally by a **Precis** of the entire article. This format was chosen to help researchers figure out as quickly as possible whether a particular essay really contains what they are looking for. It goes without saying, reading the precis is never meant to substitute for reading the article itself. At best it can supply the gist of an essay and serve as a guide to the more difficult essays.

The indexes also need a word of explanation. At the end of the text there are two separate indexes: an **Index of Topics** and an **Index of Subsidiary Discussions**. Researchers should be sure to consult both. The first index makes reference to all those essays that deal primarily with that particular topic. The second index directs the researcher to those parts of essays that treat a certain topic, but in a subsidiary way. By consulting both indexes one can be sure to have found all the relevant material on any topic. Entries in the index indicate the book (by abbreviation), the essay number, and (for subsidiary discussions) the relevant pages. Hence, **CMP.6. (222ff)** refers to a subsidiary discussion in *Christian in the Market Place*, essay number 6, pages 222 and following.[1]

---

1 When an individual article also appeared in *Theological Investigations*, the volume and essay number are cited: e.g., TI 05.12. The abstract, topics and subsidiary discussions, along with the page numbers from the corresponding Theological Investigation are provided to give the researcher a sense of the essay. These topics and subsidiary discussions are not, however, incorporated in the indexes, nor is the full precis given here. For that material one should consult my earlier work, *Abstracts of Karl Rahner's Theological*

INTRODUCTION

This book does not claim to contain fantastic original insights. In fact, I have worked hard to suppress my own views on the positions Rahner lays out in his essays. My goal throughout was merely to be an honest broker of ideas. It is my hope that by using this book in tandem with my earlier collection of abstracts of *Theological Investigations* researchers will be able to locate easily the chief contributions Rahner made on a host of important topics, and be able to write with the assurance that they have found all the relevant material from his essays available in English. I also secretly hope that in perusing this book, professors will discover other lesser known Rahner essays they might include in their course reading lists.

I wish to thank Dr. Andrew Tallon and Dr. Robert Masson of Marquette University for encouraging me to undertake this second volume of abstracts. I thank my religious community, the USA Province of the Society of the Divine Savior, for granting me the sabbatical time necessary to complete the work. And I thank the Benedictine Sisters of St. Bede Monastery in Eau Claire, Wisconsin, for providing a wonderful environment of solitude, prayer and companionship in which to finish this demanding project. I dedicate this effort to my mother and father.

Daniel T. Pekarske, SDS
St. Bede Monastery, Eau Claire, WI
August 2007

Investigations, Volume 1-23. Milwaukee, WI: Marquette University Press, 2001.

ABSTRACTED MATERIALS WITH ABBREVIATIONS

Articles from Books (AB) 11
Belief Today (BT) 25
   (appeared separately as Everyday Things; Faith Today)
Biblical Homilies (BH) 29
Bishops, their Status and Function (B) 42
Can a Christian be a Marxist? (CCM) 45
Celebration of the Eucharist (CE) 46
Christian at the Crossroads (CC) 51
Christian Commitment (CCt) 60
   (also appeared as Mission and Grace I)
Christian in the Market Place (CMP) 87
   (also appeared as Mission and Grace III)
Christian of the Future (CF) 103
Church after the Council (CAC) 110
Concilium (C) 113
Courage to Pray (CP) 126
Do You Believe in God? (DBG) 129
Dynamic Element in the Church (DEC) 136
Encounters with Silence (ES) 144
Episcopate and Primacy (EP) 148
Eternal Year (EY) 148
Everyday Faith (EF) 163
Free Speech in the Church. (FSC) 179
Grace in Freedom (GF) 181
Hominisation (H) 218
Inquiries (Inq) 230
   (appeared separately as Inspiration in the Bible,; Visions and Prophecies; Church and the Sacraments; Episcopate and Primacy; On Heresy
Is Christian Life Possible Today? (CL) 248
Love of Jesus and the Love of Neighbor (LJLN) 259

Mary, Mother of the Lord (MM) 269
Meditations on Freedom and the Spirit (MFS) 279
Meditations on Hope and Love (MHL) 288
Meditations on the Sacraments (MS) 295
　(appeared separately as Leading a Christian Life; Allow Yourself to be Forgiven; Penance Today; The Eternal Yes; The Anointing of the Sick; Marriage. Trusting and Loving; A Priest Forever; Holy Baptism. God Loves This Child; The Eucharist. The Mystery of Our Christ
Nature and Grace (NG) 307
Need and the Blessing of Prayer (NBP) 315
　(appeared separately as Happiness through Prayer; On Prayer)
New Christology (NC) 328
Opportunities for Faith (OF) 336
On the Theology of Death (TD) 360
Prayers for Meditation (PM) 373
Priesthood (P) 376
　(appeared separately as Meditations on Priestly Life)
Religious Life Today (RLT) 404
Servants of the Lord (SL) 412
Shape of the Church to Come (SCC) 435
Spirit in the Church (SC) 445
Spiritual Exercises (SE) 448
Theologians Today Series, Karl Rahner, SJ 484
Theology and the Future of Man 484
Theology for Renewal (TR) 484
　(appeared separately as Mission and Grace II)
Theology of Pastoral Action (TPA) 497
Trinity (T) 511
Watch and Pray with Me (WP) 525
Appendix 527
Abbreviations for Abstracted Materials 530
Index 533

Allow Yourself to be Forgiven: Penance Today. Denville, NJ: Dimension Books, 1975. 40 pp. *Man Darf Sich Vergeben Lassen.* Translated by Salvator Attanasio. Cf., *Meditations on the Sacraments,* MS.4.

The Anointing of the Sick. Denville, NJ: Dimension Books, n.d. 38 pp. *Bergend und Heilend.* Translated by Dorothy White. Cf., *Meditations on the Sacraments,* MS.7.

AB. Articles in Books listed alphabetically by title of article. For *Concilium* articles see below. For other articles that appeared in books but which are abstracted elsewhere see: **Appendix.**
Contents:
AB.1. "Christianity and the Future" in Karl Rahner, *et al.* (eds.). *The Future of Man and Christianity.* Chicago, IL: Argus Communications, 1969. (63-80).
AB.2. "Easter: An Epilogue" in Anita Röper. *The Fifteenth Station.* NY: Herder and Herder, 1967. Translated by Sr. M. Dolores Sablone, R.S.M. (99-108).
AB.3. "The Experiences of a Catholic Theologian" in Declan Marmion and Mary Hines (eds.). *Cambridge Companion to Karl Rahner.* NY: Cambridge University Press, 2005. Translated with Introduction by Declan Marmion and Gesa Thiessen. (297-310).
AB.4. "Ignatius of Loyola Speaks to a Modern Jesuit" in *Ignatius of Loyola.* Historical Introduction by Paul Imhof, SJ. NY: Herder, 1979. Translated by Rosaleen Ockenden. (11-38).
AB.5. "Inspiration in the Bible" in Ludwig Klein (ed.). *Bible in a New Age.* NY: Sheed and Ward, 1965. Translated by Richard Kavanagh. (1-15).
AB.6. "Leadership in the Church" in Hugo Rahner, SJ (ed.). *The Church. Readings in Theology."* NY: P.J. Kennedy, 1963. Translated by Bernard Verkamp. (40-43).
AB.7. "The Priesthood: A Sermon" in Hugo Rahner, SJ (ed.). *The Word. Readings in Theology.* NY: P.J. Kennedy, 1964. (249-252).
AB.8. "Some Critical Thoughts on Functional Specialties in Theology" in Philip McShane, *Foundations of Theology. Papers from the International Lonergan Congress 1970.* Dublin: Gill & Macmillan, 1971. (194-196).

AB.1. "Christianity and the Future" in Karl Rahner, et al. (eds.). *The Future of Man and Christianity*. Chicago, IL: Argus Communications, 1969. (63-80).
Abstract: Christianity can be understood and proclaimed as the religion of the absolute future. After distinguishing the common flawed notion the inter-mundane future from the Absolute Future, in a series of five points Rahner reframes such traditional concepts as God, grace, incarnation, and love of God and neighbor in terms of the absolute future, and argues for involvement, tolerance and democratic pluralism.
Topics: CHRISTIANITY and absolute future; FUTURE, absolute.
Subsidiary Discussions: Planning (64; 74f); Mystery (64ff); Mystery, trust in (68ff); Meaning, global (67ff); Theological Anthropology, question of man (70ff); God as absolute future (72ff); Atheism, grounds for (93); Utopia (74f); Love of God and neighbor (75f); Theological Anthropology, human dignity (76ff); Christianity, endurance of (78ff); Church, necessity for (79f); Church as "little flock" (80); Pluralism (89).

Precis: The first section (63-69) distinguishes two notions of the future. Rahner argues that the generally accepted notion of the future is only the present projected forward in time. This "vacant passage of time" disrupts our true relationship with "the real future." This future (which he describes as non-evolutionary, unplanned, non-compliant in its incomprehensibility and infinity, deliberate, silent and incalculable and unassimilable) comes to us of its own accord. And we are forced to engage it. This is the real, true, or absolute future. It reveals the finitude of our planned future and limits us. It is also silent, vast and empty. In this form it is mystery that poses for us an inescapable question. What if we could trust this oncoming future? In one sense such hope in the real future would change nothing in the world or in the absolute future. But it would open a space for love and situate the man-made future in the real openness of true history. All our plans and knowledge would be revealed as partial, and one would embrace "knowledge of our ignorance" as "the ultimate consummation of existence, as his most individual ultimate truth" (68). Such a person would be patient and modest and face the rise and fall of the man-made future with freedom. Whoever accepts life unconditionally has already accepted this oncoming future, regardless of the terms s/he might use to express it. As historical beings we are always on the lookout to know the fate of others who have trusted this absolute future.

All that has been said so far is what Christianity says about the future. All that is lacking are explicitly Christian terms. Rahner makes five points concerning Christianity and the future.

1) *Christianity is a hope for the future.* The present only has significance in light of the oncoming future. It alone allows the possibility of real development and in turn gives life meaning and reveals our transcendent nature.

2) *Christianity is the faithful hope of the absolute future.* The fundamental question Christianity posses is whether we want to see ourselves as "acting beings in the whole" who have nothing to do with the whole as such; or as "receptively active beings of the whole," who by acting in the whole to create the future, let the absolute future approach and become an event for us? Christians chooses the latter. They call this absolute future God and draw two conclusions about the nature of God: that God is not merely one object among others; and that God is inexpressible mystery [which this author translates as "secret"]. After pointing out that this is precisely what gives rise to the possibility of atheism, Rahner concludes this section by contextualizing "grace" and "Incarnation" in terms of God as the absolute future.

3) *As a faithful hope of the absolute future Christianity has no innerworldly Utopian ideas of the future.* Although Christianity sets up no ideals of the future with fixed material content, it firmly rejects as ideology any utopian claim of an absolute future completely planned by man and erected by means of what is available within his world. At the same time, Christians do contribute positively to the inner-worldly future. They see liberation from the bondage of nature and progressive socialization as their tasks. But for them only the absolute future endows individuals with value and dignity. This is made concrete in the way they identify love of God and love of neighbor.

4) *Christianity is of inestimable importance for setting genuine, meaningful earthly goals.* By means of its absolute hope for the future Christianity keeps society from sacrificing one generation to the comfort or welfare of another. It gives human relations their prop-

er gravity and preserves human dignity from being reduced to the potential of productivity. It sees each individual as an irreplaceable means of mediation for our relationship with God, the absolute future.

5) *Christianity as the faithful hope of the absolute future will endure.* Self-knowledge and self-worth grow in direct proportion. The more rational we become, the more aware we are of our dignity. The dignity of society and the importance of the individual also grow in direct proportion. But no inner-worldly change can hide forever the reality of death or eliminate our doubts concerning the meaning of the whole. Christians do not have "the answer" to this question, apart from their claim all reality participates in mystery which transmits itself to us as our absolute future. This is what is meant by faith and religion. Because the question of the whole will endure, Christianity will endure, "whose very essence lies in not confusing the question of the world with the questions in the world" (79). This enduring faith will remain institutional (i.e., a church in some form) due to the fact that the transcendent must be, and can only be, expressed in categorical realities. The church of the future will function as one segment of the world, a small, free association of believers, and not as a homogeneous national religion. For this reason Christianity is interested in creating in the world a realm of freedom of expression for itself and others. Today absolute uniformity of belief and practice is no longer the social ideal. The challenge now is to develop and defend a theory of legitimate and democratic pluralism.

AB.2. "**Easter: An Epilogue**" in Anita Röper, *The Fifteenth Station*. NY: Herder and Herder, 1967. (99-108). Translated by Sr. M. Dolores Sablone, RSM.

Abstract: Life, our Way of the Cross, has a Fifteenth Station where time sets us free into the incomprehensible love of God, and our belief in the resurrection of the body is revealed to be belief in the ultimate fulfillment of my life here on earth.

Topics: EASTER; JESUS CHRIST, Resurrection of.

Subsidiary discussions: Death (100ff); Time and eternity (100ff); Resurrection of the body (106ff); Anonymous Christian/ity (108).

Precis: Life today remains a Way of the Cross. Although we increasingly dismiss the dead from our minds we cannot in good faith dismiss the question "What happens to me after I die?" Rahner finds the claim that after death we simply "dissolve" to be somewhat weak. For doesn't life by its nature seek conclusiveness, without which the endless succession of time robs every action of significance and makes life a hell of empty meaninglessness? For this reason, life after death cannot be thought of as a space of endless duration. The consummation of death brings an end to life and to time. "In reality, 'eternity' becomes in time as its own ripened fruit which does not continue 'after' actually experienced time.... [Eternity] is a mode of spirituality and freedom achieved in time." (102). Our experiences of thoroughly disinterested moral decisions reveal to a highly developed spirituality that eternity "is buried into the time of free responsibility as the space of its becoming. Within the course of man's limited span of life it draws towards its consummation" (103). Rahner encourages those who distrust their own experiences as "too good to be true" at least to cling to Easter faith: the experience of mankind as it is given in the life of the risen Christ: that the crucified, the man who failed, is the victor in the totality of reality, the one received by God without any reservation.

We must resist the temptation to resolve the Easter experience by dissecting it. After describing the "Passover event" (104), Rahner admits it is difficult for us today to distinguish Easter from the experience of the first disciples. Faith cannot simply rely on their testimony. Because the Easter event is *sui generis*, it cannot be grasped with our own experimental knowledge. (Even an "empty tomb" is at best ambiguous.) This leads to a discussion of the differences between apostolic testimony of the resurrection and other mundane eyewitness testimonies and what they reveal about the structure of the disciples' Easter experience (105f). Rahner concludes that without the experience of the Spirit (without accepting the meaningfulness of the totality of life in faith) one cannot rely with confidence on the disciples' Passover experience. "This 'circle' needs to be and cannot be sprung open. But only the one who is called to the hope of the resurrection of the body ... [can] ... leap into this 'circle.'" (106). Why would we expect the approach to the ultimate meaning of the whole of life to be otherwise?

The essay concludes with two further considerations. The resurrection of the body is such a radically different, a-temporal reality we may as well admit we cannot even imagine it. But at root it means envisioning a completely fulfilled human being who cannot be partitioned into "authentic" spirit and merely temporary "bodiliness." Though nothing can force us to adopt the Easter experience, what allows us to remain skeptical? Life itself invites us to risk that our life has been planned by God; that it is capable of being healed and saved, and that this has been accomplished in Jesus. Gazing on Jesus we draw courage to believe about ourselves what the first disciples did about themselves. (Is it really more intellectually honest to take a skeptical stance toward life and yet to go on as if everything in life really had significance?) But many who cannot in good faith believe explicitly in Jesus' resurrection do implicitly believe that life can be healed and saved ("with body and soul") as something which temporality itself transforms.

AB.3. "The Experiences of a Catholic Theologian" in Declan Marmion and Mary Hines (eds.). *Cambridge Companion to Karl Rahner.* NY: Cambridge University Press, 2005. Translated with Introduction by Declan Marmion and Gesa Thiessen. (297-310).

Abstract: Rahner discusses four foundational experiences that shape his theology, and how he may have failed them: the analogical nature of theological affirmations; the centrality of the mystery of God's self-communication; the pluralism in modern theology; the vast amount to learn from science and the humanities.

Topics: THEOLOGY, parameters of.

Subsidiary discussions: Theological Language (298ff); Analogy (298ff); God, self-communication of (301ff); Anonymous Christian/ity (302f); Sin, importance in theology (303f); Theology, schools of (304f); Science and theology (306ff); Theology and science (306ff); Death and eternal life (309f).

Precis: Translator's Introduction maintains that the four "experiences" crucial for theological reflection are presented in order of importance. Rahner's plea for greater theological modesty is rooted in his central tenet of God's incomprehensibility.

Rahner's text. By "experiences" Rahner does not mean intimate personal happenings or encounters with great people and issues on the world stage. He means those experiences a theologian inevitably has in dealing with God's incomprehensibility– experiences which push every theologian to the limit.

Analogical affirmations: The fact that all theological statements are to some degree analogical is alarmingly overlooked. After giving a very simple description of analogy with its "strange and uncanny back and forth between affirmation and negation," Rahner concludes that analogy "comprises a fundamental and basic structure of human cognition" (299). The essence of analogy is "the negation of an affirmative statement of conceptual content precisely in its affirmation" (299). If this is overlooked, then theologians end up sounding as if they posses a great deal of positive information about the divine, whereas in fact all theological statements share the same fate as their creators: all sink into the silent incomprehensibility of God. One can only speak of God with deep humility. If we practiced this axiom people would soon realize how much is not covered by our theology. Theological affirmation serves in part to reveal the empty spaces in our knowledge. Theologians must not rush to fill these gaps. Rahner regrets that he has often neglected this axiom and has spent too much time talking.

God's radical self-communication. All too often theologians overlook the core of theology. Yes, Jesus is central, but even He can only be understood in light of God's self-communication. "For me, therefore, the true and sole centre of Christianity is the real self-communication of God to creation in God's innermost reality and glory" (301). Without this center, enthusiasm for Jesus and all work for social justice are mere humanism. We human beings can either want everything (i.e., God's divine love) or we are condemned to the prison of our own finitude. Understanding how sharing in God's love becomes a real possibility for all people (anonymous Christianity) demands much greater theological effort. For Rahner, God's saving self-communication is an even more pivotal concept in theology than sin and forgiveness. In fact, there is a great danger of taking sin too seriously. Rahner freely admits his theology never puts sin at the forefront. He always begins with God's desire to communicate Himself. If this is a weakness born of his subjective experience, who can point to any theology without similar shortcomings?

Schools of theology. In the past, the work of religious theologians often bore the imprint of a certain school: Dominican, Jesuit, or Franciscan. For many good reasons (list, 305) this is no longer the case, although Rahner certainly hopes his own work is imbued with the charisma of St. Ignatius. Nor has his work always been faithful to one school of theology. This has opened him to the charge of eclecticism. But given the pluralism of knowledge this approach, even if it may be somewhat eclectic, is unavoidable.

Theology and other sciences. Rahner admits to knowing very little of all there is to know in science and the arts. Yet, as someone who wants to know and love God, how much he should make the study of these things part of his life! The more conscious he is of his ignorance, the more shocked he is at how abstract and bloodless his theology sounds. We say God created the world, but what does one really know of the vast cosmos charted by modern science? (examples, 307f). Given all this, how modest theologians must be today! But is it really any different for professional scientists? Perhaps if theologians could humbly admit in the public forum their own woeful ignorance of the vast range of knowledge, those in other fields would have the courage to humbly admit the same. In this way today's tensions might be reduced, and perhaps a common way toward the infinite mystery of God could be found.

What is to come is a preoccupation of all Christians who hope in eternal life, a preoccupation that obviously grows more acute with age. Rahner is disappointed at the way we generally speak of this great mystery. We seem to stress the continuity with this life and to minimize the radical caesura of death. He ends his reflection with his own imaginative description of what is to come– the descent that is death as already the ascent of what still awaits us. **Notes.**

AB.4. "Ignatius of Loyola Speaks to a Modern Jesuit" in *Ignatius of Loyola*. Historical Introduction by Paul Imhof, SJ. NY: Herder, 1979. Translated by Rosaleen Ockenden. (11-38). *Ignatius von Loyola*, Freiburg: Herder, 1978.

Abstract: This meditation on the importance of St. Ignatius for our times, written imaginatively in the first person (St. Ignatius) and aimed particularly at Jesuits, concentrates on the Ignatian charism and how it has fared over history. It covers such topics as experience of God, discernment, obedience, power, etc.

Topics: IGNATIUS of Loyola, St., charism of; SOCIETY OF JESUS, history and charism.

Subsidiary discussions: God, experience of (11ff); Exercises of St. Ignatius (13ff); Grace (15f); Election, Ignatian (17f); Love of God and neighbor (18f); Jesus Christ, search for (19ff); Jesus Christ, death of (20f); Discipleship (21ff); Poverty, religious (23ff); Church, love for (26ff); Church, office and charism in (26ff); Obedience, religious (28; 29ff); Theology, Jesuit (32); Poor, preferential option (33ff).

Precis: The direct experience of God was the central fact of Ignatius' life. It led him to extend this possibility to others through the Exercises. Isn't it still shocking to claim that one can experience God?

The prelude to my own experience. Even before official approval, Ignatius began to offer his Exercises to others, to open them to this direct experience of creatures with their Creator.

Ignatian spirituality must be centered on the conviction that it is possible for people to know God directly. This must remain at the heart of what Jesuits do. The Exercises are always relevant.

The religious institution and inner experience both channel grace. One is like irrigating a garden by bringing water from outside (church, scripture, sacraments). The other is like a spring that flows from the garden of the heart. Oceans of the former, without the interior response of the latter are ultimately of no use. This is why the Exercises must remain the central concern of Jesuits.

God's love for the world is most fully revealed through the process of election (discernment) whereby the creature encounters the Creator, and the meaning of his/her freedom and love is made clear. This opens the way for a proper human response to God's personal call.

God's coming into the world is fulfilled. These are all just words, and love is only fulfilled in actions: in concrete love of neighbor. Only those who love God completely can love the world properly.

Jesus. All along we have been speaking of Jesus implicitly without using the name. However differently people today may seek and find

Jesus, they cannot bypass Him. The goal of life is to die the death of Christ.

To be a disciple of Christ takes many legitimate forms. Ignatius chose to follow Christ poor and humble, on the margins of the church and society, despite other opportunities he had and despite the trouble this brought him.

Service without power. Of course each new age must translate for itself the meaning of this poverty and humility. But it is disconcerting how elastic these ideas have become in the Society of Jesus.

Successful and unsuccessful discipleship. Despite notable examples of personal poverty and humility, in the area of discipleship the Society of Jesus has failed its founder in the last 150 years. Yet the Spirit continues to stir, and reform is always possible.

Devotion to the church. Ignatius is a man of the concrete, historical church, but not "as the egoistic, fanatically and ideologically restrictive love of power which triumphs over the conscience or as a form of identification with a 'system' which does not have any vision beyond itself" (26). To love an official church, a mere system, would be idolatry. "I loved the Church as the realization of God's love for the physical body of his son in history" (27). Such modulated devotion, which distinguishes office and charism, allows for a devout but critical attitude. It holds out the hope that conflicts between the church and conscience can finally be reconciled. This insight also guides the practice of obedience. There follows a detailed listing of conflicts between the church and the Society of Jesus (28f).

The obedience of the Jesuits. It is obvious that obedience is needed in any large, far-flung apostolic Order, however democratic its institutions may become. Though members must be willing to put the needs of the group before their own, perhaps the old Jesuit notion of obedience could stand a bit of demythologization today. In any case, Jesuits must always be selfless, sober and serviceable.

Learning and study in the Order has had positive and negative consequences for the life of the church. Scholarship should continue, but always with the death and resurrection of Christ as its focus. It should never seek a cheap compromise with the times, though its desire to encompass the full range of truth will always leave it open to the charge of eclecticism. Perfect systematization remains impossible.

The Order's potential for change. The Society of Jesus has become an Order of schools, scholars and books, though it was not always so (history, 33f). The 23rd General Congregation in 1974, repented its loss of Ignatius' broad apostolic charism and recommitted itself to "the struggle for faith and justice." What is essential here is to follow Christ, humble and poor, unconcerned over where it may lead or what effect it many have on existing institutions or social prestige.

Prospects for the future. Not everyone who experiences a deep inner conversion, not even through the Exercises, needs to become a Jesuit. Jesuits must not overestimate themselves or appear arrogant. But neither is there any basis for self-doubt, since whoever has found God can move forward with confidence. However much the times may change, Jesuit spirituality will have something to offer which transcends history and fashion, for it always addresses the individual. Will there come a time when no one will be interested in God? If that day arrives, then we will no longer be talking about human beings, but merely clever animals who no longer grasp their life as a whole. Until that day, there will always be a need for the Jesuit charism, drawing people into direct relation with their Creator, so they can judge themselves and the world without illusion and respond to love with all their hearts.

AB.5. "**Inspiration in the Bible**" in Ludwig Klein (ed.). *Bible in a New Age*. NY: Sheed and Ward, 1965. Translated by Richard Kavanagh. (1-15).

Abstract: An attempt to clarify what the inspiration of the Bible means in terms of Catholic faith.

Topics: BIBLE authorship of; BIBLE, inspiritaion.

Subsidiary discussions: Prophecy, inspired (2f); Revelation, closure of (7); Church as will by God (7f); Bible, canonicity of (13ff).

Precis: It is an amazing fact that all Christians subscribe to the authority of scripture for the reason that it is the inspired word of God. In the Catholic tradition what does this mean? The first task is to distinguish it from prophetic inspiration– someone coming forward with a message to be delivered in the name of God. Biblical inspiration is more than this, as it extends to the writing down and transmission of such prophecies as a divine initiative.

Here Rahner restates the classical Catholic teaching on inspiration, quoting Leo XIII's *Providentissimus Deus* (3f). He adds two clarifications: this concept does not try to deny the human origin of the human author; it does not imply verbal inspiration. To say that God is the author of scripture does not deny that human beings are true authors and not just secretaries. Human writing can be inspired without always calling for a direct new divine message. It is not even necessary for the human author to be conscious of being inspired (divine and human activity grow in direct proportion). Finally, God's inspiration applies to the whole of individual books and not just to some abstract religious thought contained in them. This pretty well covers the church's teaching on inspiration. Still it may seems strange to claim scripture has two real authors, or that God is in any way the author of a book. In what follows, Rahner will try to establish this concept of inspiration more fully by focusing on the New Testament, realizing it will only be comprehensible to those who already possess faith.

Since total salvation is realized in Christ, after the death of the last apostle there is no new revelation. "The Christian revelation which exists totally and completely in the primitive Church is intended for all time and for all people" (7). For it to be this enduring revelation and for this infallible norm to remain present for all time, God willed the existence of the primitive church. In this formal act of predisposition God is founder of the church, and by extension God authors scripture as the written recording of the religious consciousness of the primitive church. When inspiration is understood in this way we can see how God is the real author of scripture (10f), how human beings are true authors (11ff), and how deciding the exact extent of the canon could be a lengthy but legitimate affair (13ff). These three topic are treated in detail in the remainder of the essay.

AB.6. "Leadership in the Church" in Hugo Rahner, SJ (ed.). *The Church. Readings in Theology."* NY: P.J. Kennedy, 1963. Translated by Bernard Verkamp. (40-43).

Abstract: This condensed essay sets out a number of conclusions about individual bishops in relation to the pope, and their mutual relations to the college of bishops and to a council, along with other issues. No arguments are provided here, just citations from scripture, canon law, and Denzinger.

Topics: BISHOP/s, College of: CHURCH, leadership in; PETRINE OFFICE and college of bishops.

Subsidiary discussions: Ecumenical Council, authority of (41); Petrine Office, infallibility of (42); Diocese, nature of (42f).

Precis: After defining the word, "bishop" and listing salient citations from scripture, the main points of magisterial teaching are listed: the pope cannot abrogate the episcopacy; bishops are not deputies of the pope but have an original authority from Christ by which they govern their dioceses; the supreme teaching authority in the church is the council, i.e., the college of bishops with the pope at its head (the pope's primacy is *in* the college). This same structure sets up the parameters for infallibility. The pluralism represented by diverse bishops is a divinely willed aspect of the pluralism of the church. An individual bishop functions for the college in a particular diocese assigned to him by the pope. Proper sacramental powers are conferred with episcopal consecration.

AB.7. "The Priesthood: A Sermon" in Hugo Rahner, SJ (ed.). *The Word. Readings in Theology.* NY: P.J. Kennedy, 1964. (249-252).

Abstract: In this First Mass sermon Rahner asks the community to accept priests as the ordinary men they are; to receive from them the Word of God, however poorly communicated; and to carry priests as priests carry them. He encourages priests to endure the hiddenness of lives spent in ministry of the Word.

Topics: PRIESTHOOD.

Subsidiary discussions: Word, ministry of (250f); Word, sacramental (251); Everyday life (252).

Precis: Priesthood exists to make visible within the holy community God's own order. To fulfill this function ordinary men are chosen from the community. When the bishop imposes hands on them they receive a new power and the promise of grace to execute their office. But they remain men. Rahner asks the community to accept priests as they are: men who also need the mercy of God. He stresses that priesthood is a continuation of the Christian life. Priests are chosen to be priests *because* they are part of the community. They may be called "Father," but they remain brothers. While remaining ordinary men, priests are commissioned to speak God's word. Hence, it should be no surprise when they falter or stammer. Yet someone must proclaim this message to and for the community: that God loves and forgives us, and communicates Himself to us in Jesus Christ and in the grace of the Spirit. Rahner urges the people to accept this ancient message from priests, looking through and beyond them to God whose words they speak and perform in the administration of the sacraments. Looking into the future, Rahner foresees for the newly-ordained priest a very ordinary life demanding perseverance. It will be a life of modest success and frequent disappointments. It will be a hidden life within which the Word of God will fulfill itself in ways the priest will never know. Rahner concludes by imploring the community to carry its priests just as its priests carry them. Pray for them as they pray for you.

AB.8. "Some Critical Thoughts on Functional Specialties in Theology" in Philip McShane, *Foundations of Theology. Papers from the International Lonergan Congress 1970.* Dublin: Gill & Macmillan, 1971. (194-196).

Abstract: Without denying that what Lonergan says about the method of theology really does/or should apply to theology, or that he correctly identifies many gaps and omissions in contemporary Catholic theology, Rahner finds his discussion of theological method *so generic that it really fits every science.* Hence what Lonegan presents is not the method of theology as such but a general scientific method illustrated with examples taken from theology. In particular his functional specializations fail to identify what is specific to the method of Christian theology. Lonergan's method seems to abstract from: a) Christian theology's unique relationship with Jesus Christ, and b) the fact that God cannot be the "object" of theological inquiry in the same way as other objects in the world stand in relation to other sciences.

Topics: LONERGAN, Bernard; THEOLOGY, method.
Subsidiary Discussions: God as object of theological inquiry (195).

BT. *Belief Today.* Theological Meditations Series. NY: Sheed & Ward, 1965. 128 pp.
Contents: Preface by Hans Küng.
1. Everyday Things.
2. Faith Today.
3. Intellectual Integrity and Christian Faith.

BT.1. Everyday Things. (13-43). *Alltägliche Dinge.* Einsiedeln: Benziger, 1964. Translated by M.H. Heelan, 1965.
Abstract: On the theology of everyday things. Rahner invites readers to consider everyday events, bearing in mind four considerations: the everyday is not and should not be made a special day; God is reached in everyday activities; the significance of everyday things is revealed in moments of leisurely reflection; we must not let the littleness of things make us bitter or skeptical. By way of illustration he meditates on seven everyday events to reveal their hidden depth: **On work; On getting about; On sitting down; On seeing; On laughter; On eating; On sleep.** He summarizes these reflections in a section entitled: **On grace in everyday life.** Here he develops his idea of the experience of the Holy Spirit in everyday life– a reality he also calls "grace."
Topics: EVERYDAY LIFE; GRACE in everyday life; SPIRIT/s, experience of.
Subsidiary Discussions: Everyday Life: Work (17ff); Moving about (20ff); Resting (23ff); Seeing (26ff); Laughter (29ff); Eating (32ff); Sleep (35f). Saints (40f).

BT.2. Faith Today. (45-89). *Im heute glauben.* Einsiedeln: Benziger, 1965. Translated by Ray and Rosaleen Ockendon, 1967.
Abstract: Addressed to priests and extended awkwardly to all who share in the royal priesthood (1Pt 2:9) it insists faith is necessarily different in every age. Each has its own modes of accepting and expressing faith. Today faith must manifest fraternity, recognition of its endangeredness, simplicity, transcendence.
Topics: FAITH; nature of today; PRIESTHOOD, nature of today; UNBELIEF, sources of today.
Subsidiary Discussions: Laity, faith of (55ff); Anonymous Christianity (58ff; 85ff); Faith, *fides implicita* (63f); Faith and doubt (64f); Concupiscence, gnoseological (65f); Revelation (71ff); Mystery,

one and many (73ff); Christology (74f); Mysticism (77ff); God, transcendence of (81ff); God, proofs of existence (84f).

Precis: Faith for today contains 3 delimiting observations. 1) Faith has a constantly changing historical form. This is true because we are historical beings, and explains why faith itself has its proper history even though revelation in Christ is completed. God's one word can be appropriated in numerous historical ways. There can be a true history of faith, "if our faith, while remaining the same unique faith, constantly undergoes a change in form" (49). In fact, everyone can and should have his/her own faith. Hence, it is legitimate and necessary to ask what exactly faith is today, even though we know beforehand that we shall never arrive at the definitive answer. 2) The modes faith assumes today are not monolithic. They vary as faith is accepted and expressed in a myriad of cultures and situations. Rahner acknowledges he is speaking here to a Western European audience. 3) Just because one's particular mode of faith is very comfortable and appropriate does not mean it is the most suitable. Inherited modes of faith can become meaningless and ineffectual. Thus it is vitally important to know the mode of faith demanded of us today. This is especially true, knowing that the mode of faith we practice today is bound to pass away. Rahner proposes to present here some characteristics of the mode of faith needed today. The proof of his thesis will be clear to those who are living most fully the realities of today.

Fraternal faith. Faith today, especially for the priest, must be "brotherly." Faith presupposes and creates community. The Spirit is always given for the sake of others. The love of God is always directed toward neighbor. Priests are constantly tempted to think their faith is categorically different than that of lay people. This temptation is addressed by a humble "brotherly faith" which struggles daily against the tedium of academic theology. Rahner urges priests to set aside all pretenses. Only this will make our message credible and acceptable. Priests must manifest such brotherly faith today especially to those who seem not to believe, since our faith is part of the one world we both inhabit. Such a faith would take on a very different form without involving unconditional acceptance of the world's views.

Faith challenged. We must accept the fact that faith today is endangered. Where any particular form of faith is realized, faith is there in its fullness. Thus, for example, in truly surrendering to God one truly surrenders to Christ at least implicitly. Endangerment is an essential impulse of true faith. And since faith is a free choice, doubt is inescapable. Hence, we have no reason to conceal the fact that faith is endangered. Endangered faith puts both belief and practical action at risk. The only remedy is to find our strength and our salvation in God alone and not in ourselves. Unlike the 19th century when faith was endangered in a few of its premises by challenges from a few isolated thinkers, today the very legitimacy of faith and of the possibility of meaning are being questioned. Only the witness of authentic faith of faithful priests and lay people can counteract this new situation.

The radical simplicity of faith. Arguments for *fides implicita* aside, faith today cannot be built on appeals to a formally abstract and extrinsic view of revelation or on dogmatic positivism. Faith today is only compelling if it is shown to address the sole and total question of human existence. Theology must work to show how its historical revelation can be experienced today. A first step toward speaking today's simpler language is to realize there are fundamentally only three interrelated mysteries in Christianity: Trinity, Incarnation, and sanctifying grace. Existentially, we arrive at great simplicity by gaining new perspectives on the central content of faith, and subsequently unifying and prioritizing them. Rahner illustrates this with his theology of mysticism.

The transcendency of faith. Since God is incommensurable with any created reality, we believers must refrain from making God into an object, talking about God as if we were looking over His shoulder as His privy councilors. This transcendent God addresses all people, whether they recognize it or not. One who believes this knows that God's kingdom and the power of God's grace extend well beyond the words and powers of the church. There is no reason to be ashamed or to stay quiet about such a transcendent faith. Rahner ends praising faith, and with the words of scripture "Lord, help my unbelief."

BT.3. Intellectual Integrity and Christian Faith. (91-129). "*Glaube und intellectuelle Redlichkeit*" in *Stimmen der Zeit*. Translated by William Whitman, 1967.

Abstract: If one avoids the pitfalls of skepticism and fideism, sees the Christian message as a whole, and understands the nature of God and the human person, then one need not insist that intellectual integrity demands the rejection of Christianity. This extends even to the dogmas of Incarnation and Resurrection.

Topics: FAITH, intellectual integrity of; INTELLECTUAL INTEGRITY.

Subsidiary Discussions: Skepticism (95ff); Fideism (99ff); Hierarchy of Truths (108f); Creed, brief (109f); God (111ff); Creation (113f); Jesus Christ (115f); Theological statements (117f); Incarnation (122ff); Resurrection (127f).

Precis: Intellectual integrity is not a self-evident concept. To insure that the standard understanding is not corrupted by ideology or false authority, two pitfalls must be avoided; skepticism and fideism. **Intellectual integrity and spiritual commitment.** Skeptical reservation as an ideology must be avoided. It is never compatible with intellectual integrity, which necessarily demands "one summon the courage necessary to spiritual decision" even in the face of risk (97). **Intellectual integrity and theoretical reflection.** One must also avoid the pitfall of thinking that for faith to be intellectually honest the believer would have to think through in a detailed, scientific manner all the assumptions inherent in the faith. First, no human being is capable of such an intellectual undertaking. Second, just as there is an unbridgeable gap between thought and action, there is a similar gap between intelligence and faith. Faith, like life, calls for trust. This is difficult but not dishonest. Having dealt with the meaning of "intellectual," Rahner now attempts to clarify the intrinsic meaning of "faith."

Christian faith as a whole. Despite its seeming complexity, Christianity must be accepted or refused as a whole by the person of intellectual integrity. Rahner offers a "brief formula of the faith" (110) which he hopes sets out the essence of Christianity. **The divine God as the mystery of human existence.** The center of Christian faith is its insistence that God is not one thing among other things, but irreducible, incomprehensible mystery. This

God is a question to us only because God really already communicates Himself to us in a prior act of creation and self-divesting. Only this allows us to experience ourselves as ourselves. **His [God's] sharing of Himself with us, historically, in the person of Jesus Christ.** Christ is the center of our faith because He is the unrepeatable final event of God's free, loving, forgiving self-communication. He is the cause and meaning of creation. In Him the dialogue between God and humanity enters an absolute "Yes." Is this assertion true? Here (**The correct understanding of theological statements**) Rahner reminds us that theological statements never fully penetrate the divine reality to which they point, and that even objectively false assertions can usher us into the truth of God.

The compatibility of faith and intellectual integrity brings the essay to its final point: that understood properly, intellectual integrity cannot declare that the ultimate content of Christian faith is intellectually untenable. Of course taking such a stand demands courage and humility. This acceptance extends even to the Christian doctrines of Incarnation (**The credibility of the dogma of the Incarnation**) and Resurrection (**Intellectual sincerity and belief in the Resurrection**).

BH. *Biblical Homilies.* NY: Herder, 1966. 191 pp. *Biblische Predigten.* Freiburg: Herder 1965. Translated by Desmond Forristal and Richard Strachan.

Contents: Foreword.
1. For us no angel from heaven. Mt 1:18-21. Feast of St. Joseph, March 19.
2. He came on the side of the weak. Mt 4:1-11. First Sunday of Lent.
3. In two ways humbled. Mt 8:1-13. Third Sunday after Epiphany.
4. The denarius stands for us – and for God. Mt 20:1-16. Septuagesima.
5. The Christian and the inevitable. Mt 24: 15-35. Last Sunday after Pentecost.
6. The eternal Word of God is our companion at table. Mk 8:1-9. Sixth Sunday after Pentecost.
7. A man is born. Lk 1:57-68. Feast of the Birth of John the Baptist, June 24.
8. Love sees the world as a parable. Lk 5:1-11. Fourth Sunday after Pentecost.

9. How powerful is the seed of God? Lk 8:4-15. Sexagesima.
10. The Christian, the devil and culture. Lk 11:14-18. Third Sunday in Lent.
11. We have not far to seek. Lk 14: 16-24; Jn 6:25-56. Second Sunday after Pentecost.
12. There is something mysterious about the Kingdom of God. Lk 14: 16-24. Second Sunday after Pentecost.
13. Profiting from every situation. Lk 16:1-9. Eighth Sunday after Pentecost.
14. One small candle in the darkness. Lk 18:31-43. Quinquagesima.
15. A voice in the wilderness. Jn 1:19-28. Third Sunday in Advent.
16. Technology multiplies the loaves. Jn 6:1-15. Fourth Sunday in Lent.
17. Taken up in the eternal day of the Son. Jn 8:46-58. Passion Sunday.
18. Nature abhors a vacuum. Jn 16:5-14. Fourth Sunday after Easter.
19. The Spirit of truth accuses the world! Jn 16:5-14. Fourth Sunday after Easter.
20. God in you desires God for you. Jn 16:23-30. Fifth Sunday after Easter.
21. There stands truth. Jn 18:33-37. Feast of Christ the King.
22. A universe made to our measure. Rom 8:18-23. Fourth Sunday after Pentecost.
23. The chance of a lifetime. Rom 12:6-16. Second Sunday after Epiphany.
24. God cheerfully puts up with us. Rom 12:6-16. Third Sunday after Epiphany.
25. What we must give away. Rom 13:8-10. Fourth Sunday after Epiphany.
26. What if there were nothing more to do? Rom 13:8-10. Fourth Sunday after Epiphany.
27. We know ourselves least of all. 1Cor 4:1-5. Fourth Sunday of Advent.
28. We never know when lightning will strike us. 1Cor 9:24-27; 10:1-5. Septuagesima.
29. A thing that is transparent must be empty. 1Cor 3:1-13. Quinquagesima.
30. God's truth in search of the moment. 2Cor 6:1-10. First Sunday in Lent.

BIBLICAL HOMILIES 31

31. The past is the key to the future. Gal 4:22-31. Fourth Sunday in Lent.
32. He is the one who started it. Phil 1:6-11. Twenty-second Sunday after Pentecost.
33. We should not fear His closeness. Phil 4:4-7. Third Sunday in Advent.
34. The new style in remorselessness. Col 3:12-17. Fifth Sunday after Epiphany.
35. Forgiving each other. Col 3:12-17. First Sunday after Epiphany.
36. If the heart is alive it thinks of God. Col 3:12-17. Fifth Sunday after Epiphany.
37. The essence of Christianity. 1Thess 1:2-10. Sixth Sunday after Epiphany.
38. Morality can not just tick over. 1Thess 4:1-7. Second Sunday in Lent.
39. The supreme challenge. Jas 1:17-21. Fourth Sunday after Easter.
40. Two paradoxes. Jas 1:22-27. Fifth Sunday after Easter.
41. Thou art with me. 1Pet 2:21-25; Ps 23. Second Sunday after Easter.
42. If you can put up with him, so can I. 1Pet 3:8-15. Third Sunday after Pentecost.
43. To be sober and yet to love. 1Pet 4:7-11. Sunday within the Octave of the Ascension.
44. Why are we hated? 1Jn 3:13-18. Second Sunday after Pentecost.
45. Sealed with the seal of everlasting love. Rev 7:2-12. All Saints' Day.

Foreword. From 1953-1958, Rahner preached Sundays at the university parish at Innsbruck. Some homilies were taken down, 45 of which are presented here in hopes they still speak forcefully. The readings follow the pre-Vatican II lectionary, and are arranged here according to the sequence of biblical books.

BH.1. For us no angel from heaven. Mt 1:18-21. (9-12)
Abstract: Exegesis suggests Joseph knew of Jesus' divine origin before the angel appeared in a dream. That is why in his justice he decided to put Mary away quietly. He did not feel worthy to take a role in raising God's son. The angel's command, "Take Mary as your wife," lays on Joseph a new mission and gives him his own proper

role in the history of salvation as the guardian of Jesus. How often we too are called to assume guardianship of others.

Topics: SERMON: Mt 1:18-21; JOSEPH, St.

BH.2. He came on the side of the weak. Mt 4:1-11. (13-16)

Abstract: In his solitary prayer in the desert, Jesus excludes everything that makes up the life of man in order to identify with God. In tempting Him, the devil fastens on the discrepancy Jesus must feel between knowing He was the Son of God and feeling human deprivation. When tempted to align Himself with the divine, Jesus always identifies with the poor human. In this way He embraces our common lot and the demands of serving God. Learning from Him, we should embrace our humanity even in its weakness.

Topics: SERMON: Mt 4:1-11; JESUS CHRIST, temptation of.

BH.3. In two ways humbled. Mt 8:1-13. (17-21)

Abstract: Concentrating on the centurion whose slave Jesus heals, we see he was considered by the local Jews to be an upstanding man even though he was a foreigner. Jesus, astonished by his faith and his sensitivity to the faith of others, envisions a time when "many will come from the east and from the west to sit with Abraham." How do we view those outside the church? Do we, like Jesus, praise honesty and goodness wherever we find it? Do we entertain the notion that God's saving will extends far and wide?

Topics: SERMON: Mt 8:1-13; SALVATION, *extra ecclesia*.

BH.4. The denarius stands for us – and for God. Mt 20:1-16. (22-25)

Abstract: To find the central message of the parable of the vineyard workers we must gloss over many details. The one denarius offered for a days work is a fair wage. The generosity (grace) afforded the latecomers is pure generosity. But when it comes to our relationship to God, all is grace, even the single denarius we receive. In fact, our very life and being are grace. So there is no need to envy others.

Topics: SERMON: Mt 20: 1-16; GRACE of everything.

BH.5. The Christian and the inevitable. Mt 24: 15-35. (26-30)
Abstract: This gospel, coming at the end of the church year, juxtaposes two stories about the end and the last things: the destruction of Jerusalem and the Second Coming. Rahner emphasizes not Jesus' prophetic knowledge, but His instruction. What three things are we to do when these times come? 1) Look at what lies ahead and don't stick our heads in the sand. 2) Pray, because prayer remains meaningful even if the coming events cannot be forestalled. 3) Persevere, because it is for the sake of the elect that this time of trial will be shortened. Even at the end we have a mission and must remain faithful.
Topics: SERMON: Mt 24:15-35; TIME, end of.

BH.6. The eternal Word of God is our companion at table. Mk 8:1-9. (31-34)
Abstract: Rahner weaves three threads: the multiplication of loaves, the way in which it foreshadows the sacrifice of the Mass, and our immediate celebration of Mass. He underscores that at Mass we are like those gathered on the hillside, and that Christ gives to us gathered at Mass the strength to continue our pilgrim journey. The bread He gave them foreshadows the gift of Himself we share in the Eucharist.
Topics: SERMON: Mk 8:1-9; MASS.

BH.7. A man is born. Lk 1:57-68. (35-37)
Abstract: This account of the birth of John the Baptist makes us reflect on our own lives and ask: 1) Do I really appreciate my own existence as a gift from God? 2) Do I have a sense of wonder and awe at the fact that my life borders on holy mystery? 3) Do I give thanks that God has entrusted even me with the mission to call others into his own glorious light?
Topics: SERMON: Lk 1:57-68; EVERYDAY LIFE, gift of; JOHN the Baptist, St.

BH.8. Love sees the world as a parable. Lk 5:1-11. (38-40)
Abstract: Rahner sees this 11-verse story as the perfect scenario, lacking nothing. The concrete details speak of day and night, failure and success, bitterness and blessing. But it is the love of Christ

that joins these into a single whole. His love does the same for the otherwise disparate elements in our own lives.
Topics: SERMON: Lk 5:1-11; EVERYDAY LIFE.

BH.9. How powerful is the seed of God? Lk 8:4-15. (41-44)
Abstract: Why does Jesus tell this parable, and why does He tell it to us? He tells it first to Himself as a consolation to remind Himself that there is nothing wrong with the seed or the sower. This encourages Him to go on with His ministry. He tells this parable to us both to encourage us in our ministry and in cultivating the soil of our hearts to yield a better harvest.
Topics: SERMON: Lk 8:4-14; WORD OF GOD.

BH.10. The Christian, the devil and culture. Lk 11:14-18. (45-49)
Abstract: This healing story underscores the indisputable fact that Christians have a mission toward culture: to heal it by routing the powers of darkness, thereby heralding the arrival of the kingdom of God. Culture is not the kingdom, but a sign that God loves the world. It is not simply self-evident that ours is a divided world which needs to be exorcized. To properly appraise the world takes discernment of spirits.
Topics: SERMON: Lk 11:4-18. CULTURE, transformation of.

BH.11. We have not far to seek. Lk 14: 16-24; Jn 6:25-56. (50-53)
Abstract: The parable of the great banquet focuses attention on Eucharist, wherein Jesus is fully present– body and blood. John's Gospel uses the word "flesh" in this context to mean the whole person. In this way reception of the Eucharist overcomes the overwhelming feeling that we are so very far from God.
Topics: SERMON: Lk 14:16-24; SERMON: Jn 6:25-56; EUCHARIST, real presence.

BH.12. There is something mysterious about the kingdom of God. Lk 14:16-24; Mt 22:1-14. (54-57)
Abstract: These two versions of the parable of the wedding banquet would seem to force us to identify ourselves with the Pharisees—those who have a right to be invited but who excuse themselves—in this case who disassociate themselves from the daily grind of Christian living. This calls for serious self-examination, especially

since we can easily miss seeing just where and how we decline God's invitation.
Topics: SERMON: Lk 14:16-24; SERMON: Mt 22:1-14; FUNDAMENTAL OPTION.

BH.13. Profiting from every situation. Lk 16:1-9. (58-61)
Abstract: It is remarkable how Jesus could see enviable prudence even in this roguish nave. Can we see any good in our often mean, secular environment? Secondly, can we learn prudence from this parable insofar as this steward turned every situation to his advantage? When our hearts are truly open to God we can do this with the daily vicissitudes we encounter.
Topics: SERMON: Lk 16:1-9; EVERYDAY LIFE, prudence.

BH.14. One small candle in the darkness. Lk 18:31-43. (62-64)
Abstract: Luke stresses how the Twelve failed to understand Jesus' third prophecy of His passion. He uses three expression: they cannot take it in; it is obscure; they make no effort to fathom the mystery. Still, they remain faithful and patient, not letting Mystery separate them from Him. We must be the same.
Topics: SERMON: Lk 18:31-43; MYSTERY, patience toward.

BH.15. A voice in the wilderness. Jn 1:19-28. (65-67)
Abstract: John the Baptist is an Advent figure for whom the light has dawned but not fully. He lives in the wilderness where he finds no permanent home; he avoids the temptation of prideful self-assertion; he is a voice that seemingly vanishes in the wind but is always heard by God; he knows that somehow, the one who is to come is already with him.
Topics: SERMON: Jn 1:19-28; ADVENT; JOHN the Baptist, St.

BH.16. Technology multiplies the loaves. Jn 6:1-15. (68-71)
Abstract: We are in danger of being like the crowds in today's gospel who begin to follow Jesus into the wilderness because they are spiritually hungry for God, but after Jesus satisfies their physical hunger they seek only more bread. We are in danger of seeking God for the bread He gives rather than for Himself.
Topics: SERMON: Jn 6:1-15; TECHNOLOGY, lure of.

BH.17. Taken up in the eternal day of the Son. Jn 8:46-58. (72-75)
Abstract: Here Jesus says four things about Himself: He truly comes from God from all eternity; He tells the truth; He does not seek his own glory; He is the sinless one. Far from seeing ourselves as the exact opposite of Him, Christians should see themselves as His brothers and sisters and strive to emulate Him.
Topics: SERMON: Jn 8:46-58; JESUS CHRIST, self-awareness of.

BH.18. Nature abhors a vacuum. Jn 16:5-14. (76-79)
Abstract: After contextualizing this passage, Rahner says Jesus' departure does not *lead to* but actually *is* the coming of the Spirit. There is no vacuum. God is present in the space left by departure. We must resist the sinful tendency to cling, fearing absence which convicts the world of sin, righteousness, judgment.
Topics: SERMON: Jn 16:5-15; SPIRIT/s, present in absence.

BH.19. The Spirit of truth accuses the world! Jn 16:5-14. (80-83)
Abstract: The Spirit convicting the world of sin, righteousness and judgment can seem very remote. But it encourages us not to be sad thinking Jesus has withdrawn into death. He has gone so that the Spirit can be with us. He reveals that our sins are based in our fleeing the cross because we fail to embrace the truth of the Spirit: that Jesus has been vindicated and has already stripped the world of its power.
Topics: SERMON: Jn 16:5-14; SPIRIT/s as Paraclete.

BH.20. God in you desires God for you. Jn 16:23-30. (84-87)
Abstract: It seems untrue that God gives us whatever we ask in Jesus' name. But we ask for so much. We are a mass of competing desires. But when we focus them in Christ, praying in His name, then we pray for and receive what we most truly desire. Then He answers our prayers for He gives us Himself.
Topics: SERMON: Jn 16:23-30; PRAYER in Jesus' name.

BH.21. There stands truth. Jn 18:33-37, Feast of Christ the King. (88-90)
Abstract: The kingship of this most unlikely figure resides in the fact that He witnesses to the truth. Not to the *truths* of propositions, but to the divine truth that is the antithesis of "the world."

University people especially should not confuse these two truths, and must strive for the one truth that leads to life.
Topics: SERMON: Jn 18:33-37; JESUS CHRIST, King; TRUTH.

BH.22. A universe made to our measure. Rom 8:18-23. (91-95)
Abstract: The apex of the Letter to the Romans comes in Chapter 8 and presents a vision of man and a universe in transition ... waiting in eager longing for the revelation of God's sons. Christ is the pattern, the meaning and goal of creation and of human life. Do we share this hope for creation and for ourselves?
Topics: SERMON: Rom 8:18-23; JESUS CHRIST as meaning of creation.

BH.23. The chance of a lifetime. Rom 12:6-16. (96-98)
Abstract: This second section of the Letter to the Romans encourages us boldly to exercise our gifts, whatever they are and however secular they may seem to be, and to love the ordinary things of life.
Topics: SERMON: Rom 12:6-16; EVERYDAY LIFE.

BH.24. God cheerfully puts up with us. Rom 12:6-16. (99-102)
Abstract: At first, reading what Paul says here seems like good common sense. But have we ever really tried to overcome evil with good, to forebear just as God patiently puts up with us?
Topics: SERMON: Rom 12:6-16; CHRISTIAN LIFE.

BH.25. What we must give away. Rom 13:8-10. (103-107)
Abstract: "Owe no one anything except to love one another." Most of us are very good at giving "to each his own." But that is only the beginning since what we actually owe each other is brotherly love. We owe our neighbors our very selves, just as God has given Himself to us in the love we call *agape*.
Topics: SERMON: Rom 13:8-10; LOVE OF GOD AND NEIGHBOR.

BH.26. What if there were nothing more to do? Rom 13:8-10. (108-112)
Abstract: We must all pay our neighbors their due. But beyond this we have the mandate to love. For love "sums up" the law, i.e., gives particular laws their ultimate meaning, just as Christ "sums up"

creation. For God, love, eternity and the mystery of human life are the same thing. Thus Christians cannot just say, "Friend take what I owe you and leave me in peace." For we owe others love which has no limit.

Topics: SERMON: Rom 13:8-10; LOVE OF GOD AND NEIGHBOR.

BH.27. We know ourselves least of all. 1Cor 4:1-5. (113-116)

Abstract: Strangely, after judging himself, Paul tells us he does not judge even himself. We must examine ourselves, but leave the final judgment of our lives up to God. Some of us are too lax in judging ourselves; others are too strict. We must all do our best and then trust in God's mercy.

Topics: SERMON: 1Cor 4:1-5; JUDGMENT, self-.

BH.28. We never know when lightning will strike us. 1Cor 9:24-27; 10:1-5. (117-120)

Abstract: Paul dedicates this section of his letter to practical questions. He is level-headed and lenient, knowing that every Christian at some point will be called to make a final heroic decision for God and God's will. This will happen in the daily, grey decisions of life. We know not precisely when.

Topics: SERMON: 1Cor 9:24-27; 10:1-5. FUNDAMENTAL OPTION.

BH.29. A thing that is transparent must be empty. 1Cor 3:1-13. (121-124)

Abstract: This great hymn to love raises the question of how love and knowledge are related (something of great interest to university people). Since not even in beatitude do we fully comprehend God, our knowledge is perfected in love, in the very act of surrendering to love. So we must make love our aim.

Topics: SERMON: 1Cor 13:1-13; LOVE and knowledge.

BH.30. God's truth in search of the moment. 2Cor 6:1-10. (125-128)

Abstract: When Paul says, "now is the acceptable time," he is referring to *kairos*, the opportune time, the critical and unrepeatable moment of decision. For the Christian, every moment is potentially such a moment of decision for God. How different our daily lives would be if we took this truth to heart.

Topics: SERMON: 2Cor 6:1-10; TIME as *kairos*.

BH.31. The past is the key to the future. Gal 4:22-31. (129-132)

Abstract: This argument against circumcision employing the theological types of Sarah and Hagar can seem strange and artificial. But insofar as everything that unfolds is the product of God's providence, it is actually quite reasonable that we should see here continuity and foreshadowings of the future in the past.

Topics: SERMON: Gal 4:22-31; GOD, providence of.

BH.32. He is the one who started it. Phil 1:6-11. (133-136)

Abstract: Paul gives thanks for his favorite community in part because they associate themselves with his missionary activity, and because he is confident that the good work the Holy Spirit has begun in them will be brought to completion: that their knowledge will become more perfect in love.

Topics: SERMON: Phil 1:6-11; LOVE and knowledge.

BH.33. We should not fear his closeness. Phil 4:4-7. (137-141)

Abstract: In this intimate letter to his favorite community, Paul admonishes them to rejoice and to let the whole world see their kindness, even if the world does not know God is its source. That "the Lord is near" means He is close to us now (in Eucharist), and so we can and do put aside all needless anxiety.

Topics: SERMON: Phil 4:4-7; JESUS CHRIST, nearness of.

BH.34. The new style in remorselessness. Col 3:12-17. (142-146)

Abstract: Paul exhorts his community to forebear and forgive one another. Although the people of today have enemies in different ways than people of the past (they had blood feuds whereas we remain isolated and aloof), forgiving one another in a way that imitates the way God forgives us remains an imperative.

Topics: SERMON: Col 3:12-17; FORGIVENESS.

BH.35. Forgiving each other. Col 3:12-17. (147-150)

Abstract: To "put on Christ" means to let ourselves be transmuted by His Spirit into His very image. Not merely to imitate Him in

externals, but to practice His same virtues. Above all we must "put on love" (*agape*) which alone brings true peace.
Topics: SERMON: Col 3:12-17; CHRISTIAN LIFE.

BH.36. If the heart is alive it thinks of God. Col 3:12-17. (151-154)
Abstract: "Do everything in the name of the Lord" means acting in union with Christ, as if commissioned by Him, doing everything with a good intention. If we were truly united with Him this would naturally overflow into our actions. But most of us must cultivate this mentality by pausing each day consciously to renew our intentions to act united with Christ.
Topics: SERMON: Col 3:12-17; CHRISTIAN LIFE, good intention.

BH.37. The essence of Christianity. 1Thess 1:2-10. (155-158)
Abstract: This earliest of New Testament writings contains three essential truths of Christianity: the centrality of faith, hope and love; the Christian as God's elect; the need to turn away from idols. All three of these elements remains relevant for Christians of today, *mutatis mutandis*.
Topics: SERMON: 1Thess 1:2-10; CHRISTIANITY, essentials of.

BH.38. Morality can not just tick over. 1Thess 4:1-7. (159-163)
Abstract: Paul's admonitions strike many as pure moralizing. We find it hard to take them seriously because we have heard them all before; they are not really the center of Christian faith; they tell us what not to do without telling us precisely what to do. But God's word is always true, and we must admit that we are very good at excusing ourselves. Being truly good is hard work demanding constant attention.
Topics: SERMON: 1Thess 4:1-7; MORALITY, Christian.

BH.39. The supreme challenge. Jas 1:17-21. (164-167)
Abstract: What are we to make of James' insistence that every good thing comes from God, and that God is no tempter? We are tested by God, but for our good. Through it we achieve eternity. Thus all that comes from God is good (even the cross), although we may fail to see these things for what they truly are.
Topics: SERMON: Jas 1:17-21; CHRISTIAN LIFE, temptation.

BH.40. Two paradoxes. Jas 1:22-27. (168-171)
Abstract: James warns against self-deception. Though it may seem to be a logical paradox, it is possible. He also speaks of the "perfect law of liberty." This too seems to be both paradoxical and untrue. Yet feelings of unfreedom invite us to look deeper into our hearts and to discover there the Spirit already dwelling within us, though not yet perfectly.
Topics: SERMON: Jas 1:22-27; SPIRIT/s, indwelling.

BH.41. Thou art with me. 1Pet 2:21-25; Ps 23. (172-175)
Abstract: Peter's allusion to the Good Shepherd (an Old Testament image) begs the question whether a modern person can pray Psalm 23 with sincerity. Though the first part may seem overly optimistic, the words, "though I walk in the shadow of death" show more realism. Honest people today can pray this psalm, especially having experienced in the Eucharist the Lord's overflowing goodness and kindness.
Topics: SERMON: 1Pet 2:21-25; SERMON: Psalm 23; JESUS CHRIST, Good Shepherd.

BH.42. If you can put up with him, so can I. 1Pet 3:8-15. (176-178)
Abstract: 1 Peter says "Have unity of spirit." This reappears in the liturgical texts as "Have unity of spirit in prayer." How else can we bear with our diversity if not through prayer? And our prayer, which lifts our neighbors to God, should ask for the strength to bear with them as God bears with us and our foibles.
Topics: SERMON: 1Pet 3:8-15; LOVE OF NEIGHBOR.

BH.43. To be sober and yet to love. 1Pet 4:7-11. (179-183)
Abstract: Knowing that the end is at hand (and for us mortals it always is) Peter urges us to be sober and loving. Of course nearness of the end puts things into perspective and should make our judgments sober. Only those who have thus freed themselves from false attachments are truly able to love by offering hospitality, putting their gifts at the service of others, and thus glorifying God in all things.
Topics: SERMON: 1Pet 4:7-11; CHRISTIAN LIFE.

BH.44. Why are we hated? 1Jn 3:13-18. (184-187)
Abstract: John says, "Do not wonder if the world hates you." Yet for the most part we are not hated more than anyone else. If no one finds fault with us, except perhaps those who are disappointed to see so little from those who claim to follow Christ, then we should be suspicious of how we are living the gospel.
Topics: SERMON: 1Jn 3:13-18; CHRISTIAN LIFE.

BH.45. Sealed with the seal of everlasting love. Rev 7:2-12. (188-191)
Abstract: Beneath the complex imagery of the Apocalypse a single theme is repeated: the current struggle ends in God's victory. Among the multitudes of those sealed and gathered by God's love, we have every right to imagine ourselves and all of our beloved dead embraced by God's universally salvific will.
Topics: SERMON: Rev 7:2-12; SALVATION, God's universal will for.

B. *Bishops: Their Status and Function*. Baltimore, MD: Helicon, 1964. Notes. 78 pp. *Über den Episkopat*, 1963. Translated by Edward Quinn. Treated here as one essay.
Abstract: Rahner shares his insights on the practical effects Vatican II's teachings on the episcopacy may have on the church of the future. Where necessary he gives his own opinion on disputed questions.
Topics: BISHOP/s; CHURCH, hierarchical nature of.
Subsidiary Discussions: Church, un/changeable elements (13ff); Bishop/s, co-optation of (17ff); Petrine Office, election to (18ff; 23ff; 56; ftn 11); Cardinals, college of (23ff; ftn 15); Bishop/s, titular (27ff); Bishop/s, auxiliary (29f); Bishop/s, relative/absolute ordination (30ff); Diocese, nature of (34ff; 58ff); Church, as present in a diocese (38ff); Bishop/s and priests (44ff); Presbyterum (45ff); Bishop/s, personal prelature (57ff); Patriarchate (62f); Bishop/s, synod of (67ff).

Precis: **The question at issue.** Delivered before the passage of *Christus Dominus*, Vatican II's decree on the role of bishops, Rahner surmises with a good deal of accuracy what will be said and what will be left unsaid by the Council.

I. Background: The nature of the church's constitutional life. After a reminder that the church is constituted of changeable and unchangeable elements, Rahner addresses the question of co-optation. He asks how the co-optation of a bishop into the college of bishops is related to his appointment as bishop (and by extension whether the pope exercises his own office due to his election as bishop of Rome or his election by the cardinals as supreme pastor of the whole church). In asserting the debatable position that there is a reciprocal relationship between the two factors, he is refuting the position that membership in the college or supreme pastoral office is merely an additional consequence of other factors, including territorial jurisdiction. After laying out his justifications, Rahner concludes with a summary (22).

II. Bishops: Their status and function. Rahner now applies his position to a number of practical problems in no particular order.

1. *The College of Cardinals.* After describing the evolution of the college, Rahner concludes that as it grows increasingly international and representative of the world-church it remains the most adequate body to perform its main function: election of the pope.

2. *Titular Bishops.* Membership in the college of bishops, the supreme governing college in the church, is as appropriate for those who hold offices of major responsibility (e.g., curia) as it is for bishop with territorial jurisdiction, which is not the sole structural principle of the church. Application of this criterion renders the role of auxiliary bishop problematic. Rahner feels these appointments should be rare. But episcopal appointments should not be distributed as mere honors or diplomatic ranks.

3. *"Relative" and "absolute" ordination.* Normally "relative" betokens ordination for pastoral service in a particular place, whereas "absolute" would imply ordination without any specific territorial pastoral jurisdiction. Based on the principles enunciated above, Rahner insists this verbal distinction cannot be maintained. This is because every bishop is a member of the college, which by its nature has pastoral responsibilities, even if each bishop is not responsible for a particular territory.

4. *The nature of a diocese.* Practical questions about diocese (size, etc.) can only be answered from a theoretical stance, not on romantic or paternal considerations, realizing that even such criteria are mutable. Based on his earlier principle (that inclusion in the college

implies that one administers a considerable part of the church) a diocese should easily be seen as being "considerable." It should be a complete "church" in a proper sense – a microcosm of the universal church – carrying out all its proper functions. Only this criterion distinguishes a diocese from a parish. This section concludes with practical suggestions for determining the size of a diocese based on these principles.

5. *The bishop and his priests.* To check the danger of abusing the newly-defined role and function of bishops, there must be a lively appreciation for the theologically correct relationship between bishops and priests. Although in relation to his priests a bishop is not simply "pope" in his home diocese, some of the relationship between pope and bishop should characterize the relation between a bishop and his priests: collegiality, and the formation of a college. As a result of ordination priests are accepted into this presbyterum united locally with its bishop. They are not ordained to fill in for the absent bishop but to assist him in his presence. This college is as ancient as the college of bishops. A priest's membership in a college also explains why each parish is not its own diocese. Rahner goes on to show the difficulty in determining how much of the difference between bishops and priests derives from divine or positive law.

6. *The unity of office and powers in the church.* Rahner's argument for the unity of office and powers of particular bishops (*potestas ordinis* and *potestas jurisdictionis*) is grounded in the unity of these powers within the college of bishops itself. Although these elements can be separated in theory, in practice they are inseparable.

7. *Exemption.* The existence of "titular bishops" proves clearly that territoriality is not an essential characteristic of the episcopacy. In fact, there are important non-territorial "partial churches" in the church which fulfill the same tasks as territorial churches (e.g., military ordinariates). Exemption is an unfortunate term for this jurisdiction. Rahner suggests this office needs further regulation, and that it holds interesting ecumenical challenges for the status of reuniting churches.

8. *The bishop's function.* Each bishop in virtue of his membership in the college is co-responsible for the whole church. This often finds expression in the acts of episcopal conferences.

9. *The concept of Patriarchate.* In Rahner's view the institution of patriarchate, although rooted in the divinely authored unity of the college of bishops, remains for the most part an accidental manifestation of that unity. It is more a matter of history and terminology, insofar as collegiality can assume many contingent and alterable forms. Whether these ancient forms are retained or new forms like episcopal conferences are developed, their specific theological nature should be clarified and regularized.

10. *An episcopal advisory body to the pope.* From the standpoint of the constitution of the church, Rahner makes three points pursuant to Paul VI's willingness to consider an advisory board of bishops. 1. Such a board is *advisory.* Its decisions cannot bind the pope. In fact, it could be seen as a standing ecumenical council. 2. It is a legitimate and positive way to realize the already existing, constitutive unity of the pope with the bishops. 3. Membership in such a body need not and probably should not be limited to territorial bishops.

CCM. Can a Christian be a Marxist? A dialogue among a Marxist philosopher and two Christian theologians. Johannes B. Metz, Karl Rahner, Milan Machovec. Chicago: Argus Communications, 1969. 61 pp.

Abstract: "A Marxist philosopher and two Christian theologians explore a timely and crucial issue: Can a Christian be a Marxist? Can Marxists and Christian share similar humanistic concerns? Milan Machovec of Prague, who participated in the historic meeting of 'The Culture of Unbelief' at the Vatican, and famed theologians Johannes Metz and Karl Rahner of West Germany, take part..."(2).

Topics: CHRISTIANITY and Marxism; MARXISM.
Subsidiary discussions: Concupiscence (49); Demythology (51).

Precis: Presentation (37-41): In response to the first two presenters, Rahner expresses a desire for a more formalized synthesis of the views set forth so far, since as things stand he is not even clear what is meant by the term humanism. *A Negative Anthropology* is what Christianity seems steadfastly to maintain when it comes to humanism: it resists every attempt at a definitive, positive formulation of human being. This is the source of its liberating and redeeming pronouncements. Rahner challenges whether Metz's approach does not reduce God into a function in the service of man, and whether we cannot ultimately find some positive agreement with Marxists? *If Marxism is that.* . . . In regard to Machovec's presentation of Marxism, Rahner sees nothing to oppose, and no reason why such a Marxist could not also be a Christian.

Response (49-53): Can fully realized Marxism overcome self-alienation? Christians profess a "lasting, radical, inexorable, realistically accepted self-alienation" that leads not to the absurd, but to hope for what Christians call God and eternal life. Admittedly, this carries the danger of Christians not taking seriously the world and its problems. This tendency must be resisted by self-criticism, and Marxism helps Christians in this regard. *Love for man in the concrete.* Quite possibly Marxist love for those who suffer was an impulse of the Spirit, left untended by "unworldly" Christians. But Rahner rejects the charge that Christianity's failures arise from its being mere mythology. Although Christianity can be expressed and understood in mythological terms, it is the true reality of the inexpressible God and of our relation to God. Machovec is correct to say the history of theology is the history of formulating this mythical statement, insofar as it aims to explode all human statements about God and our salvation. But he is wrong to oppose this theology with a supposedly "demythologized" modern science.

CE. *The Celebration of the Eucharist.* NY: Herder, 1968. Index of Subjects and Index of Names. 132 pp. *Die vielen Messen und das eine Opfer. Questiones Disputatae* Series, #31. Freiburg: Herder, 1966. Translated by W.J. O'Hara. Angelus Haüssling, revisor. Treated here as one essay.

Abstract: "An inquiry into the basic principle by which to determine how often holy Mass should be celebrated" (1), occasioned by the renewed appreciation for the corporate character of the liturgy.

Topics: EUCHARIST; MASS, frequent celebrations of; MASS, nature of; SACRIFICE of the cross.

Subsidiary Discussions: God, glorification of (10ff); Sacrament as sign (20f); Sacrament, *ex opere operatum* (29ff; 66ff); Mass stipends (49ff; 114ff); Grace, sacramental (62; 85ff); *Devotio* (70ff); Intermediate state (80ff); Eucharist, concelebration (106ff).

Precis: Author's Preface: Provides the history of this article's publication and revisions since it first appeared in 1949. He thanks the revisor Angelus Haüssling, OSB. Revisor's Preface. Abbreviations.

I. **The principle regulating the frequency of Mass** has never been fully investigated. Rooted in medieval liturgical sensibilities and taking its current form in the 19th century, the principle can be summed up as "the oftener Mass is celebrated the better ... [and] it is always better for a priest to celebrate himself than for him to assist at another priest's Mass" (3). Recent growing appreciation for the corporate nature of liturgy (see interesting footnote 7 on Ratzinger's 1960 views) are leading to changes in practice which still need careful theological justification. The essay is divided into 2 parts: scrutiny of older principles governing frequency of Mass; suggestions for guiding principles for the frequency of Mass today.

II. **Some dogmatic guiding lines** offered by Rahner can seem like remote conceptual distinctions which call for the reader's patience.

1. *The honor of God.* There is a distinction between God's glory and God's glorification by his creatures. The latter is further distinguished into necessary and free glorification– a "formal" genuine and conscious glorification which can only be posited by spiritual beings such as a hymn of praise. The mere repetition of elements that give formal glorification and which are not at the same time conscious and free are in fact meaningless.

2. *Sacrifice of the cross.* After reviewing the debate over whether Christ's death is a "sacrifice," Rahner concludes, yes. As a ritual, visible sacrifice it had two constitutive, non-identical dimensions: external sacrificial action (death on the cross) and inner sacrificial attitude (obedience to the Father), the one being a sign (real symbol) of the other. The latter (the visible sign) can remain even after the former (inner attitude) is already past (summary, 16f). The third constitutive element of sacrifice is God's acceptance of it. Easter is God's acceptance of the cross. Here alone the victim offered coincides with the one who offers. The one who accepts is the one who both establishes and offers sacrifice.

3. *Sacrifice of the Mass.* The church teaches the Eucharistic liturgy is in fact a *sacrificium visibile* and no mere representation of a visible sacrifice: that the visible ritual action is itself a sacrifice (18ff). Hence, as in all sacraments a clear distinction must be drawn between the plane of the visible liturgical rite and the meta-empiri-

cal reality of Christ's saving activity which becomes present in and under the rite.

4. *Sacrifice of Mass and sacrifice of the cross.* This further explication of the nature of the *representatio* of Christ's sacrifice in the sacrifice of the Mass sides with Duns Scotus' insistence that the rite does not elicit a new act of oblation at every Mass. It is not a new sacrificial act of Christ, but a new sacrificial act of the church. The practical consequence of this view is that many Masses do not alter in any way the dignity or moral character of Christ's once and forever sacrifice (summary, 29).

5. *Sacrifice of Mass as the church's sacrifice.* The church's offering has two aspects: the ritual offering and the actual personal offering. The latter is assured by the fact that the act is always the act of the holy church in its entirety, and thus the sacrifice remains valid however lax the participation of the celebrating individuals may be.

6. *Sacrifice of the Mass as a sign.* "[T]he celebration of the Eucharist was established for the Church as the constitutive sign of its union with the Lord who gives his life for the life of the world" (33). Such signs are external actions which manifest an interior attitude. One without the other is incomplete.

III. Criticism of the average view. Here Rahner critiques in turn the three most common traditional arguments for determining the frequency of Mass (cf., 2f). *1. The sacrifice of the Mass as increasing the honor of God.* Rahner argues that the statement "every Mass increases God's glory" is true in one sense and false in another. Hence, any principle regarding the frequency of Mass must be derived not from frequency but from the nature of the Mass itself as a sacrifice.

2. *The expiatory and impetratory effect of the Mass:* Although the statement "every Mass has of itself an expiatory and impetratory effect" comes from a conditioned and restricted set of pre-scholastic concerns, it remains true that the value of the Mass is infinite precisely insofar as it is the sacrifice of the cross. Therefore, multiplication of Masses adds nothing to the value of the sacrifice of the cross. *a) Efficacy of the Mass as the church's oblation.* Here a distinction must be made between an oblation *of* the church and an oblation *for* the church. While the latter is of infinite efficacy, the former is strengthened in proportion to the quality of the church's act of offering. After analyzing and finally discounting a number of

contrary theories, Rahner concludes that any added value that accrues to any particular Mass can be applied to the church only to the extent that value is merited by the holiness of the participants. Regarding the frequency of Masses, Rahner draws this principle: "Mass should be celebrated as often as by it and in it personal participation of the faithful in Christ's sacrifice of the Cross is meaningfully promoted" (44). *b) Efficacy of the Mass as Christ's sacrifice.* The average view maintains that since the propitiatory value of any Mass is limited, Masses should be offered as often as possible. After distinguishing intensive from extensive efficacy (45-49), and looking at arguments drawn from rules governing stipends, Rahner concludes that "the reasons generally given for the extensive limitation of the intrinsic efficacy of the Mass do not therefore appear conclusive" and hence, no principles for the frequency of Mass can be drawn from this distinction (52).
3. *The celebrant's "fructus specialissimus."* Rahner dismisses this reasoning by arguing that as essential as the priest's role is in the valid celebration of liturgy, his action is not personal. He is acting for the church. Hence, the fruits of *his* participation do not differ in kind from those of any of the other Christian faithful in attendance.

IV. Fruits of the Sacrifice of the Mass. This long chapter concludes, "the fruits of the Mass cannot divide up in virtue of the Mass itself into essentially and quantitatively different benefits." The grace is essentially one "offered to each as the same but received in different ways and degrees" dependent on the level of one's *devotio* (87). 1. *The sacrifice of the Mass as application of the fruit of the sacrifice of the cross.* After an apology that the earlier discussions came perilously close to treating grace as a quantifiable thing, Rahner examines the relationship between the Mass and the sacrifice of the cross. Since the Mass is the application of the one unique sacrifice of the cross *ex opere operatum*, Mass produces no new grace of itself. God's priceless universally salvific will is made manifest in each Mass *(in actu primo)*. Thus, the limited effect of the Mass must be due to some other factor *(in actu secundo)*. 2. *"Opus operatum" and disposition.* God's offer of grace in the Mass is, *ex opere operatum*, infinite, like the sacrifice on the cross. However, the Mass is not magic. The fruitfulness of any one Mass is conditioned at least in part by the actual personal cooperation of the recipient. In Scholastic terms this subjective receptive disposition was called *devotio*. 3. *The one fruit of the sacrifice*. In establishing the claim that there is really only one unique fruit of the Mass received variously by those who participate in it due to their disposition, Rahner addresses two issues: the value of intercession for the dead (which he affirms), and the *fructus specialissimus* accruing to the priest celebrant (which he denies) based on the argument that the grace of the Mass is no *tertium quid*, but the grace of the sacrifice of the cross itself (summary, 85ff).

V. **The Principle and its application.** 1. *Definition*. Theoretical dogmatic theology cannot of itself deduce universal principles governing the proper frequency of Mass. Any norm will be determined largely by historical circumstances and cultural sensitivities. Nevertheless, any such norms must do justice to the importance of the role of Mass (avoiding Eucharistic monomania) and to the doctrines regarding the mystery of Eucharist. The desire to encompass rare and exceptional cases should not derail the effort to establish working principles.

2. *The general principle*. "Mass should be celebrated as often as its repetition increases the *fides* and *devotio* of those taking part" (92) to be "built up into the 'Church'" (94). This is only possible with deeper knowledge of the whole of Christian life, recalling especially these two facts: **i.** Mass is the common act of the church and not primarily a private act of devotion; **ii.** Mass remains the work of the Lord and not a property of the church to dispose of at will. Hence, according to Rahner, Mass should always be linked with the ongoing work of Christ in the world

3. *Its practical application in particular cases:* **a)** *Daily Mass*. There is no compelling reason for daily Mass, although it has a legitimate place in religious communities. The practice does, however, carry with it the danger inherent in routinization. **b)** *Individual celebration ("private Mass")*. Technically there is no such thing. All celebrations of Mass are acts of the church. Vatican II sees communal celebrations as the norm, although valid grounds (increase in *fides* or *devotio*) can admit exceptions. **c)** *Concelebration and assistance at Mass*. Although Vatican II prefers this form of celebration where many priests are present in order to avoid scandal and to showcase the unity of the priesthood, it is not without its theological difficulties. The solutions to some of these lie in augmenting the

juridical elements required for validity (reciting the words of consecration) with appreciation for other powerful liturgical signs. **d)** *Simple non-celebration.* Not only is there no law requiring priests to celebrate Mass daily, good reasons can be offered (increasing *devotio* and avoiding burn out) for occasionally refraining from celebrating daily Mass. **e)** *Mass stipend and stipend Masses.* This element more than any other, has determined the history of the frequency of Masses. After summarizing the history of the practice, Rahner offers two considerations: **i.** The donor of the stipend is really connected by *fides* and *devotio* with the particular Mass s/he causes to be said by reason of the gift (although these fruits for this type of ritual participation do not differ essentially from other forms of participation). **ii.** There is also a participation in the fruits of the Mass through intention. Whereas there can be many intentions without diminishing the fruits, there can be only one participation through stipend, since there is only one physical gift which actually makes a particular Mass possible. In any case, these fruits are applied by release by virtue of participation rather than by any positive act of release made by the priest. **f)** *Participation in several Masses.* There is no greater benefit to be had through assisting in multiple Masses, insofar any fruits are limited to one's subjective ability to participate. Secondly, there is no greater participation in the fruits of Masses through the practice of "uniting oneself with all Masses" by means of a pious prayerful intention in the course of the day.

CC. ***Christian at the Crossroads.*** NY: Seabury, 1975. Foreword. 95 pp. *Wagnis des Christen,* 1974. Translated by V. Green.
Contents: Foreword.
1. Fundamentals
   1. What is Man?
   2. Why am I a Christian?
   3. The Core of the Faith.
   4. What is Truth?
   5. What is Evangelization?
2. Practice
   1. The Sword of Faith.
   2. The Possibility and Necessity of Prayer.
   3. Is Prayer Dialogue with God?

4. The "Exercises" Today.
5. Penance and Confession.
6. Lent.
7. The Theology of Dying.
8. Hope and Easter.
9. The Future.

Foreword: Attempts to present the essentials of Christian faith in such a way that people today will not dismiss it as ideology or myth, and in hopes it will foster a spirit of dialogue in these upsetting times. The book is divided into two sections: Fundamentals and Practice.

1. Fundamentals
CC.1.1. What is Man? (11-20)

Abstract: Reflecting on the human person as "the question that has no answer," Rahner concludes that this question is a transcendental gift: God within, to whom we are invited to surrender ourselves in hope.

Topics: CHRISTIANITY, essentials of; CREED/s, brief; FAITH, essentials of.

Subsidiary discussions: Hope: (15ff; 21ff). Theological Anthropology: (11ff); Concupiscence, gnoseological: (13) Transcendence, human (14f); God, incomprehensibility of (15ff); *Docta ignorancia* (16f; 19); Love (17ff).

Precis: For Rahner, man is "... the question to which there is no answer" (11). He argues in turn neither experience nor natural science provides an answer. Among other reasons, there is just too much to know. Metaphysics only reveals that man is "unfulfilled transcendentality." So what are faith and theology? They are a hope in God who even in the beatific vision remains insurmountably incomprehensible. After arguing for a *docta ignorantia* (the particular form of knowledge arising from knowing one does not know) Rahner concludes that the human person is definitely a question to which there is no answer. The only answer for us to is renounce any purported final answer and surrender ourselves to this inconceivability. Love is precisely this act of surrender. The damned are those who cannot love, cannot surrender to anything greater than themselves. Yet all knowledge leads down the road to an inconceivability within and beyond ourselves. Christianly is simply "the determination to surrender to the inconceivability of God in love" (19). Here Rahner gives in one short paragraph the essence of Christianity. Those who find this explanation foolish will find themselves confronting the facts of reality with an empty "No."

CC.1.2. Why am I a Christian? (21-30)
Abstract: Rahner's description of the faith he tries to live as a Christian constitutes a brief creed.
Topics: CHRISTIANITY, essentials of; CREED/s, brief; FAITH, essentials of; HOPE.
Subsidiary discussions: God (22ff); Jesus, death and resurrection of (24ff); Church, membership in (26ff); Church, divisions within (27f); Love of neighbor (28f); Death (30).

Precis: The fact that the reflection which follows comes from a committed believer is no impediment since only the subjective has access to the objective. Rahner says he "tries to be a Christian," something only God can judge. He is a person who accepts his freedom in hope that the incomprehensibility, Who he trusts, will one day be revealed in its ultimate meaning, will be both definitive and blessed. This act of hope concerns "God" a much abused term. Hence, Rahner's Christianity is an act of letting oneself go into this incomprehensible mystery. Rather than producing more answers, such a faith actually demands living with less certitude.

This innermost movement into God by means of God is mysteriously synthesized in the encounter with Jesus of Nazareth. But who is this Jesus the Christian meets? According to the apostolic witness, we meet the one person in history in whom our hopes are realized– whose death as total surrender to incomprehensible mystery meets with resurrection. We commit ourselves to die with Him in the hope of sharing His resurrection. The community of those so committed is the church. However tragically sinful the church may be, one has a right to believe in a particular denomination if, 1) one finds there the liberating Spirit of Jesus and His truth; 2) one discovers there the firm solidarity with the apostolic beginnings despite historical change. The credibility of the believer's surrender to incomprehensible mystery is manifest in unconditional love of neighbor which, rooted in the Spirit of Jesus, is more than a mere humanitarian enterprise. This spirit of Jesus is somehow at work in other religious traditions and even in atheists. In the end there are two realities difficult to cope with: mystery (the helplessness in hope) and death, which commands us not to evade this helplessness but to endure it. The Christian identifies with Jesus' death in the hope of sharing His resurrection.

CC.1.3. The Core of the Faith. (31-36)
Abstract: Faith is very simple when its content is explained in reference to the manifold life experiences of people today instead of beginning from the multiplicity of doctrines. At its core this brief creed has three elements: God, Jesus Christ, the church. Believers know their ineluctable relationship with mystery (God) challenges them to hope and love; believers know this God has definitively and forgivingly promised Himself to us in the person of Jesus –the content and eternal validity of our imperishable lives; such believers constitute a community, the church, which attests to this message of God in Christ to the whole world for its salvation. Rahner expatiates on each of these elements in turn. **1. The comprehensive ground; 2. Promised in the man Jesus; 3. Lived in the community of faith.** He ends with summary (36).
Topics: CHRISTIANITY, essentials of; CREED/s, brief; FAITH, essentials of.
Subsidiary discussions: God (32f); Church, membership in (35f); Jesus as God's promise (33ff).

CC.1.4. What is Truth? (37-39)
Abstract: John's Gospel shows that encountering Jesus demands a response. In this situation skeptical reserve is no virtue. Rahner interprets Pilate's response to his personal encounter with Jesus in John's Gospel (18:33-38) as dismissive. His famous question, "What is truth?" points to Pilate's disinterest in looking for the truth in daily encounters, and his finding comfort in skepticism instead. Rahner feels each of us faces the same danger and we must examine our attitudes in this regard critically and honestly lest we dismiss God's invitation in Christ.

Topics: SERMON, Jn 18:33-38; SKEPTICISM.

CC.1.5. What is Evangelization? (40-41)
Abstract: Again Rahner summarizes the essentials of the faith. He defines evangelization as proclaiming the good news that in Jesus, God communicates His forgiving will and divinizes us, calling us to form the community of the church. Evangelization, where we encounter the answer to the question we are, is not mere indoctrination from without but an initiation to conversion.
Topics: CREED/s, brief; EVANGELIZATION.

2. Practice
CC.2.1. The Sword of Faith. (45-47)
Abstract: Reflection on Mary's faith as evidenced in Luke's account of the Presentation reveals the irreducibly dichotomous nature of faith: it is a sword of sorrow as well as of peace, freedom, trust and joy. We are called not to overcome but to endure this disjunction at the heart of human existence. Anything less is a form of unbelief. This is the faith of Jesus, Mary, and of each true believer.
Topics: FAITH, dichotomous nature of; SERMON: Lk 2:22-35.
Subsidiary discussions: BVM, faith of (45ff); Unbelief (46).

CC.2.2. The Possibility and Necessity of Prayer. (48-61)
Abstract: Prayer, even petitionary prayer, is possible today. It is essentially a matter of realizing and accepting ourselves in our concrete situations.
Topics: PRAYER, possibility of.
Subsidiary discussions: Science and prayer (50ff); God (52ff); Prayer, petitionary (55ff); Holy Spirit, experience of (60f).

Precis: Is it possible to pray today? If so how? **1. Preliminaries. a)** *Praying as a fundamental act of human existence* would indicate that it remains possible even today. As a fundamental act it cannot be studied from a neutral point outside itself. It must first be seen as a gift which can only be understood in its execution. **b)** *Praying as an historical constant of humanity*. Prayer is possible even today because it is a constant in human history, despite the strange and even misdirected forms it has often taken. **c)** *Praying and the exact sciences*. It would be wrong to dismiss prayer today simply because

it does not reduce to a manageable scientific datum. Any such reduction of human reality is existentially schizophrenic.
2. **Modern man's questions before prayer.** Three losses make prayer difficult today: loss of belief in God; loss of the sense that God is a person who can be addressed; loss of confidence in petitionary prayer due to our seeming insignificance. Rahner deals with each in turn. **a)** *Threatened belief.* The question of God and the question of prayer are identical insofar as prayer is nothing less than one's free act of surrender to incomprehensible mystery (i.e., God). **b)** *The mystery of God.* Even many who accept God as incomprehensible mystery are reticent to invoke him in prayer for fear of reducing God to an idol. This is commendable. Still we must try, because only when we address God as "Thou" does prayer become fully what it must be. Apart from this address God reverts to a faceless, unapproachable entity. **c)** *The permanent function of petition.* After briefly recounting the history of this problem and some of the proposed theological solutions, Rahner insists that only two things must be said to make petitionary prayer intelligible. First, such prayer is real prayer and meaningful before God only if the desire for any particular good we request is coupled with absolute surrender to the sovereign decrees of God's will. All goods sought must be made relative to the absolute Good. Second, those who surrender themselves in such a way do not become spiritualized beings. They remain regular Joes, firmly embedded in the world. Thus in petitionary prayer they are mindful not only of who God is, but of who they themselves are. How we achieve such prayer is a very secondary consideration.
3. **The experience of grace in daily life and the explicitness of prayer.** We can still pray today, recalling that prayer is not one part-time activity among others, but the expression of one's entire existence. As such, it is the most deeply personal act, but not thereby private. There is a legitimate place for common, liturgical prayer. Questions of technique are completely secondary. What is essential is the experience of the Holy Spirit which prayer struggles to acknowledge by giving it shape and voice.

CC.2.3. Is Prayer Dialogue with God? (62-69)
Abstract: Although many classical texts use the commonplace expression "talking with God," it is very difficult for people today to ac-

knowledge that in prayer one is experiencing something like a personal address on God's part. Most people today who continue to pray are more apt (often for psychological reasons) to understand the responses they hear or the inspirations they feel in prayer as talking to oneself about God. Rahner sets out on a different tack (66). The first is transcendental. What if instead of imagining dialogical prayer as God saying *something* to us *in* prayer, we rather thought that in prayer we experience ourselves as the ones spoken by God? To hear oneself as the word spoken by God and to accept that word would then constitute the dialogical aspect of prayer. The second new direction is categorical. Here, based on his experience of St. Ignatius of Loyola's Spiritual Exercises, Rahner imagines the categorical object of "indifference" giving rise to "consolation without cause" as a kind of dialogue.

Topics: PRAYER, as dialogue.
Subsidiary discussions: Spirit/s, experience of (67f); Exercises of St. Ignatius (67f).

CC.2.4. The "Exercises" Today. (70-74)

Abstract: Suggests why and how the Ignatian Exercises should be modified for use today.
Topics: EXERCISES of St. IGNATIUS.
Subsidiary discussions: *Metanoia* (71ff).

Precis: 1. While the Ignatian Exercises remain essentially a time to foster decision and choice in solitude and prayer, it is legitimate today judiciously to incorporate meetings with others. **2.** The Exercises presuppose the fundamental substance of Christianity regarding God and the transcendentality of the human person. Further, they presuppose there is an existential decision through an individual call of God to the actual person. All this must be demythologized for today. The Exercises do not indoctrinate from without. They are an initiation into one's spiritual experience and sanctification from within. This is the work of future commentaries on the Exercises: they must offer both a developed dogmatic theology of its statements and also a formal theology of the existential experience of grace itself. **3.** The perception and acceptance of the divine call in the Exercises always has two inseparable, dynamic, co-conditioning aspects corresponding to the nature of the human person: transcendental and categorical (*metanoia* and its concrete mediating realization). **4.** The one leading the Exercises must keep in mind two points that follow from this: a) Transcendentally, the situation in which the Exercises is given today is significantly different from Ignatius's time (e.g., the fundamental relationship of immediacy to God). This calls for a longer and more explicit introduction to the Exercises. b) Categorically, the multiplicity of concrete objects of choice and decision are also more varied than ever before. **5.** Any future commentaries on the Exercises must be more than pious paraphrases. They must include rigorous questioning. [Cf., Rahner's *Spiritual Exercises*, 1965, and *Priesthood*, 1973.]

CC.2.5. Penance and Confession. (75-83)
Abstract: Ten points concerning the practice of sacramental Penance in the post-Vatican II church.
Topics: PENANCE, sacrament of.
Subsidiary discussions: Metanoia (75f; 80); Sin, mortal/venial (77f); Penance services (78ff).

Precis: These 10 seemingly arbitrary elements concerning the practice of sacramental Penance in the post-Vatican II church presume the basic binding Catholic doctrine. 1) Penance is not so much a particular act but a continually renewed grace of metanoia. 2) The Christian sense of sin and the need for forgiveness stand in need of re-expression today. 3) The effective grace of metanoia is not limited to sacramental Penance. 4) There is no reason why the Sacrament of Penance cannot foster the grace of metanoia, especially if it is known and celebrated in its fullness. 5) There must be an inner unity between penitential services and particular receptions of the sacrament. 6) The yearly duty to confess grave sins must be properly understood so that it does not inadvertently contribute to one's ruin. 7) There is no reason to continue to push a pre-Vatican II rigorism, especially not the assumption that *materia objectiva gravis* was normally accompanied by subjective grave guilt and hence, must be subjected to sacramental Confession. This does not mean limiting sacramental Penance solely to confession of grave sins. Nevertheless, this attitude thrives in situations where rigorism is maintained. 8) It is legitimate for the church to insist that the need to submit grave sins to sacramental Penance is not properly fulfilled by participation in a penitential service. 9) Although the theology remains vague, communal penitential services do have the sacramental character of absolving sins and strengthening the grace of metanoia. 10) The jury is still out concerning the most appropriate form for the celebration of the general penitential service.

CC.2.6. Lent. (81-83)
Abstract: Rahner argues for a "Copernican Revolution" in the modern piety of Lent. Currently the preparation for Easter is rooted in viewing the world as two marginally overlapping worlds; the secular world of mundane human affairs, and the spiritual world inhabited mostly by nuns, priests and saints. In the season of Lent a secular person enters this spiritual world by performing certain sacred or meritorious acts. A Copernican Revolution would view the one world as the world of grace, and all its pursuits as spiritual. Then the proper celebration of Lent would entail accepting this one world in faith and hope —the new understanding of Christian asceticism as "voluntary renunciation."
Topics: LENT; SPIRITUALITY, modern.

CC.2.7. The Theology of Dying. (84-86)
Abstract: Rahner reflects on Kübler-Ross' fifth stage of dying: acquiescence or acceptance of death. The eternal destiny of the dying cannot be known by any outside observer. Whether the acquiescence accompanying the fifth stage is despair or loving trust, only God knows. The hope Kübler-Ross says accompanies this last stage could have theological significance. It could be not merely hope for some earthly change of events, but St. Paul's salvific "hope against hope" (Rm 4:18), extended even to those who are Christians only "anonymously."
Topics: DEATH; HOPE.

CC.2.8. Hope and Easter. (87-93)
Abstract: Rahner roots our particular faith in Jesus' resurrection in our own hope for achieving our own definitive state.
Topics: RESURRECTION.

Subsidiary discussions: Anonymous Christian/ity (88); Resurrection of the body (88); Jesus Christ, resurrection of (89ff); Christology, searching (89ff).

Precis: What follows is Rahner's theological reflection on his personal confession, "The Lord is truly risen!" This is a belief many people actually live without being able to reduce it to clear conceptual language, and which some people reject while they in fact live it anonymously. Both groups, by experiencing eternity in time, place their hope in man's definitiveness and in the condition for the possibility of that hope who we call God. Whoever experiences this here and now cannot consign it to future destruction. This is what we mean by hope in the resurrection, however impossible it may be to "visualize." Insofar as this hope is "for the whole man" it implies resurrection of the body.

This reflection on our human situation is the starting point for understanding the resurrection of Jesus. Our human hope forces us to scan all of history to see if ever any human person ever achieved the definitiveness we call resurrection. Christian faith finds that event in Jesus. To deny this would be tantamount to denying our own hope for ourselves. After a lengthy reflection on Jesus' resurrection, Rahner raises the final point: hope. What is the human situation if everything is based "merely" on hope? But hope needs no justification. It sustains reality as it happens. Apart from hope there is only despair.

CC.2.9. The Future. (94-95)

Abstract: Planning the future is increasingly necessary. Nevertheless, the real future remains always unknown. All we actually know is either present, still nonexistent dreams for the future, or elements of the future which are now already present. In any case, the future itself remains unknown. What are we to do? After assessing the options, Rahner advises us to exercise our freedom responsibly in the present, and to surrender to the future in hope. In this way we become aware of what is meant by God.

Topics: FUTURE; HOPE.

CCt. The Christian Commitment: Essays in Pastoral Theology. NY: Sheed & Ward, 1963. Notes. 220 pp. *Sendung und Gnade I*, 1961. Also, *Mission and Grace I*. Translated by Cecily Hastings.

Contents: 1. The Present Situation of Christians: A theological interpretation of the position of Christians in the modern world.
2. The Order of Redemption within the Order of Creation.
3. The Significance in Redemptive History of the Individual Member of the Church.
4. Mary and the Apostolate.
5. The Sacrifice of the Mass and an Ascesis for Youth.
6. Developing Eucharistic Devotion.
7. The Mass and Television.

CCt.1. The Present Situation of Christians: A theological interpretation of the position of Christians in the modern world. (3-37)

Abstract: The most important factor defining the church today and for the future is its diaspora situation. By recognizing, accepting and responding to this new truth the church will be able to unburden itself of encumbrances, refocus its energies, and accept its proper missionary apostolate as a true world-church.

Topics: CHURCH in the Diaspora; CHURCH of the future; DIASPORA.

Subsidiary discussions: Prophecy (6f); Evil (12); Governments of the future (12ff); Church, missionary nature of (27ff, 33); Church, ghettoization of (28ff); Priest of the future (32f).

Precis: Realizing this might not be the right thing said at the right time, nevertheless, Rahner opens his address to a conference on "The Theological Interpretation of the Position of Christians in the Modern World" with some theological clarifications. If the modern world is just one more particularization of that same old world addressed by scripture, then in what sense is revelation addressed to the *modern* world precisely a such? If there is such a word in Scripture then it is in the form of prophecy, not prediction or description of that "future world" in which we now find ourselves but as an "illumination" of the meaning of the future, which does not completely relieve us of our cares or responsibilities.

Before proceeding Rahner lays down two premises which seem particularly important today. No previous age can be identified with *the* Christian culture, since no one single pattern of life in the world can be deduced from Christian principles, beliefs, or morality (though certain practices can be rejected as anti-Christian). In one and the same case there can be more than one practical and justifiable possibility, the choice of which cannot be settled beforehand by recourse to Christian principles, and which demands risk. This is why there cannot be *the* Christian realization of anything. We are not bound to repeat the past out of misplaced respect. The past was one creative response to the opportunities offered by the sphere of freedom then. Today that sphere is widened and so have our options. Despite the truth of our Christian principles, they cannot tell us which of the many legitimate possibilities we should choose in any given circumstance. Two things follow: **a)** we should rejoice that the sphere of freedom and choice today is so greatly expanded, even if it means an ever-widening gap between Christian principles and the concrete proposals society demands– principles we can no longer supply in the name of Christianity (if indeed we ever could). Insisting on doing so today simply makes Christianity a target of all those who quite legitimately disagree with our concrete (but not revealed) proposals. After a note on the dangers of overstating the power of evil (12), Rahner proceeds to: **b).** To negotiate this ever-expanding range of possibilities, new institutions will necessarily arise– a new "state" with a hitherto undreamed of reach and importance. These possibilities bear great promise and great dangers for freedom.

Rahner now states his thesis: *the present situation of Christians today is best characterized as a "diaspora." This "must" in terms of salvation history is something from which we can and must draw conclusions about our behavior as Christians.* What does Rahner mean by this "must"? There are things that ought to be (e.g., Ten Commandments). There are things that are that ought not to be (e.g., crime)– things we must work to eradicate. Between these there is a third category: things that ought not be, but which are not simply contradictions of a rule. They have their own kind of validity, inevitability, value and significance for salvation. They can neither be accepted nor protested against. One must reckon with them and draw from them certain conclusions that will present us with an "ought" (e.g., "The poor you will have always with you"). The supreme moment of such a "must" in the history of salvation is the scandal of the cross (summary, 16). Christianity can fail not only by refusing to engage in the right kind of combat; it can also fail by engaging in the wrong way (i.e., with an unchristian, utopian radicalism) because it did not draw the proper conclusions about New Testament "prophecies."

Assuming all this, Rahner moves to the next thesis: our "diaspora" situation today is one such "must" in salvation history– a divinely-willed "must" (not an "ought") with which we must reckon. Rahner starts with the fact of a post-Christian, "missionary" Europe. Christianity is a minority through-out the world. Peasant and petty bourgeois Christendom is disappearing with ever-increasing speed. Much as we must desire that this diaspora situation not to be the case, it is something which we should expect: a "must" of faith (18f). The next section Rahner devotes to explaining precisely why this universal diaspora situation is a "must," (19ff). He focuses on the changes (Reformation and Age of Discovery) that impelled the church into the world arena and forced it to become a world-church. As a consequence, the work of the church today must hold in tension both its new and inevitable minority status *and* the command to defend and spread the faith.

What happens to the church when Christians live in the diaspora among large numbers of non-Christians? **a)** Faith is constantly threatened. It finds little social reinforcement and thus must increasingly become a personal decision. **b)** Culture (art, literature, science) no longer bears the stamp of Christianity. Much will be in open conflict with Christianity. Secular society will build its own institutions to replace Christian institution, but which are not for that reason simply degenerate. **c)** The future church will be a church of the active laity. Sociologically it will look more like a sect than like a national religion. A smaller church will no longer run large institutions (schools, health services) in competition with the state. Its efforts will be more focused and more strictly religious. **d)** The clerical "status" as such will have ended. **e)** Church-State conflicts will lessen as the church grows smaller and less institutional, and as its political power wanes. Sadly, most Europeans have still not awakened to these facts (26).

What are the consequences of this diaspora situation? **a)** Since this is not just a "must" that has to be accepted, we cannot cease to be missionary in the proper sense (i.e., not by fanatically intolerant frontal attacks). Though we must remain missionary we must be wise enough to focus our energies in the right places and to resist the allure of retreating into a political, cultural or religious ghetto, a move that only promotes unhealthy clericalism. **b)** Examples of steps in the wrong direction would be constructing a German-language Catholic University complete with all faculties, or campaigning to have government check the slide of moral standards through legislation. Living in a diaspora situation, we should present our principles to others and even to our fellow Christians incrementally, beginning with those issues on which we can expect some understanding; we should teach young people how to read the non-Christian materials that assail them; we should do away with desk jockey priests obsessed with statistics; we must think of ourselves as missionaries and adopt their attitudes of tolerance to cultural differences; we must speak and write with the knowledge that non-Christians are listening and have a right to comment; we must not project ourselves as a monolith devoid of a healthy diversity of opinion. **c)** Reckoning with our diaspora situation is the opposite of resignation or defeatism. Letting go of baggage from the past would free us for the real missionary adventure with apostolic self-confidence. If we demand less of ourselves and focus our energies on the right things (e.g., a battle for new members) we will be in far better shape, regardless of statistics. We would no longer be stuck on the defensive. All this, of course, takes a great faith in eternal life that is willing to endure even death (summary, 35ff).

CCt.2. The Order of Redemption within the Order of Creation. (38-74)

Abstract: This discussion of the relationship between the creative and redemptive orders begins with the ontological discussion of how things can be really different and also the same. Rahner's conclusion that the two orders co-penetrate yields six conclusions about the apostolate of the laity.

Topics: CREATION and Redemption; GRACE and Nature; LAITY, apostolate of; NATURE and supernature; REDEMPTION and creation.

Subsidiary discussions: Church, acts of (41ff); Soul and body, unity of (47f); Being, hierarchy of (47f); Religious life (62ff).

Precis: Because of the laity's special task to Christianize "the world" (i.e., the order of creation), it is appropriate at a diocesan conference on Lay Apostolate to consider the relation between the order of creation and the order of redemption, earth and heaven, nature and grace. Rahner's thesis is simply that it is best to speak of the order of redemption *within* the order of creation. This implies that divine grace penetrates the order of creation, healing and sanctifying it; that divine grace incorporates the world in the *mysterium Christi*; and that God intends this process of subsuming the world into the divine life of grace to be carried out by people in what we call lay apostolate (preview, 39).

I. The unity of the orders of redemption and creation. 1. This section concerns terminology, clarifications and distinctions without which we fall into hopeless but avoidable confusions. Our ability to draw up parallel lists of contrasting terms (grace/nature; nature/supernature; law/Gospel; church/ world, etc.) can easily mislead us into thinking that all these distinctions are simply equivalent. But for example though grace is adequately distinguishable from nature, concretely they form a unity. Grace is essentially a determination, elevation and divinization of nature. By extension, but somewhat differently, the supernatural order is related to the natural order as whole to part. In speaking of the church (41-43) things get even more complex, since it can legitimately be seen as a concrete institution or as a charismatic reality of grace taking effect even beyond the boundaries of the visible church. Attempts to define an "act of the church" are equally difficult since there are clearly Christian acts of individual members of the church which are utterly supernatural but not specifically ecclesial, since they do not actually participate in the church's hierarchical apostolate. These considerations come to a head when applied to the two terms "church/world." Very different but legitimate conclusions can be drawn depending on which understanding of the term "church" is being used. This merely goes to show how careful one must be in using terms. Many problems surrounding the Apostolate of the Laity have arisen due to carelessness with words.

2. **The fact and the more precise nature of the unity of the orders of redemption and creation: four ontological observations.**

a) These formal observations on the unity of a complex entity insist that we recognize there are entities which are really *one* though they include factors that are *really distinct* from each other. They contain a single principle constituting an ultimate unity. The exact nature of this unity differs analogically depending on the particular reality involved. A prime example is the way body and spirit are united in the one human person.

b) In addressing the question of the unity of the orders of creation and redemption, Rahner hopes as far as possible to avoid appealing to *theologoumena*. Creation, including people and their history, were originally intended by God as a unity wherein each element is related to all the rest, albeit in various ways. There is only one creation, united not simply in origin but also by communion. Within this one creation there is not only mutual relationship but also an order of superiority and subordination willed by God. Everything lower exists for the sake of the higher, and all exist for the sake of the highest: the Incarnate Word (God's self-expression in what is other than God). Hence, the order of creation, even considered *as natural*, belongs to the order of redemption. Their unity heals and endows everything in creation with supernatural meaning, while confirming the true and permanent naturalness of creation.

c) This inner openness of natural creation and of every creature to receive *a possible* divine self-communication in grace is a *potentia obedientialis* for grace. Beyond this, in the concrete order each creature *is* so ordered to this grace in such a way that it can only find its completion in the order of redemption. Hence, there is no purely natural salvation. The unity of the two orders is such that no one can simply bypass the permanently valid order of creation, since it is the condition of the possibility of the supernatural order itself. Seen in its fullness, everything natural reveals itself as more than natural. Christians especially must awaken to the depth inherent in the created order (51) which can be found in the everyday experiences of love, death, etc. This hidden depth is the only reason we can take human life with absolute seriousness. In his summary (52f) Rahner allows that we can express the relationship of unity and diversity between the created and redemptive orders as one abiding within the other (either creation *within* redemption or redemption *within* creation).

d) So far this ontology of the unity and diversity of the two orders sounds rather static. But it has a dynamic component as well. God has irrevocably ordained that this unity be realized as an historical unfolding. Hence, it is an eschatological unity– complete yet awaiting its historical consummation. It is also dynamic in the sense that it is realized over time to greater or lesser degrees, just as individuals progressively realize their human corporeal and spiritual unity to greater or lesser degrees. Creation, like the individual person is one, yet must become one. Since the event of the Incarnation, the outcome for the world at least is definitive. No drama remains since no final split is any longer possible between the orders of creation and redemption which Christ has united and redeemed. This faith in the Incarnation makes the Christian optimistic, but not in the same way as secular utopians, whose optimism centers on the potential success of their own efforts. Still, since God actually does bring about the unity of creation and redemption through our human actions, we must not live in the world as idle bystanders so long as this unity remains unconsummated in us as individuals or in the world. There are two primary ways of embodying the task of incarnational faith: asceticism and affirmation (57) properly understood (cf., II.1). For all this, the unity we desire remains vulnerable and threatened for individuals and for nations. Not threatened to the degree that Christians should simply flee its tragic dissolution (for the work of redemption has already been done by God); yet not so secure that one should enthusiastically put all one's efforts into pushing it the last few yards to the goal line (since its consummation remains the work of God). In the end, the unity of creation and redemption remains a hidden unity (a factor that also contributes to its being under threat). It is an object of faith not simply open to experience despite occasional hints. It is also hidden by the fact that God's grace for the most part remains anonymous and can easily be mistaken for worldly forces. Finally, it is hidden beneath the scandal of the cross. All these peculiarities taken together instill in faithful Christians a sense of realistic sobriety toward the world. They can neither divinize nor condemn it. Though their interventions cannot completely heal the world, neither are they completely inconsequential. Avoiding the extremes of utopianism and despair, the Christian endures in hope.

II. Application to Christian living. Given all this (summary, 62), what can we say about how Christians are to live here and now?

1. What has been said clarifies the relation of unity and difference between vowed religious life under the evangelical counsels and secular Christian life. The former is the ascetic response to the world; the latter is the affirmative response (cf., I.d). Although these two orders are really different, they are held together in a complimentary unity since the ascetic is reminded by the affirmative response that s/he cannot simply flee the world; and the ascetic reminds the lay person who affirms the world that one's own efforts are never enough to affect the unity of creation and redemption.

2. The non-ecclesial, non-hierarchical sphere of supernaturally elevated Christian life (cf., I.1) is not thereby irrelevant to human salvation or to the healing of the world. The ecclesial represents only part of what is Christian. As much as laity should be encouraged to participate in the ecclesial life of the church, their proper field of endeavor lies elsewhere. In their secular apostolates the laity are of course still members of the church. But this does not make their activities ecclesial apostolates in the strict sense.

3. The sanctification of the world is not a matter of imposing a supernatural superstructure on a sound, well-developed natural world. Christian life comes into play in the very same material sphere in which secular, profane life occurs. We must accept that the secular world has so expanded that, unlike the medieval world, it cannot easily be given an explicitly Christian stamp. But we must also allow that the presence of grace does not end at the bounds of explicit Christianity. For wherever true humanity is being lived, there Christianity is achieved, albeit anonymously. There, too, the Lay Apostolate is fulfilled.

4. Our constant experience of the world's need for healing summons a specifically Christian task and duty. We discover this supernatural call within our experience of the world as a plurality before we are confronted with the task of realizing its unity. Sometimes the experience of joy leads us forward. More often the questions

CHRISTIAN COMMITMENT 69

raised by the tragic confusion of the world prompt us to seek true fulfillment. Whatever the case, "the life of the world, if only it is experienced in its wholeness and without reserve, is itself a part of the spiritual life, and above all in its experience of the world's dire need for salvation" (71).

5. For all Christians there is an inevitable gap between a Christian attitude and an appropriate course of action in the world. As two really distinct factors in the world, there is no guarantee they will ever fully coincide. A Christian's good motivations can always lead to inappropriate action. Yet act and intention must remain united. Christians must bear with a certain discrepancy between the two as a burden laid upon them, and as their share in the cross of Christ.

6. There is always a need for a "point of contact" between the efforts of the hierarchical church as such and those Christian activities which are not strictly speaking ecclesial. After all, both are striving for the unity of the created and redemptive orders. Perhaps today this point of contact is to be found in the interface between Catholic diocesan organizations and Catholic Action (i.e., Lay Apostolate). In any case, the need to more closely unite these two orders in a way that avoids both extreme reactions of despair and utopianism is immeasurably huge today. But with God everything is possible.

CCt. 3. The Significance in Redemptive History of the Individual Member of the Church. (75-114)

Abstract: Ontological reflection on individuality reveals the church exists to promote the individual member, the increase of whose personal faith is the meaning of all rites, rules, etc. Putting individuality first radically reorients pastoral activity: ministry, church organizations, preaching, lay apostolate, etc.

Topics: CHURCH, individual in; INDIVIDUALITY; THEOLOGICAL ANTHROPOLOGY, individuality.

Subsidiary discussions: God, oneness of (78); Transcendence, human (78f); God, love proper to (84ff); Acts, religious (86ff); Church as pneumatic community (89f); Saints (92); Priesthood of the future (99f); Preaching (103f); Anonymous Christian/ity (104ff); Laity, apostolate of (106f); Church, public opinion in (110f); Church as Small Christian Community (111f).

Precis: I. Ontology of the relationship between individuality and community. Even at the level of inanimate objects, where one identical object is added to an existing set to increase its size, the analogical concept of individuality points to something mysterious. Turning to the realm of persons (77), Rahner states a principle of individuality which may at first seem contradictory: its difference from and its bond with what is other than itself vary in direct proportion. That is to say, the more something is itself, the more it is related to others. Our tendency to picture individuality in spatial terms, and to see individuals "along with" others, often obscures the real meaning of the individual. For wherever we have mind and person there is transcendence toward infinity, and there the individual knows him/herself as such in the act of opening oneself to the boundless and infinite. Hence, transcendent openness evidenced in human acts of knowing and loving simultaneously unites and individualizes the one who knows or loves. Affirming or denying this essential structure of spirit has inescapable consequences. When affirmed, I am willing to be what I inescapably am: myself united through the infinite to everything else.

In this basic structure, individuality and community are complementary and vary in direct proportion, whether in acceptance or denial. But the mistake mentioned before (thinking these factors vary in inverse proportion) inevitably leads either through fear or hubris to attempts at escaping oneself by getting lost in the group, or escaping the group by cutting oneself off from transcendent acts of love or knowledge. From within this false paradigm it may seem that one must choose community *or* individuality. But such conflicts only arise when community and individuality oppose one another on different levels (e.g., spiritual individuality vs. biological community), something that can easily happen due to the multiplicity within the human person (summary, 81). In terms of the church (to anticipate the subject), there is no problem between the individual and the community so long as they remain on the same level. But problems do arise when the pneumatic, spiritual individual comes into contact with the church which is simultaneously a pneumatic reality and a physical institution. The key to success here is never to absolutize either of the two poles, and to maintain the relative opposition between them.

II. The individual in the order of grace and the church. At the outset it must be clear: the individual endowed with supernatural grace is the highest example of individuality among created things, and the fulfillment of this individuality is what the church exists to serve. As a social, external and legal institution, the church is a lower and subordinate reality to the individual. One's *potentia obedientialis* and capacity for transcendence endow the human person with eternal validity. One is never an individual merely in the sense of being one exemplification of a general idea. Persons form an entirely special type of community. When human beings are in addition raised to the supernatural order by God's free self-communication, their very beings are elevated into an essentially higher order than that of naturally spiritual persons, and their new pneumatic individuality exceeds their natural individuality. Rahner now fills this formal concept of "grace-given supernatural individuality" with content (84ff). God's love is truly creative, transforming what it loves. God's supernatural love revealed in absolute self-communication is concrete and individual to the highest degree: absolutely unique. The concrete image which best captures the essence of this love is spousal love. Through this love the beloved becomes someone absolutely unique, something difficult to render in speech, which by its nature ranges over generalities. In calling forth the pneumatic individual, God's love is revealed as infinite not only in its totality but also in its ability to give itself to each one differently, i.e., not only in degree but also in its special character.

This supernatural elevating love of God has further consequence on free human decisions as the basis for really religious acts (86ff). They become "the realization of a genuinely spiritual, personal *and* grace-given, supernatural individuality in obedience to a completely personal call, a genuinely individual vocation from God" (86), even where it should be lived out in very mundane and even unreflexive ways. Such spiritual and religious acts, although they fulfill external laws, are more than the mere fulfillment of external norms; they proceed from the heart. Despite social and psychological influence at work in the individual, these religious acts remain free acts precisely insofar as they are individual (in the double sense indicated). They are genuinely religious acts insofar as they are individual, spiritual and concern God – acts that freely affirm transcendence by which we commit ourselves to our own eternal essence. All this is a consequence of the individuality of the act. (Rahner adds by way of warning (88) that no amount of introspection can yield certainty about the how we stand in the sight of God, how fully or freely we have responded to God's love.)

Through "really religious acts" one acquires a decisive significance in the salvation of others, for one's pneumatic individuality is precisely his/her incorporation into the church, the community of founded by the *pneuma* of God, which all the other concrete elements of the church (law, ritual, scripture, hierarchy) exist to serve. The pneumatic individual will perform these really religious acts, this essential thing, precisely *in* other concrete acts (receiving sacraments, visible worship, etc.). But the truly saving act is never the concrete, pre-personal or pre-pneumatic as such. Wherever the free, religious, pneumatic act appears, "*there* is the true individual, and there is the Church at her most real. And there it is that the individual has real significance for the salvation of others" (91). The single and unique act of redemption, Christ's solitary individual act of free total surrender to God, creates the church: community at its deepest and most all-embracing Hence, "the Church lives by the acts of individuals done within that act by which she is founded" (91). After safeguarding the fact that these salvific acts remain primarily God's doing in which we participate, Rahner finishes this section by saying the truest history of the church would be the history of the saints, i.e., those whose pneumatic existence has discovered grace-given individuality in a selfless opening of the heart toward God, and thus toward all spiritual persons.

III. **Consequences.** Rahner prefaces the pastoral consequences of this discussion with two warnings. If human nature consists of an irreducible pluralism, then any monomaniacal, one-size-fits-all pastoral approach is fundamentally false. It follows that in proposing any particular pastoral approach one is not thereby denigrating all others. Nevertheless, four basic propositions can be deduced from this discussion regarding the individual and his/her salvific significance to the church. It is useful to examine these for two reasons: first, these principles are as eternally valid as the salvific significance of the individual; second, these maxims have a special urgency today to protect pneumatic individuality in the world, and to help the church grasp ever more fully her true nature as it continues to unfold in time

1. Pastoral agents must have the courage to think in terms of the individual (95), without thereby abandoning their missionary mandate to the world and to nations. "For it is only when Christianity has reached the individual in his own unique individuality that there has been any decisive success in the pastoral field" (96). This may mean a decline in numbers, but who can say periods of mass Christianity like the Middle Ages were also the periods of greatest inner grace, or that many sacramental marriages actually betoken a great increase in sacrificial love? External religious performance, if it does not spring from personal conviction, completely misses its goal. Rahner grants that much pastoral activity will continue of necessity to take a pre-personal approach, directed as it is to children and young people. But even this must be aimed at awakening one's truly personal, grace-given depths. This can only be accomplished by "charismatic pastors" (99f). Rahner concludes by alluding to a principle: the influence of a religiously homogeneous environment on the individual's intimate personal attitude does not always increase in direct proportion: i.e., increasingly Catholic areas are not necessarily increasingly holy areas (summary, 101).

2. "The Christian life must be known and lived as real living, and not as a mere fulfillment of norms and observations of commands" (101), since it is always the fulfillment of unique pneumatic individuality. Christianity must be lived from the inside out, rather than confront us from without with its "thou shalts." Those we approach want to be treated like individuals, not merely like objects who fall under objective norms. Preaching is not indoctrination. It proclaims good news principally because it illuminates the inner reality of the hearer and helps the individual to make sense of him/herself. Any appeal to the individual from outside is always addressed to the God who is already at work within. This is equally true of the Christian mysteries we proclaim. This already-present Christian life, to which preaching appeals is not abstract but very concrete. Everyday life, rightly interpreted, is open to God. This gives us courage to hope in anonymous Christianity. For there is no completely "natural order." Everything in the concrete order is willed by God and already oriented to God. Rahner offers as ex-

amples of grace in everyday life the experiences of death, love, and loneliness (105) which also argue for anonymous Christianity. This is the heart of pastoral work: to help the individual find him/herself by assimilating the Christianity which comes from outside through the discovery of one's own grace-given inwardness. This work is equally the concern of the laity and clergy (106f). Much more could be said.

3. "If the individual has this indispensable significance for salvation, then room must be provided in the Church for this individual Christianity" (108). The amount of space allotted for individual self-discovery has varied within church history; freedom is sometimes more, sometimes less valued. The very proliferation of clubs and organizations tends to obscure the fact that they are useful or meaningful only insofar as they assist their members to stand before God as individuals. In the past, the goal of religious institutions was cultural autonomy. Religious schools, aid agencies, political parties, sports teams, etc., were set up to rival activities in the secular realm. This is no longer possible or desirable. The apostolate today must aid Christians to live their faith on their own. Finally, a church of individuals will necessarily be a church of great diversity. Not every differing opinion is *ipso facto* uncatholic. In principle all agree this diversity of opinion ought to exist in the church, but too often this is conceded only grudgingly. It is not embraced as the very condition for the possibility of having believing individuals.

4. We must cultivate a concrete intermediary between individuality at the personal, pneumatic level and universality at the social and organizational level (the latter being at a lower ontological level). This would in turn foster both individuality and solidarity. Rahner suggests this link could be called a "cell." [Perhaps the contemporary term "Small Christian Community" captures his idea better.] He goes on to show the difference between a Communist cell and his idea of a Christian cell. In the former the individual is not uniquely irreplaceable. S/he exists for the sake of the State. Whereas in the latter, the individual is of unique importance, and the larger organizations exists only to further his/her welfare.

CCt.4. Mary and the Apostolate. (115-135)

Abstract: Our new age calls for new approaches to apostolic activity. Mary should be taken as the pattern for apostolic renewal, because she held in creative tension charism and office, spirit and law, clergy and laity. She also revealed other eternal aspects of Christian apostolate: patience, endurance, humility, hope.

Topics: APOSTOLATE; BVM, and the apostolate.

Subsidiary discussions: Office and charism, unity of (121f); Priesthood, office and charism (122f); Priesthood, spirituality of (124ff); Planning (133f).

Precis: The aim of this unidentified Jesuit conference was to arrive at norms for pastoral practice— norms which though legally binding would not stifle the Spirit. The difficulties of this task mirror a fundamental dichotomy within the nature of the church: that it is simultaneously a charismatic *and* a visible incarnate entity. Rahner insists that the church, and this conference, must struggle to keep these opposites in unity and not to give way completely to the demands of one dimension or the other.

I. **The need to consider the nature and new tasks of the church.** To clarify the basic issues involved here we must turn to Mary because every fresh apostolic effort must issue from a deepened understanding of the medium and goal of all pastoral work: the church. In this rapidly changing age it is no surprise to find such unparalleled interest in ecclesiology. For the nature and task of the church, too, is rapidly changing, and only bold and uninhibited reflection on her nature and mandate in dialogue with the special character of the new age will reveal a course of concrete action.

II. **Mary— type of the church.** Reflecting on the concrete person of Mary, her acts and her destiny, will reveal more clearly what the church is than reflecting on abstract concepts. *Maria typus Ecclesia.* Mariology and ecclesiology have much to gain from each other. Because the church is not a substance but an event constantly renewed in concrete individuals, Mary provides the best starting place for reflecting on the church. Mariology, ecclesiology and Christology are three aspects of a single saving reality.

III. **Mary— type of the apostolate and of pastoral work.** In what follows, Mary will be considered simply insofar as she is a type of the apostolate and of the pastoral work of the church. A few preliminary remarks will show this is not a far-fetched comparison but has a real place in the subject matter of faith and theology. *1. Mary: the supreme instance of redemption in its coming and its acceptance.* The starting point for reflection on Mary's motherhood is not its biological aspect but the fact that it was a free act, a decision of faith. This act is part of saving history in its full, public, official sense because its goal and object was the Incarnation; and because Incarnation is already the decisive act of redemption which unfolds decisively from that act. Mary's act at the decisive point in salvation history is both official and personal. Mary's act is the supreme instance of redemption as coming and accepted. "Mary is she who is perfectly redeemed" (119). All things reach their highest fulfillment and their complementary unity in her. This is precisely what makes Mary the type of the church as such. What the church is in its functioning is shown most clearly and completely in the Mary-event wherein her personal salvation most perfectly becomes the office of salvation for others. *2. Mary: the living pattern of the apostolate.* It follows that, apart from Christ, Mary and her work are the supreme case of the apostolate of a human being. Though historically irrepeatable, her life is the archetypal apostolic event, the productive pattern of all later apostolates. Precisely in its historical uniqueness it becomes a pattern for us, insofar as every individual apostolic call is equally unique.

IV. The basic structures of the apostolate and of pastoral work. *1. Unity of the apostolate of clergy and laity.* The pattern of Mary's apostolate unites clergy and laity insofar as she was not a hierarch as such nor was she simply lay, since she held the highest office in the church. Her task was an office that claimed her entire person. She is a protest against all one-sided clericalism and laicism, a "living pattern of contradiction." She urges clergy not to be satisfied with mere office but to become completely Spirit-filled and holy. She urges the laity to resist its tendency to anarchy and anominalism, just as her life was one of submission to legitimate authority (summary, 124). *2. Unity in the apostolate between interior spirit and exterior goal.* Uniting interior holiness and external activity is a distressing struggle for all apostolic priests. Since one cannot simply abandon one for the other, it is consoling to remember these factors are related in direct rather than inverse proportion (125). We see this most clearly in the apostolate of the Virgin

Mary whose act and spirituality are one. Looking at her relieves the fear that we shall lose our souls if we become consumed by selfless service. 3. *Unity in the apostolate of Spirit and norm, of spirituality and law.* The bureaucratic aspects of apostolate often make us irritable and skeptical. But looking at Mary we must recall that she gave us the Spirit by giving us the Word in very human flesh. The true spirit of Christianity has the courage to submit to the flesh, to concrete limitations, even to death. The only way to be pastorally available is through the law. The law is the body of the spirit, and where possible we must embrace or endure it. 4. *Further basic structures in the Marian Apostolate:* a) It is from above, a service undertaken, a task which claims us and outstrips our capabilities; b) It demands the capacity to wait for the right moment, and the ability to focus our energies on what is most urgent; c) It is self-effacing; d) It demands the perseverance of a lifetime; e) It is an apostolate of the cross. 5. *Mary, the guiding pattern of pastoral work.* Rahner concedes that perhaps nothing he says here is particularly new. But he insists that if this Marian apostolic pattern is kept in mind throughout the rest of the meeting, and if each participant applies it to himself and his own proposals, better results will follow.

V. **Bold adaptation to our new situation.** We live in a new age characterized by *the breaking up of things*. This is precipitated by our ability to extend our control over nature, and by the attendant question of whether we *should* do all that we *can* do. When nature no longer limits us, we must increasingly learn to control ourselves. In such an age it should come as no surprise that pastoral work and Christianity itself assume a very defensive character. But as we adapt to this new situation we are planting the seeds and laying the foundations for a coming age when people will perhaps be more open to the message of salvation. Surely this kind of pastoral work, however partial and halting, cannot be unimportant.

CCt.5. The Sacrifice of the Mass and an Ascesis for Youth. (136-170). [*Since this pre-conciliar address presumes a very different liturgical environment than exists today, some of Rahner's concrete suggestions may no longer be relevant. But the principles he outlines remain valid and their serious consideration will be fruitful. DP*]

Abstract: Because both the Mass and the worshiper are multi-dimensional, it is legitimate to ask how the Mass could be celebrated more appropriately by a particular group. Concentrating on youth, Rahner sees "active sacrifice" as the point of connection—an acceptable seed with promise of bearing fruit in later life.
Topics: EUCHARIST; LITURGY, renewal of; MASS, participation in; YOUTH, formation of.
Subsidiary discussions: Ascesis (164ff).

Precis: Two preliminary points. 1) Because the mystery of the Mass has so many dimensions and because the human person is so complex, it will always be possible to bring the two realities together in fresh ways. History shows none of these ways can ever be considered the one final right arrangement. Though there may be one best approach for a particular time, it is discovered in devotion not prescribed by theology. **2)** The Mass is not Christianity. There is no one single organizing principle for all religious life. Even Mass is only a sign of the central thing, and not simply the thing itself. For there are other grace-giving sacraments, and Christianity is not confined to church, sacraments, and cult. Life itself confers and increases the selfsame grace. God is the only central point of religious living, and we must be careful not to fall into a liturgical monomania. This is confirmed by history and by the lives of the saints. Rhetorically exaggerated language encouraging devotion to Mary or the Sacred Heart, or even participation in the Mass in ways that neglects personal prayer, penance, service to others, is irritating, irrational, dangerous and fundamentally false. This is not meant to denigrate the Mass to the level of an Advent wreath. But its centrality should not be stressed in an overly one-sided way (summary, 143).

The Mass in the totality of Christian life. One must distinguish in the sacrament between the objective elements (*opus operatum*) and subjective devotion or personal faith. The former only has meaning, value or significance insofar as they are integrated in one's subjectivity. Sacraments affect grace in proportion to the disposition of the recipient. Objective sacraments never substitute for subjectivity, or make the demands of the sacraments less exacting. God wills the objective elements of cult "in order that man shall give Him his own subjectivity, his heart" (144). To the degree that Masses cease to do this (i.e., increase faith, hope, and love), to that degree they cease to be pleasing and meaningful to God.

The "living of life" and the "church's Mass." Education about Mass cannot limit itself to concerns over cult and community. It must be formation into the totality of Christian life (prayer, service, sacrifice, responsibility, etc.). "Unless the *res sacramenti* happens in a person's life ... the *sacramentum* of the Mass will be in vain, and there will be no appropriation through the *sacramentum* of its *res*" (146). It is artificial to draw the whole of such education in lines leading to and from the altar. Since young people must first practice things like fidelity and self-discipline in themselves in order to appropriate them, what is needed most is an awakening to the mystery of God. There needs to be a point of insertion where the reality of God touches the young person, and this point will not always be the Mass (summary, 148).

Education for interior actualization. What is required is *personal participation* in the Mass. But this means more than singing and joining in the actions of the cult, which of themselves can never achieve the necessary interior disposition. Hence, all our educational efforts must be judged by whether they serve that interior actualization. Keeping kids from being bored is not enough. Efforts toward this goal may be good and important, but they are never enough. To be educated for Mass, young people must be educated for "the Mass outside the Mass," for the whole of Christianity. Education in the *sacramentum* must always be directed towards the *res sacramenti*.

Education in the Mass and an ascesis for youth. The essay now turns to "the quest for a Christianity and an ascesis specific to young people [ages 15-25], and to identifying correspondingly specific aspects of the celebration of the Mass" (150).

The phases of religious life. The fact that there are varying stages of personal/spiritual development means not everything in religion is appropriate for every stage of life: "not everything can be performed, genuinely and spontaneously, in every phase" (151). Rahner gives the example of the experience of the vulnerability and frailty of existence, which is generally lacking in healthy youths.

Co-ordination of phases with religious truths. To show how too little attention is given these developmental facts, Rahner points to cannon law where age is practically of no account, and to other practices (list, 152). But age not only affects religious practices, it also affects our relationship to truth. "There is also a closer or more distant existential relationship to the different truths at different ages" (153). Though this may seem a platitude, Rahner questions whether religious educators have reached a stage where they could even say which Christian truths, practices or devotions are appropriate to what ages. He uses as an example devotion to the Sacred Heart (154).

Youth and its understanding of the Mass. From this Rahner concludes it is wrong to introduce the young to the Mass "by the same door we ourselves enter into it" (155), or to burden them with a great dogmatic system. We should be content to sow seeds which may sprout in later life. He concludes this section with a series of specific questions for religious educators.

The "youthful" Christian. Rahner makes some general observations on the religious life of youth. The young are optimistic, more aware of possibilities than limitations. They are ethical and oriented toward the world of measurable achievement (hence their interest in sports). They are competitive. In short they are ready for active ascesis, "for a sort of athletic, ascetical self-discipline" (158). For them, God is the absolutely unambiguous guarantee that one's optimism will prevail. Of course young people also have their doubts, insecurities and disillusionments. They are still seeking themselves, and find strength and identity in their groups of friends. An existentially appropriate spirituality would see God as the mighty Lord and ultimate ground of life who sets us a task and gives us the strength to achieve it; Christ as close to us and loving us, in whose army we fight because He is the victor, our brother and comrade; Church as the community of visionaries, fellow fighters for a better world.

Youth in the Mass. Mass for youth would stress God's covenant, thanksgiving, the brotherly community, a meal of friendship with the victorious Lord, renewal of our pledge of fidelity. Highlighting particular aspects in no way negates other equally valid dimensions of Mass. No single approach can embrace everything all at once. But how to do this [in this pre-conciliar period]? Rahner makes numerous concrete suggestions about the choice of readings, the inclusion of commentaries, the forced nature of liturgical texts. He also discusses something he calls "Mass-devotions," vernacular insertions at various points in the Mass not simply to explain what is happening, but to aid deeper participation. In any case, these suggestions all spring from his conviction that *"the liturgy in its hitherto prevailing official form is not something unalterable, but that it can and must be completely adapted to the pastoral needs of modern humanity"* (163). Since change is slow he envisions pastoral agents continuing to "celebrate Mass in a form functioning outside the official liturgy, for the sake of the people and of the young" (164).

"Youthful" sacrifice. The point where instruction about Mass and the young Christian come together is active sacrifice, active ascesis. Though denial and renunciation for the sake of something greater is not exclusively Christian (nor is it the whole of Christian life) it is a preparation for what is to come. Moreover, it can be understood and embraced by youth. "Hence, this active readiness for sacrifice can and should be combined with education for the Mass" (165). But "sacrifice" must be made intelligible to the young so they do not dismiss it as "misanthropy and secret hatred of life felt by failures who are incapable of courageously enjoying life and this world and the glory of human existence" (167).

"One's own" life in the Mass. There's no reason not to go further and relate Mass to the concrete lives of other groups: to emphasize the Word to students of language; the covenant to lawyers; healing to physicians; God the Creator to artists, etc. Without falling into the extreme of relating everything on earth to something in the Mass, valid and valuable connections can be made. But for young people today, existentially deep participation in the Mass as celebrated in the church's official liturgy is highly problematic. "When we are educating people for the Mass, from life to Mass and from Mass to life, we cannot simply rely on the official liturgy" (170) not even if it is well explained and beautifully celebrated.

CCt.6. Developing Eucharistic Devotion. (171-204)

Abstract: Rahner defends the traditional practices of thanksgiving after Mass and visits to the reserved sacrament (along with spiritual communion) by pointing to their ability to intensify and prolong the subjective dimension of Eucharist, without which the sacramental *opus operatum* remains ineffective.

Topics: MASS, thanksgiving after; EUCHARIST, visits to; SACRAMENT/s.
Subsidiary discussions: Eucharist, real presence (179ff); Altar Devotion (194f); Eucharist, Spiritual Communion (195ff).

Precis: Thanksgiving after Mass. 1. The Mass properly celebrated is the highest form of thanksgiving, presupposing worshipers make as full use as possible of the opportunities the *opus operatum* contains within itself for offering their subjective thanksgiving for redemption in Christ.
2. Nevertheless, thanksgiving after Mass is still meaningful and commendable. The fact it cannot be imposed as a duty does not make it superfluous. It can be meaningful for several reasons: **a)** For many priests this is their only form of Eucharistic adoration. **b)** The Roman liturgy is somewhat severe. It does not give full scope to the expression of feelings and emotions, making subjective participation somewhat difficult. Creating a proper disposition within oneself through "recollection" takes time that is not afforded in the current rite. For this the liturgy must be supplemented. Historical practice in the West bears this out (174f). Of all the possible supplemental devotions, "thanksgiving" is certainly one of the most meaningful and obvious. In addition, since liturgy is meant for the sanctification of everyday life (cult is not meant to be a sealed off sacral realm) it is indispensable to create an intermediate zone where Christians can bring together liturgy in its hieratic objectivity and the harsh reality of daily life. (This zone would also provide a reasonable space for a priest's daily meditation). Summary, 177. Subjective participation in the richness of the liturgical action (list, 177f) should not suddenly break off at the conclusion of the Mass, but should realize its tendency to carry on and sweep forward to confront the facts of concrete life. This points to the proper content of such thanksgiving: a prolongation of that inner attitude and disposition which ought to have been actualized during Mass. The need for such thanksgiving is even clearer today when one leaves Mass only to enter a more fully secular sphere than existed in the past. **c)** Thanksgiving should not be based on taking maximum advantage of the duration Jesus' physical presence in us, as if that presence increased His effect within us *ex opere operato*. Rahner argues that insofar as Jesus is

present for us precisely *in bread as food,* He remains present in the sign as long as the bread itself remains edible bread. Jesus' abiding presence to which thanksgiving is directed is His *pneumatic* presence. In any case, the duration of one's thanksgiving should not be tied to notions of the duration of Christ's somatic presence in one's stomach. Yet none of these considerations eliminates the true ground of thanksgiving or radically reorients it. The effective grace of the sacrament remains dependent on ones' disposition, the existential depth of the living faith with which one eats the Bread of Life. (Can this be properly realized by one who runs out of church immediately after Mass?) Though one must not to use external behaviors to judge the state of another's faith, they can be helpful points for self-criticism. All attempts to use external factors (e.g., the time of the actual reception of communion) to set the proper length of one's subjective response in thanksgiving are misdirected. Optimally, the act of reception and the act of thanksgiving should meld into one act of unbroken worship.
3. When it comes to the proper duration of thanksgiving, personal intensity and depth are paramount. But time also matters. Rahner suggests Ignatius' personal norm: "until one is satisfied," thus leaving the matter open to personal experiment and discovery. A proper thanksgiving, one that leaves the worshiper ready to face the world bolstered by grace, is not an appendage to Mass but the completion of one's spiritual response to the sacramental Word of God, a response that belongs to the celebration itself. Given the importance of this element of liturgy we might consider whether the aid of the whole community might somehow be enlisted either near the end or after the conclusion of the liturgy itself.

"Visits." 1. Rahner suspects that today's anti-visit arguments are a cover supplied in retrospect by those who chaff at the demands of being called constantly to bring themselves into the presence of God in calm, quiet, silent abandonment, and of enduring the correction and purification of God's silence.
2. One cannot use arguments drawn from history (which clearly did include some excesses and aberrations) to contradict the clear teaching of Trent (186) concerning reserving, exposing, or in other ways honoring the Blessed Sacrament. Nor can the actions of the earliest centuries simply be taken as the standard for cur-

rent or future practice. Such an attitude fails to recognize both the one-way character of history and the progressive development of our understanding.

3. The meaning of "visits" cannot be drawn exclusively from notions concerning the real presence of Christ or from the sacrament's worthiness to be adored. The nub of the theological difficulty is this: what is Christ present *for*? The fact that Christ is present *for eating* must be the theological starting point. Here we and Protestants agree that the basic proposition of Eucharistic theology is "Take and *eat*, this is my body" which contains in itself the real presence of Christ. The difficulty is getting from this point to the practice of reservation, which even Trent only justifies as keeping the sacred species available for the sick to eat. Yet scripture is not completely silent. It refers to what is offered for eating as "body and blood," i.e., the whole of our Lord. What He gives to eat is *Himself*, the whole of Himself as food. Hence, adoration is legitimate, not of a thing, but of the person here present. This food does not lose its character due to an interval between its confection and consumption. As long as the bread is bread, we have Christ offering Himself to us as food to be eaten, something which would seem to call for adoration. Wherever Christ is present He points back to the sacramental event of sacrifice and forward to the event of our final appropriation of that event by reception of the sacrament.

A "visit" is nothing other than making ourselves present "before the sacramental sign of Jesus' sacrificial death for our salvation; it is a subjective prolongation of the Mass and a beginning of one's next communion" (193). Hence, everything said earlier about thanksgiving applies here. Adoration done in this spirit keeps this devotion from turning into a strange, problematical duplication of our adoration of the one omnipresent God and our actualization of the pneumatic self-communication of Christ which can be accomplished anywhere at any time. Those who make visits might also do well to recall that before them is the sacramental sign of the unity of the church. This may help keep these visits from becoming purely "private" in an unhealthy way.

4. This whole issue can be approached from another angle: "altar devotion," the even older practice of reverencing the site of the sacred action, the seat of the Godhead, which recalls for us the sacrifice

of Christ. But today, especially insofar as reservation takes place upon the altar, there would be little distinction between "altar devotion" and visits to the Blessed Sacrament, "tabernacle devotion."
5. This links "visits" and "spiritual communion." The unanimous teaching of tradition is that spiritual communion "is in very truth personal, actualized communication, in faith and love, with the Lord in his *pneuma*" (196), in which one receives the *fructus* and *utilitas* of the sacrament. Spiritual communion is no less "real" than are perfect contrition or baptism by desire. What happens in spiritual communion "is a conscious affirmation, in a personal act of faith, in love, and with reference to sacramental communion, of that real pneumatic unity with Christ which is given by the sanctifying grace of the Holy Ghost; one's acceptance of it in the personal center of oneself is renewed, and thus its ontological reality is increased and deepened" (196). It needs no explicit reference to previous or future physical communion. The determining factor is our belief and loving acceptance of our union with Christ by grace. When better to achieve this than during a visit before the reserved sacrament? Summary, 198f.
6. The same point made in number 4 above concerning "altar devotion" transfers equally to visits to churches, even those in which the sacrament is not reserved, since these spaces, too, recall to mind Christ's saving work for the holy people of God represented by that building.

CCt.7. The Mass and Television. (205-218). From *Apparatur und Glaube, Überlegungen zur Fernübertuagtng der heiligen Messe*. Würtzburg: Werkbund-Verlag, n.d.

Abstract: Rahner's argument against the legitimacy of televising Mass is based on the existence of a "zone of intimacy" enjoyed by all free spiritual beings, to which they control access. Indiscriminate broadcasting denies this "metaphysical modesty." It also abandons the church's long tradition of *disciplina archani*.

Topics: DISCIPLINA ARCANI; EVERYDAY LIFE, privacy; MASS, broadcast of.

Precis: "Does the television camera have in principle, from the outset, the same rights as the eyes of a believing Christian?" (206). This must be answered theologically, not by appeals to good taste.

Preliminary. Rahner answers emphatically, "No." His argument begins by recalling two points of logic. Some argue that broadcasting Mass will have an apologetic value on unbelievers "peeping through the keyhole." But this allure will fade once broadcasting is allowed. The logical point here is that what may happen *per accidens* does not justify its existing in principle, "*in se.*" The second argument is metaphysical: quite unassimilable essential difference can exist between things even where there is an apparent continuity of transition between these radically different entities. Next come the positive proofs.

First thesis. There are things that can only be shown if the person showing them permanently retains free consent or refusal, and which can rightly be seen only within this sphere by anyone else when s/he personally participates and cooperates in the event being shown, not when there is only the naked curiosity of the mere spectator (208). If this is true, then certain events must never be televised (especially since the seeing by television is a real seeing). It belongs to the essence of the spiritual person as a free, self-possessed individual to enjoy an "intimate zone" into which others enter only with permission. This admission needs to be answered by an equivalent response of participation. The more personal a thing is, the more it will lie within the zone of personal intimacy, and thus be the object of a spiritual sense of modesty. Since such acts as personal love, the adoration of God, etc., are at a person's core, they are essentially reserved and limited from view. They demand for themselves a kind of *disciplina archani*, which extends from these personal acts to their enactment by the group.

Second thesis. Holy Mass is the highest degree of those intimate acts described above– a matter for that metaphysical modesty which protects the personal center and its object from mere curiosity. This can especially be seen from the fact that even those performing the ritual only have the right to do so if they themselves have the proper inner disposition. The same conclusion is arrived at by considering the object itself, since televising the *cultus* would be a complete denial of the *disciplina archani*. Here Rahner goes into an historical excursus on the concept, ending with a summary (212). To the objection that in the Incarnation Jesus condescended to let Himself be seen indiscriminately by all, Rahner replies we must not simply arrogate to ourselves what our Lord chose to do in His divine freedom. Secondly, it should be remembered that after His resurrection Jesus was particular about those to whom He chose to reveal Himself. Excluding some participation in cult is not a judgment about the state of grace of those excluded.

The microphone and the television camera. One cannot argue that because microphones are brought into the liturgy cameras should also be permitted. Hearing is not seeing. Being allowed to hear about an event is not the same as being allowed to see it. Rahner compares the way a sound broadcast reports an event to the way books (which are surely permitted) describe events. Still, it is not permissible to broadcast everything that is audible. [At this time the words of the Eucharistic Prayer were recited in a way that kept them inaudible even to the congregation.]

Conclusion. Televising Mass indiscriminately to everyone, "offends against the commandment that our most intimate personal acts, and that which is holy, are to be made accessible to another only in the measure to which he is able and willing to participate in them with a personal response; while he who is showing these acts and this holy thing must retain throughout free control over the whole showing of them" (215). By way of further objections, Rahner states that if the Mass were broadcast then even otherwise intelligent people would have to be instructed on how to view such holy events, to keep the broadcast from degenerating into mere exoticism. Arguing for the legitimacy of broadcasting from the fact that it would be advantageous to the sick and homebound is also absurd since one must first prove the legitimacy of broadcasting before extolling its merits. Finally, one should beware of the rush to be too modern, since everything old is new again.

CMP. *Christian in the Market Place.* NY: Sheed and Ward, 1966. Appendix; Notes on Sources. 184 pp. *Sendung und Gnade III*, 1959. In England, *Mission and Grace III*. Translated by Cecily Hastings.

Contents: 1. Paul, Apostle for Today.
2. Railway Missions.
3. Parish and Place of Work.
4. The Prison Pastorate.
5. The Parish Bookshop: On the Theology of Books.
6. The Theological Meaning of Devotion to the Sacred Heart.

7. Ignatian Spirituality and Devotion to the Sacred Heart.
8. First Mass.
Appendix: A Basic Ignatian Concept: Notes on Obedience.
Notes on Sources.

CMP.1. Paul, Apostle for Today. (3-18). July 24, 1958 paper to *Paulus-Gesellschaft*, Frankfurt am Main.
Abstract: Defends and develops two theses: all Christians are apostles; every situation is potentially an apostolate.
Topics: APOSTOLATE; LAITY, apostolate of.
Subsidiary discussions: God, universal salvific will of (6ff); God, experience of (8ff).

Precis: Every Christian an apostle. Speaking to the *Paulus-Gesellschaft*, Rahner maintains that one is an apostle to the degree s/he is a Christian. It is not easy to link this idea directly to St. Paul. Neither he nor his communities used the word "apostolate" as they went about fulfilling their "mission." But despite opposition and failures they never lost courage. Many Christians today are discouraged at the opposition they encounter. For some reason they assume Christianity ought to be completely obvious in today's world; that whoever encounters it should automatically convert. We should see things as St. Paul did: that Christianity is a sheer miracle of grace, the precise opposite of obvious or natural. *Three Difficulties.* 20th Century believers cannot simply adopt the mind of St. Paul. Many subsequent developments in the church have strongly limited the apostolic impulse within us. 1) People today cannot be so pessimistic about the salvation of non-Christians; 2) We experience a greater gulf today between ourselves and God; 3) Today believers themselves present one of the greatest obstacles to belief. We often fail to assume our responsibility for the salvation of our neighbors. *Meeting Each of the Three Difficulties.* The fact that my neighbor has the possibility of salvation without me does not absolve me from my responsibility to engage in apostolic activity. Quite possibly God's plan for my neighbor includes my apostolic intervention. As regards the second difficulty, Rahner insists we must preach a visible Christianity. It is up to each of us to make his/her faith as clear and realistic as possible. Here the laity will often have to call theologians to task. About our own sinfulness, each must strive to become a better Christian, and hence a better apostle.

Every situation an apostolate. Every concrete situation in which lay people find themselves (job, marriage, family, society) has to be seen as a positive opportunity for their own Christian life and their witness to it. God is always present. The question is whether we are handling these concrete situations properly. Rahner is not talking here about engaging in some kind of surefire "technique" for mass conversions. Gains will be slow, maybe imperceptible. But we make it easier by beginning where we are. The given situation possesses everything required for God to shine forth (summary, application, 18).

CMP.2. Railway Missions. (19-40). April 25, 1955 paper to a conference of societies for the protection of young girls. *Aus unseres Arbeit,* 3, Freiburg (1955) 1-13.

Abstract: an attempt to set in a wider context the aims and work of this particular apostolic effort to aid vulnerable young women, roots it in the sacrificial love Christians share with the pierced heart of Christ.

Topics: APOSTOLATE, railway.

Subsidiary discussions: Society, contemporary situation (20ff); Theological Anthropology, task of man (26ff); *Caritas* (31f); Evangelization (38f).

Precis: At this 60th jubilee celebration, Rahner feels inadequate to offer practical advice or to properly recount the history of the assembled organizations. But he can comment on the origins of this apostolate insofar as it is rooted in God, who unites its past, present and future.

The new historical situation. As free human beings we must consult the past to create our future. Our modern age has been given many names (list, 21). Whatever their truth, today's situation is different from all past ages in one particular: in the past nature both constrained and protected us. But today, with our capacity to plan and our technology to transform nature, we have simultaneously freed ourselves from nature and delivered ourselves defenseless into our own hands. Only God can now protect us from ourselves (summary, 26). Today we must be our own guardian angels.

The unchanging task devolving upon the church and the Christian. Despite this radically altered social situation, people still have the same essential task: to become themselves. "That is the task, ever old and ever new: man himself, the Christian, in his eternal destiny, which is always one and the same: the living, eternal God, who has given Himself to us in Jesus Christ our Lord, in his Spirit, and His one Church" (30).

The new service. What has all this to do with this jubilee celebration? Only by brining together the old task and the new situation will we be able to chart a true course to the future. The task of this organization is the task of Christ and of the church: in protecting even one young girl it sees the whole human being who belongs to God. Such love is the basis of *caritas*, and as such is always religious (31f). This organization must never detach itself from its religious source and goal. But as has been said, this old task encounters a new situation. Today this organization must supply in part the lost controls of nature– protecting us from ourselves. The railway station itself is a symbol of this new age, of technology, freedom, mobility, and rootlessness. The railway station has replaced the spire as the locus of Christian existence. The continuing necessity for such an organization is underscored by the fact that today we are all somehow pilgrims in transit. It should also be the aim of this organization to recreate many of the "natural ties" that can no longer be taken for granted today. By its nature, such work is one-on-one, always an exercise in hope, always beginning anew. It is difficult to build it institutionally.

The church is not an end in itself. It exists to serve real people in their actual situations (38). Christianity is a religion of self-forgetful love. "... the more we can convince a person, in deed and in truth, that we are serving him because we love him in God and are seeking for nothing besides, the more we shall convince him of Christ, of God's grace and love in the community of those who love, which is the Church" (38). This is not some modern theory. It is the truth of the gospel. "There would be no use in having the churches open if the railway missions were closed. The gateway into the Church is the pierced heart of the Lord, and of those who share in his destiny and sacrificial love" (38f). This is the spirit in which this organization must continue to perform its apostolate (summary, 39f).

CMP.3. Parish and Place of Work. (41-60). 1953 paper to a conference of *Betriebsmännerwerke* in Düsseldorf; *Seelsorge und Betrieb*, Cologne (1953). Published in *Stimmen der Zeit* 153 (1954) 401-12; *Anima* 10 (1955) 180-188.

Abstract: Assesses limitations of the Parochial Principle and argues for the legitimacy of the Place-of-Work Principle as a criterion to organize pastoral activity based on historical and other considerations.

Topics: PAROCHIAL PRINCIPLE; PASTORAL ACTIVITY, organization of.

Subsidiary discussions: Work (55ff); Force (57f).

Precis: Changes in how we live and work today indicate that the church should abandon its completely one-sided way of allocating its efforts in caring for local communities (i.e., parishes). One alternative is the *Betriebsmännerwerke*, a workplace apostolic group to whom this talk is addressed. Clearly, the gospel is addressed to all people. But because people are fundamentally social, the further question is, "*Which* community, *which* social pattern, is the one in which the Christian message comes seeking for men?" (43). "*Where* does the message seek out human beings for their redemption?" (44).

Historical observations. The missionary work of the Apostolic Age was in the highest degree flexible, making use of every conceivable point of contact to spread the good news. Such outreach presupposed and used the existing social structures so long as they offered access to individuals. The genius of St. Paul was his recognition of other sociological bases beyond the synagogue to reach Gentiles. Later, after widespread Christianization, the local community did become the chief organizing principle for apostolic activity. But this territorial principle of organization has never been exclusive (examples, 46f). "[B]esides the territorial basis there have always been other sociological facts forming the natural foundation for Christian communities, for a 'church' and its apostolate" (47). Cannon law itself is open to the resultant "federal principle" in pastoral and apostolic work.

Considerations of principle. There is nothing supernatural about territory-based parishes or dioceses. They exist because the church addresses itself to localized human beings. Any social factor can be a natural point of entry for the church's missionary activity and a natural basis for Christian community and for the apostolic activity of individual Christians, since people belong simultaneously to many social organizations. The assumption that the neighborhood community is the most religiously significant of these (hence that the local parish is the best organizing principle) is simply false.

The working community as an object of pastoral care. If follows that the work community can be in principle the natural basis of a church community in a threefold sense: as an object of missionary activity of priests, as an altar community, and as a field for lay apostolate. An argument follows to establish the *natural basis* of such a work community, which in turn legitimates its religious participation in the church as a whole. Rahner adds two further considerations: **1.** In neighborhood parishes the residential community no longer coincides with the work community. Parishes today are less like villages and more like police precincts. This leaves the church with two choices: ignore this reality and keep pumping up territorial parishes hoping God will supply what society lacks, or reach out to the new sociological realities found in work communities. **2.** This is not an attempt to justify this state of affairs. It simply states that the workplace is increasingly assuming the functions of a community, and it will continue to do so. After a 2-point summary (52) Rahner defines the "Place-of-Work Principle" and underscores the legitimacy of such free associations which do not owe their existence to the hierarchy.

Limits of the "Place-to-Work Principle." This principle has three limitations. **1.** It cannot be seen as replacing the parish, nor is it in competition with it. Objectivity and public spirit among the various pastoral ministers (parish priests, chaplains, religious) and lay apostolates are required for the proper and peaceful functioning of the church. There is enough work to go around. **2.** The human significance of particular workplaces is variable, fluid, and a matter of dispute. In addition, the motives for industry to support such all-inclusive community-like forms may simply be to prevent falling production. But Catholic social principles insist that work is for God, not religion for work. Chaplains in the work place must work to advance the goals of humanization not merely of production. **3.** Catholic associations in the workplace, such as *Betriebsmännerwerke*, must have a specifically Christian objective. Although it is the responsibility of Christian workers to participate in economic, socio-political or otherwise secular goals, these cannot be the direct concern of a Catholic association. Nor, despite the beneficial fellow-feelings such associations may inspire, can the association have for its purpose the furtherance of romantic paternalism. Workers retain their right to use justifiable force [strikes] to further their legitimate demands for change in the workplace. (Notes, 58ff, include bibliography.)

CMP.4. The Prison Pastorate. (60-79). June 23, 1959 paper to prison chaplains in Innsbruck. *Der Seelsorger*, 29 (1959) 460-469.

Abstract: Chaplains must strive to see Christ in prisoners by approaching them with reverent humility, not running from the abyss opening before them. They see their own sinfulness reflected back to them by not running from the truth of themselves. This is their path to holiness.

Topics: APOSTOLATE, prison; LOVE OF GOD AND NEIGHBOR; PASTORAL MINISTRY, holiness in.

Subsidiary discussions: Love, *agape* (65ff); Humility, reverent (68ff); Incarnation (69f); God, experience of (70ff); Freedom (73ff); Everyday Life, routine (78f).

Precis: The focus of such a day must be how a prison minister can find God. Selfless service does not automatically fill us with love of God and neighbor. Distracted as we are, we must work on our nearness to God if we are to be able to serve our neighbor, and we draw near to God by serving our neighbor. Each depends on the other, but the two are not the same thing (preview, 62). We must find Christ in the prisoners entrusted to us, and in them we also encounter what we conceal about ourselves.

Christ in the prisoners. Christ is to be found in prisoners in such a way that our encounter with them will also be for our salvation and happiness. Daily close encounter with evil and bitter experience challenges the way prison chaplains understand Matthew (25: 34-40). Our first reaction is to rejoice, since scripture addresses few vocations so directly. But the next response is terror that we are being charged to find Our Lord in these prisoners. Daily realities would have us interpret Jesus' command to act toward prisoners *as if* we were dealing with Christ. But "Jesus rejects all our realism as unreal" (65). In identifying Himself with prisoners, Jesus is not announcing a legal fiction. He is manifesting God's love: *agape*. We must think about this truth, and accept it in faith against our own "experience," that the Lord has chosen these lost individuals we meet in prisons; "that he is in them by his will to love, which calls nothingness and that which is lost by its name and creates it" (66). But even once we think this is true, how do we find Jesus in them? In this time of faith, this will only occur in a hidden way. It is not easy.

"What does it mean to find Christ Himself in his brothers in prison? First and foremost, it means a reverent humility in face of this other human being" (68). Trusting God's universally salvific will, we hope for God's merciful grace for us, and have the same duty of hope on behalf of all our neighbors. Although we may know this, with prisoners so much stands in the way. Yet we must see through it to seek and find that which is most real and ultimate in this other person: God with His love and His mercy. This way of seeing and meeting is reverent humility, in which we realize that our highest dignity is no loftier or holier than what is present in him. To see him like this is to see Christ in him. This is the practical dimension of Incarnation. There is a second sense of finding God in our humiliated brother. Precisely in his vacant stare, his cold reception, his ingratitude or ridicule, God is there. This hopeless experience will be the abyss of God Himself, communicating Himself to us, which feels like nothingness because it is infinity. Gradually learning to find God in this forsakenness does not thereby change our neighbor into a means to an end. For none of this happens unless we truly love and accept the person. We really die of this love. But to die without despair we must die into the infinite life of God (summary, 73).

Ourselves in the prisoners. We find ourselves in prisoners when we see in them the hidden truth of our own situation, something we constantly flee: the truth that we are sinners and are unfree unless the Spirit of God sets us free. The prisoners we visit are an image of our own unfreedom. The prison in which we work is an image of our unredeemed world. We can claim to have been redeemed, but we only possess this status in faith and hope. Even the redeemed bear the heritage of past sin, of concupiscence, lust

and pride. "Should we not then recognize and acknowledge that we are not so essentially different from the poor sinners we visit in prison?" (77). We must take care that our attitude upon encountering them is not that of the proud Pharisee but of the humble Publican (Lk 18: 9-14).
The deadly enemy in every life is routine. It blunts the heart and often keeps us going long after the fire of love has been extinguished. Routine gives us a good conscience when in fact we should not have one. Hence, we must fight against such deadly routine. Precisely when we endure our hard and bitter experiences, God's grace is at work in us. These moments force us out of our mediocrity and habit; they force us to ask again what we are doing in a job like this. Meditating on these hard experience can bear fruit in us: the fruit of encounter with Christ in these prisoners, and encounter with our sinful selves as well. It may increase humility within us and narrow the gap between the high priestly office we hold and our own personal holiness.

CMP.5. The Parish Bookshop: On the Theology of Books. (81-103). "Theology of Books," March 16, 1959 paper to a conference of the book apostolate in Cologne. *Kölner Pastoralblatt,* 11 (1959), 144-8, 205-11, 229-31.

Abstract: Praises the Borromeo Society's work in promoting books, religious and secular. Rahner ties the value of books to their relationship to the Bible and to the role they play in personal becoming in terms of theological anthropology. He argues that even a seemingly completely secular book can be religious.

Topics: APOSTOLATE, books.

Subsidiary discussions: Bible as a book (82ff); Incarnation (83f); Preaching (88ff); Theological Anthropology (90ff); Grace and nature (96ff).

Precis: Valuable as books are, one must not see promoting them as the single most important apostolate for building up the church. Yet they are significant and meaningful in the work of salvation. One obvious point of departure for this talk about books is Holy Scripture. Upon reflection it should really be *shocking* that a *book* holds such a place in the history of God's self-revelation. Obviously, for long ages of human history there were no books.

Hence, salvation is not essentially dependent on them. But the consecration of the book was only a final preparation for the incarnation of the Divine Word. God has willed that it is now no longer possible to encounter God's Word apart from the book. This is the source of the dignity of all books. To say the church will always exist is to say at the same time that the book will also exist.

Transmission of the Bible, reading, disseminating, explaining and defending it are an essential part of the church, *jure divino*. All subsequent "religious writing" is in the service of this Book and thus participates in its dignity, indispensability, and permanent validity. This is true even of books with no claim to being divinely inspired. This is especially true in the Catholic tradition that upholds the necessity of interpreting and actualizing scripture afresh, to the degree that even theologizing about scripture can come to be considered a definitively valid utterance making an absolute claim on faith [e.g., Patristics]. By extension the work of this Borromeo Society is essentially part of the service of The Book. After some comments on the relation of books to authorized preaching and the need for imprimaturs (88f), Rahner argues that even the promotion of non-liturgical books meant for private, solitary readers can and does promote the Word of God and hence shares in its dignity. For the Spirit also addresses us as individuals.

The theological meaning of books can be approached from the angle of theological anthropology. Human fulfillment has a dual movement: one must both go out and return to oneself. No one does this all at once, but in a rhythm alternating between solitude and society, silence and speech, work and leisure. No one pole can be absolutized, and there are many ways of actualizing these alternating moments of scattering and gathering. To withdraw into oneself without fear, one must take along something of the world. The book is such a point of leverage outside of oneself, providing "this concentrated, muted, manageable presence of the world in the solitude in which man enters himself" (94), not technical books, which are a mere extension of the world, but humane literature which leads one to his/her inner world. Such books as these are furnished by the Borromeo Society. Here two things should be considered: these books are clearly about the human world and are not strictly religious, though they may have religious significance. Secondly, the Catholic teaching on nature and grace disallows any strict separation of sacred and secular in art or in literature. There is no one path to achieving Christian perfection. In fact the "secular world" (the anonymously Christian world, 97) is precisely the arena where salvation is achieved. Hence, whatever mediates a genuinely humane understanding of life and of the world is mediating the indispensable prerequisites of Christianity. Hence, those who promote humane literature (even if it is not Christian in the strict sense) are performing a valuable apostolate (*praeparatio Evangelii*). Rahner concludes with some remarks about the mid-century state of publishing in German, the rise of mass markets and the industrialization of publishing (100ff). Although these developments do present dangers and difficulties, he applauds societies such as this which struggle so God's word will continue to be heard.

CMP.6. The Theological Meaning of Devotion to the Sacred Heart. (105-118). Cf., TI 08.11. June 12, 1953 talk, Canisius College, Innsbruck. Published in college newsletter no. 88 (1953) 1-10.

Abstract: The "Sacred Heart" is a key religious term which has the power to unite the diverse facets of Jesus Christ and the many dimensions of people today who can only find the existential unity they crave by possessing Him.

Topics: GOD-TALK; JESUS CHRIST, Sacred Heart of.

Subsidiary discussions: Metaphysics, one/many (217f); Incarnation (218f); Dogma, development of (219f); Heart (222ff); Mystery (224ff); Word, primordial (224ff); Transcendence (227f); Knowledge (227f).

CMP.7. Ignatian Spirituality and Devotion to the Sacred Heart. (119-146). June 1955 talk, Canisius College, Innsbruck. Published in college newsletter no. 90 (1955-56) 5-17.

Abstract: The three central elements of Ignatian spirituality (that it is indifferent, existential, and ecclesial) harbor dangers which find their corrective in devotion to the Sacred Heart. Hence, Ignatian spirituality and devotion to the Sacred Heart form an essential unity to be seriously examined and appropriated.

Topics: LOVE, dynamics of; SACRED HEART, Devotion to; SPIRITUALITY, Ignatian.
Subsidiary discussions: Indifference, religious (123ff, 131f); Vocation (141ff).

Precis: Characteristics of Ignatian spirituality. *I. Preliminaries.* 1. It is difficult for any religious order to retain its charism over time, and each member only manifests this charism to a greater or lesser degree. Rahner asks that this time for meditation be directed inward and not be used to judge the lived spirituality of other Jesuits. 2. No charism in the church is completely unique to any particular order. The whole variety of spiritualities makes sense only in the context of the church. 3. Today there is a certain leveling of the charisms of the various orders. One must accept the benefits of this development and resist its dangers. 4. We must accept as providential the various spiritual impulses that enter our lives. As part of our destiny, we must work to master them and build upon them in a way conducive to our own character and temperament. *II. The essential features of Ignatian spirituality.* Regardless of whether each of these characteristics is always manifested by every particular Jesuit, Rahner lists three: 1. Indifferent: a refined sense of the relativity of all that is not God, and the conviction that God is always greater. 2. Existential: sums up the practical ramifications of indifference. It is that detachment which makes an individual always open to God, however God may reveal Himself in emptiness or fullness. Such a person is "Jesuitical:" a skeptical, disillusioned, here-and-now, calculating, planner. 3. Ecclesial: Ignatian love of the church is not naive. One loves the unambiguously visible church despite its weaknesses and failings, loving whatever finite thing God has willed, knowing all the while it is not God.

Devotion to the Sacred Heart as the interior counterbalance to Ignatian spirituality. What is special in any charism is not the whole story. In fact what is special is sometimes very dangerous in its chemically pure state. Strange as it may sound, one must often work to develop offsetting virtues to counterbalance otherwise unrestrained and therefore destructive elements of a charism. Indifference can be perverted to pure functionalism; existentialism can lead to heartlessness, and love of the church can lead to glorifying the church as an end in itself (129f). "Devotion to the Sacred Heart of Jesus is the requisite antitoxin, produced out of Ignatian spirituality itself, to these dangers inherent in it" (130). In the three subsections that follow, Rahner treats in turn indifference, existentialism, and love of the church, how they can be corrupted, and how "love," is the antidote. "But the ultimate source of love is the Heart of the Lord. Hence, Ignatian spirituality can only be healthy if it loves that Heart and loves in union with it. Otherwise all that is most sublime in it becomes most deadly" (137).

Ignatian spirituality as a true flowering of devotion to the Sacred Heart. Since any effective antidote must be genuinely related to whatever it counteracts, devotions to the Sacred Heart and Ignatian spirituality must be intrinsically related. The Sacred Heart is at once the source and safeguard of the three characteristics associated with Ignatian Spirituality. In the next 3 subsections, Rahner turns his attention to why and how the divine-human love venerated in the Sacred Heart functions this way with regard to indifference, existentialism, and love of the church. In each discussion the move is the same. Rahner shows how each of the three is a product, an intrinsic moment of love. Only when it is lived radically to its end does it avoid its attendant dangers. We who are animated by the blessing of having the Spirit of love flowing from the pierced Heart of Christ "shall understand how, in the death of indifference, we die in order to live; how we attain to our own lonely uniqueness only that we may, in love, discover the other person and serve him; and how we love the Church in order to love all men" (146).

CMP.8. First Mass. (147-154). October 11, 1955 address, German College, Rome. Published in college newsletter no. 63 (1956) 26-31; *Salzburger Klerusblatt*, 88 (1955) 221f.

Abstract: At this First Mass, Rahner offers a word of encouragement to the newly-ordained and a word of blessing and advice to their families. Together they offer to God the sacramental Word of limitless grace.

Topics: PRIESTHOOD; SERMON, First Mass.

Precis: Though earthly words only faintly echo the Divine sacramental Word spoken these past days, still it is important to use them to reflect more deeply on what God has done and will do. Rahner joyfully extols these newly-ordained and invokes the Spirit upon them. He urges them to be true servants, to stand fast, not to grow complacent in luxury, not to hold onto the past through laziness nor to jettison it out of impatience, humbly to admit the limits of their competence and to share their struggles with faith in a way that edifies the faithful. They should support their brother priests and take initiative especially in their work with separated brethren and with the poor. Continue to study! Don't be content to minister to the choir, but reach out to convert people of the present and future. Above all, strive for love! Upon the parents and families he invokes a blessing: that God may reward them for letting their sons and brothers follow this path. He reminds them how important it is to continue supporting these new priests with their encouragement, comfort, and advice. To God the final word of thanks will be said at the altar, the focus of the newly-ordained's future life.

CMP.9. Appendix: A Basic Ignatian Concept: Notes on Obedience.

(157-181). "*Eine ignatianische Grunghaltung*" in *Stimmen der Zeit* 158 (1956) 253-267. Translated by Joseph P. Vetz in *Woodstock Letters*, 86, no. 4 (1957) 291-310.

Abstract: After addressing 3 misconceptions, Rahner argues that true obedience must be approached not from particular commands but from its ground. It is one element in a particular way of life, sanctioned by the church and dedicated to bringing about the Kingdom of God, which makes God's grace visible.

Topics: OBEDIENCE, religious; RELIGIOUS LIFE.

Subsidiary discussions: Surrender (179ff).

Precis: Essentially, Jesuit obedience does not differ from the obedience found in other religious orders of the church. The comments that follow do not claim to be original or complete. **Various misconceptions.** Rahner offers three considerations to preserve religious obedience from misconceptions and excesses. 1. Religious obedience is adult obedience. It is not the obedience of children to parents or students to teachers, which is merely provisional.

Since religious superiors are not by nature or by office more intelligent, moral or wise than those they govern, they should make no such claims, and let wither any customs which reinforce these attitudes. Because no superior today is omni-competent, s/he must rely on consultors more than in the past for objective information. This in itself is not a democratization of obedience. 2. Religious obedience is not mere "observance of traffic laws" (161): rational prescriptions for the smooth running of any social organization. Although this too is a necessary part of religious life, it is neither the central nor the most profound element of religious obedience. In the effort to demystify religious obedience, religious superiors should make clear when a directive is merely such a "traffic law," the tedious kind that is part and parcel of social life. 3. Not all initiative in religious life should come from the superior. Legitimate authority has no right to monopolize all effort and personal decision, nor does it have the duty to approve every initiative before it is enacted. Relations within a community should run on the principle of subsidiarity. The aim of religious obedience is not to make passive subjects. Each member has a right and a duty to suggest good alternatives, and superiors have the duty to elicit and implement them. It would be pure hubris for a superior to strive for absolute authority which only God can command. Even the superior is part of a developmental process, all the details of which are known only to God. So he too must be an obedient listener. There are many forces at work, including the power of the subjects who must not abdicate their role in the process nor the burden of personal responsibility. When each part is co-responsible the orders received are a synthesis.

True obedience. What makes religious obedience difficult to define is pinpointing the intersection of the thing commanded and God's will. For legitimate commands can be objectively wrong, and there is no moral value in pure subjection of the will to another who is not God. There is the further problem of the subject not knowing how a superior has received the commission to be the expositor of God's will. At least celibate chastity and religious poverty have clear warrant in scripture and church history as part of the imitation of Christ. Granted, Jesus and the apostles were obedient. But they were obedient to God and not to mere human authorities

(169f). Rahner sums up by asking whether in fact religious obedience is a concrete prolongation of obedience to the will of God. According to Rahner, the legitimacy and meaning of obedience, along with the other evangelical counsels is grounded in freely and permanently binding oneself to a definite church-sanctioned mode of life, renouncing the world's most precious goods for the sake of building up the Kingdom of God (171f). Obedience to particular commands in the context of a particular mode of life makes visible and historically tangible the essence of the church as the manifestation of God's other-worldly grace beyond the reach of earthly merit, to be accepted by faith alone, despite all human impotence. Rahner insists there is no sense to canonize an abstract notion of obedience as the doing of another's will. Such obedience is owed only to God. Nor do we obey for the sake of obeying, nor to make of our wills a "holocaust." Only his own approach explains why religious obedience is specifically religious, and why it is approved and sanctioned by the church. It undergirds the moral goodness of specific commands that are morally neutral in themselves, and makes clear the context of the higher good, only in reference to which any vow can be made. This being said, Rahner offers a concise definition of religious obedience (definition, 174).

Rahner maintains that those who attack this notion are in fact attacking the church. He shows how religious obedience is a legitimate imitation of Christ (175f) who embraced the risks of an unforeseeable destiny in the hope of bringing about the Kingdom fo God. Nor can one protest that the irrationality of a mistaken command frees the subject from his contract. This is because religious obedience is a share in Christ's mission, which was itself subject to such seemingly irrational demands. This leads to a discussion of the relation between obedience to commands and personal morality. Rahner warns, "The just 'presumption' that the command of a superior will be morally unobjectionable not only subjectively but also objectively does not constitute a simple dispensation from the essential obligation of every man to attain moral certitude as to whether a free action is morally licit before it is undertaken" (178f). Just because an act is commanded does not make it any less one's own, an action for which one remains responsible. Rahner concludes with a meditation on the anxieties of later life with regard to obedience in particular, but also in regard to the whole question of what if any selfless actions one may ever have undertaken in life. His advice is to stop concentrating on our ambiguous acts of obedience and to look rather at the Reality we serve– the one Person who alone is worthy of all our love and service. "Perhaps the truly obedient man is simply the lover, for whom the sacrifice of self-surrender is sweet, a blessed delight. Perhaps we should not talk so much about obedience, for it is already threatened when we praise or defend it" (181). For all religious life grounded in obedience is merely a rehearsal for our total surrender to God in death– our participation in the death of Christ and the life concealed in Him.

CF. *The Christian of the Future.* NY: Herder, 1967. *Questiones Disputatae* Series #18. 104 pp.

These four essays appeared in *Schriften zur Theologie VI.* Einsiedeln: Benziger, 1965, but not in the English edition. They are translated here by W.J. O'Hara.

Contents: Preface: gives a brief description of each essay and Rahner's reason for writing each.

The Changing Church.

Situation Ethics in an Ecumenical Perspective.

The Church's Limits: Against Clerical Triumphalists and Lay Defeatists.

The Teaching of Vatican II on the Church and the Future Reality of Christian Life.

Notes (on sources incorporated here with each essay).

CF.1. The Changing Church. (9-38). "*Kirche im Wandel*" 7 January, 1965 lecture in Cologne, in *Stimmen der Zeit* 90 (1964/65) 437-454.

Abstract. These thoughts on the limits of change in the law of the Catholic Church warn against heedless progressivism while arousing courage to discover new ways forward for the church.

Topics. CHURCH, un/changeable elements; DOCTRINE, development of; LAW, divine/positive; VATICAN II.

Subsidiary Discussions. Canon Law, mutability of (12ff); Theology, Moral (26ff); Church, dissent within (30f); Theology, pluralism in (34f); Priesthood, need for courage (37f).

Precis. The way Vatican II disturbed many "conservative" Catholics calls for a review of the changeable and unchangeable elements in the church. Obviously, this discussion presupposes the valid distinction between divine law and positive law.

Changes in the law of the church. What can be said of the im/mutability of cannon law (abstaining from meat, marriage law, cremation, etc.) is clear in principle: divine law cannot be changed, positive law can be. But in practice it is difficult to discern which is which. This principle has always been known by the church, but at times laws have been promulgated as if all were divine. When people mix the divine authority of the church to make positive law equivalent to divine law itself, the resultant change brings confusion. Despite disillusionment, adaptation remains necessary. Although some such changes must be made by central authority, their unforeseen consequences may be very different in the cultures into which they are introduced. Timing is a great factor. In these days of transition people legitimately differ in their assessment of whether the church is moving too fast or too slowly. This gives rise to nostalgia in some. But those who understand the mutable nature of positive law interpret these stresses and strains as a sign of the church's vitality (summary, 21).

The mutable element in the doctrine of faith. The magisterium has the duty and authority to declare dogma as absolutely binding without regard to the history of its development. Once established such dogma cannot be revoked, even if it remains unclear how the new dogma is related to others. Old dogmas can be restated in new ways with surprising benefits. The problem today is not so much these defined dogmas (Immaculate Conception, papal infallibility, etc.) as it is the other doctrines and positions of moral theology taught authoritatively but which cannot be considered as defined or irreformable.

Non-defined doctrines taught authoritatively are necessary, given the mysterious nature of the ways in which God interacts with us over time. In fact dogma relies on such non-defined doctrine to be at all intelligible. These magisterial teachings deserve respect and the appropriate degree of internal assent. This is especially true in the realm of moral theology (examples, 28). The church must find answers for the faithful, and often these answers are highly one-sided, conditioned as they are by the historical situation in which they were formulated (examples, 28f). Clearly, in this process the pilgrim church can and does make mistakes. Yet even the mutable and potentially erroneous can be binding insofar as the church offers it as the safest path forward at present. Progress in revising one-sided teachings often comes from discerning individuals, and the church recognizes their right to engage in such speculation when properly conducted. Nevertheless, distinguishing dogma from doctrine remains difficult.

Development in the direction of leaving matters open and encouraging people to decide many issues for themselves is justified by the complexity of life today. This openness refers not only to concrete situations (examples, 33) but extends also to theological statements and to theological language itself. Hence, future theology will of necessity be more pluralistic and "de-controlled," a switch from official church regulation of the individual and his/her conscience.

Courage to change. The church is a living, changing reality. "Whatever the changes, however, one thing endures; the nature of the Church as the presence in social form of God's grace *in Christo*, in doctrine, worship and life" (35). Since healthy change is threatened more by fear of change than by greater involvement with the world, what is needed by each Christian in this situation is the courage to change. This is especially true of priests.

CF.2. Situation Ethics in an Ecumenical Perspective. (39-48). *"Zur 'Situationsethik' aus ökumenischer Sicht"* May 1965, West German Radio broadcast.

Abstract. An illustration of how ecumenical dialogue might proceed, using the important contemporary issue of situation ethics. This essay also highlights the church's limits in coping with secular situations.

Topics. ECUMENISM, advancing dialogue; ETHICS, Catholic/Protestant;

Subsidiary Discussions. Conscience (43ff); Society, current situation (44ff).

Precis. Ecumenical dialogue would have a greater chance of success if Catholics and Protestants concentrated less on the historical circumstances which gave rise to their differences than on the similarities they face in the current historical situation. Metaphors, too, play an important role in understanding one another's positions and overcoming differences. Rahner illustrates this point by looking at divisions between Catholics and Protestants over situation ethics.

After leaving aside radical situation ethics, which neither Catholics nor Protestants can condone, Rahner proceeds to sketch characteristics of the classical Protestant Situational Ethics (40) and the Catholic universalistic position (41). Confessing that it is too complicated to reconcile these positions on the historical or theoretical levels, he directs his attention to the changes in the concrete situations that affect both kinds of Christian morality. It seems to Rahner that in this arena both systems fail to offer believers adequate assistance in ethical decision making.

What accounts for this situation today, which throws people back on the resources of their own conscience? Rahner attributes it to the ever-increasing pace of social change. There are more choices and at the same time less socially sanctioned support for the choices we make. We are increasingly "on our own." In this concrete historical situation interdenominational differences are bridged. Catholics increasingly see the value of a situational approach to ethics, and Protestants see the value of a more universalist ethics. Rahner is not sure that ethics is the best illustration of his principle for promoting dialogue. But unless we attend to the actual situation people face today, the positions represented by both faith traditions risk becoming completely irrelevant.

CF.3. The Church's Limits: Against clerical triumphalists and lay defeatists. (49-76). "*Grenzen der Amtskirche*" 29 February, 1964 address to Catholic Academy of Bavaria, in *Wort und Wahrheit* 19 (1964) 249-262.

Abstract. These thoughts on the limits of the church's capacity to give directions in the social sphere arose as a response to the preparation phase of *Gaudium et Spes*, Vatican II's "Pastoral Constitution on the Church in the Modern World."

Topics. CHURCH, social function of.

Subsidiary Discussions. Church, triumphalism in (50ff; 71); Church, defeatism in (51ff; 71); Society, current situation (58ff); Economics (67f).

Precis. In early 1964, many Catholics were eager to hear what the church legitimately had to say to the world on matters of economics, history, culture, politics, international relations, etc. But no one should overestimate the possibilities of the church taking social positions. Rahner labels "triumphalists" those who overestimate the church's influence in the social sphere, those who imagine all would be well if the church just spoke out more, and if people just listened and obeyed. He calls "defeatists" those who see the church theoretically powerful, but in practice almost completely ineffectual. Where does the truth lie? What are the limits to the church's power to influence the social sphere?

Four preliminary considerations. 1. Since salvation is gained or lost within the social milieu, the church can and must continuously proclaim principles of action– moral maxims with specific content. **2.** One must distinguish between the church as its official ministers (hierarchy) and the church itself. Each has its own possibilities and limits of action which should not be confused. **3.** "What cannot entirely be dealt with in didactic propositions is not *ipso facto* morally indifferent." Just because a moral position cannot be stated in clear propositional language does not mean it is unimportant. The cultivation of holiness can be as important as theoretical reflection in the process of discerning what is morally good. **4.** The rapidly increasing tempo of change has completely altered the socio-historical context the church must address. Culture is no longer a seemingly stable product of nature, but is itself a social creation. Almost every aspect of human life today "is more complicated and intractable and inaccessible to the understanding of the individual than was ever the case before" (62).

Universal doctrine and individual decision. The gap between the moral principles proclaimed by the church and concrete applications and prescriptions has grown so wide today as to make the two practically different in kind. This situation is not completely new. The church has always left a realm of freedom for many concrete personal choices. The new social context has effectively changed the nature of this gap. After a summary (66), Rahner provides an example: the organization of economic life. The reason the church cannot adopt a specific position in these areas is not cowardice, but a genuine inability given the complex realities. Although the church retains the right and duty to give positive concrete prescriptions, in these social matters the church is more effective when it issues negative injunctions to its own members (e.g., don't vote for this, don't join that). But these injunctions carry their own limitations (69). Rahner adds in a theological note that the church has often failed to speak definitively on many concrete issues of great social importance. The fact that it would have contradicted its very nature if it had been able to speak out but did not, argues for its incompetence in such matters (70f).

Rahner insists this analysis disposes of both triumphalist and defeatist claims, insofar as both positions exaggerate the church's power to address concrete social reality. Both undervalue the proper religious function of the church: baptizing, preaching the Word, celebrating the Lord's Supper, living in faith, hope and love. The church does not offer a complete pattern for living, but the strength to endure a life without patterns. It is enough for the church to be the church, even though Rahner is aware that living true to its religious vocation will not magically resolve all disputes even within the church. What has been said here regarding the official ministers of the church does not apply in the same strict sense to individual believers who are conscience-bound to put their faith into practice in the social sphere, each in his/her own way as led by the Spirit.

CF.4. The Teaching of Vatican II on the Church and the Future Reality of Christian Life. (77-101). *Konziliare Lehre der Kirche und kunftige Wirklichkeit christlichen Lebens.* June 1965 talk in Freiburg im Br., in *Der Seelsorger* 35 (1965) 228-241.

Abstract. This preview of the post-conciliar epoch highlights those elements of *Lumen Gentium* which will have to touch the hearts of believers if they are to live their faith in tomorrow's world.

Topics. CHURCH; *LUMEN GENTIUM*; SALVATION, *extra ecclesia*; VATICAN II.

Subsidiary Discussions. Church of the future (78ff); Church, as sacrament of world's salvation (81ff); Anonymous Christian/ity (85ff); Church, mission of (85ff); Sin (91ff); Bishop/s of the future (97ff).

Precis. Rahner offers some "marginal comments" on the Dogmatic Constitution on the Church, *Lumen Gentium*, "probably the most important product of the Council." **The Situation of Christians in the future.** Rahner asks what the situation of the ordinary Christian will be in the future. He sees the future church as a much less institutional "little flock" of personally committed believers living in a diaspora among non-Christians, with no state sponsorship. To such a church, what will be the most salient elements of *Lumen Gentium*? **The church is the sacrament of the world's salvation.** This central teaching of Vatican II will undergird the diaspora church's self-understanding in the increasing religious pluralism of the future. **New understanding of the mission: Anonymous Christianity.** This vision of the church as *sacramentum salutis totius mundi* will also refine the church's understanding of its mission: to encourage and make explicit the grace of God already at work in the hearts of those who do not profess the same faith or any faith at all. The believer of tomorrow will see **The church as the visible form of what is already interiorly binding,** the historically concrete manifestation of what all people are called to be even prior to baptism. From this point of view, is **Sin reduced to insignificance?** Rahner says certainly not, as the church is precisely the effective sign of sinners actually being saved.

Rahner moves to a second related point: **God's salvific will includes all who seek him with upright heart,** a statement he sees as a truly remarkable development in the church's thinking. Bold as this statement is, it leaves many unanswered theological questions in its wake (list, 95ff), most prominently the problem of revelation (96). A third point Rahner considers is **The collegiality of the bishops and the solidarity of the faithful.** Here he sketches his vision of the role of bishops in the future church, necessary but greatly reduced in power and serving in more collegial ways with regard to laity as well as fellow bishops, stressing "fraternity in Christ."

Growth of the new seed. What is important is not the letter of *Lumen Gentium* but its spirit. It may take a long time for this vision to be fully implemented, there may be setbacks along the way, but in the end its seeds will grow. The Lord of History will bring it about (summary, 101). **Notes** (103-104) gives the source and the full history of the appearance of each essay.

CAC. *The Church after the Council.* NY: Herder and Herder, 1966. 106 pp. Translated by Davis C. Herron and Rondelinde Albrecht. Three essays commenting on the accomplishments of Vatican II and the work of implementation remaining to be accomplished.
Contents: The Council–a new beginning.
-The Church–a new image.
-Theology– a new challenge.

CAC.1. The Council – A New Beginning. (11-33)
Das Konzil– ein neuer Beginn. Freiburg: Herder, 1965.
Abstract: Rahner offers his hermeneutic for understanding Vatican II. For all its accomplishments, the hard work of implementation is just beginning. Its essential goal is to increase faith, hope and love in the hearts of all people.
Topics: VATICAN II, implementation of.
Subsidiary discussions: Faith, hope and love (30ff).

Precis: 1. A council of liturgy and the missions. What was the Council? First, it was a gift of the Holy Spirit to the church. Working collegially, and thus retaining their mysterious unity, the bishops tackled many problems facing the church in a spirit of love and freedom. Its proceedings were a lesson to the world. Second, as a Roman Catholic council it remained faithful to its inherited faith, while searched for new ways to express it (not easy given the range of issues and the many participants). **2. The beginning of the beginning.** What now? Is the church finished? No. Now is the beginning of the beginning, the time to implement the council in the spirit of the council. A new, deeper, future-oriented theology must be created which does justice to this spirit. Rahner warns that despite the continuity evidenced by the council, one cannot simply proceed with business as usual. Proper implementation will take a number of generations. **3. Towards the future.** The main goal of the council was not the production or implementation of "churchly" documents, directives, reforms, etc. To stop with these would be a travesty. Its main work was to increase faith, hope and love among all people, a process Rahner equates with refining 1 gram of radium from 10 tons of ore– labor intensive but worth the effort.

CAC.2. **The Church – A New Image.** (37-73). *Das neue Bild der Kirche*. Wurzburg: Echter-Verlag, 1966. (*Geist und Leben*).

Abstract: The focus of Vatican II was fundamentally ecclesiological. Here Rahner briefly presents some council-inspired images of the future church.

Topics: CHURCH, images of; CHURCH of the future; ECCLESIOLOGY, post-conciliar; VATICAN II, ecclesiology of.

Subsidiary discussions: Church as local altar community (44ff); Church as sacrament of world's salvation (51ff); Salvation *extra ecclesia* (51ff); Anonymous Christian/ity (56ff); Church as community of love (66ff).

Precis: 1. A church reflecting on her nature. A review of its documents (37-38) leaves no doubt that Vatican II primarily concerned the church, reflecting on its own nature. Was this a good idea? After discussing the pros and cons, Rahner concludes it was, because in the last analysis the human person's relationship to God (one dimension of which is the church) is the "ultimate problem." Such reflection prepares the church to discern the *kairos*, the moment of grace, as it faces the future. He concludes with a note about the word "new" as applied to "new images" of the church. None of the images to be discussed here are new in the sense of innovations. All these images have existed in the past. They are new in the sense of revitalized and of potentially even greater vitality for the future.

2. The presence of the church in the local community. Tucked awkwardly into *Lumen Gentium* #26 (for reasons given 46f) is the statement: "This Church of Christ is truly present in all legitimate local congregations of the faithful which, united with their pastors, are themselves called Churches in the New Testament." In this new image where Christ Himself, His gospel, His love, and the communion of the faithful are present in the local church, it is clear that the church *is* the local altar community and not merely a diocese– an administrative unit of some larger entity. This moves beyond Bellarmine's Tridentine theology of church as "perfect society." In fact, the church constitutes a society in the very act of gathering to celebrate sacramentally the Pascal Mystery of Christ. How this will be realized in practice and articulated theologically

is a task of the future. In any case, this new image of church will strengthen it to work in an increasingly small, poor, diaspora community of the future.
3. **The church as the sacrament of the world's salvation** is another new image taken from *Lumen Gentium* #1, 9 (48). This image, however is in tension with *Lumen Gentium*'s other statements on the possibility of salvation for non-Christians (#14), along with many other statements in other documents. Since there is no backing away from the view that the church as salvific reality has now an actual and positive relationship to the non-ecclesial world, how is this dichotomy to be overcome? Rahner finds the key in the sacramental nature of the church (54). The church is the vanguard, the visible sign of the salvation to which God is now calling all people, and as a sacrament it also brings about what it symbolizes. This opens the possibility of seeing those outside the church as "anonymously Christian." Rahner applies this insight to the missionary activity of the church (summary, 65f).
4. **The community of love** is another image of the church reinforced in a special way by the bishops' display of collegiality during the Council. Such love is always concrete and focuses on real people rather than on administrative units. As the coercive power of the church continues inevitably to wane in the future, it is this new image that will serve to guide and sustain the members.
5. **Other features of the new image of the church.** Vatican II offers many other new images of the church as the pilgrim people of God gathered by His grace, an outgrowth of grace, the fruit of salvation (list, 72). Such images do not replace but balance and correct an older one-sided image of the church as an authoritative institution of salvation. It will take time before these "new" images transform the ecclesial piety of the individual and the practice of the church.

CAC.3. Theology – A New Challenge. (77-106). *Die Herausforderung der Theologie durch das II. Vaticanische Konzil.* Freiburg: Herder, 1966.

Abstract: Vatican II has presented theology with significant new themes and tasks, and has highlighted the responsibility of theologians to expand and restructure the very make-up and methods of theology.

Topics: THEOLOGY, post-conciliar VATICAN II, theology of.

Subsidiary discussions: Theology, historical (82ff); Theology, biblical (86ff); Theology, systematic (90ff): Theology, moral (92f); Theology, dogmatic (95ff); Theology, ecumenical (97ff); Theology, pastoral (101ff).

Precis: Vatican II has been a gift and a challenge to theology in many ways: to clearly formulate the theological underpinnings of its pronouncements; to expand and restructure its own make-up and methods; to explore questions left open by the Council. All this is to be done in a new spirit of freedom and mutual respect. In addition, in opening itself to greater dialogue with the world (*Gaudium et Spes*) the church has opened for theologians a whole new horizon of legitimate exploration.

Rahner looks at the effects of these changes and challenges in various areas of theology: historical (where scholars must look beyond questions of "what happened," to "where are we going"), biblical (to reconcile the Jesus of history with the Christ of faith, to help ground systematic theology, and set the program for priestly formation), systematic (to fill out the ecclesiology of Vatican II, and address the perennial issues of God, Christ, and man), moral, dogmatic (to explore hope and the hermeneutics of eschatology), ecumenical, and pastoral. This renewal of theology should be encouraged by bishops. Theologians themselves should organize even internationally. Theological experts should be more widely consulted, mindful that in the end theology always remains a gift of the Spirit to the church.

The Church and the Sacraments. NY: Herder, 1963. *Questiones Disputatae* Series # 9. 117 pp. *Kirche und Sakrament,* Translated by W.J. O'Hara. **Cf.,** *Inquiries,* **Inq.3.**

C. Concilium Series (*abstracted here)
C.3. "Observations on the Episcopacy in the Light of Vatican II." **Cf., TI 06.21.**
C.6. "Christianity and Ideology." **Cf., TI 06.04.**
C.23.1. "What does Vatican II Teach about Atheism?" **Cf., TI 09.09.**
C.23.2. "In Search of a Short Formula of the Christian Faith." **Cf., TI 09.07.**

* C.26. "Evolution and Original Sin."
* C.33. "Demythologization and the Sermon" (with Preface).
* C.43. "What is the Theological Starting Point for a Definition of the Priestly Ministry?"
  C.46. "Pluralism in Theology and the Oneness of the Church's Profession of Faith." **Cf., TI 11.01**,
* C.66. "Orthodoxy and Freedom in Theology."
  C.99. "Experience of the Spirit in Existential Decision." **Cf., TI 16.02**.
* C.153. "Christology Today (instead of a conclusion)."
* C.163. "Dimensions of Martyrdom: A Plea for a Broadening of a Classical Concept."
* C.170. "'In Season and Out of Season.'"

C.3. "Observations on the Episcopacy in the Light of Vatican II" in *The Pastoral Mission of the Church*. NY: Paulist, 1965 (15-23). **Cf., TI 06.21** as "Pastoral-Theological Observations on the Episcopacy in the Teaching of Vatican II."
Abstract: Six pastoral-theological ramifications of *Lumen Gentium*'s teaching on episcopacy, and the related tension between local and episcopal churches.
Topics: CHURCH, office in; EPISCOPATE; VATICAN II, *Lumen Gentium*.
Subsidiary discussions: Bishop/s, conferences (19f); Bishop/s senate (19f); Diocese (20f); Parish (21ff).

C.6. "Christianity and Ideology" in *The Church and the World*. NY: Paulist, 1965 (41-58). **Cf., TI 06.04** as "Ideology and Christianity."
Abstract: Contrary to appearances, Christianity is not an ideology. Humility and tolerance must always guard against its tendency to become one.
Topics: CHRISTIANITY; IDEOLOGY.
Subsidiary Discussions: Metaphysics (47ff); Pluralism (47ff); Experience, transcendental (49ff); Grace (50f); History (51ff); Anonymous Christian/ity (54ff); Society and responsibility (55f); Tolerance (56f).

C.23.1. "What does Vatican II Teach about Atheism?" in *The Pastoral Approach to Atheism*. NY: Paulist, 1967. Preface (1-3); (7-24). Cf., TI 09.09 as "Atheism and Implicit Christianity."
Abstract: Atheism was treated peripherally at Vatican II. For the church to fulfill its mission it must resist introversion and take up the challenge of modern atheism. Atheists come to share supernatural salvation not simply by obeying natural morality but by accepting their own supernaturally elevated nature.
Topics: ANONYMOUS CHRISTIAN/ITY; ATHEISM; VATICAN II.
Subsidiary Discussions: Supernatural existential (146, 162); Faith, *fides quae*/qua (152ff); Knowledge (153ff); Freedom (157f); Mystagogy (159).

C.23.2. "In Search of a Short Formula of the Christian Faith" in *The Pastoral Approach to Atheism*. NY: Paulist, 1967 (70-82). Cf., TI 09.07 as "The Need for a 'Short Formula' of Christian Faith."
Abstract: Argues the need for a short profession of faith more meaningful to modern people. Concludes with a sample creed.
Topics: CREED/s, brief.
Subsidiary Discussions: Mystery (122f); God (119f, 122f); Love (122f); Theological Anthropology (122f); Jesus Christ (120, 123f); Trinity (124f); Church (125); Sacraments (125f).

C.26. "Evolution and Original Sin" in *The Evolving World and Theology*. NY: Paulist, 1967 (61-73).
Abstract: Rahner argues it is neither certain nor necessary to maintain that only a monogenistic original group can explain the first sin or ground the dogma of original sin. Polygenism can do the same, so long as the original group is a biological and historical unit which is significant for salvation history.
Topics: EVOLUTION; MONO/POLYGENISM; SIN, original.
Subsidiary discussions: Jesus Christ as source of all grace (69).

Precis: **I. The starting point of the discussion**: does the doctrine of original sin exclude polygenism? **II. How far is monogenism a theological certainty?** or what theological value must be attached to monogenism? 1. *The data of the Old Testament* does not tell us anything about or prove monogenism. Any genuine teaching about original sin is rooted in the New Testament. 2. *The data of the New Testament* repeat the direct statements of the Old Testament, although in St. Paul (according to Trent) there appears a real teaching on original sin. Hence, the question becomes, does the magisterial teaching on original sin demand the acceptance of monogenism? Careful attention must be paid to Paul's insistence on "one single first man." 3. *The dogmatic situation.* Monogenism is not a dogma defined by the church, although in relation to original sin, Trent presupposes an "Adam who is physically one." Thus monogenism could only be binding if it could be shown that the church's teaching on original sin could not stand without it. 4. *Can monogenism be proved philosophically?* Is polygenism (even if false) compatible with the doctrine of original sin? **III. Position according to the natural sciences** accepts evolution and generally presumes monogenism. Given its methods, one should not be surprised if science is not concerned about the rise of man as a personal and spiritual being.

IV. A theory proposed. 1. *Thesis.* Since it cannot be proved that the teaching on original sin precludes polygenism, the church should refrain from censoring polygenism (method, 65). The theological question is whether the original free decision that explains our lack of sanctity is only thinkable as the decision of one, single man, or by presupposing that mankind originated from only one couple? 2. *Adam and Eve.* Can the church logically allow belief in evolution and condemn polygenism? a) One cannot accept the evolutionary origin of Adam but not of Eve. b) How could these two beings, if one assumes there were only two within an evolving population, find one another? 3. *Polygenism and the bodily, historical unity of Originating Man (humanitas originans).* It is doubtful whether a bodily, historical unity of the first human beings can be understood in terms of monogenism, whereas polygenism can retain what science generally hypothesizes as a biological historical unity. Rahner provides five reasons for this (a-e, 67) and warns against accepting polyphylism (summary, 68). 4. *The sin of one couple or the collective sin?* The question whether original sin originated with only one couple and that mankind was deprived of sanctifying grace only though this one couple can be broken into two parts: a) Does it not seem arbitrary in a polygenetic but unified origin of mankind that the whole group should be punished for the failure of one couple in that group? b) Can this group, which can represent a real unity, unite to commit a *pecatum originale originans*? 5. *"Adam" understood as a single man, though in a polygenetic situation*. In answer to the first question Rahner asks, "Why not?" Since we are intrinsically social, why can't the sin of one part of a group block the experience of grace in others (leaving aside a physicalist notion of original sin being "genetically inherited"? Rahner also argues back from the dogma that all grace originates from Christ. For if the grace of one is able to effect all, the sin of one is also capable of the same effect. This section concludes with reflections on the social nature of man and the possible effects of the sin of one on the transmission of grace to all (70f). 6. *"Adam" as the collective expression of the general guilt of the original group*. Regarding the second question (4b), Rahner maintains a collective sin of the original group is quite conceivable, and that "Adam" is a concrete expression for the group. **V. Conclusion.** It appears neither certain nor necessary to maintain that only a monogenistic original group can explain the first sin or uphold the dogma of original sin such as we profess it. Polygenism can do the same, so long as the original group be a biological and historical unit which is significant for salvation history.

C.33. "Demythologization and the Sermon" with Preface, in *The Renewal of Preaching: Theory and Practice*. NY: Paulist, 1968 (20-38); Preface (1-5).
Abstract: "The problem of preaching" is the enduring problem of "translating" unchanging salvific truth into a secular language and idiom beyond the control of the church. Rahner offers some general rules and then some particular considerations for preaching the events of saving history.
Topics: DEMYTHOLOGY/ -IZING; PREACHING; THEOLOGY, task of.
Subsidiary discussions: Language, religious and secular (20ff); Salvation history, preaching of (29ff).
Precis: Preface. One of the great practical concerns in the church is "the trouble with preaching," a problem that grows more vexing each day. Too often the text of scripture becomes either a springboard for discussing unrelated issues, or a sterile lesson in exegesis. More intimate contact with the texts of scripture today exac-

erbates people's confusion, and exegesis alone will not solve the problem. The homily must draw its strength from the heart of the Christian faith. This volume (*Concilium* 33) intends to return to the sources of faith to offer some practical help, realizing there is no recipe for good preaching. The essay proper begins with Rahner setting out what he will *not* cover.

I. **Demythologization as a method of "translation."** *1. The need for a constantly new explanation.* In approaching the question of *how* one should preach today, Rahner separates content from form. Content never changes. It is the message of the Gospel, although at different times different elements may be stressed. The form of preaching changes and must change from age to age. In the body of the sermon, the Gospel must be re-translated to make itself credible. *2. Revelation in secular speech.* The language of the church, even though it embodies revelation, is still the ever-changing language of the world. When it changes, the language of the church must change too (e.g., transubstantiation, person, heaven, blood, God). The homily must translate these terms. *3. Modes of speech and intelligibility.* "The question of 'demythologization and the sermon,' then simply means for the preacher the question of what principles should guide him in the translation from the language of Scripture and tradition into a language that can be understood today" (23). This is a complex problem but not a new one. We must remember that no definition of a word is ever final, and that no language is ever completely subject to our control.

II. **General rules for translating the message in the sermon.** *1. Demand for serious theological preparation.* Because language keeps changing, preparation is never finished. In addition, one cannot use the same words for the explanation and for the thing being explained. The theology we have today is already an explanation, a translation. *2. Hearing as the world hears.* Since the sermon generally mixes many modes of speech (religious and secular dialects) the preacher should work to hear his own sermon with the ears of his actual audience. *3. The need for self-criticism.* The preacher must produce the *right kind* of translation. To insure this he must stay in humble contact with magisterial teaching. But simply repeating it does not insure orthodoxy or even comprehension. *4. How freely should he translate?* How a preacher mixes traditional with translated language depends largely on the group being addressed and on his own discretion. 5. *Should theological problems be discussed in the pulpit?* No. The Gospel should be proclaimed. The goal of the sermon is to "edify" (28). The preacher should be familiar with theological controversies but not burden the congregation with them.

III. **Special rules for preaching events from salvation history.** *1. Events should not be reduced to mere conceptual or existential abstractions* because the human family works out its salvation precisely in history. God actually works in history in such a way that what happened once can still have salvific consequences for us today. Proclamation must unite the historical with our present existence. 2. *No need to be archaic or to "harmonize,"* and yet merely repeating the stories without translating them can give the false impression that the events of salvation history are strict empirical history. 3. *The combination of "historical" report and theological interpretation.* The way historical events were presented in biblical times (i.e, their genres) led to their being properly interpreted. The preacher today must not only understand this, he must also find new ways of presenting these same facts so they can be properly interpreted. 4. *A modified way of looking at the event of revelation.* Today we must find new ways of expressing the faith precisely in order to preserve it. Modern people, for example, appreciate God's incomprehensibility and find it difficult to see God reduced to historical categories. They have a deep religious sensibility which often finds little resonance in the traditional theological formulations. Preachers must carefully avoid the twin pitfalls of explaining all saving history by simply referring it to divine ways, or by excluding the divine dimension altogether. 5. *Understanding the various dimensions of the realities of salvation.* Modern theology with all its critical methods is working to disentangle today's various dimensions of the image of revealed salvation from those of the past. Preachers must be aware of this struggle, without necessarily making it the topic of their homilies. Therefore, today we must again pass through the New Testament history of christology. We cannot begin where each author of scripture left off, but must begin by re-experiencing Jesus as one like us. For God communicates Himself to us, and not merely propositions about Himself. 6. *This change involves a slow and uneven process.* 7. *The task of all proclamation remains the same.* Rahner offers the preacher this criterion for self-criticism: "how would he tell the story if ... he presented the event as if it had happened here and now, and not in the past?" (36).

IV. **The specific idiom of the language of proclamation.** *1. Christian proclamation of preaching to the "heathen."* Since the preacher must "translate" into the speech of the public actually in front of him, he must first of all preach to the "heathens" among us in their own language. This will also help the "good Christians" because they too are people of the modern age. The preacher cannot justify using "simple language" because the people before him are not theologically trained. They may not know theology, but they know instinctively what is credible to a modern person. *2. Secular and sacred language.* No matter how good the translation of religious truths into secular language may be, it never does away with the need for religious language— a language that can communicate the transcendental depths of the human person in a way that scientific-empirical language cannot. Not every archaic reference must be scrapped. "The Lord is my shepherd" still has meaning in a secular world.

C.43. "What is the Theological Starting Point for a Definition of the Priestly Ministry?" in *Identity of the Priest*. NY: Paulist, 1969 (80-86).

Abstract: The essence of orders lies in the unchanging mission of the church. The priest is commissioned by the church to preach the Word of God with the highest levels of sacramental intensity of this Word. Clearly the priest is no mere cult official and his call involves the whole of his life. Priesthood has a fundamental missionary character that relates it to a community, and it assumes many forms over time.

Topics: PRIESTHOOD, theological foundations.

Subsidiary discussions: Priesthood and mediation (82); Word, ministry of (84).

Precis: Rahner intends to address the present crisis in the priest's self-understanding by examining the theological foundation of Catholic priesthood leaving aside social and historical factors, although these do serve as the background to the question. The first step is to identify the starting point for defining the theological nature of priesthood, as this will allow us to separate its enduring nature from his historical changes. **I. Negative preliminary remarks.** Power to administer the sacraments of Eucharist, Penance, Anointing is not the place to begin, as this has no scriptural foundation. The same is true of the concept of mediation. **II. Positive presuppositions.** *The oneness and divisibility of "office" in the church.* One should not start with the taken for granted three-fold division of hierarchical office, but from the nature of the church as the sacrament of God's self-communication which implies the need for office, the nature of which is determined by the church and its divine mission. Office is primarily one, but its distribution actually has been and is very fluid. The current three degrees (bishop, priest, deacon) do not imply there cannot be further degrees. This sheds light on why "priesthood" can have various functions assigned to it by the church over time. *The operative character of the Word in the church* cannot be forgotten as we try to find a practicable theological starting place. Here "Word" must be taken in its broadest, biblical sense which includes both proclamation and sacramental administration. **III. The starting point itself.** *Attempt at a definition:* "the priest is he who ... preaches the Word of God by mandate of the Church as a whole and therefore officially, and in such a way that he is entrusted with the highest levels of sacramental intensity of this Word" (85). This definition makes clear the priest is no mere cult official, and that his call is more than a mere job. It involves the whole of his life. It has a fundamental missionary character that relates it to a community. (Again, this does not rule out the possible existence of other ways of serving the Word which are official and can be bestowed sacramentally.) *What can, and what cannot, change in the Catholic priesthood?* This definition allows for a wide variety of concrete applications, none of which should be identified *a priori* with the priest's proper theological nature. The rapid changes taking place today call for the church to review the various tasks it currently assigns to priestly office using this theological criterion (summary, 86).

C.46. "Pluralism in Theology and the Oneness of the Church's Profession of Faith" in *The Development of Fundamental Theology*. NY: Paulist, 1969 (103-123). Cf., **TI 11.01** as "Pluralism in Theology and the Unity of the Creed in the Church."

Abstract: In this new age of insuperable theological pluralism, creedal unity is assured more by unity of practice (table fellowship, sacramental celebrations, care for the poor, etc.) than by agreement on theological propositions.

Topics: MAGISTERIUM and theology; PLURALISM; THEOLOGY.

Subsidiary Discussions: Theology, history of (104f); Philosophy (106); Ecumenism (106, 109f, 122f); Eucharist, transubstantiation (109f); Propositions (114ff); Dogma, development of (119); Orthopraxis (121f).

C.66. "Orthodoxy and Freedom in Theology" in *Perspectives of a Political Theology*. NY: Paulist, 1971 (90-104). Translated by John Griffiths.

Abstract: Rahner takes the opportunity of defending the work of a young theologian to discuss the recent changes in theology (especially the relationship of fundamental and dogmatic) and the difficulties and risks theologians must take when they attempt to address contemporary issues and remain "orthodox."

Topics: ORTHODOXY, judgment of; THEOLOGY, method in; THEOLOGY, teaching of.

Subsidiary discussions: Theology, recent history of (94f; 98f); Theology, relation of fundamental and dogmatic (98ff); Revelation, theology of (100).

Precis: Note: This is a real letter, somewhat edited, written by Rahner to attest to the suitability of an unnamed professor (N.N) to continue teaching on a university theology faculty. **I. Preliminary notes.** *1.* Remarks to comments on the lecture which gave rise to complaints. *2.* Apologies for not treating the theological content of the disputed lecture with complete thoroughness. *3.* Strong protest against the attached negative remarks of N.N.'s colleague whose approach left Rahner "amazed and horrified."

II. On the problems of dialectics in theology. *1.* A new method of theology is required today. The old scholastic manual relied on demonstration; the new method proceeds by synthesizing scripture, history doctrine, etc., in dialogue with issues of the present age. *2.* The complexities facing theologians today is unprecedented. Should they present these difficulties to their students and risk being called too demanding? Or should they shield their students from these things and leave them poorly prepared for the world they will face? The simple fact remains: the old theology no longer works and we have entered a new age of pluralism and experiment. 3. Rahner judges N.N. to be an experimental but nevertheless qualified teacher of theology in today's milieu. He is clearly on the right track, but perhaps should be helped by his senior colleagues to be more self-critical.

III. **On the problem of orthodoxy.** 1. *a)* Because the lecture under discussion is not a complete system and theology today lacks a common vocabulary, it is impossible to judge the orthodoxy of this lecture. b) Rahner suggests that if an impartial judge were to read the entire work in relation to N.N.'s objectives, a final judgment would be in his favor. 2. Even if one grants that not everything in this work is completely beyond objection, does not every theologian have the right to choose his authorities? And what theologian is not to some degree one-sided? This does not make a writing heterodox. 3. One must seriously consider N.N.'s starting point and intention. *a)* His basic intention is to theologize within a new relationship between fundamental and dogmatic theology, basing the credibility of the former on the latter. Every dogma must be shown to have significant foundational meaning. *b)* This project (summary, 100) cannot be carried out by traditional dogmatic means. It must start from "an original appeal to man's most primal understanding of his existence, to an ultimate will to make sense of things" (100), proper exploration of which leads to a grasp of what faith means by God, grace, revelation, etc. *c)* Hence, it should not be surprising that in N.N's work one finds few references to "positives sources of revelation." *d)* This approach also explains N.N.'s "minimalism." *e)* N.N.'s method of deriving his starting point from the "secular nature" of human beings and his wedding of grace and nature are not the Modernism Pius X condemned (although N.N. could be asked to show how well his approach is able to embrace the complete scope of propositional belief). Rahner concludes that the situation and the criteria for judging theology today have changed. A professor who "addresses himself to the contemporary spiritual situation and its problems, ultimately contributes more to the strengthening of his audience's faith than does a professor who exhibits a ghetto-like and sterile orthodoxy" (103). Of course a theologian should try to be both modern and orthodox. But this seldom ever happens, and theologians must take calculated risks. Students today need professors like N.N.

C.99. **"Experience of the Spirit in Existential Decision"** in *Experience of the Spirit*. NY: Crossroad, 1974 (38-46). Translated by Francis McDonagh. Cf., **TI 16.02** as "Experience of the Spirit and Existential Commitment."

Abstract: Faced with a number of worthwhile possibilities one can only come to an existential decision before God by assuming a synthesis of the transcendent experience of Spirit and the encounter with the categorical object of choice.

Topics: FREEDOM and choice; SPIRIT/s, experience of; SPIRIT/s, discernment of; TRANSCENDENT/ CATEGORICAL.

Subsidiary Discussions: Commitment, existential (38ff); God (39); Anonymous Christian/ity (39f); Nature, pure (39f); Freedom (40f).

C.153. **"Christology Today (instead of a conclusion)"** in *Jesus. Son of God?* NY: Seabury, 1982 (73-77). Translated by Francis McDonagh.

Abstract: Modern christologies must wed the classical formulations with modern insights into what Jesus means for us. This can employ compelling new idioms. They must be christologies of ascent and must include Jesus' unique role in God's self-revelation made irrevocable in Jesus' victorious death.

Topics: CHRISTOLOGY, modern.

Subsidiary discussions: Theology, method in (73ff); Christology, method in (73ff); Christology of ascent (75); Jesus Christ as absolute savior (76); Jesus Christ, death of (76f).

Precis: To conclude *Concilium* Vol. 153, Rahner offers a few items which come more from the heart than from the head. **I.** Contemporary theologians should not simply ignore the classical christological formulations of Catholic theology. They must be cool and self-critical. They must always be learning and must never leave the Christian faithful (including the bishops) behind. At the same time they must always be looking for more intelligible and compelling ways to express the ancient faith. One fruitful approach would be for dogmatic theologians to use the old formulations to convey new important experiences and ways of expression. Dogmatic theology cannot be left to exegetes! Although they have a crucial role to play, their method and sources cannot set the parameters of the entire theological enterprise. **II.** Any present-day christology must be a "Christology of ascent." i.e., it must hold fast to fundamental theology and take history seriously. It must begin from an encounter with the man, Jesus of Nazareth. It must center on the question, what does this man mean for us? **III.** The many contemporary christologies must inevitable contain two insights: a) Jesus must be seen as the unsurpassable access to the immediacy of God in Himself. In their efforts to maintain this, Rahner insists it will be possible for modern theologians to wed their understanding of what Jesus means for us with the classical christological formulations. b) It is only conceivable for Jesus to be God's victorious self-pledging in history if Jesus' death and resurrection are seen as His irrevocable acceptance of this divine offer. A full christology must also do justice to our individual relationship to Jesus, which Rahner summarizes as "a dying with Jesus (in absolute hope) in a surrender to the incomprehensibility of the eternal God" (77). Reflection on this formulation would reveal Christ at the heart of all human and religious longing.

C.163. "Dimensions of Martyrdom: A Plea for a Broadening of a Classical Concept." in *Martyrdom Today*. NY: Seabury, 1983 (9-11). Translated by Francis McDonagh.

Abstract: The church should expand its criteria for martyrdom to the embrace the possibility of including those who die in or as a consequence of active resistance (e.g., Oscar Romero or Maximillian Kolbe). After presenting the classical definition of a martyr (9f) and upholding the real distinction between passively accepting death vs. accepting a death that results from prior active resistance, Rahner underscores their even greater similarities. He argues a case could be made that Jesus Himself "died because he fought" (10). A legitimate political theology should concern itself with enlarging the concept of martyrdom.

Topics: MARTYRDOM, criteria for.

C.170. "'In Season and Out of Season.'" in *20 years of Concilium: Retrospect and Prospect.* NY: Seabury, 1983 (88-89). Translated by Francis McDonagh.

Abstract: Established to respond to the rise of the world-church, *Concilium*, other journals like it, and regional journals are more necessary than ever to preserve and foster healthy pluralism in the church.

Topics: WORLD-CHURCH.

CP. *The Courage to Pray.* With J.-B. Metz. NY: Crossroad, 1981. 87pp. *Ermutigung zum Gebet,* 1977. Translated by Sarah O'Brien Towhig.

Contents: One: "The Courage to Pray:" by J-B Metz (not abstracted here).

Two: "Prayer to the Saints:" by Karl Rahner. (Though subdivided, treated as one essay here.)

Abstract: Because today many people find prayer to the saints highly problematic for theological reasons (the mediation implied by intercession) and human reasons (our indifference toward the seemingly remote dead) many think such prayer is completely optional. Rahner disputes this and argues not only for the legitimacy of venerating saints, but for the centrality of solidarity with the dead for completing Christ's saving work. These reflections follow basic church teaching but extend beyond canonized saints to all the faithful departed, and indeed to all the dead.

Topics: MEDIATION; SAINTS, Communion of; SAINTS, veneration of.

Subsidiary discussions: Dead, indifference toward (37ff); God, experience of (46f); Acts, religious (49ff, 54ff); Love of God and neighbor (53ff); Saints, patronal (73ff, 77ff); Death, solidarity in (82ff); Poor Souls (85f).

Precis: 1. Is it "good and beneficial" to pray to the saints? While imposing no duty on the faithful, the church's teaching can easily be summarized: "It is permissible and beneficial to venerate the saints in heaven and to ask them for their intercession." But in the developed West today this practice is looked upon with skepticism, an attitude neither inevitable nor self-justified. This essay challenges this modern aversion to venerating saints.

2. **Why is it difficult today to pray to the saints?** The modern reticence to pray to saints is rooted in a prevailing attitude of indifference to the dead, itself stemming from a widespread lack of belief in life after death. This indifference even among Christians is a big problem. Far from being a sign of the "glorious progress achieved by our times in defiance of the ancient primitive traditions of the past" (44), forgetfulness of the dead threatens our very humanity. After expressing wonder at how little this problem engages modern theologians (44), and suggesting future African theologians may one day have something important to say on the subject (45), Rahner moves to a second, more theological reason for today's reticence to venerate saints. Where does the veneration of concrete, particular saints fit in with worship of an ineffable Mystery we call God? How can we actually address those who have died and become thereby immersed in God's infinity?
3. **Praying to the saints as intercessors with God.** Since the experience of God is direct, not mediated by finite realities, and because in all strictly religious acts (e.g., prayer) everything finite must vanish, where does the intercession of saints fit in?
4. **Love of God and love of neighbor closely linked.** The radical unity of love of God and neighbor is rooted in the fact that only when loving another human being absolutely, unconditionally and freely is God being loved at least implicitly as the source of such love. Those we love form a direct line of communication to God. The world and concrete human beings are always our starting point for experiencing God, without ever becoming direct mediators of God in a graduated or hierarchical sense. All the many possible variations in approach and intention do not affect the essential unity of love of God and neighbor. It would be unnatural categorically to exclude other human beings from our relationship to God or to exclude God from our relationship with the world. True self-forgetfulness in the act of loving others is closer to religious truth than is forgetting others in the performance of the religious act.
5. **Venerating the saints by loving our neighbor in and with Christ.** God has willed that individuals are suitable subjects for His direct self-revelation, provided they are firmly united with their fellow humans who triumphantly acknowledge God's revelation through Christ. The Communion of Saints (and their subsequent venera-

tion) is nothing other than the expression of human solidarity with Christ in His solidarity with all humanity. It never actually comes between God and humanity, because it is itself the condition for the possibility of receiving God's revelation (summary, 61f).

6. **Venerating saints is synonymous with the adoration of God.** All this does not yet explain how we can salvage veneration without invoking mediation. After suggesting and dismissing a number of possible approaches, Rahner focuses on the possibility of there being a basic religious act aimed directly but only implicitly at God, the lasting significance of which should be sought in the innumerably different ways human beings have of fulfilling themselves. Seen in this light, venerating the saints along with many other various human acts which express our essentially and irreducibly diverse nature are in the end caught up and united in the one act of our lives. Hence, venerating the saints is a genuinely religious act without disrupting the immediacy of our relationship to God.

7. **How do we petition the saints for intercession?** Reference to a past encounter with Barth leads Rahner to suggest that we do not so much *pray to* the saints as we *pray with* them. We believe the saints are constantly praying for us. Our prayers do not get this process started. Rather they connect us (by uniting our prayers with the saints') to the beneficial effects of their perpetual intercession.

8. **The salvific role of the saints.** United with God in the beatific vision the saints do not lose their individuality. They continue to differ among themselves in the importance of their function in salvation history and in their degrees of blessedness, without thereby setting up grounds for envy. This lasting individuality justifies the practice of identifying patron saints for groups and individuals.

9. **Commemorating a saint as a patron.** Patrons are seen as concrete symbols of our solidarity with the dead in heaven, united before God. However, any extremism in venerating particular saints can deteriorate into superstition and must be avoided.

10. **Cultivating our solidarity with the dead.** Realistically, these theoretical explanations do not completely overcome our feelings– the sense that the dead are so terribly remote from us. Our solidarity with all humanity in the final religious act of death, when we hand over ourselves and the whole of humanity, is implicitly union with

Christ's submission to the Father. Veneration of the saints, the expression of our solidarity with them, is essential if *humanity* is to hand itself over to God. The real difficulty in praying to the saints is not theological, but a lack of human solidarity with the dead. But solidarity is an attitude we can and must cultivate. We should concentrate primarily on two groups of the dead: our deceased relatives to whom we owe so much, and the forgotten dead, "the poor souls." The simple act of wordlessly remembering them is an act of solidarity and hence a powerful, beneficial prayer, compared to which praying to individual saints is quite secondary.

DBG. *Do You Believe in God?* NY: Newman, 1969. Translated by Richard Strachan. 114 pp. *Glaubst du an Gott?* Einsiedeln: Benziger, n.d. (* abstracted here).
Contents: I. Can We Still Believe? **Cf., TI 05.01.**
II. The Believer amid Non-believers. **Cf., TI 03.23.**
III. Intellectual Honesty and Faith. **Cf., TI 07.03.**
* IV. Is Faith Possible in Today's World Picture?
* V. Science and Faith.
VI. Is Faith an Ideology? **Cf., TI 06.04.**
VII. Healing and Salvation through Faith. **Cf., TI 05.18.**
* VIII. Faith Today.
IX. Can God be experienced? **Cf., TI 11.06.**

DBG.1. Can we Still Believe? (3-16). **Cf., TI 05:01** as "Thoughts on the Possibility of Faith Today."
Abstract: Rahner discusses in turn the obstacles to belief today, and suggests that some of those who feel frustrated by these very obstacles may in fact possess an implicit, albeit anonymous faith.
Topics: CHRISTIANITY, belief in; FAITH.
Subsidiary Discussions: God as mystery (7f); Anonymous Christian/ity (8f, 11, 20f); Skepticism (8ff); Christology (11ff); Hypostatic union (12ff); Church of sinners (15ff); Church, controversy in (18ff).

DBG.2. The Believer amid Non-believers. (19-30). **Cf., TI 03:23** as "The Christian among Unbelieving Relations."
Abstract: Christians must responsibly endure the permanent diaspora situation of faith today, even as it touches their own families.

Rahner sets out various grounds for continually hoping for the salvation of all, recalling that our personal impotence does not establish the limit of God's mercy.

Topics: ANONYMOUS CHRISTIAN/ITY; SALVATION/DAMNATION.

Subsidiary Discussions: Church, diaspora (358ff); Ignorance, invincible (362f); Fundamental option (365f); Eschatology, *apokatastasis* (371f).

DBG.3. Intellectual Honesty and Faith. (33-41). Cf., TI 07:03 as "Intellectual Honesty and Christian Faith."

Abstract: If "intellectual honesty" is not fear of commitment or irrational scrupulosity disguised as chaste skepticism, and if love for truth demands we contemplate the whole of reality, then we will encounter absolute mystery, which grounds the quest for meaning, and justifies our surrendering to it in faith.

Topics: CHRISTIAN LIFE, intellectual honesty; FAITH.

Subsidiary Discussions: Skepticism (48ff); Faith (55ff); Creed, brief (59ff); God (60ff); Creation (62f); Trinity (63); Jesus Christ (63f); History (63f, 69); Language (65); Incarnation (67ff); Resurrection (70f).

DBG.4. Is Faith Possible in Today's World Picture? (45-59)

Abstract: Today we no longer simply endured nature. We actively intervene to transform it. This has religious ramifications. Negatively, God seems more distant. Positively, we experience more deeply our finitude and God's absolute transcendence. These are preconditions for a more personal, adult faith.

Topics: FAITH and modern world view; SECULARISM/-IZATION.

Subsidiary discussions: God and nature (45ff).

Precis: We are at a new stage. Our environment and world view are no longer the products of nature to which we are hostage, but of our own logical planning and ingenious technological input of which we are masters. This has religious consequences. Formerly, God was seen to speak through nature. Its uncontrollability was a direct experience of God. Today we no longer feel as though we live *in* nature; we transform it. Nature has become the material and tool of our creative activity. "Thus in a real sense, not a merely spiritual one, man is left in his own hands, and to that extent the world which surrounds him is very largely his own image" (48). Different people experience this change and its dangers to different degrees (the church probably most slowly). This development is not only inevitable, it is the inevitable product of Christianity. "For nowhere is man *more* God's free partner than in Christianity" (49). Hence, the challenges this evolution poses for Christians are at the same time a defense and vindication of the Christian's dignity as a creature of and a partner with God.

What implications does the present situation have for religion? (50) First it makes dealing with God more difficult since, divorced from nature, God seems to be father away. (Here appeals to scripture don't help.) In fact, "this godless, hominized world does mean that God is remote, that the idea of him has grown dim and unreal, alien to earth, that God has dropped out of our categories" (51). Is there any positive religious significance to this development? First, despite extended control, we experience the world as remaining ultimately uncontrollable. Despite all our accomplishments, we remain subject to control as we venture into a future of impenetrable darkness made even more so by its having been turned into a world of man. The more powerful we become, the more we subject nature to ourselves, the heavier grows our responsibility, the more serious life becomes. Those who accept and implement this new responsibility unconditionally have a genuine relationship with "God," even if they don't use that word. "For the ultimate, absolute principle of all responsibility is called God" (54). A further positive element in today's situation is that today's human creativity is capable of nurturing religion. For patiently enduring this reality over which we have little control *"is a participation in the sufferings and death of Christ"* (56). In addition, our new status is the only basis on which God achieves his own stature in our eyes as the creator, infinitely exalted in His own inaccessible glory, and not some part of the world.

We have no right to disdain this world view as being any more evil or dangerous than previous ones. It, too, has its ways of drawing us to God. We must remember two things: the *whole* world with which we interact in all its dimensions is already a *sanctified* world. God's absolute nearness precedes the explicit action of the church. And the church itself continues to evolve as it dialogues with this new world view. In this changing environment the laity has a special mandate to witness in a "supra-secular" way to this secular world (conclusion, 58f).

DBG.5. Science and Faith. (63-77)

Abstract: Because the source and object of faith is deeper than scientific reflection, science cannot judge faith. In its attempts to speak of reality as a whole, religious language must rely on analogy and thus will forever lack the precision of science. This factor gives rise to most disputes between science and religion.

Topics: FAITH and science; GOD, knowledge of; SCIENCE and faith.

Subsidiary discussions: World view (63ff); Atheism (68f, 71f); God-talk (70ff); Demythology (73ff).

Precis: How are science and faith related? To begin with, all of us enter a pre-established world and inherit a metaphysical and historical world view we can never completely cast off. It is filled with antecedent structures of thought and historical presuppositions. Ours is not a mere world of facts. This truth extends even to the scientific world view. Every world view "is the mirror reflecting a limited being who is conditioned by many factors" (65).

Since faith springs from a loftier and more primal kind of living than science, it is not the place of the scientific world view to judge religion. Man has a relation with his own finite world view, and in that very act also has a relation to what does *not* belong to that sphere: the ungrasped and ungraspable background, the unutterable source of all utterance, which is really present without forming part of our world view. We call this God. Christian philosophy has always struggled with the problem that God can only be known indirectly and can only be spoken of in analogies, despite the fact that it has often presented this truth in a more apodictic way. The truth of atheism is often no more than a proper correction of this overly glib way of taking about God. Atheism often insists only on what theology has obscured: that the world is not God. What we are really dealing with here is an altogether proper maturing of the image of God: that God is always greater (summary, 70).

There is no harm in admitting the anguish of faith. God is not dead. God is simply great, nameless and incomprehensible. "God is," is not simply one proposition among others. Science speaks of the finite, calculable world of creation, and of the truth proper to it; religion speaks of God, the absolute truth which cannot fit within the world's coordinates. Religious knowledge possesses less exactitude than science, not because it is hazier or less reliable, but because it has an undeterminable object. But today as God increasingly appears to us as ever greater, He seems to recede. Increasingly alone and responsible, we feel filled with dread. Yet Christians know in the depths of their hearts "that everything is embraced, sustained and beheld by the necessarily unutterable mystery which we call God" (72). This is the truth of truths which sets us free. The courage for such trust is a deed whereby we affirm our inmost being.

Of course all that has been said so far is, in a way, pre-Christian. Christianity rests on the know-ledge of God communicated by the God-man Jesus Christ, living on in Word and sacrament in the institutional church. It is especially on this level of concrete religious dogma, law and devotion that most conflicts with science have arisen. In great part this is due to theology's reliance on human concepts and on the analogical nature of religious language. The essay next discusses theological language. Here Rahner says a number of interesting things: "To stammer about God, to be able to stammer about him in his presence, is more important than discoursing accurately about the world" (74). It is not our responsibility to dispel the mystery; "it would be a sign that the theologian has fallen into a rationalist interpretation of divine truth" (74). He also argues that the modern push to "demythologize" religious language is overstated, and that there are no dogmas that stand or fall based solely on the strength of a pre-modern world view or its pictorial ways of expressing itself.

Rahner concludes by saying that the 19th Century's naive elevation of science to the status of a religion of pure reason is finally playing out. Science cannot be the explanation for everything. The scientific world view depends on a picture of humanity which comes antecedently from history and metaphysics, and is ordered to freedom. If science today is not to become an aimless or poisonous distraction, it must not cut off contact with the root of our primal, unarticulated understanding of and connection with life. Science "must grow deeper into its source and ground in proportion as science branches out into the vastness of the empirical" (77).

DBG.6. Is Faith an Ideology? (81-87). Cf., TI 06:04 as "Ideology and Christianity."

Abstract: Rahner argues that faith is not an ideology. First he refutes the claims of skeptics that all metaphysical reasoning is unjustifiable. He ends by showing that Christianity rests on more than ideas. It is essentially a matter of history and of personal experience of communion with God.

Topics: CHRISTIANITY; IDEOLOGY.

Subsidiary Discussions: Metaphysics (48ff); Pluralism (48ff); Experience, transcendental (50ff); Grace (51f); History (52ff); Anonymous Christian/ity (56ff); Society and responsibility (55f); Tolerance (56f).

DBG.7. Healing and Salvation through Faith. (91-97). Cf. TI 05.18 as "The Saving Force and Healing Power of Faith."

Abstract: Like all truly human realities, illness and death are a mix of psychic and somatic. Principally, faith addresses the psychic. People of faith view sickness as stages of assent, opportunities to surrender ever more completely to God. Faith does not abolish the uncontrollability of our lot; it overcomes it.

Topics: CHRISTIAN LIFE, illness; DEATH; FAITH.

Subsidiary discussions: Miracles (465ff).

DBG.8. Faith Today. (101-107)

Abstract: Faith today must be fraternal. Our personal struggles to believe in a God who seems so distant should increase our empathy with those who do not profess an explicit faith. Remembering that God, who is always greater, grants faith beyond the visible church encourages us to approach all as brothers.

Topics: FAITH, fraternal.

Subsidiary discussions: God-talk (104f); Anonymous Christian/ity (105f); God as always greater (106).

Precis: Faith today must be fraternal. It must identify itself with all those who struggle to believe. It must witness only to what we ourselves actually live (or try to live). Here theologians have no advantage over simple believers. Fraternal faith draws no distinctions between those who profess the faith and those who feel they really do not believe. Spirituality today, though it may draw sustenance from many sources, poses the one same question to human freedom about the mystery of God.

But in today's environment, marked as it is by our ever-increasing sway over nature (cf., DBG 4), we can feel as though God has retreated. This puts personal faith in jeopardy. Still, faith remains the foundation of our life. Admitting the truth of this new situation (which threatens faith itself more than it does particular doctrines) is a first step towards vindicating the Christian belief in God. The important truth embodied in this new situation is that the world is not God, nor are we. God is *God*, the incomprehensible mystery, complete surrender to whom is the grace of faith. "And in this grace, the believer experiences God's forgiving, self-communicating intimacy" (103). People today find it easier perhaps to believe in an essentially transcendent God than to imagine God actually revealed in myriad specific standards for human living. But Christianity teaches only 3 absolute but interconnected mysteries: God; Incarnation; and divinizing grace. For a Christian, faith means opening oneself to the mystery of the unutterable loving God by following Christ. It also means personal growth, prioritizing our values and putting them into perspective.

One obstacle to faith is the fact that all statements about God are cloaked in analogical language drawn from the world of concrete experience. But God is not part of this world, and His mystery outstrips all concepts. Unfortunately, people too often do not mature in this understanding, and give up faith in God altogether when they encounter the failure of language. In addition, faith is often explained poorly. Explanations stress ideas about God rather than personal encounter with God, a self-communication that is not confined within the parameters of the visible church. For this reason, Christians should approach all people as already pardoned and only lacking explicit incorporation in the visible church. Such an assumption will make our faith more generous, patient and confident. Such faith allows God to be greater than our minds, with wonderful personal consequences. Rahner ends with a brief history of faith (106f).

DBG.9. Can God be experienced? (111-114). **Cf., TI 11:06** as "The Experience of God Today."
Abstract: The only genuine experiences of Spirit are acts of renunciation— acts of self-forgetfulness done with no hope and no expectation of return. Eternal life dawns as we surrender to the mystery of God.
Topics: GOD, experience of; RENUNCIATION.
Subsidiary discussions: Nature and grace (154); Mystery (155f); Atheism (159ff); Jesus Christ (164f).

DEC. *The Dynamic Element in the Church.* NY: Herder, 1964. *Questiones Disputatae* Series #12. 170 pp. *Das Dynamische in der Kirche*, 1964. Translated by W.J. O'Hara.
Contents: Introduction.
I. Principles and Prescriptions.
II. The Charismatic Element in the Church.
III. The Logic of Concrete Individual Knowledge in Ignatius of Loyola.

Introduction (7-12). The common thread in these three separately written essays is a theoretical distinction with significant practical implications: whether the particular and individual can be reduced to the general. If, as Rahner maintains, it cannot be, then there must be a difference in kind between principles which express a universal essence, and prescriptions which are directed to a concrete individual (essay 1). It is this distinction which legitimates the charismatic element in the church (essay 2), and which provides the key to understanding personal discernment of spirits (essay 3).

DEC.1. Principles and Prescriptions. (13-41). *Wort und Wahrheit* 12 (1957).
Abstract: Rahner distinguishes in kind principles from prescriptions. Both are a permanent and legitimate feature of human choice. He laments the church's over-reliance on safely repeating principles, and suggests a greater role for the laity in articulating prescriptions to shape public policy.

THE DYNAMIC ELEMENT IN THE CHURCH 137

Topics: MORALITY, choices; PRINCIPLES/PRESCRIPTIONS.
Subsidiary discussions: Angels, nature of (17f); Everyday Life, prudence (23f); Preaching, weakness is (32f); Laity, role of (38ff).

Precis: 1. The distinction between the two concepts. Distinctions can be useful. Although both express to some degree what "should be the case," principles as universal propositions bearing on some nature or essence cannot offer solutions to every particular individual situation. Even allowing that the individual can be the object of a universal moral imperative, Rahner argues that individuals are not simply "cases," instances of the universal. It is possible they may be subject to unique individual obligations. (Here Rahner makes a scholastic argument based on the nature of angels.) Summary, 18.

Principles and prescriptions come to be known in very different ways. Natures are subject to experiment, and can be expressed in general concepts; but individual acts of knowing, loving and deciding cannot be. Rahner gives the example of vocational choice: should I become a doctor or a priest? Once all the moral principles have been observed, is it not possible that there is a morally binding individual requirement attached to this otherwise morally neutral choice? After addressing the objection that such "ineffable" commands to individuals remain "ineffable, and not open to analysis," Rahner adds that such prescriptions apply also to collective entities: nations and epochs. He further argues that appealing to prudence only makes sense if the distinction between principles and prescriptions holds true, otherwise prudence would be nothing more than the application of universal propositions. The proclamation of universal truths is the proper pastoral task of the magisterium, along with working to see that they are put into practice. In doing this, the church itself must invoke prescriptions, knowing full well that it is not in infallible possession of them all. Clearly, the choice among possibilities that do not contradict moral principles is not morally indifferent. But even here, the church is not fully competent and can prescribe in error. Hence, prayer for enlightenment is not the same as asking for knowledge of principles knowable by the general exercise of reason.

2. Practical consequences of the distinction [Cf., EF.3.3]. Today there are too many principles and too few prescriptions, and often these principles are not followed. Why? Because principles are often mistaken for prescriptions. Prescriptions must be concrete and particular, but too often preaching simply rehashes seemingly bloodless and vague principles. Our pronouncements are too cautious, anxiously detached and measured. They are correct but sterile. Decisions today must be made in a quite different style. But having been burnt in the past, the church feels most secure defending itself with old maxims. In addition, takes more effort to come up with new prescriptions than to recycle old principles.

Rahner offers three suggestions (37-41). The first is to cultivate a sort of modern "probabilism" or "tutiorism." Granted that every prescription cannot perfectly embody every principle, those who argue against a particular prescription should be held accountable to offer a better prescription. Second, granted it is the task of the official hierarchy to teach principles in an authoritative way, perhaps it is the task of the laity to suggest practical ways that fit the modern age. Finally the laity should exercise the courage to unite not only on principles but also on concrete prescriptions, fully aware the solutions they suggest, while not morally wrong, may be less than perfect.

DEC.2. The Charismatic Element in the Church. (42-83). *Das Charismatische in der Kirche*, revised 1964. *Stimmen der Zeit* 160 (1957).

Abstract: Charism in the church takes two legitimate forms: institutional charism associated with office, and non-institutional charism generally associated with individuals. This permanent, divinely-willed state of affairs has definite consequences and creates a tension in the church only the Lord can regulate.

Topics: CHURCH, Charism in; OFFICE/CHARISM; SPIRIT/s, gifts of.

Subsidiary discussions: Petrine office (44f; 75f); Church as "absolute" (48f); "*Mystici Corporis*" (50ff); Religious life, regularization of (59ff; 78); Anonymous Christian/ity (64ff); Church, democracy in (69ff).

Precis: The church is a society whose nature contains a hierarchical structure with its various offices, and the Spirit in its various manifestations. **1. The charisma of office.** The permanent fidelity of the church to its Lord is guaranteed solely by the Spirit's promise to abide in the church. Without this the church would not be itself. Such fidelity is not a juridical construct but a gift (*charismata*) pertaining to office and not to individual office holders. This is why there can be no appeal against official authority in the church. (Note, charismatic means non-juridic, not occasional.) Summary, 46. The point is that office and spiritual gifts are not two totally distinct elements occasionally united in one person more or less by chance.

2. The non-institutional charismata. *a. The thesis.* It is a church doctrine that there are charismata, impulses and guidance of God's Spirit for the church, in addition to and outside her official ministry. *b. The church's teaching* is set forth in Pius XII's encyclical *Mystici Corporis*. These gifts do not minimize or negate the charism of office. The general principle that these charismata should function in harmony is no protection against either charism or office overreaching their prerogatives. The only effective safeguard is the Lord of both (53). Following St. Paul (54ff), Rahner notes that these gifts do not necessarily assume extraordinary forms, though all are given for building up the church. Theologians are a clear case (56). A final argument for this doctrine is the fact that the charismatic has always existed in the church. Rahner takes issue with those who claim the Spirit has been asleep or absent since late Apostolic times (57f).

3. The possibility of institutional regulation of gifts of the Spirit. The institutionally organized transmission and canalization of the gifts and graces of the Spirit (e.g., the impulse to live the evangelical counsels) legitimately belong to the charismatic component of the church. Rahner argues this from the historical fruitfulness of such intervention by the official church in the case of the Franciscans. He also argues the Sixteenth Century reformers erred in seeing the official church as merely a secular form of organization with no power to administer the charismatic gifts of the Spirit.

4. Lesser and greater spiritual gifts (summary, 62). Rahner expands the scope of what constitutes a spiritual gift to embrace what might appear to be simply "human acts" of fidelity, love, wisdom or self-sacrifice. That one finds such actions being preformed outside the boundaries of the visible church should not surprise us, insofar as God's salvific will extends to all. Such charismata, when they occur among the Christian faithful, constitute a compelling argument for belief in the church.

5. **The consequences.** *a. Toleration of a charisma by official authority.* Church authorities do not rule the church. The Lord is in charge. Listening to charismatic voices from "below" is not a favor but a duty of leadership. *b. The "democratic" church.* The church is democratic not in the sense that it operates by the principle of majority rule, but insofar as God wills that power and authority within the church be distributed. It is not a totalitarian system. *c. Inevitable disagreement in the church.* Needless to say, this legitimate diversity of power and authority which leads to opposition within the church is more than a necessary evil. On the human level, love (itself a gift of the Spirit) is the only thing that can give unity to the church. Until error has been established, the church must exercise patient tolerance. This in no way lessens the need for the church to warn or even to condemn once error has been clearly detected. But this is always a judgment that calls for courage and wisdom. *d. The burden of charisma.* Charisma always involves suffering. It demands the ability to withstand give-and-take, and the patience to wait for its proper moment (*kairos*), believing that it may actually be the Lord who is creating the force of resistance to help purify an immature enthusiasm. But opposition is not *ipso facto* proof that a charism is illegitimate; and the fact that charism involves suffering is no license for church authorities to inflict needless suffering. *e. The courage to receive new gifts.* Admittedly, new charisma when they first appear can seem shocking. Nevertheless, it is the duty of the church to recognize and encourage new charismata as early as possible— a stance seeming contrary to its nature. But scripture is clear: "Do not stifle the Spirit."

DEC.3. The Logic of Concrete Individual Knowledge in Ignatius of Loyola. (84-170). In Fritz Wulf, *Ignatius von Loyola. Seine geistige Gestalt und sein Vermächtnis.* Würtzburg, 1956.

Abstract: In general, systematic theology is still unable to do justice to the spiritual insights of St. Ignatius' Exercises. Rahner suggests his own theology of the experience of God makes significant advances in this direction. This essay assumes familiarity with Ignatian method and terms. [Cf., SE; P].

Topics: ELECTION; GOD, knowledge of; SPIRIT/s, discernment of; THEOLOGY, Ascetical.

Subsidiary discussions: Spiritual literature (85f); Angels, multiplication of (111f); Universal/particular, ontology of (111ff); Causality, secondary (119ff); Transcendence (123ff); Mysticism, Ignatian (155f).

Precis: 1. Introduction. We are still far from possessing an adequate theology of Ignatius' Exercises, something not uncommon for spiritual literature which is not fully deducible from abstract theological principles. A fresh approach must allow that the Exercises may contain new elements inspired by Spirit.

2. The problem of election in the Spiritual Exercises. The nature of the Exercises is determined by the fact that they are aimed at decision, election, determining God's will. How is this done? Although a particular choice cannot contravene revealed principles of the faith, neither can it simply be deduced from them. Ignatius candidly assumes that God can communicate His particular will to individuals (94). What would be the sense of working to discern spirits or of the Spirit speaking if the object of decision could simply be known by rational reflection or reduced to a psychological impulse? But what keeps this thesis from throwing open the doors to unbridled mysticism and illuminationism? (101-104). Since election cannot contravene the objective principles of faith, the field of possibilities is *a priori* restricted. In addition, election must proceed according to the rules of rational reflection. (Here Rahner moves into the three modes of election, 105f). Hence, election is apprehended in a distinct kind of cognition, in some sense directly due to God (though it is neither the beatific vision nor revelation strictly speaking). God speaks, making known what otherwise would remain unknown by use of other methods. (Return to the modes of election, 107ff). After repeating his assertion that scholastic theology has so far failed to answer the questions raised by the Exercises, Rahner summarizes (110), this time framing things in terms of universals and particulars. Any adequate theology would have to legitimate the existence of an individual element which has its own positive content and originality, and which is fundamentally and absolutely unique, Furthermore this would have to be grounded in ontology.

3. **The logic of the knowledge of religiously important concrete particulars in Ignatius.** How can any important particular be known if it cannot be inferred from general normative principles? This is the unique goal of the Exercises. Rahner offers some fragmentary insights, moving between the text of the Exercises and theological responses to the questions it raises.

   a. *The existence of divine influences and the problems of their recognition.* Ignatius maintains there are psychological experiences arising in consciousness that originate from God. These cannot be known as such simply because they are good or produce good fruit. Ignatius insists on determining their source. Most theologians with their notions of secondary causes would balk at this (119), as would most contemporary people (120) and most commentators on Ignatius. The options to explain such a motion coming from God would seem to be one of three: supernatural, preternatural (a miracle), or some other created reality. Yet the first would seem to be non-conscious, the second mystical, and the third stays trapped in the realm of created realities. Here Rahner concentrates on his understanding of transcendence (123-127) and its being "conscious," as long as that does not imply susceptibility to being known by deliberate, explicit reflection. But even if one allows that there exist certain "self-evident" experiences of a divine origin, the question remains how to distinguish them from others, and hence to legitimate them?

   b. *"Non-conceptual" experience of God.* In this "epistemological section" Rahner asks whether Ignatius' rules for discernment of Spirits do not presuppose a fundamental evidence and certainty which performs the same function as the first principles of logic and ontology. Rahner says there is such a claim in Ignatius' Second Week. Rahner next explains Ignatius "*consolatión sin causa precedente*" (132-137). He sees this movement as congruent with his own teaching on the conscious experience of God beyond all objectification in moments of human transcendence (135). He uses this insight to critique Suarez and other commentators (137-142) whose misinterpretation of "absence of motive" misleads them into concentrating on the "suddenness of the experience."

c. *Nature and certainty of this experience.* Ignatius does not say precisely how such experiences serve as general principles in the abstract domain of logic and ontology. Rahner begins his analysis with the assumption that even within this kind of awareness of supernatural transcendence, one can admit to different degrees of purity and duration. The lowest is Ignatius' "consolation *sin causa*" (146). Leaving many questions aside, differences in extrinsic causes do not affect inner certitude. After recapping the nature of this transcendent experience (148, 149) Rahner asserts that pure and simple transcendence cannot deceive; pure openness and receptivity is always genuine as it always refers to the true God who cannot be falsely circumscribed. God is given as coming and not as having come, and can be possessed in this mode. This is by definition "consolation." All this is at the first level and leaves aside mystical states, infused contemplation, etc. Rahner now comes at this from "another angle" based on another Ignatian text (152-154), and ends with an observation on a presumably higher state of Ignatian mysticism.

d. *The grace-given experience of transcendence as a criterion for recognizing an individual instance of God's will.* But this is not the end (recap)."How is the divine consolation of transcendence and immediacy inserted into a criterion in order to arrive at the particular knowledge which cannot be imparted by an ethics of the universal alone?" (157). The will of God is known through interpreting consolations and desolations in regard to their origin by means of the Rules of Discernment of Spirits. But note, the concrete object of choice is never itself the goal. God, the starting point for both the consolations and election, is the goal. One looks to see if these two elements cohere and still leave the pure openness to God intact. This of course takes time. Rahner now backtracks a bit to show how his view sheds light on other issues in interpreting Ignatius: experiences of consolation and desolation not coming from God (160-163); the crucial importance of determining the source of various impulses (163-164); the possibility of discerning election by people unable to make the Exercises (164-169). All of these applications underscore the one process at work under very different forms. The essay concludes (169) with an insight that any complete explication of Ignatius' spirituality would have implications far beyond ascetical theology into moral theology.

ES. *Encounters with Silence.* Westminster, MD: Newman Press, 1960. 87 pp. *Wort ins Schweigen.* Translated by James M. Demske, SJ.
Contents: Translator's Foreword.
I. God of my Life.
II. God of my Lord Jesus Christ.
III. God of my Prayer.
IV. God of Knowledge.
V. God of Law.
VI. God of my Daily Routine.
VII. God of the Living.
VIII. God of my Brothers.
IX. God of my Vocation.
X. God who is to Come.

ES.1. God of My Life. (3-10)
Abstract: This meditation serves as a primer on Rahner's understanding of God as incomprehensible yet personal, infinitely transcendent yet infinitely close, etc. Without using any difficult theological terms, this meditation addresses God as "God of my life," a title that implies a complex relationship. The meditation divides roughly into two parts: a reflection on God's infinity vs. human finitude (which illustrates Rahner's notion of the "supernatural existential);" and a reflection on the command to love God. In the end it is the human capacity to love which bridges the gap between the finite and the infinite.
Topics: GOD.
Subsidiary discussions: God, incomprehensibility of (3ff); Love of God (8ff).

ES.2. God of My Lord Jesus Christ. (11-17)
Abstract: Unlike humans who must moderate and choose among their attributes, God possesses and expresses all divine attributes at once. This overwhelming thought terrifies anyone who meditates seriously on God's total love being at the same time total justice, etc. Rahner begs God to speak a word accommodated to human beings . . . something comprehensible and not everything at once. God speaks this word in Jesus. The love present in his

human heart is indeed God's divine love. Rahner ends with a prayer that God will work to conform his own heart to the heart of Christ.
Topics: GOD, attributes of.
Subsidiary discussions: Jesus Christ, as Word of God (16ff); Heart (17).

ES.3. God of My Prayer. (19-25)
Abstract: Isn't God asking too much from us to remain faithful in prayer when He remains silent? Or is God simply waiting to answer us once we finish saying everything, our whole lives? But how is prayer possible if it is a lifting up of my entire self to God? What if I cannot make my whole self present to God this way? Yet it is not God we flee when we run from prayer, but the terrifying barrenness of our own souls which we encounter most profoundly in God's silence. To pray is to wait for the decisive moment of surrender. Mystics call this moment of decision the "dark night of the soul" after which comes the endless day of God's love.
Topics: GOD, silence of; PRAYER.
Subsidiary discussions: Death (21, 24f); Love of God (22ff); Fundamental Option (20f, 24f); Soul, dark night of (25).

ES.4. God of Knowledge. (27-33)
Abstract: Most of what we learned we have learned "in order to forget." Forgetting is good. What a horror, the prospect of remembering, or having to remember all we ever knew! Though some people say knowledge is our perfection, and even call God the God of knowledge, knowing seems superficial and completely inadequate for grasping reality, which is really only grasped through love. We only know God because God has first seized us. We meet God in the joys and sufferings of life. We actually know God and not just vague words *about* God because through baptism the living Word of God, God's Wisdom, God's Light, lives in us.
Topics: GOD; KNOWLEDGE and love; LOVE and knowledge.
Subsidiary discussions: Baptism, infant (30f); Word (31f); Death (32f).

ES.5. God of Law. (35-44)
Abstract: Is God the Spirit of freedom? The God of Laws? Or both? God's commands may be freedom and truth, but what about human laws, church laws? Are they not simply a burden? Perhaps it is only my self-will that makes them seem like such a burden. Not every one of my likes is a moral imperative. And clearly, a visible church needs concrete laws. But is God the God of these laws? Is God present in them? Do I really meet God when I fulfill them? If they were only the equivalent of spiritual traffic laws, they would be no burden at all. But when they require my inner assent ... then there is the danger of legalism. The only way to meet God in fulfilling the law is precisely to look beyond the law to God in the very act of obeying the law, and in this way we avoid the mistake of idolizing the law.
Topics: FREEDOM and law; GOD and law; LAW.
Subsidiary discussions: Obedience (43f).

ES.6. God of My Daily Routine. (45-52)
Abstract: How can I redeem my life from its wretched humdrumness which invades even my performance of the most sacred rites? Truth be told, it is not my daily activities that make me dull, *I* make *them* dull. Hence, I cannot escape the monotony of routine by escaping my everyday life. If there is a path to God, then it is found through the everyday. But is this path simply the growing disillusion with what life has to offer, the pagan's *taedium vitae*? No, the disillusioned heart is no closer to God than the joyful heart. What is the way through the everydayness of the everyday? If it is true that I can lose God in everyday activity, why is it not equally true that I can also discover God precisely there? Only the grace of God's love, which overcomes all opposition can reveal the transcendent in the everyday.
Topics: GOD; EVERYDAY LIFE, routine.
Subsidiary discussions: Death (46f); Ruysbroeck (50f); Work and leisure (50f); *Coincidencia oppositorum* (52).

ES.7. God of the Living. (53-59)
Abstract: How dead the dead seem, especially those I have loved deeply. What does their silence mean? In what meaningful sense can I say I remain bonded to them and they to me? How do I ask

God about this? God seems just as silent as the dead. Is it possible that God's silence is the answer to my complaint, since any completely clear utterance which I could comprehend would be less than God, and therefore would not really be the answer to my deepest desires? Truly, the silence of the dead mirrors the silence of God. Their silence is a summons to the infinite.
Topics: DEATH, life of the dead; GOD, silence of.
Subsidiary discussions: Love of our dead (54f).

ES.8. God of My Brothers. (61-68)
Abstract: God has sent us out to minister to others, and not just to our friends. Many of these do not welcome me. Many who do welcome me don't really want the One I have come to share. In fact, they seem to want to be protected *against* being touched by God. It seems I am condemned to sow the seed and watch it wither in the stony hearts of others. But I also know that when I complain like this I am no better than they. How can I assume the burden of others when my own heart is already so overburdened? Might it not precisely be by going out to others that we find the path to God, since my only way into the deepest recesses of any other human heart is found by drawing close to God? The choice is not between God and our fellows. God sends us to them to draw us closer to God.
Topics: LOVE OF GOD AND NEIGHBOR.

ES.9. God of My Vocation. (69-77)
Abstract: Rahner rejoices that God uses the concrete world to be revealed, but he comes up short at the thought that God uses him as a priest to be such an instrument of revelation. "How can people possibly recognize God in me?" Though he takes comfort in the fact that his own ministry is fully legitimated by the true church, he wishes he could somehow separate his official life from his private life. But this commingling is unavoidable. And this is the real burden of this vocation. He concludes with fervent prayers that God will help him bear the inevitable burden of his vocation.
Topics: PRIESTHOOD.

ES.10. God Who is to Come. (79-87)
Abstract: Why in the Advent season do we continue to pray "Come Lord Jesus"? Hasn't He already come? Or is God really the eter-

nally receding One, lost in the infinite distance of eternity? But if they say God has come in the person of Jesus, then why would He embrace precisely what we humans seek to flee? How does His sharing our burden dispel it? Or is it like this: that my free surrender to what Jesus undergoes is my "Amen" to His human life, and my way of saying "yes" to His coming? Have You made my life the starting point of your coming? (85). Christ is still in the process of coming. There remains now only one period of history: His Advent. It is misleading to say He will come again. We should rather say He will finally, fully come. He will be progressively more manifested.

Topics: ADVENT; GOD, infinity of; REDEMPTION.
Subsidiary discussions: Eschatology (85ff).

Episcopate and the Primacy. Montreal: Palm Publishers, 1962. 135 pp. Cf., *Inquiries,* Inq.4.

EY. *The Eternal Year.* Baltimore, MD: Helicon, 1964. 144 pp. *Kleines Kirchenjahr,* 1953. Translated by John Shea.
Contents: Translator's Preface.
 Advent.
 Christmas.
 New Year's Day.
 Epiphany.
 Shrove Tuesday.
 Ash Wednesday.
 Lent.
 St Joseph.
 Good Friday.
 Easter.
 Ascension.
 Pentecost.
 Corpus Christi.
 Sacred Heart.
 The Assumption.
 All Saints Day.

Translator's Preface (7-11). Rahner focuses here not on exegesis but on specific aspects of the liturgical year asking, "What does it all *really* mean?" Of course the core of Christian existence is the eternally valid Pascal Mystery of Christ proclaimed in the church and celebrated in her sacraments (quintessentially in the Eucharist) until He comes again. But as this mystery is too rich and complex to grasp all at once the church year breaks it down, like a prism separates the light passing though it. Rahner emphasizes the paradox embodied by the church (glory through the cross; already and not yet; eternity in time) which only faith resolves. Hence the title of this book.

EY.1. Advent. (13-18)
Abstract: The Advent readings, like our Advent faith, weave the saving events of past and future into the one eternal now. We rejoice that God has redeemed time and has sown His Advent-faith in our hearts.
Topics: ADVENT; FAITH; TIME.

Precis: The Advent liturgy weaves together past, present and future (expectation, Incarnation and Second Coming). Since the work of God in Christ has redeemed time itself, time is no longer a bleak succession of moments or an eternal return leading ultimately nowhere. God has forever become its source, its focus, its direction and goal. This is at the core of Advent-faith. Too often we think of faith as a series of events, facts on a list, some of which have happened, some are yet to come. But fundamentally, all these saving events endure simultaneously, and we live in their midst. "Faith is God's grace working to assimilate the very reality of the event thought about" (15). Through faith and the power of the Holy Spirit, the salvation we contemplate actually takes place in us. The past comes into the present. Christ lives in us. We live and die with Him. In being granted a share in the destiny of the Incarnate Word, the future becomes present. In a hidden way, Christ's future becomes our own. And all this takes place in the eternal now. Rahner closes with an application addressed to the heart (16ff). He reflects on the changes we see in nature as we move from autumn to winter– changes that can look like a procession to death or like the tedious cycle of eternal return. But just as life lies hidden beneath the snow, so the Advent-faith God planted in our hearts lives and gives us joy in this wintry season.

EY.2. Christmas. (19-26)

Abstract: The joyful mood of Christmas is but an echo of the Incarnation, that holy night which redeems time, gives meaning and purpose to life, and assures us that God is now and forever here.

Topics: CHRISTMAS; INCARNATION; TIME.

Precis: The cheerful mood of Christmas is only a faint echo of the fact that God has changed the night of our darkness into a holy night. Celebrating Christmas, this transforming event should also become a reality in our hearts and remain there to shape our entire outlook on life— our *Christian* outlook. Our human outlook judges that nothing of real meaning ever happens in the world. Life aimlessly circles in upon itself, and people hide their purposelessness with frantic activity. But adopting the Christian outlook and saying "It is Christmas" means that an event has burst into the world and into our lives that changes all that by providing a goal and a purpose to everything (21). Our fearful, cold, bleak night has become the holy night. For the Lord is there.

The Incarnation changes time and humanity (21f). What ensues is the stillness while God awaits our response— our free answer to His final word. This pause is human history, our chance to speak. One should not talk, but "silently give himself to the love of God that is there because the Son is born" (23). Christmas, the Incarnation, has transformed everything. We need no longer fear. The night of the world has become bright. This feast is not poetry or childish romanticism, but the avowal and the faith with alone justify us: that God has come and has spoken the final Word. And in speaking our "Amen," God's Word is then born in our hearts as well. The essay concludes with a recapitulation (24ff), God addressing and encouraging the human heart with the assurance, I am there. I am with you forever.

EY.3. New Year's Day. (27-39)

Abstract: New Years and advancing age are occasions to take stock. But what we find is not good. Our only consolation lies in doing, not in thinking, adding to the balance and leaving the reckoning to God.

Topics: EVERYDAY LIFE, aging; NEW YEAR'S DAY.

Subsidiary discussions: Consolation, spiritual (32ff).

Precis: New Years is a time for taking stock, especially for the elderly whose past is long and whose future is surely shorter. In old age we find ourselves changed in many ways (28f): unfeeling towards reality, unenthusiastic, tired. But the alarming question of old age is whether "the inner man" has not also grown old and tired. What has happened to our youthful wish one day to be holy? We seem no longer even to have the *will* to wish it. Sure we have become *holier*, but not *holy*. We have never loved God as we should. Have we wasted our best hours and are left irretrievably sad? What is left apart from prostrating ourselves at God's feet in abject resignation? Is this the answer? Is despondent confession (33) our only consolation? Rahner thinks not, since such consolation is too subtle, too crafty. It too easily becomes a game: repenting to please God so that He may have the joy of being merciful. Consolation observed is no consolation at all. Figuring such repentance into our reckonings already corrupts it, and there is no neutral vantage point. "Whoever desires to take hold of his consolation *and* of God's grace spoils it" (25).

Since we never succeed in taking hold of ourselves to insure what we now possess, and figuring that at this age probably not much will be added, what is left for us to do? "Nothing, except to add further entries to life's credit sheet, to the figures that God will tally up!" (36). This is the only way to true, unconditional surrender. In our deeds alone does the heart possess itself because in them alone does it forget itself. Consolation for the elderly lies not in thinking, but in doing what we can (list, 37f). "Thus the balance becomes a dropping of the balance— I forget what lies behind me. The balance becomes a running after the prize of eternal life in the bittersweet difficulties of the Christian daily life" (38). Time is passing, God is nearing. Action alone dispels fear. "Let us, therefore, run forward, singing!" (39).

EY.4. Epiphany. (41-48)
Abstract: To the Christmas message that God has come, Epiphany adds a summons to the heart to bestir itself, and like the Magi leave its native land and make pilgrimage to the blessed Absolute.
Topics: EPIPHANY; GOD, search for.

Precis: As a continuation of Christmas, Epiphany announces the same message: the grace of our God and Savior Jesus Christ and his love for us has appeared. But Epiphany adds its own proper theme: people themselves go out to God who has come down to them. "So this day is the feast of the blessed pilgrimage, the journey of the man who seeks God on his life's pilgrimage, the journey of the man who finds God be-cause he seeks him" (42). The story of the Magi is, or should be, *our* story. Do we accommodate ourselves to the inexorable flow of time (our native country), or do we look to find a goal on this journey? God, the goal of time, immense and incomprehensible, still promises that He will be found by those who seek Him. So do we set out as the wise men did? "They sought him; but he was already leading them because they sought him" (45). Despite their fear they obeyed their ears and set out. They sought Him in sincerity, despite the pain of the seeming disinterest of their neighbors to do so. Because they were expectant they heard good news in what others dismissed as banal information. And when they found Him, "they brought before the face of the invisible God now made visible the gold of their love, the incense of their reverence and the myrrh of their suffering" (46). Then they disappear as quietly as they came, like those who die. The essay ends with an impassioned address to the heart to imitate these Magi, never despairing, never looking back in regret while on our blessed pilgrimage to the Absolute.

EY.5. Shrove Tuesday. (49-55)

Abstract: Heartfelt laughter suits the spiritual person for four reasons. Christian laughter praises God by acknowledging that we are simply people (50ff); yet loving people (52f). Our laughter is a reflection of God's own laughter (53f); and laughter itself is promised in the victory of final judgment (54f).

Topics: EVERYDAY LIFE, laughter; MARDI GRAS.

EY.6. Ash Wednesday. (57-63)

Abstract: The dust of Ash Wednesday along with the reminder "You are dust," tells us everything we are: nothingness filled with eternity, because in the Incarnation, the Word has assumed this very flesh.

Topics: ASH WEDNESDAY; MAN as dust.

Subsidiary discussions: Incarnation (61f).

Precis: The ashes traced on our foreheads today are a visible sign of what we are: people of dust and of redemption. This is no Platonic dualism indicating the body is dust but the soul has another destiny. The words of Genesis, "You are dust" are spoken to the *whole* person. What does this powerful but pessimistic sign tell us about ourselves? Dust is commonplace (58f), indistinguishable, nothing. All of us are such dust, but we are also more. Always dying, lost sinners, able perhaps "to measure the finite with an infinite norm, only to perceive with horror that the eternal cannot be reached" (60). The self-hatred this engenders is reflected in scripture (list, 61) which also uses the term "flesh" to capture this same essence.

But the Word becoming flesh also heralds our salvation. This *caro* becomes the *cardo salutis*; flesh becomes the pivot of salvation. For those with faith and love, Incarnation transforms the terrifying judgment, "you are dust." Those who die with Christ and descend with Him into the dust ascend with Him to heaven. Christianity does not liberate us from the flesh and dust, nor does it bypass them; it goes right through them (62). These words of Ash Wednesday tell us everything we are: nothingness filled with eternity; death teaming with life; futility that redeems, that is God's life forever. Easy to say but hard to endure in the boredom of daily routine in anxious times! Yet incorporated with Christ in baptism, this ever-recurring descent to into the dust is only the beginning of the splendor and glory hidden therein.

EY.7. Lent. (65-72)

Abstract: Why fast today when God Himself seems so remote? But what is remote is an idol, the God of security and easy answers. Only by accepting and enduring this remoteness in a radical way will the true God dawn in our hearts. This is only possible for us because Christ once did the same with and for us.

Topics: GOD, remoteness of; LENT.

Subsidiary discussions: Atheism (67f); Jesus Christ, Agony in the Garden (71).

Precis: Doesn't the church's proclamation of a season of fasting seem at cross-purposes with reality today? People would gladly endure a season of fasting if they weren't already starving. We suffer because *God* seems so far from us. To boast of this situation would be a sin, both stupid and perverse. But many people do feel it as a pain and as a fact that demands explanation. Feeling God's distance is not the same as denying or ignoring God's existence. Believers often experience God's remoteness most acutely. It seems to be a mark of the age, like a collective dark night of the soul. Atheism is the false reaction to such a situation— impatient and mistaken (summary, 68).

How are we to deal with this God-distance of a choked-up heart which embitters the fasting season of our life? How are we to celebrate Lent? *First* we must stand up and face this remoteness. Endure it. For what is remote is NOT the living God, but the God who does not exist— the tangible God of earthly security, an idol! Rahner's advises, "Let despair fill your heart. . . . In despair, despair not" (69). Accept the finitude and futility of everything. Block off every escape route. Then the silence you hear is God's silence telling you He is there. *Second*, notice that God is with you. Know with faith that He is there, and has been awaiting you for a long time. Relax your hold on yourself, and you will perceive, as if by a miracle, that you are with God. If we do this, then peace comes and life rises through death.

This remoteness of God would not be the rising of God in our choked-up hearts if Christ "had not suffered and done just this with us and for us and on our behalf in his own heart" (71) in Gethsemane. Since that moment our despair is redeemed. If we pray with Christ, repeating His prayer, "Your will be done" our strength will suffice. This cannot be realized in thought. It must be won through bitter daily practice in our bitter season of fasting.

EY.8. St Joseph. (73-77)

Abstract: Celebrating St. Joseph as the patron of the church is only possible for those who believe in the Communion of Saints: that the blessed are not swallowed up in God but retain the individuality born of their personal histories. The link between us and each of them is unique and irreplaceable. But can modern people still see themselves reflected in St. Joseph? Yes, if they are still seemingly small, hardworking people of few words, simple and sincere. And scripture tells us that Joseph was such a humble man who silently fulfilled his duties, righteous and God-fearing. But this seemingly insignificant life had great significance! It had one meaning: God and his incarnate grace (76). Nations need more than great men and women. Today they also urgently need simple, loyal, dutiful people. Joseph is a worthy patron of many (list, 77). The question is whether we are worthy of him.

Topics: JOSEPH, St.
Subsidiary discussions: Communion of Saints (73f, 77).

EY.9. Good Friday. (79-86)

Abstract: Good Friday veneration of the cross points to an ongoing reality: that the sight of the cross continues to call for decision about this crucified man from the hearts of those who see Him. As always, some pass by, others stay and adore. In which camp do I find myself?

Topics: GOOD FRIDAY; JESUS CHRIST crucified.

Precis: A reflection on Good Friday liturgy when the cross is slowly unveiled to the refrain, "Behold the wood of the cross on which hung the Savior of the Word; come let us adore!" This ritual is a gesture of what once happened and is still happening. This moment contained the hidden meaning and goal of all previous time. But it remained hidden, because before the word was spoken from the cross no one knew definitively and unequivocally what answer God would give all the words and deeds of human history.

Since then people have been advancing in procession to that unveiled cross. "Many pass by, and many remain" (81). Those who pass by quickly surmise that a crucified man cannot possibly be the symbol of the meaning of their lives. Bacchus perhaps, but not Him. They pass by angry or disappointed. Am I one of them? Then there are those who remain because here they have found everything. They stay and they adore, each group for its own reasons: sinners, the dying, those who weep, children, the old, the homeless, the lonely, widows and the bereaved, scholars and sages, priests, even those who think they cannot believe. "Before his Cross 'I' kneel" (84). Incomprehensible to myself, the cross reveals the incomprehensibility of my destiny: that God is really love. So I am silent. What can I say? And what can I do but surrender to His love? All who have come to know God's mercy kneel before the cross and adore. They want to be close, to hear, to see. "For only light and happiness can come after this, the lowest depths of all calamity and terror." They wait until He speaks to them His word of mercy and love. Do I wait too?

EY.10. Easter. (87-95)
Abstract: To us "children of the earth" torn between loyalty to her and frustration that she cannot provide the infinity she promises, Jesus' resurrection reveals that He has become the one path to both the infinite God and to this earth, by displacing the nothingness of her barren womb with His own resurrected body.
Topics: EASTER; RESURRECTION of the body.
Subsidiary discussions: Creed, He descended into hell. (90f).

Precis: The Easter mystery is the most difficult to express due to the secular bias that all things religious are a matter of inner thoughts and feelings. But Easter announces God has done something. In raising His Son from the dead God has conquered death, not in the realm of inwardness but in the realm where we experience our essence as mortal "children of the earth." But our status is a painful paradox: "The earth bears children of infinite hearts, and, alas, what she gives them is too beautiful for them to scorn and too poor to satisfy them fully, for they are insatiable" (89). We call this muddy mix of life and death "every-day life." Looking for more than the world offers is not an act of cowardice but of loyalty to our natures. It is to such children of the earth that the news of Jesus' resurrection comes. What does it signify? Why is it a blessing?

The eternal Word, who was no less a child of the earth than we are, has died. This does not mean His soul was released from His body and escaped to some Platonic heaven. The creed states: "He descended into hell" which Rahner interprets as, "into the heart of all earthly things where everything is linked together and is one, where death and futility hold sway . . ." (90), that is until now when He Himself displaces them and becomes Himself the divine heart at the heart of the world. He has not risen to escape the barren womb of the world. He has risen in his *body*, indicating that He has now begun the transformation of the world beginning in Himself. His body remains part of this earth forever as a share of her reality and her destiny.

Jesus' resurrection is not His private destiny. It is the first visible indication of an already changed reality at the heart of things. But because it begins at the root and not on the surface, it can seem to everyday experience that nothing has happened. Nor does His ascension change any of this. It is only the withdrawal of His tangibly transfigured humanity which announces the final closing of the gap between God and the world. Christ remains present here in many forms (list, 93). He is the heart of this earthly world and the mysterious seal of its eternal validity. That is why we children of the earth can and must love her, even though the specter of death makes us tremble. For our faith tells us that Christ has penetrated and transformed her very core. Christ is the one path to both the infinite God and the familiar earth. For His resurrection is the beginning of the resurrection of all flesh. All that remains is for us to accept this blessed news and rise from the graves of our hearts. "He must rise from the core of our being, where he is as power and promise" (94).

EY.11. Ascension. (97-104)

Abstract: Ascension celebrates how, when Christ left and took with Him all that we are, He established heaven and overcame once and for all the distance finitude imposes on us, but which masquerades as closeness. We are consoled that His physical absence is the condition for His presence with us in Spirit.

Topics: JESUS CHRIST, Ascension of; RESURRECTION of the body.

Subsidiary discussions: Beatific vision (100f); Pantheism (101); Heaven (102).

Precis: Why does Jesus' departure from us not leave us inconsolable? This good man who revealed his "Father" and who was for us God incarnate is gone in his bodily tangibility. Why are we indifferent? Do we think perhaps He could not stand being around us? (Even we cannot endure it here forever. That would be an eternal hell.) In fact, there was nothing left here for Him to do. All was fulfilled. Now He has taken away with Him this frail human flesh, this nature of ours. "What I am, he assumed" (99). He has taken it to a place where it is easier for us to imagine that it would dissolve, than to picture how such a finite spirit could endure in the presence of God. It outstrips even our power to imagine. It is a mystery.

"And so my faith and my consolation are centered on this: that he has taken with him everything that is ours." Not even the beatific vision bypasses the corporeal humanity of Jesus. He, Jesus of Nazareth, abides forever. Hence, we too must be more important than we thought, of more permanent value and substance. Christianity teaches that even with all our pride, we are more prone to undervalue than to overvalue ourselves. For our finitude "can endure in the midst of God, in the midst of this fire, in the midst of this incomprehensibility" (101). This is the message of ascension.

This is what beggars the imagination. At least the ancients had a place for heaven in their science. But their heaven is fundamentally unchristian since it pre-existed Christ who we believe *established* heaven, and did not simply open its gates. In any case, we would have failed even to attain the level of the insight of the ancients if "we were to act as if we could not take the ascension seriously simply because we could not picture it in our imaginations" (103). But what are near and far in personal terms? Are people near us just because we can touch them? Or is the body with its finite limitation actually what keeps us from ever being really close? We are like prisoners, each in his/her own cell tapping out code to our unseen fellow inmates. Earthly nearness is ultimately really distance. Hence, Christ's death and glorification put Him right in our midst through His gift of the Spirit. Because He has come close He has gone away from us. Because we do not notice the transforming effects of His resurrection already at work at the core of the world, we experience His resurrection as separation. Like resurrection, ascension too must recur in each individual through grace.

EY.12. Pentecost. (105-112)

Abstract: Pentecost is both the final event of Eastertide and its goal: that we should possess the Spirit. This requires baptism, conversion and prayer. Often we miss the Spirit because we search in the

wrong places or confuse Him for something else. Experiencing the Spirit demands daily conversion and prayer.
Topics: PENTECOST; SPIRIT/s, experience of.
Subsidiary discussions: Baptism (107f); *Metanoia* (108ff); Prayer to Holy Spirit (110ff).

Precis: Pentecost completes the feasts of Eastertide. All these events had one goal: to redeem the world and to give the world God Himself in the Holy Spirit who is with us here and now. The center of God has become our center. Eternal life lives in mortal flesh. God himself is *ours*. That is the glad news of Pentecost. But has this message really penetrated our hearts in its fullness, or is it mere rhetoric? Do we live by it? So what must we do? We must be baptized and repent (Acts 2:38).

Already we have been baptized. God has touched us not only in our inner moods and ideas, but in His own incarnate, sacramental action. God has already poured His Spirit into our hearts. The second demand is repentance. Because we can quench the Spirit, grieve and obstruct Him, we must turn to the Spirit each day and be converted. But even good Christians often feel more of the spirit of the world at work in themselves than the Spirit of the Father. Rahner maintains that this feeling arises from our being ensnared in false ideas about how God is at work in the church. This is what calls for daily reflection and conversion. For what we seek "ostensibly" is not really the proper work of the Spirit (list, 109f). Daily reflection will make clear that the problem is not so much the absence of the Spirit as our looking in the wrong places and confusing Spirit for something else. When we see aright, we shall see "he is there."

Daily conversion enjoins a second activity: prayer to the Holy Spirit. Prayer for the Holy Spirit begins once we give up praying for Him, for we cannot compel Him; Spirit is a gift. "He comes not because we pray but because God wills to love us" (111). The Holy Spirit is within us as the strength of our weakness. Rahner concludes with a prayer invoking the Holy Spirit (111f).

EY.13. *Corpus Christi.* (113-119)

Abstract: A *Corpus Christi* procession is a sign of the abiding presence of Christ, in whom our guilt and salvation, our source and goal, merge and become the source of the community's unity.

Topics: CORPUS CHRISTI; JESUS CHRIST, abiding presence of.

Precis: From medieval times the *Corpus Christi* procession has represented the intertwining of the various spheres and activities of life, "a visible expression of man's movement through the space of his existence toward his goal" (114). The Holy One Himself supports this procession, accompanies it steadfastly, and leads it to its goal. So what is its significance? First, it proclaims that we are pilgrims on the earth (114). But we are no mere throng. We are a holy movement of united people, inclusive and non-threatening (115). Its peace and unity come from the Holy One who sustains it.

In addition, it tells us of the eternal presence of guilt in human history, as it carries through the streets the Crucified. Our procession is both a confession and a symbol of redemption. For it tells of the abiding presence of Christ, our reconciliation, on the paths of our lives. He is here. Remarkably, Christ our future is also with us as the goal toward which we advance. Procession is a mysterious moment when past present and future, God and man, meet and co-penetrate. The procession also says something about the unity of those who march. Their unity is a gift bestowed freely by the One toward whom they advance. This is what it means to carry the body of the Lord in holy procession, the sacrament of the unity of the church and of the redeemed. "We are pilgrims of an unending motion towards the goal and in the goal, pilgrims of a single goal, who are one in love through the one bread of eternal life" (118).

EY.14. Sacred Heart. (121-128)

Abstract: The heart is a deep mystery. What is at its core, fullness or nothingness? Be careful of saying "God" too quickly, for the true God terrifies us. Our hearts can rest only in Christ, the finite heart of God.

Topics: HEART; JESUS CHRIST, Sacred Heart of.
Subsidiary discussions: Knowledge of self (122).

Precis: Rahner first describes the heart as an image of the whole person, the ultimate ground of one's original unity, of one's character, uniqueness, individuality and solitariness. For one's heart belongs only to oneself and to the God who created it. That is why only the heart *knows* in the full sense of the term. But what is this human heart? Life or death? Fullness or nothingness? It seems the innermost misery of the human heart lies in its unmasking the finitude of all that it collects in itself. The quick answer is that God, the primal unity, and not emptiness, life and not death, is at our core. But does this really answer our question? Does it confirm that we have really overcome our despairing loneliness, or have we merely named our ultimate need? After all, is it not most frightful to have God as the center of our center? (125). Wouldn't God's unbearable infinity overpower us, and God's inexorable justice condemn us? God's heart cannot be less than it is, and we cannot know how God would respond to us if God came.

The center of our hearts must be God. But it must not be that infinite heart that fills our hearts with dread. That is why "He has to let His heart become a finite heart" (127) so it can enter us without destroying us. This is precisely what God has done in Jesus Christ– the finite heart that is still the heart of God. Jesus' single message of love calms our hearts, for the mystery of God has loved the world in its destitution. Only in this heart do we know who God wills us to be, and we know the one fact without which all knowledge is vain. For now in the heart of Christ our hearts know that they are one with the heart of God (summary, 128).

EY.15. The Assumption. (129-136)

Abstract: Mary's life, too, was ruled by the transitoriness of time. She achieved her eternal validity the same way we do. But her freedom from all guilt makes her entire life radiant. This alone sets her apart from us. Celebrating her living, present, eternal validity fills us with the hope of our future bliss.

Topics: BVM, Assumption of; SOUL, eternal validity of; TIME and eternity.

Subsidiary discussions: Saints, veneration of (133ff).

Precis: This reflection focuses on "the mysterious moment when time and eternity, transitoriness and immortality, touch one another in the existence of one human being, the moment when man enters the house of his eternity" (129). In light of the fact that we are all subject to time, how vain and puny all our activities seem since everything ends in death. The immortal soul seems to exist for the sole purpose of announcing that all living is dying. Yet despite appearances, there is something in these events that does not pass away, something full of meaning and eternal: good and evil. This is a comforting and frightful mystery: that the goodness and evil of our actions gives an eternal shape to the soul. In the end time ceases, transitoriness ends, and what is revealed is the eternal face of the soul.

Mary's life story is the same story of transitoriness as ours (131f). But in one respect it was entirely different. Our life story is so paradoxical and confused because of guilt, because our actions are a mix of good and evil, the evil actions empty and irretrievably gone, having produced nothing. But Mary, the Immaculata, need not disclaim any moment of her life; no part of it is empty or dead. This life did not end with her death, her whole life entered eternity. Nothing was abandoned. Everything lives on in the eternal goodness of the soul that has returned home. This is a joyful, consoling feast for us as it makes personal what would otherwise be mere information about objective possibilities concerning life after death. God calls by name each of those who rest in the heart of God. They have not disappeared but live on. Venerating the saints celebrates love's imperishability, and the closeness of God and the saints. So it is with Mary. Her tender humility, bright spirit and boundless submission to God are always present and new. She too is near, and her bliss prefigures our future blessedness.

EY.16. All Saints Day. (137-144)

Abstract: Remembering our dead in these days we ask, do they remember us? Their inscrutable silence puzzles us. But it is an echo of God's silence, the only proper condition for our love to express its act of faith in His love. The silence of the dead reinforces this invitation, that we may one day share their glory.

Topics: ALL SAINTS DAY; ALL SOULS DAY; DEATH, silence of.

Subsidiary discussions: God, silence of (140ff).

Precis: We celebrate this feast in memory of all the unknown dead of every age by lovingly remembering our own dead. In recollection we let all who we have loved rise from the grave of our breast. Only those who have never loved, and are therefore dead themselves, harbor no such memories. Those who have journeyed with us and have now slipped into the silence are irreplaceable. Who could forget those they have loved? We know from experience that we are always united with the dead in the bond of love. But are they also with us?

The dear ones have departed. They are silent. What does this silence mean? God, too, is silent. And the silence of the dead is an echo of His silence. Why? Because "God's silence is the boundless sphere where alone our love can produce its act of faith in his love.... He has veiled his love in the stillness of his silence so that our love might reveal itself in faith. He has apparently forsaken us so that we can find him." (140f). Our dead imitate this silence, through which they speak to us clearly. It is we who live a dying life. That is why we experience nothing of the eternal life of the holy dead. This silence, wrapped in the silence of God, "commands us to relinquish all things in the daring act of loving faith to find our eternal homeland in his life" (142). This is how the dead are close to us. This is how they speak to us. By their silence they summon us into God's life. Celebrating these feasts by recalling our dead, we who are dying begin to enter and share their eternal life with God, the God of the living.

The Eternal Yes. Denville, NJ: Dimension Books, n.d. 31 pp. *Ewiges Ja,* translated by Salvator Attanasio. **Cf., Meditations on the Sacraments, MS.8.**

The Eucharist: the Mystery of Our Christ. Denville, NJ: Dimension Books, n.d. 53 pp. *Das Geheimnis Unseres Christus,* translated by Salvator Attanasio. **Cf., Meditations on the Sacraments, MS.3.**

EF. *Everyday Faith.* NY: Herder, 1968. 217 pp. Sources are integrated with each essay title below. *Glaube, der die Erde liebt.* Herder, 1966. Translated by W.J. O'Hara.

Contents:
THE YEAR OF THE LORD
  Advent: The Judgment of the Son of Man.
    The Festival Time of Grace.
    Patience with the Provisional.
    The Stumbling-block of the History of Redemption.
  Christmas: The Answer of Silence.
    The Great Joy.
    Holy Night.
    Grace in the Abysses of Man.
    God's Coming into a Closed World, Feast of St. Stephen.
  New Year's Eve and New Year's Day:
  Spiritual Balance Sheet of a Year.
    In the Name of Jesus.
    New Year Meditation.
    Easter: Beginning of Glory.
    A Faith that Loves the Earth.
  Corpus Christi
    Feast of the Daily Bread.
    On the Way with the Lord.
    Prayer.
LOVE OF GOD AND THE NEIGHBOR
  The First Commandment.
  The New, Single Precept of Love.
  "Forbearing one another and forgiving
    one another."
ONE SPIRIT, MANY GIFTS
  Pagan Christians and Christian Pagans.
  The Prophetic Person and the Church.
  Do not Evade Decisions!
  The Christian in the World according to the Fathers.
  The Divine Mystery of Marriage.
SAINTS' DAYS
  The Feastday of a Holy Beginning.
  "Take the child and his mother."
  Thomas Aquinas.
MYSTERIES OF THE APPARENTLY INSIGNIFICANT
  An Ordinary Song.
  Seeing and Hearing.

Prayer for Hope.
Note concerning the contributions in this book.

1. The year of the Lord.
1.1. Advent.
EF.1.1.1. The Judgment of the Son of Man. (11-13). *Der Volksbote*, 49 (1949) no. 47, December 24.

Abstract: It seems strange for Advent to begin with readings about the final judgment. But Advent marks the start of an irreversible process, still ongoing and awaiting fulfillment. Then we shall see Him as the Son of Man, as one like us. He will judge or justify our lives. We already see the face of our judge in the faces around us, especially in the faces of the poor and of our enemies. Shall we be able to raise our heads and look into His face when we hear the words, "Whatever you did to one of these ..."?

Topics: SERMONS: Luke 21:25-33; ADVENT; JUDGMENT, final.

EF.1.1.2. The Festival Time of Grace. (14-16). *Der Volksbote*, 48 (1948) no. 48, December 1.

Abstract: Christians must believe, and take risks for the unseen Kingdom of Heaven. John the Baptist is what we should be each day of our Advent lives: a prophet, in prison, awaiting certain death, but still interested in reports of miracles which are of no help to himself. He believes despite everything. He sends for news and hears back "I am coming, and blessed the one who is not scandalized in me."

Topics: SERMONS: Matthew 11: 2-10; ADVENT; JOHN the Baptist, St.

EF.1.1.3. Patience with the Provisional. (17-19). *Der Volksbote*, 49 (1949) no. 49, December 8.

Abstract: The question put to John, what are you doing if you are not he who is to come, reveals the greatest danger to Advent faith: impatient religious radicalism. We all long for God. But all we get are precursors: human beings, words, events, gestures, never the reality. The impatient wander off into nature mysticism or political schemes that never satisfy. Ours is essentially an Advent church.

All we have is provisional. And God only comes to those who patiently love his forerunners and the provisional.

Topics: SERMONS: John 1;19-28; ADVENT; JOHN the Baptist. St.

EF.1.1.4. The Stumbling Block of the History of Redemption. (20-22). *Der Volksbote*, 49 (1949) no. 50, December 15.

Abstract: The historicity of Christianity is scandalous, along with its very concrete worship, sacraments and teaching. True, God can find us anywhere. But this does not mean we have a right to tell God where to look for us. God has marked out a clear and concrete path for us; and Christ Himself has walked that path here on earth in a specific time and place. For many, Christianity is too human and historical. They would rather be something other than human. For them Christ's incarnation is a stumbling block.

Topics: SERMONS: Luke 3:1-6; ADVENT; INCARNATION.

1.2. Christmas.

EF.1.2.1. The Answer of Silence. (23-27). *Die Presse*, December 22, 1962.

Abstract: What does it mean to celebrate Christmas? In order to find out, prepare to celebrate Christmas. Have the courage to be alone, for the real gifts are the fruit of solitude. In solitude, be still. Wait. Whatever is experienced there, bear it. If you sense a void, do not be quick to call it "God." Concepts can kill religion. If one perseveres in silence and allows it to speak, one hears something ambiguous: fear of death and promise of infinity; remote yet close; familiar and mysterious. The proper interpretation of this inner experience is grace. In our solitude we encounter God in man – the heart of the mystery of the Incarnation when God becomes man (summary, 27).

Topics: CHRISTMAS; SILENCE.

Subsidiary discussions: God, as mystery (24f); Grace (25); Incarnation (25ff).

EF.1.2.2. The Great Joy. (28-30)/ *Der Volksbote*, 49 (1949) no. 52, December 29.

Abstract: God's incarnation reveals our true nature: we are not some unsuccessful experiment; it must be worthwhile to be human; we are a sacred family; human history must have a blessed outcome. Since God became man we need not become supermen. The only thing we may *not* do is will to be less than brother and sister of the Eternal Word who became flesh. In this season especially, let us be kind to one another.

Topics: CHRISTMAS; INCARNATION.

EF.1.2.3. Holy Night. (31-36). Previously unpublished.

Abstract: Why do Christians associate Christmas with night, holy night: (*Weih-nacht*)? Night is ambiguous. It has two aspects: "promising and threatened and threatening at one and the same time, something provisional which may still set off for distant goals but which is still uncertain of arriving" (32). Nothing is more like this nocturnal beginning than Christmas. Hence, we celebrate Christmas in silence, with hearts expectantly open.

Topics: CHRISTMAS; SILENCE.

Subsidiary discussions: Everyday life, night (31ff); Incarnation (33f); God as mystery (34f).

EF.1.2.4. Grace in the Abysses of Man. (37-42). *Die Zeit* 17 (1962) no. 51, December 22.

Abstract: It is indisputable that after Christmas life goes on with its inexorable descent to death. But does this negate the value of Christmas? Is it possible the real meaning of Christmas already lives in the hearts of those who do not even think of themselves as believers? Mystery permeates our existence. Over and over it compels us to face it. This incomprehensible mystery is God, whether we call it that or not; and those who engage it are already in relationship with God. Such people already have Christmas within them. Since this truth became concrete in the historical Jesus, those who surrender to mystery are also accepting Jesus, even if they do not realize it (40). In loving our neighbors we are loving God.

Topics: ANONYMOUS CHRISTIAN/ITY; CHRISTMAS; GOD as mystery.

EF.1.2.5. God's Coming into a Closed World: The Feast of St. Steven. (43-46). Previously unpublished.

Abstract: Although the proximity of St. Steven's Day to Christmas is coincidental, the two feasts are intimately connected. After a brief character sketch of Steven drawn from Acts 6-7, Rahner concludes that Steven, "when he saw the heavens open," becomes a good interpreter of Christmas. In the incarnation the infinite does come close, and the finite opens out onto infinite expanses. The only satisfying goal for us is one wherein we encounter both ourselves and the infinite. Anything less is an idol. If we call ourselves "man," and if we call infinity "God," then the goal we seek would have to be "God-man." This is the Christmas revelation where God meets us in search of Him.
Topics: SERMON: Acts 6-7; CHRISTMAS; STEVEN, Martyr.
Subsidiary discussions: Self-Transcendence (45f).

1.3. New Year's Eve and New Year's Day.
EF.1.3.1. Spiritual Balance Sheet of a Year. (47-51). *Geist und Leben* 30 (1957) 406-408.
Abstract: Taking leave of the old year is different for everyone, yet also the same. But to whom can we pass off this eternally irrevocable year? Who preserves it? Christians answer: "God." This year, whatever its successes or failures was a gift from God. In accepting even its hardships we were also accepting God, albeit implicitly. What we return to God in gratitude, He redeems and liberates. So we can shoulder once again our old tasks and fears, but heartened now, remembering that God surrounds us with goodness, love and fidelity. Whatever may happen in the year ahead, God's strength will triumph.
Topics: NEW YEARS; TIME.

EF.1.3.2. In the Name of Jesus. (52-53). *Der Volksbote* 49 (1949) no. 52, December 29.
Abstract: Since we shall live the new year in God's presence, let us begin it in His name. Time presses on not to destruction but to God, So onward! The proper name of Jesus names the incomprehensible God. We know Christ's actions reveal God's will in our regard. If we forget this name then God recedes into incomprehensibility and we are lost again. So onward, in Jesus' name! [Formerly, January 1 was the Feast of the Holy Name of Jesus.]

Topics: SERMON, Luke 2:21; GOD, name of; JESUS CHRIST, name of; NEW YEARS DAY.

EF.1.3.3. New Year Meditation. (54-70). *Stimmen der Zeit* 82 (1956/57) 241-250.

Abstract: New Year provides the opportunity for this lyric weaving together of Rahner's major themes: time and eternity, fundamental option, everyday mysticism. The new year will bring opportunities to posit oneself in the fullness of time. But these opportunities will come in the garb of the everyday, and will be embraced, if at all, only in faith.

Topics: FUNDAMENTAL OPTION; MYSTICISM, everyday; NEW YEARS; TIME and eternity.

Subsidiary discussions: Sacraments and fundamental option (58ff); Grace (61); God as eternal future (64f); Renunciation (66f).

Precis: What will the New Year bring me in terms of eternity (as that is all that finally matters)? When will be my fullness of time: the moment I fully possess myself in an act of perfect self-giving and dispossession? Rahner considers and discards a number of possibilities: we cannot seem to act so whole-heartedly while still on pilgrimage (56). Even to ask the question implies we have not achieved it (57). Yet it must occur somewhere in my life. It is not necessarily in the "greatest moments" (e.g., overtly sacramental events) for even these can be halfhearted and erode. In fact it may well occur in a completely ordinary moment of graced self-renunciation: in an act of forgiveness, simple decency, or prayer (62).

The question, "has this decisive hour of fullness of my time already occurred," is a foolish one, since any act in the past can be made relative by a future disposition. The appropriate question is "where is such an hour coming from to me out of what is still to come?" (64). And what is coming toward us is God as the eternal future, and our making that future our own. Decisive moments will come to me in the new year. But they will come in simple garb, and may easily be overlooked (examples, 66). When we seriously attempt to do commonplace kindnesses with intention, we soon realize we are the losers. But this itself is a gate to the eternal. For when the reward for virtue in this world is nothing, "then God is present as that 'nothing' and finite loss is infinite gain"

(67). Rahner calls this the "mysticism of everyday life." Few everyday situations will be decisive turning points for us. But some can be, and we cannot know in advance which are which. So let us embrace the New Year with its load of everyday situations which have the potential to open me to God in the fullness of my time. [Although the concept of "death" is not explicitly developed here, one can see it throughout as a kind of subtext.]

1.4. Easter.

EF.1.4.1. Beginning of Glory. (71-75). *Der Volksbote* 56 (1965) no. 14, April 1.

Abstract: Easter does not celebrate a past event but a beginning which has already decided the remotest future. Everything is in motion (nature and human history). But wither? Into nothingness? Christians claim God is the goal of all history, and that in Easter resurrection the definitive future has already begun. "The place at which such a beginning of the end and completion has appeared is called Jesus of Nazareth" (74). Although people prefer to escape commitment, reality compels us to give an answer: meaning, or meaningless? If we affirm life and meaning whole-heartedly, we have already said Easter.

Topics: CREED/s; resurrection of the body and life everlasting; EASTER; RESURRECTION.

EF.1.4.2. A Faith that Loves the Earth. (76-83). *"Freue dich, Erde, deines himmlischen Lichtes"* in *Gesit und Leben* 23 (1950) 81-85.

Abstract: Our faith in Jesus' resurrection and his going down into the earth, signal our faith that Jesus did not abandon the earth but transformed it at the deepest level. Being essentially "children of the earth" this faith fills us with hope and permits (in fact demands) that we continue to love the earth.

Topics: EASTER; ECOLOGY; JESUS CHRIST, death of; RESURRECTION.

Subsidiary discussions: Creed: He descended into hell (79ff); Jesus Christ, Ascension of (81f).

Precis: Easter faith is difficult for many because it is not "spiritual" enough. What God did to raise Jesus from death seems too physical. But we are children of this earth. We belong here. We cannot wish to cast off from here forever, however painful life on earth may sometimes be. The gap between what we desire and what the earth can give becomes the ground of our guilt (summary, 78). What are we to do? What does the resurrection mean for such children of the earth? Here Rahner makes much of the fact that the death of the Son of Man was immediately followed by his "descent into the realm of the dead," i.e., "into the heart of all earthly things where all is linked into one" (79). By doing this Jesus became the divine heart of the earthly world, "where time and space sink its roots into God's omnipotence" (80). Jesus rose not to escape the earth. Rather he rose bodily and transfigured to begin the transformation of the world into Himself. His resurrection, far from being something strictly personal is like a volcano, hinting at the presence of earth's real but hidden molten core. Even His ascension does not signal absence, but the overcoming of any distance between ourselves and God. "Consequently, we children of this earth may love it, must love it. Even where it is fearful and afflicts us with its distress and moral destiny" (82). Its misery is only temporary, a test of our faith. We do not experience this. We believe this. All that remains is for Christ to open the tombs of our hearts and to rise from the center of our beings.

1.5. *Corpus Christi.*

EF.1.5.1. Feast of the Daily Bread. (85-89). *"Mahl der Pilger"* in *Gottes Wort im Kirchenjahr* (1955) 19-21.

Abstract: This strange feast celebrates in a festive way what we celebrate each day: the meal of those who are pilgrims to eternal life. After extolling the greatness of the mystery of the Eucharist (86-87), Rahner bemoans the fact that it often becomes too commonplace (87-88). This days' festive celebration should open our eyes and give us renewed enthusiasm and gratitude for the great gift we partake of each day.

Topics: CORPUS CHRISTI; EUCHARIST.

EF.1.5.2. On the Way with the Lord. (90-95). Previously unpublished.

Abstract: How can I join wholeheartedly in the procession of this day knowing, "it is death they are celebrating with such jubilation" (91), the death of the Word of God made flesh? Where are these

pilgrims going but forward to their deaths? It is strange that on their way they sing and carry with them the body of Him who was slain. Why do they do this? Because in this sign of death they see "the life which made of death itself the victory of life" (93). And this procession is like every path we take in our everyday lives. For in truth, every path leads to the incalculablity of God.
Topics: *CORPUS CHRISTI;* DEATH.
Subsidiary discussions: Jesus Christ, death of (92f).

EF.1.5.3. Prayer. (96-98). "Whitsun Prayer" in *Offen sei Dein Herz zur Welt* (1954) 72-74.
Abstract: A Pentecost prayer to the Holy Spirit, begging for His gifts and fruits.
Topics: PENTECOST; SPIRIT/s, gifts of.

2. Love of God and the Neighbor.
EF.2.1. The First Commandment. (101-103). *Der Volksbote* 50 (1950) no. 38, September 24.
Abstract: Today's stress on loving neighbor should not overshadow the First Commandment: Love of God. Yet who loves that "distant God" as s/he should, with all one's tired, worn out heart? On our own we cannot love God as we should. "Only he who demands it of us can give it to us" (102). We must pray for this love. Humble alarm at our lack of love toward God is the God-effected beginning of our love.
Topics: SERMON; Matthew 23:34-40; LOVE OF GOD.

EF.2.2. The New, Single Precept of Love. (104-117). May 1965 lecture to Catholic Welfare Organization for Girls, Women and Children, in Cologne. *Korrespondenzblatt* 35 (1965) 206-216.
Abstract: A reflection on the unity of the love of God and neighbor, a bond which is much greater than it appears in the common view. Rahner approaches this topic from three angles: the scholastic understanding of the Theological Virtues, the fundamental option, and the Incarnation.
Topics: LOVE OF GOD; LOVE OF NEIGHBOR.
Subsidiary discussions: Theological virtues (108ff); Anonymous Christian/ity (110, 113f); Fundamental Option (110ff); Incarnation (114ff).

Precis: People today in their need to demythologize and break through taboos have a hard time believing in God, more less loving God. It seems only the sincere and heartfelt love of neighbor can convince others of the existence and love of God. The unity of love of God and neighbor is already found in scripture, especially in Paul and John (106f) leaving us with the thesis (108) that in loving God we are also loving neighbor. But how is it possible to maintain this thesis?

Rahner's first line of argument centers on the scholastic discussion of Theological Virtues (faith, hope, love): the three fundamental acts of the human person. He claims these are the selfsame theological gifts by which we love both God and man. But he takes it one step farther, arguing that the absolute self-abandonment experienced in love of neighbor has already arrived at the inexpressible mystery of God. Grace alone gives love of neighbor its saving meaning.

Rahner then approaches the question from another angle (110ff): theological anthropology. He weaves together two important themes: Fundamental Option and Anonymous Christianity. He argues that we can and do dispose of ourselves radically through our everyday acts of love, and thereby say a final yes or no to God. Christian do this with explicit reference to God. Others, however, might do the same thing but only implicitly. These latter we might think of as anonymously Christian.

From another angle: Christology (114f). What does it mean when Jesus says, "what you did to one of these you did to me?" Far from being a juridical fiction, Rahner argues that we actually do meet the Incarnate Word of God in the other human being we love, because God Himself is there. This is no more than a full understanding of Incarnation. "The only condition is that we allow the innermost specific movement of this human love to come to its ultimate radical goal and essential fulfillment" (115). We know nothing of God if we know nothing of man. And love is at the core of both (summary, 116f).

EF.2.3. "Forbearing One Another and Forgiving One Another."
(118-123). June 18, 1965 sermon at Northern Catholic Congress in Hamberg. *Geist und Leben* 38 (1965) 310-312.

Abstract: Rahner gives three interpretations of this text, each one deeper. Though a superficial reading seems clear and simple, a closer reading questions our seriousness as Christians. Do we really love as we should? Then we fear. A fearful reading of the text reveals that on our own we cannot love as we should. Only God's love loving within us can fulfill the demands of this text. A third reading shows the text to be one of judgment and encouragement for everyday Christians. We must stand the test of everyday life that comes from God, conscious that we can do so only with the grace of Christ.

Topics: SERMON: Col 3:12-17; LOVE OF NEIGHBOR; MYSTICISM, everyday.

3. One Spirit, Many Gifts

EF.3.1. Pagan Christians and Christian Pagans. (127-129). *Der Volksbote* 50 (1950) no. 3, January 19.

Abstract: Church membership is no guarantee of salvation. "In some respects we are all pagan Christians who refuse our Lord faith... We ought to keep a lookout for 'Christian Pagans', i.e., people who are near God without realizing it, but from whom the light is hidden by the shadow which *we* throw" (129).

Topics: SERMON: Matthew 8:1-13; ANONYMOUS CHRISTIAN/ITY.

EF.3.2. The Prophetic Person and the Church. (130-134). *Münchiner Katolische Kirchenzeitung* 41 (1948) no. 7, February 15.

Abstract: Popes and bishops seldom herald new charismatic impulses in the church. This is often the task of more obscure "prophets." The duty of church leaders is to evaluate these voices. Rahner gives many examples of such public voices and of their personal errors. Fidelity to the church during times of trial is a sign of a prophet's authenticity. The church, for its part, must be careful not to stifle the Spirit.

Topics: CHURCH, prophets in; SPIRIT/s, discernment of.

EF.3.3. Do not Evade Decisions! (135-141). M. von Galli & M. Plate (eds.), *"Kraft und Ohnmacht. Kirche un Glauben in der Erfahr-*

ung unserer Zeit," 1963, 84-91. [Cf., DEC.1. "Principles and Prescriptions" for original fuller context.]
Abstract: The church is good at enunciating principles and general moral norms. These are the ideals on which there is often consensus. But what we need to guide concrete actions are specific "prescriptions." Allegiance to abstract principles is not enough to justify a Christian. Rahner suggests it may be the special task of the laity to provide such needed prescriptions and to forge coalitions in contemporary society.
Topics: LAITY, role of; THEOLOGY. Moral.

EF.3.4. The Christian in the World according to the Fathers. (142-153). Introduction to *"Kirchenväter an Laien. Briefe der Sellenführung,"* 1939, 1-17.
Abstract: How to realize one's Christian ideals in the world is once again a hot issue. Rahner looks to the writings of Clement of Alexandria (150–215) for guidance, insofar as he was one of the last to explore this issue fully in a cosmopolitan, pre-Constantinian, pre-monastic age somewhat similar to our own. He advocated direct involvement in the concrete affairs of the world (rather than flight from the world) in order to make all things holy. The details of how to do this are left to the genius of each new generation.
Topics: CLEMENT of Alexandria, St; LAITY, spirituality of.
Subsidiary discussions: Martyrdom (145); Monasticism (148ff).

EF.3.5. The Divine Mystery of Marriage. (154-159). *Geist und Leben* 31 (1958) 107-109.
Abstract: Most discussions of matrimony as a mystery of Christ's love for the church merely transfer the mystery from one realm to the other without ever explaining how the two realms converge. Entrusting oneself wholly to another person may seem commonplace, but in fact doing so brings one implicitly into the presence of God. This only becomes fully explicit in the sacrament. Matrimony like every other sacrament conveys grace –not simply "divine help," but a communion in divine life (presupposing one's interior consent). It is fitting that the liturgy of matrimony moves from the couple's exchange of consent to the holy sacrifice of the Mass, underscoring as it does the sacrificial nature of the love of

both Jesus and the couple. In matrimony a couple enters an even deeper relationship with God in His love.

Topics: SERMON: Eph 5:32; MATRIMONY, Sacrament of.

Subsidiary discussions: God in marriage (155f); Grace as divine life (156f); Cross as source of grace (158).

4. Saints' Days

EF.4.1. The Feast-Day of a Holy Beginning. The Feast of Mary's Immaculate Conception. (164-168). *Korrespondenzblaat des Collegium Canisianum* 94 (1960) 13-16 (meditation outline 08.12.1959).

Abstract: A very dense treatment of the Immaculate Conception centering on the notion of beginnings.

Topics: BEGINNINGS; BVM, Immaculate Conception of.

Subsidiary discussions: Sin, original; (167f).

Precis: Rahner considers the Immaculate Conception under three interrelated aspects: **I. Beginnings as such.** A beginning is not empty nothingness or mere indeterminacy. It is the radical ground of the whole history which is to come. The beginning as such is the plentitude of God. To look forward in hope to the future is to anticipate the fulfillment of the beginning. **II. Mary's beginning.** In the case of Mary, it took the church centuries to complete the journey from consequence to origin, and finally to proclaim the Dogma of the Immaculate Conception. In Mary one cannot posit a guilty difference between God as beginning and beginning as posited by God, for such a rift is subordinate to the saving work of Christ, and Mary is an integral element of that work. **III. Our own beginning.** Although it remains hidden until we arrive in God, we know our beginning contains certain elements: earth, ancestors, Jesus, church, baptism and eternity. All are encompassed by God's knowledge and love. All must be accepted. But even the power to accept is already a grace which alone can overcome the gap our human will imposes between God's will and human will, something already encompassed from the beginning by God's love.

EF.4.2. "Take the Child and his Mother." On Devotion to St. Joseph. (169-184). *Geist und Leben* 30 (1957) 14-22, heavily revised. Also in *Theology Digest* 6/3 (1958) 169-173.
Abstract: It is not enough to say we honor St. Joseph because he was a just man related to Jesus and Mary. Proper exegesis of the first chapter of Matthew shows he was incorporated into the history of redemption as such. We venerate him as a member of that family no longer born of the will of the flesh but of spirit.
Topics: SERMON: Matthew 1; JOSEPH, St., veneration of.
Subsidiary discussions: Salvation History, official (170ff).

Precis: What justifies the growing veneration of St. Joseph? Mere kinship cannot be enough, since others more closely related to Jesus are not so honored. **Position in official sacred history and inner holiness:** Salvation history has two facets: what is revealed, (i.e., public and official) and what remains hidden. The first is somehow sacramental, uniting office and holiness (*charis* and *charisma*). Does St. Joseph belong to the former category of sacred history or to the latter? **On the exegesis of Matthew 1:** This careful textual analysis questions many former pious interpretations of Joseph and Mary, their thoughts and motives. According to Rahner we can say with confidence that Joseph knew the heavenly origin of the child and for that very reason wanted to withdraw, not wishing to claim for himself the one who God had claimed (179). **Joseph the officially appointed father of Jesus:** Granting this, it becomes clear that being appointed husband and father and entrusted with the care of Jesus and Mary, he was also being officially incorporated into the history of redemption as such. Hence, in him task and requisite holiness united. His birth is not of flesh but of spirit. This is the starting point to understand and justify his veneration.

EF.4.3. Thomas Aquinas. (185-190). *Korrespondenzblaat des Collegium Canisianum* 95 (1961) 25-28.
Abstract: I. When it comes to venerating saints, Catholics today are not as Catholic as they suppose. For proper veneration is not mere historical remembrance but a real genuine relationship with a person who has attained perfect fulfillment and hence remains present and powerful. The saints find their fulfillment in God but are

not thereby swallowed up or simply lost in God. **II.** We honor Thomas Aquinas as being sober and objective. He is a systematic thinker who sees and presents everything in light of the whole, without losing his love and respect for the particular. In him, his theology and spiritual life merge. He is a mystic who adores the mystery he studies, but without ever making the incomprehensibility of mystery a grounds for fuzzy thinking or laziness.

Topics: SAINTS, veneration of; THEOLOGY; THOMAS AQUINAS, St.

5. Mysteries of the Apparently Insignificant.

EF.5.1. An Ordinary Song. (193-195). *Orientierung* 23 (1959) 93-94.

Abstract: Rahner asks whether there is no longer a place for ordinary church music for simple people which expresses everyday sentiments, and which one might even be tempted to whistle at work.

Topics: MUSIC, liturgical.

EF.5.2. Seeing and Hearing. (196-204). K. Pawek (ed.), *Panoptikum oder Wirklichkeit. Der Streit um die Photographie.* 1965 (75-81).

Abstract: This analysis of two senses, hearing and seeing, moves from sense organs to cognition as a fully human act, and ends with contemplation: training the eyes and ears to really see and hear.

Topics: COGNITION, *conversio ad phantasma.*
Subsidiary discussions: Contemplation (203f).

Precis: Banal philosophy regards hearing and sight as two faculties that connect external objects with human subjectivity. They are limited but serviceable, like an old AM radio. But this overlooks the metaphysics of sensation: that we do not simply have senses, we *are* sensibility. Here Rahner delves into implications of the Thomistic doctrine of cognition, *conversio ad phantamsa* (198f). Two other realities are co-given in the human act of seeing and hearing: 1) contact with the necessary horizon against which any particular thing is seen or heard (200); 2) the practical moral dimension which raises the question of human intention connected with a corporeal experience (201). After discussing whether people today are increasingly attracted to one sense or another, Rahner concludes that reliance on either sense can end up being so much distraction, mere sound and fury, if we do not develop a capacity for contemplation which alone helps us make true sense of what we see and hear, and which ultimately leads us back to God.

EF.5.3. Prayer for Hope. (207-211). Previously unpublished.
Abstract: This prayer asks three things of God: to strengthen our hope by conforming our lives with Christ's; to help us share in the prayer of Jesus; to recognize our sufferings as a share in the cross.
Subsidiary discussions: Hope (207f); Jesus Christ as the source of hope (207f); Jesus Christ, prayer of (209); Jesus Christ, Cross of (210).

Everyday Things. London: Sheed and Ward, 1965. Theological Meditations Series 5. 41 pp. *Alltägliche Dinge.* Translated by M.H. Heelan. **Cf.,** *Belief Today.* **BT.1.**

Faith Today. Hans Küng (ed.). London: Sheed and Ward, 1967. Theological Meditations Series 9. *Im Heute Glauben.* Einsiedeln: Benziger, 1965. Translated by Rosaleen Ockenden. **Cf.,** *Belief Today,* **BT.2.**

FS. Free Speech in the Church. NY: Sheed and Ward, 1960. 112 pp. *Das freie Wort in der Kirche,* 1959.
Contents: 1. Free Speech in the Church.
2. The Prospect for Christianity.

FS.1. Free Speech in the Church. (9-50)
Abstract: "... there is and should be something like free speech within the Church as there is outside it, and consequently even people who have nothing more to offer than their own private and personal opinions have a right to express these and to be given a favorable hearing when they do so" (50).
Topics: CHURCH, public opinion in; LAITY, rights and responsibilities of.
Subsidiary discussions: Theologians, freedom of (27ff); *Sensus fidelium* (18f; 24ff).

Precis: The essay begins with 3 questions: Is there something akin to "public opinion" in the church. What is it? Is it legitimate? (9-20). Rahner argues that though the church is a divine institution it is also human. It is neither totalitarian nor simply democratic. People have feelings about what the church does and teaches, and expressing these feelings is not only legitimate, it is essential for a healthy church. There are, however, limitations (27-32). People may vary greatly in where they might set these limits (Rahner thinks they are set too narrowly today). But free expression and setting limits entail a subjective judgment (34-39) which takes time and discipline to learn and exercise. In a transitional time such as ours, these differences are exacerbated. Rahner concludes (39-50) by pointing out some of the ways Catholic laity today can and must make their opinions known in the church.

FS.2. The Prospect for Christianity. (53-112)

Abstract: Seen with the eyes of faith, the distressing "facts of modern life" in no way support "apostolic defeatism." Though the forms of Christianity will change and we may become more defensive, theology and history argue that Christianity will remain *the* world religion of the future.

Topics: CHRISTIANITY, future of; CHURCH, future of; FAITH.

Subsidiary discussions: Laity, missionary task of (53ff); Neo-paganism (59ff); Faith and doubt (75ff); Jesus Christ, Second Coming of (90f); Grace of election (91ff); Man, religious propensity of (99ff); Christianity and other religions (102ff).

Precis: 1. The "facts of modern life" seem to support a sense of "apostolic defeatism" among Christians (dwindling numbers, loss of power in secular affairs, mere toleration by neo-pagans, seeming doctrinal irrelevance, internal fatigue. Summary, 64-69). Can the church be "a light to the nations," if its actual position in history is in decline?

2. Even granting the truth of all these "facts," from the faith perspective defeatism is completely unjustifiable. Faith accepts the truths of these "facts," but comparing them to the grounds for faith they lose their force, though we may rightly remain anxious.

3. How then do we understand the "facts of modern life"? Rahner cautions that even these "facts" are subjective. The church need not remain unchanging to fulfill its mission. The public significance of the church may change without canceling its essence. Rahner supports this with two arguments: an *a priori* theological argument (81-84) and an *a posteriori* historical-empirical one.

4. Are these defeatist indicators really "facts" or are they highly dubious interpretations? Rahner begins by recalling two theological doctrines: the Second Coming, and the grace of election. He then considers history which is ever-changing. This period of transition which we view as catastrophic may be seen by future generations as a time when something new and great was being born. But is it possible Christianity as a world religion may not survive the present crisis? Rahner argues No, for two reasons: a) man's indestructible religious propensity; and b) the "empirical fact" that Christianity has no formidable rival, since it alone among world religions is transcendental, universal, realistic, and historically mature.

5. Despite his faith, Rahner does not envision the flowering of a new "Christian Era" within the foreseeable future. Societies move slowly. Hence, for generations perhaps, Christians will be in this distressing situation, on the defensive. This calls for patience and grim determination. The deciding factor will be whether we perform our tasks with devotion, self-sacrifice, holiness, penance and sincere prayer. For this we must be capable of absolute faith and absolute selfless love.

GF. *Grace in Freedom*, NY: Herder, 1969, adapted with Sources. 267 pp. *Gnade als Freiheit: Kleine theologische Beitrage*, 1968. Translated by Hilda Graef.

Contents:
I. Responsibility in the Post-conciliar Church.
  The Christian's Responsibility for the Church after the Council.
  Advice to a Worried Catholic.
  To an Impatient Catholic.
  Compulsory Alternatives.
  Present Tasks.
II. Christian Faith – the Deliverance of the World.
  Faith and Culture.
  The Christian Character of the Secularized Ethos.

III. Religious patterns.
  Is Christianity an "Absolute Religion"?
  Visions.
  Medical Ethics.
IV. Ecumenical Perspectives.
  The Question of Justification Today.
  A Catholic Meditation on the Anniversary of the Reformation.
V. Free Acceptance of Creaturliness and Cross.
  "Remember, man, that thou art dust."
  The Passion of the Son of Man. Words for Holy Week.
VI. Commitment to the Church and Personal Freedom.
  Institutional Spirituality of Church and Personal Piety.
  Prayer of the Individual and the Liturgy of the Church.
  Democracy in the Church?
  Theology's New Relation to the Church.
VII. The Little Word "God."
  Meditation on the Word "God."
  God is no Scientific Formula.
  God, our Father.
VIII. True Freedom.
  The Theology of Freedom.
  Origins of Freedom.
  The Test of Christian Freedom.
  Fate and Freedom.
Sources.

I. Responsibility in the Post-conciliar Church.

GF.1.1. The Christian's Responsibility for the Church after the Council. (9-26). June 6, 1966 lecture in Munich. *Stellaner Nachrichten* 12, no. 8 (1966) 3-14.

Abstract: The Council's goal was to produce faith, hope and love in the hearts of today's faithful. This is the ancient faith. A responsible laity must study the council documents, embrace their proper apostolate in the world, commit themselves to their local churches, dialogue, and patiently endure these new times.

Topics: CHURCH, post-conciliar; VATICAN II, post-conciliar concerns.

Subsidiary discussions: Laity, apostolate of (20f); Church as local altar community (21f); Dialogue (23); Everyday Life, patient endurance (24ff).

Precis: Preview. I. *The ancient tradition is also the very latest.* Hoping not to sound reactionary, Rahner begins by saying the first duty in this post-conciliar period is faithfulness to the old, which is also the new. Despite its characterization by journalists, the main work of the Council was to preserve the ancient faith. The apostolic faith was never in danger of being changed, even though the ways we express it may need renewal. The old faith remains, as do the old problems of loving unselfishly, and the old revealed moral principles, despite the fact that human laws may need updating. The Christian faithful must continue to preserve the old faith, to pray, to fulfill their vocations, and to transmit this faith to a new generation.

II. *A transitional period is now beginning.* The future is already upon us. Much as we might like the church to be our refuge, the Council affirmed, "she must serve men and will courageously take upon herself all the risks of this service and enter the changing history of our time" (13). Since much is controversial and we are rightly attached to the old ways, we must approach the new and untried with courage, and bear with these uncertainties and with one another. At first things will get worse rather than better. But this is the church in which God has placed us. We have the inescapable duty to endure the uncertainties of this transition. Neither retrenchment nor reckless experimentation are the true way forward. In addition, we must avoid provincialism, recalling that we are members of one, very pluralistic church, and that our decisions must meet the needs of all (summary, 15).

III. *The cooperation of the laity is demanded.* One major insight of the Council is that we all constitute the church. Much of what people criticize in the clergy (short-sightedness, fear, or recklessness) is also rife among the laity. But because we are the church we have both the right to criticize and the duty to correct our own inadequacies. First and foremost, this must take the form of personal study of the Council documents. From *Lumen Gentium*, one learns the nature and true constitution of the church and one's role in it, and that all of us are called to holiness, each in his/

her own way. Rahner continues to name other documents and suggests their importance to the laity (17ff). Second, laity must grasp their true apostolate which they must exercise in everyday life: fulfilling one's familial, professional and civic duties. The fact that the Council teaches that those outside the church may "in a way known only to God" achieve salvation does not absolve lay people from the missionary task of spreading their faith wherever they find themselves. Third, since the church actualizes itself in its highest form in the local church (the altar community) the laity must invest themselves more fully and consciously in the life of the parish community. This calls for dialogue with our fellow parishioners (whether we particularly like them or not) and with church authorities, who may or may not rejoice in our common priesthood. Finally, we need to endure our current diaspora situation in a post-Christian, neo-pagan world.

IV. *The need for the patience of life.* The various social factors impinging on us today give rise to a new kind of disappointment in life. Despite the many opportunities modern life offers there is still so much colorless boredom, along with the ultimate *angst* of life. Especially now Christian have the duty not to escape through frivolous, empty or immoral diversions. We must endure with faith, hope and love, relying on prayer and God's grace. We can endure only if from the very center of our hearts we begin to believe in God, in Jesus Christ, in his grace, and in eternal life –our constant, ancient faith.

GF.1.2. Advice to a Worried Catholic. (27-33). North and West German Radio broadcasts. *Oberrheinisches Pastoralblatt* 68, no. 5 (1967) 129-32.

Abstract: Though the church is a community of love and truth, it remains difficult for us to accept one another. Yet as a world-church we must move forward. This calls for change. Those who truly love the church must be helped to endure this time of change. Unity and not division is the way forward.

Topics: CHURCH, post-conciliar; VATICAN II, post-conciliar concerns.

Precis: How to answer Catholics who think "The Council is of the devil"? Progressives must take such worries seriously. For despite our sinfulness we are all brothers and sisters in one church. No one has a right to gloat, and not all the worries of conservatives are figments. Their concerns are a needed counterweight. The church is pluralistic, and no one faction can claim to speak for the entire church. Conservatives should be bolstered by this and participate fully, charitably, and tolerantly in ongoing dialogue. Worried Catholics should be told: not everything has become uncertain. Remain loyal to the true church, and distinguish between its unchanging truths and the changing historical ways in which that truth is presented (i.e., in liturgy and on moral issues). Remember, the darkness in life has always been with us and must still be borne with patient endurance. The church's caution is not cowardice. And honestly, many of the irritating peripheral questions of theology, especially in liturgy, are mere matters of taste. They cannot be solved by appeals to theory. Still the church must decide; it cannot move in two directions. When one option wins over other cherished ways of doing things, one must remember the final decision must make sense in a global church, not just in one's own region (summary 32f).

GF.1.3. To an Impatient Catholic. (34-39). West German Radio broadcasts. *Oberrheinisches Pastoralblatt* 68, no. 5 (1967) 161-164.

Abstract: Progressives disappointed in the results of the Council must demonstrate "holy impatience," staying loving and generous toward their opponents. "Holy impatience is the fruit of patient love."

Topics: CHURCH, post-conciliar; IMPATIENCE, holy; VATICAN II, post-conciliar concerns.

Subsidiary discussions: Theology, task of (36).

Precis: The Council left many impatient and disappointed. They see nothing like the new Pentecost they had expected, but everywhere they see quarrels and alienation. What can we say to these impatient progressives? There is such a thing as holy impatience, legitimately expressed. The church needs it to move forward. But it must truly be holy: unselfish, loving one's opponents as brothers, giving no cause for scandal. For one party is never wholly right and the other wholly wrong. Theologians must be admonished to make their impatience holy. Good modern theology will build on tradition, and the proper work of the theologian "is not to destroy traditional taboos but to build up a living authentic faith" (36). Holy impatience is required since it will take a long time for the Council to penetrate everywhere. It will encounter setbacks and hesitations. Hybrid solutions will arise that please no one. Impatient Catholics must not simply assume that their views are the definitive voice of divine wisdom. In the church, love must unite all, whatever their views. Finally, progressives must be reminded that ours is a pilgrim church, always sinful, always in need of reform. We ourselves build a holier church wherever we bear with even the sinful and unholy in patient love, recognizing our own shortcomings and limitations. Holy impatience must be the fruit of patient love (summary 38f).

GF.1.4. Compulsory Alternatives. (40-44). December 4, 1967, German Radio broadcast.

Abstract: The principle of "compulsory alternatives" applies to decision making where there is always a choice to be made among alternatives, only one of which can be chosen if there is to be common action. Most likely, each alternative has something in its favor, and choosing one means losing the benefits of the other. But today many disputants proclaim their view is the only right and sensible one, and denigrate all others. Knowing that only God is completely good, disputants should be more self-critical, admitting the weaknesses and dangers in their own views. Though each party must show how its opinion corresponds to Christian principles, it is likely that both will. In real life, appeals to theory are never effective in making practical decisions which always have a moral element: love, respect, tolerance. Framed in this way we can see that not every compromise is a betrayal of reason. Disputes between conservatives and progressives would be enhanced if this principle were practiced (summary, 44).

Topics: CHURCH, decision making in; CHURCH, post-conciliar; VATICAN II, post-conciliar concerns.

GF.1.5. Present Tasks. (45-68). "*Blick in die Zukunft,*" in N. Greinacher and H.T. Risse (eds.) *Bilanz des deutschen Katolizismus* (1966) 487-508.

Abstract: Suggests strategic and tactical principles the church in the West should embrace in this post-conciliar decade, humbly aware that they are no panacea, and that God alone directs the outcome.
Topics: CHURCH of the future; CHURCH, post-conciliar; VATICAN II, post-conciliar concerns.
Subsidiary discussions: Theology, post-conciliar task of (54f); Laity, formation of (55f); Magisterium (57f); Obedience (58f); Morality, post-conciliar (59ff); Birth control (59f); Error, invincible (60f); Divorce (61f); Conscience (62f); Laity and clergy (63ff); Priests shortage (66f).

Precis: Rahner insists the church must set strategic goals, however tentative, realizing that what is most essential is the ancient yet ever-new message of Christianity (description, 45f). Neither rigid formalism nor radical social activism marks the way forward. Though God alone directs history, the church must still form a plan to meet the future. This can only be done in open dialogue between hierarchy and laity.
General remarks: *The Church of Personal Faith.* It is simply a fact that the church of the future will no longer be the traditional established church. It will increasingly become a free association of believers expressing their personal faith within a pluralistic society. How to make this transition cannot be settled by recourse to eternal principles but must be hammered out with prudent practical considerations. *Concentrating Ecclesiastical Action.* Because the church cannot do everything, it must find the courage to concentrate on definite points. It should not concentrate on addressing "the people" but the educated, because they are the ones who shape and will shape society. *Courage and Self-confidence of the Preacher of the Gospel.* Those who preach must see themselves differently. They must get off the defensive and take courage from the fact they still proclaim the precious saving message the world desperately needs.
How the suggestions of the Council are to be realized. All the Christian faithful, bishops, priests, religious and laity, must strive to carry out the spirit and letter of the Council, each within his/her own competence. Rahner identifies the unfinished challenges set forth by the documents of Vatican II (list, 51ff). He ends by specifically mentioning the new task of theologians (54f) to ex-

plain and justify the teachings of Vatican II. They must return to the central themes of Christianity: God, Incarnation, grace, eternal life. Their theoretical work must also assist with today's practical pastoral needs.

Educating mature Christians. How do we address the danger uncovered by the Council: that many Christians are tempted to deny the infallibility of church doctrine and dismiss its practical directives? *a. Unchangeable Principles and Changeable Directives.* Laity must be taught to distinguish between unchangeable principles and changeable directives, something that in the past was often obscured by blanket appeals to authority. *b. A Right Understanding of the Teaching Office.* Laity must be taught how the Magisterium arrives at binding decisions. There is always a human element, and it is wise to leave many unsettled issues open– something irksome to both conservatives and progressives. *c. Responsibility in Free Obedience.* We must all learn to bear responsibility for the church and not to oppose it secretly, to bear with the church in this historical moment in freely given obedience. We must not simply go on vacation and return once the dust settles. Priests and laity cannot let their impatience degenerate into fundamental opposition.

Individual morality rightly understood. *Difference between Theoretical and Real Morality.* In the realm of practice, there will always be a gap between the official morality the church proclaims and the actions of average believers. Sometimes the church has no choice but to announce the hard message. But when the gap is too great (e.g., on birth control) the church must have the wisdom to ask herself whether she has done everything to work out her doctrine in pastoral practice. More must also be done practically to explore the moral ramifications of a whole society gripped by invincible error. *Objective and Subjective Guilt.* Not every objective failure to live up to the church's moral teaching constitutes subjective guilt. What is the church to do when an individual's or the society's capacity to realize a moral precept subjectively remains below the objective demand? *The Problem of Divorce.* Theoretically, too, the church has not yet figured out what to do in cases of an insurmountable difference between theoretical and practical morality. In marriage for example, what subjective conditions must be present to constitute a valid marriage, and what is the church to do in cases where the objective good of marriage it teaches encounters the subjective decision of conscience that a particular union is irretrievably broken? *Necessary Conditions and Dangers of a "Morality of Conscience."* In seeking answers more and more cases will have to be left to individual conscience guided by the norms of the gospel. Many will object to this, fearful that most people will take the easy way out for themselves. But if this it the case, it is a product of prior poor religious formation. This state of affairs must be tolerated while we work to do a better job of forming a new generation of Catholics.

The future relationship between the "estates of the church." *Clergy and Laity.* One element of bright promise as the church transforms from an established church into a community of faith in a pluralistic society, is a new relationship between clergy and laity. Increasingly they will encounter one another as "brothers" in a common religious mind and heart. Old "power struggles" will subside. While retaining their proper roles, clergy will cede as much power as possible to the laity who will be treated not as mere objects of the church's saving activities but as subjects and partners in discerning and deciding. For mutual protection and to avoid misunderstanding, these newly acquired rights and duties should be encoded in law. *The Problem of the Shortage of Priests.* When the laity assume their full stature and do all they can within the church, the priest shortage will lessen somewhat. In addition, one must question the current pattern of distributing priests, based as it is on the territorial principle. This pattern seems to discriminate against more "charismatic" free associations. Might it not also be possible to expand the pool of future priests to include men of tested virtue, similar to elders in the early church, whose training might not be as academically rigorous as that of traditional candidates? (Conclusion, 67f.)

II. Christian Faith – The Deliverance of the World.
GF.2.1. Faith and Culture. (69-77). June 11, 1967, Southwest German Radio broadcast.

Abstract: Christians can and must contribute to secular culture. But what? Religion assists people to endure the changes, limits and frustration of increasing mass culture. Its hope in the absolute future keeps it from absolutizing existing structures or plans, and emboldens it to be a constant social critic.

Topics: CULTURE and faith; FAITH and culture; HOPE.
Subsidiary discussions: *Praxis* (75f); Future, absolute (75f).

Precis: Rahner begins with a reservation: faith, transcending as it does the realms of beauty, truth and holiness, has no need to justify itself before the bar of utilitarianism. This being said, what is the positive mutual relationship between faith and culture espoused by Vatican II (GS 53-62)? After offering a brief definition of culture (70) Rahner restates the question: "What can and should the Christian faith achieve for a contemporary culture such as it should be?" Faith demands responsibility before God even for the secular culture. For Christians, involvement with culture, however secular it becomes, is not optional (GS 59). Transforming secular culture is among the elements of a Christian's vocation and mission.

Today's increasingly unified mass culture is a Christian concern. The church approves of "a more universal form of human culture," stronger international institutions, and full participation of both sexes of all social classes in developing this culture. The church renounces the idea that culture presupposes a permanent large number of poor, socially weak, exploited men and women. This "socialist tendency" is based not on ideology but on the Christian view that each person has the right to participate in culture because s/he is endowed by God with human dignity. Mass culture is not embraced happily as the ultimate goal, but soberly as a simple necessity fraught with dangers. Faith has a role to play in helping people adjust to and endure the changes, limits and frustrations of mass culture. At the same time religion must guard against being co-opted into becoming a mere agent for the forces of social change.

Christians have the duty to imbue the structures of secular life (i.e., culture) with their eschatological hope (GS 35). "Hopeful expectation" should drive cultural activities. But for Christians this is hope for the absolute future, hope for eternity. Far from being a conservative force, the church, grounded in hope, embodies a revolutionary attitude. True *praxis* is never the mere implementation of sure plans. It risks the unplanned, rooted as it is in hope for the absolute future. Christian hope refuses to absolutize any human structure. It calls everything into question and accepts even the passing away of the "form of the world." This Christian surrender is neither the proud revolt that absolutizes the immediate future nor the despair of the hopeless over the transience of the world. One form of Christian hope is constant, fearless criticism of secular structures. This stems from seeing all things as provisional, in spite of the fact that Christianity lays no claim to having a grand theory for an ideal future. Grasped by primordial hope, Christians are willing to risk. Having had their personal lives transformed by such hope, it becomes easier for them to extend this same hope to the structures of society.

GF.2.2. The Christian Character of the Secularized Ethos (78-79).
"Das eigene Zeugnis" in *Spektrum* supplement of *Presse*, Vienna (24/25 December, 1966) 3.
Abstract: Growing secularization is a fact. And "there will be ever more man-made reality which is neither 'numinous' nature nor profane in the bad sense" (78). Dramatizing secularization only makes it worse. And really, in less secular times were people that much more imbued with faith, hope and love? In fact, today's secularized ethos draws it power from Christianity. Most private works of mercy are still undertaken by Christians and not by "humanists." It is much more important to witness to our faith in the market place by our words and deeds than to compile statistics and make forecasts.
Topics: SECULARISM/ -IZATION.

III. Religious Patterns.
GF.3.1. Is Christianity an "Absolute Religion"? (81-86). *Orientierung* 29, no. 16 (1965) 176-178 (see: TI 05.06 "Christianity and the Non-Christian Religions).
Abstract: What dogmatic sense can Catholics today make of non-Christians? Their religions must be seen as legitimate, divinely-willed and divinely-permitted social avenues of saving grace. And since all salvation is salvation in Christ, we must view the adherents to these religions as anonymously Christian.
Topics: ANONYMOUS CHRISTIAN/ITY; CHRISTIANITY and non-Christian religions.

Precis: "Open Catholicism" (definition, 82) imposes the duty to understand and embrace the pluralism of religions in a higher unity. Today's inter-religious situation is far different from the past. Globalization has made every religion a question and a possibility for every man, and a challenge to the absolute claim of Christianity. What follows is a "dogmatic Catholic interpretation" of non-Christian religions.

Christianity claims to be an absolute, unparalleled religion destined for all people– *the* religion which binds all people to God. But it is also an historical religion. This raises the question of when this religion makes its existentially real demands on people. Is it at the same time for all? If the answer is no, then we can understand the first thesis in a differentiated way– a way that leaves open the question of time. Also, since religion is a social entity, we can ask whether paganism continues to exist because it has not yet had an impressive encounter with Christianity. Until this encounter takes place we can acknowledge that even flawed non-Christian religions are legitimate religions in different gradations.

(Reprise, 83ff). The first part of this thesis states that non-Christian religions contain supernatural elements of grace, but that the salvation to which this might lead is specifically Christian, for there is no salvation apart from Christ. These statements can only be combined by saying that all people are exposed to the influence of divine grace made fully manifest in Christ. The second part of the thesis goes further, maintaining that non-Christian religions have a positive meaning (even those religions containing errors). Hence, we must give up approaching these religions by asking whether they are wholly of divine origin or merely human. In these religions people have a saving encounter with God, and this happens in a social context. Hence, these religions are expressions of God's salvific will. If this thesis is true, then whenever a Christian confronts a non-Christian s/he is meeting a person who may already be regarded in certain respects as anonymously Christian (85).

It must be possible to be not only an anonymous theist but also an anonymous Christian for two reasons: the one to whom the missionary goes out may already have encountered salvation; and this salvation must be salvation in Christ, as there is no other. Hence, missionary activity does not transform a forsaken soul into a Christian, but an anonymous Christian into an explicit Christian. This higher phase of development is not superfluous since it is demanded by the Incarnational and social structure of grace and Christianity, and because this greater explicitation offers a greater chance of salvation. It follows that the church today "will not view itself as the exclusive community of candidates for salvation, but as the avant-garde, expressing historically and socially the hidden reality which, Christians hope, exists also outside her visible structure" (86). However non-Christians may view our position, Christians cannot but regard them as anonymously Christian.

GF.3.2. Visions. (87-89). Previously unpublished. Cf., *Inquiries,* **Inq. 2.** "Vision and Prophecies" (Parts II &III).

GF.3.3. Medical Ethics. (90-93). *Fortschritte der Medizin* 85, no. 24 (December, 21, 1967) 1029-1030.

Abstract: Objectivity, the capacity and will to see and admit objective facts, to be guided by objects and not by prejudices, is the moral virtue underpinning modern medicine. At first blush it may seem that the more medically objective physicians become the less they are required to make decisions of conscience. But not even the principle of objectivity can be derived from objects, which can only determine means not ends. Hence, the medical paradox: is the patient before you a biological mess or a person worth keeping alive? What grounds the absolute demand to preserve life? Is it a wild exaggeration of the biological zest for life and hence itself not objective? Or is it a genuine absolute ethical demand? And if so, what grounds this demand? Many physicians profess the dignity of man but without considering its ultimate ground which Christians call God. Doctors are paid to be objective and they are expected to be humane. Theirs is not merely a profession it is a vocation to be a person for others. Hard work indeed!

Topics: ETHICS, medical; MEDICINE, vocation of; OBJECTIVITY as a virtue.

IV. Ecumenical Perspectives.
GF.4.1. The Question of Justification Today. (96-100). November 5, 1967 lecture in Soest i.W. on the 450th anniversary of the Reformation.
Abstract: This sketch of a Catholic dogmatic understanding of justification/salvation intends to show how this once decisive Reformation issue is no longer a legitimate cause for continued separation.
Topics: ECUMENISM; JUSTIFICATION; SALVATION.
Subsidiary discussions: Theological statements (97).

Precis: There were many diverse, complex reasons for the Reformation-era rift. Many other factors arose later which are indicative of pluralism but do not justify continued separation. To make this case, Rahner presents the contemporary Catholic understanding of justification (the decisive theological reason for separation) from a dogmatic perspective. Catholics confess as a fundamental truth of faith the solely justifying grace of God. Justification/salvation comes to the sinner as a completely free and unmerited gift of God revealed through Jesus' meritorious death and resurrection. Accepting God's offer in freedom, all our subsequent saving activities are simply a response to God's prior initiative. In fact, this very power to respond is itself God's gift. The bestowal of this gift of justification is an "event" and not a constant dialectical state. It is appropriated in hope as a promise, not in knowledge as a possession. Thus we never cease to rely on God's merciful judgment. If we follow St. Paul's lead and call this "event" of grace "faith," then we can say we are justified by faith alone. However, our justified status, seized in hope, remains inaccessible to theoretical reflection. This leaves us always under the threat of the world's power of sin. In this sense we remain *simul justus et pecator*, and must again and again turn away from ourselves and toward God's offer of saving grace. This justifying grace frees us from the powers of death and the external demands of the law, and presents us with the demand to love and bring forth the fruits of the Spirit, all without giving us any claim on God (conclusion, 100).

GF.4.2. A Catholic Meditation on the Anniversary of the Reformation. (101-111). *Stimmen der Zeit* 180 (1967) 228-235.

Abstract: Despite great theological progress, church leaders lack courage and imagination in the ecumenical arena: the will to "give way" that comes from love. They let our many small differences obscure our great common faith. Uniting in our common task to witness to Christ may prove the best way forward.
Topics: ECUMENISM.
Subsidiary discussions: Conscience (104f).

Precis: It is difficult for Catholics, and indeed for any Christian, to speak about the Reformation. It is a complex historical event which never should have happened, and for which all bear some inexcusable guilt. We can only trust in God's mercy. Rahner offers some provisional opinions. Careful study of Reformation history will bring home to Catholics the dreadful guilt we bear for these sad events. They will be horrified to realize how easily the church once did, and still can, succumb to the spirit of the times and become guilty without noticing it. Secondly, the Catholic Church confesses the *sola gratia* (*sola fide*) of the Reformers. Both parties must now work to see that secondary theological differences are not allowed to become a cause of continuing separation. Third, especially since Vatican II's promulgation of *Dei Verbum*, which makes clear that the church is "the servant of scripture" the Reformer's principle of *sola scriptura* ought no longer to separate the churches. On a fourth point (responding to a conference presenter, Bishop Lilje) Rahner takes issue with the claim that the church and its magisterium are the first and fundamental factor in the faith of Catholics. Catholics believe the church (not *in* the church) because they believe in God and in God's grace. Faith is a decision *for* the church, and not one derived *from* the church. Catholics, too, retain a lively respect for solitary conscience, despite the fact we often mounted a legitimate defense of the magisterium with overly paternalistic and feudal understandings of authority. Hence, ministry today must be more self-critical and never give the impression it has any other end but to strengthen the faith of the individual believer in the free exercise of conscience.

For all this, we are still divided after 450 years. Though theoretically we appreciate our duty to seek ecclesial unity, practically many view separation as a natural fact. Clearly, church leaders today are not completely devoted to the cause of ecumenism. They need greater courage, and the wisdom to see that pluralism does not justify separation. Here Vatican II's teaching on the "hierarchy of truths" could be of great benefit. These times call for courage and imagination, and the humility to "give way" which only comes from love. Catholics especially must be more self-critical.

Rahner also has questions for his Protestant partners. Who speaks authoritatively for them in ecumenical dialogue to insure that it does not disintegrate into private theological conversation among individuals? (107f). Why do many Protestants feel they cannot for the sake of their faith and conscience join in the same church and Eucharist with Catholics, yet they easily form unions with other Protestants who have hardly anything left of the ancient creeds of the Reformers? (109f). This leads to the question, what is it that the Protestant churches today actually do believe? Clarifying this would be very helpful in furthering dialogue. Christians today have a new common task: to bear witness to Christ in a world that does not want to hear it, and to proclaim this message intelligibly and credibly. Despite our differences we do have a common faith. In today's environment it becomes increasingly clear that it is more important to tell the world what is meant by the word "God" than to rehash the controversies over Vatican I. Engaging in this new common task may be the best way to progress in ecumenical dialogue.

V. Free Acceptance of Creatureliness and Cross.
GF.5.1. "Remember, man, that thou art dust." (113-116)
Ash Wednesday sermon, 1967 in Munich. *Geist und Leben* 40 (1967) 1-3.

Abstract: Theses words, "Remember, man . . ." when we hear them as spoken to us by Christ are our truth, our indictment, and our comfort. They promise hope and demand our response.

Topics: SERMON: Ash Wednesday.

Subsidiary discussions: Incarnation (114f); Death (116).

Precis: Rahner insists that even in our bleak existentialist age, we still need to hear the words, "ashes to ashes, dust to dust." But there is a difference if we hear these words coming to us from ourselves (in which case it is protest or self-pity) or from Christ mourning for us (in which case it is a real word of comfort). Christ's and the church's mourning for us allows us to mourn for our sorrows, to weep at our powerlessness and bewilderment from which not even complete surrender to God frees us. Christ speaks to us in our sorrow and reminds us that through His Incarnation He bore the same grief, yet to an even more intense degree. Nevertheless, the mourning of Christ and of the church also bear a note of accusation. Much of what we suffer we have brought upon ourselves by the guilt of unredeemed lusts and rebellious despair. The words of Ash Wednesday are simultaneously our truth, our comfort, and our indictment. In these words God reveals the abyss of our origins. But in the fact that *God* speaks these words to us, He promises us Himself as the abyss of our future. This is our hope against hope. It remains now for each one to apply these words to him/herself. The death implied in these words can take many concrete forms (list, 116). Each must identify and embrace his/her own. What matters is that we do it willingly– that the passion of Christ is also our own deed though which we receive grace.

GF.5.2. The Passion of the Son of Man. Words for Holy Week. (117-125). March 20-25, 1967, Holy Week sermons broadcast on Bavarian Radio.

Abstract: This Holy Week aid for sharing in the Passion of Christ concentrates on bearing the cross in our daily lives, and thus mysteriously lightening the burden of mankind as we move toward Easter glory.

Topics: SERMONS, Holy Week; SERMONS, Holy Thursday; SERMONS, Good Friday; SERMONS, Holy Saturday; CROSS.

Precis: I. *Monday.* During Holy Week, Christians desire to participate more deeply in the Passion of Christ. They do so by bearing everyday burdens bravely and without show. This in turn gives us a share in the sufferings of all humanity, whose burden is thereby mysteriously lightened. Christ's own passion "is the unique acceptance of the passion of mankind, in which it is accepted, suffered, redeemed and freed into the mystery of God" (118). II. *Tuesday.* The cross confronts us in our everyday life. It is present to each of us in a unique way in the everyday activities of life in which we confront the limits of our natures. III. *Wednesday.* The cross is inescapable. The only question is how we accept it: grudgingly, protestingly, or in faith, hope and love for our salvation. Each of us does this in our own way depending on the contours of our everyday lives. In doing so we cry out with Christ, "My God, my God, why have you forsaken me," and immediately, "Father, into your hands I commend my spirit." **IV.** *Holy Thursday*. It is wonderful how on this day all Christians celebrate the Eucharist of the Lord, even if we interpret this event differently. Though the meaning of this sacred feast is manifold and diverse (list), it does not reach its ultimate truth and fulfillment short of "communion." This takes place in everyday life when we recognize and respond to Christ in the least of our brothers and sisters. We must live the Eucharist if it is not to become judgment against us. **V.** *Good Friday*. Today in the folly of the cross we witness the eternal wisdom of God. Hence, it is good for us at least on this one day to stand beneath the cross and consider freely the terrors of life, and in the words of Christ, "Father, into your hands I commend my spirit," once again surrender ourselves to God. **VI.** *Holy Saturday*. This transitional day, set between the terrors of Good Friday and the glories of Easter, is symbolic of the Christian's everyday life. Neither put off by horror nor entranced by glory we move toward Easter, maintaining our infinite claim, our persistent hope for the joy of eternity revealed in the death and resurrection of the Lord.

VI. Commitment to the Church and Personal Freedom.

GF.6.1. Institutional Spirituality of Church and Personal Piety.
(127-136). January 31, 1967 lecture to lay theology students, University of Munich. *Christophorus* 13, no. 1 (1967) 23-28. Abridged.

Abstract: As faith becomes increasingly personal and free, how can spirituality remain free from stale tradition? Recalling that all freedom is limited and that Christians must accept and transform these limits, Rahner calls on all Christians to develop new forms of spirituality without simply abandoning the old.

Topics: FREEDOM and spirituality; SPIRITUALITY and freedom.
Subsidiary discussions: Theology, dangers of (132).

Precis: Today as the formerly institutional faith increasingly gives way to a more personal faith, questions arise about spirituality.

What is the relationship between older forms of institutional piety, which often feel like limits imposed by external laws, and the unique spirituality that expresses my freedom?

Freedom related to the situation. All human freedom is inescapably enacted in a pre-existing sphere of time, space and circumstance. Hence, an essential element of human freedom consists in accepting these given conditions in order slowly to change them (*amor faiti*).

The norm as freedom's way to itself. In addition, we are not simply free, we *become* free. It is a process and the achievement of a lifelong struggle against a norm, the truth of my life, which often strikes me as imposed, and which I often deny or suppress. The same is true in the realm of spirituality. Hence, I protest against the rules of fasting, religious laws and customs. Yet there remains a proper legal, institutional piety, even though it may not meet the full expectations of my personal freedom.

Christian spirituality as permanently dependent on its own history. This institutional material bears within itself a rich spiritual tradition including writers and practices. Why should these be *a priori* denigrated beneath newly-encountered Eastern mystical practices? Modern exegesis does not replace the need of prayerfully reading scripture, and theology never replaces prayer.

The free acceptance of the spiritual order. Spirituality is impossible without discipline of some kind, just as one cannot become a pianist without practice. The system we employ may be quite modest but it must exist, since spirituality is never a mere matter of momentary religious feelings. Of course system is never enough. Theologians especially must take care not to confuse scholarship for holiness.

The obligation through the personal call over and above the law. The unique and free dimensions of spirituality can never be commanded or completely institutionalized. This is because there is in religious experience an "individual ethic." God calls me to encounter and express Him in a way unique to me – in a way I cannot deny. This is in fact the origin of all spirituality.

Seeking new forms of spirituality. In this time of transition how can we remain genuinely devout without practicing a stale, irrelevant piety? Currently, theologians are too abstract and have little to offer practically speaking, although they, along with bishops and all

Christians, are obliged to seek new patterns of spirituality. The necessary experimentation this calls for does not legitimate simply abandoning the old ways.

Self-criticism as regulating the claim to freedom. The best proof of an authentic synthesis between Christian freedom and a serious affirmation of external law is a self-critical attitude. For true love of peace and unity always make us more cautious and humble. In the end there is no law against those who genuinely love their neighbors and thereby surrender themselves to God in faith, hope and love. In this love, law and freedom merge into grace.

GF.6.2. Prayer of the Individual and the Liturgy of the Church. (137-149). In H. Schlier, et al., *Strukturen christlicher Existenz: Beiträge zur Erneuerung des geistlichen Lebens* (1968) 189-198.

Abstract: Liturgical prayer must not be understood in a way that denigrates private prayer. In fact, the latter is the source of the former. "Official authorization" adds nothing to the value of liturgical prayer.

Topics: LITURGY and prayer; PRAYER, personal.

Subsidiary discussions: Sacred Heart devotion (145).

Precis: Vatican II marks the high water mark for liturgy by putting it at the center of the life of the church. But this moment of triumph comes at a time when people are asking themselves whether they are still even capable of worship and liturgy. This is part of the greater danger of losing entirely the personal relationship to God in prayer. Indeed, heightened emphasis on liturgy may inadvertently be making private prayer seem superfluous and fueling the danger to private prayer.

I. Vatican II teaches explicitly: a) there is non-liturgical prayer, strictly speaking; b) Sacred Liturgy has a "higher dignity" than non-liturgical pious exercises; c) This higher dignity does not abolish the need and duty of private, non-liturgical prayer which remains highly recommended when practiced correctly (SC 12-13, art. 7).

II. Leaving aside the problems entailed in defining "liturgy" (141), theologically what does it mean that liturgical prayer "far surpasses" (*longe antecellere*) private prayer? Since it would seem the answer lies in liturgy's being performed "in the name of the church," Rahner asks what can be said theologically about private prayer?

Is liturgical prayer (excluding of course Eucharist and the sacraments) really always preferable? What would such a preference mean in Christian life? The prayer of all Christians, even when not strictly commissioned by the church, is an act of the church insofar as those who pray are her members. It would be wrong to assume that only "officially sanctioned acts" are acts of the church. It is the holiness or sinfulness of members that makes the church holy or sinful. So why is liturgical prayer so surpassingly privileged? First, *"longe antecellere"* is perhaps a kind of pious exaggeration, which would be wrong to take in an exclusive sense. Second, it could be seen as redressing the trend of "desacralization." But care must be taken not to overplay this elevation of cult. Finally, modern ecclesiology, which views the church as the People of God, emphasizes its charismatic origin manifested in liturgy over its social structure. But "a liturgical order of prayer exists because prayer itself exists, the former does not create the latter, but on the contrary presupposes it" (147).

What then is the advantage of liturgical prayer over private prayer (leaving aside Eucharist and sacraments)? Quite simply, any advantage is *small*. Not only do they share the same essential characteristics, but official authorization of itself adds no superior value. It simply validates and encourages it. Hence, some non-liturgical prayer may well be holier and of greater value than liturgical prayer, and not simply *per accidens*, for God imparts grace as He pleases. Of course the real threat to personal prayer does not come from liturgy, but from the real or apparent lack of religious experience.

GF.6.3. Democracy in the Church? (150-168). May 3, 1968, lecture in Freiburg i. Br. *Stimmen der Zeit* 182 (1968) 1-15.

Abstract: Despite important difference between church and state, there is a basic inner relationship between what is meant or realized by democracy and the church, which has nothing to fear from a greater democratization of its forms, few of which are *jure divino*. Rahner furnishes current examples.

Topics: CHURCH, democracy in.

Subsidiary discussions: Heresy (157f); *Jus divinum/jus humanum* (155ff; 161f); Parish Councils (162ff); Bishop/s, election of (164f); Parish of the future (166f); Public Opinion (167f).

Precis: Leaving aside a full discussion of the nature and value of democracy (that form of society which grants its members the greatest possible freedom and participation in its life and decisions in accordance with their intellectual, cultural and social conditions), Rahner discusses in Part A some principles concerning the possibility and desirability of democracy in the church. In Part B he examines the concrete possibilities of greater democratization in the church in accord with her own doctrines.

A. I. *The basic relationship between democracy and the church.* A fundamental inner relationship exists between what is meant or realized by democracy and the Catholic Church. To understand it one must keep in mind that membership in the state is compulsory whereas membership in the church is voluntary, although both contain elements which are not the product of the free decisions of its members. Democracy in the state works to insure the free allegiance of its members, whereas in the church such allegiance is presupposed. A second element of the inner relationship between democracy and the church is her essentially charismatic nature which cannot be institutionalized, and which we believe the Spirit will preserve indefinitely. A final characteristic which at first seems undemocratic is the fact that *jure divino*, ministry is represented in individual persons. This has the effect of insuring that all the members know who is making responsible decisions, and deciders cannot hide behind committees. This makes it easier for all to cooperate in decisions. **II.** *A fundamental difference in applying the concept of democracy to secular society or to the church* lies in the fact that the "constitution" of the church is given her in the divine revelation of Jesus Christ, and is not subject to the will of the people. This limits the question of democracy in the formal sense, but leaves much open in the material sense. In addition, a member who freely and knowingly contradicts the dogmatic faith of the church can no longer be a member in the full sense of the word, even if s/he would still like to be thought of as a member. Finally, the ministers of the church do not receive their powers simply from the members but from Christ whose ministers they are. **III.**

Despite this radical difference the question of democracy in the church can be posed, because human nature is an element of grace, and human nature at this point in time demands democracy. In fact, little of the church's constitution is a matter of immutable divine law. Much in the historical forms the church has assumed can easily be changed to be more democratic.

B. On the possibility of democratic development of the church. I. This discussion centers on social institutions which would enable the People of God come of age to take an active part in the life and decisions of the church. Here one must be careful not to think that every human law is simply arbitrary and hence changeable. Rahner holds that some things previously determined *jure humano* may in fact now be justly considered *jus divino*. The two are not easily distinguished. **II.** Parish and diocesan councils are a good example of expanding democratization. But this development also raises the thorny question of just representation. Both election and appointment have drawbacks. A second problem is precisely how such bodies will be able to develop their own initiative and remain in harmony with ecclesiastical authority. This will demand great virtue on the part of all. **III.** Another possible path to greater democratization would be the election of ministers by the faithful. This too raises difficulties given the size of modern dioceses and the question of who would participate (nominal members, etc.). **IV.** Another possibility is seen in the growth of non-territorial Christian communities, which might in time present for ordination their own "elders." These might not have the traditional seminary training, but their virtue would have been proven to the community. One could imagine there being much less tension in such communities between the minister and the faithful, and between the community and the hierarchy. **V.** Finally "public opinion," so long as it remains within the framework of the faith and ready to obey legitimate authority, could have an important role to play. Both sides must accustom themselves to the fact that disagreements are inevitable and even healthy, so long as they are aired with the respect befitting God's holy people.

GF.6.4. Theology's New Relation to the Church. (169-181)
May 14, 1968 lecture in Münster. *Geist und Leben* 41 (1968) 205-216.

Abstract: Theology is essentially an intra-ecclesial dialogue which remains fruitful only so long as theologians presuppose the church's dogma. In this context theologians critically question what these dogmas mean in an ever-changing socio-historical horizon of knowledge. They speak both *for* and *to* the church.

Topics: CHURCH and theology; DIALOGUE; THEOLOGY, ecclesiality of.

Subsidiary discussions: Bible and theology (173f); Theology, dissent in (176ff).

Precis: Theology is only itself and interesting when it is "ecclesial" and not merely personal. Theology must remain within the church's reflection on the Word of God. One's private opinion, despite the fact that it cannot be completely excised from theological speculation, is not particularly important. In fact, one must be more distrustful of one's own opinions than of others'. In principle, the opinions of others must be as important as my own. Subjectivity lives only in constant give-and-take with the truth of others through permanent dialogue. This presupposes the existence of a deeper unity between the interlocutors. Without this common ground there could be no dialogue. All this is particularly true for theology which examines man as a whole. Such truth is necessarily institutional, a characteristic which insures that the truth remains free and not subject to my fanciful manipulation, i.e., that it remains independent of me.

For individual theologians this means there must be a concrete and independently acting authority which we allows to have a truly determining influence in our theologizing, and with which we carry on a constant dialogue. Neither scripture nor the Spirit can be this partner in dialogue until they become active partners opposing one's own theological opinions within the institutional community called the church. Until this occurs, engagement with scripture and the Spirit remain a monologue. Nor does discussion among theologians by itself, however necessary, constitute this authentic dialogue because such an exchange is not the forum of decision. Theology not only discusses the church's confession of faith, it is bound by it. Hence, the institutional church is theology's active and properly constituted dialogue partner. This ecclesial confession which confronts the theologian "must always be considered anew; it remains, and it changes in order to remain" (175).

This being said, how do theologians today view the ecclesiality of Catholic theology? Theologians do not merely repeat the magisterial teaching by which they are bound. They perform a critical function by examining what this teaching actually means. Since the church herself does not possess the pluralism in human knowledge it needs to explain itself in a fast-changing world, theologians have the duty to represent this knowledge to the church in respectful dialogue. "For theology speaks not only from but also to the Church.... Theology has a true [and inalienable] dialogical relation to the Church and her confession." (175). Hence, theologians will produce creative controversy in order to reconcile what is still unreconciled. They must want to be troublesome. At times they will even have to dissent, albeit in a rule-governed context. In any case, the dogma of the church remains the presupposition of any intra-ecclesial dialogue. To reject this, or to insist that in an academic discussion everything is open for discussion, results either in a monologue or in a merely human dialogue. True intra-ecclesial dialogue which is always conducted in the hope of an ever new reconciliation between the individual and the collective consciousness, is always in danger of slipping into a monologue (recapitulation, 180). The example of this ongoing struggle to achieve dialogue within the church that respects both the theologian's freedom of conscience and institutional faith may be instructive to society at large, which in the future will be faced with similar questions as it attempts to establish a common social ethos.

VII. The Little Word "God."
GF.7.1. Meditation on the Word "God." (183-190)
March 3, 1968, South German Radio broadcast.
Abstract: Meditation on the existence of the word "God" and its possible future reveals the uniqueness of this word. It calls into question and grounds all other words and all of language. If it were to disappear we would have reverted to being clever animals. This word constitutes our essential humanity.
Topics: GOD-TALK; MAN, nature of.
Subsidiary discussions: Language (188f).

Precis: Meditating on the word "God" is difficult because it seems unavoidably to slip into a broader discussion of what the word signifies: the reality of God. Yet it is a meaningful discussion precisely insofar as discussion of this word makes real what it signifies. In addition, we must begin here because we have no direct experience of God as we do of external realities like rocks and trees. Leaving aside its future and the objections of atheists, we can say this simple word contains our spiritual existence. Of course we are not interested in the *word* (*Gott, Deus* or *El*) but in the fact that such a word exists at all. Since none of these words says anything about God, we must seek is meaning from another source. Its very indeterminacy is well-suited to its meaning since it reflects what it signifies: "the Ineffable, the Nameless One, who is not part of the definable world, the Silent One that is always there yet always overlooked, and . . . can be passed over as meaningless" (185). All other words become intelligible only within the complex of other words. But this word is the last word, the foundation of all others.

As for the future existence of this word, there seem to be two alternatives. First (186), supposing the word disappears without a trace with no replacement, then we will no longer be confronted with the one whole of reality as such, nor with the whole of our own existence. Having thus forgotten our wholeness and our ground, we will have ceased to be human and will have returned to the state of an animal, albeit a clever one. The second alternative (188) is that the word remains embedded in the reality of language. There it continues to function in a special and unique way. It is the word by which language apprehends itself and its ground. Ultimately it makes no difference whether we embrace or reject this word-event, "which wants to force us, who are part of the world, to confront the whole of the world as well as ourselves without being the whole or being able to rule it" (189).

Finally, we do not first think the word "God" which only then enters our existence. The word precedes thought. Our relationship to God pre-exists passively and is engaged when language enters consciousness. We do not create the reality of "God" simply because we create the phonemes that constitute the word "God." Rather, it creates us because it makes us into human beings. It has the same origin as we and the same future. It is the last word before the silent worship of ineffable mystery.

GF.7.2. God is No Scientific Formula. (191-195)
December 24, 1965 article in various West German newspapers.
Abstract: Not being a thing, God cannot be reduced to a formula or given a place in a set of coordinates. God is the ground, the silent, ineffable mystery behind all phenomena which we experience in moments of transcendence. Does scientific honesty compel us to shrug off these moments or to engage them?
Topics: GOD as mystery; SCIENCE and God.

Precis: God is not present in the realm of science the way other things are: as something to be integrated into a homogeneous system. Nor is God simply an hypothesis temporarily filling the gaps in science. God is incomprehensible mystery, not the sum of phenomena, but the whole of its origin and ground. Hence, God cannot be imprisoned in an exact formula or assigned a place within a system of coordinates. Though speech fails, believers do not remain silent. They understand how the unease expressed by troubled atheists may be a more authentic expression of faith than the creed of an untroubled believer. We experience this God, this secret ground of being, whenever we encounter our own transcendence in facing inescapable responsibility, profligate love, or joyless death. The questions raised by these experiences are themselves blessed experiences of the incomprehensibility of God. The one who has experienced these moments as communications of protecting forgiveness is no mere "theists." For s/he has experienced the personal God, what Christians call divine grace, "the primeval event of Christianity has already taken place at the center of his being: the direct presence of God in man in the Holy Spirit" (194). Although much must still transpire before such a person professes explicit faith in Jesus Christ as the full meaning of this experience, Christianity only has meaning if it really introduces us to the trusting, holy surrender to the holy nameless mystery. Of course scientists may reject all this as poetry or cheap comfort. But even they are at times confronted with moments of transcendence. Do they just shrug? Is that really such an honest reaction? Or might it not be a betrayal of the ultimate dignity of both daily life and of their own research, to turn their backs on the infinite? "We must have sufficient courage to experience this abyss as the holy mystery of love – then it may be called God" (195).

GF.7.3. God, our Father. (196-202)
Christmas supplement of *Presse*, Vienna. December 24, 1964.
Abstract: Despite its paternalistic trappings we are still able to call God "Father" both because of our personal experience and because of the courage the example of Christ inspires in us. Christmas is the feast of the coming of the Son with the message, "God is near," the one we dare to call "Our Father."
Topics: CHRISTMAS; GOD as Father; INCARNATION.

Precis: Are we still able to call God "Father"? Certainly the God of the philosophers, of those who see God as incomprehensible mystery, is no Father. But is this the only way God exists, in the necessary distance that keeps us from reducing God to a mere idol? No. God is more. For we too experience this abyss as protecting, the silence as tender, the distance as home, the mystery as pure blessedness, and this we call Father. Despite the paternalism and inhumanity that often attach to it, "Father" remains a fitting word for many reasons (list, 197f), and to some degree it approximates our personal experience. But our life is also communal. And in our common history we encounter one who called Himself the Son, and who touchingly called the abyss of mystery "Abba." His example also encourages us to believe this great improbability. Those who believe in the Fatherly truth must celebrate four festivals: *Christmas* (that the Son has come); *Good Friday* (when faced with the absurdity of death He said "Father"); *Easter* (that He arrived at the Father in the whole reality of His being); *Pentecost* (when He gave us the courage of His heart to say "Father.") The rest of the essay concentrates on Christmas and the meaning of Incarnation.

Christmas is the feast of the coming of the Son, who makes the Father accessible in everyday life when we too say, "Father." The message of this feast is "God is near." God only seems distant or absent because He has always been there. Incarnation means: trust the nearness because it is not empty. The infinite mystery which silently surrounds us does not betoken judgment but grace. Those who meet this message with open, longing, hope-filled hearts are able to call this mystery "Father." Then, if we ourselves are good, full of fatherly love and childlike trust, "we shall be embraced and supported by the strength of the sacred secret of the world and of our own existence which we call God" (202). Only those who believe in the holy origin can believe in the infinite future, in final salvation.

VIII. True Freedom.
GF.8.1. The Theology of Freedom. (203-225)
In O.B. Roeggele (ed.), *Die Freiheit des Westens* (1967) 11-40.

Abstract: True freedom remains a mystery because it participates in the mystery of God at the core of the human person. Freedom is not the capacity endless to choose this or that. Rather it is the capacity to be-come one's definitely valid self, finally saying Yes or No to God through the mediacy of the finite world.

Topics: FREEDOM, theology of; THEOLOGICAL ANTHROPOLOGY, freedom.

Subsidiary discussions: God as the "Wither" of transcendence (205ff); Fundamental Option (213f); Love (214ff); Love of neighbor (217ff); Jesus Christ and freedom (224f).

Precis: Freedom in history. We objectify our ultimate and permanent human characteristics such as freedom throughout life, often without realizing it. Hence, we often do not know what true freedom is, and not all of us mean the same thing by the one word. Freedom has a history. First it is seen as freedom from compulsion— the opposite of slavery. Later, shaped by interiority, freedom comes to mean self-determination, often achieved through detachment. The final eschatological stage of freedom is reached with Jesus Christ who reveals the true freedom to accept absolutely the absolute mystery we call God. The essence of freedom is not the capacity arbitrarily to make and remake particular finite choices because God is not one finite object among others. Every free human act is necessarily played out in reference to the "Wither" of transcendence (avoiding here the words, "God" and "object" for fear of evoking misplaced concreteness).

Freedom is possible only through God. Freedom is theological by its very nature, since God is present in every free act, however implicitly. In each free act, the Wither of our transcendence is present in the mode of rejection and absence proper to itself – as mystery. For this Wither is never experienced directly, but is implicitly co-experienced in every act of transcendence. It is the condition of the possibility of transcendence.

Freedom towards God. What moves Christian freedom far beyond mere indeterminism is this decisive element: it exists both *from* God and *before* God. This implies the possibility of freedom saying Yes or No to its own horizon — a possibility constitutive of Christian freedom even when the categorical choices do not explicitly concern God. In this sense, we encounter God everywhere radically as the basic question put to our freedom in everything, especially in regard to our neighbor.

The paradox of human freedom. Because the Wither of transcendence is both the condition for the possibility of freedom and also its real "object," the act of freedom which denies God is the absolute contradiction: God is affirmed and denied simultaneously. But at the same time this decision is rendered relative by the fact that it occurs in the finite material of our life. Still, this paradoxical rejection remains a real possibility without which we as subjects would not be free.

Freedom and grace. Our capacity for transcendence is not merely natural. It is a product of grace pointing to God's nearness. Hence, God is not only infinite distance but also intimate presence in deifying grace. This is what transforms our freedom into the power to say Yes or No to God as such.

Freedom for salvation or damnation. Freedom by its nature is concerned with the freely chosen final end of the subject. This is the core truth beneath all talk of salvation, damnation, responsibility, and judgment. In daily life it may seem freedom of choice is merely a quality of human acts for which we will be held accountable. In this view, more or less free acts would be attributable to a neutral human freedom which could continue to pick and choose among options as long as life held out. But in the Christian view, through the use of our freedom we are able to determine *ourselves* wholly, definitively and completely. Through free acts *we become* good or evil, not accidentally but in the depths of our being.

Freedom as self-realization. Freedom is not the quality of an act. It is the transcendental qualification of being human. Whatever happens to me becomes important for my subjective salvation only if it is freely understood and accepted by me in a very special way as a free subject. The "I" of my personhood can never be replaced or explained by another. I can never shift responsibility for myself onto others. Freedom is not the capacity to choose this or that, but to say Yes or No to *myself*. It is my self-realization brought about in the choices I make. It is an inescapable burden.

Freedom – the capacity of the eternal. Freedom is realized in time. Although not every free act is capable of bearing our radical self-expression (our *option fondamental*), each act does add to the whole of the one free act of the one finite life. This fundamental act is never the mere sum of our free acts, nor is it the final quality of our last act before death. It is the unity in difference between the formal *option fondamental* and our free individual human acts. Freedom is the capacity for the eternal; the result of freedom is the true and lasting necessity.

Freedom – the capacity of love. Since this self-perfecting of freedom into the eternal moment is its self-realization before God, salvation and damnation cannot be seen as externally applied rewards or punishments. They are the accomplishments of freedom. The destiny of the whole person is "the capacity of the heart," the capacity for love. Only love of God is the total integration of human existence. Only there are we completely whole. We have understood the dignity and all-encompassing greatness of human existence only if we sense that love must be the content of eternity.

The risk of love. This love is not an achievement that can be exactly defined. It is known only when accomplished. We do not know what love is, or what we are sacrificing or gaining until after we have actually loved. Hence, love cannot be calculated in advance. I cannot know what is demanded, for I *myself* am demanded, and until I have loved I do not know myself. Love is always a risk.

Love has no measure. The Christian ethos is not primarily concerned with respecting the various structures of reality, since the only ultimate structure of the person is the basic and measureless power of love. All sin is the refusal to entrust oneself to this measurelessness. Of course to discover what is meant by this we need the many objective commandments. But they are all partial compared to the norm of love. We can talk about a "command of love" as long as we remember that it does not command *something* but *someone*: ourselves. We do this by receiving God's love which is not a thing, but God's very Self. God is no impersonal "it." God is the living God, and all human activity is a response to God's call.

We only take ourselves and our history seriously once we know ourselves as integrated into the sovereign freedom of God. This is our creatureliness.

Love of one's neighbor. Human freedom is always actualized in and among categorical objects. If God's word is to appear in this world at all, it must appear as a finite word of man. All relation to God is mediated by inner-worldly communication. Hence, the original relation to God is love of neighbor (218). In love of neighbor, freedom enters history even more deeply by personal decision. For practical freedom cannot simply be deduced from theoretical norms. That our freedom always remains creaturely freedom is evident from two things: that our transcendental nature is always experienced as given and not as self-authoring; and that it is necessarily mediated by the surrounding world. Creaturely freedom is conditioned by the situation, and the situation is always determined in part by guilt (i.e., original sin and concupiscence). Dependent on foreign material to express itself, freedom will always be alienated from itself. Hence, it will never be clear how much of any free act is our free objectification, and how much springs from nature. Unable ever to know for certain the status of its Yes or No to God, freedom must trustingly surrender to God's judgment, something for which our wounded freedom needs divine help: prevenient grace. Freedom remains a mystery (summary, 221).

Freedom is subjectivity. As has been said above, the free act participates in the mystery of its origin and goal insofar as it is never absolutely objectifiable. This truth is also explicitly emphasized in scripture and doctrine, both Catholic and Protestant.

Freedom and moral judgment. Though one cannot make an absolutely objective statement about the exercise of one's own freedom within a given act, one is both able and obliged to judge one's moral state objectively and to arrive at a well-founded opinion about how one uses freedom. This yields a kind of binding certainty, even though it realizes it is not final. In this objectified knowledge one accepts oneself and surrenders to the mysterious judgment of God. Yet freedom remains a mystery.

Freedom through Christ. Because in Christ, God has made known His irrevocable decision to set freedom free, the history of freedom is salvation history. However scripture may describe it (list,

224), what happened in Christ's free act of self-surrender to God is repeated in us as we live out our own freedom: "God himself has given himself to the freedom that surrenders itself it him" (224). The Christ-event reveals that God has permitted our "No" only in order to communicate Himself to the freedom of His creatures, and thus His "Yes" remains victorious (conclusion, 225).

GF.8.2. Origins of Freedom. (226-247)

July 29, 1965, lecture in Cologne to *Evangelischer Kirchentag*. In M. Horkheimer, et al., *Über die Freiheit* (1965) 27-49.

Abstract: Freedom originates in God, and its proper actualization leads back to God. Free acts, because they are always material, are essentially social/moral. The problem of freedom is not how to insure no one's freedom is ever restricted, but how to extend the one sphere of freedom most fairly to all.

Topics: FREEDOM; FREEDOM, sphere of.

Subsidiary discussions: God as the ground of freedom (226ff); Liberalism (240ff).

Precis: Formal characteristics of Christian freedom. True freedom born from human transcendence is always freedom before and towards God. The free act is our meeting point with God. God, the infinite horizon of our transcendence is the condition for the possibility of freedom and also its goal, even if this should remain only implicit. The free human act is diffuse and constitutes the one act of human life. In our free acts we become ourselves. The finite choices we make constitute a fundamental Yes or No to God through the acceptance or rejection of our natures. The innermost essence of freedom is the possibility of absolute self-commitment.

Grace and freedom. Properly understood, the doctrine of Christian freedom need not be a point of contention among Christian denominations. Any notion of "natural freedom" conceived apart from God, the essential ground and goal of freedom, is impossible, and the *Deus absconditus* present in the "natural" free act is never simply the *Deus revelata*.

Freedom as demand and possibility. Because freedom has three aspects (as decision relative to God; as finality; as final self-commitment) it is an accomplishment to be realized – a demand and not merely a fact. It is not a quality of actions or states but of persons. This has many consequences (list, 231).

The corporeal nature of freedom and its sphere. There is a dialectical character in our relationship to our own freedom and to the freedom of others. It becomes clear in light of the specifically human creatureliness of freedom. All free personal acts are accomplished in the material realm since subjective freedom can only be realized in objects not identical with itself. Hence, all freedom is realized in the common sphere of the unity of historical subjects. In realizing my own freedom I partially determine the sphere of freedom of others, enlarging or restricting it. Hence, freedom is intrinsically moral. It necessarily involves the distribution of freedom. This continually gives rise to controversy and must continually be renegotiated. For this reason, action in society always implies risk from which Christians in particular can never escape. Rahner next offers some theoretical considerations on how to handle concrete dangers and duties faced by Christians in the one sphere of freedom.

The change in the sphere of freedom in the last centuries has been simultaneously enlarged and restricted by such factors as technology, automation and the development of human relations.

The Christian's Yes to the enlarged sphere of freedom. Christians embrace this enlarged sphere of freedom since such a space is required for freedom to realize itself. This is true even when it implies the possibility and danger of perverting freedom. It cannot be the duty of individuals or of society to restrict the sphere of freedom, except in special circumstances (237). The subsequent erosion of formerly homogeneous "Christian societies" and the rise of greater social pluralism must be accepted and respected by Christians as allowed by the Lord of History. Freedom consists first in the courage to accept its larger sphere in spite of dangers. In fact, this enlarged sphere of freedom has it origin in Christianity, despite the fact that church history shows it has come into being only slowly and painfully. The Western passion for freedom is a Christian passion rooted in the principle of human dignity – the Christian knowledge that all are children of God and have eternal value as such. For Christians not to respect the freedom of all would betray Christianity itself.

Freedom and its limits. Nevertheless, in regard to freedom Christians are reasonable liberals and not social libertines who promote arbitrariness and license. Christians represent personalism not libertine individualism. They do not see the problem confronting freedom that some individual rights are restricted (this is an inevitable consequence of exercising freedom), but how to distribute freedom fairly in the one sphere of freedom (241). No one can claim a sphere of freedom for him/herself. The libertine principle of unlimited freedom for everybody to claim absolute freedom for everything does this, and thereby actually denies the sphere of freedom for others (summary, 242f).

Freedom as the courage of commitment. Any concrete social policy to establish the largest possible sphere of freedom for all people demands the courage to affirm the need for commitment (even to coercion and to the authority that limits the freedom of some for the sake of others) despite the clamor of libertines. Legitimate power is not sinful, and not everyone has the right to everything. The common good limits freedom for the sake of freedom itself, and is not an alien element. No permanent concrete distribution of the sphere of freedom is ever possible. There will always be struggle and compulsion, victors and vanquished. The social order will always stand in need of correction. But in this process the church must never claim for itself any special help from secular powers to further its own special mission.

Freedom and the demands of the time. Christians have the duty to participate in shaping the actual distribution of the one sphere of freedom. Though this distribution will be based on theological principles, it cannot simply be deduced from them. It will always be a creative decision demanding courage and wisdom. Still, not everything can or should be legislated. Freedom must be allowed to others even when there is a good chance they may abuse it; and the church must never make special claims for her own way of life. Social controls will always be needed to defend the freedom of all, even when that means restricting the sphere of freedom of others. Material regulations will also be necessary. To protect true freedom, Christians must always find a new relation to the dialectical unity between the largest possible sphere of freedom on the one hand, and its perhaps compulsory distribution on the other.

Finding this balance is a task not of theoretical but of practical knowledge

GF.8.3. The Test of Christian Freedom. (248-261). January 14, 1967 lecture in Frankfurt to *Katolische Erziehergemeinschaft* of Hessen.
Abstract: The eccesial and social ramifications of Christian freedom are great. As the will to the necessary it accepts the finite; as the will to truth it is self-critical; as the will to extend itself to all it is tolerant and dialogical; as the will to the unlimited it takes risks. Christian freedom is the ground of true humanism.
Topics: CHURCH, freedom in; DIALOGUE; FREEDOM.
Subsidiary discussions: Truth and freedom (250f); Church, dissent within (251ff); Church as pilgrim (258f); Humanism (259f).

Precis: After setting out the broad dynamic of Christian freedom, which is graced human freedom oriented to God, Rahner tries to say a bit more clearly what freedom is as such. First it is *"the will to the necessary."* By this he means the free acceptance of oneself as a finite human being. He also calls this *amor fati*. Freedom is the capacity to change what is foreign into oneself, the possibility of acceptance and love. However much control we may be able to exert today over the material world by means of planning and technology, freedom always remains finite. At times freedom protests. But rebellion is never the last word of freedom.

Genuine freedom is *"the will to truth,"* as only truth frees us from the interior dangers of shortsighted pride and egoism. Truth undergirds the self-criticism needed to temper freedom of thought and expression. This is no less true when it comes to theological discussion in the post-conciliar church (251ff), which must allow freedom of discussion without allowing that everything is open to debate. On the one hand, church membership is voluntary; and on the other hand the church has the right to define when one's opinions have put him/her beyond the pale.

By extension, Christian freedom exhibits *"the will to give freedom to all."* It respects the freedom of others, is tolerant and seeks open dialogue with all. Finite freedom must always objectify itself (e.g., in the choice of one's religion). But for the Christian it is decisive *how* this objectivizing comes about. Only if it occurs through freedom is it personal and hence conducive to salvation. Christianity imposed through indoctrination or social pressure would deny its own nature. To successfully propagate itself, Christianity must will to create and enhance the sphere of freedom, even if that should mean setting the ground for its rejection. The decisive factor is this: "The church herself must will a sphere of freedom for all men, because without it free human beings and also Christians cannot exit" (255). Tolerance is not a "tactic" but an essential demand of the church which has no other way to accomplish its purpose. The church cannot work to prevent what is wrong at any price, including the price of freedom. The church should be the first to make the defense of the freedom of others its own.

The will to extend freedom to all also signifies something deeper (256): devotion to responsible freedom and unconditional respect for the dignity of others. One must be willing to assume that others, even those most unlike us, share the same will to love, even though this desire may be objectified in quite different ways. "Such an attitude contains implicitly and germinally the essentials of Christianity, namely faith, hope and love of God" (256). Christians who will the freedom of all must believe that others are capable of dialogue, and that they will the good even where it is realized in wrong and threatening ways. They must also believe that because there is common ground for dialogue there is also hope.

Freedom is also *"the will to the unlimited"* – the courage to risk the unforeseeable future. Despite our best efforts at planning, there are always unforeseeable and unintended consequences. Risk is possible only in transcendence: when a particular finite choice is grounded in an anticipation of the absolute good. Hence, transcendence is both the condition of free action *and* that which free action must accept and confess. Thus, finite freedom is also historically creative. This also applies to the church as a pilgrim people making its way through history. "Her constancy in the risk of her historical freedom is guaranteed by her Lord, by her Spirit" (259). Such a stance demands courage.

"Realized freedom is the unique event of the personal uniqueness of every man in his finality before God" (259). It is the final act of commitment of the spiritual subject, an event of eternity in time, a final acceptance or rejection of God. This ultimate capacity, this freedom, constitutes our highest dignity and is the foundation of true humanism. Humanism is not a product of the Western way of life. "It is rather the confession of the absolute future of man which is God himself" (261). Freed from allegiance to any finite cultural objectifications, the church can discuss with all others how to harmonize secular activities with our eternal task and destiny (conclusion, 261).

GF.8.4. Fate and Freedom. (262-264). March 1, 1967, Bavarian Radio interview on the problem of astrology.

Abstract: All attempts to combine fate and freedom must begin by fully recognizing and remaining open to both. Although in the end the finite person cannot reconcile them, the attempt to do so gives us the courage and humility to accept both in the infinite mystery of God. Fate exists in a twofold sense. We experience life as a single chain of causes and effects. But we are unable to distinguish which causes, or even how much of any given cause, is due to freedom or to fate. Such judgment is reserved to God. But those who believe in God will also experience fate in a deeper sense: as lives wholly borne by God precisely as this unity of freedom and fate. However much one may know of fate, the burden and dignity of freedom is inescapable. Only accepting destiny in faith and hope as coming from infinite love reveals the true character of life. One may never abdicate the responsibility of shaping one's life with the excuse "whatever is going to happen is going to happen." For this decision, too, is part of what will happen.

Topics: FATE and freedom; FREEDOM and fate.

Happiness through Prayer. London, Burns Oates & Washbourne, 1958. 109 pp. *Von der Not und dem Segen des Gebetes.* **Cf.,** *The Need and the Blessing of Prayer.* **NBP.**

Holy Baptism. Denville, NJ: Dimension Books, n.d. 40 pp.
Gott Liebt Dieses Kind, **Cf.,** *Meditations on the Sacraments,* **MS.1.**

H. Hominisation. The Evolutionary Origin of Man as a Theological Problem. NY: Herder & Herder, 1965. Notes and Bibliography. 120 pp. "*Die Hominisation als theologische Frage*," from K. Rahner

and P. Overhage, *Das Problem der Hominisation*. Freiburg: Herder, 1958. *Questiones Disputatae* Series, #13. Treated here as one essay.
Contents: Preface.
I. The Official Teaching of the Church on Man in Relation to the Scientific Theory of Evolution.
II. What the Sources of Revelation State about Human Origins.
III. Theological and Philosophical Questions.
Notes and Bibliography

Abstract: Although the scientific and theological views of human origins cannot be completely reconciled, they are not completely contradictory. By applying metaphysics to such concepts as matter and spirit, becoming, causality, self-transcendence, Rahner tries to create common ground for dialogue.
Topics: BECOMING; CAUSALITY, divine; EVOLUTION; SCIENCE and Theology; THEOLOGICAL ANTHROPOLOGY; THEOLOGY and Science.
Subsidiary Discussions: Truth, oneness of (11ff); Soul/Body, unity of (19ff); Magisterium, competence of (24ff); *Humani generis* (24ff); Angels (51f); Spirit and matter (46ff); Transcendence, horizon of (81ff); Cognition (81ff); Soul, creation of (93ff).

Precis: Preface (7-10). By indicating the topics that cannot be covered here Rahner clarifies the topic of revelation and human evolution. He then briefly outlines the contents of this 3-part essay:
I. Official Teaching of the Church on Man in Relation to the Scientific Theory of Evolution. (11-31)
1. Formal pronouncements on the fundamental principles governing the relation between revealed doctrine and secular knowledge. It is the Catholic position that since all particular truths derive from the same font of all reality, they cannot conflict. Christian scientists must acknowledge the more comprehensive authority of the magisterium and not affirm as established any position that contradicts defined doctrine. Notwithstanding, not all conflicts between science and Catholic teaching can be avoided beforehand on the principle that each discipline has its own material object and hence its own area of unchallenged competence. The magisterium claims for itself (even if only *sub resepctu salutis*) competence even over empirical events. Though real, objec-

tive conflict between these two authorities is never possible, real tensions may appear which for a time do not seem to admit of resolution. Nevertheless, the church teaches that because people have a plurality of cognitive powers, from a certain point of view secular knowledge has a certain priority over revealed doctrine. Revelation aims at initiating dialogue with people who have already attained responsible self-awareness. It has no intention of supplying a comprehensive principle for the whole of reality and thus abrogating all human intellectual history. The ensuing dialogue is surprising and unpredictable; it affects both partners and there is no principle that can adjudicate all their differences beforehand. Hence, at most we can say that revelation and theology provide a *norma negativa* for natural science (16f), realizing that more remains to be said.

2. **Positive theses of sacred theology important for the scientific theory of evolution.** The church warns against two things: 1) falsely transposing scientific knowledge to all other domains in a facile attempt to explain all reality by appealing to the concept of "development" or "evolution" which ends up as a kind of dialectical materialism; 2) casting doubt on the essential difference between spirit and matter. Man is a substantial unity. This unity is ontologically prior to and comprises a real and genuine, irreducible plurality of essential composition. Consequently, no statement can be made about anything in man (e.g., body or soul) apart from this unity. Every statement about one part implies a statement about the whole. Because this is both a defined truth of faith and a fundamental presupposition of Christian theological anthropology, it is easy to see why theology was not eager to accept the idea of harmonizing science and belief by delivering the body to science and retaining the soul for itself.

There is also a genuine, irreducible plurality of realities within man. Neither materiality nor spirituality can simply be deduced from, or reduced to, one or the other. Body and soul are different in kind. And despite the unity of man, the soul is intrinsically independent in being and meaning from matter. Of its very nature it is immortal. Consequently, the soul can only come into being by the divine act of creation. At the same time, man as a corporeal being stands in causal connection to the whole material world. The fact that the whole of man originates from the earth makes us the proper object of science. This fact has greater theological significance than is often allowed and calls for greater attention. In any case, a proper study of man cannot be undertaken without reference to our original and substantial unity, and to the truth that the soul is not a thing on its own that could be understood independent from matter. This alone keeps true anthropology from becoming mere "somotology."

As to *how* man is connected to material reality, nothing in church teaching forbids us from conceiving of a real ontological connection between the animal kingdom and our corporeal nature. The encyclical *Humani generis* only insists that we avoid claims that any such evolutionary theory is already quite certain, or that such a thesis is completely outside the range of the competence of revelation. Obviously, church competence does not extend to the intrinsic scientific probability of a theory. But it is competent to reject a scientific theory if it is at odds with revelation. Furthermore (26), although *Humani generis* presents its position as subject to revision, this is not to be expected due to any new scientific data (which in itself is never the basis of church teaching) nor to development of doctrine which, although it may at times pronounce previously held positions as false, never adopts previously false positions as now true. This applies both to the scientific argument itself and to the exegetical principles set forth for the proper interpretation of Genesis (history of, 29f). This section concludes with a summary of the current state of affairs (31).

II. What the Sources of Revelation State about Human Origins. (32-44).

1. **The new formulation of the question.** What intrinsic reason is there connected with the very essentials of the message of faith which impels the church to draw boundaries and to grant permissions allowing the theory of evolution? To determine what scripture actually says on the matter (Genesis 1-3) we must look to its literary character, which in this case is historical aetiology.
2. **Preliminary reflections on method: direct and indirect revelation.** Even about a revealed proposition we must be free to ask whether it was revealed directly or was only implicit in a primordial revelation concerned with something else. Though revealed, it may have a derivative character and thus it remains possible to ask

about its source: from whom was it known, how was it revealed and in what respect? Negatively it can be said the creation narrative is not a firsthand account. If it were, its figurative language would be meaningless and impossible to justify. The real question is what is the source of the knowledge the writer of Genesis reports? Rahner's answer is "historical aetiology."

3. **The concept of historical aetiology.** Aetiology broadly means assigning causes for another reality. It is of two kinds: mythological (the narrower sense) and historical. *Mythological aetiology* (favored by Protestant exegetes) assigns an earlier event as the reason for an observable state of affairs, whereby the cause is known. Its often vivid language is meant to impress on the mind the present state of affairs. In *historical aetiology* (favored by Catholic exegetes) the reference back to an earlier event may be genuine, a successful inference of an historical cause from a present state of affairs. Almost inevitably the inferred cause is expressed figuratively, something which does not belong to the earlier event but derives from the aetiologist's world of experience.

4. **Its application to Genesis.** After going more deeply into the difference between the Protestant and Catholic uses of aetiology (37f), Rahner maintains that with divine assistance the historical aetiology found in Genesis may well be valid concerning the special creation of man, equality of the sexes, unity of the human race, etc. (list, 38). He concludes with a number of arguments in favor of this approach based on its explanatory power, (e.g., it explains the use of figurative language, the enduring relevance of the language, its value in drawing distinctions, its positive relation to a theory of original revelation).

5. **Content of the Genesis account on this view.** According to Rahner, historical aetiology provides the axiom for separating the content of Genesis 1-3 from its figurative mode of presentation. What it affirms is what is truest and most vital in our present situation: that we are unique partners with God, radically distinct from animals; that the existence of two equal sexes is something intended by God from the beginning; that human life is threatened by the powers of this world; that relationship with God is an inescapable feature of human existence. Rahner finishes this positive listing (40) by recapping the theory of historical aetiology.

Negatively, nothing is said or can be said regarding the manner of immediate creation by God (apart from the fact that the creation of man bore on a previously existing world). Historical aetiology cannot say anything about matters which are simply past and have no connection to life here and now. It leaves them as open questions for secular inquiry. Their answers (e.g., our connection to the animal kingdom) have no significance for theology as they do not bear on salvation as such. What we must know from Genesis 1-3 for our salvation is already confirmed through historical aetiology. People who in the past thought they saw in Genesis details about how humans were created were simply ignorant of the genre employed, and misread the text. A "more literal" reading of the text is one which takes genre more seriously, not one which attends only to the words (42f). Rahner concludes this section by arguing for the superiority of historical aetiology because it avoids mythological retrojection, upholds church teaching, and does greater justice to the notion of beginnings than does the rival theses.

III. Theological and Philosophical Questions (45-109). The present truce established between science and theology is no more than the precondition for continuing dialogue. There are still many unanswered questions regarding hominisation. This section does not so much seek to answer all these questions as to set them out and clarify what is at stake in each.

1. Spirit and matter. In the debate over evolution, Catholic teaching presupposes many things about matter and spirit (list, 46). But only a rigorous investigation of these terms can justify its position.

a) On the distinction between spirit and matter. For Rahner, what is spiritual is more immediately known than what is material. To insist otherwise is scientific ideology. When a materialist claims that all is matter, the key term, "matter," has no assignable value. It extrapolates beyond the competence of science, and it is open to the wildest forms of Idealism. But if by "matter" the materialist means "being," then it is quite true to say that nothing exist except being, and as a corollary that regarding everything that can be thought, some statement can be made which is common to and valid for all beings. It would also have to be added that there exist essential and irreducible differences among realities, which in turn raise the question of their original unity, which Rahner argues is primordial (without becoming mere pan-psychism). Hence, it is not appropriate to subsume under the term "matter" the subjectivity we meet as part of the primordial unity, as this would obscure the fundamental difference between subject and object encountered in that unity (50). So the decision to employ the terms matter and spirit derives from analysis and is not merely borrowing from Plato.

Christian belief in God in no way settles the question of the dialectical unity shared by matter and spirit since God is not a part of the world but rather the ground of all reality, and hence different in kind from whatever we can meet in the world. We apply the word "spirit" to God only analogously because of the infinite openness we attach to spirit in the world, as opposed to the limitedness of matter. Leaving aside the question of angels (51f), we are not obliged to begin all inquiry with the proposition that every-thing individual is material, since in the act of cognition, through which we are able to inquire into the nature of the things we experience, we already encounter the primordial unity between cognition and the object manifesting itself. This returns Rahner to his initial point: knowledge of matter (that which is closed to a dynamic orientation above and beyond itself to being in general) is derived from our more immediate grasp of spirit (a primordial datum in transcendental experience in which we know ourselves as one single spiritual and corporeal being, underivative, which is either present totally or not at all).

b) *On the unity of spirit and matter.* After briefly recapping the arguments for the distinction between spirit and matter (53), Rahner now refutes claims that the two are absolutely heterogeneous from a metaphysical point of view, since this would annul the real unity of man. His first argument is based on cognition which, in presupposing an actual communication between reality and the knower, must exclude their complete heterogeneity. What they share is called by Christian philosophers "being." (Rahner bolsters this argument by reference to creation. Were matter not created by God essentially for the sake of spirit and oriented to spirit (its purpose and finality) it would be meaningless— itself an ontological impossibility.) Hence, one cannot say that Christian philosophers have stressed only the differences between matter and spirit.

But maintaining their distinction does mean that it is impossible to argue that matter can somehow, of itself, shed its essential limitations and change into spirit. Limits are removed from what is limited, but only in mind and spirit, i.e., in man. And what is liberated this way is precisely "the spiritual reality of matter." This is ultimately not "'something or other' objectively known as alien to the spirit, but a factor significantly related to spirit and the latter's plentitude of being" (57). This alone can explain how the soul is *per se ipsam* the form and act of *materia prima*. Matter is a limited component or factor in spirit itself, which spirit distinguishes from itself and posits as that which renders possible the achievement of its own identity. Finally, two other specifically Christian doctrines are enlisted to refute the absolute heterogeneity of spirit and matter: the nature of final beatitude in which matter and spirit are both perfected (unlike a Platonic sloughing off of the flesh), and the nature of the Incarnation which entails Christ's eternally maintaining the material reality of his flesh (summary, 61).

2. **Philosophical problems connected with the concept of becoming.** *a) The problem itself.* The fact that Christianity can embrace a moderate theory of evolution (definition, 62) does not settle all theological problems and turn the field over to science. For given the substantial unity of man, anything science says about the body has reference to soul; anything theology says about soul carries implications for the body. Theology must insist, therefore, that anything science says about evolution towards man is really a statement about the pre-history of the soul. This brings into focus the question of how to conceive the development of a being that consists in producing as its goal something higher than itself, or at least something oriented to self-transcendence (64). After an excursus on the right way to consider divine causality which avoids making God part of a train of causes (albeit the first), the initial problem arises in a new form. Does not the insistence that at a definite point in time God creates a spiritual soul in the animal form which has appropriately developed on its own, suddenly replace the closed series of secondary causes with God Himself? (Variations on the question, 66f). It in no way helps to say this happens daily with the genesis of each human being. In fact this only widens the problem. Rahner focuses the question (69f): does divine creation of the soul contradict everything we

understand of the relation of primary to secondary causes, or can the general concept of becoming be employed to show that this event exemplifies the accurate and fully-developed concept of the relation between the two? All this leaves open whether the relation between God and the origin of the spiritual soul does not also occur in nature and history. "To facilitate progress," Rahner concludes this section with a preview. In what follows, he will address how God's enduring active support of cosmic reality actively enables finite beings to transcend themselves by their own activity in a way that holds good in general and "for the creation of the spiritual soul." He will also show how finite becoming is 1) the approach to those things that are higher than themselves through active self-fulfillment of their own natures, and 2) an active transcending of their own natures wherein an individual moves actively by its own activity beyond and above itself.

b) *Suggestions from scholastic philosophy and theology.* This very dense metaphysical subsection intends to indicate a few points in the scholastic philosophy of change that might help provide a starting point in this discussion of becoming. The first concept Rahner reviews is *eductio e potentia materiae*: the drawing forth of the form from the potentiality of matter (70-76). On this principle, creatures can produce new reality. But it leaves open whether this change is a matter of *becoming-more* or of *becoming-otherwise*. He illustrates this by reference to motion as an example of becoming-otherwise (72). He goes on to say that modern science operates on the principle of the absolute equivalence of functionally linked phenomenon. So is becoming-otherwise inconceivable, and can its sufficient cause be found within the cosmos? Rahner maintains that "if a new substantial form appears in an *eductio e potentia materia*... something really new in the sense of 'being' appears" (73). But can finite active power be the sufficient cause of such an increment of being? If one holds to the axiom of sufficient reason and maintains that what is more cannot simply come from what is less, then one must admit of a perspective open for endless becoming, the idea of infinite Being as the ground of the very possibility of any becoming that involves an increase of being. Although this ground cannot simply be part of the efficient cause, it must be linked to the finite agent and belong to it though transcending it (summary, 76).

The second scholastic concept reviewed here is divine *concursus* (conservation) and the related notion *praemotio physica* (76-81). Rahner argues that the introduction of these concepts does not simply supply the kind of sufficient cause required. They harbor the danger of either becoming too immanent (just another finite element within efficient causality) or too transcendent, in which case they do not explain the actual becoming of the finite object. Rahner summarizes the special kind of cause needed to explain becoming within the context of sufficient reason, and then asks whether this notion is valid and demonstrable, "or only a paradoxical and intrinsically self-contradictory construction which can only conceal the fact that our thought has reached an impasse" (82f). The answer to this is found by a review of even more basic fundamentals.

c) *The transcendental source of a genuinely metaphysical concept of cause.*
Two presuppositions: the validity of genuinely ontological propositions is proved by transcendental deduction (by showing that the proposition is implicitly confirmed as a condition of the possibility of inquiring into the thing); for human beings the ontological paradigm of a being and its fundamental properties is found in the being him/herself who knows and acts. Since all the transcendental properties of being are ultimately experienced in the activity of the knowing subject, a genuine concept of becoming must be attained in the operation of cognition itself. (This must not be dismissed as merely a mental event.) What do human beings discover is transcendentally necessary in their acts of cognition? They discover their openness to being in general, and hence to absolute being, as the condition for the possibility of reflective self-awareness, and for discriminating between and uniting other objects. He calls the term of this orientation a horizon (not an object). This horizon possesses three more precisely determined aspects: 1) it is an essential factor in all intellectual knowledge, an immanent component of transcendence; 2) its imminence is expressed in an irreducibly paradoxical (dialectical) way. Its imminence is only possessed in virtue of its transcendence; 3) this horizon sets cognition in motion. "The orienting term of transcendence moves the movement of the mind" (86). Cause and action are only known in light of this movement. All other efficient causes are deficient modes of this causality.

d) Ontological theses on the concepts of becoming, cause, and operation. Based on all that has been said, the following affirmations should now be intelligible [!]. **1.** Becoming is always an advance, a going beyond, and not merely a reduplication or repetition of the identical in a self-transcending movement toward being as such. The resultant possession of being qualifies the affected subject in the most radical way. **2.** This self-transcendence takes place because it has within itself absolute Being as the cause and ground of its self-movement (but not in such a way that it causes movement within absolute Being). For this reason it can be said that finite being can affect more than it is. **3.** Hence, the "essence" of a self-transcendent being does not determine what it might produce beyond itself, but can indicate the goal of a process of becoming that has yet to come. Everything cannot become anything. **4)** Self-transcendence that rises above the essence of the agent must not be ruled impossible from the start. This is due to the grades of limitation of being (90) which in turn explains the direction of self-transcendence and some of its limits (conclusions, 92). What has been said about the unity and differences between spirit and matter can be applied to the development of material things toward spirit, which is not an inconceivable idea, providing this self-transcendence can only occur in the direction of spirit.

3. On the creation of the spiritual soul. According to Rahner, the concept of becoming set forth here overcomes some otherwise intractable problems surrounding the coming into being of the first human and subsequent individuals as well. It has something to add to the current [1963] discussion about potential "pre-human" states of the human biological organism.

a) The problem. The church teaches that individual spiritual souls do not pre-exist and are directly created by God at a time before birth. But how is one to conceive of God's operation without reducing it to one of many seemingly natural intra-mundane causes, but still something completely miraculous and as a matter of course quite different from all other divine interventions explained through secondary causes? Here Rahner revisits the question of whether the soul is multiplied with the increase of individuals of the species, or whether one and the same soul "which, unfolding its formative power at various material points in space and time, manifests itself more than once in space and time" (96f).

He argues for the second option, [a kind of world soul?] as both reasonable and closer to the scientific view. For what we experience as a plurality of living, discontinuous things is no proof of an ontological plurality of living beings in respect of their formal principle. In this view, individuals and species would be a reality proper to the "noosphere" of personal minds rather than to the biosphere of naturally occurring things.

b) *Towards a solution of the problem of God's "predicamental" operation in the creation of the individual human soul.* This section reiterates the claim that Rahner's view of self-transcendence which demands that God be seen as a constitutive part of the process (the condition of its possibility) without thereby simply becoming part of the finite actor, is the best way to guard against reducing God's participation in becoming to a "predicamental" [categorical] operation (i.e., a discrete miraculous intervention in the coming to be of each individual human soul). The fact that this is uniquely operative in the creation of the human soul does not mean that it is confined exclusively to this activity (99). Summary, 100f.

4. **The biblical narrative of man's origins and the theory of evolution.** The reason for the great gulf between the scientific and religious views of the origin of man is that religion sees Paradise at the beginning, whereas science sees it at the end. Science sees man starting from a zero point and gradually ascending, whereas religion sees man beginning in plentitude, descending, and now on a path of slow recovery. Can these two views be reconciled?

a) *The biblical statement.* Church doctrine on human origin says no more than scripture. Because it belongs to the form and not to the content of revelation, we do not know the concrete details of proto-history. The church teaches only three truths: man was created by God to be His partner; concupiscence and death did not belong to the first man; the first man was the first to incur guilt before God, making it an intrinsic part of our entire subsequent historical situation. But *how* this happened we do not know. Metaphysics tells us that "original sin" was man's first original act of freedom, since if the first act had been good, as an act of complete integrity it would have completely determined the doer, making any subsequent bad act impossible. Thus proto-history cannot be thought of as taking place over a protracted period of time. Initial integrity is posited as the only explanation for such a radical decision determining the situation of man ever after. But the loss of this original integrity, such that it no longer applies to each of our actions today, does not mean that none of our actions today can contain a similarly definitive decision about ourselves. Indeed, within the parameters of the church's teaching there is no reason to assume Adam's empirically tangible situation before sin was essentially different from our situation today. For even then, man faced a real future to be actualized through genuine, free self-development. This potential future must not be confused with his actual pre-lapsarian situation, as some medieval thinkers mistakenly did. Hence, religion would say Adam began in a state of "potential" Paradise.

b) *The scientific statement.* Nor is science able to form a complete picture of the first man. No concrete dividing line between man and animal may ever be found. But the dynamism of self-transcendence does separate us. Wherever there is such intellectual transcendence, man is there, and there is knowledge of God, however inchoate.

c) *The relation between the two.* It is quite possible the statements of science and theology will never directly and positively coincide to form one concrete picture of our origins. But it cannot be said that the two sets of statements simply contradict one another. Every statement about origins is deduced aetiologically from a later state still in the process of change. All such statements must affirm that the beginning, as mere beginning, was less than what was to come; and that what did come is intelligible from the point of view of the beginning. There is no danger that an evolutionary view properly understood will make us think less of the first Adam. Man as we know him today was there when man began to exist. "And what now is historically and externally manifest, was then present as a task and as an active potentiality. Because now his biological, spiritual and divine elements are present in him, they are also quite plainly and simply to be affirmed of the beginning" (108f). All this shows that when it comes to human origins only a very complex answer on many levels can be the correct one, and that oversimplifying the problem can only lead to error.

Inq. ***Inquiries.*** NY: Herder,1964. Acknowledgments; Abbreviations; Author's Preface. 463 pp.

Contents: Inspiration in the Bible.
Visions and Prophecies.
The Church and the Sacraments.
The Episcopate and the Primacy.
On Heresy.

Inq.1. Inspiration in the Bible. (10-86). *"Über die Shriftinspiration."* Freiburg: Herder, nd. *Questiones Disputatae* Series, #1. Translated by Charles H. Henkey. 2nd edition revised by Martin Palmer.

Abstract: In this pre-Vatican II reflection, Rahner replaces the Two-Source Theory's failed attempt to defend development of doctrine (so obvious in the development of the canon) with his idea that God remains the author of scripture in the sense of willing ("authoring") the church, and by extension willing all the means necessary for the church to fulfill its mission (among them scripture). This frees the human writer to "author" scripture in the more traditional sense.

Topics: BIBLE, canonicity of; BIBLE, inspiration; DOCTRINE, development of; REVELATION, Biblical.

Subsidiary discussions: Bible, authorship (11-24); Revelation, two source theory (34-38; 76ff); Church, as absolutely willed by God (40ff); Church, apsotolicity of (43ff); Revelation, closure of (71ff).

Precis: Introduction. The general neglect of this central topic has allowed the church's teaching to accrue suspect material content. Without denying the doctrine of inspiration, Rahner's systematic thesis proposes to explain inspiration and related questions more elegantly, comprehensively and accurately. Behind all this is an attempt to justify a theory of development of doctrine vis-à-vis scripture.

I. The problems. After reiterating the outlines of pre-Vatican II teaching on inspiration (10-12, n.b., ftns.) Rahner examines four associated problem areas. Each discussion ends with a brief summary. **1. The two authors.** How can the current definition of inspiration explain and support the real divine and human authorship of scripture? **2. Some problems concerning the concept of inspiration.** What theory of inspiration safeguards this dual authorship? **3. How the inspiration of the Bible is ascertained by the church.** What theory of canonicity does justice to our historical knowledge of the history of the development of the canon? **4. The inspiration of the scriptures and the teaching authority of the church.** What justifies and rectifies the relationship of an infallible magisterium and infallible scriptures without making one or the other redundant (with special attention to the limitations of the Two Source Theory)?

II. The thesis is developed systematically starting from statements on the theology of the church. (In Part III, Rahner will return to four questions raised in Part I.) **1. God founds the church** in a unique way (i.e., as opposed to God's will to create). God founds the church through an absolute predefined act of will within the context of salvation history, thus giving it an irreversible and eschatological character.

2. The apostolic church (the church in the first generation) is subject to God's intervention in a unique manner distinct from its mere preservation, thus endowing it with a singular and irreplaceable function for the rest of the future of the church. Hence, the church has an institutional character and is not simply an ever-recurring event of faith. Evolution and development in the church derive from its origin, which is not simply God or Christ, but the apostolic community (summary, 45f). In this way God is the author of the church, and the apostolic church is the permanent ground for all that is to come, recalling: **a)** this first generation had a specific duration; **b)** the church had and forever retains the capacity to express its essence, and to distinguish its true nature from foreign elements within itself. The highest expression of this faculty is the apostolic church's ability to produce the norm by which she is to measure herself.

3. The scriptures as constitutive elements of the church is fundamentally the apostolic church's self-expression of her faith intended as the permanent source, the canon and norm for the later church.

4. The thesis. Inspiration of the Bible is simply God's willing the existence of scripture as a constitutive element of the very church which God wills absolutely. Hence, divine authorship of scripture

is rooted in, and is analogous to, God's prior will to author the church.
5. **Inspiration and the Old Testament** is a special question. After a word about the mutual relation of inspiration and canonicity, Rahner maintains that ultimately God effected the production of the Old Testament books to the extent they were to have a certain function and authority in the New Testament. God authors and inspires the Old Testament insofar as it is the authentic crystallization of the church's prehistory, hence, as an element in God's formally predefining production of the church.

III. Conclusions. 1. Does Rahner's thesis sufficiently safeguard traditional doctrine? After formally restating his thesis, Rahner argues it does preserve divine "authorship" of scripture in a special sense of the term. This leaves aside all discussion of God's exact method of authorship, something that is not an essential part of the doctrine, and something his thesis does not address. It also encompasses interior inspiration, leaving open the exact point at which such impulses operate within the writer.

2. How does Rahner's thesis supply more satisfactory answers to the problems posited in Part I? **a.** Rahner maintains his theory is better able to account for divine and human authorship by taking inspiration out of the realm of efficient causality or metaphor, and centering God's contribution in willing the church as such, and scripture as one of its constitutive parts. **b.** It also allows for a better explanation of the human author's consciousness of being inspired by focusing more concretely on the human author's awareness that he was committing to writing the church's self-awareness of God in Christ. **c.** It also supplies a better, more historically realistic approach to canonicity, "by distinguishing between the fundamental revelation as such (as process) concerning the inspiration of a book on the one hand, and the reflex propositional conception and formulation of revelation on the other" (69). Rahner also offers a more nuanced interpretation of the closure of revelation with the "death of the last apostle." **d.** His theory clarifies the relation between inspired scripture and the church's teaching authority by emphasizing their mutual dependence. The eschatological, hierarchically structured church infallibly expresses its own self-definition. This character attaches to both the *content* and to the very *act* of teaching. Hence, arising together, the two neither cancel one another out nor collide. "... the infallible teaching authority of the Apostolic Church ... consists in the capacity for creating the Scriptures, while the infallible teaching authority of the later Church consists in the authentic interpretation of Scripture" (77). The Two-Source Theory, which was an attempt to explain the development of dogma, actually failed to do justice to the material sufficiency of scripture. Rahner's thesis safeguards the sufficiency of scripture in the following ways:(i) It does not eliminate oral tradition but demands such "tradition." (ii) It does not allow one to jettison developed dogma with a claim that "it is not in scripture" since scripture is the unique beginning but not the end of theology (which is itself evident in scripture). (iii) In fact the Two-Source Theory does not make development of dogma easier to understand. (iv) The difficulties concerning development of dogma raised by the Two-Source Theory stem largely from an excessively narrow conception of how dogmas are explicated in history. **e.** Other corollaries of Rahner's basic thesis shed light on other important issues: (i) How Christian scripture relates to other religions and to their inspired books; (ii) why we find particular literary genres in a book ascribed to God; (iii) the relation of literary forms and inerrancy; (iv) the relationship between inspiration and canonicity; (v) the legitimacy of various "non-apostle" authors of scripture; (vi) hermeneutics which must take into account that the human author writes as a member of the church. Recalling that the author is a member of society helps account for his particular point of view; recalling his affiliation with the church helps us see him in canonical context.

Inq.2. Visions and Prophecies (89-188). Translated by Charles H. Henkey and Richard Strachan. *Visionen und Prophezeiungen.* Freiburg: Herder, n.d. *Questiones Disptatae* Series, #10. Also excerpted in GF.3.2; SC.2; SC.3.

Abstract: Despite the close of public revelation, prophecy retains unique importance in the church. It cannot be replaced by a general theory of theology, the natural or supernatural wisdom of the hierarchy, or by mysticism devoid of images. Hence, it is urgent to set forth criteria to identify authentic visions.

Topics: PROPHECY; REVELATION, private; VISIONS, criteria for.

Subsidiary discussions: Causality, supernatural (126ff); Parapsychology (174ff); Miracles as proof of prophecy (184ff).

Precis: I. The possibility and theological significance of private revelations and visions. Especially in troubled times, people look for reassurance about the future. This makes them both more gullible and more genuinely receptive to true messages from above. Belief in visions can either strengthen or weaken faith. Hence, it is important for Christians to have criteria to authenticate the claims of visionaries. Rahner uses as a rule of thumb that any claim which can be explained in natural terms cannot be considered to have established its supernatural character. **1. The possibility of private revelations** (definition, 95) is for Christians evident in principle, and to deny it is an offense against faith. Scripture is a witness to this (96-98). Rahner distinguishes mystical and prophetic visions. The former are personal, while the latter contain some communication meant for the broader public. **2. Observations on the theological significance of private revelations.** In what follows, Rahner concentrates on prophetic visions, but from a theological rather than a psychological perspective. The average theological views of private revelation are simultaneously too negative (they are not taken seriously) or too positive (they fail to appreciate the essential difference between revelations before and after Christ). Post-apostolic, private revelations, "do not reveal an objective affirmation as such which would either form an 'accidental' supplement to public revelation or simply be identical with it, but private revelations are essentially imperatives showing how Christianity should act in a concrete historical situation: not new assertions but new commands" (108). This section finishes with a recap and a discussion of the practical importance of private revelation.

II. The psychological problems of visions. 1. The imaginative vision as normal case. What is happening when the BVM "appears" to someone? After dismissing "the naive view," Rahner goes on to distinguish three kinds of visions: corporeal, imaginative, and purely spiritual. Of these, corporeal visions raise the most difficulties (115-120) but they also establish some negative criteria: e.g., the impression of reality, or physicality alone are never proof of authenticity. Here Rahner sides with St. Theresa who minimizes the value of corporeal visions in favor of imaginative visions, despite the claims of whole groups sharing a seemingly corporeal vision. Two things can be said of imaginative visions: 1) they must largely conform to the psychic laws determined by the intrinsic structure of the seer's spiritual faculties (123-124); 2) they must be caused by God (124-128). Summary 128-129.

2. **How the *species sensibilis* is produced.** It is not presented to the senses as a material object. Rather God, mediately or immediately, presents to the subject a *specie sensibilis impressa*. For this reason it can appear in manifold forms.

3. **Objectifications of the object of sense consciousness.** The seeming reality of this object of consciousness is not actually a fact but a judgment, and thus can be erroneous. Misjudgment is not a case of God deceiving us with false sense data, rather we are the ones who have misconstrued it. The only way to prove the divine origin of such visions is if the concrete content of the vision greatly exceeds the powers of the seer's sensible and intellectual faculties. This is rare. Theologically, authentic visions are supernatural due not to their content but to their source. All this calls for great reserve.

4. **The point of contact of the divine action on the visionary.** If the impetus for such imaginative visions is not presented to the sense organs, where does it touch the seer? Rahner proposes that God touches the seer at a deeper level in infused contemplation, and that what is encountered in visions is "a radiation and reflex of contemplation in the sphere of the senses, the incarnation of the mystical process of the spirit" (139). Hence, God is at most the indirect cause of imaginative visions. This helps explain 5 things: 1) why classic mysticism is generally indifferent towards visions; 2) why skepticism surrounding visionary claims is justifiable; 3) how even authentic visions remain subject to normal psychological laws; 4) the traditional emphasis on the seer's humility and other inner virtues; 5) how the particular content of a vision is conditioned by various factors in the seer's environment. It is practically impossible to tease apart those elements of a vision that derive from the subjectivity of the seer from those which may be infused. But their overlap does explain the many erroneous elements that occur even in the visions of saints (146-155). This

state has a positive consequence (it counsels leniency in judging visionary claims) and negative consequences (even an authentic vision cannot compel one to accept its every detail, or to reject it because of a few errors).

III. **Some criteria for genuine visions** (158-170). Unsatisfactory or least adequate criteria are: piety and personal holiness, which though required of real visionaries, are no proof of authenticity. The same is true of generally good physical and mental health, which can be discreetly altered. Clarity, stability and apparent objectivity can at times indicate the opposite of a true vision. Parapsychological manifestations should be disregarded as neutral at best. Personal integrity has the same status as personal holiness.

Positive criteria fall into two categories: those for the visionary, and those for the observer. Visionaries may be conflating certitude over the original mystical phenomenon of infused contemplation with the reality of the vision itself. (Visions themselves are generally considered by experts to be of relatively little importance.) Observers may rely on this same criterion, but since we have no experience of the visionary's inner state its value for us is greatly diminished.

In practice (barring external evidence of a miracle) alleged visionaries should be treated respectfully. But we are left free to judge the degree of importance we assign them in our own spiritual lives. The maxim remains true, supernatural agency is not to be presupposed but proved. Where visions claim to contain an element of prophecy demanding others to follow it, only a miracle is corroborative. Without this the vision can lay no claim to the assent of others. The most the church can do after investigation is to say a vision may be believed with human faith. This is not, however, an infallible statement, and it imposes no duty on the Christian faithful. One has a right to be skeptical about any private revelation that offers a way around the cross. Although it may be an invitation for others to take their faith seriously, we should not limit our appreciation for the faith to such devotions. God speaks to us most clearly in the church; and Christ appears to us most certainly in the faces of the poor. Rahner concludes (168-

170) with a lengthy list of investigated visionaries who turned out to be illegitimate.

IV. Prophecies (171-188). What was said about apparitions in general (including psychology, etc.) implicitly includes the most important theological data on prophecies, since any prophetic information is usually conveyed in visions. Rahner proceeds with a rough taxonomy of 5 kinds of prophecies. 1) Soothsaying, divination, and all forms of superstition rely on magic: the notion that God can be manipulated into giving answers about the future. 2) Parapsychological: dreams, clairvoyance, second sight. Much remains unknown about these experiences but they do not necessarily imply divine intervention, even if they sometimes are identified with saints. Parapsychological visions of the future are generally simply that: like discrete film clips without context or meaning. They do not lead necessarily to action. This distinguishes them from divine prophecy that communicates a meaningful "word" (177). 3) Anticipations of the future. These are generally due to the perspicacity of a great mind reviewing events in light of history or philosophy. Generally these deductions are based on an insightful analysis of the present. 4) Fabricated prophecies, frauds, illusions. 5) Genuine supernatural revelations with God as their immediate cause. These are attested to in scripture, and along with miracles are proof of God's action in history and motives for credibility.

Rahner next examines the theology attached to each of these five types. 1) Divination is morally wrong and participating in it is condemned. 2) Parapsychological phenomena being involuntary have no moral content. 3 & 4) Anticipations of the future, if they pertain to theology must be assessed on their theological accuracy. 5) Real God-given revelations of the future are attested to in scripture, and as part of the personal endowment of the church will never die out. This does not mean all prophecies are authentic or correct. Miracles are the only corroborative proof of the genuineness of a prophecy, provided the two are intimately connected. The purpose of all prophecy is to inspire confidence in God as Lord of History. They are calls to penance, conversion, prayer, trust in the victory of Christ, hope in God's eternal promise. Still, according to 1 Corinthians, prophecy remains a mere fragment in comparison to love.

Inq.3. The Church and the Sacraments (191-299). Translated by W.J. O'Hara. *"Kirche und Sakramente."* Freiburg: Herder, 1963. *Questiones Disptatae* Series #9.
Abstract: Part I tries to overcome a way of thinking about the church and sacraments as extrinsically connected and replace it with a deeper connection based on seeing the church as *Ur-sakrament*. In Part II each of the seven individual sacraments is presented as a particular manifestation of the church's nature.
Topics: CHURCH as *Ur-sakrament*; SACRAMENT/s.
Subsidiary discussions: Church as People of God (193ff); Christ as sign of God's grace (198ff); Salvation, outside the church (203ff); Sacrament/s, *Opus operatum* (206ff); Reviviscence, sacramental (215f); Causality, sacramental (216ff); Sacraments as instituted by Christ (223ff); Real Symbol (219ff); Marriage (227ff; 289ff); Holy Orders (230ff; 254; 277ff); Confirmation (233ff; 272ff; 272ff); Sacraments, number of (238f; 252ff); Anointing of the Sick (240ff; 294ff); Death (249f; 295f); Sacraments, development of (260ff); Eucharist (264ff); Baptism (269ff); Penance (275ff); Church as local altar community (267f; 293f); Baptism, character of (270ff); Priesthood, holiness of (280ff).

Precis: Introduction: a proper explication of the nature of the church as *Ur-sakrament* sets the stage for grasping more deeply the particular nature of each of the seven sacraments. **I. The Church as the Church of the Sacraments. 1. The church as fundamental sacrament.** Understanding church as "People of God" demands a look at the role of Christ: "the historically real and actual presence of the eschatologically victorious mercy of God" (196). Incarnation already signals in principle mankind's being accepted for salvation in Christ its head, who is irrevocably united with God. Incarnation decides the open fate of the world, and forms the People of God. The church is the continuance in the world of God's salvific will revealed in Christ, affecting God's utterance by itself uttering it in sign. The church's intrinsic sacramental structure comes from Christ its source. Hence, this church can never

become a meaningless symbol. It always brings about what it symbolizes. It is the primal, foundational sacrament (recap, 200).
2. **Explanation of the sacramental structure of the church and its actualization in the seven sacraments generally.** *a. Various levels of the church's activity.* The church is fundamentally a community of persons. It exists precisely in the act of fulfilling its function: bearing witness to Christ. *b. The actual fulfillment of the church's essence as the sign of an individual's sanctification.* Salvation is offered and promised to individuals by their entering into positive relations with the church. But the gap between church as "People of God" and as "the juridic constitution of the People of God" safeguards the fact that all salvation comes from Christ through His continuing presence in the church, without at the same time demanding one's explicit recognition of the church. All grace is only available sacramentally, but these sacramental moments of grace are not limited to the church's official sacraments. Rahner can now define a proper sacrament (204) and what he means by the church as fundamental sacrament (205-206).
3. **The nature of a sacrament in general, viewed in relation to the church as fundamental sacrament.** This view of the sacraments allows us to grasp the deeper meaning of five traditional church teachings. Each area raises special questions. *a. Opus operatum.* The old approach makes it difficult to discern why every grace-filled act (e.g., prayer) is not *ipso facto* a sacrament, and to distinguish Old Testament rituals from the church's sacraments. The section ends with a clear recap of what Rahner means by *opus operatum* (214-215). *b. The reviviscence of the sacraments. c. Sacramentum and res sacramenti. d. How sacraments cause grace.* All other attempts to explain sacramental causality (moral, physical, intentional, etc.) share a fundamental defect: some one factor, adequately distinct from another, must produce the latter. Viewing the individual sacraments as "intrinsically real symbols" which actually make present what they signify (i.e., the church as Christ's abiding presence) overcomes these difficulties. *e. The institution of the sacraments by Christ.* Rahner's basic move here is to ground the legitimacy of individual sacraments in the sacramentality of the church itself rather than in some instituting words of Christ recorded in scripture or purportedly passed on orally (224-230). He looks closely at four sacraments and to

unique issues raised by each: Matrimony (and the limits of the argument for oral transmission); Holy Orders (the relationship of ritual gesture to institution); Confirmation (the legitimacy of partitioning sacraments); Anointing of the Sick (distinguishing official sacraments from other grace-filled work of the church, e.g., prayer). Even allowing Rahner's thesis, one cannot thereby simply "deduce" the sacraments. Each has a unique, unfolding history that can only be understood *a posteriori*. The same is true of the church itself (summary, 254-256). *f. Sacramental and personal piety* can be reconciled in this view by developing the well-accepted distinction within the church itself between the church as a visible society and the church as a community of faith and grace.

II. The Various Sacraments as Acts in which the Church's Nature is Fulfilled. 1. General considerations. Rahner begins with a recap of his general theory of sacraments and a question: why is the actual history of the institution of the sacraments so seemingly haphazard? Here Rahner offers a brief, organized account of the genesis of the sacraments (260-263) as they arose from the efforts of the church coming to express itself, rather than from the evolution of specific rites. He ends by highlighting the ecclesial aspects of each of the seven sacraments, often developing issues specific to each.

2. Eucharist. Narrow concentration on individual communion with Christ at Mass deforms the faith that tells us Eucharist is always the sacrifice of the church. In an unparalleled way at Mass we participate in the Mystical Body, the church, for here everything that goes to form the church is found fully and manifestly present in the act of the particular community gathered around the altar (list, 267).

3. Baptism. Little needs to be said here, insofar as it is well understood today that baptism signifies and affects incorporation into the church and its faith. There follows a discussion of the indelible "character" of baptism, which Rahner sees as the church's express and enduring claim to the baptized person springing from the historical fact of baptism.

4. Confirmation, whereby the Holy Spirit imparts charismata for building up the church, clearly reveals its ecclesial nature. Rahner suggests a rationale for partitioning the sacraments of Baptism and Confirmation based on the double direction of grace: the dying with Christ to this world (Baptism) and the rising with Him manifested in our commitment to building up the Kingdom of God (Confirmation).

5. Penance. This sacrament with its binding and loosing is best understood in terms of the church's work to reconcile sinners with itself (sinners being those who have grievously failed as members of Christ to manifest God's salvific will in their lives). Reconciliation through the church is reconciliation with the church.

6. Holy Orders. Rahner returns to a point he left unsettled in his earlier discussion of Orders: how the sacramentality of the transmission of ministry in the church follows from the principle that the church is the fundamental sacrament (cf., Part I. 3e). Rahner answers that God who gives the command must also provide the means. Two further questions arise: why is the transfer of spiritual power a fundamental action for the church, radically involving her very nature; why does this sacrament necessarily extend to the sanctification of the bearer of this office (280-288)?

7. Matrimony. Rahner returns to answer a question left hanging in his earlier discussion: why marriage is a sacrament, and how this can be shown from the sources (cf., Part I .3e). Rahner focuses on Ephesians 5, and outlines a far-ranging argument for the sacramentality of marriage based on the deep content of the "symbolic" character of the two relationships: love of husband and wife, and love of Christ for the church. He ends by drawing a parallel: a married couple is to the parish as the altar community is to the church. The smaller unit contains the essentials of the church. Indeed it is the church in miniature.

8. The Anointing of the Sick. Eschatological expectation is an essential component of the church. The Sacrament of Anointing manifests this in a radical way when individuals are confronted with their own mortality. Rahner concludes (298f) by listing some related questions which he did not explore here, and with the observation that the ecclesial nature of all the sacraments thwarts any attempts to carve out a purely private realm of Christian life or holiness, since none of us lives for ourselves alone.

Inq.4. The Episcopate and the Primacy. (303-400). *"Episkopat und Primat"* in *Stimmen der Zeit,* 161 (1958) 321-36. Also *Questione*

Disptatae Series #4. Freiburg: Herder, n.d. Translated by Kenneth Barker, Patrick Kerans, Robert Ochs and Richard Strachan. Part I appeared in *Sendung und Gnade*; Innsbruck: Tyrolia Verlag; *Mission and Grace, Essays in Pastoral Theology, Vol. II.* London: Sheed and Ward, 1964. Translated by Cecily Hastings and Richard Strachan; and *Theology for Renewal. Bishops, Priests, Laity.* NY: Sheed & Ward, 1964.

Abstract: Believing that a deeper, more conscious knowledge of the church's nature contributes to the ever purer realization of that nature, Rahner undertakes this examination of the relationship between episcopacy and primacy, which moves from theoretical considerations to very practical applications.

Topics: BISHOP/s; PETRINE OFFICE.

Subsidiary discussions: Church as local altar community (312ff); Eucharist as summit of church actualization (318f); Spirit as guarantor of church unity (326ff); Apostolic succession (340ff); Council, supreme power of (349ff); Church, unity in diversity (370ff; 374ff); Ecumenism and episcopate (381f); Diocese (388ff).

Precis: I. The Episcopate and the Primacy. 1. The state of the question. The church can always benefit from deeper reflection on its nature. After outlining the textbook teaching on the nature of the church, Rahner asks whether the relation between its hierarchic-episcopal and monarchic-papal structures is as clear as it can be. Because the church is human as well as divine, Rahner feels justified tin comparing the church with other human institutions.

2. The constitution of the church. The church is a monarchy of a kind, different in that its monarch is elected not hereditary, and not simply "absolute," insofar as there exists a divinely instituted episcopate not even the pope can abolish, though he can limit the powers of individual bishops.

3. Primacy and episcopate compared with the relationship between universal church and local church. Some might argue that this divine right of the episcopacy is today vestigial, merely verbal, having no real meaning insofar as the episcopate has no way to exercise its authority apart from the pope. Rahner begins his response with a reflection on the relationship between the local and universal church itself (and by extension the relationship between individual apostles and the apostolic college). He notes that the church as a whole becomes "event" in the full sense and "tangible" only in the local church. The church is itself *in* the event of witnessing to Christ. This can happen concretely only in the local church, and does happen to its highest degree in Eucharist. From this Rahner concludes that episcopate exists by divine right and must have (no less than the pope) all the powers of jurisdiction and order required to fulfill its divine mandate of witnessing to Christ. This equality is not the result of an arbitrary command but springs from the nature of the church. Hence, it is a complete misunderstanding to think of bishops as mere tools, loudspeakers of the pope.

4. **The episcopate and charismata.** Bishops are at once independent and subordinate to the pope. "In his initiative, subject to the immediate guidance of the Spirit of God, the individual bishop must always assure himself of permanent unity and of the assent . . . of the universal Church and the pope" (324). But in all this the bishop retains his own charism and is not simply carrying out the directives of the pope (examples, 326). Needless to say, it is very difficult or impossible to formalize these relationships in a clear constitution. The only guarantor of a practical, balanced relationship between these two powers is the assistance of the Holy Spirit.

II. On the Divine Right of the Episcopate. 1. Preliminary remarks. The theology of the relationship between papal primacy and episcopate has yet [1958] to find its final form. It is immediately evident that the church's official statements (330f) on episcopate and primacy [prior to Vatican II] are not compatible in theory or in practice. Most attempts to harmonize them end up relegating bishops to the status of mere papal functionaries.

2. **Necessity and precise definition of the problem.** Although it is impossible to define completely the material limits of the rights of pope and bishop by listing inalienable particular episcopal rights, this does not mean it is impossible to define the more exact content of episcopal *jus divinum*.

3. **The *jus divinum* of the whole episcopate is the material and cognitive ground of the *jus divinum* of individual bishops.** Any more exact definition of episcopal powers must proceed from the nature of the universal church and (more decisively) from the

nature of the episcopate as a college – successor to the college of apostles. Here Rahner points out that the powers a pope may have, for example to suspend a particular bishop, do not simply by extension apply to the whole episcopate such that he could suspend the entire college. In fact, the pope must take care to protect the prerogatives of the college which it has *juris divini*. But how can these episcopal powers be more precisely defined?

4. **The theological nature of the college of apostles.** A proper understanding of the rights and duties of bishops and of the pope is grounded in their being members of the episcopal college which succeeds the apostolic college. "Jesus founds a college" (341). This explains their powers ontologically and juridically. The college pre-exists them. They do not constitute the college by surrendering prior individual prerogatives. Peter's primacy is primacy *within* the college. Rahner comes at the same reality from two other angles: that real unity is prior to its parts; that the college corporately represents the twelve tribes of the New Israel. This complicated relationship cannot be fully reduced to legal terms (345). The ultimate guarantor of this structure is supra-juridical: the Holy Spirit. The responsibility of the members of the college is essentially charismatic, active and non-transferable. It implies a moral and legal duty among the members both to teach and to listen to one another. "All primatial rights are rights of the head of the college as such" (348). Finally, the concern of each member extends to the whole church, not merely to one territory over which a particular bishop has been given special care.

5. **The college of bishops as successors of the apostolic college.** *a. Priority of the college of bishops over the individual bishops.* Rahner seeks to prove the priority of the college over the individual bishop by pointing to intractable dilemmas that otherwise arise in attempts to understand where a council derives it's supreme power. He concludes: ". . . the college of bishops, as such, exists as the supreme subject of governmental power in the universal church prior to the individual bishop as such. The individual bishop is primarily a member of the universal episcopate as the collegiate ruling body of the Church, which *jure divino* finds in the pope its permanent unity and the possibility of concrete activity" (352).

b. Possible objections. The main objection claims that from the start bishops governed territorially limited communities, making it hard to imagine them as originally conceived of as a college. Rahner sees this as an attack on the very notion of bishops as successors to the apostles. Though history itself argues against this, it does raise the interesting question of how membership in the college and territorially limited episcopal office are related. The "normal" bishop enjoys both, but membership in the college is not dependent on territorial jurisdiction, as there are auxiliary bishops and purely administrative bishops who nonetheless are called to participate in councils as full members of the college.

c. *The subject/s of infallible teaching authority.* Rahner argues in detail from the constitution of the church that there are *not* two inadequately distinct subjects of infallible magisterium in the church. Any such theory leads to illogical conclusions, or denies explicit church teaching on the divine right of the episcopacy or of the Petrine Office. After defining the one infallible magisterium as residing in the college of bishops united under the pope as its head, Rahner reframes the meaning of the pope acting "alone" (360ff), and the notion of "full power" (363ff).

d. *"Para-canonical" influences on the episcopate.* However valid Rahner's thesis may be, it does not make possible or even desirable a complete, written, systematic legislation to regulate the relationship of the pope within the college (nor does the absence of such legislation indicate the absence of the rights and duties of bishops). There are many legitimate ways for bishops to influence the pope, although they have only moral authority to do so, not legal right.

e. *Why a "college" to rule the church?* The wisdom and efficacy of Christ's decision to have the church ruled by a college can be appreciated from many angles. Rahner sees great strength in a church constituted by many qualitatively different members. It can thereby guard the unity of the church as a unity in diversity at all levels.

6. **Conclusions from the nature of episcopate.** a. *The "jus divinum" of the individual bishop.* The best way to understand the legitimate authority of a bishop is not in terms of presumption or subsidiarity, but charismatically insofar as the local bishop embodies and safeguards the divinely-willed pluralism of the church. Given this charismatic pluralism, individual bishops should not be faulted for making decisions that would not be appropriate to implement in the universal church. They should be allowed to exercise more autonomy over local affairs and have a greater voice in universal

governance. A more pluralistic episcopacy in theory and practice could also have significant positive ecumenical impact.

b. *Organization of "para-canonical" customs according to this divine right.* Rahner makes a case for the value of examining both the positive and negative "para-canonical" practices which have arisen in the church with the idea of keeping the good and reforming the rest. As examples he cites the absence of rules governing the relation between bishops and the curia, the rise of bishops' conferences, the role of Primatial Sees, rules for general councils, and the possibility of more frequent universal or local councils.

c. *Position of auxiliary bishops in the universal episcopate* could be clarified, distinguishing "real" auxiliaries who assist in governing territorial dioceses from bishops *honoris causa*.

d. *Some consequences for the structure of dioceses* include proper sizing, neither too small (as in Italy) nor too large. Such decisions should be based on the ability of the local church to realize its nature and to embody the whole universal church.

e. *The office of bishop as service of the universal church* should be emphasized and strengthened.

f. *Concerning the possibility of an election of the pope by the whole episcopate.*

7. **A distinction: legal and moral norms.** Every papal decision has two facets: legal and moral. It is possible for a decision to be legally valid but "morally illicit." Protests against such decisions by the episcopate are justifiable, even though there is no judicial recourse. The Holy Spirit is the final guarantor that the powers entrusted to the church will not be abused.

Inq.5. On Heresy (403-463). Translated by W.J. O'Hara. "Was ist Häresie?" in *Häresien der Zeit*, A. Böhm (ed.), Freiburg: Herder, n.d. *Questiones Disptatae.* Series #11. Translated by Karl-H. Kruger. **Cf., TI 05.19.**

Abstract: The unavoidable pluralism and ambiguity of today's social and intellectual situation insure the existence of a new kind of "cryptogamic" heresy which appears even within the church itself. .. diffuse, pervasive, ambiguous, and thus extremely hard to combat.

Topics: HERESY; TRUTH.

Subsidiary discussions: Apostasy (470; 484ff); Revelation (469ff); Truths, hierarchy of (474f; 490f); Anonymous Christian/ity (474f); Propositions (478ff; 506ff); Pluralism, gnosiological (493ff); Magisterium (505ff).

CL. *Is Christian Life Possible Today? Questions and Answers on the Fundamentals of Christian Life.* Denville, NJ: Dimension Books, 1984. Translated by Salvator Attanasio. 140 pp.
Mein Problem: Karl Rahner Antwortet Jungen Menschen. Freiburg: Herder, n.d.

Contents: Preface
1. Where is happiness for a human being?
2. Sometimes everything bothers me!
3. Does God know beforehand if I do or don't believe?
4. Grateful to God, with so much misery in the world?
5. My biggest bottleneck is prayer.
6. When everyday life becomes a torment.
7. I don't need a church in order to love God.
8. Anxiety before each and every decision.
9. The prison of internalized conformity.
10. Paralyzed by my dark moods.
11. Life is life straggling along a mountain precipice.
12. It's so difficult for me to go to church.
13. Beautiful resolutions, but then it comes to action.
14. Confess – yes, but why to a priest?
15. I never had any guilt feelings afterwards.
16. Two possibilities for giving a meaning to life.
17. Is trust in God enough?
18. Life is unbearable without illusions.
19. Bidding farewell over and over again.
20. I almost never think about God.
21. Called into life in order to come under death's control.
22. The dishonest Christian?
23. Can one always remain a child?
24. I can't be alone.

Preface. (4-6). These authentic letters from a parish youth group, slightly edited, cover many problems and give a valuable insight into the lives of young people today. The answers are necessarily limited and incomplete. Rahner learned something from struggling with these letters and hopes the reader will also.

CL.1. Where is happiness for a human being? (7-14)
Abstract: *Norbert, black sheep of his family, feels like a nobody. Happiness seems an illusion. Is it real? What is it?* Rahner is astonished by Norbert's honesty and shocked by his self-loathing. Why can't he simply admit he wants a different life with real standards? Why does he glory in his shame? Because he is demanding too much of happiness he is continually disappointed. Behind his exaggerated demand lies a secret unbelief. Because he really does not believe God is his fulfillment he frantically tries to maximize happiness here and now. His family he disparages for being content with bourgeois happiness and for trudging along each day, may actually be people of faith who await their fulfillment when life reaches its consummation. They may seem boring to him but only because unlike him they are not driven by illusions. Having admitted that he is tired of his current life why can't Norbert take the next step and admit that his stubborn pursuit of life is not heroic but the last ditch cowardice of one who cannot embrace the everydayness of life. Fulfilling one's duty is actually the courage to go beyond the idols of momentary happiness, and to move forward to that one happiness which alone deserves the name.
Topics: EVERYDAY LIFE, pursuit of happiness.

CL.2. Sometimes everything bothers me! (15-21)
Abstract: *Marie writes that she is unhappy with her lack of self-direction and expresses this by isolating herself in her black moods.* Rahner observes that spiritual writers call this behavior "disconsolation." They also set up rules to counteract it: replace irritability with patience, etc. He also recommends prayer, and waiting till such moods subside before making serious decisions. Although he knows it is easy to view his advice as outmoded, prayer is always possible and helpful. He also recommends thinking of others, doing small kindnesses, or exercising. One must resolve not to make those around us suffer from our moods. Persevering in the face of depression often brings success. Humor also helps. Depression need not lead to despair. Though one cannot do everything, still one can attain the joy of being a good person.

Topics: DESOLATION, spiritual; EVERYDAY LIFE, depression.

CL.3. Does God know beforehand if I do or don't believe? (22-28)
Abstract: *Christiane wonders about predestination and freedom.* Rahner is happy to know young people still think about such things. Because God is incomprehensible, we cannot expect a crystal clear answer. The true answer might involve accepting a number of propositions we cannot deny, even if we cannot fully reconcile them. Christians must profess that freedom and responsibility are givens, and also that an infinite, incomprehensible God knows the history of my freedom in His eternity. But His knowledge does not annul my freedom. Even if I cannot reconcile all this logically, I must live in such a way that I accept responsibility for my freedom, and also let God be God. It would be arrogance to reduce God to fit my system, as many thinkers often do. The point is not to understand God completely, but to love God fully.
Topics: FREEDOM; GOD, incomprehensibility of; PREDESTINATION.

CL.4. Grateful to God, with so much misery in the world? (29-34)
Abstract: *Alexander volunteers in an old age home in contact with many embittered and suffering elders.* Their question has become his own: "How can God let good people suffer?" Whenever we stand helplessly before the unfathomable dimensions of life we are standing before the cross. Alexander should remember that the bitterness and indifference of these seniors may be quite inculpable in God's eyes. But as to suffering, it can never be fully answered. It is part of the incomprehensible mystery of God Himself we must accept in hope. We are never satisfied by what we can grasp and always reach beyond. But when we do, we touch the incomprehensible God, and the question of whether we can love such a God. It is quite possible these old people once did and now no longer can reach out to God. But God has already embraced them in love long ago. Don't let their current bitterness unnerve you or destroy your optimism.
Topics: EVERYDAY LIFE, aging; GOD, incomprehensibility of; SUFFERING.

CL.5. My biggest bottleneck is prayer. (35-39)
Abstract: *John writes that he is lazy and inconsistent in prayer. He knows it is important and wants to know how to pray better.* Rahner congratulates John on the fact that he prays, and encourages him with a reminder that no matter how old we get we always remain novices in prayer. There are many methods of prayer but they all demand some collectedness and distance from the thousand daily cares. He suggests reading some of Ignatius' suggestions or trying the rosary. The quality of prayer is determined not by content but by recollected presence before God. Like skiing, one learns by doing. Persevere!
Topics: PRAYER.

CL.6. When everyday life becomes a torment. (40-44)
Abstract: *Robert's relationships with his family and his girlfriend are rocky, he feels he has no faith, and after the suicide of a friend he now fantasizes about suicide.* Rahner urges Robert to let go of his suicidal ideas. Suicide never solves problems, it only finalizes them. Drinking, too, is no help. If he has separated from his girlfriend, he should not just go blithely on, but should ask himself what he learned from this relation-ship. Only this can transform a mistake into a "blessed blunder." Robert should keep his ideals and fight his way to faith, which is no simple matter, not even for an old priest like Rahner himself.
Topics: FAITH; PERSEVERANCE.

CL.7. I don't need a church in order to love God. (45-51)
Abstract: *Gregory believes in God but has no time for the church and its rituals (Mass, rosary or confession). He scoffs at those he sees praying by rote at Mass. Still, sometimes he wishes he had staunch faith in the church.* Rahner responds affably that he cannot understand today's young people, "socialists" who yearn for structured community and service to neighbor, but cannot see these elements in the church. Like a family, the church only meets our needs once we have accommodated ourselves to it. Seeing God in nature is great, but isn't it possible that God wants to reveal more of Himself, and this can only be done in church? It is simply silly to say "authentic believers" do not need symbolic actions. As incarnate beings we must express ourselves in concrete symbols. Why should prayer

be any different than love? (It is also silly to overrate Jesus' saying about not praying on street corners when there are many other more important sayings.) Since human beings are meant for community, why should God not intend that believers should also have the community of the church? Try approaching the church with kindness and patience, rather than with judgment. Though faith in God and faith in the church are not precisely the same, the church is certainly a privileged instrument pointing to God. Be a bit more patient and self-critical. Do not think that your experiences with the church so far have exhausted all it has to give.
Topics: CHURCH, need for.

CL.8. Anxiety before each and every decision. (52-55)
Abstract: *Barbara, age 17, writes she is disgusted with herself— with her laziness, inconsistency, and susceptibility to peer pressure. She feels trapped by her failures. Rahner addresses her perfectionism, telling her the pressures she faces are normal. We all make mistakes and mustn't take them too seriously. Whatever trap she feels caught in, it is a trap with an open bottom, since we can always atone tomorrow for today's failures. The trick to Christianity is how to take responsibility for our acts* and *remain joyful and serene.*
Topics: EVERYDAY LIFE, perfectionism; EVERYDAY LIFE, serenity.

CL.9. The prison of internalized conformity. (56-59)
Abstract: *Marianne is inspired by the life of St. Francis of Assisi and falls into a dark mood because unlike him, she cannot simply trust in God and break out of the prison of internalized conformity.* Rahner answers that although St. Francis is a great saint and role model, each of us must be holy in our own way. Most likely she is not called to be a second St. Francis. There is no shame in that. But if she works slowly, step by step, she will find the way. We cannot simply construct our own path in life. "Carry on, cheerfully!"
Topics: FRANCIS of Assisi, St; HOLINESS, personal.

CL.10. Paralyzed by my dark moods. (60-66)
Abstract: *Harold struggles with his melancholic disposition in every aspect of his life. Even those close to him fail to understand who he really is.* After summarizing Harold's situation, Rahner admits there is

no easy way to undo one's fundamental disposition. But at this young age isn't there still a chance his melancholy will moderate? In any case, one cannot simply surrender to moodiness. Luckily, it seems that in his life, Harold has many positive elements to build on (intelligence, sensitivity, loving family, etc.), although Rahner warns him against the fantasy of finding a girlfriend "on whose lap I can lay my head and cry out loud." We must learn to stand on our own two feet. Rahner is confident Harold can make something beautiful of his life. He encourages him to build on his belief in God. "Take the statement seriously and fill it with life!" Maybe God does demand from him a serious and difficult life. So why not? When we honestly, courageously and hopefully accept ourselves, we are also accepting God.
Topics: EVERYDAY LIFE, melancholy; EVERYDAY LIFE, self-acceptance.

CL.11. Life is life straggling along a mountain precipice. (67-72)
Abstract: *Frank says he doesn't believe in God or the claims of Jesus. Having been sick once himself, he sees why the poor and weak are attracted to the church. But affluent people also suffer. Why does no one reach out to them?* Rahner recalls Frank is a scientist. As such, he will have to work hard to overcome his ingrained empirical prejudices when approaching the mystery of life. Suffering can as easily lead people to God or to atheism. In addition, it misrepresents the church to say it preys upon the weak and needy. But Frank is more insightful than he realizes when he says the rich also suffer. Anyone can experience the seeming meaninglessness of life. In both the rich and poor, this is an opening to God. To aid Frank in the hard work of finding faith Rahner recommends his own book, *Foundations*. He also encourages Frank to stay in contact with the community of the church to discover that it is more than lovely rituals and cheap solace.
Topics: CHURCH and the poor; FAITH and science.

CL.12. It's so difficult for me to go to church. (73-79)
Abstract: *Bernard was raised by a loving father who hopes he will become a good Christian. Bernard has faith, but hates attending the "dead" Sunday Mass. Can't a good Christian skip all that and communicate to God directly?* Rahner asks Bernard whether he has shopped

around for a Mass celebrated more meaningfully. Though Mass is routine, what gives him the right to impose his preferred Jazz Mass routine on others? Has he really worked hard to find meaning in the routine way Mass is celebrated? Isn't there some value to going through the motions even when one doesn't feel like it (as we do when we are courteous at home)? Of course one can (and should) pray in one's room. But we should also cultivate authentic community and community prayer. Inwardness and community are not opposites. One reinforces the other. Yes, one can escape routine by abstaining from participation. But that is a dangerous slippery slope.

Topics: EUCHARIST, routine celebration of; SUNDAY OBLIGATION.

CL.13. Beautiful resolutions, but then it comes to action. (80-89)
Abstract: *Matthew at age 21 fears he lacks the will, courage or strength to master himself. He is lazy and habitually fails to fulfill his resolutions. He lacks empathy for others and clings to the few friends he has out of desperation. He affects a cool attitude and only talks seriously if he is drunk. He is also a soft touch and cannot say no. His once active adolescent faith is gone, though he still believes in God and toys with the idea of becoming a priest. He is just drifting, waiting to hear something from God, but afraid to make any real choices for himself.* Rahner asks why the many good experience Matthew has had do not inspire a more optimistic view of his future life. Why does he cave in to every setback? Why not get up and try again? Make small, achievable resolutions and stick to them? Since drinking only makes all this worse why not quit? Matthew seems mercurial, setting too high goals and then falling into depression when he fails. Why not aim for the middle? Accept everyday life more soberly and modestly. One doesn't have to become a saint all at once. Small steps are enough. Rahner senses there is nothing serious lacking in Matthew, he just needs to get his act together. What he is going through may well be only a phase.

Topics: EVERYDAY LIFE.

CL.14. Confess – yes, but why to a priest? (90-97)
Abstract: *George cannot see the need for sacramental confession. Why isn't talking directly to God enough?* Rahner answers that certainly

there is no value in a mechanical confession without contrition. Although one is only obliged to confess mortal sins, not foolish pranks, one must be careful not to dismiss small faults too quickly, for it is often difficult to perceive their subjective meaning. George should trade in his childish assessment of this sacrament for a more adult understanding. The fact that we can turn to God directly for forgiveness does not render the sacrament meaningless. He is surprised to hear George's wholesale dismissal of the sacrament, especially given how people today try so hard to make sense of themselves through various kinds of psychological therapies. George should ask himself whether he has ever really made a heartfelt confession of sin aimed at repentance. Perhaps if he does, he will not be so smug about his own transgressions or as blasé about the value of the sacrament. He should remember, too, that all sins, no matter how seemingly private, have social consequences.

Topics: RECONCILIATION; SIN, social.

CL.15. I never had any guilt feelings afterwards. (98-102)

Abstract: *After describing his sexual history, the young theologian David asks about the church's position on premarital sex, whether it is finally changing to catch up with the times. Rahner's answer avoids discussing theology. David can read that anywhere. Instead he focuses on the gap between David's "honest confrontation" with his former girlfriends and his lack of guilt feelings. Has he honestly confronted his past acts, or has he dismissed them too easily? If these relationships were deep, why were they not also sincere? David should not confuse his own lack of guilt feelings with a radical change in the church. Rahner ends by encouraging David to examine moral theology earnestly along with his own life.*

Topics: MORALITY, pre-marital sex; RECONCILIATION.

CL.16. Two possibilities for giving a meaning to life. (103-105)

Abstract: *Charles, a budding philosopher, proposes two options for the meaning of life which he infers from his "system." One should either accomplish some world-altering feat or be satisfied to pass away with the knowledge that one has contributed to the objective meaning of some other dimension. Rahner congratulates Charles for his philosophical interest. But he would have him add to his system the fact that* human consciousness is different. It is able to view and respond freely to the "system" as a whole, and relate to the ground of that system: God. This completely recasts the question of meaning and Charles' proposed alternatives. Rahner encourages Charles to keep thinking. In the end he will come to the same realization Christianity offers.

Topics: GOD as ground of being; MEANING, question of.

CL.17. Is trust in God enough? (106-108)

Abstract: *Gabriel doubts her choice of vocation: religious education. Although she loves the idea of communicating the faith, she worries about the job becoming routine.* Rahner encourages her. Every job will have some elements of routine. That is inescapable. But her desire "to communicate God's love to us mortals" is the most important prerequisite for church work. With this she can overcome all other difficulties.

Topics: DISCERNMENT, vocational.

CL.18. Life is unbearable without illusions. (109-113)

Abstract: *Christine prefers a world of illusion to the world of renunciation and self-discipline the church enjoins on us (somewhat hypocritically).* Rahner remarks on her changed status as a new mother. He wonders whether now, looking into the eyes of her newborn, she does not see things differently. Now embracing hard responsibility is no longer a theoretical option, but a concrete decision flowing from love. Now real happiness can no longer be found in escape but only in meeting the concrete demands of love. For one who embraces the daily challenges of life, there is no fear of failure. Regarding the church, Rahner merely counsels her to approach it more as a community and less as an idea. For now she should settle into motherhood and be guided by the glimmer of light that radiates from her child's face.

Topics: CHURCH as community; EVERYDAY LIFE.

CL.19. Bidding farewell over and over again. (114-118)

Abstract: *Clement feels overwhelmed with the farewells of change, separation and death. What lessons should he be drawing from these?* Rahner observes that farewells differ depending on how close we were to the person from whom we separate. The real question is

whether our leave taking is culpable. If it is, can it be for-given or amended? Non-culpable farewells are part of life, growing up and becoming independent (e.g., marriage). Even scripture recognizes these. Rahner advises: "Learn to weep and take off, nevertheless!"
Topics: CHRISTIAN LIFE, maturity; EVERYDAY LIFE, endings.

CL.20. I almost never think about God. (119-121)

Abstract: *John writes that he can expend great effort launching his career, but when it comes to God he seems unable to muster any energy at all. Is this wrong?* Rahner tells Johan not to worry. Yes, we are told to love God with undivided hearts, but we are still on the way. At this stage in life, giving his career priority is not evil. But it is never enough just to honor God in the abstract. We must try to love Him. A great part of the Christian task is precisely to love God from within this great jumble of heavenly and earthly. We are inescapably creatures of earth and children of God. Be both, and trust that God can rectify the balance.
Topics: EVERYDAY LIFE; LOVE OF GOD.

CL.21. Called into life in order to come under death's control. (122-127)

Abstract: *Robert has decided to embrace atheism because to do otherwise would mean accepting an all-powerful God who is a sadist and misanthrope.* The existence of suffering is the only motive for atheism Rahner takes seriously. But does atheism really make suffering more bearable? Doesn't real compassion finally demand meaning and a blessed annulment of suffering? Is it possible Robert's conception of God might be a bit primitive. Might a really incomprehensible God be able to make even the suffering of the world somehow meaningful? Atheists must concede that in the end suffering has no meaning; it is ultimately inconsequential. It is only believers for whom suffering is at all problematic precisely because of their belief in a loving God. (Nor must Robert escape into thinking that God is not all-powerful.) Is it Christians who offer an opiate by hoping in God, or is it Marxists who ultimately must dismiss suffering as altogether meaningless? Finally Rahner asks Robert what he makes of our experiences of joy, meaning, and happiness. Or has he so absolutized his own bitterness that these realities mean nothing?

Topics: ATHEISM; GOD and suffering; SUFFERING and God.

CL.22. The dishonest Christian? (128-130)
Abstract: *Renata is disconcerted. She is able to do big public acts of charity like working with handicapped children, but falls woefully short in doing small acts of kindness at home.* Rahner answers that no one can immediately realize *ideal* love of neighbor. It takes persistent hard work to accept our duties anew each day.
Topics: LOVE OF NEIGHBOR.

CL.23. Can one always remain a child? (131-135)
Abstract: *Irene wonders about growing up. She is often chided by her friends for her childish sympathy and sentimentality. Must one let go of all this to become an adult?* Rahner sides with Irene against her friends. He warns that not everyone who "grows up" actually grows into a good adult. She should retain and develop her sense of compassion as a gift from God. It is better to be confused about one's true feelings than to deny them out of peer pressure. Adulthood and genuine childlikeness are not mutually exclusive.
Topics: CHRISTIAN MATURITY.

CL.24. I can't be alone. (136-140)
Abstract: *20 year-old Maria is studying to be a pastoral assistant. She lives alone and finds herself so inundated with friends visiting that she has little time for sleep or studies, and no time to pray as she would like. On the other hand, she can't stand when no one comes to visit!* Rahner sees this as a problem of freedom. Sometimes choices present us with a clear either/or. But the life Maria has chosen is mixed. She has chosen two goods, and while pursuing one she will often find herself longing for the other. What is required of her is self-discipline. There is no single recipe for everyone. She will have to experiment her own way forward.
Topics: EVERYDAY LIFE, mixed; FREEDOM.

Leading a Christian Life. Denville, NJ: Dimension Books, 1970. **Cf.,** *Meditations on the Sacraments*.**MS.** Six essays printed separately under their separate titles complied in MS with their original pagination.

LJLN. *The Love of Jesus and the Love of Neighbor*, NY: Crossroad, 1983. 104 pp.
Contents: What Does it Mean to Love Jesus?
Who are Your Brother and Sister?
Epilogue: The Mystery of Unselfish Communion.

LJLN.1. What does it mean to love Jesus? (9-46). *Was heisst Jesus Lieben?* Freiburg: Herder, 1982. Translated by Robert Barr.
Abstract: This essay argues that the simple Christian's unconditional love of Jesus, contextualized in terms of a "christology from below," encompasses and clarifies the classical Chalcedonian doctrine of the hypostatic union and *communicatio idiomatum*, and serves as a complement to descending christologies.
Topics: CHRISTOLOGY ascending; JESUS CHRIST, Hypostatic Union of; JESUS CHRIST, love for.
Subsidiary discussions: Love, human (16ff); Jesus Christ as Messiah (26ff); *Communicatio idiomatum* (30ff); Love, human (40f); Mystery, surrender to (41ff, 44ff); Anonymous Christian/ity (43f); Meaning, global (49ff); God as mystery (52f); Jesus Christ, humanity of (54ff).

Precis. Preface: Part I of this essay appeared in the Vienna monthly *Entschluss: Zeitschrift für Praxis und Theologie* 36 (1981): 3-18, 23-24. Part II appeared originally in *Geist und Leben* 53 (1980): 405-416, based on an address given to Austrian physicians. This explains the overlap and some difference in styles and subheadings.
Introduction. What does it mean to love Jesus? A book on this subject can be read on two levels: as information or as invitation. Rahner hopes readers will take the second approach and put his words in dialogue with their human experiences. Only in this way will they be able to make up for the inexactitude of the words he uses – an imprecision that attends every attempt to speak of ineffable mystery: God.

Part I. On Love for Jesus. 1. Some preliminary clarifications. *Mere human being? Abstract idea?* In our complex relationship with Jesus there are two misunderstanding to avoid: that Jesus is just a person ("Jesuanity"), or that he is just the concrete realization of an idea. *The risk of a relationship.* To avoid these misunderstandings we must meet certain theoretical and existential conditions. First, we only find ourselves in the act of unconditional abandonment to another. Though reasonable, responsible self-abandonment requires grounds, none of the relative antecedent grounds available to us justifies absolute commitment. We *must* venture more than the grounds seem to warrant. Just so, despite whatever we know, our loving relationship with Jesus is fundamentally a risk. *Bridge to someone far away.* Can we love someone far away without turning him/her into a mere idea? It is not merely enough to say that Jesus is risen, He lives today and we find Him with God. Nor is it enough to reconstruct Jesus in an act of hero worship. *Diversity as task.* So how do we make the relationship with Jesus (or even with saints) comprehensible today? We humans seek nearness, direct physical presence, to exchange our love fully and reciprocally. But what happens when two people love? Do they really become *one*? Actually they do remain diverse and distinct. Since this very difference is the precondition for love, we cannot say that distance simply makes love impossible. Hence, it is possible to love Jesus, acknowledging of course that He is risen and living with God who takes the initiative to love us and gives us the grace to respond. *The courage to throw your arms around him.* The distances between us and Jesus do not make it impossible for us to really love Him, "on the condition that we *want* to love him, and that we have the courage to throw our arms around him" (23). Two further observations: love of Jesus does not constrict our love for others. It is in fact a prerequisite and a spur to such love. This love for Jesus must grow and ripen as the result of patience, prayer, and immersion in scripture. It remains always a gift of the Spirit.

2. **Our relationship to Jesus.** *The modernizing of christology.* There are two ways to go about describing our relationship to Jesus: start with Him and what we know about Him and slowly move toward our relationship with Him; or start with us and our relationship with Him and move toward Jesus. Whichever path we take, the results will not be radically different. For "love and the beloved condition each other mutually, and the description of one implies a proposition about the other" (25). Rahner begins with the first approach, and presupposes everything that normal Catholic christology is able to say about Jesus (greatly abbreviated here). Such an investigation could begin either with Jesus' authentic self-

presentation in scripture or with the church's subsequent faith-understanding. *The Messiah: God become a human being.* After a number of disclaimers and presuppositions, Rahner states that Jesus understood Himself as Messiah: the one with and through whom the definitive Kingdom of God has come. He further argues that properly understood, the title Messiah says about Jesus all that traditional christology seeks to say with its talk of divine Sonship, incarnation, hypostatic union, etc. This suggestion has the apologetic advantage of bringing together Jesus' self-understanding in scripture with the christological faith of the magisterium. *A God who gives himself.* Implicit in Jesus' self-description as God's definitive unsurpassable Word is an identity with God which is impossible for merely finite creatures. Not only is God's self-disclosure unique in Jesus, unlike prophets before or since, He makes this claim about Himself. Thus, if what Jesus says about Himself is true, then His tangible human reality must be the very reality of God, without diminishing in any way that struggling humanity in which God is present.

Problems of a traditional christology. Traditional christology uses the term "hypostatic union" and the concept of *communicatio idiomatum* to describe the singular relationship between God and the reality of Jesus. For all its value, this communication of attributes has disadvantages. People often confuse the *unity* between human and divine as simple *identity*. *The dogmas of unity and distinction.* The problem with *communicatio idiomatum* centers on the word "is," which in common parlance indicates identity, but which here refers to a unity occurring nowhere else. This little word "is" both reveals and obscures. Despite the difficulties we have to grasp this unique unity and the sense in which Jesus is one "person," this unmixed unity of two natures in the one person of Christ is not a theological opinion. It is a dogma taught by the Council of Chalcedon. *Tolerance for modern christologies.* Here Rahner makes some observations apropos to theology itself [which lay readers could skip]. The notion of hypostatic union is not so plain and simple that the only question is whether one accepts or rejects it. Thus, new attempts are always needed to say more clearly what it means. But how? People may rightly reject the explanations offered by Küng, Schillebeeckx or Schoonenberg, but what can they offer in their place? To say that it is a mystery does not excuse us from thinking. Of course new explanations must be tested. But just because one or two highly placed theologians may find these explanations wanting is not *a priori* evidence that they are. In this intellectual environment much greater mutual tolerance is demanded in the church. *In Jesus, God has come absolutely close to me.* From all this complicated theology the average Christian could extract the following: if I am really convinced that in Jesus, God has personally bestowed Himself on me, then I have embraced and covered the whole of christology. This is the faith-consciousness the church must continually reflect on, develop, clarify and purify. This insight is what makes sense of the long history of christological reflection, and we have a right and duty to consider things using new approaches (list, 38). This section ends with a restatement of the simple, basic, unassuming christological faith implicit in the insight: in Jesus, God has come absolutely close to me (38).

What happens when we love Jesus? Rahner now looks from the other pole of this relationship: from us to Jesus. Keeping in mind that our love and even the power to love is only possible because God's initiative precedes, and that Jesus' love for us and ours for Him are co-conditioning, is this radical love beyond space and time possible? Rahner argues, yes, citing the very fact that it occurs (*ab esse ad posse*). *Unconditional and definitive.* What actually happens when we love Jesus is essentially what happens in every act of love. What is particular to this love is its lack of any inner sense of threat or reservation, in spite of the fact that from our perspective it always remains a striving, reaching out for unconditionality. Our love can make this claim because in Jesus it "knows the Ground of this unconditionality to be given in indissoluble conjunction with him: the God of faithfulness, his *own* unconditionality" (41). *A love of total surrender.* Such love demands certain prerequisites both in us and in Jesus. From the human being it requires the same prior, prevenient power of love required in the act of loving God. From Jesus, such love requires that He enjoys absolute and definitive union with God. Only the one who is so associated with God that God's own purity, clarity and boundlessness are His own, deserves our unconditional love. We know this about Jesus because it is signaled in the fact of His resurrection. *Jesus loved anonymously.* One could object that we human beings can express such unconditional love directly to God, i.e., that no relationship with Jesus or His hypostatic union is necessary. But upon what does the definitiveness of the human being's supposed unmediated union with God rest? Concrete, absolute, irreversible affirmation is found, at least "anonymously" only in Jesus who is "co-loved" in every unconditional act of self-surrender to the other (summary, 44). *Sinking into the incomprehensibility of God.* Unconditional love for Jesus culminates in the radical act of human existence: surrender to God as incomprehensible mystery. Those who love Jesus seek to share his destiny and so they surrender to Jesus' destiny of death, "illuminated by a final, secret light, humbly received as Jesus received it in his abandonment when he said, 'Father'" (45). Unconditional love for Jesus alone, along with our unconditional surrender to God (which alone constitutes the absoluteness of human existence), are at bottom one, due to what scholastic christology calls the hypostatic union of the eternal Word with the human reality of Jesus.

Part II. Jesus Christ as the meaning of life. Knowing whether and in what sense Jesus is the meaning of our life will further clarify what it means to love Him. In answering this question Rahner admits that he will necessarily package the orthodox Christian truth in his unique theology. His conclusions may disappoint insofar as they indicate the limits even of Christianity to answer this question, and they end in the invitation to surrender to the mystery of God. Finally any global, formal answer still leaves to the individual the task of discovering meaning in the particulars of our lives.

The search for meaning. By "meaning" Rahner intends the one, whole, universal, definitive meaning of human existence, realizable in the act of existence. Christians believe this meaning is both a gift from God and a task they must actualize. Two observations on global meaning: **1.** *Searching for a meaning with concrete consequences.* Global meaning cannot be a patchwork of partial meanings. Christians seek total meaning as the fruit of human history but outside the course of history, as everlasting life bestowed by God Himself. They seek a "transcendent" meaning whose validity has real and tangible consequences for life here and now. The object of this search is God and not an element of everyday experience. **2.** *Meaning become Mystery.* The God we seek remains the everlastingly mysterious One we approach only through surrender, and not though comprehension which reduces God to the scope of our ken. This leads to a curious crisis. The kind of meaning we long for is an illumination that would subsume everything within the capabilities of our perceptions. But what we get is mystery that encloses us in its grasp. It satisfies us only when we affirm and love this holy mystery for its own sake and not for ours: when we surrender.

The search for Jesus. We saw above that "God" alone is the meaning of human life. Yet Christians also say "Jesus Christ" is the ultimate answers to our search for meaning. The real question here is in what sense Jesus of Nazareth (*qua* incarnate Word, yet as a human being in human history) has constitutive significance as the total meaning of our lives. *Jesus' humanity and the total meaning of the human being.* Realizing that Jesus Christ in his humanity is not simply God, and yet that God alone is our ultimate goal and meaning, pointedly raises the question of what Jesus' humanity betokens for salvation. Scripture and Christian proclamation formulate this in many ways (54f). In the end there are two schools of thought on this matter: Neo-Chalcedonian, and Pure Calcedonian. Neo-Calcedonians tend to see the *communicatio idiomatum* as an identity of attributes, and they attribute salvation to the fact that in Jesus, God died and redeemed us. Pure Chalcedonians insist more firmly on the non-confusion of the two natures with the consequence that they see Jesus accomplishing salvation by undergoing human obedience, suffering and death, while the divine nature remains impassible. *From "Christ for us" to "Christ in Himself."* But Pure Chalcedonian theology also has its limits. It is unable to explain the function of Jesus' death after it asserts that God's impassible blessedness has been the formal cause of redemption. This excursus highlighting the inadequacies of the hypostatic union was not meant to deny it. It was merely offered to suggest there is a different and better starting place. We should not begin with the reality of Jesus *in Himself* and then proceed to the reality of salvation. We should begin with the saving significance *for us* of Jesus and His history, and from there begin our search for the meaning of the hypostatic union.

Jesus Christ, the meaning and salvation of human existence. Rahner briefly sets out his "christology from below" showing how

Jesus' unshakable two-way solidarity with God and man leads to death on the cross and definitive affirmation such that we experience Jesus as The Risen One (58). This gives the fate and person of Jesus a special meaning above and beyond their ordinary human character. The resurrection seals Jesus' self-interpretation: that through him the Kingdom of God has irrevocably come. To accept Jesus as God's definitive, irreversible self-bestowal on us is to confess Him as consubstantial with the Father – the content of the doctrine of the hypostatic union. How is this to be explained? Because nothing finite can transmit to us the unsurpassable self-communication of God. Yet Jesus does just this. Therefore, he must somehow share in God's own reality. "Only a finite reality that is assumed by God as his own reality can make God's commitment in the world irrevocable" (59), however difficult it may be to explain this oneness without their being one and the same (summary, 60).

Faith in Jesus Christ. Rahner claims to have shown how a "christology from below" can proceed quite readily to embrace the propositions of classical christology. It complements "high christology," and clarifies "how and why a seemingly innocuous relationship of unconditional trust in Jesus can be charged with the whole of classical christology" (60f). It also shows how such a relationship is altogether available to the ordinary Christian who is not a professional theologian. (Brief christological formula, 61).

LJLN.2. Who are Your Brother and Sister? (49-104). Translated by Robert Barr. *Wer ist dein Bruder?* Freiburg: Herder, 1981. November 10, 1980 address to the Catholic university community and Catholic academics of Graz for a diocesan day of recollection on *Brüderlichkeit*. Appeared originally in *Geist und Leben* 53 (1980): 405-416, based on an address to Austrian physicians.

Abstract: Taking seriously the intimate connection between love of God and love of neighbor (fraternal communion) in the new situation of today's world-church, would lead to far reaching changes in how we live out our personal Christian spirituality and our corporate witness in the world.

Topics: LOVE OF NEIGHBOR and love of God; LOVE OF NEIGHBOR as communion.

Subsidiary discussions: Love of God (69ff); Humanity, oneness of (76f); World-church (77ff; 85ff); Communication, interpersonal (79f); Petrine Office, as world conscience (87f); Church, missionary activity (88f); Politics, Christian participation in (89ff); Parish, as community (93ff); Evangelization (95ff); Theological Anthropology (100ff).

Precis: Introduction. This essay is about *fraternitas*, in German *Büderlichkeit*, and in English the Christian communion of brothers and sisters. The three-part essay goes from general theological observations to the new contemporary situation, and ends with practical conclusions for Christian living.

1. Preliminary considerations. *Love for God and human beings.* The relationship between love of God and love of neighbor is generally viewed too superficially, as if love of neighbor were merely one rule, a "test case" that proved one's love for God. *Love of God as the only thing and everything.* We must begin with a full appreciation for what love of God really is. Just as God is not simply one thing among others, so love of God is not just one more command among others. Loving God for His own sake is the totality of the free fulfillment of our human existence. It is the basis and goal of all individual commands. This love, this self-abandonment to God, is simultaneously self-evident and incomprehensible. Its ability to blast us out of the narrowness of our existence dawns upon us as a miracle, a grace only God can bestow. It is to be hoped for despite our sinfulness. *The reciprocal relationship between love of God and love of neighbor* is intimate: they are co-conditioning. Love of neighbor not only flows from love of God, it is also antecedent to it. There is no love of God that is not already love of neighbor, and vice versa. Only those who love God (albeit anonymously) can abandon themselves to other people for their own sakes. *The unity of disposition and act.* Catholic anthropology distinguishes act and disposition. The two are neither identical nor separate. Disposition is always and only actualized in definite acts. These in turn reflect disposition without thereby ever fully revealing it. With love of neighbor, this unbreakable unity invalidates any would-be choice between either an ethics of acts or an ethics of disposition. *The historical guise of love of neighbor.* Because love of neighbor is essentially historical it is constantly confronted with new situations to which it must respond. Hence, it is full of surprises. Despite what some traditionalists may think, simply opening and reading the Bible cannot tell us concretely today what love of neighbor demands.

2. **Addressing a new situation.** *A new situation for Christian communion.* "The Christian communion of brothers and sisters today has entered a new phase" (75), but the persistence of tradition and the slow pace of change often mask its dawning. The new world situation the church faces has two characteristics: a globalized humanity, and a new kind of human interiority. *A humanity gradually becoming one.* There is a centripetal force at work in humanity today driving individual cultural and historical spaces together into a single, common existential space for all human beings. This itself deserves greater theological reflection. *Christian communion in a new Word Church.* This changing situation demands the church become a real World-Church and live its communion in an altogether new way. After a brief history of the modern missionary effort (78f), Rahner maintains that in this new situation insistence on uniformity must give way to greater respect for pluralism, and paternalism must bow to greater respect for the equal rights of all members. *A world of intercommunication.* Today's new situation which presents greater opportunities for free communication among people also affects the church. Our subsequent greater knowledge of the world and our enhanced ability to express ourselves bring with them greater responsibility. The church has been slow to take advantage of this new situation. *Brotherly and sisterly encounter.* In today's new situation there is a greater potential for a fraternal exchange of personal spirituality, for discernment, and for consoling and encouraging one another through common prayer, etc. Of course this in no way abrogates or diminishes each individual's inalienable responsibility to actualize his/her own holiness. In this new situation we are, however, moving from a rather exclusively private, interior spirituality to a spirituality of greater communion.

3. **Consequences.** *Dangers of true communion.* Taking seriously the intimate link between love of God and "communion of brothers and sisters" would subvert much of what currently passes for respectable Christian spirituality and Christian living. It would raise radical and difficult questions for each individual. *The open-*

ness of communion. Genuine fraternal communion will challenge us to transcend a sectarian and self-aggrandizing mentality in our religious subjectivity. *Communion within the church.* Life in a world-church does not suit the current Western mentality of neo-individualistic subjectivism. Accepting the validity of points of view and practices quite different from our own may be painful but necessary. Why should everything in the church have to suit *me*? Reciprocal tolerance is a virtue greatly needed in a world-church. *A brotherly digression.* Regarding the papacy, Rahner suggests it could assume a new function today: a kind of world conscience for a single humanity without regard to dogmatic differences. *Christian mission of communion.* A further consequence of today's new situation is the greater involvement it demands in world mission, albeit in a new way which, while spreading the good new of salvation also addresses human social needs without the ulterior motives of conversion. *Social dimension of communion.* Properly addressing the new world situation would also involve greater political activism on the part of Christians. Despite its recent 200-year history, the church is not essentially conservative. In any case, it is not enough for today's Christians merely to conserve old social structures. Informed by the gospel they must also participate in civil society to bring about reform and to develop new ways for meeting new challenges. Unfortunately, Christians today still lack a developed "political theology" to help them fulfill their civil and political responsibilities. *Communion in the parish or local community.* Today's enhanced possibilities for greater shared subjective interiority manifest themselves in a greater longing among Christians for deeper forms of community. Their search for more authentic ways to live their Christian commitment changes fundamentally what people expect from their parishes to help them overcome the isolation and loneliness of modern life in the West. This longing will continue to transform the church. *A confessing communion.* The new situation makes possible and imposes a duty on Christians to overcome our excessive individualism and publicly to profess our faith with joy— uninhibitedly bearing witness to and sharing with others the inmost power and brilliance of our own lives. Why today is every public display of piety automatically suspected of indiscrete religious exhibitionism? What makes it so wrong today to offer to pray for others, or actually to pray with them?

Epilogue: The Mystery of Unselfish Communion. A reprise of the unfathomable mystery of fraternal communion which is identical with the totality of human existence. Love of neighbor is the compenetration of two mysteries in which Mystery *simpliciter* (i.e., God) is present to man and thereby ultimately renders all boundaries between the two lovers unrecognizable. There may be other anthropologies that hold up this same love as the pinnacle of human life. But for them it remains a rare human achievement. That view is elitist. The anthropology of Christian communion is different. With improbable optimism it sees this mystery of infinite love as possible for everyone. It can, must, and does occur. Salvation or damnation are nothing more or less than the fulfillment of this potential. A few considerations bolster this optimism: first, the fact that it need not be accomplished in explicitly reflexive terms; second, that in everyday life and in many different ways people do indeed glimpse infinity (list, 102f) and do take unfathomable risks for others, risks that, whether they know it or not, are occasioned, made possible, and encompassed by what we call God's grace (summary, 103f).

Marriage: Trusting and Loving. Denville, NJ: Dimension Books, n.d. 26 pp. *Glaubend und Liebend.* Translated by Dorothy White. **Cf.,** *Meditations on the Sacraments,* **MS.6.**

MM. *Mary, Mother of the Lord. Theological Meditations.* NY: Herder, 1963. 107 pp. *Maria, Mutter der Herrn,* Freiburg: Herder, 1962. Translated by W.J. O'Hara.

Contents: Preface.
A Short Outline of the Teaching of Faith about Mary.
Mary in Theology.
The Fundamental Idea of Mariology.
The Immaculate Conception.
Mary the Mother of God.-The Virgin Mary.
Mary without Sin.
Assumed into Heaven.
Mediatrix of Grace.
Mary (A Prayer).

Preface: This Part II of a university parish lecture series on Mary concentrates on doctrinal instruction.

MM.1. A Short Outline of the Teaching of Faith about Mary. (9-20)

Abstract: This essay sets the stage for what follows by securely tethering all the particulars of Mariology (Immaculate Conception, perpetual virginity, sinlessness, Assumption, mediatrix of graces) to the central mystery of God and God's love for the world manifested in Jesus Christ, the God-man.

Topics: BVM, doctrines.

Subsidiary discussions: Jesus Christ, hypostatic union of (11f); BVM in scripture (16f): BVM, hyperdulia (18f); Doctrine, development of Marian (18f).

Precis: I. All that can said about Mary flows from the meaning of this statement: Mary is the virgin mother of Jesus Christ. In unfolding this truth, Rahner takes a long running start. He begins with a systematic overview of God and God's relation with the world (9f) and moves on to God's self-gift to the world in time: Jesus Christ and the mystery of His hypostatic union— two nature in one person (11f). Finally we arrive at Mary, the virgin mother of Jesus Christ, the God-man. This relationship must not be viewed in a narrowly biological way. Her divine motherhood is the result of her faith, which is not merely her private history, but is the central event in salvation history. In Mary, her central role in salvation history and her own personal holiness coincide. As such she is the radical case of redeemed humanity. From this flows all the church's Marian teachings: her Immaculate Conception, her perpetual virginity, her sinlessness, her assumption into heaven, and her unique position as "mediatrix of all graces." (14f). **II.** All we know of Mary's earthly life comes from scripture, and its accounts are very spare. **III.** To honor Mary properly is to praise God's grace at work in her, and how this work has benefited the human family. We call such legitimate praise not adoration but hyperdulia. The history of venerating Mary unfolds over time as the implications of the church's faith develop and clarify. Personal growth in Marian devotion is a gage of how well our abstract belief in God has become a concrete reality.

MM.2. Mary in Theology. (21-31)

Abstract: Rahner justifies Mariology by rooting it in a "theology of man." Christians cannot think of God apart from "God with us" revealed in Christ. In addition, God wills that we achieve our salvation in a community in which Mary plays a decisive role. Hence, we cannot praise God without also praising her.

Topics: BVM in theology; MARIOLOGY, justification of.

Subsidiary discussions: Theological Anthropology, foundation for (23ff); Salvation as rooted in community (26ff).

Precis: Catholics deepen their reflection on Mary by returning to scripture which we interpret properly with the assistance of the magisterium. But what has faith to say about Mary? Yes, Mary is mentioned in scripture, but isn't she incidental? Shouldn't we be concentrating on God and on Jesus? (22f). To answer these objections we must first establish whether in addition to a theology of God there is not also a legitimate "theology of man." It is legitimate because God Himself, in the life of the Trinity has taken us into this eternal life and is the center, indeed the condition for the possibility of our personhood. In addition, God has willed directly to interact with us, and so became flesh in the person of his Word. "Consequently, no doctrine of God is possible any more without a doctrine of man, no theology without anthropology" (26). In glorifying man we are praising God. This is why Mariology is possible, and why her life is not merely a private story, "but an affirmation of faith itself concerning a reality of faith, without which there is no salvation" (26). There is a further consideration that stems from that fact that we are not merely atomic individuals but members of one community: physical, biological, cultural, social, and spiritual— a community of nature and of grace. The salvation of each is mediated through community. Because Mary is of decisive importance in the story of salvation, she is important to each one of us and must have a place in theology. *What does this signify for us?* (29ff). First, there is a "theology of man." In other words theology, even Mariology, is existential. Second, we all belong together. The love of God has called us from isolation into community. The fact that Mary is our common mother makes me concerned about the welfare of my neighbor.

MM.3. The Fundamental Idea of Mariology. (32-41)

Abstract: Rahner proposes this statement "Mary is the perfect Christian" as the touchstone for under-standing and honoring her. Mary does most perfectly what all Christians are called to do (i.e., accept God whole-heartedly and radiate God's love to all). The joys Mary enjoys now will one day be ours.

Topics: BVM as perfect Christian; MARIOLOGY, fundamental idea in.

Subsidiary discussions: Christianity, essential (35f); Jesus Christ, hypostatic union of (39).

Precis: Is there one fundamental principle from which the many Marian truths follow self-evidently, a basic statement to which we can always return to sum up all we believe about Mary and her importance to our own lives? After suggesting many (list, 32ff) Rahner proposes this one: "Mary is the perfect Christian." But what exactly is prefect Christianity? It is basically God Himself coming to man, and influencing us in such a way that we open our hearts to God. It is God's love for us and our love for God overflowing into love of neighbor. The perfect Christian receives the gift of God in grace-given freedom with all our hearts, and what occurs there in the depth of the soul is put unconditionally at the service of others. If this is so, then we must say that Mary is the perfect Christian, purely accepting salvation, accepting it body and soul into herself, and thereby assuming the central role in the salvation of all. As the perfect embodiment of Christianity she is the second Eve (37), not in a biological sense but through spiritual motherhood (summary, 28). Even allowing for her unique dignity, her redemption in the most perfect manner, Mary remains one of us. Whereas Jesus Christ is both human and divine, Mary remains completely human. What she now enjoys is ultimately also ours. What she is, we will become. She comes with us before God, and in so doing is our mediatrix. Mary's perfect Christianity should guide us in our future reflections and assist us in honoring her more sincerely and with greater faith.

MM.4. The Immaculate Conception. (42-52)

Abstract: Mary's Immaculate Conception sets her apart from us only insofar as she enjoyed God's sanctifying grace from the beginning.

It stands as a proof of the power of the Incarnation overflowing for mere humanity as love and fidelity, grace, divine life, and the eternal value of each individual existence.
Topics: BVM, Immaculate Conception of.
Subsidiary discussions: Grace, sanctifying (48f).

Precis: After outlining what the Immaculate Conception is not, Rahner summarizes the definition made by Pius IX in 1854 (43). But what does it mean? First, it points to the importance of the beginning of each spiritual being. Despite all human freedom, the beginning laid down by God also contains the end which we can only embrace or sinfully protest. Second, it means that God surrounds each life with redemptive love, despite the mystery that envelopes God's irrevocable summons. Such was the summons Mary received. And since it was true for her it is true for all, since all of us are implied in her summons to be the mother of Jesus. Third, The Immaculate Conception means that God surrounds the human family with loving fidelity. The beginning was made blessed in light of its end, and God will not renege. Our egoism keeps us from seeing much of ourselves in this glorious beginning. What does Mary's Immaculate Conception, her possession grace from the very beginning, signify to someone who has sanctifying grace– the gift of God's own self? In this we are the same as Mary. She differs only in having had this gift from the beginning and incomparably. But the grace she enjoys was intended for all. We differ in that her holiness from the beginning is didactic, pointing out how grace is a gift, neither a merit nor an accomplishment. Finally, the Immaculate Conception shows that God's call is a summons to what is most individual because it encompasses our human freedom to dispose of our lives as we will. Mary's Immaculate Conception is a kind of proof that the Incarnation of the Logos actually does overflow for mere humanity as love, and fidelity.

MM.5. Mary the Mother of God. (53-62)
Abstract: Honoring the divine motherhood of Mary, we focus not on the physical fact of generation but on her act of faith, her free and complete consent to God that opened the way to redemption.

This consent is the central moment in salvation history through which Mary becomes the mother of all the faithful.
Topics: BVM, Annunciation; BVM, motherhood of.
Subsidiary discussions: Freedom as dialogue with God (56ff).

Precis: The church has nothing to say about the life of Mary from her conception until the appearance of the Annunciation angel. Flowing from the church's reflection on the nature of Jesus, the God-man, in 431 the Council of Ephesus decreed that Mary, the mother of Jesus Christ, is the mother of God. In some ways this is a logical extension of the apostolic faith, "born of the virgin Mary," the shared faith of the whole church, Catholic and Protestant. Scripture rightly situates Mary's high dignity not in the physical fact of her motherhood, but in her obedient consent to God in faith– free, personal and grace-inspired. Through this faith her act emerges from the private sphere and she becomes a figure in sacred history, like Abraham, on whom our salvation likewise depends (summary 56).

The drama of human freedom is a dialogue between God and us. From God's side it was always open; from our side it was always ambiguous. But in the Word made flesh everything changes. God has spoken definitively and irrevocably, drawing the world into his eternal mercy, and bestowing on it a proper goal: Himself. Mary, through her *fiat* (the grace for which derives from God), is the portal of this eternal mercy. But the fact that this graced disposition was a gift from God in no way diminishes the fact that Mary's consent remained her free act. What God freely gives us is most truly ours (60). Unlike gifts from parents or friends, what comes to us from God constitutes our very individuality. Therefore, the divine motherhood of Mary is God's grace alone, *and* her own act, inseparably. It is not merely a physical fact, but an act of personal faith belonging to the history of redemption in which she plays an active role. Rightly understood, this makes Mary truly our mother, as she is the mother of salvation.

MM.6. The Virgin Mary. (63-72)
Abstract: Though Mary's perpetual virginity was a grace that radiated from her divine motherhood, it underscores for us that God's grace is freely-bestowed, not compelled by nature. Mary's com-

plete openness to grace is the exemplar for consecrated virginity in the church and a model for all believers.
Topics: BVM, virginity of; VIRGINITY, Christian.
Subsidiary discussions: Renunciation (71f).

Precis: It is part of the ancient faith that Jesus was born of a virgin. But how can we understand her virginity before, after, and also in His birth? Without going into detail, Rahner suggests that one born free of original sin and its attendant concupiscence might undergo the same physical events as others (childbirth, etc.) but experience them existentially in a different way. But a more central concern for Rahner is the significance of Mary's virginity, and why God chose the vehicle of virgin birth for the Incarnation. Certainly it was not to disparage marriage or the goodness of conjugal love. Rahner maintains that Mary's virginity must always be viewed in tandem with her divine motherhood. The grace of her virginity radiated from within, as a consequence of her vocation to divine motherhood. "Her will to virginity is in a true sense fully comprised in the readiness of the Blessed Virgin to submit absolutely and unreservedly always and everywhere to the decrees of God's holy will in whatever form; it was implicit in her freedom and her love as she said: Behold the handmaid of the Lord" (66f).

The question of the meaning of this virginity shifts, however, when viewed from this perspective: why did the Son of God will to become flesh without having an earthly father? For Rahner such a virgin birth makes plain in the clearest fashion that the Son came wholly by God's decree and not from any claims or intrinsic potentialities arising from the world. Mary's virginity and the origin of our Lord without a human father signify one and the same thing: God is the God of freely bestowed grace (69). As for Mary's perpetual virginity, Rahner maintains that because her whole existence was totally absorbed in her role as divine mother, she was ever a virgin, ever obediently receptive of grace.

Is this merely a special privilege radiating from Mary's divine motherhood? What if anything does this have to do with us? Besides serving as the exemplar of consecrated virginity, Mary's virginity contains a message for all Christians who should have "this attitude of expectation, of readiness and receptivity to grace from on high, this awareness that the ultimate thing is grace and grace alone.... For ultimately none of us work out our salvation by our own power" (70f). We are really only Christians when we approach God with this same virginal attitude of mind found in the Blessed Virgin Mary. This alone empowers us to renounce not only evil things, but whatever is not completely from God's grace.

MM.7. Mary without Sin. (73-82)

Abstract: The church's confidence in Mary's sinlessness comes from centuries of reflecting on her divine motherhood, and the slowly dawning realization that freedom from sin is compatible with a very ordinary life. This gives us courage to hope that God's grace is also transforming our ordinariness.

Topics: BVM, sinlessness of.

Subsidiary discussions: Church, holiness of (76f); Doctrine, development of (78ff).

Precis: In 1546, the Council of Trent expressly affirmed that Mary was always sinless. This might seem surprising when one recalls that scripture says that all people stand in need of God's mercy, and that whoever says he has not sinned makes God a liar (1Jn 1:8). In addition, how can Mary be the object of redemption if she never actually sinned? But the grace of redemption is not linked to sin but to mercy. Who can say that being preserved from all sin is not an even more splendid redemption than being redeemed from the sins we have committed? To affirm Mary's sinlessness the church does not need to carry out a canonization inquiry. It needs only to meditate deeply on what it means to be the mother of God, to know that in her, redemption was perfect and utterly triumphant. The possibility to make such a proclamation flows from the very nature of the holy church as the tangible presence of the victory of grace. In addition, the church knows that in praising Mary's sinlessness it is not ascribing to her an excellence she acquired by her own power, but the pure and dazzling mercy of God.

But early on, some Church Fathers saw in scripture hints that seemed to them to argue against Mary's sinlessness (list, 78f). They, however, were confusing a sinless life with an extraordinary life, a life somehow free of confusion, tedium, misunderstanding. It took many years of reflection to see that the pure grace of God enjoyed by Mary could be "hidden in the sober, unassuming, ordinary ways of a human being such as we know only too well, and suffer from" (80). Surely we must take sin seriously, aware that we may be deceiving ourselves, even misconstruing the evil we see in ourselves as holy. But at the same time, the example of Mary can also embolden us to hope that perhaps underneath what we see in ourselves as sinful, the goodness of God may actually be at work, bringing about in us and our poor, insignificant lives the same blessedness it accomplished in Mary.

MM.8. Assumed into Heaven. (83-92)

Abstract: Despite its long development, Rahner practically deduces the truth of Mary's Assumption from her being the perfect fruit of redemption. Since beatitude must include resurrection of the flesh, and since Christ's resurrection proves this is possible, for Mary to enjoy full beatitude she must have been assumed.

Topics: BVM, Assumption of.

Subsidiary discussions: Doctrine, development of (84f); Resurrection of the body (86ff).

Precis: The church confesses, among other things, Mary's consummation. Its knowledge does not derive from history but from her motherhood and the fact she is the most perfect fruit of redemption. This teaching, too, is the product of centuries of reflection guided by the Spirit. Knowing Mary's identity and her role in salvation history, it is no surprise that the church should attest "that Mary, with the whole reality of her life –with body and soul–, has entered into that perfect fulfillment which every Christian hopes for from the grace of God, as the one outcome and fruit of his own human life" (86).

In many ways this is consonant with our human nature: with the fact that we are a substantial unity of body and soul, whose perfection can only be realized in the presence of God as a spiritual/corporeal unity (86f). Of course it is impossible for us fully to imagine or describe this consummation without falling into contradiction. Yet we know by faith and the use of reason that we are called to enter with body and soul into God's life and glory. The resurrection of Christ's flesh, which shares in our humanity, proclaims that such eternal glory is already possible. Mary, the perfect achievement of redemption who has left this realm of time and space through death, has been gathered into God's eternity and attained perfect beatitude. And since the resurrection of Christ attests that this beatitude must and can include the body and soul, we must confess that Mary was assumed body and soul into heaven.

What is the importance of this mystery of faith for us? First, this highest praise of her is nothing less than the hope we all rightly harbor for ourselves: the resurrection of *our* flesh and life everlasting. In an existential age which is intensely concerned with the self and which often tends to denigrate the body, this doctrine proclaims the fact that this flesh is saved. It begins for us in Mary. The flesh, therefore, is neither a wall the separates us from God nor something to be eliminated, though it must be transformed.

MM.9. Mediatrix of Grace. (93-103)
Abstract: To us, Mary is the mediatrx of grace, though her "mediation" differs radically from that of Christ. Called to salvation as a community, we all mediate grace to one another. How much more the saints, above all Mary, due to her unsurpassable role in salvation history! Since even average Catholics can differentiate between Christ's mediation and Mary's, we do not fear cultivating veneration of Mary.
Topics: BVM, Mediatrix of grace. MEDIATION.
Subsidiary discussions: Communion of Saints (97ff).

Precis: Does anything remains to be said about Mary? Yes and no. So far in these essays we have spoken about Mary in herself. We have yet to speak about Mary as she really is for us. We can say simply that she is our mediatrix. Though this is not a defined doctrine, it flows naturally from belief in the communion of saints and our knowledge that they intercede for us. One might object that Jesus Christ is the one unique mediator (94f). Here we must allow that due to the limitation of human speech, we are using the same word to bear two similar but radically different notions of mediation. In reference to Mary's mediation we must recall that we are called to salvation as a people. By bearing one another's burdens we help one another achieve salvation. In this way we are all intermediaries of grace for each other. And how can what is true for us on earth be any less true of the saints in heaven? By calling these saints mediators, we are not saying they stand between us and God like sentinels barring our access to Christ the one mediator. Rather they stand beside us and intercede for us (reprise, 98f).

Hence, the only question can be how deeply and radically important is any one individual for another; in what way and to what degree is s/he a mediator of grace for his neighbor. Although there are differences of degree and kind, Mary's importance is equal to the unsurpassable role she played in salvation history. And her absolute unique "yes" of consent spoken once, remains her eternal "Amen," her eternal "Let it be done" to all that God wills, for the whole plan of salvation. In this area there is no fear of confusion. Even the average Catholic easily grasps the difference between the mediation of Christ and that of the Blessed Virgin, though one might not be able to express it in well-chosen theological concepts. Thus there is no need to be nervous, sparing or niggardly when we honor Mary. Love for her and veneration is a sign of a truly mature Catholic life.

MM.10. Mary (A Prayer). (104-107)
Abstract: This concluding prayer to Mary summarizes all that was said earlier. It is a prayer of praise and thanksgiving for Mary's *fiat*. It also implores her intercession, and serves as an act of consecration: a profession of our desire to be what we already really are.
Topics: BVM.

MFS. *Meditations on Freedom and the Spirit.* NY: Crossroad, 1978.
115 pp. Originally three separate essays: *Glaube als Mut; Freiheit und Manipulation in Gesellschaft und Kirche; Toleranz in der Kirche,*
Contents: 1. Faith as Courage.
2. Freedom and Manipulation in Society and the Church.
3. Toleration in the Church.

MFS.1. Faith as Courage. (7-29)
Glaube als Mut. Benziger, 1976. Translated by Rosaleen Ockenden.
Abstract: Christianity is fundamentally simple. It is the practical expression of radical courage. This courage is at root Christian faith, insofar as the dynamism to hope for God (however implicit) is a

gift of God, an impulse of the Spirit. Courage to hope finds its highest expression in the resurrection of Christ.

Topics: ANONYMOUS CHRISTIAN/ITY; COURAGE; FAITH as courage.

Subsidiary discussions: Word, *Urworte* (9ff; 12ff); Theological Virtues (12ff); God, revelation of (19ff); Christianity, essential (25ff); Jesus Christ, resurrection of (27).

Precis: Words as keys to existence. Words are of two kinds: simple denominators like "hydrogen," and inexhaustible words that hold the key to reality and human existence, like, "love" and "justice." These words that are concerned with the whole of man are no less legitimate than the more precise scientific words. Fleeing from such words is the same as fleeing from the mysterious core of our human existence.

Courage in hope. No such "key-word" (faith, hope and love are the theologically most well known) can be understood in isolation from the others. The proper meaning of one touches on the meanings of all others. At different times in history certain words have had greater resonance and popularity. Today the world "courage" engages our attention.

Radical total courage. For all the reasons mentioned above, courage is not easy to define. It comes into play when we confront the inevitable gap between what we know and can plan, and what we must face and address. This becomes especially acute and courage becomes "radical" when we face the question of our existence as a whole. For we not only *have* tasks, we *are* a task. This is the meaning of our freedom. The gulf can only be bridged by absolute hope "of an absolute future offered as real possibility, a future we call God and which we first really know only in hope" (18). But hoping in God, trusting in God's saving freedom, demands courage.

Courage as faith. Although such radical hope often appears in non-religious acts, often with no explicit reference to "God" (list, 20), this does not render religious acts superfluous. Rahner argues that this courageous hope is already revealed faith in the truly theological, albeit rudimentary sense. How is such implicit hope revealed faith? Because in radical hope our freedom does not merely reach out for one more thing, but for God Himself. This dynamism of the heart is itself a gift. "In making himself the dynamism and the goal of our hope in this grace, God is truly revealed to us" (22). "It is the work of the Holy Spirit, no matter whether it is put explicitly into words or not" (23). It is the basis of what Rahner calls anonymous Christianity.

Courage as Christian faith. Rahner next addresses the distinction between this faith and the faith required to accept Christian doctrine. As different as they seem they are related as seed to flower . . . religious faith being the explicit realization of radical faith. To see this, Rahner points to the heart of the Christian message. It tells us first that we can and must have the courage to hope, despite our sin and guilt. Here the anonymous courage for life and explicit faith are one. Second, it points to the cross and resurrection of Jesus Christ, where absolute hope is triumphant and attains it goal. Believers see realized in Jesus what they hope in courage to accomplish with their own lives. Hope for their own resurrection gives them the courage to believe in the resurrection of Jesus, and vice versa. All the rest of Christianity's dogmatic and moral claims are ultimately derived from the Risen Lord. When confused over particular religious claims or teachings, Christians should focus their attention on Him (summary, 28f).

MFS.2. Freedom and Manipulation in Society and the Church. (33-71). *Freiheit und Manipulation in Gesellschaft und Kirche,* Katolische Akademie, Bayern, 1976, and a paper on Freedom and Manipulation given at Paderborn. Translated by David Smith.

Abstract: The dynamic relation of freedom and coercion in society and the church, which as a product of concupiscence can always be sinful, stands in constant need of being reinterpreted to expand legitimate, true freedom. Though Christianity is rightly skeptical of utopian claims it is not essentially conservative.

Topics: CHURCH, freedom in; FREEDOM and constraint.

Subsidiary discussions: Concupiscence (44f); Skepticism, Christian (49ff; 66ff); Utopia (50); Revolution (53); Church, democracy in (63ff); Theology, pluralism in (65f).

Precis: Foreword (33-35). Though this is a sociological topic and Rahner admits he is no sociologist, it also has legitimate theological ramifications. (Preview) **The concept of freedom.** Rahner analyzes first the concept of freedom (36ff), then manipulation

(41ff), and finally the two together (45ff). *Freedom* itself, and the relation between religious and social freedom, are not simple concepts. Theological freedom is our orientation to God through the Spirit in Jesus Christ. It is freedom from the slavery of sin, death and selfishness which keeps us from loving God and neighbor as we should. Theological freedom is closely interconnected with the scope of social freedom for two reasons: it is only in the concrete, social realm where we realize religious freedom; these very acts of freedom are what become irreversibly definitive in eternity. As we expand our control over broadening the realm of social freedom, Christianity has an increasingly important role to play, insofar as the extent of social freedom greatly conditions the very possibility of religious freedom. *Manipulation.* [Rahner also calls this "violence" and seems to mean coercion, force or constraint.] Though human freedom is finite, this finitude is not manipulation, which occurs only when the free acts of others impinge on our freedom. Of themselves, such constraints are inescapable and are morally neutral. Coercion can become institutionalized in a number of ways (list, 43) which are often sinful, an ongoing effect of concupiscence. The situation in which we find ourselves as the result of both personal and social concupiscence is not innocuous and must be abolished. It cannot be overcome merely by appealing to theory. *Freedom and manipulation* form an inescapable and ever-changing unity within us. One is never absolutely free from manipulation nor completely manipulated with no possibility of freedom. Confronting and changing whatever is sinful in the dynamic of freedom and manipulation is the legitimate task of human freedom. The fact that this ever-changing dynamic can never be rendered completely clear to theoretical reasoning contributes greatly to its difficultly.

Freedom and manipulation in society. From what has been said above, Rahner concludes: the work of redressing the balance between freedom and constraint falls within the purview of human freedom, despite some of its attendant necessity. It is essentially an open history and not an inevitable or completely graspable process. Not even God's promise of the eschatological kingdom guarantees that freedom will be victorious in this world. Although this does not mean that improvement is impossible, Christians remain skeptical about the history of social freedom. This explains in part the anxious conservatism of the church during the recent age of revolutions. Knowing that God's definitive victory must pass through death, it is skeptical of all utopian claims. This does not mean Christians cannot or should not participate in the struggle here and now of freedom against sinful manipulation. In fact, Christian hope can embolden us in the struggle since our attachments to earth are provisional. Despite its recent track record, there is no necessary reason for the church to embrace a sterile form of conservatism while rejecting a revolutionary utopianism. This fight to optimize social freedom (properly understood, 54f) is increasingly becoming a Christian task in today's world. But are Christians up to the task?

Freedom and manipulation in the church. All that has been said about the interplay of freedom and coercion in society can be applied *mutatis mutandis* to the church, which is also a human society. For many reasons there exit both sinful and legitimate manipulation in the church and amidst the interpersonal communication of its members (list, 58). In the church, too, this sinful manipulation can be institutionalized, *juris humani*. Freedom (in both a transcendental religious sense and a social sense) also exists in the church in a constantly changing, dialectical relation to coercion. This ought not to be. The history of the church should be the history of ever-increasing freedom even in the social sphere. Today the secular history of freedom has become an inescapable element of the church's own history (61). As clear as this may seem, the church must humbly admit that often we are not self-critical, that we feel instinctively threatened by an increasing realm of freedom, and are more comfortable opting for more law and order, tradition and institution. Whatever the cause of this reactionary impulse, the church must become more self-critical and redefine the balance within itself between freedom and coercion.

Freedom and love. This final section attempts to illustrate what has been said so far. Insofar as one finds a close connection of theory and practice in how the church expresses its teachings, there will also be in the church a sphere of freedom and coercion. This connection is both positive and negative. But there must always be a legitimate realm of freedom in the church because faith cannot be coerced and because much of what the church teaches is itself provisional. Failure to promote this sphere of freedom will have a detrimental impact on the teaching authority of the church. Not only is there is a legitimate pluralism in theologies, but Rahner warns that church appeals to authority should always be secondary to clear and compelling theological explanations. Theory, however true, cannot simply be applied to practice. And freedom in the church should be presupposed rather than denied.

What practical conclusions can be drawn from these theoretical considerations? Authority in the church (*potestas jurisdictionis*) should be reinterpreted. "The feudalistic and paternalistic models of office and those invested with office must be broken down and give way to an understanding of office as a function" (67). Church officials should be made more accountable for their actions (69), and those appointed to office should be suitable candidates the Christian faithful feel they can trust. Rahner also calls for an extension of the checks and balances on authority already found in the church (list, 70). As positive steps in this direction he points to more autonomous national synods, and increasingly more independent conferences of priests and pastoral workers. Reinterpreting the balance of freedom and coercion in the church is a legitimate and important task for becoming the church of the future.

MFS.3. Toleration in the Church. (75-115)
Toleranz in der Kirche, 1977. Translated by Cecily Bennett.

Abstract: With many examples, Rahner shows the need for tolerance in addressing conflicts that arise in the church (dogmatic, doctrinal, pastoral) as the inevitable result of human pluralism. Tolerance, the virtue of Christian patience, is enjoined on all parties in a conflict, not only on the magisterium.

Topics: CHURCH, toleration in; THEOLOGY, dissent; TOLERATION in the church.

Subsidiary discussions: Concupiscence (83); Church, sinfulness of (83f); Conscience, dignity of (85f; 112f); Freedom and coercion (86f); Everyday Life, patience (96); Magisterium, mandate of (98f); Heresy (99); Obedience, religious (110ff); *Epikeia* (113); Schismatics (113f).

Precis: Foreword. Because "toleration" is a socio-political term (history, 75f) we must exercise caution in applying it within the church.

A second cause for caution is the fact that unlike civil society, the church is a community with a common ideology— shared convictions freely held. Hence, when competent authority judges that people have put themselves beyond the pale of orthodoxy, this cannot simply be labeled as intolerance. Despite these difficulties, it is legitimate to import this term into discussions on the church because over the centuries toleration has been one of the ways the church has actually overcome internal conflict. To show there has always been conflict in the church, Rahner reviews the past hundred years (list, 78f). Since such inescapable conflicts can seldom be resolved simply by recourse to theoretical principles, the church of the future will have to increase its capacity for toleration.

Conflicts. 1. What causes conflict in the church? The first reason is the unintegrated plurality of human consciousness in the world at large and therefore also in the church. This is the source of both human limitation and human dignity. Pluralism is a God-given dimension of the church and has the right to exist. In practice it cannot be subsumed by the application of any general principle. Hence, toleration means, "patiently and hopefully bearing with the unintegrated and unintegrateable historical contingency of a Church which is not yet the perfected Kingdom of reconciliation and unity" (83). In this way, the church is like a concupiscent individual. The second cause of conflict is the sinfulness of the church which effects all the members. A third cause is the disparity of cultural or social consciousness (generation gap) among the members. A final point is the irreducible strangeness that adheres to a church where people exhibit widely diverse and at times mutually incomprehensible charisms from the one same Spirit. **2.** What principles can be applied to meet all such conflicts in a Christian way? First is respect for the dignity of individual conscience, although no appeal to conscience can justify an individual laying claim to say or do anything s/he wants. The church can never deny anyone the freedom to leave the church. Decisions concerning orthodoxy are left to competent authority (summary, 88f). It is legitimate to work for change in the church. But when anyone attempts to use force to co-opt church teaching in a revolutionary way, the church retains the right to defend itself by force, expelling would-be manipulators. In the community of faith, such self-defense is not intolerance. This principle is obviously very general and the discussion leaves open its exact interpretation and application. A second general principle for overcoming conflict by means of toleration is that all those concerned must adhere to Christian virtues: love, unselfishness, humility, readiness to serve, respect (list, 91). Of course reason and logic should be employed to solve conflicts as far as possible. But often logic does not extend to the heart of the matter. Sadly, it is at such points that sinfulness on the part of those in authority often makes itself felt. Here the appeal to virtue comes in. This leads Rahner to describe tolerance as "the attitude required on both sides of the conflict, by which they endure to the end the impossibility of a fully adequate rational solution in the hope of that ultimate reconciliation which still awaits us" (93). **3.** Sensible and sanely applied modern techniques for dealing rationally with conflicts must increasingly find their way into the church. These include consultative bodies, dialogue, transparency, due process, right to appeal (list, 93f). **4.** Rahner refutes the faulty utopian vision of a conflict-free church which would supposedly render formal authority unnecessary. Conflict results from pluralism, and Christ himself willed both this pluralism *and* the authority to regulate it. Not even adopting more democratic processes will render decision making in the church totally easy or painless. Toleration is nothing more than Christian patience.

Doctrine and authority. The essay now focuses on the role of toleration in doctrinal conflicts within the church. It is an old discussion with many facets (list, 97f) regarding which Rahner offers a few partial comments. **1.** Rahner summarizes the church's formal self-understanding: that it has the duty to proclaim the faith authoritatively in morally binding (albeit reformable) propositions. Guided by the Spirit, recognized church authorities can speak and teach infallibly. Whoever freely and knowingly contradicts such dogmas puts him/herself outside the church, which has the right and duty to defend itself against such heresy. **2.** But not even in the sphere of purely dogmatic conflicts do these formal principles solve every problem. Rahner gives the example of theologians using different terms or approaching a topic from within differing world views (100f). Here there is a need for caution, patience, keeping the dialogue open, and toleration on both sides. He outlines in some detail the kind of toleration demanded of both church officials (101ff) and of theologians (103ff). **3.** The next set of difficulties arises when theologians counter doctrinal statements the magisterium "proposes" as authentic but does not define infallibly. (Rahner does not discuss here the many grades of teaching authority and requisite assent.) History clearly shows that in making such authoritative declarations the magisterium can err. So here, too, toleration is called for. Although theologians must receive such statements with respect and open minds, the critical discussion must go on. And conscious of its own fallibility, the church must enter these discussions and not merely impose *silentium obsequiosum*. In this fast-changing world, Rahner finds that what *Lumen Gentium* 25 says on this issue needs further refinement. Where it is not clear whether the conflict is over dogma or doctrine, the church would do well to exercise patience and wait for the matter to clarify itself (109). Rahner ends this section expressing the hope that the organs for dialogue in the church such as the Congregation for the Faith and the International Theological Commission would become more transparent, more diverse, and more tolerant.

Practice and toleration. The discussion now turns to non-doctrinal conflicts on pastoral matters such as canon law, liturgy, or personal clashes. To what has already been said, Rahner adds only one thing: the fact that these conflicts usually involve the ecclesial obedience a priest owes to his bishop. There are many cases where such obedience does not rise to the level of conscience (e.g., distributing communion in the hand) and where one can justly apply the principle of *epikeia*. But when such conflicts do become matters of conscience, then the church has the duty to respect the conscience of the subordinate and to be tolerant. The subordinate must refrain from acting in such a way as to denigrate or dispute the legitimacy of church authority. If such accommodation cannot be found, there may be a small number of cases where the subordinate would have to be disassociated from the community. Such a schismatic is separated *in corpore*, though not necessarily *in corde*. Rahner summarizes (114f) that conflict arises unavoidably from the nature of human freedom. In such a world everyone is enjoined to be tolerant and to seek to respect and preserve freedom in an attitude of peace and reconciliation. When toleration is no longer possible (and everything possible must be done to avoid coming to such an impasse) this too should be accepted in patience, leaving the final judgment to the Lord of History.

MHL. *Meditations on Hope and Love.* NY: Seabury, 1977. 85 pp. *Was sollen wir jetz tun?* 1974; *Gott ist Mensch geworden.* 1975. Translated by V. Green.
Contents: PART ONE:
The Last Days and the Lord's Coming.
Making Ready the Way.
What Shall we Do?
God is with us.
PART TWO:
The Power of Birth.
Obedient unto Death.
God Made Man.
Lighten our Darkness.
PART THREE:
Faith, Hope and Love.

PART ONE.
MHL.1. The Last Days and the Lord's Coming. (9-14)
Abstract: I. 1. Jesus' description of the end of the world is not a report of the future but points to the transience of all things by use of pictorial language. These images recall our own suppressed experience of disillusion with the world. We celebrate Advent by accepting these indications of the end, but with the hope that the absolute end will be the blessed resolution of all things. **2.** That end is identified with the coming of the "Son of Man," not some localized event, but the end of the process of the irreversible triumph of Christ as the fulfillment of history. **3.** Cf., MHL.3.

II. Advent as a whole is a wintry season. But secretly, below the surface, a deathless life is growing. We share this life now because we have faith in the advent of God's time which is victorious over fleeting time, filling us with modest joy and faithful hope.
Topics: SERMON: Luke 21:25-28; 34-36; ADVENT; JESUS CHRIST, second coming of.
Subsidiary discussions: Faith (13f).

MEDITATIONS ON HOPE AND LOVE

MHL.2. Making Ready the Way. (15-20)
Abstract: Like John the Baptist, we are "forerunners." We preceede without clearly knowing who or what we are serving. What we await and expect overtakes us without really catching up with us, in the sense of our having seen clearly what we were aiming at. This gives our Advent celebration its special spirit.
Topics: SERMON: Luke 3:1-6; ADVENT; JOHN the Baptist, St.

MHL.3. What Shall We Do? (21-26)
Abstract: Pressed for specifics about how to live their radical conversion, John the Baptist offers his listeners seemingly everyday moralistic platitudes. But it is precisely by faithfulness to these small duties, in season and out, that we help bring about the Kingdom of God. For in fulfilling these dull, tedious, everyday demands we fashion and test our absolute "Yes" to God. More than this, remaining faithful to our everyday virtuousness, even when it no longer pays, becomes a kind of "forerunning" of the God of salvation and freedom (24), an experience of God's saving wilderness. Advent calls for a surrender in hope to the hidden meaning and innermost power of this everyday life of ours.
Topics: SERMON: Luke 3:10-18; EVERYDAY LIFE; JOHN the Baptist, St.
Subsidiary discussions: God, experience of (24f).

MHL.4. God is with Us (27-32).
Abstract: "Emmanuel," God is with us, points beyond God's presence in finite realities to God Himself being within us: to "uncreated grace." We must overcome our inclination to think of ourselves finitely and to live moderately. We must instead accept and surrender to this absolute closeness. This closeness is what makes Christian morality radical. Surrender means salvation; rejection means sin and estrangement.
Topics: SERMON: Matthew 1:18-24; GRACE, uncreated.

PART TWO: These four interrelated essays approach the mystery of Christmas in four ways: from ascent christology; from the point of view of the end (death and resurrection); from descent christology; finally in terms of how we live the mystery of Christmas today.

MHL.5. The Power of Birth (35-51).
Abstract: Even in a christology "from below," Christmas is the coming of God's Word to us – the word through which God communicates His reconciliation in a unique and unsurpassable way.
Topics: CHRISTMAS, message of; CHRISTOLOGY, ascent.
Subsidiary discussions: Freedom (39f); Jesus Christ, self-consciousness of (42ff); Kingdom of God (44ff); Jesus Christ, more than a prophet (47ff).

Precis: Experience with Jesus: experience with ourselves. For most people today, the traditional way of describing the Christmas mystery in terms of a descent Christology (the preexistent Son came down from heaven . . .) is just too mythological to be compelling. Rahner suggests starting from the same perspective of Jesus' original hearers: that He was first and foremost a man. If it is true that "Jesus is the answer," He is no less also the question, just as we are all mysteries to ourselves.

Birth, the beginning of a history (summary, 38). The meaning of Jesus' birth can only be appraised in light of its totality, though here for the time being Rahner sets aside Jesus' unique end: His death and resurrection (cf., MHL.6). However valid the New Testament tendency may be to interpret Jesus' beginning in light of the resurrection, this approach tends to obscure certain things. So in this essay Rahner moves more slowly, asking: **What does Jesus' life say about his birth?** This methodology of Christology from below, attempting to inquire into Jesus' birth from the empirical aspect of His life, is very difficult.

The Word of God entered the world. Rahner offers a preliminary proposition: "in Jesus' life, person and proclamation seen as a whole, we find the ultimate, irreversible and of itself victorious word of forgiving and liberation self-communication of God to us in historical tangibility" (42). Christmas marks the event of His coming into the world.

Jesus' self-consciousness. Contrary to our Monophysite tendencies, Jesus did have a human self-consciousness at some distance from God. This self-consciousness had a history, and over time Jesus expressed the growing awareness of His unique relationship to His Father as the "immanent expectation" of the coming of God's

Kingdom. This may or may not be viewed as "error" on Jesus' part (44).

The core of Jesus' proclamation was the Kingdom of God in a special sense (defined, 44f), and not Himself. Anything Jesus says about Himself reveals His "self-oblivion for the sake of God and humanity. In this way "his function reveals his nature" (45). Jesus' awareness of this closeness to God and His eternally-valid call for decision on our part is unique, something which first appears in Him.

The newly-proclaimed nearness of the Kingdom of God. The pre-Easter Jesus' proclamation that the new nearness of the Kingdom will appear *through* Him is the connection to Christmas. Here Rahner discusses problems associated with identifying Jesus' preaching with the Kingdom's unique nearness.

Jesus' new unique relationship to God. What is new in Jesus' preaching is His proclamation of a radically new relationship with God which is only present through His preaching. The pre-Easter Jesus saw His unique relationship with God as an example for others, and proclaimed the Kingdom of God as it had not existed historically before, "and as it was there *through* and *in* him"(50).

God's definitive word to the world: this is the meaning of Christmas as revealed even in the pre-resurrection Jesus. Christmas marks the birth in the world of the unique, unsurpassable "Son" of the eternal God in His person and in His proclamation (summary, 51).

MHL.6. Obedient unto Death. (52-56)

Abstract: The cross and resurrection reveal the radical perspective of what was said above (MHL.5). They constitute God's seal on Jesus' self-understanding. Hence, Christmas becomes not only the beginning of the life of Jesus but also the start of His death – His total obedient surrender to God.

Topics: CHRISTMAS, message of; DEATH; JESUS CHRIST, death and resurrection of.

Precis: How does the word of God really enter into history without thereby simply canceling it out by fulfilling it? **God's word – man's answer.** For this to be the case, God's word directed to our freedom must be fully united with our response – an act both human and divine – without which we would never know if that offer had been accepted in an unsurpassable way. But given our nature, the only act that encompasses man as a whole and gives an ultimate and supremely valid response to God's offer is death. In turn, God's acceptance is signaled as resurrection. **Submission to God.** Rahner lays out in more detail here the relation between death and resurrection as our response to God's invitation, and as the sign of God's acceptance of that response. Furthermore, he links Jesus' resurrection with us, insofar as from the start Jesus identified Himself with a message of God's forgiving self-communication to *us*. **Life and death as destiny** (summary, 54f). Hence, we can look at Christmas as the onset of Jesus' death and resurrection, "the beginning of the fulfillment in which Jesus, unconditionally and without support from anything other than God, cast himself into the inconceivability of God as his own fulfillment, a fulfillment he himself did not ordain" (55). Christmas is the beginning of the man who was to die in this culminating act of faithful obedience – not one act at the end of life, but a life of surrender and dying in obedience to God.

MHL.7. God Made Man. (57-64)

Abstract: An analysis of traditional descent christology shows it compatible with the more existentially compelling ascent christology. Both proclaim the single message of Christmas: that the eternal Word of the Father has appeared in human flesh, has taken on our reality and history as His own; and has communicated Himself to us victoriously and irrevocably.

Topics: CHRISTMAS; CHRISTOLOGY, descent; JESUS CHRIST, Hypostatic Union of; TRINITY, ecconomic.

Precis: If all that was said above (MHL.5&6) is true, then we must confess that a unique and definitive union exists in Jesus between Jesus and God: a unity from the beginning. This is the traditional doctrine of descent christology enshrined in the formulas of Ephesus and Chalcedon (summary, 58). **Eternal Son of the Father.** Hence, Christian dogma states boldly that Jesus "is" God. This is not a plain identity of subject and predicate, but a mysterious, "unmixed" unity of divine and human reality. **God's "influence" on Jesus.** To avoid Monophysitism we think of "an active centre of freedom with a free finite personality of a kind appropriate to human being, set at an infinite distance from God, and [if we] use the term 'person' in a human sense, then of course Jesus has created human personality; in that sense he is a human 'person.'" (59). **God in Jesus.** Clearly, traditional formulas expressing our Christmas faith can be misinterpreted. It might be wise to update them. But they are also true when properly understood: "that God in himself has communicated himself to us as our absolute future, reconciliation and forgiveness, and that he had done so in the one whole reality and history of Jesus, from the beginning to the end of his own eternal definitiveness" (60). **The mystery of the Trinity.** Despite the tri-thesitic errors we can easily make in formulating the doctrine of the Trinity, there is a proper way to describe the three aspects of God's self-communication to us – God as the economic Trinity (62). To avoid the heresy of modalism, Rahner underscores that these are true modalities *in* God and not simply modes of human reception. **The Trinity of God's self-communication.** Rahner returns to the theme of the economic Trinity as the best way to understand the immanent Trinity (summary, 63). Understanding the Trinity in this way lends credence to descent christology. Nevertheless, descent christology is not the only or even the best or most complete way to describe the mystery of Christmas.

MHL.8. Lighten Our Darkness. (65-75)
Abstract: "Christian realists" celebrate Christmas as the start of a life that ends on the cross. Rather than mask "the miserable reality of life with pious words," this celebration of surrender to mystery accurately assess our life in the face of death and offers true hope. Celebrate this "Holy Night" with sober joy.
Topics: CHRISTMAS.
Subsidiary discussions: God as mystery (66ff); Anonymous Christian/ity (68f).

Precis: The world's celebration of Christmas is for the most part a sham. The true Christian sees on this day the birth of the one who dies on the cross, who faces death forthrightly, and sparks that improbable courage which alone resists despair. **The mystery.** Despite our intellectual protests, the common, everyday movement of life is to hope. Beneath our daily concerns lie the unfathomable depths of unutterable mystery. **Trusting in mystery.** To celebrate this thinking, hoping existence means opening and giving ourselves to God. When we allow ourselves to be encompassed by this intimate, forgiving "grace," then Christmas has already come. But as concrete historical beings, we require God's coming in a conceivable, tangible, irrevocable form. This we have in Jesus Christ, in whom question and answer become one, and culminate in His death. **Celebrating Christmas with sobriety and good cheer.** Both those who have the courage to believe expressly in the truth of Christmas and those who silently accept the unsurpassable depth of their own existence with hope can celebrate Christmas together: that God has indeed come, and that God celebrates with us. They can set aside the bourgeois hoopla that surrounds the season and move more honestly and profoundly into the truth of their lives. People like these celebrate the day soberly and joyfully. **Birth in the night.** The birth of Jesus is always associated with night in all its ambiguity – as a sinister time of danger and death, or as a watchful time of calm serenity and recollection. It is a time of promise under threat; "a forerunner with access to the most distant future, but one we are not certain will come" (72). Christmas is the "Holy Night" precisely because it is the absolute beginning whose victorious outcome is assured. In Christ, God is with us. **Celebrating Christmas.** In quite poetic fashion Rahner goes on to describe how Christmas should be celebrated by those who have faith: quietly, peacefully, recollected and gentle in heart. **God is close to us.** There is a beautiful and appropriate way to celebrate Christmas. But in means facing that lonely place inside each of us where no one but God can dwell, and listening there to the God who sings to the solitary soul.

PART THREE
MHL.9. Faith, Hope and Love. (79-85)
Abstract: Looking on the cross, faith sees inevitable suffering and asks us to search out the crosses we hide from; hope sees the Crucified and spurs us to hope beyond hope of any concrete thing; love affirms, yes, Jesus does love me in His absolute love, and I can love Him in sacrificing myself for my neighbor.
Topics: CROSS, meaning of.

Subsidiary discussions: Faith (79ff); Hope and despair (81ff); Jesus Christ, love for me (83f); Love of neighbor (84f).

Precis: Faith looks at the cross and sees inevitability. In life there are only the vanquished. Our life is a Way of the Cross into death; into life's loneliness and inconceivability. We are strongly tempted to veil the harsh reality the cross speaks to us. Hence, we must all ask ourselves: Where is the cross in my life that I don't want to see, that I would not willingly take up? **Hope** looks at the cross and sees the one who keeps us from dropping despairingly into empty meaninglessness. For Christian hope is never hope for any concrete thing, nor is it simple resignation. Christian hope begins when there is nothing left to hope. It has two aspects: letting oneself fall into the inconceivability of God, into unutterable blessedness *and* recognition of the victory of Jesus in His mortal defeat. **Love** looks at the cross and asks two questions: "Did He really love me?" and "Can I really love Him?" The answers, difficult as they are to explain, are "Yes." Jesus' love was absolute, and as such in death it penetrated the very depth of all reality (which we call God) – the point at which we are all united, the point at which He loved us. And "Yes," we love Jesus but only by loving our neighbor unreservedly. In risking our whole lives for love of neighbor, with no assurance of return, we are following the path of Jesus. We are united with Him in saying "Yes" to God.

MS. *Meditations on the Sacraments.* NY: Seabury, 1977. 105 pp. *Die sibenfältige Gabe.* Munich: Joseph Mueller *Ars Sacra Verlag,* 1974. Also appeared singly and partially collected in *Leading a Christian Life.* Denville, NJ: Dimension Books, 1970.

Contents: Preface.
Introduction.
1. Baptism: God Loves This Child.
2. A New Baptism in the Spirit: Confirmation Today.
3. The Eucharist: The Mystery of the One Christ.
4. Penance: Allow Yourself to be Forgiven.
5. Orders: Vessels of Clay.
6. Matrimony: Trusting and Loving.
7. Anointing of the Sick: Saving and Healing.
8. Final Vows: The Eternal Yes.

MS.Intro. Preface and Introduction by Karl Rahner (ix-xvii).
Translated by James Quigley

Abstract: Sacraments today are seen as "ecclesial manifestations and historical incarnations of that grace which is at work everywhere in the history of mankind and manifests itself historically, though in highly diversified ways, wherever men are striving to do good and thereby in some inexpressible way striving for God Himself in faith, hope and love" (xvi).

Topics: GRACE, sacramental; SACRAMENT/s.

Subsidiary discussions: Grace, experience of (xiii); Jesus Christ as *Ur-sakrament* (xiv f); Church as sacrament of world salvation (xv); Eucharist (xvi f).

Precis: Preface: These eight meditations on the sacraments (and religious profession), written over many years and in many styles, hope to provide a better understanding of sacraments. This is also the purpose of the non-systematic "Introduction," which attempts to lay a foundation for sacraments in general.

Introduction. *Preliminary thoughts about the sacraments in general.* A "Copernican Revolution" has taken place in the modern understanding of sacraments. Formerly, Christians saw themselves living in a profane world oriented to God but remaining empirically profane. We and the world were put into proper relationship with God by discrete quantities of a mysterious quality of divine grace coming to us from the outside through the sacraments. Thus, "A sacrament is thought to be a single act by which God reaches into space and time to confer grace under signs instituted by Christ. Without this grace we cannot be saved. But because this grace is supernatural, it cannot be the object of profane awareness" (x).

The new understanding of sacraments begins with two propositions: 1) grace is everywhere, as the inmost primordial divinely implanted entelechy of world and human history; 2) grace is not so much a "thing" as a comprehensive, radical opening up of one's total consciousness in the direction of God's immediacy, brought about by God's self-communication. We experience grace whenever we experience our human totality in freedom. Whether we accept or reject this experience of grace is of utmost importance.

Whether we do so in thematically religious terms is a very secondary consideration.

Though grace is everywhere, it also has a history of acceptance and rejection which points towards its goal. The personal acceptance of grace is a salvific act. And all such acts are mediated through taking a position toward worldly reality. Our yes or no to God is always mediated through our response to concrete reality. Yet these acts remain ambiguous and do not need to have an explicitly religious theme.

Two more points must be added to help understand sacraments. The first involves Christ as the primordial sacrament of salvation (definition, xv). The second involves the church as the basic sacrament of the salvation of mankind (definition, xv). When this church (as the basic sacrament) at decisive moments in the life of an individual or group, pledges itself with an absolute commitment of its being as the basic sacrament of salvation, and when it does so historically and palpably, and when we in turn accept this pledge of salvation and live it out *as* the manifestation of our interior graced dynamic, then we have what is meant by sacraments of the church (xvi). This will be illustrated in the essays that follow.

Two things about Eucharist call for emphasis. 1) What we see in the sacraments, therefore, is precisely "the inmost being of the history of mankind in the world, inasmuch as history's inmost entelechy [Christ], by being God Himself, makes history the history of God Himself" (xvi). 2) Sacramental signs are efficacious. The sign is the cause of what it signifies, just as conversely it is the effect of what is signified. A real understanding of Eucharist lets us see it as the manifestation of that mysterious grace which inconspicuously governs our whole life.

MS.1. Baptism: God Loves this Child. (1-15). *Gott liebt dieses Kind.* Translated by Dorothy White.
Abstract: Explains "what happens" in baptism, justifies the practice of infant baptism, offers short treatises on sanctifying grace and love of neighbor, and describes the role of each one present at baptism.
Topics: BAPTISM; BAPTISM, infant.
Subsidiary discussions: Grace, sanctifying (7ff); Man, mystery of (9f); Love of neighbor (10f).

Precis: The distinguishing characteristic of baptism is that here God is dealing with a human being, initiating a dialogue that invites him/her to salvation. God deals with adults as partners and with infants directly. But what happens in the baptism of a child? "What is always happening for our salvation is here more clearly revealed." But what God is doing under these outward signs is difficult to describe because it is the act of an unimaginable Supreme Being and because, despite original sin, through the mystery of Christ's Incarnation this child has already been loved by God from all eternity. We have confidence in the sacramental sign of baptism precisely because the glory of the divine Word enlightens all people and extends to them God's universally salvific will. But God's pre-existing love does not render the sacrament redundant because for us God's grace must appear concretely in time. Baptism marks that moment which now marks every future moment as its secret essence. When an adult is baptized we can see more clearly how faith is already at work in the believer even before s/he receives the sacrament.

But the question returns, "What happens in baptism?" (6). It is the act of the church by which a human being joins the visible company of the church of Jesus. Divine life signified in this membership is freely bestowed by God. Later the baptized person must decide what to do about it. Being born into the church is no more arbitrary than being born. In neither case is consent required or expected. But even if one later rejects church membership, s/he remains bound to the church and to the grace bestowed at baptism. Rahner now offers a brief treatise on sanctifying grace derived from one grasping him/herself as mystery called to infinite perfection (9ff). The gospel teaches the twofold truth: that our fulfillment is the boundless love of God; that this fulfillment is already here in our possession of the Spirit– saving grace. In baptism this child receives this grace. Here words fail and, "we must listen within ourselves to the silence of unutterable longing and let the mysterious truth speak from the depth of our hearts" (9). This is nothing less than the mystery of man calling out to the mystery of God.

Finally, Rahner turns his glance to those others celebrating the baptism. What part do they play? We want to continue loving this child but know that human love must navigate the twin dangers of suffocating closeness and deadly distance. Only by loving others in the love of God united in Christ can these dangers be overcome. The essay concludes by describing the role of each participant at the baptism: priest as agent of the church; godparents as witnesses to the action and future exemplar witnesses to the faith; the Christian faithful, who accept this child into the community, commit themselves to raising him/her in the faith, and who use this occasion to remember and renew their own baptismal promises.

MS.2. A New Baptism in the Spirit. Confirmation Today (16-28). Translated by Salvator Attanasio.

Abstract: This very scattered meditation reflects the current status of the sacrament. Rahner suggests the future of the sacrament may lie in the charismatic renewal's emphasis on Baptism in the Spirit (properly understood) or on a renewed appreciation for the lay vocation to the world in witness and mission.

Topics: BAPTISM in the Spirit; CONFIRMATION.

Subsidiary discussions: Sacrament, as instituted by Christ (21); Grace, experience of (23ff); Spirit, experience of (23ff).

Precis: Confirmation stirs up little enthusiasm among most Catholics. But two factors point to hope for its brighter future: charismatic renewal and its interest in "baptism in the Spirit" (16f), and a contemporary revival of the belief that each Christian has a special charism in the church for the world: a unique mission which is never completely profane.

Confirmation as the Sacrament of Witness. In this context Confirmation could have a new future as a sacrament of *mission* and *witness*, the fulfillment of the task of the church for the world. The current limbo in which Confirmation finds itself is due primarily to the difficulty in distinguishing it from baptism, which is also a communication of the Spirit to strengthen us in our individual tasks.

Confirmation. A communication of the Spirit. This section comprises a collection of somewhat disjointed academic reflections on the sacrament including such issues as: the church's irreversible decision that there are precisely seven sacraments (making baptism and confirmation forever distinct); the suggestion of seeing

Confirmation as primarily a sacrament increasing and strengthening the Spirit; a second look at the history of the sacrament; the sacramentality and irrepeatablity of Confirmation insofar as it confers a permanent "status" (character).

Confirmation today. We cannot start with the idea that sacraments are simply ritual events which affect and dispense something which otherwise does not exist in daily life. We must ask where we experience grace in our daily lives. The sacraments are precisely the churchly embodiments, the promise and fulfillment of this everyday grace. Wherever in my life the Spirit of God's grace is concretely at work, there is the true Baptism in the Spirit, however humble or mundane its manifestation.

The presence of the Spirit. Whenever the difficult but unavoidable experiences of life are welcomed with joy as challenges to our freedom and not as fearful specters against which we try to barricade ourselves (list, 25), there we truly find God and God's liberating grace, and experience the Holy Spirit. Though each person undergoes this experience differently, Christians know this experience in a special way (description, 26), and together they form a church. First in Baptism and later in Confirmation this church imparts its saving Word and invites us to choose life. Why should we not want to hear and receive this Word a second time in Confirmation, knowing that this Spirit is our inevitable fate? We should desire to accept and profess this Spirit in our effort to achieve our fullness. No matter the age at which we are confirmed, it only marks a beginning. Baptism in the Spirit, which must spread over a lifetime, need not appear in spectacular ways. Wherever we hold to our duty or struggle against despair, there is Baptism in the Spirit of Life which leads us to profess our faith.

MS.3. The Eucharist: The Mystery of the One Christ. (29-41). *Das Geheimnis unseres Christus.* Translated by Salvator Attanasio.
Abstract: Rooted in theological anthropology and the "mystery of man," this recap of Catholic doctrines surrounding our celebration of the Lord's Supper (one sacrifice, real presence) also serves as an apology for certain extra-sacramental devotional practices (Eucharistic reservation, adoration, processions).
Topics: EUCHARIST.

Subsidiary discussions: Jesus Christ, death of (29ff); Eucharistic, real presence (32ff); Eucharistic devotions (35ff); Man, mystery of (40f).

Precis: What happens when we celebrate the Eucharist? The Lord's Supper becomes present among us and for us. On the eve of His passion (the opening act of His single passion-death-resurrection) Jesus accepted His death, surrendered Himself totally to God, and gave Himself to His disciples in the event and the symbol of a meal. His acceptance of death and everything that goes with it is the redemption of the world, our salvation, the revelation that we are loved and accepted (summary, 31). All that is missing at this stage is the disciples' individual, full incorporation into Jesus' acceptance of death. Hence, through the power of His creative word Jesus becomes manifest and manifestly operative under the sign of a meal. In this way He truly belongs to the disciples and enters the center of their being.

The Lord's Supper becomes His presence among us and for us in the church's Eucharistic celebration, its *anamnesis*, its recalling what Christ did once and for all. This does not repeat the actual past event, but "what happened then enters into our place and our time, and acquires presence and redemptive power within our own being" (33f). Eucharist is not an event of the past. Jesus' definitive act of surrender to God gives it eternal validity by virtue of the pure essence of the decision itself. The actual presence of Jesus' act embraces our lives, confronts us, and demands a decision about the eternal validity of our own lives. It calls forth our faith and at the same time sustains it. This is why the church celebrates the Lord's Supper in a ritual and concrete way. Here Jesus is present to us in many ways: as promise, power, and friend (list, 34). All that is demanded of us is our "Amen," our response to His invitation which unites our lives and our sacrifices with His eternally valid sacrifice.

Rahner concludes by justifying certain Eucharistic devotions common among Catholics: reserving the sacred species (35ff); private adoration of the Blessed Sacrament (36f); Eucharistic processions on *Corpus Christi* or during Eucharist Congresses (37f). All these extra-sacramental practices underscore in concrete ways our belief that Jesus accompanies us through daily life, confronts and challenges, comforts and sustains us. It would be a shame for Catholics to remain childish in their faith, and not to grow in their knowledge, appreciation and union with Jesus through the mystery of the Eucharist. The more fully and honestly we plumb the mystery of our own human lives, the closer we come to understanding the meaning of the mystery of the Eucharist (40f).

MS.4. Allow Yourself to be Forgiven: Penance Today. (42-59). *Man Darf Sich Vergeben Lassen:* Munich: Joseph Muller, *Verlag Ars Sacra*, 1974. Translated by Salvator Attanasio.

Abstract: The forgiveness offered in sacramental reconciliation, far from being something extrinsic, is rooted in theological anthropology, and answers the deepest longing of the human person.

Topics: FREEDOM and guilt; GUILT; PENANCE.

Subsidiary discussions: Salvation/damnation status (43ff); *Metanoia* (49f); Sin, mortal/venial (53ff); Conscience (54); Church as agent of forgiveness (55f); Baptism (53f); Sin, social aspect of (56ff); Contrition, im/perfect (57f).

Precis: The essay has six parts. **1. The obscure mystery of guilt.** In striving for our irrevocable finality we are capable of a final, free "No" to God, which is at the same time a rupture of our relationship with ourselves and with the things of this world.

2. What is guilt before God? Mysteriously, this "No" to God comes about through the use of our freedom in search of the good. We must admit that our freedom is more than the neutral faculty endlessly to choose among things. It is the capacity to posit ourselves as whole persons. Hence, our "No" to God is never merely the sum of mistakes or infractions of particular rules, however legitimate.

3. The totality of factors in guilt before God. The mysterious nature of this guilt means, furthermore, that no one can ever know absolutely the exact status of his/her guilt before God, nor that of anyone else. And even though judging others is a legitimate part of dispensing justice in this world, how often we minimize our own guilt and yet condemn others! The very obscurity of our guilt before God keeps guilt itself from ever becoming simply innocuous.

4. The hopelessness of guilt. The mystery of our "No" to God contributes to the hopelessness of ever affecting forgiveness ourselves.

Since our relationship with God is dialogical we cannot restore it simply with our own efforts.
5. **The word of forgiveness** becomes possible only when, neither minimizing nor exaggerating the "eternalness" of our free acts, we trust in the "eternalness" of the miracle of God's love. This alone can cancel guilt. We hear this word of forgiveness in conscience, the pre-existing ground of conversion. This internal word has become manifest in space and time in Jesus Christ, who in the throws of His own death accepted both the darkness of our guilt and the word of God's forgiveness. This word of forgiveness remains efficaciously present in the church in its creed, its prayer and its sacraments (especially Baptism and Penance). In reconciling penitents with itself, the church is reconciling them to the forgiving word of God as an extension of the effect of Baptism.
6. **The teaching of the church.** For forgiveness to be effective it is necessary to recognize and realize two things as best one can: 1) that all sin is social to some degree. Liturgical rites alone never dispense us from the prerequisite need for true conversion or from working to restore love and justice. 2) Penance is never simply a matter of "confessing sins." Rather it is the act of surrendering oneself as completely as possible to God's merciful judgment. Summary: in the end, there are only two possibilities: to remain imprisoned by the hopelessness of our guilt, or to find the courage to be forgiven by the incomprehensible mystery of God. "Christianity is this message: we should allow ourselves to be forgiven. And the Church offers us the means: the Sacrament of Penance" (59).

MS.5. Orders: Vessels of Clay. (60-68). *Die Gnade wird es vollenden.* Translated by James Quigley, SJ

Abstract: Speaking at a priest's First Mass, Rahner rehearse the essentials of Catholic priesthood: that a fellow human is entrusted to preach and administer the sacraments as efficacious signs of hope to all.

Topics: PRIESTHOOD.

Subsidiary discussions: Preaching (63f); Sacrament/s, administration of (64ff).

Precis: At a First Mass we do not so much celebrate the newly-ordained as we do the priesthood and the church as the body of

Christ, which glimpses in this man the holy dignity of all. **What is a priest?** *He is a man:* God sends men to men, to others who are weak, sinful and struggling, as if to encourage all not to be offended, but to see in this one man the promise of grace God extends to all. *A messenger of God's truth:* God's truth longs to be proclaimed to all, to take root and produce much fruit. Priests are entrusted with God's word – simple, monotonous, but divine and eternal. The priest stutters the word and is amazed to find hearers who welcome it. *A dispenser of divine mysteries:* The Word entrusted to priests is God's efficacious, sacramental word which actually incorporates, reconciles and heals. People in the world prefer something else. But those who accept it find time in eternity, life in death, light in darkness, and the true presence of God. *Entrusted with the sacrifice:* Because Eucharist is at the heart of the body of the church we rightfully celebrate the First Mass of a priest where everything is brought together: "men, the Church, God, Christ, the sacrifice of the Cross, the living and the dead, the poverty of earth the blessings of heaven" (66). Here, authorized by Christ himself, the priest celebrates the sacrifice of eternal reconciliation in the name of all, with all, and for all – a daily action that will shape the priest's own future life of sacrifice. Everyone has a divine calling. The priest's, with its intimate union with God, is especially happy and terrifying. Hence, we are filled with a fear which is only relieved by our knowledge that only grace can and will bring this vocation to perfection.

MS.6. Matrimony: Trusting and Loving. (69-78). *Glaubend und Liebend.* Translated by Dorothy White.
Abstract: The adventure of human marriage is part of the mystery of God insofar as it is a moment of free, total self-disposal in the unique miracle of love. God is the silent companion in every true marriage not only as assistance, but as "divine life, eternal power, a share in the divine nature, a pledge of future blessedness, a seal and an anointing, the beginning and foundation of a life grafted on God's own life as worth living forever" (71). In short, grace, God Himself. This is why marriage is a sacrament. Wherever marriage is present, God is present. Hence, marriage is fruitful, producing the courage and wisdom to love truly, and the miracle of children, a new eternity in God's sight. Since every marriage is

unique, what advice can we give to this new couple other than to repeat the words of scripture concerning this great mystery (list, 75ff)? It is most fitting to celebrate this sacrament in the context of the Eucharist since all grace comes from the pierced heart of the Redeemer. The grace of marriage also bears the mark of this origin: the grace of self-sacrificing, faithful, fruitful and forgiving love.

Topics: SERMON: Ephesians 5:32; MATRIMONY.

Subsidiary discussions: God as grace of married love (70ff); Marriage, children as fruit of (73f).

MS.7. The Anointing of the Sick: Healing and Saving. (79-93).
Bergend und Heilend. Translated by Dorothy White.

Abstract: This essay beautifully describes the sacramentality of the Catholic practice of anointing from an existential perspective. In so doing it provides an apology for including it among the seven sacraments.

Topics: ANOINTING, Sacrament of; DEATH; EVERYDAY LIFE, sickness.

Subsidiary discussions: Prayer, efficacy of (83ff); Grace, presence of (90ff).

Precis: Serious illness as a messenger and portent of death forces a choice: to hide from the full reality of human life or to accept the full pain of dissolution. "Illness brings us face to face with ourselves, and is therefore a part of the history of our salvation" (80). Sadly, illness confronts us with this most difficult decision at precisely our weakest moment. Only the grace of God can help us pass this trial. At such moments we feel so alone, but we are not so. God is with us, along with the whole community of believers united in the church by the death of Christ.

Rahner now turns to the famous passages (Js 5:14f) to see how the early church responded to this existential human crisis (83f). There we see how in time of grave illness the official representatives of the church (elders) were summoned to pray and anoint. This leads to a short excursus on the efficacy of prayer (84f) and the custom of anointing (85ff), and a recap of official church teaching (86f).

Rahner concludes with a summary showing the divine wisdom of this seventh sacrament. By its very nature, grace must be particularly evident whenever, "in the most critical events of human and Christian life, a person is brought starkly face to face with himself, and the dread but blessed mystery of his existence forces him to come to a decision" (88). Illness is a consummate moment of such *kairos*. So it is only reasonable that God should be especially present in sacramental form at this juncture, uniting the suffering member with the entire believing community, and thus with Himself.

MS.8. Final Vows. The Eternal Yes. (94-105). *Ewiges Ja.* Translated by SalvatorAttanasio.

Abstract: What is the meaning of final vows? A human being is giving his life a definite form and direction, once and forever. We have gathered to praise the fact that there are still such men willing to do this. But we fear it may not even be possible today, and so we humbly pray that God will help these men with His grace. The heart of this act and of every Christian act is the mystery of God (95ff). But doesn't the structured, institutional life of monasticism threaten to kill this essentially charismatic, eschatological call to leave all and to follow Christ single-heartedly? This danger does exist, and so we pray.

After describing the three monastic vows (*stabilitas, converatio morum, obediencia*, 99ff), Rahner celebrates the fact that monastic profession is an act of the church. It is nothing less than an event of the church's own actualization, since the church becomes itself when her members publicly proclaim the victory of the Lord. Hence, the church prays that God will bring to completion what begins today.

Topics: RELIGIOUS LIFE, final vows.
Subsidiary discussions: Vows, monastic (99ff); Church, event of (103f).

Mission and Grace: Essays in Pastoral Theology, Vol. I. London: Sheed and Ward, 1964. *Sendung und Gnade.* Munich, Tyrolia Verlag, 1961. Translated by Cecily Hastings and Richard Strachan. **Cf.,** *The Christian Commitment: Essays in Pastoral Theology.* **CCt.**

Mission and Grace: Essays in Pastoral Theology, Vol. II. London: Sheed and Ward, 1964. *Sendung und Gnade*. Munich, Tyrolia Verlag, 1961. Translated by Cecily Hastings and Richard Strachan. Cf., *Theology for Renewal. Bishops, Priests, Laity.* **TR.**

Mission and Grace, Essays in Pastoral Theology, Vol. III. London: Sheed and Ward, 1966. *Sendung und Gnade*. Innsbruck: Tyrolia Verlag, 1959. Translated by Cecily Hastings. Cf., *Christian in the Market Place.* **CMP.**

NG. *Nature and Grace: Dilemmas in the Modern Church*, NY: Sheed and Ward, 1964. Notes. 149 pp. Chapters 1, 2, 3, 5 were originally published as "*Natur und Gnade*" in *Fragen der Theologie heute.* Einsiedeln: Benziger, and in *Grefahren im heutigen Katholizismus*, Einsiedeln: Johannes-Verlag. These same chapters were first published in English as "Nature and Grace." London: Sheed and Ward, 1963. Translated by Dinah Wharton.

Contents: I. Dangers in Catholicism Today.
1. The Individual in the Church.
2. The Appeal to Conscience.
3. A New Form of Heresy.

II. Faith Seeks Understanding.
4. The Sacramental Basis of the Layman's Position in the Church. **Cf., TI 08.04.**
5. Nature and Grace. **Cf., TI 04.07.**

PART I. Dangers in Catholicism Today

Introduction to Part I (5-8). Though the church is guaranteed to withstand all dangers, individuals within the church enjoy no such assurance. The greatest dangers arise when the spirit of the age almost imperceptibly meets with an existing weakness in the church. Saints and prophets oppose such dangers by witnessing to the power of the Holy Spirit. Theologians oppose them less effectively and with cruder tools. Admittedly, the three chapters of Part 1 are the work of a theologian not a saint. They point out three different dangers facing the church today: individuals seeking shelter and justification in the group; radical individualism in moral decision making; a new form of "cryptogamic" heresy.

NG.1. The Individual in the Church. (9-38), *Friedliche Wewägungen über das Pfarrprinzip. ZKT*, 70 (1948) 169-98.

Abstract: There is a private sphere in each individual (touching even on personal morality) over which the institutional church cannot exercise direct control. This is the realm of Spirit who distributes diverse charisms to individuals to build the church. Discerning and exercising charism takes great spiritual effort.

Topics: CHURCH and individual; INDIVIDUAL.

Subsidiary Discussions: Theological Anthropology (12ff); Trinity (13ff); Conscience (20); Discernment of spirits (31ff); Church, charism and office in (35ff).

Precis: After centuries of battling the tendency toward unbridled individualism, the church now faces the rise of collectivism. Clearly, both extremes present dangers. This essay, which attempts to explore the "both-and" position of the church in dealing with this modern dilemma, focuses on the individual within the institutional church.

I. The individual. What does it mean to say, and why must it be true, that there is and should be an individual in the religious sphere? *1. Philosophical and Dogmatic View of the Individual.* Individual is not simply the opposite of common. The terms are correlative, increasing and decreasing in direct proportion. Conflicts arise only when at one ontological level either concept declares itself to be absolute. Following Aquinas, Rahner distinguishes three ontological levels conjoined in human individuality: we are material, spiritual, and theological (children of God) whose destiny is a share in Trinitarian life. Hence, the real question is not individual or community, but what is the proper balance between individuality on one level and community on other levels. *2. Religious View of the Individual.* In a sense, Christianity discovered the individual as one who achieves an eternal destiny with the tools of space and time. Christ and the church do not mediate the individual's relationship to God, they make it immediate. *3. Ethical and Moral-Theological View of the Individual.* Since the individual is truly unique and not merely an instance of the universal, there is a legitimate individual, "private" sphere of morality and religion. This is not the realm of arbitrary choice. It is the realm of conscience where the art of "discernment of spirits" is necessary to distinguish between individual morality and universally binding norms.

II. **The individual in the church.** 1. *The Church.* "The church is the community of the redeemed bound together in spirit in Christ Jesus, and at the same time a visible organized society with rules and founder's charter" (21). These two dimensions, charismatic and institutional, invisible and visible, exist inseparable but unmixed. The church is simultaneously a graced community and an organized society. In what follows the term church will indicate its institutional sphere, and the term individual will indicate personal, spiritual individuality. 2. *The Individual in the Church.* Within the church the individual retains a truly and essentially *private* sphere that cannot be immediately reached by the church as a lawgiving society. Some matters are too unimportant, and hence above legislation; others are too intimate, and are beneath legislation. (What makes these matters difficult to separate is the fact that all the different metaphysical levels in the one person are actualized in one's actions.) Rahner illustrates this (25-26) by pointing out that the church cannot make a final determination of anyone's salvation/damnation status; the church cannot command internal acts (e.g., forced baptism); the church actually prescribes very few religious duties.

III. **Conclusions and applications.** (1) The individual in the church must have the right and the duty to make choices, even individual moral choices, not directly governed by church law. The church cannot relieve individuals of their burden and duty to be individuals and to decide matters. Individuals cannot use the church to hide from themselves in an ecclesiastical collective. The great danger among Christians today is not militant collectivism assailing the church from outside, but an internal collectivism that arises on the inside; not from the church overstepping its limits, but from our own weariness which would happily give up responsibility for making decisions. Here the issue of individual moral imperatives cannot be discussed fully. It is enough to say they exist, they must be discerned, and that to do so takes the help of others. (2) The individual in the church is also the bearer of God-given charism, often difficult to distinguish from natural personal individuality. The church is in essence both institutional and charismatic. The Spirit is always at work in the church, bringing about something new, and the church ignores charismatic voices to its peril. (3) The individual in the church is related to others. The private sphere is not asocial. Since the Spirit brings people together in movements or "free groups" to work and to pray (e.g., Benedict and Francis) the church should not raise obstacles to their community life. It should strengthen and nurture them. Of course the best thing is for charism and office to exist in the same person, as will be the case in the kingdom of God.

NG.2. The Appeal to Conscience. (39-63)
Abstract: Although conscience is an absolute and final element of each human being, it is under threat from two trends in contemporary society: situation ethics, and the mystique of sin. Rahner describes each threat in turn, and then counters each with the true Christian doctrine of conscience.
Topics: CONSCIENCE; MORALITY, situation ethics; SIN, mystique of.

Precis: I. The tendency towards an extreme situation-ethic. Many factors today (list, 40) make it extremely difficult to know clearly and to do the morally right thing. Life in former times was simpler. What were formally rare borderline cases are today almost the norm. So much of the complexity around us and in our personal experience (list, 41f) contributes to a sense that everything is relative to time, place and culture. The very possibility of material moral norms is doubted. We want to be responsible moral agents, but we despair of the complexity. We give up on discerning the rightness or wrongness of definite actions and retreat to the "motive" for our actions. *What* we do is not as important as *why* we do it. If our motive is good our conscience is clear. "We retreat to conscience" (44). But today the norm for conscience is no longer the objective nature of the act but conscience itself. Conscience is no longer the interpreter of a binding norm but the legislator issuing decrees valid just for me, and from which there is no appeal. This kind of situation ethics recognizes no universally binding moral law beyond conscience. Even priests often throw decisions back onto the consciences of their penitents because they themselves are too lazy to clarify the difficulties involved.

II. **The tendency towards a mystique of sin.** A second danger to Christian conscience today Rahner calls a generally latent "mystique of sin." In brief, it allows that since we are all sinners and seem unable to avoid sin, the best we can do is to throw ourselves on God's mercy. Abject surrender, and not the effort to fulfill the commandments, is what pleases God who saves us unchanged. There is the additional danger that one may come to see sin as a necessary stage in a person's life – a condition for the possibility of salvation. This mystique of sin participates in the Gnostic error of separating the God of Redemption from the God of Creation, and acting as if flesh were essentially unredeemable.

III. **Situation-ethics.** Yes, a person must obey conscience, even if it is objectively wrong. Even though conscience is not infallible, it cannot be bypassed. Yet it remains very difficult to discern the true voice of conscience from the many other voices within (passion, self-will, etc.). Thus we have a duty to conform our conscience to objective moral law as taught by the magisterium. Although there is such a thing as individual morality, it takes place within and never outside the framework of a universally normative morality. Christian conscience should be mature. But this means being able to apply universal norms to oneself, and even being able to see obligations applying to oneself beyond those imposed by universal norms. Furthermore, Catholics see morality, fulfilling the Commandments, as an essential part of Christianity. Moral laws are also truths of the faith taught either through the ordinary or the extraordinary magisterium. They need not be solemnly defined to be binding.

Though moral norms are universal, precisely as such they are to be the rule for the individual case. To argue that such norms are universal "except in my case" would be tantamount to metaphysical nominalism that would eviscerate every universal norm. It is more honest to admit that we have sinned in making ourselves an exception to a universal moral norm than to insist that we are the exception to it. We can only succeed in deceiving ourselves by suppresses God's truth. Especially in this age of psychology we should all be acutely aware of how easily we deceive ourselves. If in addition we take seriously that Christian life is lived in the shadow if the cross, we should not be at all surprised to discover that following moral norms will often lead to inconvenience and even to death. What then becomes of the freedom of the children of God? Does this not put us back under the law? Law is superseded only when the Spirit within us is powerful enough to bind us immediately with God in a relationship of fully personal love. But the Spirit can be lost. And we can deceive ourselves. The safest route for conscience is to remember that those who love God keep the commandments (summary, 58f).

IV. **The mystique of sin.** It goes without saying that the grace of salvation is offered to sinners. But those who honestly confess their sins must also say, "I will arise and go to my Father." A comforting voice which calls sin unavoidable or allows sin by urging us to trust in God's mercy, is not the voice of conscience but of self-delusion. Presuming on God's grace is hubris. Contemporary novels notwithstanding, Christian existence calls for more than deliverance. It entails striving for the sanctification of the world, for the gifts of the Spirit to bring about the Kingdom of God. The Word became flesh not to save us from our flesh but to save the flesh itself (summary 62f).

NG.3. A New Form of Heresy. (64-80).

Abstract: Greater clarity over doctrine and church authority make old forms of heresy difficult to sustain. In their place a new form of latent, cryptogamic heresy has arisen. It is best combated with new measures: not administrative censorship, but renewed magisterial teaching which makes sense to people today.

Topics: HERESY, cryptogamic.

Subsidiary Discussions: Theological Language (76ff); Censorship (78f).

Precis: Heresy is "the distortion of the word of God preached by the Church into human error, by a Christian who makes his own fancy and his own standard a measure of the word of God and suits it to himself instead of himself to it, and so sets up his own Christianity against the Church's" (64). Heresy is inevitable. It "must come" both because of our sinful nature, and also as part of the mysterious plan of God, so that no one can boast before Him. Hence, Christian are never surprised to encounter heresy. In fact, absence of heresy makes the Christian nervous as this may signal growing indifference to the truth of faith. What heresies must we guard against today? It is not the anti-Christian spirit of the world because, being publicly non-Christian, it cannot really constitute a heresy. Heresy today has a new form due in great part to the increased clarity with which the church expresses her doctrine, and the increased recognition of who speaks authoritatively for the church. All this actually makes it harder to be a public heretic within the church (summary, 69). Does this mean there are no longer heresies in the church?

If one starts from scripture and assumes there *must be* heresy in the church, what form must it take in this new church environment? Whereas in the past heresy was overt, today it is hidden, "a sort of cryptogam" (70), hard to see and diagnose precisely because it is not spoken openly, clearly or precisely. Thus heretics can escape detection, confrontation, condemnation and expulsion. Latent heresy employs two principle methods: it remains vague, and its writing concentrates on unsolved problems, passing over in silence any truths that contradict it. Here Rahner notes he is not talking about contumacious heretics, but simply material heresy that can be present in attitudes and behaviors that pervade one's thoughts and actions. It poses a danger precisely because it is a lack of truth, and it can exist even in those who earnestly will to believe correctly. It can exist both in the *hearing* church and in those who represent the *teaching* church, especially when the latter distort the truth by narrowing it, obstinately promoting the factional hair-splitting, or when through their hardness of heart they preach the gospel in a way people today cannot sufficiently grasp or appropriate. And who can deny this has happened?

So, do these postulated hidden heresies actually exist in the church? Rahner says, yes, they do. He points to Benedict XV's condemnation of an "*occulta oppugnatio*" and to an anonymous challenge to the church that advocated "Reformed Christianity." But more dangerous and pervasive is the contemporary feeling of mistrust and resentment of the magisterium, the sense that people cannot say what they are thinking— attitudes often hidden beneath works of historical theology or passed on by word of mouth, or by avoiding topics one does not fully agree with— unfashionable topics like purgatory, fasting, the devil, etc. Another form of this heresy is plain indifference (76). True, God's truths are rendered in words and propositions, but freezing the form in which these gospel truths are expressed is a dangerous sign of indifference, indicating a lack of power to assimilate the truth existentially and express it in new terms.

Whoever takes what is said here as an invitation to open a witch hunt for heresies has missed the point. Whoever wants to draw practical conclusions should look first to him/herself. Combating this new kind of heresy calls for new tools. In fact, reliance on the old tools (*administrative measures* like Pius X's Syllabus of Errors) only makes things worse. What are needed are *magisterial measures:* positively formulating true doctrine so as to uproot whatever is false. Officially suppressing even unripe theological efforts to express the ancient truth in new and compelling ways only makes the real situation worse by driving heresy and potential heresy further underground.

PART II. Faith Seeks Understanding.

NG.4. The Sacramental Basis of the Layman's Position in the Church. (83-113). Not in British edition. Translated by G. Richard Dimler, SJ. **Cf., TI 08.04.** Translated by David Bourke.

Abstract: By sacramental consecration every Christian in the visible church is authorized, empowered, and equipped for the task of actively cooperating in the church's supreme task: witnessing to the victory of Christ. Enumerates how each of the post-baptismal sacraments specially equips one to fulfill this task.

Topics: CHURCH, membership; LAITY; SACRAMENT/s.

Subsidiary Discussions: Baptism (55ff); Anonymous Christian/ity (55; 58f; 62ff); Eschatology (63ff); Confirmation (68); Penance (69); Eucharist (69); Orders, sacrament of (69f; 73); Marriage (70); Anointing of the Sick (71).

NG.5. Nature and Grace (114-149). Translated by G. Richard Dimler, SJ. **Cf., TI 04.07.** Translated by Kevin Smyth.

Abstract: This theoretical analysis of nature and grace necessitated by advances in philosophy and history improves on the scholastic theory and makes significant contributions when joined with metaphysical anthropology.

Topics: GRACE and nature; NATURE and supernature; THEOLOGICAL ANTHROPOLOGY.

Subsidiary Discussions: *Potentia obedientialis* (167f; 186f); Thomism, transcendental (169f); Sin, *simul justus et pecator* (173); Trinity (175ff); Incarnation (176f); God as horizon (178); *Pneuma* (179); Anonymous Christian/ity (179ff); Dialogue (185f).

NBP: *The Need and the Blessing of Prayer.* Introduction by Harvey D. Egan, SJ Collegeville, MN: Liturgical Press, 1997. Translated by Bruce W. Gillette. 101 pp. Originally eight sermons on prayer given at St Michael's Church in Munich, Lent, 1946. *Von der Not und dem Segen des Gebetes.* Also as *Happiness Through Prayer.* London: Burns Oates & Washbourne, 1958; and *On Prayer.* NY: Paulist, 1968.

Contents: Introduction.
Note on the translation.
Foreword.
1. Opening Our Hearts.
2. The Helper-Spirit.
3. The Prayer of Love.
4. Prayer in the Everyday.
5. The Prayer of Need.
6. Prayers of Consecration.
7. The Prayer of Guilt.
8. Prayers of Decision.

NBP. Intro. Introduction. (vii-xviii)

Abstract: After personal reminiscences (vii ff), Egan says prayer is a central, lifelong concern of Rahner's. It is rooted in his theological anthropology to the degree that he can say the human is essentially the one called to pray. He also equates prayer with the human act of surrender for which Christ is the paradigm. The remainder of the introduction discusses "everyday prayer" and covers such themes as banality, longing, joy, and sanctity. He suggests that Rahner is more interested in describing negative experiences, not because miserable people are somehow closer to God, but because it is when the lights go out and all the props are removed, in darkness and silence, that surrender is most pure (xv).

Topics: PRAYER, everyday.

Subsidiary discussions: Rahner, biography (vii ff); Supernatural existential and prayer (ix ff); Surrender (ix ff); Trinity and prayer (xi f); Saints, unknown (xvi ff).

NBP.Trans. Note on the Translation. (xix-xxi)
Abstract: Discusses the richness of the German language and Rahner's idiosyncratic use of it, with particular attention to the word *die Verschütteten*, "rubbled over," a word that would resonate in the hearts of the Munich citizens he addresses immediately after WWII. The translator is more interested in fidelity to Rahner's German than in achieving smooth English. Rahner and others considered this an important theoretical work on prayer. Many have found them profoundly moving.
Topics: GERMAN LANGUAGE (xix ff).
Subsidiary discussions: Germany, Post-war (xx).

NBP.For. Foreword (xxiii).
Abstract: These eight sermons from 1946 are not a systematic treatment of prayer. "If we are not supposed to cease praying, then perhaps one shouldn't cease speaking about prayer; speaking about it as well and as poorly as it is given to one."
Topics: PRAYER.

NBP.1. Opening Our Hearts. (1-13)
Abstract: A candid appraisal of our "rubbled over" hearts can lead to despair. But those who have the courage to stand firm miraculously discover God within those very hearts. Tranquility follows, and then our hearts spontaneously open up in prayer.
Topics: EVERYDAY LIFE, despair; HEART, human; HOPE; PRAYER, genesis of.
Subsidiary discussions: Transcendent/Categorical (3ff); Surrender (7ff); God (7ff); Jesus, Agony in the Garden (11f); Prayer, Our Father (13).

Precis: Finite creatures involved in many things desperately long to do one thing wholeheartedly, something fully worthy of human dignity. But just because this thing is so important and necessary does not make it easy, natural or free. Like love, prayer is such a seemingly simple, necessary and self-evident activity which may only be achieved at the end of a lifetime of struggle. Prayer is not easy to understand. Much of what passes for prayer is actually nothing but "the corpse and the lie of a prayer" (2).

In prayer we open our "rubbled over" hearts to God. For Rahner, the finite human heart is like a citizen cowering trapped in a dark bomb shelter, terror-struck that already the escape routes have been rubbled over with debris (3ff). We long to flee but cannot escape. Optimism fails. We despair. Rahner describes the many forms of modern despair, Stoic and Christian (5ff).

But the situation of the rubbled over heart is not hopeless. One can open such a heart by means of prayer. How? First one must stand firm and submit (7f). One must learn how to despair correctly. Second one must notice that God is already there with you (8f). Then tranquility comes of itself (9f), and finally the heart begins to speak on its own (9f). What does it say? It utters itself. No one can force another to pray. No one can give assurances beforehand that surrendering to the hopelessness of our human condition will yield an overwhelming experience of God within. But why should the body and the voice not try to do what the heart most deeply desires: to pray? None of this would be true if Jesus had not "suffered and done all of this in his heart with us, for us and before us" (11) in the garden. (Recap with a prayer gloss on the Our Father, 12f).

NBP.2. The Helper-Spirit. (14-24)

Abstract: When we pray we simply repeat the words spoken by the Holy Spirit who resides in our hearts. The Spirit's praying within us is what gives us the courage to pray.

Topics: PRAYER, role of Spirit; SPIRIT/s and prayer; HEART.

Precis: Where do we find the courage and strength to pray? Our first aid to prayer is our union with Jesus Christ, the Son. But we also pray in the Spirit of God. Here Rahner analyses two things: the place for the Holy Spirit in our hearts, and the fact that the Spirit prays with us and in us. The human heart in the modern person is something quite new. Seemingly freed from the tethers of custom and religion, we have fallen prey to every possible idol and have become for ourselves an impenetrable question. One benefit to this is that we can now glimpse the hidden depths, the vast extent of our inner being. But have we really plumbed the abyss within – that true infinity where God lives within us? When we finally do, there we discover the Holy Spirit filling the depth of our hearts (hymn, 20). Beautiful words! But are they true? Do I possess such depths? Certainly all have seen the profound evil that erupts from the depths of the heart! But the good news of faith is that the human heart is also the seat of the Holy Spirit. This is the secret of our being. Rahner now returns to the second question on prayer (21). This Spirit is not only the God before whom we kneel, this same Spirit also prays within us. The Spirit is the depth of our prayer, what gives our prayer dignity and direction. For when God hears our prayer and looks into our hearts, there He sees and hears the Spirit moving and praying within us. Our groanings are the groanings of the Spirit. In this way the Spirit is our helper in prayer, praying within us and consecrating our prayer

NBP.3. The Prayer of Love. (25-36)
Abstract: Love of God and prayer are intimately connected. In fact, true prayer *is* love. By extrapolating from our experience of selfless human love, we come to know love of God. We predispose ourselves for love by attending to quiet stirrings of the heart, by cultivating single-mindedness, and by praying for it.
Topics: LOVE OF GOD; PRAYER as love.

Precis: Love of God and prayer present the same two dangers. First, when we analyze these intimate human acts, they cease to be themselves, and we are left considering not the things themselves but our own subjectivity– a prison which can be broken through only by the self-forgetfulness of love and prayer. The second danger lies in how we seek to escape this deadening self-reflection. To avoid mistaking our thoughts and feelings about God for God, some people abjure all overt references to God. Preferring a chastened silence, they cease to pray. But this response, even if well-meant, closes the door to the only way the infinite can reveal itself: through the finite. An imageless approach to God not only denies the very core of religion. But faith inevitably evaporates into atheism. "The mystery must be named, called to, loved, so that it remains here for us" (27).

"Every uplifting of the heart which intends this God himself directly, is prayer" (27), and the pure fullness of this prayer is love. In such prayer the Christian does not say some*thing*, but says himself by surrendering to God. To say what prayer is, we must know what love of God is. It is not just beautiful words or merely observing commandments. To know the love of God we must proceed from what happens in selfless human love. Love is not mere egotistical desire. The passion of love is the desire to break through egotism and to lose oneself, to squander oneself on what is higher. God is already in such love. If only people would cling to God with such love, and lose themselves and everything in God! Then they could live openly, without shame or defenses, without fear of betrayal, knowing they are infinitely loved. Love is the highest act of which we are capable, for God is the only proper object of such love. In loving God we love the One who first loved us. But this impulse so to love God is not yet love for God. It becomes Christian love only after it is redeemed by grace. This implies: 1) God must preserve this highest faculty from becoming pride and presumption, since the proper love of God is humble adoration. 2) Our capacity to draw near God is not our accomplishment. It is the act of His love made possible when God poured the Spirit into our hearts. "We do not ascend up to him, rather he descended down to us" (32).

Does this love live in us? We know from experience that our love is a weak and partial thing at best. "However, one thing is certain: whoever wants honestly to love God already loves him" (33). We must continually pray for the love of God in our hearts, that the object of our love will visit us, while we do all we can to remove the obstacles to this love. The very tedium we feel at the pleasures life offers is an unconscious stirring of this love of God to which we should pay careful attention. And when God does draw near we must not drown out His voice with business and diversions. Although what we contribute through our own efforts to the ebb and flow of God's love within us is small, almost inconsequential, still we must avoid filling with the rubble of sin the springs of this love. Only the pure of heart, the single-minded will see God. To grow in love we must not only attend to the quiet stirrings and prepare a pure heart. We must also pray. "Increase, O God, your love in us!" No greater grace can be granted a human being. It comprises our true life, our happiness and peace. Rahner concludes with a sample prayer.

NBP.4. Prayer in the Everyday. (37-47)
Abstract: We must pray every day, and not simply await grand moments. Daily prayer is a prerequisite and a consequence of lofty prayer. We must pray the everyday, allow ourselves to be transformed by the daily tedium that, if experienced in prayer, breaks down egotism and opens us to greater love of God.
Topics: EVERYDAY, prayer in; PRAYER, everyday.

Precis: Scripture exhorts us to pray constantly. But since prayer is such an exalted activity, how can it also be the business of the everyday? Rahner makes two points: *Pray in the everyday*: A regimen of prayer should be part of the fabric of everyday life (morning prayer, meal prayer, Angelus, etc.). But these old styles of prayer are eroding in today's fast-paced society. Even for those who do pray in this way, it is often mechanical. Many people suffer from an inner paralysis. They want to pray but can't. So they wait for those occasional grand moments of heartfelt prayer and avoid daily prayer which often feels forced or sterile. Despite these difficulties we must heed the traditional wisdom and pray daily. Not all moments of prayer are equally satisfying. But daily prayer prepares the ground of such lofty moments. Without it we risk becoming deaf to God in our daily routine. And how will the fruit of lofty moments be translated into daily life without daily prayer? "Everyday prayer is the prerequisite and consequence of the great hours of grace in Christian life. And therefore it is vital and indispensable" (41f). An even weightier motive to pray each day is to extol the glory of God, which does not wax or wane. We must not focus on our own subjective moods in prayer but on the objective reality of the One we address. Rahner concludes with an exhortation to daily prayer and a list of suggestions (list, 43). "Such and similar tactics of one who wants to pray in the everyday can be learned and practiced. You can learn them too!" (44).

Pray the everyday: But not even daily prayer will completely overcome the sufferings of the spiritual person. Despite prayer, life continues to feel so "everydayish" and weighs us down. "[T]he everyday cannot be overcome through flight but only by steadfastness and by a transformation" (45). God must be sought and found *in* the world. Going out into the world must become a going inward with God. Every day must be prayed. How? Through selflessness and prayer. Everyday monotony, humiliations, misunderstandings, disappointments, etc. are a divine pedagogy. They invite us to let go of our egotism which blocks out the love of God. They knock down our defenses and free us to love expansively. "Everything depends on how we bear the everyday. It can make us everyday. However, it can also make us free from ourselves as nothing else can" (46). Everyday dying can become an everyday rising in love.

NBP.5. The Prayer of Need. (48-59)
Abstract: Conscience answers the case against petitionary prayer with an indictment of its own against those who question God. God's silence is broken only by Christ, who prays our petitions and models petitionary prayer: completely human and divine, uniting expressed need with complete submission.
Topics: PRAYER of petition.
Subsidiary Discussions: Sin and prayer (52ff): Jesus Christ and prayer of petition (55ff).

Precis: Petitionary prayer stands on trial. The prosecution begins with a list of bitter complaints brought forward by those who throughout the centuries prayed but were not answered (list, 48ff). They *did* pray, but God never answered. So why pray? Yet these plaintiffs are not all the same. While some conclude there is simply no purpose to such prayer, others conclude it is useless because God *cannot* intervene in worldly affairs. Therefore, such prayer is childish. Finally, others conclude that prayer of petition is justified but only for important matters, not for my petty daily business (summary, 51).

God remains silent. But we who hope, we who have been given the mandate to offer petitions in the Our Father feel compelled to speak. How do we answer this charge? When we silence our lust for life and our hunger for happiness the voice of God arises in our conscience and indicts us. *"Are not many of the things you seek my help to escape simply the consequences of your own sins? Hypocrites! You are concerned now that you are suffering but neglected the suf-*

ferings of others. You minimize your own sins and along with it you minimize my glory. Does God have to prove his goodness to you, or you to God? And by what standards do you judge what is evil? You complain that life has no meaning simply because it does not support the meaning you want for life." Petition must be transformed into question: not I want this, but, what should I want, this or that? This is how conscience could answer.

Incarnation also provides an essential answer to our complaints. Jesus Christ, the eternal Word, became the cry of human need in time and dwelt among us. He does not come to teach metaphysics but "to pray the prayer of petition for us" (56). As long as God remains silent in this time of faith, Jesus is our only answer. His prayer of petition is our 3-fold model: a word of realistic petition ("Let this cup pass"); a word of heavenly confidence ("I know that you always hear me"); a word of unconditional submission ("Your will be done"). Jesus' prayer unites what is most divine with what is most human. Truly Christian prayer is both totally human and quite divine, lifting earthly concerns into the light of God and thus transforming them. True prayer of petition only becomes possible and comprehensible in the mysterious unity of the human and divine found in the God-man (57). Our prayers of petition join with His only insofar as we ourselves have entered into the will of God which burns away all egotism. Does all this explain the mystery of prayers of petition? No. It remains a mystery that reflects the true mystery at the heart of Christianity: the childlike unity of expressed need and complete submission. Is this highest human act really possible? Yes. It is as possible as Christ.

NBP.6. Prayers of Consecration. (60-74)

Abstract: What happens in prayers of consecration? They are attempts at expressing ourselves completely in a total definitive and irrevocable act of human freedom. When they succeed these graced acts of love have not simply done something, they have done *everything*. Even if they fall short, still they ennoble us.

Topics: FUNDAMENTAL OPTION; PRAYER of consecration.

Subsidiary Discussions: Freedom (64ff); Death (66f); Eternity in time (68); Freedom and grace (70f); BVM, consecration to (73f).

Precis: Since it is neither a resolution nor a public vow, does anything actually happen in a prayer of consecration, the free streaming of love from one heart to another? Aren't we doing what has always been our duty, and just what we are always doing anyway: loving God? Rahner argues that a true, successful act of consecration completely expresses us such that *we ourselves* become stated and promised. He begins by pointing out that in the spiritual life acts do not simply follow one another, the current act canceling out all previous acts. Rather the past is preserved in the present act (62f). Similarly, one can anticipate the future in a present act of grace (63f). This occurs not simply as a plan or resolution, nor as an inevitable outcome of a prior act (e.g., marriage). But if the present act can decide the future, then what of freedom? Rahner now lays out his notion of human freedom (64ff). He maintains it is not a neutral capacity endlessly to choose this and then that, but rather the capacity to become something definitive. In fact, this is the goal of freedom and of human life. Although in a lifetime thousands of free acts may fail to achieve this, it remains possible that "there can be one such moment when freedom really effects what it always actually wants: to decide about everything at once and for ever" (66). There is clearly one such moment: death. Rahner asks whether our past experiences, even where they disappointed, don't prove this (67). He calls this momentous hour of realized freedom "the moment of eternity in time" (summary, 67).

Having established the formal character of freedom, Rahner now asks what this moment must be filled with so that it can be the eternity of salvation, the pure and ultimate yes. He answers it is the act of the love of God. But this may not be apparent for two reasons. First, because of its rarity and our innumerable experiences of failing to love God with all our hearts; second, it is not so clear that love is capable of integrating the whole of our lives. But the love of God, and it alone, is able to encompass everything (69f). As much as this act of love which achieves eternity in time must be seen to be called the most sublime act of freedom, yet it remains grace since God has first loved us. In fact it is a double grace: the grace to receive it and the grace to fulfill it.

Now one can more clearly see what happens in prayers of consecration, "The basic act of consecration is the act of love" (71). It is our attempt at a definitive act of freedom. If it succeeds it is ultimate and irrevocable. Though we can never know whether it has succeeded, God knows. Only a few points remain to be clarified. Regarding the *manner* in which we undertake an act of consecration, it is not a daily event nor should such acts be endlessly multiplied. Does the act of consecration really do something? Yes. In fact, if our attempt succeeds it does *everything!* And even if it does not succeed completely, it has accomplished at least a part of our human task: it has brought love into the everyday. So the very attempt is salutary for us whatever the outcome, leaving completely aside what effect our act of love may have on God (73). A final concern remains about the meaning of acts of consecration directed elsewhere than to God, e.g., to the BVM or the saints. These figures are loved by us because they are loved by God. And our love directed to them does not aim to end with them, but to go through them into God (summary, 74).

NBP.7. The Prayer of Guilt. (75-90)

Abstract: Attempting to say how we can pray, "Forgive us our guilt" without evasion, exaggeration, or excuses, quickly becomes a deep discussion of the elements of justification: personal sin, venial sin, fallen human nature, *sola gratia*, and the possibility of knowing our salvation/damnation status.

Topics: JUSTIFICATION, knowledge of; PRAYER of the sinner; SIN.

Subsidiary Discussions: Forgiveness, grace of (79); Sin, venial (79ff); Uncertainty Principle (87ff).

Precis: Christ instructs us to pray, "Forgive us our guilt." This refers not just to past sins, but to the guilt we bear now, always, and ever anew. But how can we pray this? Are we not redeemed? And what if we don't feel sinful? Rahner sketches the story (75-79) of people, baptized and forgiven, yet still burdened with the task of struggling with the powers of darkness throughout life. Most find themselves to have guiltily drifted away from God in a thousand ways. We only return to right relationship when we admit this without minimizing or excusing our fault. We must admit that we ourselves are sinners, and we have intended evil in our deepest hearts. This insight and the power to confess are themselves gifts of grace. To deny our sinfulness is to refuse the grace of conversion. And so we pray, "Father I have sinned against you. Forgive my guilt!" But the question remains, can the redeemed honestly pray this way each day? It is possible, in the sense that the grace of God's forgiveness remains a gift which I dare not presume, and the truth of God's goodness is magnified when I proclaim my sinful truth. But here we must go slowly.

Tradition could reply, yes, even good Christians pray daily for forgiveness of their daily weaknesses and mistakes (79-81). After all, "venial sins" are still sins. But can one earnestly repent of sins we ourselves categorize as merely "venial"? If they are technically venial and do not issue from the core of a person, is it not disingenuous to repent for them "more than they deserve?" Doesn't such an approach also blur the line between venial and serious sin? Although venial sins must be taken seriously, they do not lie at the heart of the sinner's prayer "Forgive us our guilt." Before moving on to greater clarity about how this prayer for forgiveness can be said seriously even by saints, Rahner distinguished the Catholic from the Protestant understanding of sin and justification (82-84). For Catholics, although everyone may in fact sin, sin is not inevitable (i.e., not the outcome of our nature). More to the point, *I* freely sin. And whenever I manage to avoid sin it is always due to God's grace (*sola gratia*).

If (following 1 John) no one can say he has not sinned, and since sin is not inevitable, must one say he *has* sinned? Rahner suggests it is better to leave the judgment to God and merely to say, "I cannot say I have not sinned." Nevertheless, most of us can safely confess we have often sinned and continue to do so. We must say so forthrightly. But can those who are not conscious of any sin claim to stand justified before God? No, for who knows whether the good of which we boast is at most a fig leaf covering our shame? Knowing how ambivalent we are in so many other areas of life, who among us dares to say unequivocally that s/he is justified in God's sight? It is safest to confess ourselves sinners.

It may even seem to some observers that we actually flee the knowledge of our true status in God's eyes in order to escape responsibility for ourselves. Here Rahner is cautious. Ignorance of how we stand in God's eyes cannot simply be reduced to an act of bad faith on our part. Self-reflection cannot yield certain knowledge of how we stand before God because there is a kind of "uncertainty principle" at work (87-89). The moral act of self-examination and our reaction to what we see in ourselves in fact changes the status of what we are evaluating. As a result, in principle we can never know our state of grace: how we stand in God's sight relative to our salvation/damnation status. Yet we also seem to possess a faculty, call it conscience or what you will (list, 89), at the innermost center of acting that seems to possess a sure sense (we dare not call it knowledge) of what one's actions mean and intend. And since we cannot reduce our self-awareness to words we are left to groan, "Have mercy on me a sinner." Rahner concludes with the analogy of running. One cannot both run a race and be one's own sideline coach, knowing and judging precisely where one is on the course. One can run only by forgetting the fact that one is running. This is how it is with us and our justification status. We cannot judge ourselves in mid-course and say "I am in your grace." We must just keep running and say, "Have mercy on me a sinner" (conclusion, 90).

NBP.8. Prayers of Decision. (91-101)

Abstract: Rahner highlights 3 prayers of decision: temptation, this historical moment, and death. In these moments we say yes to God's invitation in love. Only prayer defeats temptation, when our desire for God eclipses all other desires; the best preparation for death is to pray now as we would desire to pray then.

Topics: PRAYER of decision; TEMPTATION and prayer.

Subsidiary Discussions: Germany, post-war (97ff); Death, prayer at the time of (99f).

Precis: Not all moments in life are equal. Some can determine a life and an eternity. These are moments of decision (e.g., choice of profession, marriage partner, a vow made to God). Whether they arrive amidst fanfare or quite unheralded, they are all are irrevocable. At such moments, one stands "eye-to-eye" with God, and God with us. These are moments of grace as God awaits our answer to his invitation. Such moments are moments of prayer, for if we have answered correctly they are moments of love. In what follows, Rahner considers closely three such prayers of decision: prayer during temptation; prayer in the decision of contemporary time; prayer for the decision of death.

Life on earth is trial and temptation (93-97). These must be seen, accepted and endured. They strike when we are weak and find in us an ally who would pass off evil as something good. Succumbing to temptation is never inevitable, whatever rationalization we may make. We will never win the battle over temptation armed only with the resources with which it finds us. We must grow during temptation by taking the battle beyond ourselves and unto the field of eternity. Only the one who fights temptation as a true soldier of God deserves the victory. How does this change take place? Only when we pray. During temptation one must not speak to temptation but to God, and not *about* temptation but to God *about* God, His grace, His love, His life! (95). Only the one who prays survives temptation because only through prayer does one become that child who finds no allure in sin and despises it. Temptation is overcome when the desire for God crowds out every other desire. So we must pray during temptation. We must develop a sensitivity which warns us immediately when our inner joy and spiritual health decrease. The one who fails to pray in moments of temptation fails to recognize its deepest nature. For temptation is always an invitation of divine love. And the answer to this invitation is always love (97).

Next comes the prayer of decision of contemporary time (97-99). [These were 1946 Lenten sermons delivered in post-war Munich.] It would seem the West has betrayed its mandate from God to bear the faith to all people, and as a result even now its scepter is being passed to others who will bear good fruit. But the future remains open. Even today the Lord says to us as he did to the people of the Exodus: "I place before you life and death. Chose life that you may live." Much depends on our response, our decision. To choose well we must pray.

Finally there is the decision of death (99f). Our death is the moment of decision pure and simple. It is the definitive moment when time becomes eternity. But will our last word be a beautiful prayer of decision, saying to the bridegroom, "Yes, come Lord Jesus"? We do not know. For death comes like a thief in the night. Meanwhile, the best we can do is to stay alert and to pray often the prayer of decision we *want* to speak at the hour of our death (example, 100). To think now of one's death is a good prayer. It is a prayer of decision.

Rahner ends with what might be considered a conclusion to the whole series of eight sermons on prayer. He realizes there is much he has not said about prayer. Especially lacking is any talk of prayer and our reaching out to the poor. But whatever he has said or left unsaid, talking *about* prayer doesn't matter. Only the words we ourselves actually say to God matter. If only they come from the heart, and if only the Holy Spirit prays them with us, then they are heard by God. And God will never forget them, for God cannot forget the words of love. Does this not make us want to pray?

A New Baptism in the Spirit: Confirmation Today. Denville, NJ: Dimension, 1975. **Cf.,** *Meditations on the Sacraments.* **MS.2.**

NC. *A New Christology.* NY: Crossroad, 1980. Revised. 239 pp. *Christolgie – Systematich und Exegetisch,* Herder, 1972. Translated by David Smith and Verdant Green.
Contents: PART I. "Jesus Christ and Christology" by Karl Rahner.
1. Christology Today.
2. The Provenance of the Church in the History of Salvation from the Death and Resurrection of Christ.
3. The Death of Jesus and the Finality of Revelation.
PART II. "New Testament Approaches to a Transcendental Christology" by Wilhem Thüsing, not abstracted here.

NC.1. Christology Today (3-17).
Abstract: Sketches in broad strokes "searching christology:" that when our desire for salvation searches history it finds there the definitive validity of Jesus, dead and risen, who meets with our hope for our own resurrection. Specific discussions of resurrection, Communion of Saints, anonymous Christianity.
Topics: CHRISTOLOGY, searching; JESUS CHRIST, resurrection of.
Subsidiary discussions: Communion of Saints (14f); Propositions, theological (15f); Anonymous Christian/ity (15ff); Incarnation (17).

Precis: Preliminary remarks: 1) This study is not exhaustive, and the topics it covers are to some extent arbitrary. 2) This issue can only be studied in the context of the whole person with our ultimate mystery (God) and the question of our salvation which we often suppress. 3) There are many valid possible points of departure in christology, and all of them could lead to the searching christology which finds its answer in the orthodox confession of the church. 4) This study cannot incorporate all of the church's teachings on christology. It only aims to indicate where modern people can find within themselves a starting point for such a christology.

What is "searching christology"? One is (or should be) concerned with oneself as a whole. This is salvation. But since it seems that this cannot be done in the context of history which can only present particular details of life, one turns to mysticism, metaphysics or skepticism, none of which satisfies. But if one comes to see that the answer must lie in history, since this is the sole realm in which freedom realizes itself, then one will begin to look for another person in whom salvation has been successful and one who we can experience as such. We can call the person being sought in this way the "absolute bringer of salvation." This of course presumes that the one being sought exists in absolute solidarity with us and we in him (6). Yet such salvation as has already succeeded in the one we seek can only have taken place in death, since only in death does freedom become definitive. At the same time this death, because it is also God's promise of salvation extending to us, must become tangible to us in an absolutely unique way. We call this the resurrection of the person. And it must follow that the life and self-understanding of this person must be such that somehow such a resurrection is fitting and believable. "This person who is sought, however, is only the absolute bringer of salvation if his fulfillment through his death and resurrection in the power of God in solidarity with us is the irrevocable sign of the fact that God has promised himself to us as the fulfillment of our salvation" (7).

According to Christian teaching, we have found this absolute bringer of salvation. He is the Christ of God, the Son of God, Jesus of Nazareth. Have we sufficient reason and the right to make this claim today? How is it legitimate? Despite the fact that the earliest historical sources are testaments of faith, this does not mean we have no historical knowledge of Him. We must also insist that Jesus did more radical things than just preach about God.

He proclaimed Himself to be the definitive Word of God to us in history. His proclamation contains a new turning of God toward humanity. More than a mere offer, it was made irreversibly victorious in Jesus' death and resurrection. In answer to the question *how* Jesus knew all this, we can only answer that He was so equally united in the unconditional solidarity of love with both God and humanity that He never felt forced to choose between them, "but understood his own salvation to be that of the whole of mankind" (10, with summary).

Rahner now makes four points concerning the resurrection of Jesus (10-13), the confirmation and appearance of what was given with Jesus' person and message. "It was the historically visible victory of God's promise of himself to mankind" (10). These four elements are indissolubly connected: 1) Resurrection is a statement about the whole person, his definitively saved nature and history. It is not a return to spacio-temporal biological life. It is incommensurable with other events but remains historical. 2) We are only able to understand this unique event in light of our own hope of resurrection which is manifest every time we act out of real faith, hope and love. 3) Even granting the difficulties the apostles had in expressing this unique experience of resurrection, can we offhandedly refuse to believe their testimony? 4) There is a personal experience of the risen Christ (albeit dependent on the testimony of the apostles) when in history our transcendence is alive to the immediate presence of God in grace and freedom. In grace we experience ultimate, unconditional freedom. Keeping these four point in a unity it should be possible for Christians today to believe in Jesus' resurrection.

Rahner now considers the individual Christian's personal relationship with Jesus (13-17). For all the reasons given earlier (summary, 13f), Christian should have "a personal relationship of hope, trust and love with this Jesus, who has been saved, in the uniqueness of his human reality" (14). It is a real possibility which should be cultivated, since the dead have become definitive and hence do exist. What we believe in general about our connection with the dead in the Communion of Saints must certainly apply in specific to the living Jesus. Our vivid relationship with Him in turn invigorates our own faith in our own resurrection, our achieving our definitive validity one day.

Clearly, many people today reject the orthodox formulae of classical christology. Yet they remain able to believe authentically in the incarnation of the Divine Word. Christological propositions, however objectively true they may be, are never the final word on faith. Here Rahner summarizes the essence of christological faith (16), and maintains that whoever holds such faith believes what the church believes regardless of theological formulations. Rahner goes further, saying that people have in fact encountered Christ without knowing it whenever in faith, hope and love they have ventured the whole of their lives on something immeasurable. Rahner concludes with specific remarks on the Incarnation. He sees in this deep mystery a certain inevitability. How else but in man (*the* mystery) could God have expressed Himself? If our longing for absolute nearness to God (itself an incomprehensible gift) should reveal to us that this nearness is to be found not in the realm of spirit but in the realm of flesh here on earth, then we shall find it nowhere else but in Jesus of Nazareth.

NC.2. The Provenance of the Church in the History of Salvation from the Death and Resurrection of Christ. (18-31)

Abstract: Did Jesus intend to found a church? Rahner argues yes, insofar as He willed the permanent and ongoing witness to His acceptance of God's offer of self-communication made definitive in His death and sealed by His resurrection. The church is this witness, which institutionalizes itself to perform its mission.

Topics: CHURCH as founded by Christ; SALVATION.

Subsidiary discussions: Jesus Christ, imminent expectations of (21ff); God, universal salvific will of (24f); *Jus divinum* (27ff); Church, structure of (27ff).

Precis: After some comments on the present form of the text, Rahner makes two preliminary remarks concerning whether Jesus ever intended to found a church. First, this is such a broad field the following remarks will be rather arbitrary; second, these remarks are those of a systematic theologian. Exegetical considerations are covered in Part II of this volume. This essay has the following outline: comments on the whole question and in particular on the traditional solutions in Catholic theology and the attendant problems of each; Rahner's thesis and how it supplies better solutions to standing problems.

The question is: "Can we really say Jesus founded the church?" Immediately this raises the question, "Which Jesus?" pre- or post-resurrection, a question that would never have occurred to theologians of a previous age. Today it is hard to maintain Bellarmine's Counter-Reformation approach of grounding the foundation of the church in explicit, objective, juridically interpreted statements of Jesus, which see Peter as the first pope, the apostles as the first bishops, etc. The first challenge to this institutionalist Tridentine approach came with Pius XII's *Mysici Corporis*, in part a belated response to the challenges posed by Modernism. These arose from two main sources. The first is in the seeming collapse of Jesus' imminent expectation of the coming of the Kingdom of God (24). It is argued that having expected the end, Jesus would hardly have thought of founding a church. The second challenge is sociological. It argues that the wide diversity of organization in the apostolic church argues against its being founded by Jesus. (Rahner addresses the argument at the end of the essay.) Allowing that he cannot offer a full response to the argument from the collapse of Jesus' imminent expectation, he admits that today's reaction must be different from the hostile rebuff given it by Pius X.

Rahner's first suggests substituting the term "provenance" for "foundation" with its juridical/ institutional implications exegetes can scarcely justify. Next he turns to the implications latent in the title of the essay. The death and resurrection of Jesus has great eschatological significance within the history of salvation that extends to the provenance of the church. Succinctly, through the crucified and risen Jesus, "God's victorious eschatological and definitive self-communication finally appeared" (24). Rahner now lays out the core of his thesis (24-27) starting with the fact that until Jesus' death and resurrection the status of God's universal salvific will, the free offer of His self-communication, remained obscure, open and questionable. The resurrection, however, is the unambiguous seal that salvation history will end well through the power of God's grace. Jesus' unconditional solidarity with God and humanity victoriously unites God's self-communication in the mode of offer with the mode of real success as a lasting promise made to the world. But Jesus can only be this insofar as this victorious offer of God is always present in the world. No ongoing community of faith in the world would mean no permanent presence of God in the world, and hence Jesus would not be what He claimed: God's definitive promise of Himself. But the church *is* God's eschatologically definitive and lasting victorious promise of Himself to the world in Jesus Christ. This is what links Jesus, God and the provenance of the church. The church owes its existence to Jesus' self-understanding of His unique role as the absolute bringer of salvation (summary, 26f).

Yet some would claim that none of this, however true, justifies a claim that Jesus sanctioned a particular structure for the church (popes, bishops, etc.). This problem in particular was very difficult for Tridentine theology (27f). So what does ground the traditional claim that the church's structure is justified by a *jus divinum*? There is a *jus divinum* governing the structure of the church at least to the degree that for it to fulfill its function throughout time (i.e., witness to salvation in Christ) it must have a structure. Rahner argues that it was not necessary in the Apostolic Age for this *jus divinum* to have been unambiguous, irreversible and concretely binding. And although it became such over time, this does not mean these human choices are therefore simply arbitrary and reversible. After all, not everything that is freely chosen is simply reversible (e.g., marriage, one's choice of profession). This one-way movement of history that ends in subsequently irrevocable decisions is at work in the church *juris divini* (summary, 29f). Yet the church continues to have a completely open future in the sense that its concrete organization may be reformulated in fidelity to its permanent mission to the world. The church's structure has changed enormously over time. Today some say the pace of change is too fast, others too slow. Whatever the case, the church has remained true to her history and mission through it all (summary, 31).

NC.3. The Death of Jesus and the Finality of Revelation. (32-41)
Abstract: When did revelation end? With the death of Christ? Of the last apostle? At the close of the Apostolic Age? In this dense essay, Strictly speaking the cross marks the end of revelation, since it alone is the definitive deed of one person in radical solidarity with both God and humanity, who saw the universal effect of His

acceptance of God's offer of self-communication on the salvation of others.

Topics: JESUS CHRIST, death of; REVELATION, close of.

Subsidiary discussions: Christ-event, insurpassability of (34f); Word, eschatological (36); Death, theology of (38ff); History, meaning of (40f).

Precis: The Catholic axiom is "Christian revelation, insofar as it is 'publicly' and 'officially' directed to all men and women in a binding way, closed with the death of the last apostle" (32). This is true even though theologizing and the history of our understanding continue to unfold. Yet *Dei Verbum* mentions only the insurpassability of Christ and not of the apostles. Despite the difficulty pinpointing the close of revelation the meaning of the axiom remains clear: God's revelation in Christ was a unique historical event, circumscribed in time and history, but nevertheless valid for all subsequent ages. Nothing more that is truly new can now happen in the history of revelation (33). But can we connect more precisely Jesus' death and the fullness of revelation? This notion disturbs modern people since it would seem to rob history of its ultimate profundity; its dignity seems to disappear if the history of revelation has ended. Rahner argues this difficulty can be overcome by focusing on the ongoing nature of our understanding of revelation, and by stressing the insurpassiblity of the revelation manifested in the Jesus-event. Notwithstanding, here Rahner restricts himself "to the question of whether and how the *death* of Jesus as such relates to the insurpassability of the revelation-event in Jesus Christ, and how from that point we can eventually reconcile the new spirit of an open future with the dogma of insurpassability and the 'finality' of Christian revelation" (35).

Thesis: Jesus' death as such (completed in the resurrection) has an essential and unique meaning in regard to the insurpassability of Christian revelation. "Only by the cross of Christ as such can the insurpassability of the Christian revelation be constituted, and only thus is it constituted" (35). Only the death of the one who is simultaneously the bearer of revelation and the revelation-event can offer the "end" of revelation. This assumes that revelation history continues since human history itself must continue. It follows that the finality and insurpassability of a revelation-event in ongoing history can occur only in the historical appearance of the absolute self-promise of God as such, and as the goal of history itself. Any other word or cessation of speech on God's part would be completely arbitrary. And any other act on the part of man would still be open to change, hence, not a definitive acceptance of God's offer of self-communication. This is what distinguishes a *prophetic* from an *eschatological* word (36). The eschatological word is a definitively realized possibility which to some degree affects what it announces.

How is this to be conceived as an eschatological and unsurpassable word of revelation? [Note: the dense argument to follow takes the form of a transcendental deduction: since X and Y are the case, whatever is the necessary condition of their possibility must also be the case.] Since this revelation must be realized by words and deeds sharing an inner unity, and since this revelation must be able to affect all humanity, then it can only be given in one man who has through his deeds accepted the word of self-promise freely and definitively in tangible history. A mere word of self-promise addressed to the world is never enough (37). Acceptance must happen through an historical event of an individual whose self-understanding holds that his acceptance in obedient freedom affects the salvation of the whole world (the starting place of classical christology). Summary, 38. To explain why only death offers the condition for the achievement of definitive, irrevocable and unambiguous validity, Rahner sketches his theology of death (38ff). It explains why Jesus' death as such forms an essential constitutive element providing the finality of the eschatological word of the self-promise of God to the world. Properly understood the cross, then, marks the end of public revelation because there God pledged himself irrevocably to history. The history of this revelation includes both scripture and the ongoing history of our struggle to articulate and submit to this revelation. There is a special sense in which we can also say public Christian revelation ended with the Apostolic Age (40).

Rahner ends by returning to the aversion some modern people feel toward the notion of a closed revelation which seemingly puts an end to meaningful historical development in an unlimited future. He points out that people today, like all those who came before them, will always find their creative efforts for a new future thwarted by death. This irresolvable conflict between our will and our accomplishment can only be reconciled if death itself is not the annihilating end of history but the event by which history is saved by God's action. This is the definitive message of Christianity that assures the outcome history and closes revelation. Far from annulling human history, only this message assures its validity.

OF. *Opportunities for Faith: Elements of a modern spirituality.* NY: Seabury, 1974. Sources. 229 pp. *Chancen des Glaubens.* Herder, 1970. Translated by Edward Quinn.
Contents: Abbreviations and Acknowledgments.
Author's Preface.
1. The Gospel Claim.
   Righteousness in the New Testament.
   Radical faith in ordinary life.
   Man's possibilities and God's.
   Shrewd stewards of life.
2. Mysteries of Faith.
   Advent as antidote to Utopia.
   The cross – the world's salvation: Meditations of Good Friday.
   Risen victorious from the tomb: Meditations for the Easter Vigil.
   Easter.
   Fear of the Spirit: Thoughts for Pentecost.
   Our faith is only theoretical.
   Mary's Assumption.
3. Faith and Prayer.
   Theses on the theme: faith and prayer.
   On prayer today.
   Prayer too is action.
4. The Message for Today.
   What is the Christian message?
   Theses on the problem of revelation and history.
   Epochal mutation of Christian key-concepts.
   "Sins" and guilt.
   Peace as mandate.
   Ordinary virtues.
5. Living Testimony.
   Teresa of Avila: Doctor of the Church.

Thinker and Christian: obituary of Romano Guardini.
A man at play: Panegyric for Hugo Rahner.
Confidence and composure in sickness.
The doctor and Good Friday.
6. Priesthood and Religious Life in Upheaval.
Current discussion on the celibacy of the secular priest: an answer
7. The Pilgrim Church.
Trust within the church.
The duty of discussion: a plea for Cardinal Suenens.
Experiment in the field of Christianity and the church.
The church's Eucharistic celebration and the Christian's Sunday obligation.
Sources (integrated with each essay title below).

Author's Preface: "Opportunities for faith" means "opportunities for proving or testing our faith. Rahner hopes these articles highlight some of these opportunities, which generally call us to loving service in our everyday activities.

1. The Gospel Claim
OF.1.1. Righteousness in the New Testament. (3-6). July 7, 1968 address to theology students at St. Charles Borromeo College, Münster.
Abstract: Understanding the Sermon on the Mount demands calling oneself into question, giving up self-righteousness, and surrendering to God. This alone frees us from ourselves. Such "capitulation" does not reject our adult self-reliance, just our self-defensiveness. Only then can we encounter God. The call to priesthood is a special call to this radial life of surrender.
Topics: SERMON: Matt 5:20-24; RIGHTEOUSNESS; SURRENDER.
Subsidiary discussions: God as incomprehensible mystery (5); Priesthood (5f).

OF.1.2. Radical Faith in Ordinary Life. (7-10). July 5, 1970 sermon to Catholic students' community at Münster.
Abstract: People are "scandalized" when the message or the messenger is too close to the "everyday." They expect or want a breakthrough to another world. But faith justifies itself and does not

require anything more than the everyday. Rather than replace the everyday, faith reveals the radical roots of freedom, responsibility, love, hope, guilt, forgiveness, and their ultimate ground: God. Preaching that does not return us to the everyday runs the risk of offering an unsustainable ideological superstructure. Faith does not require authorization by means of premature glorification.
Topics: SERMON: Mk 6:1-6; EVERYDAY; FAITH.
Subsidiary discussions: Preaching (9f).

OF.1.3. Man's Possibilities and God's. (11-12). February 7, 1969 sermon to lay theology students at Münster.
Abstract: Neither the rich nor the poor can enter the kingdom of God on their own. The desperation this realization should enkindle in us is meant to return us to our roots: to God for whom all things are possible. But most of us do not want God, or what God wants. We want some *thing*. Occasionally we must let the horror of this realization touch us: that we cannot save ourselves. This insight is the prerequisite to encountering and surrendering to God.
Topics: SERMON: Mk 10:23-27; SALVATION.

OF.1.4. Shrewd Stewards of Life (13-17). July 28, 1968 sermon in St. Michael's, Münster.
Abstract: However we interpret the action of the steward, Jesus concentrates on his shrewdness. Finding himself in a winless situation the steward has the courage to risk everything. Children of this world are more bold and resolute than children of light. Do we realize we are only stewards of our lives and may suddenly be called to give an account? Do we have the courage to risk all, or are we content to cling to the status quo, despite knowing better? Wise stewards are looking for the moment to break through and change. They watch and are ready. Recognizing that we are always in a life-or-death situation makes it easier for us to give up superfluous things. But this divine prudence seems like folly to those without faith. It is the folly of the cross, which teaches us to embrace our own death with faith, hope and love.
Topics: SERMON: Lk 16:1-9; WISDOM, divine.
Subsidiary discussions: Cross, wisdom of (17); Death (17).

2. Mysteries of Faith
OF.2.1. Advent as Antidote to Utopia. (21-24)
Abstract: Christians are people of the future – the infinite God. Hence, they are not fundamentally conservative because they realize the present is provisional. Utopians, who are also people of the future, often strive frantically to create here and now an intra-mundane perfection. Despite their reactionary proclivities, Christians with their "faith in Advent" are less dangerous than utopians, who are impatient with the present and hate everyone who impedes material progress. Those with Advent faith love the present because they see God at work here; and they meet the future with composure. Only they can voluntarily accept death and surrender to it. But there are utopians scattered among Christians, and Christians scattered in among utopains.
Topics: FUTURE; UTOPIAS.
Subsidiary discussions: God, as future (22f); Death (23).

OF.2.2. The Cross – the World's Salvation: Meditations on Good Friday. (25-30). March 27, 1970 Bavarian Radio broadcast.
Abstract: The passion-death-resurrection of Jesus is the salvation of the world insofar as it dispels the otherwise ambiguous darkness of human death with God's eternal "Yes" to the world, which becomes historical, unambiguous and irrevocable in Jesus' cross and resurrection.
Topics: SERMON: Good Friday; DEATH; JESUS CHRIST, death of.
Subsidiary discussions: Non-conformity (25f); Causality, final (29f).

Precis: I. Jesus' death is first of all death, a dying. But it is of a particular kind. It is a political-religious murder brought about by Jesus' nonconformity. All nonconformity is a gateway to death. When nonconformity becomes hopeless it opens onto the folly of the cross. **II.** What can we learn from the death of Christ? First, what do we learn from any death? Someone disappears in utter powerlessness. He went radically alone, yet we are untied with him, seeing our fate in his death. Has he fallen into emptiness or into holy acceptance? It seems so ambiguous. **III.** The Christian doctrine surrounding Jesus' death sounds so mythological . . . appeasing an angry God, etc. But to interpret such formulas correctly we must remember three things: Jesus' death does not change God's mind toward us; it does not rein in a world run beyond God's control; it did not render God's original grace superfluous. In the death of Jesus, God's eternal "Yes" to the world becomes historical, unambiguous and irrevocable.

OF.2.3. Risen Victorious from the Tomb: Meditations for Easter Vigil. (31-36). March 28, 1970 Bavarian Radio broadcast.

Abstract: Hope for our own resurrection prepares us to discover the resurrection of Jesus, an event in history which does not force us to believe but makes our own belief in resurrection intellectually honest.

Topics: JESUS CHRIST, Resurrection of; RESURRECTION.

Subsidiary discussions: Empty tomb (32); Body/soul dualism (31f); Christology, searching (33f); Hope (34); Everyday Life, joy (35f).

Precis: I. To understand what the mystery of Jesus' resurrection means to us, we should leave aside the unhelpful division of body and soul. Resurrection means simply the redeemed finality of an integral human being. It is a general term that says nothing definite about our materiality. Our own claim to our own resurrection ("I shall be") makes it possible to believe in the resurrection of Jesus. **II.** My hope for my own resurrection impels me to scan history for any sign which might validate such a hope. Jesus of Nazareth is that sign. Easter does not compel us to believe, but it does permit us to believe with intellectual integrity. When we look to Jesus we see reflected both the substance of our hope and the very factor that calls it into question: sin. But to hope at all is to hope for resurrection. **III.** Why do Christians not exhibit more Easter joy? The light of Easter shines only for those who have endured to the end the darkness of Good Friday. Fearful of such a denouement, we experience an empty Christian joy, a longing for joy that prepares us to receive joy whenever and from whatever quarter it may come.

OF.2.4. Easter. (37-39). April 6, 1969 Easter sermon at St. Ignatius Church, Frankfurt-am-Main.

Abstract: (abridged version of OF.2.3.). Proclaiming the resurrection entails witnessing to an objective fact (the Lord has risen) and a subjective truth (His resurrection is the firm basis of my own life). Resurrection is not about revivified bodies. It is about the whole person being eternally redeemed – a mystery beyond comprehension which implies that neither Jesus nor His cause are forever done with. The same factors which allow us to be intellectually honest in accepting the hope of our own resurrection (38) allow us to be honest in professing Jesus' resurrection. Faith in the two resurrections are co-conditioning.

Topics: SERMON: Easter; JESUS CHRIST, Resurrection of; RESURRECTION.

Subsidiary discussions: Jesus Christ, empty tomb of (35); Body/soul dualism (38).

OF.2.5. Fear of the Spirit: Thoughts for Pentecost. (40-45). *Publik,* no. 20, May 15, 1970.

Abstract: Our allegiance to the Spirit is mostly theoretical. Basically, we fear the Spirit who opens before us the incomprehensible and uncontrollable. This calls for courage and trust.

Topics: SERMON: Pentecost; SPIRIT/s, fear of.

Subsidiary discussions: Holy Spirit, gifts of (44f).

Precis: Even Christians have little room today for the Holy Spirit if looked for as just another kind of causality. But when we envision the Spirit as that which grounds the depth of our human experiences of loyalty, love, commitment and forgiveness, then the Spirit is quite real and dynamic. **Our faith is only theoretical.** It would be easier to discover and experience the Spirit if we were not afraid of Him. But we fear the Spirit because we fear what we cannot control. Even the church fears the incomprehensibility into which the Spirit would like to throw us. **Fear among "traditionalists" and "progressives."** Both camps fear the Holy Spirit. The one because He fosters change; the other because they cannot control the change He fosters. Yet it would be a terrible mistake to imagine the Spirit as some kind of golden mean, a mediocrity. He is not just one more vector in the play of forces. **Readiness for the incalculable.** Surrender to the Holy Spirit means readiness to admit the incomprehensible into our lives. It means living with hope, not with certitude. It demands boldness and experimentation We must have the courage to exercise whatever gift the Spirit has given us, confident that He alone can and will harmonize them.

OF.2.6. Mary's Assumption. (46-50). August 15, 1968 sermon on Bavarian Radio.
Abstract: Though Mary's start in life is different from ours, our destinies are the same: face-to-face immediacy with God. In her Assumption we see the hope we harbor for ourselves. But does she not differ from our own beloved dead insofar as she already enjoys the bodily consummation of her resurrected state? Here Rahner speculates on two points: the possible nature of a resurrected body (47) and how time may be altered in eternity (47-48). He ends by admitting: "We simply don't succeed ... in uniting in a higher synthesis and thus balancing off against each other the concepts and models of time and the concept of eternal finality" (48). Nevertheless, this feast renews our hope in our own resurrection as one complete human being despite the harsh transformation of death.
Topics: SERMON: Assumption; BVM, Assumption of; DUALISM, body/soul; RESURRECTION of the body.
Subsidiary discussions: Time (47f); Death (49f).

3. Faith and Prayer

OF.3.1. Theses on the Theme: Faith and Prayer. (53-61). *Geist und Leben* 42 (1969) 177-184.
Abstract: A 16-point guide to help religious superiors understand the difficulties this new generation of religious may have in faith (#1-7) and in prayer (#8-16), and so to assist in their formation.
Topics: FAITH; PRAYER; RELIGIOUS LIFE, formation.
Subsidiary discussions: Vocation, criteria to accept (55); Doubt (56); Prayer, education for (59f).

Precis: Faith: 1) Understanding the pluralistic and secular environment from which new vocations come encourages us to approach faith more existentially and less dogmatically. 2) The doubts and questions of the young are not vices, nor is the inability of the old to have such doubts a virtue. 3) The distinctions we find between an individual's developmental appreciation of faith and the collective faith of the church is legitimate, so long as the individual is open to growing into the faith of the group. 4) Faith today, insofar as it is not publicly supported, must constantly be realized and defended by personal decision. 5) Lapses of faith (and vocation) are more common today. We must be careful how we judge these and what we ascribe them to. 6) Lists criteria of faith required for acceptance to religious life or priesthood. 7) The present situation corresponds to the inner nature of faith. Experience is essential to appropriate the conceptual contents of faith. In the process, honest faith is vulnerable, open to question and doubts.

Prayer: 8) Prayer is an essential aspect of religious life. Routine prayer is never enough. It prepares us for deeper forms of formal prayer. 9) Self-denial (surrender to God) is a better measure of spiritual maturity than the amount of time spent in routine prayer. 10) In determining the amount of time to be spent in private prayer, we must consider other modern "spiritual" disciplines young people may be engaged in (therapy, study, support groups, etc.). 11) Over-regulation of spiritual matters leads to hypocrisy. Zeal should be the measure. Long hours in prayer are not necessarily good. Nor is brief prayer bad. 12) In religious life today, prayer is endangered. But legislation is not the answer. 13) A new theology of prayer should take us out of the realm of mythology and help us to develop new styles of prayer. 14) Spiritual directors must be trained in psychology. 15) Education in prayer is needed. Here Rahner lists five specific areas. 16) Christ is the center of all Christian prayer, and the center of the service to neighbor that leads to deeper formal prayer.

OF.3.2. On Prayer Today. (62-73). December 6, 1968 notes for a lecture to Benedictine nuns, Holy Cross Abbey, Herstelle.

Abstract: Private and liturgical prayer do not carve out a separate sacral sphere where God is found. Rather they express explicitly God's saving work unfolding at each moment in our everyday lives.

Topics: LITURGY of the world; PRAYER.

Subsidiary discussions: God, nature of (64ff); Transcendent/Categorical (67f); Sacrament: *sacramentum/res sacramenti* (67ff); Religious Life (72ff).

Precis: Both liturgical and private prayer seem endangered today. This danger takes the form of the question, "Can we pray at all?" God seems so far off. And in this secular age, prayer is often interpreted as psychological immaturity. Yet these very dangers bear within them two important truths which far from destroying our spiritual life reveal its ultimate depth: a) that in His incomprehensible, distant and silent mystery God is *nowhere*; b) that in His free, loving act of self-communication God is *everywhere*. Precisely from these preconditions both personal prayer and public worship assume their true nature.

Humans can only realize what is deepest, most transcendent in themselves by brining it to concrete, categorical expression. In this way human history is the history of God, some moments of which are definitive, irrevocable and eschatological. The greatest of these moments is the cross of Christ (68). Sacraments are privileged moments of connection with the grace of Christ. But salvation, radical surrender to God, can be mediated both there and elsewhere. Liturgical events and moments of formal prayer are not always our most radical encounters with God. This is because sacraments are signs, and are not identical with the thing signified. Formal liturgy is the explicit incarnate form of the hidden mysterious liturgy we celebrate in the mundane secularity of everyday life.

Rahner concludes (70-72) that both liturgy and prayer are revivified when they are *not* seen as respites from the secular world, or worse, as an alternative world to live in, but as the events within which the unfolding work of God in the world is made articulate in its identification with the unfolding work of Christ. Religious (like Benedictines) also live in the real world, and they have the same duty and privilege of any Christian: to make God's saving work explicit in prayer and worship. Religious do this in a special way: through living their specific founding charism, in season and out.

OF.3.3. Prayer too is Action. (74-75). Letter to Carmelite nuns, in *Christliche Innerlichkeit* (Vienna) Jan.-Feb. 1969, 1f.
Abstract: No concrete life can actualize every dimension of the Christian call. Trying to do so leads only to mediocrity. Each Christian has unique gifts and talents. Far from being provisional,

God, prayer, self-denial, renunciation are the realities that sustain love of neighbor. The question is not, therefore, whether the contemplative form of life should continue to exist, but what form it will take in the future. At times, opposition is an indispensable service. Contemplatives today should not let themselves be discouraged by loose talk. Their life is a unique element of ecclesial life to which people are still called. It is not provisional, despite the countervailing fashion of the current activist age.

Topics: PRAYER; RELIGIOUS LIFE, contemplative.

4. The Message for Today.

OF.4.1. What is the Christian message? (79-82). September 1970 working paper for *Concilium* conference.

Abstract: Changing times urgently demand new articulations of faith. Here Rahner briefly suggests the basic elements of access to, and the content of the Christian message.

Topics: CREED/s; FAITH, formal statements of.
Subsidiary discussions: God (81f).

Precis: Every religious group must put its self-understanding into words. This becomes especially urgent in fast-changing times like ours. Rahner gives some brief disclaimers and assumptions. **Formal statements on the Christian message:** The unavoidable and completely valid pluralism in theology and proclamation today affects the conceptual objectification of the Christian message. But it retains a basic unity because it is grounded in certain factors (list, 79f). Hence, certain common elements of any future formulation can be indicated (list, 80). **The contents of statements of the Christian message:** *Preliminary observations:* There are two considerations: access to the message and content. Though Rahner focuses here on content, he does mention that any approach is legitimate so long as it has a certain understanding of man and God, and is open to validation by proper church authority. **The necessary unity and the unity of what is necessary in these statements:** *Content of the Christian message:* The core of the Christian message is God: a) as mystery, b) communicating Himself, c) definitively in Jesus of Nazareth, d) thus revealing the Trinity, and e) establishing the church which hopes for the future, who is God. This message is both simple and necessary. **A**

message open towards the future, due to its incomprehensibility, and its participation in the death of Christ which radically dissolves every system.

OF.4.2. Theses on the Problem of Revelation and History. (83-85)
Lecture to Evangelical-Catholic dialogue group.
Abstract: An extremely terse and dense string of 11 points focusing on "word," probably meant to aid in Evangelical-Catholic dialogue.
Topics: WORD, theology of.

Precis: 1) A word is never simply what is stated. 2) Some words are simply statements; others are events. 3) Not even the word of salvation is identical with the salvation event. 4) This is particularly true of God's self-communication. 5) A human word can be received as the word of God only when it is heard with the ears of faith (the Spirit already at work in the hearer). 6) The word of God always has categorical and transcendent dimensions which remain together but unmixed. 7) The transcendent element of divine self-utterance always appears in the here-and-now. 8) The relation of the categorical and transcendental is not static. 9) God's self-utterance reaches its irreversible climax in Jesus of Nazareth, died and risen. 10) This eschatological word directs the world to its hoped-for future as word of promise. 11) This word continues to be expressed in the church. Its proclamation is productive, hence, "sacramental."

OF.4.3. Epochal Mutation of Christian Key-concepts. (86-91)
Abstract: When words are applied to human acts they always convey more than their verbal content. For the human acts so named are in reality the subject's attempts to posit his/her entire self. Hence, it is not surprising that often one word merges with another (e.g., faith with hope with love), or that all words prove to be partial at best. [Elsewhere Rahner calls them *Urworte*.] History shows that over time these words (e.g., sin, nature/person, *pistis*, faith) may gain or lose their evocative force. This is something over which the church has no control. Applying these insights to former theological controversies could aid dialogue with Evangelicals by revealing whether in the last 400 years these old terminological disputes have been displaced.

Topics: THEOLOGICAL LANGUAGE.
Subsidiary discussions: *Urwort* (86ff); *Metanoia* (88; 90); Dialogue, ecumenical (90f).

OF.4.4. "Sins" and Guilt. (92-93)
Abstract: Mature people today find more resonance in the tern "guilt" than "sin." All of us have discovered guilt in our lives. Guilt is not something we did. It is who we are when we deny our very nature and say "No" to the ineffable mystery which is the ultimate meaning of our existence.
Topics: GUILT; SIN.

OF.4.5. Peace as Mandate. (94-107). November 12, 1968 lecture to German Women's Circle.
Abstract: Since peace is the work of justice, there can be no peace in the private or public sphere when others are wronged. Rahner lists concrete decisions, attitudes and actions to bring about peace.
Topics: JUSTICE and peace; PEACE and justice; UTOPIA.
Subsidiary discussions: Force (94ff); Hope (105f); Future (106f).

Precis: Peace is the work of justice. We fool ourselves to think peace is a self-evident reality or that the way to peace is clear. Force is legitimate in civil society, although we must always take care not to apply force unjustly. Even if the time has come when the foolish wisdom of the gospel is our best way forward, when it comes to practical actions there can still be legitimate differences of opinion. **The institutionalized injustice of our society:** Those who would work for peace must train themselves to see the injustices in society. They are everywhere. We benefit from them. Awareness puts us into the arena of choice and hence of sin. **Temptation to take refuge in privacy:** Anyone who retreats from the "dirty business" of politics has already betrayed peace. We must engage. **Improving the political climate:** Rahner urges moving beyond the insulated frontiers of party and social group. **Breaking down the front:** we should renounce slavish party identification which is often just a way of selfishly protecting our vested interests. **Examples of our responsibility:** *Overcoming group selfishness:* The selfishness we encounter in politics is simply our own selfishness (the selfishness of "the man on the street") writ large.

Responsibility for the Third World: in a globalized world our fate and the prospects for peace are tied to all nations. Do we take this seriously? *Right of conscientious objection.* Inaction on these fronts reveals that we may want peace, but we don't want to pay for it. **When are we peace-loving?** Rahner gives a long list of very practical attributes of true lovers of peace who were praised in the Sermon on the Mount. **Creative hope and peace:** Peace cannot be attained without creative hope which does not just expect but who also acts. Peace must start with individual actions but it cannot be won in the private sphere. It is a group effort demanding radical change. **Peace of a new future:** Peace is just another name for the whole future successfully achieved. It is both an act of freedom and a gift of history and its Lord. Those who hope for this peaceful future but do nothing are liars. The future will need small personal steps, and large revolutionary ones. Even merely overcoming our personal selfishness has social ramifications.

OF.4.6. Ordinary Virtues. (108-120). *Geist und Leben* 43 (1970) 46f.

Abstract: Deeply reflecting on "ordinary virtues," which are generally taken for granted and anonymous, has theoretical and practical benefits. It clarifies the workings of human freedom and provides a valuable platform for monitoring our moral lives.

Topics: EVERYDAY LIFE; FUNDAMENTAL OPTION.

Subsidiary discussions: Sacred/secular (109ff); Sin, mortal/venial (112f, 115f); Freedom (117ff).

Precis: Suspicious as the tern "ordinary virtues" may sound, they do exist – things like punctuality, politeness, good humor. Though we take them for granted, they merit deeper reflection. **Ordinariness of grace.** There is no sacral sphere of life where salvation is achieved. All time and activities are graced, and we forge our eternal relationship with God in the most ordinary, mundane events. **Littleness of ordinary life:** Nevertheless, ordinary life remains ordinary. Rahner draws a parallel to serious and venial sin. Ordinary virtues would be comparable to "venial" good acts. Yet this would seem once again to reduce their theological importance. **Dialectic of the littleness of ordinary life and the basic decision of freedom:** Inevitably we make a final option for or against God. This may be done in a big, thematically religious act, or in a seemingly very small ordinary act that sums up our final disposition. We cannot know absolutely. Summary: despite the valid distinction between slight and grave acts, ordinary virtuous acts can be either. **Waiting for the coming of the Lord:** Ordinary life generally only provides scope for slight actions. The *kairos* of life-decision is a gift from God for which we must hold ourselves in readiness. We do this precisely in our fidelity to ordinary virtues, hoping that by being faithful in small things we may be faithful in great trials. **Liberation for the objective task and for the obvious:** The moral realm is always the realm of personal freedom. Though every free human act has an objective and subjective pole, in any particular choice one may fully eclipse the other. The value of ordinary virtues is their objectivity (concreteness) which makes them more accessible to reflection. They can more easily reveal how self-forgetful, how altruistic we are becoming. **Anonymity of ordinary life:** To be more practical it might be good to draw up a list of ordinary virtues. But this is impossible, especially in a changing world. In fact they are only the concrete form of the higher virtues lived out in ordinary life. Ordinary virtues are the sum total of contemporary morals, and as such they are anonymous, merely taken for granted.

5. Living Testimony

OF.5.1. Teresa of Avila: Doctor of the Church. (123-126). *Ecclesia* (Madrid) 30 (1970) September 26, 1970 (23f).

Abstract: Taking seriously the church's declaration that St. Teresa of Avila is a Doctor of the Church invites us to reexamine the nature of mystical experience and mystical theology.

Topics: THEOLOGY, Mystical; THERESA of Avila, St.

Subsidiary discussions: Women in the church (123); John of the Cross, St. (126).

Precis: If declaring Teresa of Avila a doctor of the church was not just a "handsome gesture" to women, what do her great teachings on mysticism teach the universal church? **Teacher of mysticism:** First it raises some old questions about mystical visions and prophecies (list, 124) with fresh urgency. These questions are far from being answered today, especially with the modern development of comparative mysticism which takes seriously the phenomenon of mysticism in other faith traditions. **Mysticism within the present horizon of understanding.** In an age when some question the very possibility of having a personal experience of God, the classical mystics are particularly adept at making such an experience intelligible. They point to the "mystical" climax of all human life in contemplation. Of course, in order to be fully understood and appreciated their teachings must be expressed in contemporary terms. Perhaps Teresa with her more frankly visionary (concrete) mysticism and earthy practical wisdom might be a more sympathetic guide today than the more negative, unworldly St. John of the Cross.

OF.5.2. Thinker and Christian: Obituary of Romano Guardini. (127-131). October 2, 1968 Bavarian Radio broadcast.

Abstract: After presenting a brief biography of Guardini, Rahner mentions some of the areas of his work. How one interprets his output depends on how one interprets the times. Rahner gives his interpretation, suggesting that the church won the struggle against Modernism, but lost insofar as the defenses it erected could not be sustained in the long run. Guardini and a few men of his generation provided alternatives to the church's pre-WWI reactionary stance. Guardini was a representative of *Kulturkatholizismus* insofar as he had a deep conviction that Catholicism could have a mutually fruitful dialogue with contemporary culture. In this way he and others like him set the stage for Vatican II. We must be grateful for his fidelity.

Topics: CHURCH, pre-conciliar situation; GUARDINI, Romano; VATICAN II, pre-conciliar generation.

OF.5.3. A Man at Play: Panegyric for Hugo Rahner. (132-134). *IHS* (Zurich) 1969, no. 2.

Abstract: Rahner gives a panegyric tribute to his recently deceased brother.

Topics: RAHNER, Hugo.

OF.5.4. Confidence and Composure in Sickness. (135-138). June 21, 1970 sermon at the teaching hospital at the University of Münster.

Abstract: After conceding how difficult it is for those who are well to address the sick, Rahner states that sickness is just one more of the great questions with which the mystery of life is filled. Sickness demands from us a response to the mystery of life. Hence, sickness is not simply a fact, it is a task. It requires simultaneously confidence and resignation. We can never capitulate to the creeping powerlessness of death, "... we should let God's providence overpower us" (136). Part of the task of sickness is to remain grateful to those caring for us. If this sounds preachy, Rahner excuses himself for appealing to the sick as still being capable of actions such as confidence, resignation and love. Sickness remains a question, a mystery. Whoever accepts this question thereby participates in the death of Christ, simultaneously acknowledging one's God-forsakenness and yet surrendering to God in faith, hope and love.
Topics: DEATH: EVERYDAY LIFE, sickness; SURRENDER.
Subsidiary discussions: Jesus Christ, death of (137f).

OF.5.5. The Doctor and Good Friday. (139-144). *Tribuna Medica* (Madrid) March 25, 1970 (14f).
Abstract: Good Friday raises special questions for doctors. The first surround the actual death of Jesus and its special meaning. The second concerns the links between the death of a patient, Christ's death, and the doctor's own. Failing to examine these links, the doctor is turning his back on the meaning of life.
Topics: DEATH; JESUS CHRIST, death of.

Precis: The kinds of questions forming in the mind of a Christian physician celebrating Good Friday are of two types: **1) The medical facts:** yet in light of historical science we can scarcely say more than Jesus was scourged and died on the cross. **2) Pious exaggerations:** there is no need to insist (as some do) that Jesus had a special capacity to suffer and so underwent a uniquely excruciating death. What is unique is not the length or acuteness of biological pain but the degree of his free acceptance of death. **A sublime example:** Though Jesus' death is consubstantial with our own, yet it remains a sublime and ultimately unique moral example. One should stay close to scripture to understand where this uniqueness lies (list, 142). **The doctor and death:** Doctors are present to death more frequently than most others. The death of others confronts us with our own mortality. But the Christian doctor is called on to interpret these events more profoundly as mysteriously united with the death of Christ. A doctor would be missing the boat to say that s/he is interested in patients only insofar as they are alive. To do so actually bypasses life.

6. Priesthood and Religious Upheaval
OF.6.1. Current Discussion on the Celibacy of the Secular Priest: An Answer. (148-167). August 1, 1948 lecture to German-speaking rectors; *Geist und Leben* (1968) 285-304.

Abstract: Reviews the main arguments for and against priestly celibacy, and shows the relative strengths and weaknesses of both positions. He views the present crisis over celibacy as fundamentally a crisis of faith and asks whether young people today are capable of renunciation for an eschatological good?

Topics: CELIBACY; PRIESTHOOD, celibacy in; RENUNCIATION.

Subsidiary discussions: Faith and renunciation (148ff); Marriage, dignity of (151f; 159f); Church, order and charism in (157ff).

Precis: It is important to state the question of celibacy correctly, and to keep in mind that in the future it may take a very different form.
The ultimate reason for the present crisis of celibacy: Though many factors contribute to the crisis surrounding celibacy, it is basically a present-day lack of faith. It must be asked whether young priests and candidates for priesthood have really appropriated a faith that is capable of renouncing the goods of this present life. In this nexus of faith, renunciation and public witness, priesthood and celibacy, are intrinsically if not essentially related.
Mechanisms of the arguments for and against celibacy: The arguments for and against celibacy are often rife with unexamined assumptions: *Celibacy more highly esteemed as a result of devaluing marriage:* although this appeal was made in the past, in fact the higher the value placed on marriage the better we can understand the radical renunciation in celibacy. Though marriage can be an obstacle to full surrender to God, we must not make the absurd claim that non-celibate clergy are incapable of such surrender. *Purely verbal with respect for the recognition of renunciation of marriage in scripture:* People today do not fully appreciate the

evangelical council to celibacy, however much lip service they may pay to it. *A decision of practical reason:* No one can argue there is a necessary connection between celibacy and priesthood. But it is also possible that in the church things that were once optional can over time become binding (e.g., the number of sacraments). Few human issues can be solved by an appeal to theoretical reasoning. Practically, celibacy is no panacea. It will have its own frustrations and drawbacks.

Arguments and objections against celibacy: *The psychological arguments:* healthy psycho-sexual development is imperative and the church has not always done all it could to promote it. But there is no essential link between celibacy and neuroses, so long as celibacy is lived as renunciation and not as repression. Renunciation can be a healthy choice.

Practical considerations: Every form of life has practical, daily hardships. Abandoning priestly celibacy is not the only way to mitigate these difficulties. Rahner suggests more communal living and heightened fraternity among priests.

The argument based on legalized compulsion and the juridical institutionalizing of celibacy: the church is wrong to insist on linking celibacy and priestly ministry. It cannot legislate a charism. Rahner responds first that no one has a "legal right to priesthood." Also, it is not illegitimate that someone might simply endure a particular disfavored condition (celibacy) for the sake of possessing a greater good (priesthood). Those who completely separate the two dimensions of the church, charism and order, and claim that the church cannot require a charism for admission to orders, fail to understand the church, and reduce it to the status of civil bureaucracy. Finally, to insist that people are not capable of making such a life-long commitment is to deny the essence of both marriage and priesthood.

The argument based on the possibility of a personal vocation to pastoral work without the charism of celibacy: Although there may be many such talented people, Rahner reminds the reader that no one has a moral claim to priesthood. The challenge is to find other ways to use the talents of such people, a move that could free priests from responsibilities which are not properly theirs.

Shortage of priests: How deep the priest shortage is depends in part on assumptions about how priests are actually being utilized.

Perhaps redistribution is a more obvious solution than making celibacy optional. Also those available to serve today in a non-celibate clergy are an "oddly mixed type" – a peculiar generation that may well soon pass from the scene. Rahner can imagine a very different ecclesio-social picture in which celibacy would again be highly prized (164).

The argument based on statistical investigations: Much helpful information can be gleaned from sociological surveys. But the church is directed by the Holy Spirit, not by polls. In any case, it remains imperative that priests and candidates for priesthood be examined closely on whether they have a faith that can embrace renunciation.

Rahner concludes with apologies for the way he has presented his case. In passing he also mentions two other important considerations: the church must do better to minister charitably to those who have come to the conclusion that they cannot bear the burdens of celibacy (166); to him it is axiomatic that if the priest shortage were to become acute and a relaxation of the rule of celibacy were the only way to supply pastoral needs, then the divine prescription that requires the faithful to worship takes precedence over the counsel of celibacy (161, 162).

OF.6.2. The Meaning and Justification of Priestly Celebrations.
(168-176). *Mitten in der Gemeinde.* Munich (1968) 13ff.

Abstract: As the mental horizons of the church and world shift, so do the criteria for the nature and appropriateness of "priestly celebrations." Although they are still proper, they must be redesigned.

Topics: CHURCH, nature of; PRIESTHOOD, celebrations of.

Subsidiary discussions: Church as local altar community: (172); Priesthood and mediation (173f).

Precis: Great public celebrations, including ordinations, First Masses and jubilees, are problematic today. **Change in the Christian mental horizon:** In fact, much of what was celebrated in the past and the ways it was celebrated were actually pagan, relying on a split between sacred and secular. Happily, this world view is irrevocably gone. **Celebration and feast:** People today have little appetite for celebration. They prefer escape (cinema, travel, carnivals). Yet public celebrations rightly remain as needed opportunities to bring to explicit expression important existential realities about life and society. **Celebrating church:** The church, too, must celebrate feasts to make explicit her communal nature. These feasts are not primarily "priestly" but "ecclesial." They focus not on the church itself but on what God is doing in the world. **Eucharistic celebration:** Some "priest-centered" celebration is justified, even if in going beyond the strictly liturgical it tends to separate the "object" of celebration from the central elements of salvation. For it simultaneously reinforces the truth that the essential social character of the altar community extends beyond the bounds of any "sacro-liturgical sphere." **Priestly celebration and priesthood:** Any priestly celebrations today must take into account contemporary sensitivities. While remaining warm and personal, they should celebrate priesthood and not a particular priest. This means especially taking into consideration the purely *sacramental* mediation of a priest, and not dwelling on those functions which "only the priest can do." For whatever a priest does is done in service to the church. **Acceptance by each of his own mission:** In the church of the future, marked by the individual's exercise of a freely chosen faith and not by social mores, the proper role of the servant priest will be better understood, appreciated, and even celebrated.

OF.6.3. The Future of Religious Orders in the World and Church of Today. (177-193). September 23, 1970 lecture to Jesuits.
Abstract: Former supports of religious commitment are gone forever. Our unknown future calls for an ability to live with insecurity, greater faith, more experimentation, loyalty, and reassessment of the vows. Social activism is not the complete answer. The world will still look to religious for authentic spirituality.
Topics: CHURCH, future of; RELIGIOUS LIFE, future of.
Subsidiary discussions: Church, pre-conciliar (177f); Future, *docta ingnorantia futuri* (181ff); Faith, essence of (182f); Religious Life, experimentation in (184ff); Holy Spirit, testing of (186); Religious Life, vows in (188ff); Spirituality, need for (191f).

Precis: The present situation: No longer can anything in the orders (or the church) be simply taken for granted. The church and our religious orders no longer support us; now we must support them with our free commitment. They are no longer the producers of our life decisions but the products.

The future situation: This situation, in which life is no longer shaped by the weight of tradition but by my individual free choice and expression, is likely to persist. It will bring in its wake more controversy, disagreement, and pluralism. We should just get used to it and to the insecurity it brings!

The way of faith into an unknown future: Concretely, we cannot know what the future will hold and we must be ready to endure this *docta ingnorantia futuri*. But if our faith is rooted in an embrace of the incomprehensibility of God as our future, then what have we to fear? Knowing that in the future the expression of religious life may change radically does not justify abandoning it.

The necessity of experiments: Times like these demand experimentation (properly understood). Some is justifiable, even when not sanctioned from above. Experiments can succeed even when they fail. But all healthy experimentation demands dialogue, tolerance, and self-criticism (185). In short, the Spirit can blow without our official permission. We must be on guard not to stifle the Spirit.

Loyalty in the midst of change: Though these times may call for experimentation, orders are already set on a path and are doing good work. Loyalty is also called for in this wintry season. The order represents and will continue to stand for some specific thing (187). It is not right to hijack an entire order to realize one experimental goal, however good it may be.

The three vows: *Poverty:* Between the two orientations: penury or the requirements of sustaining a common life, Rahner opts for the latter as offering a better chance for the future. He suggests that perhaps "poverty" is a misnomer. *Celibate Chastity:* If approached realistically and dispassionately in the light of everyday life, an individual can effect such renunciation as a participation in the death of Christ (a precursor to our surrender in death). Mixed motives for choosing a celibate life do not simply negate the choice. *Obedience:* Pious mythology aside, essentially nothing more is required here than can generally be asked of any human being accepting to some degree the incomprehensibility of sharing the lot of Christ. It makes no significant difference that this sharing is sometimes imposed.

Social commitment or more: The mission of an order cannot be reduced to the social horizon. All we do must originate in an explicitly grasped relationship to God, and in the church's mission of salvation. Rather than divide our hearts, these relationships make our commitment more radical. In any case, Rahner feels sure that what the world needs and will need most in the future is not social activism so much as "old fashioned" spirituality.

OF.6.4. "Making Sacrifices:" or Everyday Renunciations. (194-196). "*Opfer und Opferchen*" in *Jetzt* (Munich) I (1970) 3ff.
Abstract: Don't be too quick to disparage small sacrifices made for others. Excellence in any human field (arts, sports) demands discipline and practice. So too in Christian life. These small moments may not constitute life's decisive turning point (our final yes, or no to God) but they do prepare for them. They are small gestures of hopeful faith in the grace of God and should be cultivated, not disparaged.
Topics: EVERYDAY LIFE; RENUNCIATION.

7. The Pilgrim Church
OF.7.1. Trust within the Church. (199-203). June 25, 1968 sermon to lay student of theology at Münster.
Abstract: The focus of this article is not trusting the church, but trusting individual people (office holders) within the church. Trust (like love) means "surrendering oneself to another person without an ultimate reassurance." Trust demands: 1) giving others the benefit of the doubt and assuming their good faith; 2) the capacity for self-criticism. This is only possible in those who are truly willing to serve.
Topics: CHURCH, trust within; EVERYDAY LIFE, trust.
Subsidiary discussions: Everyday Life, self-criticism (201ff).

OF.7.2. The Duty of Discussion: A plea for Cardinal Suenens. (204-213). *Publik*, June 12., 1970 (23f).
Abstract: A frank exchange between Suenens and Paul VI on the topic of priestly celibacy presents Rahner with the opportunity to comment on collegiality (the pope cannot unilaterally interpret the mind of Vatican II), and dialogue within the church (that new forms of national dialogue are needed).

Topics: BISHOP/s, collegiality; DIALOGUE.
Subsidiary discussions: Priesthood, celibacy debate (passim).

Precis: Preliminary historical remarks: The context of this discussion is the exchange between Cardinal Suenens and Paul VI centering on the appropriateness of further collegial dialogue on the topic of priestly celibacy, even after the pope called for an end to the discussion. **What is a bishop to do?** With empty seminaries and priests departing, Suenens was caught in a dilemma between loyalty to the pope calling to end the discussion on celibacy, and sensitivity to his own people among whom the discussion continues regardless. To fulfill his proper role as bishop, the cardinal chose to speak and not remain silent, believing there are times when even a pope's position needs further discussion. At times true obedience may call for infringing the letter of the law. **The theology of dialogue:** Rahner frames the dispute in terms of collegiality, and who has the prerogative to interpret the mind of Vatican II on this issue. There are many open questions. But the way to proceed on these matters should be set out in canon law and not left simply to the prudent judgment of the pope. Suenens makes a further recommendation: bolder and more intense dialogue among all members of the church including priests and the faithful. On such complicated issues, Rahner sees this call for broader dialogue as quite reasonable. But he questions whether the structures in place today (Synod, etc.) insure this upward flow of information. The primary rationale for this broader dialogue is the very presence of the Spirit throughout the Mystical Body of Christ. **On dialogue in the individual churches:** Rahner sees Suenens' call for a new kind of more intense dialogue on the local/national levels as quite in keeping with the charismatic nature of the church as presented by Vatican II (GS 92).

OF.7.3. Experiment in the Field of Christianity and the Church.
(214-222). *Internationale Dialogzeitschrift* 3 (1970) 360ff.
Abstract: Properly understood, experimentation in the church is a permanent state.
Topics: CHURCH, experimentation in; EXPERIMENTATION.
Subsidiary discussions: Planning (218); *Conversio ad phamtasma* (219f).

Precis: Many documents of Vatican II call for "experimentation." But what is it? **Experiment – transitory happening or permanent state?:** Generally when we speak of experimentation in the church we assume it is a temporary event. Rahner hints it is actually a permanent state. **Experiment in natural science and in the church:** Experimentation in the church differs from scientific experiments in that: 1) Experiment in the church has an existential dimension. All church experiments are carried out on herself, and their effects cannot be rescinded; 2) The desired result of a church experiment is not to gain a fact or know-how, but a goal which is not known beforehand, despite the existence of certain parameters. **Church history as the radical experiment:** Beginning with the "experiment" of Christ's surrender on the cross, and continued by the Spirit, "church history is either the most radical experiment" or it is not the real history of the church. **Planned history:** Today we no longer merely endure our life and history. We promote and accelerate it by planning. Experimentation is precisely the point where our surrender to God as incomprehensible mystery meets our duty to plan the future. **Creative experiment:** In general, church leaders do not see things this way. They have much greater reservations, often based on a conditioned Thomistic model of human understanding. Experimentation is not essentially disrespectful. If the church is a pilgrim, then experiment in the church is a permanent state. **Plea for responsible experiments:** This is not an invitation to arbitrariness. In fact, theology, the attempt to express truths of the faith in new ways, is itself experimental. There are also para-canonical experiments going on all the time. Whether these are arbitrary is a judgment that cannot be made by higher authority prior to the experiment. The church cannot be reduced to a bureaucratic reality, for the living Spirit guides the church.

OF.7.4. The Church's Eucharistic Celebration and the Christian's Sunday Obligation. (223-226). November 10, 1970 public lecture at the University of Münster.

Abstract: 1. Celebrating Eucharistic rightly has a privileged place in the church. But one must not confuse the sacramental sign for what is signified, and fall into apotheosis. Existentially, the celebration of liturgy is not always the highest expression of one's life of faith. **2.** Nothing in the essential nature of Christianity or the church imposes any particular frequency for individual participation in Eucharist. Weekly Sunday worship is a positive law of the church. In Europe, weekly participation should not be the sole criterion for church membership or Christian existence. **3.** Since the realm of the operation of grace extends well beyond the sacraments, it is justifiable to consider whether some activity other than the sacraments might be a more efficacious Sunday activity. **4.** A proper understanding of sacraments might lead us to view and celebrate Eucharist as *one* privileged moment in the ongoing redemptive work of Christ.

Topics: SACRAMENT/s, nature of ; SUNDAY OBLIGATION.
Subsidiary discussions: Liturgy, sacramental nature of (223f).

On Prayer. NY: Paulist Press. 1968. Cf., *On the Need and the Blessing of Prayer.* NBP.

TD. *On the Theology of Death*, NY: Herder, 1972. With "On Martyrdom." 127 pp. *Zur Theologie des Todes*, Freiburg: Herder, 1961. *Questiones Disputatae* Series, #2. Translated with Preface by Charles H. Henkey.

Contents: Preface.
Introduction.
On the Theology of Death. (Treated as 3 independent essays.)
  I. Death as an Event Concerning Man as a Whole.
  II. Death as the Consequence of Sin.
  III. Death as Dying with Christ.
On Martyrdom.

TD.Intro. Preface by Charles H. Henkey; Introduction by Rahner.
Abstract: The *Preface* offers a word on the task of theology today and on Rahner's contribution as a theologian, his life and method. The *Introduction*, after discussing the relationship of theology to faith and to the magisterium, justifies the outline of the essay and explains its obvious limitations.

Topics: THEOLOGY, method.
Subsidiary discussions: Rahner, biography (9ff); Theology and faith (14f); Theology and magisterium (16f).

Precis: Preface. Theology must do more than conserve the past. Basing itself on scripture and magisterial teaching it must constantly occupy itself with questions raised by the world today. Henkey concludes with a brief overview of Rahner's career, and defends Rahner's preferred genre, the essay. **Introduction.** After discussing how faith and theology condition one another while remaining distinct (14f), Rahner proceeds to discuss the method he employs here. He will first present as objectively as possible what is immediately and explicitly contained in proper sources of faith concerning death. Then he will seek to formulate a proper "theology of death." One must not be surprised to discover that many formal church teachings are relatively clear and simple, but at the level of theoretical theology they contain many unclear, inchoate and problematic points. This is often due to theoretical theology's reliance on many metaphysical methods, concepts and theories extrinsic to theology itself. Finally, to some it may seem misguided to treat the mystery of death in such a cool and analytical fashion. But without such reflection how can we face death with open eyes? The essay itself begins with asking what the church clearly teaches and then develops a more systematic, but by no means complete, theology of death. The three division of the work are suggested by the topic itself: those church teachings which are: I. Existentially neutral and address every human death; II. Death as the decisive event for sinful man; III. Death insofar as it is the highest act of appropriation of salvation based on the death of Christ.

TD.1.1. I. Death as an Event Concerning Man as a Whole. (21-39)
Abstract: A look at death's "existentially neutral" elements as they affect the whole person: the universality of death insofar as it affects all people; the effect of death on the whole person insofar as it affects the substantial unity of body and soul; the finality of death insofar as we achieve definitiveness.
Topics: DEATH, existential elements of; MAN, substantial unity of.
Subsidiary discussions: Death, universality of (21ff); Death as separation of body and soul (24ff); Angels, relation to the cosmos (31f); Purgatory (32f, 35); Resurrection of the body (33f, 35). Time and eternity (36); Man, historicity of (36f); Judgment, final (37f).

Precis: Preview. Because humans are a substantial unity of nature and person, our death possesses both personal and natural dimensions. By the natural aspect, the church means the definitive end of our state of pilgrimage. This, together with a reflection on the universality of death, rounds out Part I of the essay. **1. The universality of death.** All people are subject to the law of death. This divinely revealed statement says more than the mere syllogistic or biological statement. It posits sin as the spiritual origin and cause of death. Only from this spiritual viewpoint can one ever fathom the meaning of universal death.

2. Death as the separation of body and soul: this is how Catholic doctrine describes death. Though this is not a biblical expression, it is found from the early Fathers to the latest catechism. It is true insofar as it says that in death the soul (one's spiritual life force) assumes a different relationship to the body, and it underscores the imperishability of the soul. But the statement is not fully adequate insofar as it does not satisfy the demands of metaphysics (25f); it does not explain whether this separation is accidental or the result of some deeper dynamic; the concept of "separation" remains unclear. Of special concern to Rahner is whether the separated soul's new relation to the world is "a-cosmic" in a Neoplatonic sense, or "all-cosmic" (26ff). Rahner concludes this discussion by saying it is permissible to suppose the separated human soul "will, in some way or other, maintain its relation to the world" (29), becoming all-cosmic. Although this obviously happens in a special restricted sense, it is conceivable that the soul would continue to have a real ontological influence on the whole of the universe. Here the deeper study of angels and their relation to the world might prove helpful (31f). It might also shed some light on the doctrines of Purgatory (32f) and the resurrection of the body (33f).

3. Death as concluding man's state of pilgrimage. This third proposition is directed more to "person" than to "nature." It attests to the coming to finality of man as a moral-spiritual being— a kind of consummation of one's decision for or against God, leaving open the possibility of development after death (Purgatory and bodily resurrection), since even beatitude must be viewed as a never-ending movement of the finite spirit toward God. This points to our essential historicity, which achieves its eternity in time through death. Although this perspective answers certain questions, it leaves open many questions about divine judgment (37f). At any rate, because death is personal it must also be understood as a human act, as a deed originating from within. It is not merely suffered passively. In this final act the soul itself achieves the consummation of its own personal self-affirmation. When we take with full seriousness the substantial unity of man, then the effects of death cannot be assigned to either the body or to the soul, thereby dissolving man's very essence. This ontological unity of acting and suffering in death has a meaning which will be shown later. [TD.1.2. begins with an excellent summary of TD.1.1]

TD.1.2. II. Death as the Consequence of Sin. (40-63)
Abstract: Though death is a consequence of sin, its natural essence contains a positive meaning. The sting of death is its obscurity: our inability to know if the end we achieve in death (consummation) is fullness or emptiness. Sinful approaches to death dismiss one or the other dialectical dimension of death's mystery. This affects our understanding of the original sin of Adam, personal mortal sin, and the sin of the angels.
Topics: DEATH; DEATH of Adam; SIN and death.
Subsidiary discussions: Salvation/damnation status (46); Fundamental Option (51f); Sin, mortal (51f, 57f); Sin, original (55ff); Death and devil (59ff); Angels, sin of (60ff).

Precis: After summarizing the first three propositions set forth in TD.1.1, Rahner examines a fourth: "death is a consequence of sin" – our death as the death of Adam, as the death of a sinner. He begins with a recap of the basic teaching of the church that death is the visible demonstration of the fact that man has fallen away from God as a consequence of the sin of Adam, and the subsequent loss of original justice.

1. Adam's freedom from death. It is incorrect to infer from the statement that death is a consequence of sin that had Adam not sinned he would have lived this life endlessly in Paradise. In fact, he would have experienced an end to this life, but in a different way: in an act of pure, active, self-affirmation. This "death without dying" would have been without suffering any violent dissolution of his actual bodily constitution through a power from without. This points to the fact that not every aspect of death can be considered a consequence of sin that ought not to have been.

2. **Death as guilt and as a natural consequence.** Death as consummation cannot be completely a consequence of the fall. It is a doctrine of faith that the death we actually do experience also has a natural essence with positive meaning in itself. As a natural event it must contain the potentiality of dying in either of two directions: as a punishment for sin (the death of Adam) or as a dying with Christ (the death of Christ). Since in the individual case this direction is determined "by the attitude with which man as a person, sustains this natural essence" (44), objectively we can never know which death any particular individual died. In short, death is never *merely* a natural process, though it must also be a natural element of human nature. Were this not the case, then death could not be an event of salvation or damnation and still remain one in all people.

3. **Further exploration of the essence of natural death, in virtue of which it can be an event of salvation or of damnation.** What is the natural essence of death that allows it to bear this ambiguous character? The answer is its darkness. This requires further explanation. We experience death as an end affecting both body and soul. But "end" is a varying, highly analogous concept we often misapply when dealing with different levels of reality. Applied to humans, "end" constitutes an irreconcilable, real-ontological contradiction (48). As a spiritual person death is our active, immanent consummation; but as a biological being it is our destruction, an accident that strikes us from outside . . . a thief in the night. To suppress one or the other dimension of death misrepresents it. The problem here is not *whether* man does or does not continue after death, but *how*. Due to the dual nature of death, however, it is never possible to say whether the fullness, the "end" reached in death may not prove to be an emptiness which had previously been concealed in a busy life, or whether what had previously seemed emptiness may not prove to be true plenitude. "No human experience will ever be able to reveal whether death is truly a pure perfection or a pure end of the man who died. Death is indeed hidden" (summary, 50).

The death of Adam before the fall would not have been hidden in darkness. That we experience death as suffering, visibly manifests the absence of divine grace and proves death is the penalty of sin. Understanding death as an act of consummation and not as an isolated act at the end of life allows us to see how, implicitly or explicitly, death can be mortal sin. Rahner concludes by contrasting the proper human way to face death with two false ways, each of which denies the complete dialectical mystery of death in its own way. We should face death as an act of complete self-surrender with unconditional openness to the disposal of the incomprehensible decision of God, since due to the darkness of death we cannot dispose of ourselves freely and knowingly. The sinful understanding of death insists it is simply natural. This manifests itself either in despair or in inflating the spiritual or the corporeal meaning of one's own essence. The first faulty "autonomous interpretation" of death sees it is liberation from materiality; the second sees it as a biological process that heralds our silent return to impersonal nature.

4. **Death as a penalty for original sin.** After the sin of Adam, the death we experience is veiled in a darkness which can hide either salvation or damnation. But this darkness of death is a moment proper to death itself. It belongs to death as a natural process and is the immediate result of our spiritual-bodily nature. The punishment-dimension of death which we feel is not this darkness, but a demand for that superiority over death which Adam once possessed. This is what makes me experience death as something against my concrete nature and against myself as existing in this concrete nature, and hence as an actual loss or penalty. Since Adam's fall we no longer possess a pure nature, although we retain our supernatural destiny as a gift, obligation and task [supernatural existential] with its tendency toward consummation from within. Hence, we currently experience a death "that should not be," a consequence and punishment of a loss which is ours due to the sin of Adam. This death is no punishment imposed extrinsically by God. Rather it is the expression and manifestation of sin itself. Here Rahner links the punishment-dimension of death to both original sin (56) and to concupiscence (57).

5. **Death as personal mortal sin.** Death is not only the expression in body and soul of our alienation due to Adam's sin. Scripture (especially St. Paul) insists it is also a consequence of our grave personal sin. "As in the case of original sin, so here too, death is an intrinsic, essential expression, the visible appearance of these per-

sonal sins in the entire reality of man, body and soul"(58). Saints are no exception.

6. **Death and the devil** seem related by the fact that the devil tempted the first man to sin. But this leaves open two questions: the relationship of the devil and death in the sub-human world (not explored here), and the degree of intimacy between the devil and the sinful death of man, which is assumed here. This leads to a discussion of the relationship of non-material beings to the material world (60f) which infuses the cosmos with a drive toward death as consummation (but in the fallen angels to a death without grace). Human beings ratify this cosmic evil consummation with their free, sinful acts.

Summary (61ff). Metaphysics alone cannot explain why natural death inspires dread. Theology insists we rightly fear death because we should not die, insofar as we are oriented to share divine life. Our experience of death is the consequence of the sin of Adam which we ratify with each personal sin. Though such a death contains the note of divine judgment, it is primarily the revelation of the emptiness of sin itself, and we rightly shrink from this mysterious horror. To deny this horror by misinterpreting death we really only pursue that which we most dread: a beginning of eternal death. Death and our attitude towards it will only be transformed in the light of the death and resurrection of Christ.

TD.1.3. III. Death as Dying with Christ. (64-88)

Abstract: Christ's death shares many characteristics with ours, chiefly its darkness. Rahner supplements Anselm's satisfaction theory of redemption to show why it is precisely the *death* of Christ that redeems us, and how His death transforms death. Participating in His death (visibly in sacraments) transforms our deaths in faith hope and love, without thereby ridding death of its darkness.

Topics: DEATH; JESUS CHRIST, death of.

Subsidiary discussions: Creed, He descended into hell (65, 71f, 74); Redemption, satisfaction theory of (66ff); Theological Virtues and death (79f); Sacraments and the death of Christ (80ff); Baptism and the death of Christ (82f); Eucharist and the death of Christ (83ff); Anointing of the Sick and the death of Christ (85f).

Precis: The previous section attempted to show that death (as a neutral, natural phenomenon) can equally be an event of salvation or damnation. This section tries to show how death can be a revelation of our saving participation in the death of Christ (preview, 64). **1. The death of Christ.** Christ dies our death. His substantial identity with human death is indicated in the creed, "He descended into hell." It has already been shown that death has many dimensions. Christ's death does also. And it is not clear on which of these dimension/s of Jesus' death our redemption is based. This leads to a discussion of Anslem's satisfaction theory of redemption (66f), its positive contents (67f), and its shortcomings (68f). Among these shortcomings are its inability to explain why it is precisely through the act of death that redemption comes about, and whether it embraces the full biblical meaning of Christ's death (active and passive). In assuming the "flesh of sin" Jesus assumed an existence that could only reach its consummation by passing through death in all its darkness in the emptiness of the bodily end. In an act of absolute freedom He enacted and suffered death as the revelation of sin in the world, "and as an act of the revelation of that divine grace which rendered divine the life of his humanity and which, by reason of his own divine person, belonged to him of natural necessity" (69). Through His death, death becomes something absolutely different from what it might be for us. The very darkness of death which Christ also endured becomes the condition of the possibility of an absolute Yes to the will of the Father. The real differences between how Christ and how we face death are not so great as to destroy their intrinsic similarity (70f). This explains, according to Rahner, why it is precisely through His death that we are redeemed.

This leaves two questions: why Christ's death is *our* redemption, since we are different persons than He? What might be added to the theology of death to complete the usual satisfaction theory? Here Rahner returns to the idea he developed in TD.1.1 (21ff) on the possibility of the separated soul establishing a new, open, unrestricted relationship with the cosmos, not unlike that of angels. Applied to the death of Christ we can say the spiritual reality He enacted in His life and brought to consummation in His death "becomes open to the whole world and is inserted into this world as a permanent destiny of a real-ontological kind" (71).

In support of this position he refers to his interpretation of the doctrine of Christ's descent into hell (72). Rahner reiterates his anti-Gnostic stance that in death the soul does not lose its relationship with the spatio-temporal dimension of the world but is for the first time rendered open to it. Christ's death transformed the world when His reality, consummated by death, was grafted unto the cosmos and became its destiny– something that could only be done through death. Rahner finds further confirmation of his interpretation in the widely held doctrine of the physical instrumental causality of Christ's humanity with respect to grace for all people after Christ (74).

2. **The death of the Christian as a dying with Christ** is different from the death of a sinner –not just the outcome, but the death itself. According to Trent, for the Christian in the state of grace death no longer has the mark of punishment. It is simply the consequence of sin (*poenalitas sed non poena*) which serves for purification. But this is obscure. The New Testament goes much farther: "our assumption of Christ's death begins in principle with Baptism and faith, while the process of dying with Christ, and winning the new life it offers, penetrates our life here on earth" (76). But how does this take place? What is particular about the death of Christ is that, as the manifestation of sin, it was transformed in Him into a revelation of grace: "the emptiness of man into the great event of God's fullness.... Death was changed into life" (78). "His death, as an act of grace, helped to offer to God the 'flesh of sin' –which death really is– transforming it into a flesh of grace; so that we now can, through his grace, belong to God and to Christ in death, despite the fact that death, in itself, means remoteness from God" (79). What then do Christians achieve in death through the grace of Christ? We experience the true darkness and bitterness of death, but in a surrender in faith, hope and love. These theological virtues transform death itself, making it the highest act of believing, hoping and loving, They change the dread of my heart from "My God my God, why have you abandoned me?" to, "Into your hands I commend my spirit."

3. **The sacramentally visible union between the death of Christ and the death of a Christian** constitute privileged encounters with Christ through the church, but without exhausting the range of such encounters. This union occurs much more broadly every

time a person in the state of grace freely accepts God's grace which always intends the transformation of the entire person. Still the sacraments do incarnate and make visible the most basic and decisive cases of the encounter of God and man in Christ. The appropriation of the death of Christ which transforms our own death happens not in a moment but over a lifetime. Three sacraments in particular aim at this appropriation, and Rahner discusses in turn Baptism (82f), Eucharist (83ff), and Anointing of the Sick (85f), ending with a summary (86).

Grand Summary (86ff). For all that has been said about death, Rahner fears he has actually said very little. He has tried to show how nothing in the world is more important than the death of Christ. Since we have received the vocation to die with Christ, our earthly death is raised to the level of a divine mystery. "In order to understand this mystery and to perform it worthily in the liturgy of our life, we must contemplate the death of the Crucified" (87). Rahner uses the analogy of the two crucified thieves at Golgotha to illustrate how Christians must surrender to God's promise, but always in fear and trembling.

TD.2. On Martyrdom. (89-127)

Abstract: Rahner restores martyrdom to its central place in Christian life. He shows its intrinsic connection to the theology of death, to freedom, and to the essential holiness of the church. Along the way he addresses a number of ancillary problems including salvation outside the church.

Topics: DEATH, martyrdom; MARTYRDOM.

Subsidiary discussions: Death and freedom (93ff); Freedom and death (93ff); God, universally salvific will of (98ff); Salvation outside the church (98ff); Death of unbaptized infants (98f); Sacraments and grace (100f); Church, holiness of (108ff); Baptism by blood (110f); Sacrament, martyrdom as a (110f); Church and martyrdom (112f); Death, good or bad (118f); Anonymous Christian, death of (120ff).

Precis: Martyrdom and its relation to Christian death should not be left on the margins of theology. What is the fundamental connection between witness to Christ and death? Is it accidental or intrinsic? There are many superficial ways to connect them (list,

90f). But the mystery of martyrdom is generally concealed in the incomprehensible mystery of death. This leads to a discussion of death as more than a mere biological ending, which is not well expressed as the separation of body and soul. For death is fundamentally an inescapable, voluntary act. Here the instant of death must be seen as the end of the process of death– the death of death. Whether it opens to a second death or to the victory of life remains hidden. Seen properly, death is the free act of living. Our freedom does not encompass the power *not* to die, only the power to choose *how* we die, the attitude we take toward death. The choice is to run the course of life toward this end either protestingly or lovingly. Our answer is seldom theoretical, but becomes clear in our actions.

What then is the correct Christian interpretation of death? First, the Christian must accept death freely but as an inescapably "imposed liberty." This attitude separates us from animals, "for wherever there is free liberty, there is love for death and there is courage to face death" (95). Secondly, this liberty is freedom to abandon ourselves, to say "yes" both to death and to the full meaning of existence. It allows us to embrace death as consummation, an "endless end." This can only be done in an act of faith made in light of the seeming destruction of everything. Such faith allows the Christian to interpret the "downfall" of death as the surrender to the "Father" in faith, hope and love. This faith can only be guaranteed and enacted by the grace of Christ. Such a death is no longer the death of Adam but the death of Christ (96).

These statements involve theological difficulties. Chief among them is the prospect that one could live a life of meritorious acts that failed to rise to the level of supernatural moral acts. Such a death would then be non-sinful but also non-salvific (96f). Is this possible? Bracketing certain borderline cases, Rahner follows Ripalda in arguing against the possibility of morally significant but supernaturally neutral acts (97-103). His argument centers on understanding God's universally salvific will, and points to the problems that stem from confusing the condition of salvation with historical comprehensibility and visibility (100), for grace and sacrament are not coterminous. How then can we envision the basic human situation whereby we, through our free decisions, can be brought to attain a supernatural act and thus salvation (even outside the historical reality of the church)? In brief, Rahner argues that whenever we arrive at a free decision about ourselves, we are capable of a *fides virtualis* that can be elevated by interior grace (102). Furthermore, Straub argues that it is possible that whenever we are forced to make a moral decision, we are always deciding between salvation and damnation *within* the supernatural order as such. Since death certainly is such a consummate moral act, Rahner concludes: "Christian death is the free liberty of faith, which in reality and in truth presides over the whole of life, and leads us to accept the rupture of this moral existence as the most wise, loving disposition of God" (104).

The nature and hence the outcome of such a death, however, remain veiled to human eyes here and now. The act is ambiguous. In fact in the act of death, freedom reaches its highest point of ambiguity since the deed and the doer disappear from view into the mystery of God's sole judgment. But is there *any* death whose appearances do disclose this reality? Such a revelatory and self-explanatory Christian death would also be the most perfect Christian witness since it would manifest visibly and comprehensively the consummation of Christian life. This "beautiful death" which reveals the Christian essence of death is the martyrdom of the faithful (105). To reveal itself as an act of free liberty it must be concretely avoidable *and* be imposed by external violence (vs. suicide), just as when Jesus freely laid down his life (summary, 106). But when and how is death that act which reveals faith? This is not so simple when one considers the general law that every death remains ultimately enigmatic in the eyes of human judgment. So how can we discern the martyr's death and distinguish it from that of a fanatic?

To know why a death in faith, a witnessing death, is also a martyrdom in the eminent sense we must study the background: the holiness of the church (108-115). In the witnessing death of martyrdom the essential holiness of the church is manifested in a precise and certain manner as the highest expression of faith and love. Here, in order to sanctify the church and to make her appear holy, divine power overcomes the gap between human existence in God's eyes and in the eyes of the world, between supra-historical truth and historical appearance, between interior spirit and empirical fact. Because the martyr's death belongs to the essence of the church, and because the church must be forever the visible sign of grace in the world, there will always be martyrs. This explains the ancient link between martyrdom and baptism (110). Though martyrdom is not a sacrament in the strict sense, this is not because it is *less*, but because it is *more* than a sacrament. It is "supra-sacrament" insofar as it unfailingly brings together the sign and the thing signified, overcoming the ambiguity that attaches to other sacraments. Here we have perfectly consummated the indissoluble unity of the testimony and the thing witnessed. "Church and martyrdom testify to each other reciprocally" (112). Given all that has been said about martyrdom, death and the church (summary, 113f) the question remains whether, in order to be a real testimony and a motive for faith, martyrdom must not manifest visibly the sign that it is a witnessing act. Rahner is content to say that in such an act a miracle of grace can be distinguished from fanaticism, but only to those who are helped by the grace of God to see in martyrdom the grounds of faith (115).

Clearly this does not exhaust the topic of martyrdom. Other questions could be raised, other approaches could be taken (list, 115f). Rahner looks particularly into the question of voluntary death and what separates the "good death" of martyrdom from the "bad death" of suicide or fanaticism. Here he insists that motive, what one dies for, is not enough. Scholastic morality rightly maintains that in a good act, intention is always wedded to concrete action. Intention implies an entitative difference. And when it comes to the act of total self-consummation this difference must be recognizable. This leads to a further discussion of the difference between a good and a bad death (118f). He concludes that a truly good death, one that is loved and embraced and not merely endured, should be verifiable by observation (119).

One further point: in martyrdom, death is loved in itself as a sharing in the Lord's death. It is not merely endured or loved for what it affects. Does such a death occur as an historically demonstrable reality outside Christianity? Rahner says, no. Because only Christianity justifies in theory what one does in reality (121). (Here Rahner includes "Christians in spirit" though not in name.) This good death of consummated freedom "draws its strength from that for the sake of which the man dies. In other words: this death is good, because it occurs for the sake of the crucified and dead Christ" (121). Rahner realizes that the martyr's death which may engender credibility is not logically compelling. The act of martyrdom always retains the possibility of an equivocal interpretation. It is recognized for what it is only by one who in his heart is already a Christian. But it can still provide a motive for faith insofar as it can be known naturally (empirically) in the presence of two factors: one's insuppressible human nature, and God's grace which continually reveals things we would just as soon suppress.

Being what it is (summary, 124) martyrdom's high esteem in the church (list, 124f) comes as no surprise. Future attention should be given to the modes of martyrdom, especially to modern, practically anonymous and dehumanizing deaths —deaths of anguish and weakness— that aim at breaking the spirit, killing victims before they die. Rahner suggests that perhaps these deaths are closer to those of Jesus' death than are those of any past martyrs. Rahner concludes the essay by exhorting the reader to pray for a faithful heart ready to follow Christ even by sharing in His death.

PM. *Prayers for Meditation.* With Hugo Rahner. NY: Herder and Herder, 1962. 71 pp.
Gebete der Einkehr. Translated by Rosaleen Brennan. (* authorship by Karl Rahner)
Contents: Foreword
A Blessing on our Beginning.
*Before God.
Christ as our Choice.
Sin and Conscience.
*Between Grace and Judgment.
*The Imitation of Christ.
*The Life of Grace.
*The Holy Ghost.
*The Sacrament of the Altar.
Study and Daily Life.
*Christ all in all.
*Dedication to the Blessed Virgin.
Return to Everyday Life.
*A Blessing on our Ending.

Foreword (7-8). The form of these prayers before the Blessed Sacrament reveals their origin: first given at a university retreat to sum up each day's conferences. They can also aid everyday Christians in their common and private prayer.

A Blessing on our Beginning. (Prayers contributed by Fr. Hugo Rahner are not abstracted.)

PM.1. Before God. (12-19)
Abstract: A sinner comes into God's presence and falters, not knowing how to address God or what to say. Sorting out the relationship, the petitioner (mediocre even in his/her sins) knows all s/he can ask for is pity and mercy. This is the only stance that gives one the confidence to face the darkness of one's sin.
Topics: GOD, prayer to; MAN, as sinner.

Christ as our Choice
Sin and Conscience

PM.2. Between Grace and Judgment. (30-33)
Abstract: This post-reconciliation reflection, after praising God's inexhaustible patience, reads like an examination of conscience, the penitent asking whether s/he will use well the time remaining till final judgment. S/he asks the Lord for His continued companionship now and at the hour of death.
Topics: JUDGMENT; PENANCE, fruits of.

PM.3. The Imitation of Christ. (34-38)
Abstract: In the mystery of the Incarnation, Jesus shares our human lot completely, and shares with us all He has from the Father. We desire to imitate Him in our prayer, and witness to His truth in the world.
Topics: INCARNATION; JESUS CHRIST, imitation of.

PM.4. The Life of Grace. (39-43)
Abstract: A hymn of praise to the Holy Spirit – God's grace dwelling within us – and a prayer to Jesus present in the Blessed Sacrament to fill us now and always with that Spirit.
Topics: SPIRIT/s.

PM.5. The Holy Ghost. (44-48)
Abstract: A prayer for discernment and for the Spirit's many gifts and fruits.
Topics: SPIRIT/s, discernment of ; SPIRIT/s, fruits of.

PM.6. The Sacrament of the Altar. (49-53)
Abstract: A prayer before the Blessed Sacrament, the Sacrament of the Lord's Supper, where Christ continues to proclaim His sacrificial death which unites us with God. We pray that our communion with Him will consecrate and strengthen us for the task of witnessing to Him fearlessly in the world.
Topics: EUCHARIST; JESUS CHRIST, death of.

Study and Daily Life

PM.7. Christ all in all. (58-59)
Abstract: Prayer to Jesus as: Eternal Word of the Father, Eternal High Priest, Life of Mankind, Source of Grace, Savior of Sinners, Bond of Love, Victor over Suffering, Lord of Eternal Glory.
Topics: JESUS CHRIST, our all.

PM.8. Dedication to the Blessed Virgin. (60-64)
Abstract: An act of consecration to Mary, recounting all her attributes and her contribution to salvation history. This dedication is nothing other than the wish to be what we already are, and to imitate in our own lives the life and the sufferings of Christ.
Topics: BVM.

Return to Everyday Life

PM.9. A Blessing on our Ending. (68-71)
Abstract: This prayer marks the end of the retreat and the students' return to everyday life. Self-knowledge makes us mistrust our enthusiasm, good resolutions, and strength of purpose. So we pray for only one thing: that Jesus would stay with us and bring to completion with His grace what He has begun.
Topics: EVERYDAY LIFE, endings.

A Priest Forever. Denville, NJ: Dimension Books, n.d. 30 pp. Translated by James Quigley, SJ. *Die Gnade wird es vollenden,* Cf., *Meditations on the Sacraments,* MS.5.

P. *The Priesthood.* NY: Herder, 1973. 281 pp. Also appeared as *Meditations on Priestly Life. Einübung Priesterlicher Existenz.* Freiburg: Herder, 1970. Translated by Edward Quinn.

Contents: Preface.
  1. Experience of God and Image of God.
  2. Man and the "Other Things."
  3. Nature and Achievement of Indifference.
  4. The Triple Sin.
  5. Our Own Sins.
  6. The Kingdom of Christ.
  7. The Incarnation.
  8. The Hidden Life of Jesus.
  9. The Catholic Priesthood.
  10. Priestly Office and Personal Holiness.
  11. Priesthood and Religious Life.
  12. The Priest and his Superiors.
  13. The Priest and Men.
  14. The Priest of Today.
  15. Dangers for the Priesthood Today.
  16. The Two Standards.
  17. The Three Classes of Men.
  18. The Three Kinds of Humility.
  19. Eucharist.
  20. The Passion of Christ.
  21. The Cross of Christ.
  22. The Risen One.
  23. Spirit, Church, Mary.
  24. Love.

Preface (1-3). Though many factors may contribute to the crisis in the priesthood today (list, 1) this book is not concerned with theory but with practice. It is an initiation into the mystery of priesthood. Though it emerged from a 1961 retreat to seminarians (cf., *Spiritual Exercises*) it is essentially different. There are still good reasons to read a pre-conciliar meditation on priesthood. There is continuity in change. Tradition can help us discern substance from mere fashion, and the priesthood remains a venture in faith and love.

P.1. Experience of God and Image of God. (4-15)

Abstract: To minister credibly today, priests must plumb the modern sensibility of God's remoteness. Setting aside their "ideas about God" they must experience God in the deepest realities of spirit (silence, loneliness, love, death). Confronting false images, we discover God as incomprehensible, greater than our hearts, and outstripping the parameters of human language.

Topics: GOD, experience of; GOD, nature of.

Subsidiary discussions: Mysticism (9f); God, attributes of (13ff).

Precis: Today God is not simply taken for granted. Even believers tend to feel God is quite remote. People who deny this generally do not have deeper faith. They are merely repressing the truth. To minister effectively, priests today must learn to bear God's apparent remoteness. This is the goal of the Exercises. **1. Experience of God.** It is the greatest mistake to substitute theology (secondary ideas about God) for the primary experience of the living God. But we can only bring out this primal relationship with God if we stop living in the world of ideas and face the deeper realities of the spirit (silence, fear, love, death, etc,). Failing to do this we will never be credible to people of today. We must open ourselves to those primal experiences where "object, ground and horizon and all that we see in these, merge –so to speak– into one another. Wherever these things happen, God is really already present and available to man" (9). All we say about God can do no more than point to this primal experience. We can call it mysticism. Because it is constantly being buried under the rubble of daily life it takes constant tending. **2. Images of God.** Even we carry around within ourselves false images of God (list, 10f). Religion itself can be used to prop up such false idols. We must examine ourselves to find these idols within us (list, 12). **3. The true God.** What do we know of this true God, not merely conceptually, but insofar as what we say corresponds to our primary experience of God? For only then are we speaking of the true God. Then we mean the

God beyond our minds and "greater than our hearts," infinite in all His attributes. Rahner invites us to contemplate what it means to say God is incomprehensible, personal, forever living . . . that God loves me. Yet whatever we say, whatever words we use, God remains *Latens Deitas.*

P.2. Man and the "other things." (16-29)

Abstract: Ignatius' anthropocentrism is surprisingly modern. To be a creature is not the same as being insignificant. Rather it underscores one's unique relation to God and reveals the underpinnings of human freedom and the possibility of my eternal validity. "Other things" are not simply expendable. They mediate my immediate relation to God in a way Rahner alternately describes as sacramental.

Topics: THEOLOGICAL ANTHROPOLOGY, anthropocentrism.

Subsidiary discussions: Man as creature (19ff); God as goal of life (23ff); Creation, as mediating God (28).

Precis: This meditation focuses of the first half of Ignatius' "Foundations." Its value does not lie in any of Rahner's comments as much as in the reader's grappling with the text. **1. Modern anthropocentrism.** This surprisingly modern text follows Aquinas and puts man and not the cosmos at the center of concern. "This is not in opposition to theocentrism, but precisely in order also to provide scope for the conceptual expression of man's real theocentrism" (17). For man is what God intends, not the world. Man is the meaning of creation. This perspective is not self-evident. Whereas it may strike us today as a truism, in Christianity it marks the beginning of modern times. **2. Man: the creature.** We must not misunderstand the claim: "Man is created." Here "man" means "I," the unique, irreplaceable individual God loves and to whom God speaks. Nor must creation be seen as a past fact. Even now I am being created and held in existence by God. Furthermore, to be a creature means I am radically finite and I know it. Yet as such I am always directed away from myself and towards the incomprehensible God. Hence, I never become totally clear to myself. Priests must make the consequences of this clear to people (list, 22f): as creatures the incomprehensible God is the sole meaning of our existence. **3. Man's goal.** Ignatius says man is, "Created to praise, reverence, and serve God our Lord, and by this means to save his soul" (23). This *pati divini* equates with the self-forgetfulness of love. Praise, reverence and service are not extrinsic things we occasionally do. Rather in accepting our true creaturely nature we become, we exist as an act of praise, reverence and service, something fit for eternity. In this we affect our salvation. But that does not mean we praise, revere and serve God as mercenaries, pursuing a means to an end. We praise God so that God may be praised. **4. The other things.** "The other things were created for man's sake" (26). This includes all the grandeur of nature and of human history. But what have these other things to do with our immediacy to God? They are not merely to be passed over or renounced. They mediate God's presence to us in a "mediated immediacy" which Rahner also describes as a dialectical, sacramental mediation. Nor must we see "the other things" as merely means, for they include other people, and the *Logos* himself, who have eternal validity. Admitting that "mediated immediacy" is not perhaps the most elegant or lucid formula to express what it means to use things and yet be free of them, Rahner summarizes (28f).

P.3. Nature and Achievement of Indifference. (30-38)
Abstract: Indifference toward "other things" is the only proper attitude of the creature who has found in God his/her greatest good. This indifference appears naturally, as it were, in every act of knowing and judging. But the resistance it meets from our radical egoism must constantly be opposed.
Topics: INDIFFERENCE.
Subsidiary discussions: Self-transcendence and indifference (30f).

Precis: Follows the second part of Ignatius' "Foundations" (quoted, 30). **1. Indifference as basic structure of mental life.** Before looking at indifference in its moral aspects, Rahner locates it squarely within the structures of mental activity. For every act of knowing and judging involves a kind of transcendence wherein the individual dissociates him/herself from what is apprehended and thus becomes "indifferent" in regard to the individual thing. This alone reveals the finite as finite, the good as provisional, and the individual as contingent. **2. Attainment of indifference.** Ignatius says we must make ourselves indifferent by keeping ourselves open to ever-greater reality. We cannot satisfy ourselves with idols. But this is painful, a kind of death. It meets the resistance of a deep radical egoism that would find bliss in the attainment of one particular thing. The death of sinful egoism takes the courage to accept our own nature as creatures, and to live the obedience of Christ. Turning from what we understand to the incomprehensible is a task imposed on us anew each day. We never attain indifference. We are constantly coming to be so. **3. Dimensions of the exercise of indifference.** There are three ultimate and basic dimensions for the exercise of indifference: corporeality (indifference to sickness and health); self-assertion (honor and dishonor, wealth and poverty); existence as such (a long or short life). Rahner asks the retreatant to ask himself where he meets resistance to indifference in his life, remembering we are not all that different from the people around us whom we often criticize. Indifference is never fully rational or conscious. Often we sacrifice the big things without being able to surrender the small. **4. The "more"** is a constant theme in Ignatius. It involves our relations with discernable things: the duty and desire to love God ever more fully, and the desire to find a better and more direct way to do so. But no single means is ever absolute, and we are forced constantly to seek indifference anew, each for him/herself.

P.4. The Triple Sin. (39-51)
Abstract: Meditating on the sin of angels (primal sin), of Adam (original sin), and of the redeemed is no mere historical analysis. For these set the parameters of our world and make clear that sin is and remains a real possibility for us all. Only the experience of God's mercy permits us to acknowledge our sinfulness.
Topics: SIN.
Subsidiary discussions: Angels, sin of (45ff); Freedom, finality of (46f); Adam, sin of (48f); Sin, of the redeemed (50f); Freedom, dualism of (50).

Precis: Sin and mercy are inescapable realities with which a priest must engage. **1. Preliminary remarks.** Sin is a mystery— the incomprehensible that should not be and does not have to be. But sin admits of no dualism. God remains the Lord even of sin, for God's mercy encompasses even sin. The abyss of our sin serves to reveal the even greater depths of God's mercy. Hence, we are allowed and even required to hope. The first week's meditation on sin is not meant to focus on the pre-history of sin, but on the concrete possibility of my freedom to sin deliberately even now. Our greatest threat comes from the sins we commit but do not admit– the sins we minimize, rationalize, excuse or deny. Nevertheless, I am bound to admit that sin does exist, if nowhere else, at least in me. Then the existentially difficulty returns: that I cannot judge where I stand in the sight of God in relation to sin or justification, and can only throw myself on God's mercy. **2. The sin of the angels.** This meditation and the next focus not on past events but on those things that constitute the historically free character of the situation in which we live– the pre-history of our own existence. The angels are part of the world, and as such their sin is part of the structure of the world we inherit. Their sin is their desire to be emancipated from God, and our sin emulates this false notion that things could be perfect if they were liberated from God. The fact that theirs was a sin in the mind and not in the flesh, underscores that danger for us. Like all sins theirs too was a sin against Christ the eternal Logos, and it reveals the finality and irrevocability of sin that stem from the nature of freedom. Their sin continues to be felt in the dynamism of our memory, intellect and will (summary, 47f). **3. The sin of our first parents.** Adam and Eve are not just anybody. They are the permanent ground of my existence. They are me. Redemption does not nullify their sin or its consequences. Rather their sin is radically incorporated into the divine context. Sin does not thereby become inevitable, although now it remains a perpetual possibility. **4. The sin of the redeemed.** Even those incorporated into the life of Christ can sin and bring about their own damnation. This reveals the dual nature of our freedom: it seeks to involve the whole person, but in doing so is resisted as something that feels imposed: like a divine judgment. **5. Colloquy of mercy.** Only the revelation of the grace of God's mercy found when we stand beneath the cross enables us truly to know sin. Grace alone gives us the power to admit our sinfulness.

P.5. Our Own Sins. (52-63)

Abstract: We must "demythologizing" the way we talk about our spiritual lives to get an honest look at ourselves. We are the worst judges of our own salvation/damnation status. We are prone to think we are fine so long as we only discern "venial sin" within us. Grace alone gives us the power to admit our sin.

Topics: SIN, salvation/damnation status.

Subsidiary discussions: Sin, venial (58ff); Fundamental Option (59ff).

Precis: 1. Demythologizing the ascetical life is essential because complicated terminology often stands in the way of taking a cool look at our spiritual reality. When we see the faults of those around us, how can we honestly think that somehow we have escaped these faults ourselves? Of course it is a great mistake to believe that we can judge someone else's status in the eyes of God simply from his/her external behavior. Yet we are even worse judges of ourselves. In addition, it does little good for a priest to tell someone what to do or to avoid without telling them *how* to do so. **2. Sin, venial sin, and fundamental decision.** Having demythologized sin and admitted it is a permanent possibility and a real danger for me, a second danger lies in claiming that I cannot hope to avoid venial sin. We are tempted to assume venial sin is innocuous, whereas it can in fact be the visible tip of the iceberg of a fundamental cowardice or refusal to give ourselves to God. Simply avoiding mortal sin never establishes someone as justified before God. **3. Sin as reality encompassed by God's grace.** Nevertheless, God's will to salvation in Jesus Christ, God's grace, is always really greater than our sin. This must be preached in such as way as to avoid Pelagianism on the one hand and presumption on the other. **4. The Triple Colloquy.**

P.6. The Kingdom of Christ. (64-72)

Abstract: A human life only becomes great in the service of a greater person. Christ is the greatest. We imitate Him first by accepting the decree of God. But even pagans do this. What sets the Christian apart is anticipation: voluntarily reaching out to embrace the cross.

Topics: JESUS CHRIST, imitation of.

Subsidiary discussions: Anonymous Christian/ity (68f); Cross (70ff).

Precis: The second week of the Exercises is aimed at coming to a choice, not of ends but of means. Insofar as priests have already chosen both the end and the particular means (perfect imitation of Christ), the point of this meditation is to prepare ourselves for the right attitude of choice. **1. Jesus Christ is Lord.** No human life is great unless it serves a greater cause . . . a greater person. There is none greater than God revealed in Christ, who is still coming and who calls us in the midst of our own history. This is the tremendous yet obvious truth of our Christian faith. **2. The call to imitate Christ.** Jesus invites all Christians to follow Him, to let Him become the meaning of their lives. **3. Imitation in a life of effort.** This life of imitation is difficult, toilsome, arduous and narrow. It means death and pain. It requires constant effort. **4. Obedient acceptance of God's decree.** The life to which Christ invites us, to voluntarily endure the struggles of everyday life, participates in human life in general (something non-believers often do even better than we). **5. The voluntary step towards the cross** is our closest imitation of Christ. This "more" and "acting against" is our way forward to what is decreed. How do I know whether I shall accept death with faith except by finding the courage in Christ to advance even a little in Him, accepting the cross even now? All this is contained in Ignatius' truly terrifying "Prayer of Oblation."

P.7. The Incarnation. (73-85)

Abstract: Incarnation must not be seen or taught as one discrete moment in the past. It is the sum and substance of creation. We enact it daily by imitating Christ, by freely accepting and coming to terms with our humanity in everyday life, as the Logos did. We thereby become united with others and with God.

Topics: INCARNATION; JESUS CHRIST, imitation of.

Subsidiary discussions: Mystery, one and many (74f); Trinity as revealed in creation (74f; 82f); Creation, meaning of (77f); BVM (83).

Precis: The meditation begins with theological principles and proceeds to historical gospel facts. **1. The Christocentrism of all reality.** It is misleading to present the Incarnation as a something secondary to creation, as a solution to the problem necessitated by sin. In fact, Incarnation was the basic intention of God for creation. Creation, God's absolutely first and comprehensive decision, is the condition of the possibility for God's self-utterance in the non-divine world. From this vantage point the Christian mysteries (Trinity, Incarnation, grace and glory) are seen as one, and the Incarnation is perceived as more than one moment in time. It is the inner meaning of the whole world and of human history. **2. The meaning of the Incarnation.** In the Incarnation, God creates by assuming. In assuming our human nature the Logos is not assuming just anything. The Logos assumes precisely that which can receive God's self-communication and thus fulfill God's eternal intention of self-communication. Hence, in seeing the Logos, the God-man, we actually see God and not merely a mask. To accept this truth about one's one human capacity to receive God's self-communication is already to understand oneself as the image of the Logos. This alone explains the unparalleled centrality of the Logos. **3. Incarnation and imitation.** Imitating Christ is not primarily a matter of practicing certain moral virtues. It is first and foremost a matter of accepting our human existence: freely accepting and coming to terms with oneself, just as the Logos did. To accept oneself is the core of all holiness. To reject one's nature is the source of all sin. Free self-acceptance, even when our nature feels imposed, is the task life sets before us. To accept our nature is to accept Christ (however anonymously). In imitating Christ we imitate even His assumption of the contingent when we accept the everydayness of our lives. Christ is the absolute standard for true humanity. **4. Persons involved in the Incarnation.** Christ is the Omega Point, the one way to the Father. In drawing close to Him the unity of mankind increases and we draw close to God. In addition, we draw closer to the Trinity and to the sinless Virgin Mary. **5. The event of the Incarnation.** The Logos appears precisely in becoming flesh. This is the tremendous paradox of Christianity grasped only in faith: the unredeemed is assumed and redeemed; life is released through acceptance of death.

Incarnation, the Logos' assumption of humanity, remains a daily activity in which we are invited to participate.

P.8. The hidden life of Jesus. (86-98)
Abstract: Little is said about Jesus' hidden life because, like our daily lives, there is little to say. Yet in assuming this common life of growth, patient waiting, poverty, work, obedience and prayer, Jesus elevates and redeems it. We must enrich our everyday lives by contemplating Jesus' ordinary life.
Topics: EVERYDAY LIFE, acceptance of; JESUS CHRIST, hidden life of.
Subsidiary discussions: Jesus Christ, self-consciousness of (87f); Priesthood, permanent commitment to (89f); Jesus Christ, obedience of (93f); Priests, life and ministry of (95f); Contemplation (97f).

Precis: In assuming the whole of human life (the normal, the everyday, the boring, repetitive and insignificant) the Logos confirms it all. The very silence of the evangelists on this dimension of Jesus' life is striking, precisely because there is not much to be said. For the most part our lives are just as common-place, but no less redeemed.
1. Growth. Setting aside questions of Jesus' self-consciousness, He grew. He accepted each phase of human life and obediently gave way to the next. Continually He moved into the unknown. Life-long commitment is only possible if our one life has continuity. This is granted by the Spirit and unfolds in the shadow of the cross. **2. Able to wait.** Jesus' 30-year wait to begin his public ministry reveals how much of life we simply have to endure. Even our legitimate ministries cannot be accomplished all at once. "The acceptance of what God plans is our life's work" (91). **3. Poverty.** To accept normal, everyday poverty is more significant and important than to endure heroic deprivations. **4. Work.** What other way of life would have suited the Son of God any better than that of a common laborer, since any great accomplishments as a scholar, artist or statesman would have paled in relation to His true identity? **5. Obedience.** Jesus is obedient even to the contingent and narrow religious, social, and political laws of his time. He respects them. **6. Payer.** Jesus prayed. **Hidden life— contemplative life.** Our Christian life is hidden within the everyday events of life.

What is most real and decisive in our lives can only be grasped by faith. This is especially true of the life of priests and in their interiority which Rahner refers to as "seclusion." There is a danger of sinking into apathy or mediocrity. We combat this with a life of lively contemplation, the content of which is "our life with Christ in God: the life of the Spirit of God in us, the life of patience, fidelity, love, prayer, of looking for and expectation of eternal life" (97). All this underscores that we can be Christians and priests today without trying to escape from our age.

P.9. The Catholic Priesthood. (99-107)

Abstract: Like the church, the priesthood too is an empirical-social and charismatic reality. Hence, the priest is both an ecclesiastical functionary who directs cult, and a charismatic prophet. In this dual role a priest carries on the one ministry of Christ without replacing it: building up the People of God.

Topics: PRIESTHOOD, nature of.

Subsidiary discussions: Jesus Christ, priesthood of (103f).

Precis: 1. Mediating functionary of a total religious system. Viewed from an empirical-sociological perspective a priest can be described as a mid-level, dependant mediating functionary within a total religious system. Failure to realize and accept before ordination that they will be working in such a hierarchical structure leads to disaster. In addition, priests are religious men who must exercise their charismatic call within the existing institution. Inevitably there will be stresses and strains. One consequence of belonging to a total religious system, one which seeks to integrate all spheres of activity into itself, is that priests have no private life. They are always on duty. **2. The risk of institutionalizing religions.** Priests are indisputably church functionaries. They cannot limit their ministry of Word and Sacrament to times the Spirit moves them. Still, they must be on guard not to let the institutional routine kill their inner spiritual vitality. **3. Continuation of Christ's priesthood** (103f) is the inner reality of the institutional priesthood which combines the cultic with the prophetic elements of priesthood. But not even in cult does the priest diminish the one, eternally valid mediation of Christ; and as prophet the priest embraces a new, full-time, apostolic way of life, distinct from other

Christians (Scripture citations, 105f). **4. Servants of the community:** this is the essence of priesthood. The priest's ministerial powers, even though they do not derive from the people, are meant to build up the people.

P.10. Priestly Office and Personal Holiness. (108-113)
Abstract: Due in large part to Donatism it became important to distinguish office from the personal holiness of the office holder. But God intends the two elements always to appear together, not as something extrinsic but as an embodiment of the essential holiness of the eschatological community itself.
Topics: PRIESTHOOD, office and charism.
Subsidiary discussions: Donatism (108f); Church, holiness of (110f).

Precis: Of course those who hold the office of priest are called to be personally holy. But because our anti-Donatist reflex often emphasizes the power of office over the call to holiness, this issue needs closer attention. **1. Love decides.** "Ultimately, what counts for God is simply and solely the personal, freely given love of the individual" (109). All the rest, church, sacraments, etc., is nothing– merely a means to an end. The two are not fundamentally opposed, but office is subordinate to charism. **2. Holy church.** To say the church is permanently holy refers not just to its institutional elements but also to its members. This promise insures that the unity of office and charism will never lapse. Such a danger exists only for the individual and never for the church itself. **3. Unity of existential and institutional holiness.** Only the priest who realizes this institutional and personal call to holiness to a high degree is the person he is actually called to be. The call to personal holiness is an essential requirement of the priestly vocation and not merely something extrinsic.

P.11. Priesthood and Religious Life. (114-122)
Abstract: Priesthood and religious life have a proper and legitimate relationship. In a special way, the life of priests living under the evangelical counsels invigorates the charismatic dimension of their priesthood.

Topics: PRIESTHOOD and religious life; RELIGIOUS LIFE and priesthood.
Subsidiary discussions: Evangelical counsels, need for (116ff).

Precis: The relationship between priesthood and religious life is neither simple nor obvious. One can wonder if the priesthood might not be able to accomplish its mission better if it were set free from the encumbrances of religious life. **1. The unity of the two forms of life.** Rahner gives four reasons why priesthood and religious life are properly related. Viewing this situation from the perspective of religious life we must admit that religious life exists for more than the sanctification of its members. It also has an apostolic function. The church must have members living the evangelical counsels to whom it can point to show it is living in eschatological expectation. Clearly, therefore, religious life can seek expression in priesthood. Religious priests also underscore the prophetic-charismatic element of priesthood. Finally, religious life in a community of priests corresponds closely with the presbyteral character of the priesthood (summary, 119). **2. Practical conclusions.** The relation between priesthood and religious life cannot be static. Despite any latent dangers, each priest must work to seek and find this unity afresh. There are many ways to realize this unity, many legitimate ways of being a religious priest. No one person can realize them all, but together the order can manifest many. Since no one knows the future, there will always be differences of opinion within orders. Stresses and strains will need to be tolerated.

P.12. The Priest and his Superiors. (123-136)

Abstract: The only legitimate theological justification for religious obedience is as a realization of faith. There are secondary ecclesial dimensions of obedience that put one at the service of the community and the apostolate. Rahner ends with practical considerations on religious superiors and their subordinates.
Topics: OBEDIENCE, religious; PRIESTLY LIFE, obedience.
Subsidiary discussions: Evangelical counsels, justification for (123ff); Authority and obedience (131ff).

Precis: There are many legitimate reasons to combine the discussion of the priest's relationship to ecclesiastical and religious superiors. **1. Obedience as realization of faith.** Religious obedience is first an ascetic factor, an evangelical counsel, not an organizational factor. As an existential actualization of faith, it is part of the life of every Christian. Religious are unique in that they anticipate the eventual surrender of all things to God in death through voluntary renunciation of centrally important goods of this world. Outside the context of supernatural faith, such renunciation makes no sense. No utilitarian benefit achieved by following the counsels can ever legitimate them. This does not, however, make the counsels easy to live. **2. Obedience in the service of the church.** Religious obedience also has an ecclesial and apostolic aspect when it puts us at the service of the community's life and the church's mission. This supports the call to the evangelical counsels but does not completely justify them. It does, however, give religious obedience a practical purpose and meaning. **3. Authority and obedience.** Renunciation is not unique to the religious, nor is it ever an end in itself. Hence, obedience can never be absolute. It can never exist without a prior and ongoing autonomous disposal by the individual of his/her freedom. No vow of obedience to the superior can release me from the absolute responsibility I have for the exercise of my freedom before God. Nor can the superior desire this. **4. Practical conclusions.** "There must be a real will to obedience as an act of selflessness in faith: the will and desire to experience in this life an absolute test of faith" (135). This can also involve taking initiative and making our own decisions in the line of duty. It is also our duty to scrutinize any orders we receive to be sure they do not involve sin. Finally, we must have the courage to be "troublesome subjects."

P.13. The Priest and Men. (137-146)
Abstract: Priests have a unique and decisive relationship with others who they exist to serve. They succeed as priests precisely insofar as they love their neighbors. They must exercise their authority humbly, since it is not properly their own, but God's. They must reach out to all classes of people.
Topics: LOVE OF NEIGHBOR; PRIESTLY LIFE.
Subsidiary discussions: Priests, authority of (139ff); Celibacy (144f).

Precis: The priest has a unique relation to others. He exists to serve them with his whole life. **1. Love and mission.** Human beings are related to others in many ways (list, 137f). But priests are related to others though the Holy Spirit whom they share, and who draws them into community. His relationships with others are infused with this supernatural love of neighbor. It is not enough to be an office holder. Priests who fail to love their neighbors genuinely fail to be priests. **2. Humble authority.** There is another factor in how priests relate: "We are ambassadors for Christ." Priests act authoritatively in the name of God. But to be effective this authority must be greeted with faith on both sides. This makes it different from any other worldly authority. But this very burden of authority, since it is not their own, should make priests all the more humble and unassuming. **3. An important, but not the sole function.** There is a dangerous tendency involved in the exercise of this authority: priests either exaggerate their own importance at the expense of others, or they become uncertain of the value of their priestly life. The role of the priest is unique and decisive without being (or needing to be) the whole show. Priests exist for the salvation of individuals and not primarily for the church. They establish the right relationship with people through love and not by the mere exercise of the power of office. **4. The priest and particular classes of men.** Priests are sent to many different kinds of people. We must examine ourselves to be sure we are reaching out to all of them, not merely to those with whom we feel an affinity. **5. The priest and women.** We have chosen a celibate life. Following it faithfully, like following any other life, will demand sacrifices. Yet celibacy is never the center of priestly life, nor is it the easiest element. It always carries the danger of desiccation, or of lapsing into sublime misanthropy or a comfortable bachelor existence. Priests must keep alive the positive ideals of their calling and care for themselves spiritually, intellectually and physically.

P.14. The Priest of Today. (147-163)

Abstract: Rahner lists a daunting number of qualities needed by priests today. These are no more than the practical extension of true love of neighbor— one flawed, limited, hopeful human being to another.

Topics: PRIESTHOOD, nature of today.

Subsidiary discussions: Faith, burdens of (152f); Christianity, limits of (154f).

Precis: This list of qualities expected of a priest today is more than anyone can fulfill. This should not surprise us since following Christ always calls for more than anyone can do by his own power. **1. Individual apostle in the mass age.** In this age of mass culture, the priest is sent to liberate and defend the individual. **2. Mystagogue of a personal piety.** The priest today cannot be a mere functionary. He must have the ability to initiate people into an authentic spiritual life. **3. Truly human.** Priests today must approach people one-on-one, like actual human beings. They must show that to be truly Christian means being truly human. They must believe in the goodness of all God has created, including human nature. No one expects priests to know everything, but they should be educated broadly in the liberal arts. **4. Fraternal companions under the burden of faith.** People should find in priests companions who can commiserate with them in their struggles to believe. **5. Credibility through honesty.** Priests should be honest about the limits of their knowledge. In knowing God as mystery, much remains unknown, including which particular course of action to take on many important moral matters. Priests who pretend to know more than they do make themselves unbelievable. **6. A loving person.** All priests like to think they are loving, selfless and good. But the test of real love is the ability to bear the sufferings of others. **7. Looking for a new language.** Though the truth of the faith remains the same, priests must always be on the lookout for new ways to express it— ways that are more understandable and compelling. **8. One who can let other minds count in the church.** God wills a diverse and pluralistic church. Priests should not suppress but should encourage and harness this diversity for the good of all. **9. Concentration on essentials** means preaching and centering parish life on God, Mystery, Trinity, Jesus, Eucharist, and not on secondary devotions. **10. A discreet man of religion.** Priests today must not be loud or pompous. Rather they should be reserved, modest and devout. Since all they have to give others is faith, hope and love, these should be their distinguishing characteristics. **11. A man of ecumenical outlook. 12. A true nonconformist.** Priests must be able to stand up when necessary, without making non-conformity a principle. **13. A man who speaks freely in the church.** One should be able to risk speaking his mind in the church without becoming quarrelsome. **14. A happy man. 15. Teacher of freedom.** Priests should train people for freedom, not making them dependent on the priest alone. The Christianity they extol does not remove mystery but encourages its loving acceptance.

P.15. Dangers for the Priesthood Today. (164-169)

Abstract: Modern priests are tempted to love change for its own sake; to succumb to the deadening effects of routine; to become mediocre. Disaffection leads to workaholism disguised as asceticism, and to intolerance of other ideas. Dread of the unknown future leads either to revolution or to retrenchment.

Topics: PRIESTHOOD, dangers today.

Precis: Priests today face the following dangers: **1. Love of danger** [sic? change] **for its own sake.** Today we cannot keep doing things as they were done in the past. But this leads some to dismiss the past uncritically as completely outmoded and to embrace change for its own sake. Since every state of affairs bears its own values and shortcomings, tolerance is needed within the church. **2. Impersonal routine** endangers the charismatic vitality of priests. **3. Ordinariness as a principle.** Adopting the average as the norm presents the danger of a mediocre priesthood. **4. Asceticism from despair.** Many disaffected priest justify remaining in ministry by means of a redoubled but desperate asceticism. Zeal without holiness often results in workaholism. **5. Intolerance in the service of the church.** In changing times there is always the temptation to canonize one's own point of view. **6. Dread of the unknown future** can lead to two opposite extremes: a revolutionary frame of mind or nervous conservatism.

P.16. The Two Standards. (170-179)

Abstract: Decision is an unavoidable dimension of life. But the ambiguous nature of things prior to decision presents the possibility of self-delusion. Ignatius calls this temptation or seduction, the core of which is falsely absolutizing any categorical object. Priests must imitate Christ and cling to God alone.

Topics: ELECTION, Ignatian; TEMPTATION.
Subsidiary discussions: Categorical/Transcendent (177f); Jesus Christ, imitation of (179).

Precis: The real meaning of this meditation comes into play when applied to important life decisions. But insofar as even seemingly small free decisions can be decisive, this meditation is valuable at any point in life. **1. The meaning of the meditation on the two standards.** This meditation focuses on overcoming self-delusion in our response to the call of Christ. The dualism implied in the two standards has a long tradition pre-dating Ignatius (171f). Its seeming simplicity should not blind us to the grandeur of this concept, nor can we be naive in how we separate the forces of good and evil in the world. For the world, like the church, has its share of weeds and wheat. **2. Necessity of decision.** Decision is unavoidable. To posses one thing always means renouncing another. We must face this truth in all its radicality, pain and harshness. Not everything can be synthesized. One cannot be a priest *and* everything else. **3. Technique of seduction.** Temptation and seduction are possible because before a decision is made everything in the world is ambiguous. After contextualizing the three grades discernable in temptation (riches, power, self-assertion) Rahner summarizes seduction as the temptation to absolutize any particular thing. One who does this is essentially unfree, and in justifying himself merely suppresses his guilt. **4. The making of a true Christian.** The true Christian is poor. He has confidence in God alone, courage for God, eschewing any other value. Only through this renunciation of categorical realities can Christians come to know in the course of daily life the transcendent reality of *Deus semper major*. **5. Assimilation to Christ.** Of course all of this can be misinterpreted by us and by others. Poverty can look like disdain of worldly goods, indifference can appear as arrogance, etc. But at its core the attitude described here is first and foremost an imitation of Christ.

P.17. The Three Classes of Men. (180-193)
Abstract: Even after election moves into the realm of love and is no longer a matter of human calculation, a certain ambiguity attaches to the concrete choices at hand. The three different types of men

respond differently. One is paralyzed into inaction; one refuses to renounce everything, but one is indifferent.
Topics: ELECTION, Ignatian.

Precis: 1. The function of the meditations on election. Rahner begins with a review of the dynamics of election through the First Week. He concludes that contact with God's transcendence ("the more") inspires love and moves us beyond the realm of strictly rational calculation of the best means. What counts now is more sublime: free, unreserved surrender to God's supreme love. Still, our response, the response of the three types of men, remains rooted in realistic, commonsense, everyday reality. **2. The men's situation.** All three classes of men considered here legitimately hold office, though they did not knowingly choose it out of love for God. We often do this, reasoning that if a choice is not morally objectionable, then it is ok with God. Hence, when we finally do elect to love God in everything, we discover much in our lives that was not consciously chosen with this criterion in mind. The men Ignatius considers here have all come to this point and are honestly disturbed the love for God does not permeate every aspect, every decision of their lives. **3. The men's reflections.** These three classes of men then ask, what should I do in my office to save my soul as God wills? But as the meditation on the two standards showed, the options available, while not necessarily sinful, are ambiguous. And the more options they consider, the more overwhelmed they can become (summary, 188). Ignatius thinks the problem can be solved in one of two ways: detachment, a heroic person's leap away from office; or assimilation, a reasonable person's melding his office into his decision for God. But all three categories of men know they lack the power to choose. **4. The men's decision.** The first man wants pure love but is lazy and does nothing. He will not risk because he is afraid to surrender himself to the immensity of God. So nothing happens. The second man wants to love God and to be loved. But he wants these things on his own terms. When invited to choose he focuses not on God but on the thing to be given up. The third man, by the grace of Christ's cross, is truly indifferent. Focused on God, he does not recoil at what must given up. **5. Colloquies.** Hence, it makes sense to pray the colloquies remembering Mary's *fiat*, Jesus' cross, and the Father's ineffable love.

P.18. The Three Kinds of Humility. (194-207)
Abstract: These three degrees of humility (indifference/love) are our response to God's love. The three degrees are not higher or lower. They interpenetrate and merge in love of the cross, whereby we actively practice what we must finally endure in death, which ultimately demands detachment from all things.
Topics: HUMILITY, Ignatian types; INDIFFERENCE, Ignatian; LOVE, Ignatian types.
Subsidiary discussions: Sin, venial (194f; 199ff); Molinism (201); Death as final renunciation (204f); Cross, love of (204ff).

Precis: 1. Humility and love. Ignatius sees three ways of responding to God and Jesus. It makes little difference whether one calls this basic election-attitude humility, indifference or love. **2. Basic decision.** In all three degrees of humility we must remember what was said previously (cf., P.5) about venial sin and not assume it is innocuous even when it does not point to anything objectively grave. **3. The three degrees** are not lower or higher. In fact they are interdependent and often merge with one another, constituting one entire healthy attitude of man to God. **a) The first degree** begins unpretentiously from below. "It is an absolute determination to accept God's will, so far as God wills himself as man's end and destines man for himself as the one, real and true end" (196). This grace of the Spirit that allows us even now to be called children of God, Rahner describes as "unpretentious." It does not race toward God in its exuberance but waits for God to integrate human reality into love (summarized in b). **b) The second degree** is "free, active indifference" that liberates us from ourselves and stokes the will to avoid even venial sin. It "produces a free gaze towards God as such. God becomes known in a radical way, existentially, transcendentally, and not merely categorically" (199) in a pre-existing synthesis between God and the things of the world. But this degree of humility is never perfectly achieved. **c) The third degree** is bold love of the cross which positively reaches out for poverty, shame, humiliation, the cross of Christ. This bold love is the best defense against failing to understand the true will of God due to unacknowledged self-love. But merely because we say we want to love Jesus completely does not make it easy for us voluntarily to seek shame or humiliation. Do we make Jesus' life the final concrete norm for our own (granting we cannot simply imitate it in detail)? If so, then we must ask how we are to go about this third degree of humility. How do we gain indifference, the ability simultaneously to esteem and renounce the world? **4. Realization of love of the cross.** Every attempt at renunciation must be an expression of the faith demanded of every Christian—the total self-surrender required in death. Just as death is imposed on each person, so is love of the cross. Ignatius' "poverty, shame, humiliation" is nothing more than a particular form of what is imposed on every person. Although what the third degree of humility imposes is not easy, it is not artificial. It arises from the inner structure of our existence. This does not, however, allow us to sit back and do nothing, awaiting the inevitable. In imitation of Christ we must practice actively what we must nonetheless endure (summary, 207).

P.19. Eucharist. (208-215)

Abstract: Is the Eucharist the center of priestly existence? No and yes. The 30 minutes a day spent at the altar *is not* the center priestly life. But the *res sacramenti*, i.e., the self-surrender, the unity and love, the grace and humanity priests attempt to manifest in their daily lives, and which finds its fullest expression in the one sacrifice of Christ, certainly *is* the center of priestly existence.

Topics: EUCHARIST as center of priestly life; PRIESTHOOD and Eucharist.

Subsidiary discussions: Church as locala altar community (212f); Jesus Christ, resurrected body of (214).

Precis: A realistic meditation on Eucharist situated among the realities of everyday life. **1. Eucharist and ordinary life.** Is it really true that Eucharist is the most wonderful and unsurpassable moment of our lives? It is true that our life of faith is sustained by the love that flows from the cross. But liturgy is not the place where we encounter the cross first or most acutely, nor is it necessarily the moment at which we relate to Christ most intimately. That generally happens in everyday life. Receiving Christ's body and blood is the effective sign of what occurs, or should occur, in the totality of human life. Though it orients and aids us, the Mass does not simply cause union with Christ. Therefore, it is not the ultimately decisive factor of this salvation-creating event. **2. Eucharist and divine worship.** How does the Eucharistic sacrifice connect to the ultimate task of human existence: surrender to God? On the cross Jesus, the God-man, committed Himself in a total surrender of absolute indifference to the incomprehensible decree of the Father. What took place on the cross, the essential goal of every human life, is present in the anamnesis of the Mass under cultic signs. The point at which the priest enters into this sacrifice is usually not when he dons his liturgical vestments, but somewhere in his actual, wretched, everyday life. Hence, his whole life is ultimately part of this Eucharist as worship of God. **3. Eucharist and growth in grace** can be linked when we receive Holy Communion in faith, hope and love. But this only sparks the real growth that occurs in real life situations of faith. **4. Eucharist as sacrament of the church.** The Eucharist requires, symbolizes and affects the unity of love within the church. This is no less true of the local altar community than for larger divisions within the church. **5. Proclamation of the death of Christ.** Participation in this sacrament is our visible "yes" to the cross of Christ in our lives. It is the sacrament of our readiness to suffer for Christ. **6. Sacrament of humanity.** Because Christ's risen body belongs forever to this earth, it makes our bodies too a sacrament of divine grace. **7. Sacrament of holiness. 8. Starting point and center of priestly life.** Mass in the sense of the celebration of the liturgy is not the center of priestly existence. But it is the center in the sense that the *res sacramenti* is celebrated in the whole of our lives. Do our lives manifest the meaning of the liturgical sign we celebrate?

P.20. The Passion of Christ. (216-226)
Abstract: Focusing in turn on the various distinct aspects of Jesus' passion (futility, betrayal, beating, imprisonment), Rahner draws lessons we can apply to our own lives and sufferings.
Topics: JESUS CHRIST, passion of.
Subsidiary discussions: Renunciation (216f); Jesus Christ, hypostatic union of (217f); Sin of the world (218ff); Futility (221); Sin (225f).

Precis: **1. The disciples in the garden of Gethsemane** is a vivid description of voluntary Christian renunciation on the part of Christ. It is the freedom with which we go out to meet our true cross. At the same time it is a scandal to the disciples and to the world– the scandal of faith and love. Here we must take the mystery of the hypostatic union seriously and affirm that truly in the Garden, the divine Logos bore human weakness and suffering, and thus wrought our redemption. **2. The sin of all.** The same disciples who experienced the Transfiguration and expected to see the fulfillment of the Law and the Prophets now see their complete breakdown, when the Faithful One is conquered by sin. Yet only when sin takes the upper hand are the Law and the Prophets fulfilled. Jesus experiences the incomprehensible wickedness, the mystery of the sin of the world, and at the same time identifies with the sinners. His particular agony comes from suffering evil at the hands of those He loves. We, on the other hand, generally protect ourselves from this by despising the evil doer. **3. Futility.** In His passion the Lord fell unconditionally into the abyss of futility. This is the source of His agony at being abandoned by God. **4. The chalice.** The dark chalice Jesus dreads to drink is the very cup we raise at Mass. Having accepted it He says "Rise, let us be going." Miraculously, impotence gives way and strength flows out of the void of the heart. **5. Betrayal** signifies the abandonment Jesus felt in the breakdown of his personal relationships, mirroring his felt-abandonment by God. **6. Profession.** In professing his identity to the Sanhedrin, Jesus, the norm of our life, seals his fate to be sacrificed to religious and political propriety. **7. Imprisonment.** Jesus was truly imprisoned but we are not. By descending into my prison of helplessness Jesus has opened it so we can advance into the freedom of God. **8. Rejected.** Jesus is rejected by all– by the Jews as a scandal and by the pagans as a fool. **9. Beaten.** With this beating the fatal breaking down from the outside begins. The scandal of death becomes clear. What makes it worse is that this death was freely inflicted by others who justify their cruelty by the pitiful weakness they themselves inflicted.

P.21. The Cross of Christ. (227-237)

Abstract: The cross is neither scandal nor folly. Its wisdom, found in faith, reveals love to be the meaning of the world. The cross is

mission and revelation. For his own sake and the sake of those he serves, a priest must constantly ask 2 things: Is he able to embrace the cross? Where is the cross in his life today?
Topics: CROSS and sin; JESUS CHRIST, cross of.
Subsidiary discussions: Jesus Christ, hypostatic union of (233f); Death and Anonymous Christian/ity (235ff).

Precis: 1. The cross – and the Jews, Hellenes and Christians. When we look concretely at the cross of Christ we can ask who are the Jew, the Greek, and the Christian of today. The "Jew" is the follower of the Law. He knows God absolutely and follows God's norms closely, sure of his safety now and his final reward later. To such a one is the cross of Christ not a scandal? The "Greek" is the aesthete who could never imagine that the meaning of life is found in the cross. That is sheer folly. By nature we are one or the other. We must pray for the gift of faith, which alone can embrace the cross. Only these will recognize the folly of love is the meaning of the world. Only these can embrace both life and death. **2. The cross in the life of Jesus.** The cross is at the same time a mission. For Jesus it was the culmination of his mission. Hence, every situation (even death) can be for us a mission and a task. Yet we cannot die such a dark death as Jesus died on the cross. For darkness and evil are a part of us, and not a senseless contradiction. Only Jesus can praise God as he falls into the abyss of death; all others can do so only in Him. **3. The universal significance of the cross** lies in the fact that it reveals the insane blindness of sin. Yet it is also the culmination of divine love which redeems the world from both sin and death. **4. The cross of Christ in my life,** what does it mean? The fact that our lives are a conscious participation in the death of Christ gives us no warrant for cowardice or self-pity. Even unbelievers face the reality of death, and often more courageously than we. No death can be completely mastered with worldly bravery. And all those who obediently and silently accept death in all its futility can be said to have died in the redeeming death of Christ. "In the life of the Christian the cross of Christ should mean a continual act of faith and hopeful endurance" (236) even when the cross comes overpoweringly in death. Am I really able to recognize these signs of the death of Christ in my life as signs of election? The second important question is "Where do I find my cross today?" This is so important both for the priest and for those they serve because the unrecognized cross, the cross denied, is the source of all inward twisted neurosis.

P.22. The Risen One. (238-248)
Abstract: Christ's death, resurrection and ascension are three phases of one complete act. His death and resurrection, whereby He enters God's infinity with our humanity, are our absolute and unsurpassable future. His victory fills us with courage and allows us to face this suffering world with calm assurance.
Topics: FUTURE, absolute; JESUS CHRIST, resurrection of.
Subsidiary discussions: Resurrection of the body (239); Death (241f); Jesus Christ, Ascension of (244ff); Liturgy, cosmic (244f); Utopia (247f).

Precis: Christian life as a whole is always sustained by the death and resurrection of the Lord, whose death, resurrection and ascension are phases of *one* integrated event. **1. The risen victor.** The whole *one* reality of Jesus is taken up into His conquest of death where we can no longer distinguish body from soul. **2. The exalted Lord.** For all the dizzying advances we see around us in the world, Christ's resurrection remains the unsurpassable human achievement, for He has surpassed all human possibilities by entering into God's infinity. "This means then that the absolute future has already arrived: for us indeed it is still only present in faith and veiled, but truly present" (240). We reach this future only through the narrow gate, death, which only the resurrection of Jesus can explain. Though the horror of the world continues, at a deeper level Christ has cut it off like a stream at its source. It continues to flow, but because it has already been stemmed its effects are secondary and provisional. Christ's ascension, *sedes ad dexteram patris*, is the improbable apotheosis of man in Jesus our brother, whose glorified humanity we share. This is what makes every liturgy a participation in the cosmic liturgy. **3. The Christian's courage for victory.** This exalted Lord is still remote. We await His final coming, the real, true future. This is the source of the Christian's courage for victory (scripture citations, 245f). We must constantly remind ourselves that love and mercy are final. Though a struggle remains, the outcome is certain. Christ is victor and nothing can separate us from His love. This confidence, however, does not give us the plans for any future utopia here on earth. We cannot render death or suffering superfluous, for Christ conquered first on the cross. Keeping this in mind helps us to see the world's fate calmly.

P.23. Spirit, Church, Mary. (249-264)

Abstract: Priestly life is life *of* the Spirit, *for* the Spirit, *in* the Spirit of the church. Christ's outpouring of the Spirit in the church proves His glorification, and the church is the concrete realization of that Spirit in the world. Mary is the fullest human actualization of that Spirit in her unique role in salvation history.

Topics: SPIRIT/s, experience of: CHURCH and the Spirit.

Subsidiary discussions: Spirit, in Ignatius (253f); Church, love for (257ff); Church, service to (260f); BVM (263f).

Precis: 1. The Spirit. By pouring out the Spirit, Jesus proves He sits at the right hand of the Father. Since this realization *is* the church, the two necessarily belong together (scripture citations, 249f). We possess this Spirit, although often it is impossible to distinguish the boundlessness of the Spirit from its absence. Nor can we clearly demarcate what is "natural" and what is divine in our own acts of transcendence. Since all grace is supernatural, when we divide things into natural and supernatural "we tear apart the very unity of the supernatural mental life in the Spirit of God" (251), and everyday life becomes a spiritual wasteland. Not surprisingly, when we see the Spirit shaping every part of our daily lives the "supernatural" becomes difficult to distinguish. We know only through faith that we possess the Spirit. Faith elucidates our experience, and experience shapes our faith. After discussing the central importance of the Spirit to St. Ignatius (253f), Rahner turns to the experience of the Spirit's absence. He attributes this to our creaturely-pilgrim status, to the primitive state of our spiritual lives, and to our guilt. He even suggests this may be a divinely-willed note of our time in history. After posing a number of questions (list, 256) he insists that those imbued with indifference, who have the courage to seek God in all things, will certainly find the Spirit somewhere.

2. The church. When priests love and serve the church we bear testimony to its divine mission. But how do we love the church? We can and must distinguish believing *in* God from believing God. But when it comes to the church, because it is not a person, we cannot simply believe it. A distinction must be made between the church and her members, although this is not absolute since for better or worse the church *is* her members. "True love for the church is a love coming from the Holy Spirit, as grace of faith in the inner reality of the church which cannot be perceived directly or empirically" (259). The most decisive factor in the church is and remains her Holy Spirit who is poured out in the members as faith, hope and love. This obviously means not only love of the spirit of the church but also humble service to its members. After offering priests a set of questions for self-examination (261f) Rahner summarizes by saying a priest is a man of the church. He is never more himself than when he is serving her, and his ability to distinguish the church (which exists to serve mankind and not simply to be served) from the Kingdom of God keeps him from discouragement.

3. Mary. God's salvation is completely personalist. Salvation is carried on by people and by their freedom. Hence, our relationship to the church is given shape in our relationship to Mary who represents the pure church. In her we see the completely redeemed person; the complete identity of office and holiness; perfect surrender to God; complete sinlessness and transfigured humanity. She is no private individual who has made good, but an irremovable fact of salvation history. What she did is forever a factor in our own salvation. Hence, she is part and parcel of every Christian life (summary, 264).

P.24. Love. (265-281)

Abstract: This dense meditation underscores that our love expressed in service is a continuation of God's descending love for the world. We find God (the ever-greater) only when our love of the world is characterized by indifference. Burning with love for God alone, priests find God specifically by living their priestly life to the full.

Topics: LOVE.

Subsidiary discussions: Election, Ignatian (267f); Love as service (272); Love as *imago trinitatis* (275); Love in Ignatius (275f).

Precis: **1.** *Foundation* **and meditation on love.** The first and last meditations of the *Exercises* sum up the whole. Finally what has been driving the whole can be given its proper name: love. **2. Immediacy of creator to creature** is essentially what comes to the fore in the *Exercises*. We seek God's particular will for ourselves which, like any true love, cannot merely be deduced from formal principles. It is a New Testament love accessible to everyone. Over the course of the Exercises it becomes clear that the only true election is "being elected" to experience God's personal and unalterable love for me. It is my grasp of this love that is purified step by step through the weeks of the *Exercises*. **3. Nature of this love.** The theme of this meditation is really God's love for me, to which I should respond with the love made known to me through Jesus. All the things of this world only find their proper place and meaning in light of the love of Christ crucified, an insight that is only possible now in the Fourth Week of the *Exercises*. **4. Descending love** is how we describe God's love, though we also speak of creatures returning to God in an ascending love. But in the end "this ascending love which we have for God is always part of the realization of God's descent into the world" (271). **5. Service.** Our response to God's self-emptying love is to imitate it in service to others. It is this same descending love which alone anchors our ability to find God in all things. **6. God in all things** can be found only because God has given himself to the world precisely as eternal glory never to be confused with this world. This is no mere philosophical or mental activity. The Christian who shares in bringing about God's descent into the world can love the world truthfully, radically with this love in a way that would otherwise be impossible and inconceivable for man. Only such self-forgetful love can encompass the great mystery that submitting to God and realizing our selfhood grow in direct proportion. **7. Love as** *"imago trinitatis"* embraces the powers of memory, intellect and will. Since this love is truly God's self-communication we should expect that its fullness would manifest a Trinitarian structure. **8. The specifically Ignatian love** is really this "serving God in all things." Loving God never means bypassing the world, since the descending love of God in Christ has redeemed the world. But this love is only possible for those who have achieved true indifference, and love all things with God's own love for them. It comes about through renunciation and mortification. **9. The four points of the meditation.** The meditation's four co-penetrating points reduce to this: "finding God in all things, looking to God through all things, since the redeemed world and the redeemed subject are transparent to God and God thus approaches us in all things" (278f). So armed, Ignatius sends the retreatant back into the world to find God, who is always greater. Rahner adds a series of specific questions for priests (279). **10.** *Suscipe* of Ignatius is equivalent to the *"adsum, mitte me"* of the candidate for diaconal ordination. We can say quite simply that where priests find God is in their priestly lives.

RLT. *The Religious Life Today.* London: Burns and Oates. 1977. 88 pp. Freiburg: Herder, 1974. Translated by V. Green.
Contents: 1. The Setting of the Religious Life: The Christian message now.
2. Religious Life Today and Tomorrow.
3. Calling and Vocation.
4. Being the Church Together.
5. Life in the Christian Community.
6. Prayer and the Religious.
7. Obedience and Freedom.
8. Enthusiasm and the Religious.
9. The Challenge of Growing Old.
10. A Successful Death.

RLT.1. The Setting of the Religious Life: The Christian message now. (1-6)
Abstract: This pluralistic age especially calls for a non-technical restatement of the basic religious convictions which ground our Christian hope. **The need for a statement.** Creeds ground the unity of the church. Shared convictions undergird its missionary activity. Although such creeds can have a wide diversity of starting places and take many legitimate forms, they must include two points: that human salvation depends on Jesus; that the church is fundamental and essential. **A statement in history.** Any creedal formula must take its historical audience seriously. It can do this without endangering its essential message. Much of what is officially orthodox is no longer effective because it fails to take the

current historical realities into account. **The content of the message.** Any adequate Christian message must start with God and how God is known, although particularly today this term "God" is difficult to define. It must include Jesus Christ as the culmination of God's saving intervention in the world, and the church as the community of those who believe the message of Christ.

Topics: CHRISTIANITY, essentials of; CREED/s, need for a brief formula.

Subsidiary Discussion: God, definition of (4); Jesus Christ as savior (4f).

RLT.2. The Religious Life Today and Tomorrow. (7-21)

Abstract: True religious life is timeless. Its essence, witnessing in concrete, practical ways to the enduring mystery of faith, hope and love in the face of evil, sickness and death, never goes out of fashion.

Topics: HOPE; RELIGIOUS LIFE.

Subsidiary discussions: Anonymous Christian/ity (11f); Tolerance (13f); Cross (14); Love of God and neighbor (15ff); Mystery (15ff); Death and sickness (17f).

Precis: The future of religious life is uncertain. But the more that religious are who they are and what they want to be, the greater the chance that religious life will both survive and prosper. **1. Essential Christianity.** According to Vatican II, what Christianity itself ought to be (i.e., ultimate faith, hope and love) should be alive and evident in religious life. Essential Christianity is simply hope. Hope is simply another way of saying God. Because this hope must become tangible, we are drawn to the church. Religious should be numbered among those in the church who make hope tangible in simple and practical acts of love. Thus they proclaim and attest to the fact that the world is saved, and they become signs of hope themselves. **2. Religious life and change.** Religious life is undeniably changing: numbers are decreasing and the workload is increasing. This change, which affects the whole church and threatens the self-confidence of religious is necessary. But there will always be Christians who organize themselves in various ways to live out the gospel demands. Though new times may call for new orders, this does not mean dismantling the old. Even old orders can reform. One need not despair if his/her order is changing too quickly or too slowly, in too liberal or too conservative a fashion. Accommodating change requires selfless love. The plurality of gifts found in religious life demands love-inspired toleration. Adapting to change calls us to carry our cross each day in cheerful hope. **3. The life-style of a nursing nun.** To those who say Christianity boils down to love of neighbor, Rahner insists that only those who really know what is meant by "God" can truly love their neighbor. He illustrates this by pointing to the "mystery" at the heart of the life of a nursing nun: the identity of love of God and neighbor in dedicated service amidst the sober bitterness of life, especially sickness and death. Such a practical, living proclamation of hope will never become unnecessary or outmoded. **4. The modernity of daily life.** True religious life is as timeless and urgent as death itself.

RLT.3. Calling and Vocation. (23-27)
Abstract: Rahner begins with a list of presuppositions. He insists that every particular call is merely a concrete specification of the one universal divine call to salvation. This remains true even when we are not alert to the fact. To the three classical notes of a true calling to religious life (personal suitability, proper motivation, acceptance by the order) Rahner adds a fourth: the grace of genuine attraction. But one's freedom cannot completely determine the outcome of one's life and promises. Even after final vows made in good faith, it may become apparent that the preconditions for a vocation are no longer present. Such a person should be free to leave his/her order. Ecclesiastical dispensation simply recognizes the facts. Perpetual vows can only bind us to shape our lives each day as best we can in conformity to the life we have chosen. But we must never mistake the inevitable presence of the cross in religious life for an incontrovertible sign we are not called to the particular life we embraced with our vows.
Topics: VOWS, perpetual.
Subsidiary discussions: Freedom (25f).
RLT.4. Being the Church Together. (29-42)
Abstract: Rahner discusses the essential characteristics of the church today. He locates them in the grass-roots, voluntary affiliation with an institutional community united with the universal church,

and committed to faith, hope and love. He sees no reason existing parishes could not become such realities.
Topics: CHURCH, nature of; PARISH.
Subsidiary discussions: Church, democracy in (32f); Anonymous Christian/ity (36ff); Love of neighbor (36ff); Prayer (38); Church, dissent within (38ff); Baptism in the Spirit (41).

Precis: The church Christian. Every fully mature Christian is a church Christian: a member of an institutional church beyond the bonds of one's own family that traces its existence to the apostolic times. He refutes the modern tendency to non-denominationalism. Particular local communities united with the universal church are the *church* and not mere franchises. The parish is "the church on the spot" bringing into being the purpose of the church: the perpetuation of the Holy Spirit of faith, hope and love. Everything else in the church is only a means toward this end. **The church is all of us.** We are the church and not merely objects of pastoral attention. Because this places demands on us, legitimate criticism of the church must begin with self-criticism. **The grassroots church.** Every local church today is to some extent a church of the diaspora, existing in a profane, secularized society. This presents two dangers: 1) a "liberal sell-out" which reduces the church to an agent of secular humanism; 2) the development of a ghetto mentality of "holy remnant." The future of the church will increasingly depend on the continual creation of living, grassroots communities. The hierarchical church will increasingly depend on the people at the bottom. Christianity needs to be more democratized because people today will no longer willingly be led like a flock by the clergy. **The modern parish.** There is no reason modern parishes could not grow into such grassroots communities. All voluntary communities (parochial and non-parochial) must fight against becoming too culturally, socially, or theologically homogeneous. Christians with differences should be able to be brought together by their dedication to the fundamental beliefs of Christianity (list, 35).
Priorities for communities. A living community is "church" only where these characteristics prevail: 1) Love unites its members. This mutual loves raises a community beyond secular humanism, as it also embraces and supports the efforts of anonymous

Christians. 2) It is a community of prayer. Such prayer is both formal, liturgical prayer and informal charismatic prayer. 3) It is connected to the universal church. The parish must be missionary– willing and able to disagree with those in authority in a spirit of sympathy and support. 4) It openly and courageously proclaims the whole gospel. Even those people of good faith who do not measure up to our own particular orthodoxy should be given responsibilities commensurate with their dignity and interest. 5) Ultimately the church is undergirded by an unknown group of Christians who have broken through to true freedom in faith, hope and love. Rahner lists the characteristics of such people "baptized in the Spirit" (41f) and says we should all strive to be such.

RLT.5. Life in a Christian Community. (43-45)

Abstract: Whoever cannot cope with the many various disappointments of human life will never cope with community life, where the determination to live a religious life often makes one's own failures and those of others even more noticeable. Determination to serve a cause is what makes community life possible. Success in religious life calls for the courage to forget one's self and to trust another. There is a wisdom in the forms of community life which have developed over the centuries. But nothing replaces the need for an unconditional belief in, and relationship with, Jesus Christ crucified and risen.

Topics: RELIGIOUS LIFE, community.

Subsidiary discussions: Society of Jesus (44).

RLT.6. Prayer and the Religious. (46-50)

Abstract: Religious life is prayer insofar as the essence of both is the same: selfless surrender to God in faith, hope and love. Religious are called to foster their relationship with God "professionally." Prayer is a universal structural principle which they make the theme of their lives, though it is not exclusive to them. Although true prayer may enhance the life of one who prays, the essence of prayer, like the essence of love, is a certain surrender which is completely self-forgetful. It is the miracle of true freedom. Prayer faces two dangers: being reduced to activity in the service of power, or being reduced to passivity in introspection. People can engage in the true prayer of self-surrender anonymously, without even explicitly knowing they are involved in what Christians call prayer and the following of Christ crucified.

Topics: LOVE OF GOD AND NEIGHBOR; PRAYER; RELIGIOUS LIFE.

Subsidiary discussions: Freedom (48).

RLT.7. Obedience and Freedom. (51-69)

Abstract: Here religious obedience (relationship of superior/subordinate) and the question of conscience are "demystified" and redefined functionally: as the risks involved in commanding and in voluntarily promising to serve the aims of a particular society, without thereby abdicating one's freedom.

Topics: OBEDIENCE, religious.

Subsidiary discussions: Cross (57ff, 60f); Everyday life, resignation (57ff); Freedom (61f); Church, democracy in (62f); Conscience (65ff).

Precis: This essay concerns religious obedience strictly speaking (relations between superior and subordinate) with an eye to apostolic religious, without prejudice to those communities with a tradition of seeing superiors as "spiritual fathers." **1.** There is no harm in demythologizing religious obedience. a) Religious obedience is completely separate from spiritual discipleship. b) The religious superior is "God's representative" and should be obeyed only in the sense that s/he is the congregation's legitimate social authority as God wills the institute (here the church) to be structured. c) Religious obedience should not be m/paternalistic. Religious are not related to their superiors as children to parents. Such analogies are not helpful today.

2. Rahner sees the significance of religious obedience as primarily functional in an institute with a common purpose and apostolate. a) The corporate mission of the institute does not fully correspond to the private, spiritual-subjective aim of the individual. b) Religious obedience is the free decision of the member to follow the directives of legitimate authority to achieve the aims of the institute. The binding force of such instructions does not depend on the superior making them the norm of his/her own conduct. c) Religious obedience is essentially functional: it integrates the ac-

tions of the individual into the group. It regulates the common life insofar as it touches on the fulfillment of the institute's apostolate. **d)** The superior's competence is limited by this functionality. He can command only what serves the mission of the group. Where functional appropriateness is lacking obedience ceases to bind. There is no personal subordination of subject to superior. Both are subordinate to the common aim of the institute. Commands cannot be given to "advance the person in virtue: to humble or mortify him/her. **e)** Obedience is not the only factor which regulates the relationship of superiors and subordinates in religious orders.
3. Even in this restricted understanding of obedience, its spiritual essence cannot be perfectly observed. **a)** In our fallen state there will always be conflicts between the need of the individual and the needs of the group. In Christian terms this involves the cross and resignation. **b)** Suffering and the cross are inevitable in the legitimate exercise of authority, even when the subject is deeply committed to the goals of the institute. **c)** In professing vows one voluntarily risks encountering the cross entailed in religious obedience. **d)** Though the risk may intend a situation beyond what can be perceived by the subject, any legitimate command must be seen by the superior as serving the goal of the institute; **e)** Although the command can intend the good of the subject, it can backfire. The religious will try to identify his resultant sufferings with those of Christ. **f)** Thus, religious never abdicate or sacrifice their human freedom. They realize this freedom most perfectly in furthering the goals of their institutes.
4. The concrete forms of religious obedience have changed and will continue to change. **a)** The forms of exercising command, its extent, and even its material content my change without entailing a change in the essence of religious obedience. **b)** Change itself is of the essence of obedience, and superiors must not use their powers to obstruct all change.
5. Here Rahner explains why he is not treating the "vow of obedience" in the strict sense, and therefore why he is not addressing whether the vow is a promise to follow a particular way of life or to sincerely aim at following that form of life.
6. Superiors and subjects must reckon with conflicts of conscience. **a)** It cannot be denied that erroneous judgments (even inculpably

immoral ones) can be made in good faith by either subjects of superiors. **b)** Every command is subject to the moral judgment of subordinates, since such reflection is part and parcel of their duty to judge their own actions. **c)** When subordinates express their conscientious reservations to a command, the superior should: (i) remind the subordinate that not every command which is burdensome is *ipso facto* immoral; (ii) if the conscientious objection cannot be cleared up in open discussion, then the superior should: 1) if it is a slight matter, transfer it to someone who has no such reservation; 2) invite the objector to consider leaving the institute, or take steps unilaterally in that direction, since the institute has the right to maintain its integrity against counterclaims of conscience.

RLT.8. Enthusiasm and the Religious. (71-76)

Abstract: All religious today are familiar with charismatic prayer groups. Rahner offers three dogmatic principles to help religious respond to such movements with "critical sympathy." **1.** Experience of the Spirit is real and legitimate. **2.** All spiritual experiences are simultaneously human experiences. "There are no purely divine experiences of grace; there are only 'incarnate' spiritual experiences" (72). This makes such experiences difficult to prove, and explains why they call for the discernment of spirits. Not every powerful emotional experience is necessarily from the Spirit. **3.** Discernment of spirits is never easy. Separating the human from the divine in any particular experience is a minor question, since every good impulse regardless of its source can be traced back to God. In the end, whatever leads us to embrace or to intensify our appreciation of or commitment to transcendent mystery is the work of grace.

Topics: CHARISMATIC RENEWAL; SPIRIT/s, discernment of.
Subsidiary discussions: Mystery (75).

RLT.9. The Challenge of Growing Old. (77-84)

Abstract: Old age is a special challenge in Christian life, and so too in religious life. Aging affects every aspect of life. It is a special grace not given to all: a difficult mission and a venture at which we can fail. Since aging is a particular form of the universal human task of making one's life definitive, it is a very serious matter. Society's tra-

ditional attitude of respect toward the elderly is changing rapidly. This also affects religious orders in many ways yet to be reflected upon. Rahner concludes with an unsystematic list of many questions these changes pose for religious orders (80ff). He ends with an examination of conscience for religious: "Questions on the care of elderly colleagues."
Topics: DEATH; EVERYDAY LIFE, aging.

RLT.10. A Successful Death (85-88).
Abstract: Since it may be true that St. Theresa died believing, despite the mortal temptation she felt to unbelief, isn't it possible for us to hope the same is true for many if not all people? What is important to Rahner about St. Theresa's death is the fact that the church has guaranteed it as a "successful" death: an actual self-surrender in faith, hope and love to incomprehensible Mystery. The impenetrability of human freedom makes it impossible for us to judge whether or not a death has been "successful" in this sense. But in this case the church (i.e., the church of praying, calling, trusting, and praising Christians) has discerned that St. Theresa's death was successful: the ascent of light in darkness conquering all unbelief and despair. This interpretation and guarantee makes death more comprehensible to us.
Topics: DEATH; THERESA of Lisieux, St.
Subsidiary discussions: Saints, canonization of (87); Spirit/s, discernment of (87).

SL. *Servants of the Lord*, NY: Herder, 1968. Translated by Richard Strachan. *Knechte Christi*, 1967; and *Vom Sinn des kirchlichen Amtes*, 1966.
Contents: Preface.
  1. The Meaning of Ecclesiastical Office.
  2. Today's Priest and his Faith.
  3. God's Word Entrusted to Men.
  4. The Grace of Office.
  5. No Regrets.
  6. The Priestly Office and Personal Holiness.
  7. The Man with the Pierced Heart.
  8. The Spirit of Change.
  9. Christ the Exemplar of Priestly Obedience.

10. The Celibacy of the Secular Priest Today: an open letter.
11. Priestly Confession.
12. Prayer of an Ordinand on the Eve of his Ordination.
13. Prayer for the Right Spirit of Christ's Priesthood.
Related Publications of the author (a brief bibliography of mainly German sources).
Sources (integrated here at the head of each essay).

Preface (5-9). These essays treat the Catholic priesthood without being a complete theology of orders (cf., "Related Publications," 217f). It is a collection of pre-conciliar occasional pieces, revised and expanded here. If there is one theme it is demythologizing the priesthood, but in a specific, legitimate sense that holds in tension the priest's call to holiness and the distinction between office and charism (6). The first essay stresses the indispensable, singular "function" of priesthood and sets the stage for later entries.

SL.1. The Meaning of Ecclesiastical Office. (13-45). *Vom Sinn des kirchlichen Amtes*, 1966. November 12, 1966 lecture at Freiburg/Br. honoring Archbishop Hermann Schäufele's 60th birthday.
Abstract: After situating hierarchy within the broad scope of the nature and constitution of the church (II-V), Rahner examines the theological limits of hierarchy (the legitimate existence of charism in the church, VI-VII, and the inescapable sinfulness of office holders, VIII). He concludes with a discussion of how to moderate disagreements in the church between clergy and laity (IX-X).
Topics: CHURCH, constitution of; HIERARCHY, meaning of; OFFICE AND CHARISM; PRIESTLY LIFE.
Subsidiary discussions: Demythology/izing (6ff); God, self-communication of (16f); Jesus Christ (18ff); Church (21ff); Heierarchy, *munera* of (27); Causality, sacramental (28f); Hierarchy, sinfulness of (37ff); Laity, duties of (42f, 44f); Conscience (42f); Church, dissent within (43f).

Precis: I. Every essay necessarily has its own limited perspective. This one concentrates on achieving a better understanding of the hierarchical office in the constitution of the church (presuming the teachings of Vatican II, and leaving aside New Testament controversies).

II. Rahner takes the longest possible view: God the creator of all, insofar as hierarchy does not bridge some gulf between God and man for the first time, but reveals the eschatological historicity of the direct union of God and man which already exists everywhere. For Christians the world is one event: the self-communication of God — a love that beggars comprehension. **III.** This love has a temporal history, manifested fully and finally in Jesus Christ. At a thousand different points in the seeming chaos of human history, "one thing occurs which produces and sustains it all: the silent coming of God" (20). This can occur anywhere since the love of Christ embraces all. **IV.** In this world there is a community which publicly bears witness to Jesus, and to God's self-donation to the world, and to its inevitable victory. This community is the church, the oneness of whose single witness requires cohesion and order.

V. This (II-IV) is the only proper context to understand hierarchy in the church, which exists by virtue of the whole church, just as the church exists by manifesting its historicity. Rahner now enters into a very dense discussion of ecclesial office. He states that its claim to truth rests on the faith of the whole church guided by the Spirit, and that office bearers in the church are unable to disgrace totally the meaning of their office as this would mean the end of the effective witness of the church. The gradations within the one authentic witness of the hierarchy are difficult to describe (25). The church's witness issues from both *Logos* (as offer) and *Pneuma* (as acceptance), mirroring the two Trinitarian processions. These beget in us faith, hope and love (summary, 26), and in turn are reflected in the distinction of the three *munera* associated with hierarchy: the teaching office summoning faith, the pastoral office manifesting hope, and the office of sanctification as the event of love (27). The hierarchy's word of witness, (threefold and one) can be spoken either by the power of governance or the power of sanctification, both of which orders are conferred in ordination. For this reason they are one in nature. This word of witness is always effective, causing what is said to occur. Thus we call it sacramental, together with its attendant sign causality (28f). Realizing that this word spoken to and lived by the church is precisely the *Ur-sakrament*, the function of hierarchical office can perfectly well be understood as *ministerium verbi*, even though that term may rightly be used in a more restricted sense.

VI. What theological limits are there to the meaning of hierarchy? First, office is office: it is antecedent to the church and serves the church. In addition to office there is also a hierarchy of spirit, of grace, of union with God, of holiness. As much as we may wish they always coincided, one never implies or demands the other. The closeness to God indicated by office is not the same as the intimacy with God found in holiness. This is positive. It should keep clergy humble and make the laity sanguine about its clergy. **VII.** Rahner continues the discussion of office and charism, reiterating that the church works through both clergy and laity in everyday acts of love and patience. But one cannot deny the importance of office in regulating, guiding and nourishing the church. In fact, it is hard to draw the line between the two since office holders may also possess charismata. The criterion for the genuineness of any charism is the bearer's perseverance united in loyal obedience with ecclesial office. **VIII.** Another theological limitation on the meaning of hierarchy is that the bearers of office remain finite, sinful, human beings. They do not possess God, but only witness to God. Whatever good may come from their work is God's sovereign doing. "Always the authority of office will overburden its bearer, make him painfully aware that however true our doctrine, however valid the administration of the sacraments may be, inwardly we all fall short of the duties set to us" (40).

IX. Should office be criticized? Yes, but "loveless, carping criticism without self-criticism, priggish criticism, are far from being a virtue" (41). After all, each of us contributes to this church of sinners. Our criticism should build up the church, and should not expect or demand that office-bearers be angels. Both clergy and laity must avoid the unctuous hypocrisy of self-righteousness — clergy considering themselves beyond challenge, and laity quick to blame the clergy for all that is amiss in the church. In any case, office has another limit. It cannot reach conscience: the point where one's own heart begins to witness to God's grace in everyday life, despite the fact the church has officials appointed to do this (summary, 43). **X.** In the church, differences of opinion should not destroy solidarity and love. When clergy and laity realize they both serve God with the talents they have and in the posts they have been given, and that on Judgment Day they will not be asked about their status but about their faith, hope and love, the laity will come to value and obey the gift of order in the church, and clerics will come to see themselves as servants. The signs of the times, too, point in this direction. The forms of hierarchy will certainly change over time, but the witness of office will endure (conclusion, 45).

SL.2. Today's Priest and his Faith. (47-69). *Der Glaube des Preisters heute,* in *Geist und Leben* 40, no. 4 (1967) revised. July 4, 1967, Lecture to diocesan clergy of Münster, Westphalia.

Abstract: Though priests feel their faith challenged they need not panic. Real faith is always opposed. In today's necessarily confusing theological climate a return to the hierarchy of truths dispels any defeatism. To give a compelling account of their faith priests must be men of prayer and mystical contemplation.

Topics: FAITH; PRIESTLY LIFE; THEOLOGICAL LANGUAGE; THEOLOGY, task of.

Subsidiary discussions: Demythology/ -izing (57ff); Revelation History (58ff); Hierarchy of Truths (63ff).

Precis: We must accept our place in history. Today faith is no longer a matter of course. That it meets challenges on every side is neither unnatural nor bad. But it does prompt us to examine in greater detail what the faith of today's priest must be. **I.** It felt somehow "natural" for men of prior generations to become priests. But this had much less to do with the nature of faith than with sociology. Today, faith is questioned at every turn. But this situation suits a faith which always preaches the "folly of the cross." Opposition and rejection should not astonish or panic us. We can still be honest believers even without all the social reinforcement.

II. What is required in the faith of priests today is first straightforward obedience to revelation and magisterium. No priest today may harbor a faith that openly or covertly differs from the faith of the church as officially formulated by the magisterium. One cannot cover one's heterodoxy by recourse to the inevitable gap between the content of a religious truth and its formulation (although simply repeating old formulae does no service to the church). "No, we believe and preach the formulated faith as identical to the reality it conveys" (52). There is always something institutional about the truth because it is about intercommunication which is never purely private. Nor must the pluralism in scripture be used as a tool against the church, since it is the scripture *of* the church. There is no room for fanatical, unself-critical theology in the church. Those who find themselves irreconcilably opposed to a set doctrine of the church should have the courage and decency to leave it, rather than to infiltrate it with Modernist methods.

III. Priests must also try to assimilate the theology of today, a theology that is restive due to its attempt to "confront the Christian message boldly and squarely with the whole idea of life that men have today" (55) . If the world changes, then theology must change, precisely to be able to preach the "old Gospel" and not another. Given the pluralism in society there must necessarily be a pluralism of theologies. Such theological groping is a trial to be endured in Christian patience and hope. But priests must never say they, "no longer know what we believe." These are panicked reactions to difficult times. Nor should theological problems be aired from the pulpit. Failures in preaching should spur us on to fashion a better, more orthodox theology which will be new precisely because it is orthodox.

IV. One of the particular tasks and difficulties of today's new theology is "demythologization." But this program is not completely new, examining as it does the relation between the content and the form of our religious concepts. What is new is the keen sense today of the need to have the nature of redemptive history more accurately defined. We cannot read scripture or imagine salvation history superficially as the ancients did. We must have sharper eyes precisely in order not to lose what the ancient faith saw and believed. Our multi-dimensional, critical approach to revelation history must aid us in drawing distinctions (e.g., hypostatic union, yes – latent Monophysitism, no). Needless to say, this interpretation of the central task of theology today (exploring the gap in propositions between content and form) does not make it any less painful or risky.

V. Priests today must not let themselves be paralyzed by the false notion that we are fighting a rearguard action in defending the faith against skepticism and agnosticism. To keep from becoming intimidated we must return to the "hierarchy of truths" which alone keeps faith from being seen as a complicated system of individual propositions. Rahner now sets out the three quite simple notes at the heart of faith (63f): the self-revelation of the incomprehensible God finds its final and irrevocable fulfillment in Jesus Christ, to whom the church is the faithful witness. Christian faith looks death in the eye and drops the incomprehensibility of life into the even greater incomprehensibility of God, which it believes is love. All its propositions are but a thousand variations on this one theme. That the world today is too busy or too deaf to accept this message will not shake the person who has appropriated it. Secure in our belief that the church is the embodiment of the salvation of the whole world, we will never give into defeatism. But we must no longer use statistics as our "standards for success" prefaced on an outwardly homogeneous, generally Christian society. All debates over the meaning of particular propositions must be related to this inmost center of faith represented in the hierarchy of truths.

VI. Priests today are asked to give an account of faith – a faith that is their own, that is Catholic, that is living, honest and fraternal (list, 67f). Only a person of prayer is capable of such faith, which is grace, which is God Himself and the activity of the whole person. "The faith of today's priest is the faith of a man of prayer and mystical contemplation or it is nothing" (68). God will give us the grace if we wish to be such men.

SL.3. God's Word Entrusted to Men. (71-79). *Zur Primiz, in Korrespondenzblatt der Priestergemeinschaft des Collegium Canisianum zu Innsbruck,* 97 (1962) 24-28.

Abstract: Priests are human beings and fellow Christians, but entrusted by God with a divine word to share with the world in season and out. To do so faithfully they need the loving support of the people.

Topics: PRIESTLY LIFE; WORD, ministry of.

Subsidiary discussions: Word, sacramental (76).

Precis: This First Mass celebration spurs Rahner to ask what a priest actually is in God's holy community which gathers this day for two reasons: to give thanks to God for their shared salvation in Christ, and because this community of God's is an ordered community manifesting the divine order established by God Himself. This alone explains the existence of priesthood in the church.

This day of new beginnings is actually a continuation of a human life and a Christian life. The imperfect, sinful, human priest asks the community to let him accompany them along the road of their lives, to speak God's word to them and give them God's grace. This fellow Christian, whose new status derives from the community and who himself needs the grace of the church, asks to be accepted to exercise the office of ministering to their sanctification and salvation.

So we see the newly-ordained priest, who remains a mere human being and a fellow Christian, today begin to speak the word of God to the faithful by God's authority. Whatever his personal talents or shortcomings, he has a divine word to convey. He comes because God tells him to announce, "that God, the infinite, unutterable, nameless mystery embracing our existence, loves us, forgives us, gives us himself in Jesus Christ our Lord and in the grace of the Holy Ghost" (75) – an old message, ever young. At times, this word becomes the sacramental word, affecting in our lives what it proclaims. This priest is a steward of the mysteries of God. In a sense, Christ's words ring out through him. Through this seemingly ordinary word we meet the Lord face to face and encounter his grace. So the priest asks the people to accept this word from him, believe it together, and be saved.

As for the future, we know little. But assuredly this new priest's life will be humdrum and tedious, with little success and many disappointments. But if he remains faithful he will be able to say: "I am where I belong. I am doing my duty. I am not living for myself but for God's mission and grace." What more can anyone want? What comes of it all is unknown. Like every life, his, too, will one day be swallowed up in the unutterable silence of the everlasting God. But if we have accompanied each other in faith to the end, God, the true and only future will come. Then God will be all in all, the fulfillment of this priest's life and of ours. But for him to stay faithful, those he serves must sustain him just as he sustains them. When they pray for priests, patiently put up with them, accept God's word and sacramental mysteries from them, there the holy church already stands, and with us Christ, his grace and eternal life.

SL.4. The Grace of Office. (81-87). *Gnade des Amtes*, in *Korrespondenzblatt der Priestergemeinschaft des Collegium Canisianum zu Innsbruck*, 91 (1957) 19-21.

Abstract: Speaking at a First Mass, Rahner describes the priesthood by reminding the assembled priests how God has graced them; he prays that God may continue to do so, and justifies his hope that God will.

Topics: PRIESTLY LIFE; WORD, ministry of.
Subsidiary discussions: Word, sacramental (82f).

Precis: At this First Mass celebration, Rahner directs his remarks to the assembled priests. First: "*God has given us grace.*" Nothing about us poor, weak, sinful men makes us worthy of the great call we have received. It is a tremendous, unmerited call to utter God's eternal word, Jesus Christ ... and above that to speak the sacramental word and to offer sacrifice. This grace we have received is all-consuming for three reasons: 1. We are given to the church, she is now our mother, the bride of Christ, who pays the price for being human – hesitant, puzzled, slow to understand. Composed of sinful men (i.e., us) she is often unnecessarily harsh and bitter. 2. We are also given away through the church to people we must serve and who have a right to us. We cannot keep ourselves for ourselves. We have no right but to serve. 3. God has given Himself to us, and the longer we serve Him, the more we surrender to Him, the more this truth is brought home to us, the more we shall understand that the grace God whereby God gives Himself to us as his priests is an all-consuming grace. This section closes with a prayer.

Second, in these difficult times we must say "*May God give us his grace*" because we are weak and sinful men, and because priestly life is hard. And God, give us your grace because humans are a riddle, both we ourselves and those to whom we are sent, whose burdens we are asked to bear. Finally we must say, "*God will give us his grace.*" Why should we doubt that the One who has called us and brought us this far would now refuse us his grace? Does God will his priests? Yes, because God wills the church; and God wills it in irrevocably willing the salvation of all. Rahner ends with a call for prayer for the newly-ordained, for his family, for those gathered, and for the whole church.

SL.5. No regrets. (90–94). *Wir haben es nicht betreut,* in *Zur Pastoral der geistlichen Berufe* (1966) 81-88. 1957 address in Freiburg/Br. on the occasion of his silver jubilee of ordination on July 26, 1932.

Abstract: Speaking for the 25-year priest jubilarians Rahner tells seminarians they have no regrets; they continue to place their trust in God; and they encourage these young men also to "take the plunge."

Topics: PRIESTLY LIFE.

Precis: It is appropriate to celebrate this 25th jubilee of ordination in a seminary with young men aspiring to priesthood. Gathered to thank God, let me speak in a plain and brotherly way about priesthood and say simply, "*We have no regrets.*" Certainly no regrets as we consider the great truths and realities of our faith; but more so, no regrets to having said yes to God's call, though we were weak and sinful, and naive, and unequal to the task. But God never forsook us, so we have no regrets. It is useless to ask whether we would do it again. All we can say is God brought to completion what He started. The good accomplished in us remains, and the failings we brought with us into the priesthood have been engulfed in God's mercy. Secondly, we can say, "*We place our trust in God.*" However long we have left to serve, whatever we are asked to do, however well or poorly we do it, our experience spurs us to place our trust in God, confident that God will bring our poor efforts to completion in God's own way and time. Finally, we say to the seminarians here, "*You can take the plunge.*" You are human as we are; we took the plunge and have not regretted it, why not you? You have a noble calling (93), believe in it! But each day you must translate it into reality anew. "The noblest, most blessed prize is always the most hazardous and difficult to win" (94). If you are called, risk it! It may overburden you, but God's grace will surpass you.

SL.6. The Priestly Office and Personal Holiness. (95-106). *Immaculata,* in *Korrespondenzblatt der Priestergemeinschaft des Collegium Canisianum zu Innsbruck,* 89 (1955) 80-89, revised.

Abstract: For all their differences, the link between priestly office and priestly holiness is mirrored by the link in Mary's life between her office/role as Mother of the Savior and her personal holiness as enshrined in the doctrine of the Immaculate Conception. Her example calls us to strive for such holiness in our lives.

Topics: BVM, Immaculate Conception of; OFFICE, and charism; PRIESTHOOD, office and charism.

Subsidiary discussions: Donatism (102f).

Precis: The meaningfulness of linking the Immaculate Conception and priesthood must be shown. **The mystery of this feast. 1.** *God engulfs the life of man.* Respecting our freedom, God gives and plans our lives in such a way that we are what He calls us to be. **2.** *God engulfs the life of man in redemptive love.* There is no appealing God's plans or God's judgments. We rejoice to know that God's final word and judgment on us is love and mercy that does not condemn but saves. The fact that it happened once fully and finally in Christ fills me with hope that God will engulf me, too, in love. **3.** *God engulfs Mary's human life in loving fidelity.* The beginning indicated by the Immaculate Conception was blessed because the ending was to be blessed. This feast tells us that what God starts He brings to blessed conclusion, that God plans in light of the end, that God grasps totality. This is especially true of Mary but applies to all of us. Yet we are generally such dullard egotists we do not grasp this. **4.** *God's call is a call to man to become himself.* God makes us to govern ourselves in such a way that in achieving ourselves through the use of our freedom we also achieve His plan for us. Similarly, in willing a mother for the Logos, God willed her to be free in herself before God. Hence, her beginning, like ours, is the beginning of true self-discovery, the beginning of a particular history. And yet her life also deserves to be eternally valid. Since we only know God through His works, we look to what He did in the life of Mary and see there the eternal validity God also wills for us. Our task, like Mary's, is to become what we are.

Oneness of office and person. Rahner now draws a parallel between the unity of office and personal holiness in the life of a priest with the unity of Mary's office (i.e., her role in salvation history) and her personal holiness. He begins by asking why it was fitting that Mary be conceived immaculate. He answers that her consent to divine motherhood was no mere biological fact, but an historical act of personal faith. **1.** Mary becomes a mother by her assent, which forms part of salvation history itself. Her faith and her motherhood are of a piece like office and grace. Her act of faith is inseparably public and private. In short, that she was conceived immaculate indissolubly identifies "Mary's role in the history of salvation with her God-wrought personal holiness" (102). **2.** What has this to do with priesthood? Often Catholic theology is criticized for stressing the institutional and juridical at the expense of the charismatic. If so, this is to avoid Donatism, insuring the validity of sacraments independent of the holiness of those dispensing them. But this distinction is neither fundamental nor absolute. Mary's Immaculate Conception underscores just this unity of office and holiness. There follows a long and eloquent admonition from the lips of Mary to priests urging them to be holy (104f). **3.** Obviously there is a difference between the unity of office and holiness found in Mary and in us: hers is an existing unity, a duty to accomplish. But if ours is a duty, then God can grant us the efficacious grace to become holy, and the gap between office and holiness becomes merely provisional. We do not know this, but we must hope so (summary, 105f).

SL.7. Man with the Pierced Heart. Devotion to the Sacred Heart and Tomorrow's Priesthood. (107-119). June 17, 1966 lecture at *Collegium Canisianum*, Innsbruck. *Korrespondenzblatt der Priestergemeinschaft des Collegium Canisianum zu Innsbruck*, 101 (1966/67) 19-27.

Abstract: Understanding what is meant by the heart of Jesus and devotion to it can be an unutterably holy grace even for priests of tomorrow.

Topics: JESUS CHRIST, Sacred Heart, devotion to; PRIESTLY LIFE.

Subsidiary discussions: Priest of tomorrow (111ff); Heart (115f).

Precis: After reflecting on the notable silence of Vatican II concerning devotion to the Sacred Heart, Rahner concludes this devotion has reached a critical juncture. In 20 years will it have died of neglect and live only in the liturgical calendar? Many factors contribute to these dangers (list, 109) but they fail to explain fully the critical state of the devotion. History doesn't just happen. It is the outcome of our choices. Rahner maintains that "understanding what is meant by the heart of Jesus and devotion to it can be an unutterably holy grace even for priests of tomorrow" (110). After voicing two reservations (1. he is not referring here to the concrete popular piety of tomorrow; 2. such devotion *can* be a great grace but *need not* be) he proceeds to clarify this thesis.

What will a priest of tomorrow be like and look like if he is to prove himself worthy of his mission? After a long and uncompromisingly tough appraisal (111ff) he summarizes, "tomorrow's priest will be a man with the pierced heart, from which alone he draws strength for his mission" (113), and through which he is led to the core of his own existence and leads others to their core. This essence of priestly existence will become increasingly obvious to others and in demand. And the priest will have to do this on his own since society will no longer succor him. Where will this overtaxed priest of tomorrow look to find what he does not have in himself? Surely he will look to the man with the pierced heart.

Rahner now turns a bit more theological. He examines the notion of the heart as "a basic concept," an *Urwort*, indicating a person's center where one stands before God as a whole." Tomorrow's priest will find his own nature if he contemplates the heart of the Lord" (116). Rahner now describes beautifully the heart of Christ (116f), not "sweet" but "terrible." He warns that devotion to the Sacred Heart is far from old-fashioned, for much of what is old anticipates the real future. Nor is it a Baroque luxury for religious introverts. "Understanding the heart of Jesus in faith, hope and love, is the one long adventure ever new, that only ends when one has arrived at one's own heart and discovered that after all that frightful pit is filled with God" (118). Abstract theology cannot move one to this devotion. It can only point to the real questions each priest must ask himself.

SL.8. The Spirit of Change. (121-126). *Geist der Wandlung*, in *Klerusblatt*, 27/10 (May 15, 1947).

Abstract: Because the church is the church of the Spirit, it is a church of eternal unrest. Its indefectability is a promise of constantly awakening to new life; its permanence is perpetual motion. Priests (who are meant to be the living unrest of the church) often dismiss the call to change, confusing their laziness for loyalty. Yet this has always been the case, or else God's word which forever calls us to conversion would be a lie. But we barricade ourselves against the unrest of the Spirit – a spirit of eternal discontent. It is true that we priests often feel much of the spirit of the world in ourselves and little of the Spirit of the Father. But it is also false, because often we harbor false ideas about where and how the Spirit works in the church. Often when we say we are looking for the Spirit (immovable faith), we are actually looking for something else (i.e., to be absolved from the risk and responsibility of decision). But if we daily revise our thoughts about the Spirit, are honest with ourselves, and do not misrepresent our experiences, we shall find, "Here he is! He is with me!" (Payer, 126).

Topics: CONVERSION; PRIESTLY LIFE; SPIRIT/s.

SL.9. Christ the Exemplar of Priestly Obedience. (127-148).

Written in Latin for a special number of *Seminarium*. Revised and enlarged.

Abstract: Rahner seeks to clarify the meaning of clerical obedience by grounding it in an exegesis of Jesus' obedience and by comparing it to civil obedience. This reveals how legitimate conflicts may arise between superior and subject, and how Christ is a model for those who obey and for those who in conscience resist.

Topics: JESUS CHRIST, obedience of; OBEDIENCE, clerical; PRIESTLY LIFE, obedience.

Subsidiary discussions: Spirit, role in obedience (143ff).

Precis: I. Introductory observations: 1. Care must be taken in using Jesus as a model of clerical obedience. Despite the claims of some overheated spiritual writers, clearly Jesus did not and could not have formally practiced all Christian virtues as such. Hence, we "follow" Christ rather than "imitate him." The obedience we learn from him "consists essentially in ready acceptance of a limited life, one into which not everything can be crammed that is good and desirable 'in itself'" (128). **2.** Clerical obedience is a complicated reality which takes many forms. Scripture cannot yield its concrete norms, although the example and teaching of Christ do provide its ultimate justification and motive. **3.** Obedience in human society. **a)** *In the broad sense* means voluntary acceptance of necessity for whatever motive. For Christians this motive is the acceptance of God's sovereign but personal will, and hence comes close to obedience in the strict sense. **b)** *In the strict sense* it is recognition in thought and deed of the legitimate authority in a society which makes its will known in general laws and particular commands. It may include obedience to God, but unlike such obedience it does not necessarily involve an intimate relationship with the one who commands. Moreover, unlike obeying God, obeying civil law may feel like compliance with an alien will. In short, obedience to authority has a "functional" role in society. The subject does not submit to those in charge, but is directed by them to the goal and good of society. This is also true of authority in the church. Though even here, commands that clearly conflict with the good of the society must never be obeyed (though this is no license for indiscriminate "revolutionary" disobedience). Not all decisions of church authorities are simply "God's will" demanding obedience. They are fallible decisions arrived at by human means. Nevertheless, they are legitimate and do derive from God insofar as they are rooted in God's will that societies be effective and well ordered. c) *In the church*: all this explains why even in the church legitimate conflicts can arise between people of good will over the morality or immorality of particular commands. When such conflicts arise superiors must tolerate or penalize, and subjects must resist, while at the same time recognizing the superior's right to govern.

II. Rahner proceeds with a brief exegesis of New Testament terms used to indicate the obedience of Christ (list, 134) in: **a)** the Synoptics, particularly Luke; **b)** John; **c)** Paul; **d)** Letter to the Hebrews. **III.** From this exegesis Rahner, **1.** draws a twofold conclusions as to why Christ's salvific work is presented as obedience to God, which he then contrasts with Jesus' clear disobedience to Temple leaders. **a)** Although both Christ and we His followers have faith and also obey, the link between us is harder to see clearly when it is formed in terms of faith. Therefore, the New Testament writers consciously chose to highlight the obedience of Jesus, which is most clearly the fruit of His faith. **b)** Of the many terms applied to the salvific work of Christ, obedience is the most adequate: the unconditional acceptance of life in its obscure facticity as the loving will of the "Father of Life" that bears death hidden within itself and makes its way toward death. **2.** We must not overlook Jesus' refusal to obey the synagogue, not out of a sense of personal freedom, but out of His even deeper obedience to the authority of the "Father." Hence, His disobedience was obedience in the highest sense. Thus, Jesus can be a model today for those who find disobedience to church authority both a right and a duty.

IV. How is Jesus' obedience relevant to clerical obedience? **1.** Not being a cleric himself, Jesus' obedience was not clerical obedience. Hence, clerics today cannot simply reproduce His obedience and call it clerical obedience. **2.** Clerical obedience is one concrete means for priests to share in the obedience of Christ. **a)** All Christian must fashion their lives on the obedience of Christ: submitting to human authority and accepting God's will from the heart. For priests, the church itself offers ample opportunities to accept the blind facticity of life just as Jesus did. **b)** The example of Christ helps us to distinguish the "functional" from the "religious" dimension of obedience. The functional legitimately exists to order society. It must never dress itself in a pseudo-religious guise. But there is a religious dimension even to functional obedience, when, for example, in his obedience the priest experiences self-denial, sacrifice, the cross. All of this calls for greater specifically religious obedience to God. **c)** Clerical obedience requires *diakonia*, being a servant of the church and a "slave to Christ" for the salvation of all. **d)** The Spirit who works with a priest to conform him to the image of Christ is a spirit of freedom and sonship, a spirit of peace, love, gentleness and joy (list, 143f). **3.** Those who practice true clerical obedience in the freedom of the Spirit can obey the law with joy, whereas obeying the law without this Spirit is drudgery and a curse. **4.** Christ can also be the model for a cleric in conflict with his superior. Just as Christ disobeyed in order to obey his Father, the cleric must honestly examine his motives to disobey for conscience sake.

V. The issue of priestly obedience cannot be completely solved in the realm of theory. At best theory justifies the general, but it can never explain how a particular person can choose and remain faithful to a life of obedience. The concrete life of Christ is the only and ultimate norm of our lives, and it calls for no external justification. To overcome current difficulties, both superiors and subordinates must conform themselves every more closely to the obedience of Christ. Rahner ends with specific advice to superiors (146f), to clerics (147), and then reminds both groups that all our commands and decisions are governed by history which we can do little to speed up or to stave off. Not even the possession of the Spirit through sharing in the obedience of Christ will ever exempt any of us from carrying His cross. Conflicts are inevitable. But whoever, led by the Spirit, renounces his/her own advantage renders God the obedience of faith and so abides in the peace of Christ.

SL.10. The Celibacy of the Secular Priest Today: An Open Letter.
(149-172). *Der Zölibat des Weltpriesters im heutigen Gespräch. Ein offener Breif,* in Geist und Leben, 40 (1967) 122-138.

Abstract: This surprisingly frank, personal and unsystematic letter advises a young priest how to think more clearly about the practice of celibacy for Catholic priests and reveals Rahner's unvarnished opinion.

Topics: CELIBACY; PRIESTLY LIFE, celibacy.

Subsidiary discussions: Marriage (passim); Renunciation (passim).

Precis: There is no reason to pretend all is well among priests, or that priestly celibacy is not a hot issue in the church today. Jumping right in, Rahner insists there is no sense in talking to anyone who sees no more to life than sex, discounting responsibility, renunciation, pain. Much of the distress priests feel in living their celibate lives is a consequence of their commitment (not an antecedent fact) arising from their having lost a firm will to resist hunger for tangible happiness. Life itself (celibate or married) calls for brave endurance of daily routine. It is naive to think reversing the discipline of celibacy would lead to a life free from suffering. Even successful marriages are built on a capacity for solitude and self-denial.

Rahner refutes the claim that renouncing marriage is always a sign of psychological abnormality. Yes, every important human decision stems from many motives, and neither marriage nor celibacy absolves us from sorting them out. Celibacy rightly understood is a real option offered by human nature. Human sexuality is not a fixed quantity but a task, a challenge calling for renunciation. This position is found in scripture (154f). In addition, "we only live once." However difficult choice may be, we can't experience every lifestyle option and then go back and make our choice. The fact that celibacy is recommended in scripture for those who can accept it, and that many have found it to be a meaningful choice is enough for Rahner. True renunciation is as enlightening as the experience of what has been renounced. This is true of both celibacy and marriage, and Rahner finds the business of comparing the advantages of the two "a great bore." No vocation is absolute or unlimited.

People complain that priestly ministry and a call to celibacy have nothing in common and it is arbitrary for the church to link them. They also say a 25 year-old is too young to make such a life-long choice. Rahner argues the two *do* have something in common, and the church *is* right to link them (allowing the discipline to be suspended in those countries where not doing so would deprive the people access to the sacraments). Celibate priesthood is no more coercive than marriage. In both states grace is won again and again by fidelity. Nor do we insist that 25 year-olds are incapable of entering a life-long marriage. If, however, maturity is the problem, then why not raise the age of ordination to 35 rather than make celibacy optional? Every choice is made in the face of an obscure, unpredictable future. Lapses in fidelity do not render these decisions nonsensical. Making once-in-a-lifetime decisions takes faith; accepting the cross and cooperating with God's grace takes hope, obedience, prayer, prudent restraint.

It is wrong to talk about this issue in the abstract. Each of us should study *our own* celibacy. The question is not about celibacy "as such," but "Where do I stand as a priest?" (160). Rahner finds it strange that people everywhere are talking about individual choice, but on this issue they are content to take refuge in generalities. But what can shed light on *my* celibacy? Only prayer and prayerful struggle. It is disingenuous to claim people lose the will to remain committed celibates "through no fault of their own." (Something equally true of marriage.) *My* celibacy is part of *my* faith – "the free vital act that brings the life that is God himself through to me and testifies to it, by Christ's death and mine" (162). Put simply, "I relinquish a noble, awesome gift of this life because 'I' believe in eternal life" (163). Marriage is built on the same belief. "Madness? Yes, the madness of loving God and believing in the death that alone gives a man true life" (163). To dismiss all this as pious talk is to debase marriage. Ask yourself, if "I" were to marry, if "I" tried to cram all the attainable happiness of life into this one lifetime so as to miss nothing, would "I" then believe and hope more firmly, love more selflessly, take God and eternal life more seriously? For himself, Rahner says, "I could not."

Without passing judgment on anyone, Rahner sees this sudden enthusiasm for marriage among the clergy not as sign of greater faith but as a sign of weakened faith. Though he often feels besieged, his confidence in the gospel is not shaken, despite the real risks of lovelessness which dog the choice for celibacy. But every concrete life is a mixture, a compromise. It never embraces everything at once. Every Christian life calls for abnegation and self-denial – a preparation for death. The charge that celibacy is the product of an unhealthy dualism blind to the unity of love of God and neighbor is simply not true for Rahner's own celibacy, though he admits it may be true for the celibacy of others (166).

Unsatisfied with his "stammerings," Rahner begins to close the letter with personal advice to the young priest, but cannot resist throwing in a few more observations and arguments. He tells the young priest to read scripture. Keep praying your way into what Jesus says about discipleship and the cross. Think beyond yourself to those you serve. Be patient. All this will draw you nearer to the heart of Christ. And don't worry about what everyone else is saying or thinking. Focus on *your own* celibacy. See your voluntary suffering in the context of the greater inescapable sufferings in the world.

Are critics right when they predict the end of the requirement for celibacy in the near future? Being no prophet, Rahner can only say: 1) he hopes the discipline will not change; 2) he hopes the church will do a better concrete job of helping seminarians to embrace and live the celibate life; 3) the church must be magnanimous in granting dispensations; 4) he hopes the Western church will not develop a mixed system among diocesan clergy. Arguments drawn from the history of the development of celibacy in the West do not interest Rahner, nor do comparisons with the discipline of the Eastern Church (169f). He does ask, however, why the church should not continue to take the *simple priest* in the West seriously by demanding of him the same celibacy the East demands of its bishops. And is it not possible that in relaxing this discipline the church would simply be moving from dealing with the calamitous scandals associated with a celibate clergy to a host of infidelities and broken marriages? Rahner reiterates, "my celibacy" is not a barrier erected by the church. He freely chose it and will continue to choose it regardless of any changes in canon law. He has made his choice. He is sticking to it. He has no regrets (170f). Many other things could be said on this issue, but for now Rahner feels "talked out."

SL.11. Priestly Confession. (173-203). Based on a manuscript for a 1940 lecture to clergy, revised and updated in light of Vatican II.

Abstract: The pre-conciliar practice of compulsory frequent Confessions for priest, religious and seminarians is theologically justifiable. It implements and strengthens the church's teaching on the sacrament, and makes these groups more responsible for the way their sins defile the whole church.

Topics: CONFESSION, frequent; PRIESTLY LIFE, frequent confession.

Subsidiary discussions: Spiritual Direction and Confession (190f); Church, reconciliation with (194ff).

Precis: This essay focuses on one aspect of Confession particular to priests: canon law's requirement for frequent Confession. Though present day [1940/1966] practice is extremely difficult and confusing (people today shy away from "compulsory" things and many new spiritual practices have arisen) we must not summarily dismiss this practice. Due to the outmoded "ascetical" language that clings to this discussion it is difficult to assess the hidden power *and* latent dangers of compulsory frequent Confession. Hence, Rahner urges readers to pay attention to the transformation certain words used in this essay undergo like "frequent confession" and "obligation" (preview, 176).

I. Historical background of frequent confession, current legislation, current efforts at reappraisal. A brief restatement of the requirement for Confession which applies to all the Christian faithful. *1. Formal theological assessment of frequent confession in the light of history of dogma.* Canon Law's requirement for frequent Confessions for priest, religious and seminarians can be justified in light of the fact that the church sanctions and requires it. This practice is not an aberration (178), nor can the history of the frequency of Communion be played off against the frequency of Confession (summary, 179f). No priest does well to frown on a spiritual life built according to the mind of the church. 2. *Priestly Confession in the Code of Canon Law.* After quoting the old Code, Rahner observes: **a)** frequent Confession is enjoined on priests, religious, and seminarians regardless of the presence of serious sin. **b)** This obligation is imposed on bishops. **c)** Though "frequent" is not defined, less than once a month would hardly seem frequent. **d)** "Sacramental" Confession is understood here, not spiritual direction or therapy, however expedient. Rahner discusses neither the nature of the obligation imposed on bishops for monitoring this practice nor the nature of the penalty imposed on priests for noncompliance. He merely notes that neglecting frequent Confession would be a serious sin if it were the only means available to preserve one's state of grace. 3. *Theological and pastoral trends at and since the Second Vatican Council.* Because the trend in post-conciliar theology is to distinguish more sharply between morals and law (not to translate every moral call into a legal norm) one does not expect the new Code to say much more than did *Presbyterorum Ordinis* #18: **a)** It issues no law, and one trusts that any new legislation will be based on facts and not on mere formal authority. **b)** P.O. stresses the fundamental meaningfulness of frequent Confession in the life of the priest without, however, obliging it. **c)** Frequency remains undefined. **d)** The meaningfulness of frequent Confessions is seen as part of a whole spiritual program and not as isolated acts open to enforcement. Two further points. Council documents show the church desires to preserve a tradition without blocking all change. The actual practice of Confession changed over time and will continue to do so. Whatever new forms may arise, priests in the interim should take care not to discourage Confession. The Council is *not* saying no priestly life can be what it should be without regular Confession. But we must move from the attitude that sees whatever is not legislated as completely discretionary. Each priest has a serious duty to ask whether or not frequent Confession is not meaningful *"for me"* (summary, 187).

II. **The theological basis that makes frequent Confessions meaningful.** Rahner assume here the church's teaching that venial sin can be blotted out apart from sacramental absolution for serious sin. The question is whether this frequent practice is meaningful in the framework of a healthy spiritual life. 1. *Radical sinfulness* *of concrete man and the origins of frequent Confessions*. No one can object to the practice of frequent Confession by claiming that the more spiritually mature we become the less concerned we are over venial sin. Just the opposite seems to hold true. We attend to the frailty of our nature not out of a sense of childish self-absorption, but so that we may cast ourselves more completely on God's mercy. Nevertheless, this does not suffice to justify the practice. *2. Subordinate theological arguments for frequent Confession*. Some would justify frequent Confession by linking it with the value of spiritual direction. However valuable this coupling may be, there is no intrinsic link between the two activities, and we still have not justified the practice. Because there are many means for blotting out venial sin, this cannot be the justification. Hence, the justification "must be sought in the nature of the sacramental penance as an act sacramentally and directly ordered to the forgiveness of sins" (192). *3. Man's repentance and God's pardon*. What have we said so far? (summary, 193). Only submitting even our venial sins to God through the spacio-temporal, historical ministrations of the church assures the righteousness that is not one's own but which comes from God. *4. Ecclesiastical and social aspects of frequent Confession*. By restoring Confession to its theological center, it loses its private character and reveals its social and ecclesial character. Frequent Confession affirms that every venial sins defiles the visible church and does spiritual harm to all the members. Hence, frequent Confession is a unique form of love of neighbor and a means for the priest to accept his personal responsibility for the church which he must serve with his whole life. Vatican II teaches that sacramental Confession not only forgives sins committed against God, it also "reconciles sinners with the church" (LG #11; PO #5). Conclusion, 196f.

III. **How frequent Confessions can be practiced despite attendant difficulties.** Confession acknowledges that God alone blots out our sins in his sovereign mercy which we meet historically in the sacraments of the church. Frequent Confession presupposes, implements, and strengthens this attitude. *1. Confession – but how often?* This is not a matter of divine law, nor can it be dictated by the calendar. Frequency must be determined by individuals within the framework of their spiritual lives as a whole. *2. Fitting frequent Confession into one's spiritual life.* Merely going to Confession often will not insure that one is living a proper priestly life. The fruitfulness of the sacrament depends above all on one's inner abandonment to God's mercy. Repentance is difficult to achieve if we hold that our venial sins are either inevitable or inconsequential. These attitudes would seem to be antithetical to living a spiritual life seriously or to disposing oneself to true conversion. **3.** *Theological and spiritual importance of due preparation.* Preparation for Confession should be taken more seriously. Venial sins should be carefully examined not simply for the act but for the outlook they may manifest (list, 202f). Since such a heartfelt and thorough Confession takes great effort perhaps the waning of frequent Confession is not such a bad thing. But unless we manage it "fairly often," then we prove ourselves priests with hearts of stone, distorting what we should be in order to fit what we are.

SL.12. Prayer of an Ordinand on the Eve of his Ordination. (205-211). *Priesterweihe. Gebet eines Weihekandidaten am Abend vor siener Preisterweihe,* in *Geist und Leben,* 26 (1953) 66-69. Published anonymously.

Abstract: In this devotional meditation Rahner prays through some of the major moments in the liturgy of Priestly Holy Orders as it was celebrated before the reforms of Paul VI. **1.** "Is he worthy?" I am not. But here I stand. **2.** Bishop's silent imposition of hands installs me in the unbroken line of mission, and reminds me that God's hand will remain upon me. I, like Christ, will say the words of Isaiah, "The Spirit of the Lord is upon me. . . ." **3.** Being vested in stole and chasuble challenges me to bring them unstained to judgment. **4.** Anointing of hands leads me to pray that my hands will always be full of blessings to dispense to others. **5.** Receiving the chalice and patten I vow to offer sacrifice for the people. **6.** The kiss of peace reminds me that Christ will look at me, call me "friend," and remind me, "You are my friend if you do what I command." **7.** Reciting the Creed will remind me that I stand in the line of the Apostles. **8.** A second imposition of hands by the bishop will confer the power to bind and loose. **9.** Placing my hands between the bishops' hands I will vow obedience to the church. **10.** Ordination is the last great word God speaks to me in my life- the final, irrevocable call that forever shapes my life. May I be found faithful! The essay ends with the prayer of St. Ignatius.

Topics: PRIESTLY LIFE.

SL.13. Prayer for the Right Spirit of Christ's Priesthood. (213-216). Previously unpublished, 1966.
Abstract: In a devout prayer on the eve of ordination, the ordinand thanks God for his call, applies Jesus' words and actions to himself, pleads for the gifts of the Spirit, and asks especially for the grace of prayer.
Topics: PRIESTLY LIFE.

SCC. *The Shape of the Church to Come.* NY: Seabury Press, 1974. 136 pp. *Strukturwandel der Kirche als Ausgabe und Chance.* Freiburg: Herder, 1972. Translation and Introduction by Edward Quinn. Each of the three parts is treated here as a separate essay.
Contents: Introduction (Karl Rahner's Vision; Author's Preface; The Synod's Problems).
Part One: Where Do We Stand?
Part Two: What are We to Do?
Part Three: How can a Church of the Future be Conceived? Epilogue.

SCC. Intro. Introductory material. (3-16)
Abstract: Karl Rahner's Vision (3-8). Situates this book as a response to the 1971 German Synod, and to the call of some to reaffirm certain "indisputable presuppositions" (e.g., divine sonship, resurrection, virgin birth). To Rahner, reaffirming these indisputably true propositions without making them more intelligible to modern people misses the boat. The Synod is largely failing because it lacks a synthetic view (a basic concept). By appraising the modern situation and offering concrete proposals, this book takes a step towards providing such an overview. **Author's Preface** (9). Many may complain this book is too liberal or too conservative. But what is *their* vision? Though these essays focus on Germany they have broader application. **The Synod's Problems** (10-16). The future of the German church will be determined by the Spirit and not by Synodal resolutions. Still the Synod is important. So it is disappointing it should have begun its work without a clear grasp of its single task, with no basic plan. Instead, it works piece-meal on legislation and "themes." Rahner argues for the importance of a basic concept, and maintains that appeals to "the Catholic faith"

or to Vatican II are too broad to provide a meaningful focus. He defends the development of "blocks" within the Synod. After insisting that no one person can supply *the* basic concept required by a Synod, he hopes his fragmentary suggestions may be of assistance.

Topics: SYNOD, German national.

SCC.1. Where Do We Stand? (19-42)

Abstract: To plan for the future, a Synod must consider the actual situation of the church in the world. Rahner sees a church in transition from a *Volkskirche* to a free association. A future "little flock" marked by great internal diversity must strive to avoid polarization, learn to fight fairly and to compromise.

Topics: CHURCH, current status of.

Subsidiary discussions: Church in transition (22ff); Church as "little flock" (29ff); Church, diversity in (35ff); Church, polarization in (38ff).

Precis: 1. **Analysis of the Situation.** Since a Synod is interested primarily in pastoral theology, it must begin with an analysis of the current environment. Most descriptions are too one-sided. They focus on what the church is doing well and ignore those realities it is failing to address. This leads to a hybrid attitude of stubborn conservatism and unspoken despair. Rahner enumerates some features of the current situation. Intellectually, the rise of science (natural, historical, psychological) over metaphysics has led to greater relativism and a diminished role for authority. Our ability to manipulate the environment has changed our relationship to nature and to ourselves (list, 21f). Sociologically, today's church is characterized by "remnants" of a previously socially-sanctioned, traditional "Christendom." But these are slowly being eroded by an increasingly heterogeneous social reality. The formerly close ties between religion and the social order can be seen as a "grace" on which we can no longer rely. In summary, the church is in a state of transition from a *Volkskirche* (socially sanctioned, homogeneous Christendom) to a voluntary association characterized by deep, free, personal faith (23). Either the church will make this transition or there will be no future church at all. In this time of change the church must continue to win as many personally committed members as possible. This description of the situation of the German church could be greatly expanded (list, 25f). One very sad consequence of this situation is the knee-jerk defensiveness of the hierarchy which seems more interested in conserving past forms than in asking what is required for the church of the future (examples, 27).

2. **Church of the Little Flock.** Frankly, the German church is at the beginning of a period of considerable institutional and numerical decline toward becoming "a little flock." But this does not mean becoming a ghetto or a sect. The smaller we become the bolder we must become and the more open to the world. As the *Volkskirche* continues to disintegrate, the core of practicing churchgoers will no longer be surrounded and secured by large numbers of "officially registered" non-practicing Christians. In this new situation the church must be more missionary, more on the offensive in wining new converts from a non-Christian milieu than in defending past privilege. It will do this through active faith, proclamation, and convincing living. "It means more to win one new Christian from what we may call neo-paganism than to keep ten 'old Christians'" (32). Because the church's missionary forces are very limited, they must be focused. This missionary task must inform the choice of bishops and other church leaders.

3. **Church of non-simultaneity.** Like the world around it, the church is becoming increasingly heterogeneous. At one and the same time there are groups within the church who are really living in different historical ages or mind sets. This unavoidable reality calls for great patience and tolerance. Such a church must make many compromises. But these compromises must not lead to a peace of the grave. We must learn how to fight fair— how to uphold our own point of view without denigrating others' by insisting they have nothing to offer, or that Jesus is clearly on our side.

4. **Church of polarization and group-formation.** There is in the German Church today a great danger of inhuman and unchristian polarization. The problem is not the existence of different opinions, but that those who hold these opinions form groups that refuse to cooperate with others. In belonging to any group, one must boldly resist the temptation to misinterpret, demonize or dismiss others. A modest view of our own position liberates us from self-righteous and humorless fanaticism. Those in author-

ity are especially prone to experience these groups with different opinions as "pressure groups." But if the goal is proper and if the pressure is exerted honestly, there is nothing at all illegitimate about pressure groups. But woe to those who exploit such groups for their own narrow ends.

SCC.2. What are We to Do? (45-89)
Abstract: A future church would continue to be Roman, but less clerical and more attuned to serving the poor. It would present a moral vision without simply moralizing. It would be welcoming and inclusive, offer concrete directives on real world problems, and be aflame with a more authentic spirituality.
Topics: CHURCH, future of.
Subsidiary discussions: Church, planning for future of (45ff); Petrine Office, future of (52ff); Church, office and charism in (56ff); Authority in the church (57ff); Church and the poor (61ff); Church, moral teaching of (64ff); Morality, proclamation of (64ff); Conscience, formation of (68f; 77ff); Church membership (71f); Dissent and orthodoxy (74f); Magisterium, concrete directives of (76ff); Church, spirituality in (82ff); Spirituality, ecclesial (82ff); Preaching, existential imagination (83ff); God, church's proclamation of (86); Jesus Christ, church's proclamation of (88).

Precis: 1. Preliminary methodological considerations. No one knows the concrete future, and we must advance hoping in the grace of God. Still, what can be said, and on what methodological grounds? First the church must continue to offer imperatives and directives. These cannot however be unassailable conclusions derived rigorously from principles of faith and morality. Confining the church within such limits would lead to complete paralysis. The church must speak and act based on its best knowledge and conscience. Its directives will often demand a bold choice among many possible options. The church must also choose where to deploy its limited resources. Since it cannot do everything it must focus where it can have the greatest effect. This demands the courage to give up certain tasks and claims (something the church has never done well in the past to her own detriment). Our criteria should not be based on what has served us in the past, but on what we will need for the future (e.g., missions, 49). "To win one new man of tomorrow for the faith is more important for the Church than to keep in the faith two men of yesterday" (50). Plans must be made and implemented at the opportune time. For example, there are competent lay preachers now. But if the church waits 20 years to incorporate them will there be any left?

2. **Roman Catholic Church.** The future church will be Roman. The Petrine Ministry is and will remain by divine law, a constitutive element of the church. But since this office is also historically commissioned it can change. The form of the modern papacy must be examined without succumbing to the modern allergy towards it. Since the church is not a debating society, the Petrine Office must be able to issue universally binding decisions without being totalitarian. But even if the future exercise of the office becomes more collaborative, decisions arrived at by the office will not thereby please everyone.

3. **A declericalized church.** By divine law the church will always have a hierarchical component with particular functions and powers. But those who hold the highest offices in the church are never *ipso facto* the holiest (as in a chess club the president is not necessarily the best player). Simply put, a properly "declericalized" church lives and practices this dogmatic truth. What this means and its importance become even clearer when we recall that the future church will be more grassroots than institutional. In issuing their directives, church leaders will increasingly appeal to faith rather than merely to authority. More will be expected of office holders in the future by way of charism and lifestyle. Office holders of the future will have to reverse some unjust policies, apologize, seek advice, admit to doubts, be more open to criticism and explain more fully the grounds for their decisions.

4. **A church concerned with serving.** Under pressure, the church must resist the temptation to become self-absorbed and defensive. It exists for people. Its outreach is not a means to grow itself, but to help all people reach their proper end. Office holders are the most likely to become ecclesial introverts. In serving others, the church must stand for justice, freedom and human dignity even when it is to the church's own detriment. We ought to be suspicious when the church does *not* come into conflict with civil powers as it sides with the poor.

5. **Morality without moralizing** must be the goal of the future church. Taking seriously the evolution of concrete morality (64f), the church can no longer inculcate morals simply by an ineffectual insistence on concrete moral principles. By "moralizing" Rahner means "expounding moral norms of behavior peevishly and pedantically ... without really tracing them back to that innermost experience of man's nature, which is the source of the so-called principles of natural law and which alone gives them binding force; [without tracing them back to] that innermost core of the Christian message which is the message of the living Spirit, the message of freedom from merely external law, the message of love which is no longer subject to any law when it prevails" (66). Failing to do this, Christian morality will seem to modern people like so many arbitrary commands. Proclaiming a morality linked to the person also offers more stability in a quickly changing world. In this area, the church must have the wisdom not to offer concrete norms on every aspect of human life, and the courage to do more than merely repeat general moral principles, leaving the rest to conscience. It must proclaim morality in a way that contributes to the formation of conscience. But in no case should it suggest that all life's concrete problems (like world hunger or overpopulation) would be solved simply by invoking God, although a right relationship with God may help us to see these issues more clearly.

6. **Church with open doors.** Formerly the church divided people into two groups: its baptized and professing members, and the unbaptized or lapsed. Yet baptism alone does not insure real member-ship or living faith. Theologically, church boundaries are very vague and somewhat fluid. A church with "open doors" would acknowledge this situation positively and treat both groups more or less equally. It would see those who have not yet professed the faith explicitly as somehow belonging to her; as catechumens of a kind. Of course this does not rule out the possibility and the necessity of enforcing certain orthodox parameters of the faith (e.g., acknowledging Jesus as Lord, etc.), although this alone does not settle the problem of orthodoxy, a matter that must be approached with some modesty.

7. **Church of concrete directives.** Even today the church must have the courage to issue concrete imperatives and "directives" in the realm of politics and society. This is problematic today as op-

posed to the past because today there are many concrete ways to realize a general Christian principle. As a result the magisterial teaching tends to become increasingly abstract and ineffective. Rahner suggests the magisterium can get beyond merely repeating abstract principles by issuing "directives:" non-binding decisions about concrete situations addressed to the conscience of the believer. Though inconclusive, these directives are not thereby inconsequential since they do further the development of Christian conscience (e.g., Paul VI's *Populorum Progressio*). A second factor which could lead to these directives being adopted would be tracing them back to some clear charismatic impulse and avoiding pedantry.

8. **Church of real spirituality.** To stay true to itself the church and its officials must remain "spiritual" (as opposed to ritualistic, legalistic, administrative, boring or mediocre). Rahner challenges preachers to use their existential imaginations, i.e., to imagine how their homilies or explanations of the faith (God, death, Jesus) sound to average people. Where are the preachers today who preach with the joy and the power of the Spirit? Where are the Christian gurus of today who can initiate the young into the experience of God? Today's spiritual poverty cannot be turned into riches simply by admitting it– but that's a start. A church devoid of mystery and a sense of the evangelical joy of redeemed freedom becomes merely a social welfare agency. The church is first and foremost concerned with God (86f), and with liberation in Christ (88). How do we understand, live and preach our faith in the power of the Spirit?

SCC.3. How can a Church of the Future be Conceived? (93-132)

Abstract: Looking into the distant future, Rahner envisions a more grassroots church that is more open, ecumenical, democratic and engaged in social and political problems. It will be less institutional and pedantic; more diverse and with hazier borders, promoting the charisms and views of all members.

Topics: CHURCH of the future.

Subsidiary discussions: Church, ghettoization of (93f); Heresy in the church (94ff); Ecumenism (102ff); Petrine Office and ecumenism (105ff); Church as base community (108ff); Priesthood of the future (110ff); Holy Orders, relative (110; 114); Priesthood, celibate (110f); Women, ordination of (114); Parish of the future (115ff); Bishop/s, election of (119ff); Laity, consultation with (121f); Sin, social aspect of (124ff); Revolution (125f; 130f); Church, development work of (128ff); Globalization (129ff).

Precis: 1. Open church. The greatest danger facing the church is the temptation to retreat into a ghetto or to become a sect. The only antidote is to become and remain an open church. First, in regard to orthodoxy the church, although it must defend the truth, must also be slow to judge whether a formula or position is heretical. Second, it should not primarily combat heresy with appeals to authority but with reference to the innermost center of living faith. The church must recognize that today heresy (or at least rampant heterodoxy) is actually rife among the Christian faithful and can never be completely uprooted short of excommunicating almost everyone. The proper approach to take toward heresy in the church is patient teaching with the hope that all will arrive at a better understanding. All this raises the question of who belongs to the church. In this environment it is better to be a more open church and to base decisions more on ecclesial-social factors than on strict theological criteria. Though such an approach is not ideal, it is unavoidable. The church of tomorrow will of necessity be doctrinally more pluralistic.

2. Ecumenical church. The church of the future must have an honest ecumenical objective. Much has been accomplished, and few theological obstacles to reunion remain (leaving aside the Petrine Office). Most obstacles today are religio-social. Rahner suggests the way forward will not be primarily through further theological progress. He suggests beginning with institutional unification that would work its way toward full unity of faith and theology. Even now, despite the great theological difference within a particular church, the members still feel a sense of union without demanding from their co-religionists a profession of strict orthodoxy. The Petrine Office (105f) could be increasingly incorporated into such a setup as it became *de facto* responsible for unity and for vigorously defending what is essential in the faith, while allowing considerable institutional autonomy. Other churches would not be forced to accept for themselves the way the papacy functions in the Catholic church, but would not be allowed to deny the legitimacy of how it functions there. The development of the total consciousness of our shared faith could be left to history and to the Spirit. Rahner asks whether anyone else has a better suggestion.

3. **Church from the roots.** The church of the future will not draw its primary strength from its institutional character. Rather, it "will exist only by being constantly renewed by the free decision of faith and the formation of congregations on the part of individuals in the midst of a secular society bearing no imprint of Christianity" (108). This is a theological as well as a sociological reality, although precisely how such base communities will emerge is unclear (whether they will come as a result of the withering away or the strengthening of territorial parishes). Nevertheless, when they do emerge they will have the same rights and duties as traditional parishes. Among these is the right to have their leadership acknowledged by the great episcopal church. Future leaders of the community must be chosen with an eye to their relationship with the base and not to their supra-community administrative skills. The disciplinary rule of celibacy is secondary to the community's spiritual well-being. Such base communities would surely retain their strong ties to the great episcopal church, although authority would be exercised more collegially. Nevertheless, the link between community leadership and eucharistic leader must be retained (112f) without reverting to any false clericalism that would deny the existence or needlessly constrain the exercise of other charisms within the community. In this regard Rahner is quite open to the (relative) ordination of women, seeing them functioning well in cultures open to that possibility. How these base communities would interact with existing parishes remains to be seen. But they will have to resist the temptation to become inward-looking enclaves of the like-minded. Finding the way forward will demand bold experimentation (116) and there will be a great deal of diversity. Already canon lawyers should be considering the legal status of such future entities within the church and in the state.

4. **Democratized church.** Without prejudice to the hierarchical order of church governance and legitimate authority established by divine law, the process for identifying such leadership could be more democratic, certainly involving the local clergy. The laity, which

might to a lesser extent be involved in this process, can and certainly must enter more fully in the decision-making process of the church in more than a mere advisory capacity.

5. **Socio-critical church.** Among the most important activities of the church of the future is its service to the world. Only in this way do we realize the co-penetration of love of God and neighbor which always has a socio-political character. But socio-political action cannot be naive. It must take seriously the fact that social reality and institutions are marked by sin. Christianity is debased when the struggle with sin is totally confined to the private sphere, as this engenders apathy or resignation in the face of social evils. Hence, the future church must be socially engaged. Properly understood, the socio-political task of Christians is revolution. But in reducing general principles to particular actions, people of good will can legitimately differ on the means to be employed. Conflict is inevitable, and here the role of church leader-ship is not to resolve every conflict (it cannot) but to maintain unity within the community. For the church to be credible it must allow freedom and strive for justice within itself. To this end, a bishop should be prepared to tolerate even seemingly wayward initiatives.

It is distressing how few people take this socio-political dimension of Christian life seriously. Of course there are laudable exceptions. But even the German social outreach *Caritas*, which does outstanding work, leaves many thinking that its efforts absolve them from personal involvement. Today there is much that can only be done at the institutional level. But we must also engage personally. The base community will provide an excellent opportunity for such personal outreach. In this globalized age, Third World outreach is a particularly important Christian socio-political task, surrounding which there is much talk but often little action. The focus of the church must be global. Rahner offers some concrete suggestions which he thinks are far from Utopian (131). He concludes with some remarks about national political party affiliation, insisting that people of good will can legitimately disagree about the best means to a commonly agreed upon end, and thus in good conscience can belong to different political parties. There are no purely Christian parties, none of whose actions would ever offend Christian conscience.

Epilogue (135-136). Clearly, this little book has not answered all (or perhaps even any) of the many concrete problems facing the German Synod. But without a view of the whole, one risks missing the forest for the trees. Our inability to know the future absolutely is no excuse for not bravely looking into the distance with faith and hope.

SC. *The Spirit in the Church.* NY: Crossroad, 1979. 104 pp.
Contents: Part I: Experiencing the Spirit.
Part II: The Charismatic Element in the Church. **Cf.,** *The Dynamic Element in the Church,* **DEC.2.**
Part III. Some Criteria for Genuine Visions. **Cf.,** *Inquiries,* **Inq.2.III.**
Part IV. Prophecies. **Cf.,** *Inquiries,* **Inq.2.IV.**

SC.1. Experiencing the Spirit. (3-31). *Erfahrung des Geistes,* 1977. Translated by John Griffiths.
Abstract: Rahner maintains that in addition to extraordinary manifestations of the Spirit, there are also genuine experience of the Spirit in "everyday mysticism," which he proceeds to describe in some detail.
Topics: MYSTICISM, everyday; SPIRIT/s, experience of; TRANSCENDENCE in knowledge and freedom.
Subsidiary discussions: Mysticism (7ff); Spirit, baptism in 9ff); God (14f); Grace (15ff); Saints and the Spirit (22ff); God, universally salvific will of (24f); Death and the Holy Spirit (26f); Spirit/s, discernment of (29ff).

Precis: This meditation envisions the Spirit as the gift of God's self-communication.
The testimony of Scripture and the experience of the Spirit. Since Scripture describes the experience of the Spirit in personal terms (list), we are entitled to ask where/how we personally experience the Spirit.
Individual experiences and the one fundamental experience of the individual. The experience of Spirit is incommensurate with our individual experiences of other specific realities. It is one in which we encounter ourselves as a totality. Substituting appeals to authority for such personal experiences leads to ideology or mythology.

Is there such a thing as experiencing the Spirit? Questioning the possibility of such an experience does not invalidate the reality. The unconscious is also not given to direct experience, but it is no less real.

The testimony of the mystics. There always were and continue to be mystics in all religious traditions. They seem to express and explain one core experience in different ways. Though often associated with extraordinary phenomenon, at root these mystical experiences are not so far removed from us.

Longing for the power of the Spirit. Though difficult to understand completely, today we can also see charismatic movements and the phenomenon of "Baptism in the Spirit."

Can we experience the Spirit? Rahner maintains that we who are not mystics or charismatics can and must have experiences of the Spirit, but we often overlook, misconstrue, or fail to take them seriously.

Experiencing the unutterable mystery. A few preliminary remarks on human knowledge and freedom show how these are human actions precisely insofar as they connect us to the infinite, incomprehensible and mysterious horizon against which alone any particular thing is known or chosen. This inner depth of experience is not simply given in the act of knowing or choosing; it is grasped only in subsequent reflection, and hence can be ignored or repressed. Such everyday experiences of transcendence are the condition for the possibility of experiencing the Spirit.

God the inclusive but illimitable ground. Such everyday moments of transcendence (even though mediated by a concrete object) are actually encounters with God.

The unrestricted movement of the Spirit and the bestowal of grace. In transcendent experience God is present both as the goal we seek in hope (philosophically) and goal attained as grace (theologically). In short, transcendent experience is God's self-communication, and as such it is the experience of the Holy Spirit. In everyday experience this remains anonymous, unreflective and unthematic.

Everyday experience and the experience of the Spirit. The breakthrough from everyday experience to a thematic experience of the Spirit can happen positively (*via eminentiae*) or negatively (*via negationis*). Rahner is predisposed to trust and to develop to latter.

Experiencing the Spirit in actual life. Though these thematic moments of transcendence are unique to each individual, Rahner furnishes here a veritable litany of examples involving everyday experiences such as accountability, forgiveness, love, duty, courtesy, fidelity, responsibility, prayer, death, etc.

Living as people in the Spirit. This experience, a foretaste of the eternal, puts this world in proper perspective (as the saints saw it), and this very truth that seems to drain the joy from everyday life is actually the Spirit opening the way for us to cast ourselves off into eternity.

Everyday mysticism and the grace of Jesus Christ. How is this experience of God in the everyday related specifically to Jesus Christ? Evidence of the Holy Spirit at work even among those who are not explicitly Christian should not shock or surprise us, insofar as it would be evidence of something we believe in deeply: God's universally salvific will.

Sharing in the victorious death of Jesus. Ultimately, transcendence occurs when we cease to absolutize any categorical thing and surrender instead to the inconceivability of God, as Jesus did. Hence, experiencing the Holy Spirit and sharing in the victorious death of Jesus "are one and the same thing."

Experiencing the Spirit is not elitist. However charismatic or extraordinary mystical prayer or meditation may be (and Rahner does not disparage them), they do not constitute the only access to the Spirit.

Everyday mission. Since the gifts of the Spirit for building up the church are manifold, how do we discern them? Rahner gives a rule of thumb (30). In the end, we do not work at discernment so we can possess the Spirit, but so that we can abandon ourselves.

SC.2. The Charismatic Element in the Church, revised 1964 (35-73). **Cf.,** *The Dynamic Element in the Church,* **DEC.2.** In *Das Dynamische in der Kirche,* 1962. Translated by W.J. O'Hara.

SC.3. Some Criteria for Genuine Visions, revised 1963 (77-86). **Cf., Inquiries, Inq.2.III.** From *Visionen und Prophezeiungen,* 1962. Translated by Charles Henkey and Richard Strachan.

SC.4. Prophecies, revised 1963 (89-104). **Cf.,** *Inquiries,* **Inq.2.IV.**
From *Visionen und Prophezeiungen,* 1962. Translated by Charles Henkey and Richard Strachan.

SE. *Spiritual Exercises.* NY: Herder, 1965. 285 pp. Translated by Kenneth Baker, SJ *Betrachtungen zum ignatianischen Exerzitienbuch,* 1965.

Contents: Foreword.
Introduction.
  1. God and Man.
  2. Man and the Other Things.
  3. Indifference and the "More."
  4. Our Practical Attitude toward Sin.
  5. The Essence of Sin.
  6. The Three Sins.
  7. Our Personal Sins.
  8. Venial Sin and the "World."
  9. Asceticism for the Modern Priest.
  10. On the Sacrament of Penance.
  11. Death, Judgment, Heaven, Hell.
  12. The Enfleshment of God.
  13. The Following of Christ.
  14. The Kingdom of Christ.
  15. The Annunciation.
  16. The Birth of Our Lord.
  17. The Hidden Life of Our Lord.
  18. Jesus Remains in the Temple.
  19. The Two Standards.
  17. The Hidden Life of Our Lord.
  20. The Sermon on the Mount.
  21. The Three Classes of Men.
  22. The Three Degrees of Humility.
  23. The Priesthood.
  24. The Holy Eucharist.
  25. The Agony in the Garden.
  26. From the Garden to the Cross.
  27. Our Lord's Death on the Cross.
  28. Resurrection and the Ascension of Our Lord.

29. The Spirit as the Fruit of the Redemption.
30. Mary and the Church.
31. The Contemplation of Love.
32. The Grace of Perseverance.
Glossary.

Foreword (7-9). Rahner calls these "theological meditations" on Ignatius' Spiritual Exercises. They come from unedited notes transcribed by seminarians participating in 8-day retreats he conducted over the years. They provide a theological foundation to the Exercises without being too pious or too abstract. He warns readers not to mistake them for a commentary on the Exercises, and not to conclude that having read this book they have made the Exercises, which are essentially a matter of personal discernment.

Introduction (11-14). **I. The situation of the Exercises.** Only those who know they can only master their lives with constantly renewed effort and who seek to experience the truth of their individual situation are ready to make the Spiritual Exercises. **II. The essence of the Spiritual Exercises** is not a theological system. It is a choice of concrete means for living Christian life. Though these seminarian retreatants have most likely decided their path in life, it is good for them to reexamine the genuineness of that choice. For no decision is simply final– a linear extension of previous decisions. The question is always, what does God want from me now? God alone can give the answer, and an Ignatian retreat is prefaced on the belief that God can and will speak to my soul. **III. The right way to make a retreat** is calmly, not rushing from point to point, but attending to even the slightest movements of the Spirit however unimportant they seem. We must have courage and trust that God wants to speak to us. Only in this way can we escape our own desperate situation and enter the infinite breadth of God.

SE.1. God and Man. #23 (15-17)
Abstract: Reviewing the attributes of God underscores the fact that God is always greater than our minds. What we know of God is revealed by Christ: that God is a Father, a Trinity, and the love

which constitutes our being. Living on earth while knowing God as our source and destiny demands humility and courage.

Topics: GOD, attributes of.

Precis: Personal decision, our turning to God, must spring from *"The Foundation"* which contains the framework for the Exercises. But it is so hard to find God in the bitterness of this world and the obscurity of the future, and at the same time to address God as "Father" with a feeling of complete security. **I. The infinite God.** A review of God's attributes only serves to remind us that we cannot grasp God, who remains always greater. **II. The living God.** God grounds my being in such a way that my autonomy and self-direction are not diminished but firmly established. **III. The Father of Our Lord Jesus Christ.** Jesus reveals that God is not infinitely removed (as moderns think is only proper for God), but is in fact our Father who has come near us in Christ. **IV. The Trinitarian God.** The Father's Son sent the Spirit. This Trinitarian view grounds the Exercises. **V. God is love.** God's love is the foundation of human existence. It is a complete gift, but no ordinary gift, since it is God Himself. The dreadful greatness of our freedom is its ability to accept or to decline this love. **VI. The still distant God.** Though God is our source and our destiny, we find ourselves on earth. This demands of us the humility to recognize our unfinished status and the courage to strive for future community with God.

SE.2. Man and the Other Things. #23 (18-22)

Abstract: A Christian's relationship to "other things" is easy to say and hard to live. We only find God through things and we cannot simply eliminate them. Relating to them in the way that furthers our goal of union with God, demands appreciation of their goodness and the choice to subordinate them to God.

Topics: ELECTION, Ignatian; GOD and other things; RENUNCIATION.

Subsidiary Discussions: Death (21).

Precis: Note. What Ignatius says about the relationship between God and everything else is so clear and easy to say, but so hard to appropriate. And only appropriation is true knowledge. As we are always in the process of appropriating we are always becoming. Perfection comes later. We are always in danger of either choosing things and living in opposition to God, or of embracing God and not taking creatures seriously. **I. The other things** are everything that stand between my "self" and God. These include even those things which I falsely identify with myself: my possessions, friends, talents, vocation, health, etc. Separated from these, there remains only the free, self-surrendering person posited by God. Other things are not in themselves obstacles to God. In fact, dealing with them helps us to find and understand our right relationship with God. Hence, we must not try to eliminate them or to remain Stoically beyond being affected by them. We must learn to use them properly and direct them all to God. **II. Using and leaving the "other things."** Other things are absolutely necessary for a proper relationship to God. They should be used or left alone to the degree they help us attain our final end. But sin has disrupted the natural order of things and makes the proper use of things so difficult. Even Christian renunciation acknowledges the goodness of the things being given up and thus avoids bitterness. In fact "leaving" other things means entering an even more intense relationship with them: the valid relationship God desires. This demands from us a difficult choice. This whole dynamic of renunciation has the Christological structure of death and glory (21). **III. A self-examination.** This gives rise to important questions for self-examination that should transform our life into a prayer for the "more" so we may always strive for God's greater glory.

SE.3. Indifference and the "More" (23-27)

Abstract: Decision demands freedom from natural prejudices, and the spiritual perspective Ignatius calls indifference. This is never an end in itself. Rather it is freedom for decision– for embracing God's decision as my own. Once a choice is made, indifference must turn into non-indifference. True indifference is rare even among Christians.

Topics: ELECTION, Ignatian; INDIFFERENCE, Ignatian.

Subsidiary discussions: Death and indifference (24).

Precis: Note. *"The Foundation"* makes two things clear: the need for indifference and the need to choose those things that are "more conducive to our goal." **I. Indifference** is a distance from things that allows for the perspective needed to decide, despite the fact that prejudice and pre-judgments always remain a possible part of the mix. We are not indifferent by nature. We must continuously work to become so. The *active indifference* we seek to aid us in rejecting our own prejudices is accomplished in part by handing ourselves over to God (a foreshadowing of death, 24). The choice of what to hold onto and what to relinquish cannot be deduced from principles. The choice flows from my personal history and from God's will for me. We can never attain this kind of indifference by ourselves or permanently. We make our choice as best we can and then entrust ourselves to God's mercy. **II. The "More."** The distance that comes with indifference is never the end in itself. It is freedom for decision and is elevated into the decision to do "more" – not my decision, but God's. Indifference must transform itself into non-indifference. For example, once I have chosen a way of life I must pursue it with all my capacities. But to remain open to God we must remain flexible, always open to hear and respond to God's will. Hence, indifference is the opposite of apathy. We suffer it. It does not mean mediocrity or uniformity, since God's call is directed precisely to my individuality. Indifference is not the staple of most people. To be a Christian by choice is something exceptional that others will find strange. To follow this path takes courage and grace for which we must pray. **Note.** Re: indifference, Ignatius gives a few simple-sounding examples: health/sickness; riches/poverty; honor/dishonor; long/short life.

SE.4. Our Practical Attitude toward Sin. #47 (28-33)

Abstract: Sin is especially hard for sinners to see. Yet it is real. To see it we must look deep into our hearts and not judge ourselves by externals. Human freedom can accept or decline fully and finally God's gift of Himself. It is a choice we cannot escape. At its core, priestly ministry is about the forgiveness of sins.

Topics: SIN, consciousness of.

Subsidiary discussions: Fundamental Option (30ff); Priesthood and sin (32f).

Precis: Note. Meditations of Week I on sin, hell and judgment are not at all easy, since sinners are the least likely to grasp their own sinful state. Rahner proceeds slowly to insure we see all that Ignatius wants us to see. **I. Our practical attitude toward sin in the world.** The brutality and shallowness of the world repels us. But looked at more closely the evil we see becomes ambiguous. If not necessary, it seems at least to be an unavoidable expression of our reduced state. Nonetheless, sin is real! God cannot forgive everything. To grasp this we must open ourselves to revelation. **II. Our practical attitude toward sin in ourselves.** Most of us think we are pretty good, judged against external standards. But when we look into the depths of our hearts, there we can see how sin is a real possibility even for me. We must pray for the grace to see ourselves as we truly are. **III. Our attitude toward our personal human existence as a real possibility for sin.** Reflecting on sin makes clear that we are free to dispose of our lives, fully and finally, as we will. But precisely the totality of this *option fondamental* (31) makes it hard for us to see it. Hence, we never know how we stand before God. Christianity maintains this dramatic, eternal choice is inescapably at the center of each human life, not just the lives of a few. No one can decline his nature and "return his ticket" to God. **IV. Priesthood and sin.** Priests must deal with sin not only professionally but from the depths of their being. Since in some way the salvation of others depends on them, they must dedicate themselves to the forgiveness of sin. Whoever does not believe this is the most important element of his ministry is far from being a real priest.

SE.5. The Essence of Sin. (34-42)

Abstract: Sin is neither an element of our nature nor is it completely contingent. In fact, sinning makes us sinners. The unredeemed person cannot really grasp sin. Only a prior experience of grace enables us to know and see sin in its true dimensions. That is why these meditations begin at the foot of the cross.

Topics: SIN, essence of.

Subsidiary discussions: Grace manifesting sin (38ff).

Precis: Note. 1. Ignatius' meditation on sin is not rooted in theory but in concrete salvation history. He gives first place to human freedom. **2.** The suggested readings supply the psychological background for the salvation history we are about to meditate on. The

First Prelude is a particularly helpful and realistic sketch of our sinful human state **I. Sin as a personal act.** Catholicism embodies the danger of seeing sin as being merely contingent events to be confessed and forgiven. Protestantism tends to see sin as a constitutive element of human nature. The truth lies between. Although sin is not a necessary part of my nature, neither is it contingent. When I sin, existentially I become a sinner. There is an essential difference between mortal and venial sin, which must be judged objectively and subjectively. Sin can make no claim on grace. It is not one pole of a dialectic. We must also be honest with ourselves. We must not use the Exercises to whip up an artificial sin-mysticism. The point is that by sinning existentially we become sinners ontically. Since our sinful acts penetrate our being, our sinfulness is hard to see.

II. Sin as guilt. 1. *The Attitude of Unredeemed Man toward Guilt.* It is necessary to judge our sinfulness viewed from its origins. We are tempted to think we sin because we suffer. But actually suffering follows sin/guilt. Those whose lives have not been illuminated by grace use this excuse to justify themselves before God. Similarly they confuse guilt with the inevitability of fate, or worse they so absolutize them-selves that they boast of their sins and do not seek forgiveness. 2 .*Toward a Clear Knowledge of Guilt.* Through the light of natural reason we can come to know sin as a violation of God's will. But this primitive notion of sin is far from the Christian concept of sin. Knowledge of and sorrow for sin is a product of the revelation of God's grace. Natural knowledge of sin without grace ultimately suppresses sin or leads to despair. The cross of Christ alone gives us a clear picture of the essence and actuality of guilt. 3. *The Essence of Guilt.* What we are concerned with here is the guilt of mortal sin, the free act for which we alone are responsible. Sin can never be blamed on God. Guilt comes about when I deify finite reality, when I desire radically to assert myself in the realm of the finite. My sin offends against God and against myself in denying the objective structure of my life which God has willed and established. When we sin we are not merely breaking a law, we are refusing God's offer of self-communication and His Spirit. "Therefore, it is essentially the loss of grace and a falling out of the life of God" (41). Sin is an *absolute non-value*. All other value-deficiencies can have some meaning, but not sin.

There are so many question concerning sin and the possibility of sin (list, 41) that we would easily dismiss it were it not for the cross of Christ. Only those who have been touched by God's grace can admit to sin existentially in their lives. That is why Ignatius places us at the foot of the cross in this first meditation.

SE.6. The Three Sins. #45 (43-51)

Abstract: Meditating on the history of sin reveals the origin of our own sins. They occur in the sin situation caused by past events, and ratify the sin of Adam. The damning potential of each mortal sin reveals the power of my freedom, the importance of the present moment, and God's immense mercy.

Topics: SIN, history of.

Subsidiary discussions: Soul, powers of (43); Cross (45); Angels, sin of (45ff); Jesus Christ, creation in (47, 48); Adam, sin of (48f); Damnation (49f); Fundamental Option (50).

Precis: Note. 1. Ignatius relies on the traditional 3-part division of the power of the soul: memory, will and intellect. How we subdivide these powers is not important. The point of this meditation is to see that sin corrupts this Trinitarian image of God within us. **2.** As a practical, concrete thinker Ignatius is always linking concepts and images, particularly historical events. Since it is only in association with others that we come to know ourselves, this link to history helps us see ourselves as sinners. **3.** We meditate on the history of sin because sin constitutes the current situation in which I find myself, and which I ratify today with each of my personal sins. We place ourselves before the cross because only the cross both chrystalises and solves the problem of sin. Rooting my sin in the first three sins serves to keeps me from floating off into abstractions, and underscores the incomprehensible gift that is salvation.

I. The sin of the angels (#50). Though angels are incorporeal they belong to the world. Hence, their history and their choices threaten me. Given the sin of the angels, there is nothing left in the world that remains immune to sin. In addition, the fact that pure spirits *can* sin keeps us from identifying our sin as a consequence of corporality. We are quite similar to angels in that we share the same transcendental openness to God which demands a choice.

Somehow, their sin is also a sin against Christ. The point of the meditation is to realize how deeply rooted the sin situation is (47).

II. Adam's sin (#51). From the parallel Paul draws between Adam and Christ, in some way "Adam sinned as a 'Christian'" (48), i.e., his sin against the love of God manifested in creation was at the same time a rejection of Christ who is the true meaning of creation, just as the grace Adam enjoyed before the fall was also the grace of Christ. The disobedience of Adam is the source of our sinful insubordination— our turning a deaf ear to God. Each sin of mine ratifies the sin of Adam, and the history of his sin pervades my life as the ongoing history of the penance laid on him.

III. Sin of the redeemed man (#52). Every mortal sin exposes one to eternal damnation. Every sin encounters the resistance of the reality of creation. Hence, there is always a passive element to our sins I cannot completely grasp. This meditation on the fact that I can be lost due to one mortal sin raises a number of considerations: that my free acts are actually so powerful and of such consequence; that every moment of my life can be a moment of salvation or damnation; that my whole life is present in each moment of time; and how infinite God's mercy has been towards me. Yet our very familiarity with these three sins can bar us from grasping and appropriating their true importance.

SE.7. On Personal Sin. #55-61 (52-58)

Abstract: An honest inventory of our history of sin reveals who I have become and how my sin has corrupted everything in my personal world. I discover how it has reduced me to a mere source of contagion. How wonderful that God's mercy still reaches me, that God gives me space to return!

Topics: SIN, personal history of.
Subsidiary discussions: Saints and sinners (55).

Precis: Preludes. 1. Imagining my soul imprisoned in this corruptible body is no pious fancy. It accurately describes life in a body ruled by sin and thus subject to decay. **2.** Praying to grow in sorrow for our sin does not require working up a false sin-consciousness. We all know the possibilities of sin slumbering within us are legion. Often we are good not because we are holy but because we are afraid. **I. A look at the record of my sins** (#56). An inventory of my sins helps me get to know myself, the person I now am because of my sins. I also come to know my sins, their history and development. I discover that nothing in my life is as it should be. In my cowardice I have corrupted everything. I alone am responsible for this. These are *my* sins. I am *this* man. Who can say where I stand with God? **II. The seriousness of my sins (#57).** I should see my sins for the rottenness they are. **III. Who am I that sins? (#58).** 1. *Compared to other men,* my sins have made me a mere cipher. I have lost my self. 2. *Compared to angels and saints,* I am a failure. For saints are not just better persons than I, they are totally different: perfected by their love for God. 3. *Compared to God,* I am in exile from Him, alone in a wilderness, alone and despairing. 4. *In reference to my own body,* my own sin leaves me helpless, partial, unreal. 5. I am a source of contagion to myself and to others. Nothing proves this more definitively that the sight of Christ on the cross. **IV. My sins in the sight of God (#59).** Every attribute of God trumpets my sinfulness: His wisdom opposes my ignorance, His power my weakness. **V. A cry of wonder (#60).** When I consider my sin in the light of how God preserves the world, and of His saving love, I marvel. This light does more than reveal my wickedness. It gives me the possibility of being saved from myself, if only I have the courage to abandon myself. **VI. Colloquy of mercy (#61)** looks to the future: "I will resolve to amend for the future," knowing that the strength to do any good thing comes not from me but from God.

SE.8. Venial Sin and the "World." #62-63 (59-65)
Abstract: Venial sin, with its power to distract and injure, must be resisted. This work of a lifetime takes self-knowledge and often spiritual guidance. We must also resist "the World" insofar as it suffers the corrupting effects of sin. This is a special task of priests who will inevitably find their efforts opposed.
Topics: SIN, venial; WORLD (*kosmos houtos*).
Subsidiary discussions: Priests and the world (64).

Precis: Note. Ignatius' instruction to repeat the First and Second Exercises makes sense insofar as two new ideas have now been introduced: venial sin (the disorders of life, *peccata quotidiana*) and the concept of "the world." **I. Venial sins** clearly exist and should be taken seriously since they distract us from our goal and injure us in many ways (list, 61). Among other things they hinder our apostolic effectiveness. Rahner goes on to list many of the more common venial sins (list, 61). Our fight against them will vary according to their nature (examples, 61). The key to reforming our character is self-knowledge— the job of a lifetime! To overcome our tendency to concentrate on the wrong faults, the help of a spiritual guide can be invaluable. But sometimes we must simply bear our defects with Christian patience. **II. The world.** In using this word, scripture is not generally referring to creation as it came from the hand of God but to the world as it is right now, poisoned by sin. The world is a mixed bag. Knowing the world so as to be able to reject all that is bad in it is no simple matter. Priests especially must remove themselves from the world, a stance that will seem even to regular Christians a scandal, a provocation, a perfect stupidity giving the impression of fanaticism and exaggeration. But a priest must not compromise, even though the world will oppose him. **Note: The Triple Colloquy (#63)** addressed in turn to Mary and to the saints, to Christ, and to the Father.

SE.9. Asceticism for the Modern Priest.

Abstract: Asceticism is essential in the life of each Christian. It cannot be justified by an appeal to natural goodness, but only as an expression of an eschatological-transcendent love for God, prompted by God and sanctioned by the church. Renunciation is an especially important dimension of priestly life.

Topics: EVANGELICAL COUNSELS, theology of; PRIESTHOOD and asceticism; RENUNCIATION.

Subsidiary discussions: Spiritual life, definition of (69ff); Death and asceticism; (73f); Celibacy (76f); Anti-clericalism (76f); Everyday Life, self-deception (77f).

Precis: Note. I. As the meditation on sin leads directly to a reflection on how we can follow Christ better, this is a good place to discuss asceticism, character formation, self-discipline and penance. **I. The present-day situation.** Despite whatever reasons can be given, we are left to admit that our age is characterized by an alarming degree by mediocrity in spiritual matters. Nor have we always exercised due caution in this area, often throwing out the substance of asceticism along with its forms. **II. Nature and necessity of asceticism.** 1. *Asceticism in the Broad Sense* is the grace of living our relationship with and toward God. It is a life of self-forgetfulness, praise and thanks. It is also work. It doesn't just happen; it takes conscious development. 2. *Asceticism in the Strict Sense* is just a part of what was mentioned above. Here we are talking about a self-abnegation which gives up the good things in ths life, not for any practical benefit in this world, but from another motive altogether. a) *The meaningfulness of this asceticism* cannot be justified by any appeal to the natural order (71f). It can only be adequately grasped from the standpoint of charity with which such self-denial must be intrinsically connected. In fact, such renunciation is *only possible* as a direct expression of love for the eschatologically-transcendent God. At the same time it is an anticipation of the self-denial of death (summary 74). b) *The necessity of this asceticism* can only be explained ultimately by a positive call from God manifested in the institutional church (e.g., in the celebration of Baptism and Eucharist, and in sanctioning religious vows). In order for the church really to manifest its essence (list, 75), all Christians must embrace some form of asceticism. This is especially true of priests. Renunciation is one of the things that make priestly life credible in the eyes of the world. **III. Toward the practice of priestly asceticism.** 1. Celibacy is part of priestly asceticism in the strict sense. But it is only one form. Putting up with modern anti-clericalism is another. 2. With regard to asceticism in the broad sense, we must resist the danger of extremes: being overly charismatic or overly institutional. These tendencies are best countered with holy fear and trust in Divine Providence. Rahner ends by warning against self-deception, encouraging the capacity for solitude, embracing voluntary penance, and relying on traditional devotional practices like private prayer, rosary, visits to the Blessed Sacrament, etc.

SE.10. On the Sacrament of Penance. #44 (80-88)
Abstract: Ignatius recommends Confession to retreatants. After discussing the essential sacramentality of the church, Rahner insists that since each sin (especially those of priests) injures the church, each must be confessed to the church to affect a fuller participation in the redeeming cross of Christ.

Topics: PENANCE, sacrament of; SACRAMENT/s.
Subsidiary discussions: Sin, ecclesial character of (82); Sacrament as sign of redemption (85f); Penance, frequent (86f).

Precis: Note. The Incarnation makes the church essentially sacramental, underscoring the fact that we can only reach God (explicitly or anonymously) *through* the world. Among these explicit sacraments belongs Baptism (first justification) and Reconciliation (second justification). Ignatius urged his retreatants to participate in the Sacrament of Reconciliation. **I. The confession of sin as an act of a man before the church.** Every sin has an ecclesial/social character. And since every sin injures the Body of Christ, the sinner has a different relation to the church than one who is justified. This is especially true of the sins of priests. Having so injured the church by our sins, we must come to the church and confess them. In this semi-public act the church assumes a double function: penitent and reconciler. **II. Absolution and intercession as an act of the church for the sinner.** Admission of our guilt, that we are not who we should be as members of the church, sets up the condition for the possibility of becoming who we are and of being reconciled. Our very contrition is a movement of God's grace for which the church constantly intercedes. **III. Remembrance of the cross of Christ.** Like every sacrament, Reconciliation too is connected to the redemptive act of Christ: it commemorates it, makes it efficacious here and now, and points to our final redemption. It alone overcomes the sinner's self-alienation and the inner division. **IV. Confession of devotion.** All this points to the value of frequent Confessions, although strictly speaking this is not required. Rahner concludes by pointing out some of the benefits of frequent Confession.

SE.11. Death, Judgment, and Hell. #65-71 (89-96)

Abstract: Calling to mind death, judgment and hell with complete existential urgency moves us toward indifference, makes us more honest and our love for God more humble. We discover that we waiver in our love for God because this love is itself a gift to which we must recommit ourselves each day.

Topics: DEATH; HELL; JUDGMENT.

Subsidiary discussions: Indifference, Ignatian (90f); Imagination in St. Ignatius (93f); Temptation (96).

Precis: Note. I. Death is terrifyingly ambiguous because it is simultaneously a participation in the death of Adam and the death of Christ; and according to our disposition we die either one or the other. Since our death is the unique culmination of the unrepeatable oneness of our personal human existence (*hapax*), we cannot rehearse it in advance, although we can prepare for it by cultivating "indifference," or self-divestment. Rahner ends by meditating on the weakness, loneliness and finality of death. **II. Judgment.** After analyzing various meanings of the term, Rahner characterizes judgment as a kind of revelation. It adds nothing new, but simply clarifies what has always been known even if we have hidden from ourselves or others the true nature of our actions and decision. **III. Hell.** *1. Prelude*: an imaginative composition of place. *2) Application of the Senses*. The point here is not to create some great Baroque tableau of the Inferno, but to concentrate on feeling the inner bitterness of being eternally lost. *3. The Meaning of the Meditation on Hell* should make our love of God more humble, and awaken a holy fear of the Lord. This only happens when we accept the possibility of hell for ourselves with complete existential urgency. Such a meditation as this should fix the focus of our love on the cross. Our love is tempted and fickle precisely because it is a gift we must humbly accept each day.

SE.12. The Enfleshment of God. (97-113)
Abstract: In this brief but nonetheless dense christological treatise, Rahner attempts to show how christology is the beginning and end of anthropology. Christ's Incarnation, God's becoming man, reveals that our essential human freedom grows in direct proportion to our obedient nearness to God.

Topics: CHRISTOLOGY; INCARNATION; THEOLOGICAL ANTHROPOLOGY.

Subsidiary discussions: Theological Language (97f; 104; 110f); Logos, incarnation of (98f); Mystery (100ff; 112f); Obediential potency (102f); God, un/changeableness of (104ff); Creation (106f); Anonymous Christian/ity (111f).

Precis: Note. This meditation begins Week II of the Exercises focusing on Jesus' life. Rahner starts with a few theological remarks. What does it mean today to say God became incarnate, presupposing the old theological formulations but not limiting ourselves to them? Rahner sets aside the question of the precise nature of the Logos and why only this person of the Trinity is the proper subject of Incarnation. He begins with the predicate "man." **I. God became MAN,** what does this mean? What precisely is the human nature God assumed? In fact, there can be no comprehensive definition of man, though many aspects can be defined (list, 100). Essentially the human spirit is mystery, since the incomprehensible God is our final referent. Hence, we understand our basic nature only in a final, free acceptance or rejection of our own transcendence. Mystery is not something temporary or provisional but an essential characteristic of God. What then does it mean to say God assumes a human nature as his own? In short, "the Incarnation is the unique case of the perfect fulfillment of human reality— which means that a man only *is* when he gives himself away" (102). This is the essential meaning of *obediential potency*, assuming one does not hold that Incarnation 1) can be deduced, or 2) is not unique. We are free to understand ourselves in one of two ways: as utter emptiness or as discovered by the infinite, in which case one becomes a person who attains his own fulfillment only if he hopes that somewhere one like himself has surrendered completely to and been accepted by the mystery that is man. Hence, the central question is no longer *what*, but *where* and *in whom* may this have taken place? This search leads one to Jesus of Nazareth. The christology traced out here is not a christology of consciousness opposed to an ontological christology treating the substantial unity of the Word with his human nature. Rather, beginning with the metaphysical insight of true ontology that equates being and spirit, this christology tries to formulate the ontological counterpart of the ontic statements of tradition. Only this approach keeps from reducing christology to mythology.

II. God BECAME man. God becoming something is a special problem not for pantheists, but for Christians who maintain God is unchangeable, pure act, and make this tenet a dogma and no mere philosophical postulate. Traditional scholastic philosophy would seem to solve the problem by assigning all change to the humanity assumed by the Logos, thereby keeping the divine nature itself free of all change. But this separation cannot do justice to the fact that the Logos somehow did change by becoming man: "the Unchangeable can be changeable *in another*" (106) in the very act of divesting Himself, by positing the other as His own reality. Scripture defines this *kenosis* as love, whose lavish freedom is undefinable, and establishes the condition for the possibility of creaturely transcendence. (Here Rahner turns again to why of the three persons of the Trinity only the Logos could become man, 107). The humanity of the Word Incarnate originates in the Logos' act of self-divestment. "This man, precisely as man, is the self-divestment of God because God externalizes Himself when He divests Himself" (107). Otherwise His humanity would be only a mask, revealing nothing of God. Here Rahner returns to his theme that "when God desires to be non-God, then man begins to be— that and nothing else" (108). Christology is the beginning and the end of all anthropology. Due to the fact that God became man and now remains man for all eternity, man (the expressed mystery of God) cannot be taken lightly. The Old Testament God of creation is now confessed in Jesus as existing right here where we are. This new relationship with God reveals that nearness to God and human freedom increase in direct, not inverse proportion. Jesus is most fully human precisely because of, and not in spite of, His nearness to God— a proposition that avoids all mythology (110). Accepting Jesus as the truth of one's life is what is essential; how one formulates this experience is quite secondary. This leads to a discussion of Anonymous Christianity (111f). By way of summary Rahner concludes that the Incarnation of God is the absolute and also the most obvious mystery (112f).

SE.13. The Following of Christ. (114-125)
Abstract: Jesus of Nazareth is the meaning of human life and points the way to life's true meaning. To achieve our true nature, therefore, Christians freely follow Christ, each in his/her unique way, although every Christian life will somehow reproduce the material hallmarks of Jesus' life.
Topics: JESUS CHRIST, imitation of.
Subsidiary discussions: Obedience (119f); Indifference, Ignatian (122ff).

Precis: I. The essence of the following of Christ. As has been shown above, Jesus Christ reveals that the ultimate reason for human existence is to be loved by God. This grace, "which is an existential injection of the one graced into the inner life of God, is a concrete assimilation to Christ and a participation in His life. Therefore ontologically, and not just morally, it is the *grace of Christ*" (115). Insofar as this is pre-given as a metaphysical truth, it is our *nature*. Insofar as it also becomes the product of free decision, it is an element of our *person*. Since we enjoy a greater degree of assurance the more explicitly we follow the historical Jesus of Nazareth, St. Ignatius proposes meditations on the life of Christ in which we should keep in mind: **1.** Imitating Christ is not a matter of following moral maxims, but of entering His life and thus the inner life of God. **2.** Following Christ does not oppose, but is the free unfolding of our true inner natures. **II. The formal structure of the following of Christ.** True following of Christ must be a free decision to find one's own way to do so. We discover our way in concert with other people. It is no slavish imitation of the external details of the life Jesus once led. It involves risk, serving others, and obedience, just as Christ was obedient to the unique call He heard from the Father. The challenge comes when we attempt simultaneously to obey the general law of Christ and courageously be ourselves (which is simply a more radical form of obedience). **III. The material structure of the following of Christ.** Among the basic characteristics of the life of Jesus of Nazareth, Rahner lists the following: its bold everydayness that bound Him closely to reality; the element of scandal, insofar as He was not what people expected; His holy indifference. We are called to implement a similar renunciation in our own lives albeit with discretion. The meditations to follow will make this abstract discussion more concrete.

SE.14. The Kingdom of Christ. #91-100 (126-135)
Abstract: This meditation, built on the work of Week I, aims to predispose one to make a radical choice for God's will as it is revealed in the particular circumstances of one's life. This is affected by means of a parable: the summons of a great king– an image which only thinly veils Christ's call to His followers.

Topics: ELECTION, predisposition for; JESUS CHRIST, imitation of.
Subsidiary discussions: Cross, 127ff.

Precis: Note. Building on the work of the First Week, this foundational meditation for Week II of the Exercises is meant to predispose one for decision. To affect this, Ignatius brings one face to face with Christ, the concrete form of Christian living, to discover in His life the imperative that applies to me alone. The goal of this meditation is an unconditional readiness to make the choice God is asking of me (not actually to choose). To keep from deceiving ourselves and to focus our minds, St. Ignatius puts before us the suffering Christ, the man of scandal, who elicits an absolute decision from us. The core of this meditation is the parable of the summons of a great king to join him in a perilous undertaking. In the rest of this section Rahner argues for the enduring validity of this parable despite its culturally limited images of kings, royal summonses, etc. **Preludes.** 1. Mental representation of place: the Judea of Jesus, the details of which have become eternal in the glorified humanity of Christ. 2. Prayer for an open ear and responsive heart. **I. First part of the meditation: The parable of the king.** 1. Imagine a great king. 2. Consider his summons and its warning of hardships to come. 3. Consider the proper response of a good subject. **II. Second part of the meditation: The application to Christ.** 1. It is easy to imagine Christ as a greater king than any on earth and to see that following Him will entail suffering. 2. To ignore the cross of Christ at this point would be self-delusion. 3. Ignatius appeals to the "more" involved in an unconditional desire to accept the cross of Christ and to share the scandal of His life, however that will play out in any particular life. "Anyone who hesitates here should really give up the retreat right now" (134).

SE.15. The Annunciation. #101-109 (136-146)
Abstract: The Annunciation grounds our grasp of Incarnation in the concrete reality of Mary's simple but radical yes to God's invitation (her *fiat*), and so preserves it from becoming mere metaphysics. The Word becomes flesh. It is addressed to us, and we continue to proclaim and to pray in and with this Word.

Topics: BVM, Annunciation; INCARNATION; PRIESTHOOD and Annunciation (144f); WORD, theology of.
Subsidiary discussions: Angels, nature of (140f); Prayer (144f).

Precis: Note. Meditating on the Annunciation avoids reducing the truth of the Incarnation to mere metaphysical speculation. It also highlights that Jesus' human existence is not locked in a blind natural process, but is the outcome of a free, voluntary choice on Mary's part. St. Ignatius suggests that in these meditations we look at the person, hear what each is saying, and then see what each is doing. **Preludes.** The retreatant is required to perform three preludes: consider the mystery as a whole; imagine its historical setting; request a specific grace. **I. The world of the Annunciation**, the ancient world into which the word of Annunciation is spoken, is a chaotic, upside down world, much like our world today in which I play my own part. **II. The God who announces Himself.** St. Ignatius urges the retreatant to consider the Trinity who eternally conceived this world in order to assume it in incomprehensible love. Here Rahner briefly repeats his argument concerning the unique incarnation of the Logos. **III. The angel of the Annunciation.** Angels play a very small role in modern spirituality or theology. They remain vague to us as a consequence of postlapsarian disorder which imprisons us in the world and seemingly makes us more open to the influence of fallen spirits. Our life task, like the angel of the Annunciation's task, is to proclaim the Word. **IV. Mary,** in her *"fiat,"* represents all mankind. She thereby assumes her eternally valid role in salvation. **V. The Message.** Mary's lowly everydayness anticipates the scandal of over-turned expectations that will be embodied in the concrete life of God incarnate. Because Jesus fully adopted our nature He no longer resides in His unattainable otherness. Now He can be found precisely where we ourselves are, concealed in our weakness. Jesus becomes a man of sorrows, and Mary the Mother of Sorrows. **VI. The Annunciation and the priesthood.** The priest is the "official guarantee" that the Incarnation will continue to the end of time. He does this by surrendering himself to God. Rahner ends with a meditation on prayer by saying that since the Annunciation, every word the Christian prays in the Spirit participates in the fullness of the Word made flesh, and thus penetrates to the heart of God.

SE.16. The Birth of Our Lord. #110-112; 121-126 (146-150)
Abstract: This continued reflection on Incarnation highlights privation and blessedness. By assuming our everyday lowliness God answers the question that is man: the meaning of our transcendentality. The only remaining question is what will be our response to the Word God directs to the world?
Topics: CHRISTMAS; INCARNATION.
Subsidiary discussions: Time (146f); Man, question of (148ff).

Precis: I. A birth in the confinement of time. At birth we assume unalterably our place in space and time, geography, culture and politics. This is the everyday contingency within which we work out our unique finality. Jesus was born one of the many unnoticed poor. Putting on our history was indeed for Him a descent into privation. His birth inaugurates His death in utter poverty and weakness. **II. A birth for the fullness of eternity.** But His is also a blessed birth, the dawn of a new and eternal reality, through which God's *phil-anthropia* was revealed. His birth ushers in the first real possibility of human happiness, for it reveals once and for all God's attitude toward us, and fills our transcendentality with meaning. When God becomes man, all the questions flowing from our finite humanity are answered. Now the only open question is the one directed to us: how will we respond to the final Word of God directed to the world? We cannot remain neutral.

SE.17. The Hidden Life of Our Lord. #134, 271 (151-160)
Abstract: Participating in the priesthood of Christ is essentially a religious form of life demanding the whole of our existence. A holy priest is neither a functionary nor a fanatic. Only by embracing the modest and obedient hidden life of Christ in its ordinariness can we help others to live for Christ.
Topics: JESUS CHRIST, hidden life of; PRIESTHOOD as a religious form of life.
Subsidiary discussions: Celibacy (151f); Vocation (152f); Laity, vocation of (153); Everyday Life, growth, human (157); Poverty, religious (157f); Work (158); Obedience (158f).

Precis: I. The priesthood as a religious form of life is undergirded by celibacy which points to the fact that it is not merely a job or profession. It binds together the public and private dimensions of one's life. Rahner describes the young person's normal development of religious awareness and distinguishes this from a vocation: a call to a religious form of life that determines one's whole being. Despite their radical differences, one can easily mistake one for the other, especially since even those not called to a religious form of life are still expected to remain generally religious. God demands more of priests: to participate in the priesthood of Christ one must base his whole existence on Him. Given the dual nature of priesthood (from above and below) it is easy to see how false developments could occur. One could become a functionary or a fanatic (154f). But the truly *holy* priest is neither. He exhibits the grace of indifference. **II. The hidden life of Jesus as a religious form of life.** Jesus' life has three intrinsically related parts: hidden life, public life, passion. Jesus was primarily and exclusively a religious man. Most of the time, He stayed at home and concentrated on religious interests. Priests should imitate Him in this. **III. A few characteristics of Jesus' hidden life.** Luke tells us Jesus' interior life grew. We too must grow, and this requires patience with ourselves. Jesus was poor; he worked; he was obedient. Priests must imitate these characteristics. **IV. Our hidden life in Christ.** Although the life of every Christian is hidden in Christ, in the life of the priest this religious identification becomes tangible. To help others fix their eyes on heaven, priests must embrace quite unexceptionally modest and obedient lives, secluded and regular in the midst of activity. "The courage to embrace an ordinary life like that is a measure of our faith" (160). Of course, focusing too narrowly on oneself can also lead to mediocrity and dullness (160).

SE.18. Jesus Remains in the Temple. #134, 135, 272 (161-168)

Abstract: The Temple incident reveals that not all conflict is the product of sin. Here a tension arises from obedience to two goods: to follow the commandment to obey one's parents, or to follow a higher personal call to be about the Father's business. Similar tensions can arise in making our life decisions.

Topics: ELECTION, conflict in: OBEDIENCE, religious.

Subsidiary discussions: Law, obedience to (162f); God as always greater (163f); Everyday Life, conflict (164); Church, charismatic impulses in (167f).

Precis: Note. The Second Week is aimed at preparing one for a concrete decision which cannot be made *a priori* or merely by reference to general principles. These meditations are not a speculative treatment of Jesus' life. We are to place ourselves in a real relationship to these events by means of a "Salvation-historical salvation-bringing remembrance" (not unlike our participation in Eucharist) which affects the grace we need to follow Christ. **I. Jesus fulfills the law** by going to the Temple, even though as the incarnate Logos He is greater than the Law. He thus reveals a very definite side of the religious life: "the humility of even the most spiritual person to submit . . . to forms and laws coming from without" (164). **II. The conflict** Jesus encountered is real: whether to do His Father's will by remaining in the Temple, or to fulfill His duty to obey His parents and return home. This shows not all conflict is the result of sinful inclinations. It is possible for both sides to be in the right. Such conflicts must be borne with humility and selflessness. **III. The state of the commandments and the state of the evangelical counsels.** According to St. Ignatius, this meditation, insofar as it highlights the conflict in Jesus' life between obeying the Fourth Commandment or a transcendent call from heaven, should dispose the retreatant to a state of real indifference in choosing between a life of the Commandments and a life of the evangelical counsels. **IV. A few additional considerations.** We note in this story of Jesus' coming of age how He dedicates His life to serving God rather than asserting His independence over against God's will. He also shows us how lonely and painful such a valid religious choice can be on the human level. We note, too, that in returning home, Jesus opts for the ordinary. Christian life is seldom sensational. This event also manifests the validity of personal charismatic impulses within the church.

SE.19. The Two Standards. #136-147 (169-179)

Abstract: Spiritual writers have always seen the world and our hearts divided into two camps: Satan's and Christ's. Since the two camps interpenetrate, the choice we must make is difficult to discern.

Satan seduces us with possessions, honor and pride. Jesus offers the antidote: poverty, insult, and humility.
Topics: ELECTION, Ignatian.
Subsidiary discussions: Evil, reality of (171ff); Poverty, religious (176f).

Precis: Note. *1. The Decision-Character of This Meditation* centers on, "How can I distinguish a true call from God from a false impulse?" *2. Situation of a Human Choice.* Our decisions are never made from a neutral position since our pre-existing environment is already conditioned by both sin and grace. Not only the world, but also our own hearts are divided between Satan and Christ. Every great spiritual writer has seen this. The front lines are not static. The two camps interpenetrate. The church is not completely holy nor is the world completely depraved. **I. Lucifer's standard: The art of seduction.** 1. Ignatius reminds us that evil exists. 2. Evil is operative everywhere. 3. Satan's seduction begins with the lure of riches, it moves to honor, and ends in pride. Rahner transposes these three allures into a desire to possess, a desire to be somebody, and a desire to exist (in open rebellion to God). **II. The standard of Christ: His call.** 1. Consider Christ. 2. Consider those who labor for Him. 3. Christ summons us to embrace the three antidotes to Satan's seductions: poverty, insults, and humility. The attitudes desired by Christ and those desired by Lucifer can be mistaken for one another. There are false forms of poverty, insult and humility.

SE.20. The Sermon on the Mount. #161, 278 (179-186)
Abstract: Meditating on the Great Discourse from Matthew's Gospel highlights what is demanded of a priest. It serves as a kind of checklist and examination of conscience for those considering such a life.
Topics: SERMONS: Matthew 5; PRIESTLY LIFE, temptations in.
Subsidiary discussions: Beatitudes (179f); Prayer, dangers to (183f).

Precis: Note. The Great Discourse is inseparably bound with the person of Christ, and its prescriptions can only be fulfilled in the power of His Spirit. **I. The Beatitudes** (Mt 5:3-12) are deceptively simple. They do not announce a future outcome, but a present condition (the poor *are* blessed). This can only be seen by the eyes of faith. It is the wisdom of the cross. **II. The task of the disciples** (Mt. 5:13-16) is especially relevant for priests. It serves as the basis for a good examination of conscience for them. **III. The Old and the New Commandments** (Mt. 5:17ff). This diffuse reflection touches on clerical failures: legalism, jealousies, impurity, dishonesty, vengefulness, selfishness, lifeless prayer, joyless fasting, etc. The Great Discourse reveals what faithfully following Christ will demand from priests (summary, 184f).

SE.21. The Three Classes of Men. #149-157 (186-195)
Abstract: This meditation highlights the proper attitude required to make a life decision. It takes place not at the level of decision but of attitude and attachment. It surpasses indifference and even the embrace of the cross. It calls for nothing less than unreserved surrender: to will what God wills.
Topics: ELECTION, Ignatian.
Subsidiary discussions: Surrender (192).

Precis: After repeating Ignatius' descriptions of the Three Preludes and the Three Classes of Men (186f), Rahner summarizes the attitude presupposed in this meditation (that includes the "more," Ignatian indifference, and the sinner's encounter with the God of Love manifest in the cross of Christ). In this meditation this attitude is surpassed in a free and total surrender to the ever-greater love of God. This meditation exemplifies the attitude required for such a choice. Rahner changes the three men into three priests, and the 10,000 ducats into an honored post in the church. Each priest has acquired his position honestly and exercises it justly. Nothing sinful attaches to the priests' retaining their station. Yet each is aware that he has not acquired his post from a complete and unreserved love of God. It is objectively possible to integrate this job into God's love, but none of them has yet done so— as our meditation on the Two Standards would urge. All three priests in this parable desire to love God completely. They know the weight of this impediment and are looking for the best way to give up this attachment. This meditation is meant to help us avoid the two false ways of solving this problem: either by simply walking away from one's station, or by immediately deciding to keep it and to reform it by informing it with the love of God. Both of these wrong responses focus on *decision*, whereas this is a question of the proper religious *attitude* which should precede decision: surrender, abandonment to the will of God, which surpasses even the indifference of the *The Foundation*. Rahner spends the remainder of this meditation examining each class of men in turn. Those in the first class (192f) do nothing because they fear love and want salvation on their own terms. Those in the second class (193) secretly want to retain their posts and use them for good. They cannot imagine any good arising from giving them up. They cannot embrace the folly of the cross. Only those in the third class (193f) love God as God desires to be loved. They struggle not with the post, but with their own attachments. Above all, they seek to will what God wills.

SE.22. The Three Degrees of Humility. #162-168 (196-202)
Abstract: This meditation treats the now aroused decision-attitude from the angle of willingness to serve God. The three interrelated "degrees of humility" move from conditional, rationed love through active indifference, to a complete subjection to God marked by self-forgetfulness, but still calling for discretion.
Topics: HUMILITY, degrees of; LOVE, degrees of.
Subsidiary discussions: Love and discretion (200ff).

Precis: Preliminary Considerations. Here we can substitute the word "love" for "humility" recalling that for Ignatius both are essentially generous service to God. Also we should not think of "kinds" of humility but of "degrees." This meditation is meant to treat the already aroused decision-attitude from a different angle.
I. The first degree of humility is marked by a modest but rationed love of God. Ignatius likens it to those who resolve never to commit a mortal sin, but leave the rest negotiable. They never radically reassess their relation to things, and hope to use them to attain their goals. Their love of God is never unconditional.
II. The second degree of humility is more prefect. It embodies active indifference. Only those who have decided to live for God alone set their sites on the second degree of humility. Hence, we can see this as a continuation of the First Degree. **III. The third degree of humility** is the most perfect. It consists in the will to

choose the cross for love of Christ, provided it does not diminish the honor of His Majesty. Hence, it always requires discretion. At this level behavior is no longer ruled by this-worldly motives. As complete followers of Christ, Christians possessing the third degree of humility no longer consider themselves and are completely subject to the unconditioned disposition of God. **IV. The inner unity of the three degrees of humility** is quite apparent. Rahner concludes by developing the theme that even this highest degree of humility demands discretion in implementation.

SE.23. The Priesthood. (203-209)

Abstract: All the radical characteristics of priesthood can be traced back to its origin in Christ: the way it unites the human and divine, its inseparable liturgical and missionary dimensions, and the oneness of office and charism underscored in the West by the priestly commitment to celibacy.

Topics: JESUS CHRIST, priesthood of; PRIESTHOOD.

Subsidiary discussions: Word, ministry of (206); Office and charism (207f); Celibacy (209).

Precis: 1. The priesthood and the incarnation of the Word. The radicality of New Testament priesthood derives from Jesus Christ, who as the Incarnate Son of God is born a priest. From the moment He enters the world "Christ is the eternal communication center who makes possible the conversation between God and men, between God and the whole world" (204). New Testament priesthood, though it must be spoken of with modest reserve, is essentially a continuing realization of this medium between God and humanity. The unity of human and divine found in the Incarnate Word is continued in the priesthood. It fills priests with joy and apprehension that they will dispense God's grace as His and *their own*. **II. Cult and kerygma in the priesthood of the New Testament,** liturgical worship and prophetic sending, are inseparably united in ministry of the Word. Neither can be neglected, although in the concrete life of each priest one or the other function will predominate. Nevertheless, "sending" distinguishes priesthood from other modes of Christian existence. **III. Office and life** in the Western priesthood mutually determine one another. Official powers and personal charisms (like holiness) can never be completely separated if the church is to continue to exist as the holy church of God. Authority and holiness must co-penetrate. Each priest must strive to be a holy priest, despite the truth of anti-Donatism. Since office alone can never guarantee holiness, priests must execute their office with fear and trembling. After offering a few points for examination of conscience, Rahner shows how celibacy serves to bridge office and charism by working to insure that personal commitment to one's priesthood remains alive and fruitful. Jesus must not only be the exemplar but also the companion and source of strength for every priest.

SE.24. The Holy Eucharist. (210-216)
Abstract: Participation in Eucharist is the heart of Christian existence insofar as it is participation in Christ. It links our death to His, and unites us to one another and thus to the whole church concretely, not just abstractly. What is demanded of every Christian is expected of each priest in a more perfect way.
Topics: EUCHARIST; PRIESTHOOD and Eucharist.
Subsidiary discussions: Death (211ff); Priests, death of (214f); Church, unity of (215f).

Precis: Note. The Lord's Supper is a cultic, liturgical, and perfectly valid expression of the same sacrificial attitude which was realized on the cross for the salvation of the world. **I. The Eucharist as a participation in Christ** is the heart of Christian existence. We can only receive the grace of Eucharist to the degree we make real in our personal lives the sacrifice it contains. This demands at the least that we cultivate preparation and thanksgiving. Although the meditation on Eucharist in the Exercises does not demand this participation, all the elements highlighted so far (indifference, the "more," the Two Standards, the degrees of humility) point to the same thing. In a special way, Eucharist is a participation in the death of the Lord. Our liturgy does not minimize or domesticate this death, but brings us face to face with the destiny of our miserable existence: the eternal call of God's love. "In the Eucharistic celebration, therefore, we announce not only the death of Christ, but also our own death" (212). We share the same death with Christ insofar as it is the final fulfilling act of life, and is imposed without our consent. At the heart of our celebration of the Eucharist should be our earnest prayer to die our death in the Lord's death. This is especially true of priests, who should bring their own silent, long-suffering everyday lives to the altar. Of course in the Eucharist we participate not only in the cross but also in Christ's glory. **II. The Eucharist and the unity of the church.** Our participation in Eucharist also incorporates us into the life and mission of the church. To be united with Christ is to be united with his Mystical Body. It is no private affair. When we receive the body and blood of Christ it is really we who are received! There is no unity of the church if concrete unity is lacking among the individual members. This is especially true for those who through their priestly existence are sent out to others, just as the Word is sent out by the Father.

SE.25. The Agony in the Garden. #200-204 (217-226)

Abstract: Aside from a few theological conundrums which distinguish Jesus' death from ours (e.g., how to square Jesus' agony with His immediate vision of God and lack of concupiscence) this meditation focuses on the grace of surrender which reveals God's power shining through our human weakness.

Topics: JESUS CHRIST, Agony in the Garden.

Subsidiary discussions: Jesus Christ, immediate vision of God (218f; 223); Law, culmination of (220); Jesus Christ, prayer of (223ff); Jesus Christ, surrender of (225f).

Precis: I. Jesus goes to the Garden of Olives, knowing beforehand He will be betrayed there. This underscores Jesus' free acceptance of His fate. **II. The agony and the immediate vision of God** are difficult to reconcile. Our theological certainty of Jesus' immediate vision of God affords no reason to water down the Gospel account of His Godforsakenness. In reconciling the two, the vision of God must not be taken as just one attribute among many others since, as God's self-communication, it is constitutive of human existence. Furthermore, this immediate vision is not necessarily a beatific vision. It is possible that in the Garden, God is agonizingly present to Jesus in His hiddenness. Whatever the case, we can say that in the Garden, Jesus freely submitted Himself to the full terrors of death. **III. Gethsemani and Tabor** merge. The Agony in the Garden reveals the triumph of the Law in the death of the Just One and the Prophets seemingly become absurd. For in Gethsemani the final victory remains hidden. **IV. The Agony** of Jesus must somehow be reconciled with His immunity from concupiscence. Ironically, this freedom from concupiscence makes His agony worse because Jesus integrates His suffering into His total reality. Jesus *is* His suffering (221). In this regard, death for those who have grown up with concupiscence is completely different from the death of the Just One, to whom death is utterly absurd. In an application of the senses we must experience, as it were, "the negative immediacy of God" (223). But from out of the mute nothingness into which the agony of Jesus' cry disappears, comes something wonderful: God's victory is made perfect in weakness. This act of surrender is not an act of power but an incomprehensible miracle of God's grace. What was true for Jesus is no less true for us as we face the agony of our death.

SE.26. From the Garden to the Cross. (227-233)
Abstract: Meditation on Jesus' way of the cross reveals many things about Him, about us, and about the world. Among these are the nature of sin, and the various reasons for rejecting and abusing Jesus.
Topics: JESUS CHRIST, way of the cross.
Subsidiary discussions: Sin, manifestation of (227f); God, honor due (228f); Soul/body, unity of (231f).

Precis: Note. Jesus' way of the cross illuminates world history and must always be viewed against this backdrop. **I. Jesus betrayed and abandoned.** Clearly reveals the godlessness of sin, for here we see the fundamental perversion: the love of God rejected. At the same time it reveals God's faithfulness. **II. Jesus before the Sanhedrin** is condemned in the name of good order. This tendency has not completely died out even within the church of today, which too often mistakes the honor of the world for the honor of God. **III. Jesus in prison** descends into the prison of my own finitude and hopeless self-deception and throws open the gates. But I lack the courage to stand up and leave! **IV. Jesus rejected by the Jews and pagans.** The Jews reject Jesus in the name of God as a scandal. This is the attitude of the second class of men who demand that God fulfill their reasonable expectations and refuse to open themselves to His incommensurability. Pagans reject Jesus as foolishness. **V. The scourging and crowning with thorns** is a direct violation of Jesus' whole person, due to the fact that like us, He is a substantial unity of body and soul. At a certain point His pathetic state becomes the very justification for His abuse, since might makes right, and those who suffer are obviously stupid or naive. Attacks on the church today are nothing less than a continued attack on Jesus' own body. Yet this is the man we follow, and in doing so we achieve the only real humanism that has value in God's eyes— a humanism without illusions.

SE.27. Our Lord's Death on the Cross. (234-243)

Abstract: The cross is the pinnacle of Christ's glorification. In His "yes" to suffering and death Jesus says "yes" to the incomprehensibility of God. His obedient love for the Father reveals the essence of sin: our insane, blind hatred of God's love, and invites us to identify where we avoid the cross, our only hope.

Topics: CROSS; JESUS CHRIST, death of.

Subsidiary discussions: Obedience of Jesus (237f); Love (238f); Sin, essence of (240f); Jesus Christ, heart of (242); Everyday Life, despair (242f).

Precis: Note. In summary, the cross is the fork in the road of world history. It is the true *philo-sophia* of God's love which is a scandal for Jews and foolishness to pagans. **I. To the Jews a stumbling block, to the Gentiles foolishness.** In the first camp are all those who find the cross a scandal because it does not fit their rational concept of God. They cannot surrender to a God who is greater than anything they can imagine. Among the second class are those whose vision cannot extend beyond this world. It takes great courage to resist these alternatives and to embrace the true *philo-sophia* of the cross. **II. The cross in Jesus' earthly life** marks the highpoint of His mission: that which "had to be." It is also the supreme catastrophe and the most personal act of His life. For through His total obedient submission to the Father He is able to absorb into Himself and transform what is absolutely foreign to Him. On the cross, Jesus freely says "yes" both to abandonment and suffering and to the incomprehensibility of God. In doing so He accomplishes the incomprehensible act of love, losing Himself to find Himself. It is only His total love for the incomprehensible God that transforms the hell of His cry, "*My God, my God, why have you abandoned me,*" into the blessedness of "*Father, into your hands I commend my spirit.*" The cross is not the unsurpassable moral act because it can be attributed to the Word and achieves infinite value (Anselm); but because it is the personal act of the Word Himself. **III. The meaning of the cross in salvation history** reveals what sin really is. On the cross we see the world blindly devour the very Son of God in its insane hatred of God's love. Since the cross reveals these same base and hellish possibilities in us, we can truly say "He died for me." The cross does not explain the why of God's love. All we can do in this meditation is to accept it. Nevertheless, we continually try to block it out. We work to become cozy in the prison of finitude, loneliness and powerlessness we have imagined for ourselves, the door to which Christ has already opened. Rahner concludes this section with a meditation on the pierced heart of Christ. **IV. The cross in our life.** It takes courage to put up with life's sufferings and failures. But the seeming courage of the pagans, veiled in cynicism or Stoic resignation, is only the escape of those who despair. Christian courage is completely different. Born on the cross, it is not despair but a real loving surrender to God. Hence, I must examine myself to discover where I avoid the cross in my life.

SE.28. The Resurrection and Ascension of Our Lord. #218-229 (244-250)

Abstract: A proper assessment of Christian life must include Jesus' Resurrection and Ascension. His body, resurrected and glorified, points to the day our lives will become definitive; His Ascension, whereby a part of creation is irrevocably accepted by God, heralds a new, final phase in world history.

Topics: JESUS CHRIST, Ascension of; JESUS CHRIST, Resurrection of.

Subsidiary discussions: Resurrection of the body (245); World, transformation of (246ff).

Precis: Note. In Week IV we are to ask for a share in the joy of Christ risen and seated in glory– a glory only possible through the cross.
I. The Resurrection in the life of Jesus. The whole picture of

Christian life must be embraced, both the cross and Resurrection of Jesus in which He overcomes death and the world and is present to God in glory. With the resurrection of His body His whole history is taken up in glory. Nothing is lost. Not even His death is put behind Him. It is eternally present in glory. **II. The Ascension of Christ and its meaning for salvation.** With the Ascension of Christ a part of this world has been taken up forever and irrevocably in glory, and by extension the whole world is already transformed. Thus we can say the world itself has now entered its final phase. Ultimately, the world has been set right; all that now happens on earth is either an effect of His victory or a futile effort to resist it. In this way, our share in Jesus' Resurrection is not simply something that will happen in the future. It is a factor in our present existence (247). We have already risen with Christ because we already possess his glorifying Spirit. This is the source of our confidence in His victory. This we experience through faith. Hence, in spite of any evidence to the contrary we should repeatedly tell ourselves the love and mercy of God are final and nothing can separate us from His love . . . so long as we cling to His cross.

SE.29. The Spirit as the Fruit of the Redemption. (251-261)

Abstract: The glory of Christian life can be summarized: through the pierced heart of Christ we have received the Spirit of the Father and so have been filled with divine life. The Spirit abides in the church but cannot be fully contained by its strictures. Priests who accept office but reject love insult the Spirit.

Topics: SPIRIT/s.

Subsidiary discussions: Holy Spirit and the Trinity (251f); Theology and the Spirit (254f); Church and Spirit (256f); Priesthood and Spirit (258ff); Spirit, experience of (259).

Precis: Note. No account of Christian life would be complete without considering the impact of the outpouring of the Holy Spirit, then and now. **I. The Spirit in the Trinity** is the very Spirit we experience, since the economic Trinity is the immanent Trinity. We should not look to abstract concepts but to scripture, and embrace the Spirit we find there. The glory of Christian life can be summed up by saying we have received the Spirit of the Father and so have been filled with divine life. **II. The source of the**

Spirit is the pierced heart of Christ. When we complain of not feeling buoyant or enthused we should ask whether we have really accepted the cross and have let our hearts be touched. "Give your blood and you will possess the Spirit." **III. The testimony of scripture** (citations, 253f) reminds us that Christ, and not human cleverness is the source for our theology. We can do theology only because the Spirit has been given to us by God. Theology is never more than a poor reflection of our experience of God. The Spirit is the uncontrollable Spirit; the Spirit of virginity; the principle of *koinonia* and of forgiveness. **IV. The Spirit and the church.** The church came into being when the Spirit made of it a permanent home. Of course before Christ there was justification and grace and Spirit. But after the Incarnation there is a new element: God has finally assumed the world into His spiritual life. Letter and Spirit, sacraments and grace, office and holiness are now bound together as a result of the Incarnation, but without a mixing of natures. **V. The Spirit and official positions.** Despite their legitimate distinctions, office and holiness in the church are united by the Spirit of holiness who produces in priests "love, faithfulness to God and men, courage and willingness to bear the cross" (258). To accept office but reject love is an insult to the Spirit. More-over, it is the Spirit who inspires the faithful to listen to the preaching of priests and to receive sacraments at their hands. **VI. The experience of the Spirit** in our lives may seem quite different from that described in the New Testament. But wherever we find the strength daily to bear the cross, that too is the Spirit working within us. The ministry of priests should be marked with joy, and with the humility to submit to norms imposed on them. The more we allow the Spirit to take hold of us as we follow Christ on our way of the cross, the more we will taste the fruits of the Spirit.

SE.30. Mary and the Church. (262-269)

Abstract: Mary is the perfectly redeemed person. Her concrete unity of body, soul and spirit manifests the unity of office and charism, service and self-fulfillment, for which priests in particular should strive. As the incarnate prototype of the church, Mary forces us to evaluate our own love for the church.

Topics: BVM and the church; PRIESTLY LIFE and BVM.

Subsidiary discussions: Priesthood, office and charism in (264f); God and everything else (266f); Church, love for (268f).

Precis: Note. Although St. Ignatius never treats this theme expressly, he does refer to Mary throughout the Exercises. All his meditations on salvation history lead us to one question: what is my love of God supposed to look like? We find the concrete answer in Mary, the actualized ideal of the absolutely redeemed, sinless, holy, perfect person. **I. Mary, the perfectly redeemed,** realizes a perfect openness to Christ which, though unique to her, reveals the goal of our lives. Theologically, her perfect redemption flows from her being the blessed mother of our Redeemer. As perfectly redeemed, Mary is the absolute unity "of spirit, body and soul. In her everything is summed up in the act of her personal surrender to God" (263). Hence, we can say she conceives the Word in her faith, heart and womb. Her perfect redemption also indicates the perfect harmony of her beginning and end (Immaculate Conception and Assumption). This has special meaning for priests to whom she models the perfect unity of office and personal holiness, as well as the unity of service to others and self-fulfillment. Her example of humility also opposes any humanistic cult of personality. **II. Mary and the church.** Mary is the prototype of the church. Her role in the Incarnation shows how God communicates with creatures in their particularity and gives their very concreteness a religious significance. Such "Incarnational Christianity" forces us to take Mary seriously. The fact that in her we can see how all things point beyond themselves to the infinite love of God, helps us avoid the temptation of thinking we can get directly to God by bypassing His creatures. **III. The church and us.** Recalling that the church is a real community of believers and not just a teacher of abstract truths, priests especially must examine the quality of their love for the church, which grows and endures its ups and downs just like every other human love. Hopefully these trials make their love stronger and more mature. Rahner concludes with questions for self-examination (list, 269).

SE.31. The Contemplation of Love. #230-237 (270-277)

Abstract: This meditation recapitulates the entire Exercises and draws its seemingly disparate elements together in a love which inspires

ultimate commitment to the Incarnate Word. Detachment from self in turn allows one to see God in all things and to reenter the world imitating Christ in truly loving service.
Topics: LOVE in St. Ignatius.
Subsidiary discussions: Cross (271f); God in all things (273ff).

Precis: *"The Foundations"* begins and *"The Contemplation on Love"* ends the Exercises. Though strictly speaking they lie outside the body of the Exercises, they both contain the whole. The goal of this meditation is the same as the goal of the whole retreat: that as a result of decision, God in His sublime love should say something to the retreatant that surpasses mere philosophy or theology. The single dynamic of love has been operative through every part of the Exercises. This thoroughly incarnate love is also completely Christian, insofar as it cannot be realized except through the cross. Ignatius identifies this love with service, not with the abstract metaphysical *eros* of God. This love is Trinitarian (272) and reveals itself in deeds (272f). It leads to the discovery of God in all things through detachment finalized in death (272). This love is fundamentally ecclesial (274). St. Ignatius presents us with an almost kaleidoscopic view of God's love which Rahner breaks into four elements: God gives; God inhabits; God works; God descends (275f). The common element in all this is the "'finding of God in all things' so that I and the redeemed world might be transparent toward God and God toward the world" (276). Although this is nothing else than the basic truth of Christianity, it can only be experienced through an act of ultimate commitment. Those who succeed at the Exercises are able to pray the *"Sucipe"* wholeheartedly because they have broken away from themselves in the following of Christ. They are now ready to reenter the world, able to find God in everyday things. They will possess God, "not in opposition to the world, but as the only One who gives value and dignity to the world" (277). This section concludes with 1Cor 13.

SE.32. The Grace of Perseverance. (278-285)
Abstract: Perseverance is simultaneously a divine gift and an effect of our freedom. Only those who have fully and freely surrendered to God can calmly receive the future back from Him. The surest

indication we possess the grace of perseverance is the quality of our love for Jesus' Sacred Heart and for his Mother.
Topics: PERSEVERANCE, grace of.
Subsidiary discussions: Surrender and freedom (279f); Sacred Heart, devotion to (282f); BVM, devotion to (282f); Exercises of St. Ignatius, resolutions (284f).

Precis: Note. After a long quote from Trent, Rahner notes that apprehension about the unknown future is an essential part of finite spirit in matter. The theological question of perseverance is whether we shall finally be what we are now, or at least what we hope to be. **I. The essence and origin of Christian perseverance** is God alone, but worked out in concert with our own freedom. Only those who completely surrender to God can realize the full meaning of God's power and freedom, and accept their future from Him as a gift which, as a result of our free surrender, still really belongs to God. God is the only being with whom we can share our freedom. Only the gifts we accept from God have the capacity to become our own free acts. Perseverance is actual grace– a gift that comes about through our act of surrender to God in love and freedom. Sin is essentially drawing back from God because we have more confidence in ourselves than in God. Perfect loving surrender to God affects a holy fear of God that makes us happy, calm, and confident (summary, 281). **II. Signs of divine election** are those brought about by our own actions, which are signs of God working within us (e.g., constant prayer, selfless love). Rahner especially mentions those experiences, looking back on which, we can't imagine how we survived! There are also less joyful signs like those described in Francis Thompson's *The Hound of Heaven*. **III. Sacred Heart devotion and devotion to Mary as means of acquiring perseverance.** Whatever aids there may be to achieving perseverance, they all involve doing. We could profitably examine ourselves for signs of any split between our religious practices and the wholeheartedness of our participation. To Rahner it seems that personal forms of devotion are more apt to develop the grace of perseverance than habitual, institutional forms. Among the former he singles out devotion to the Sacred Heart and to Mary, both of which must be truly interior if they are to be practiced at all. Of course God is the only guarantee of the grace of perseverance. But to check the quality of our love for God, which is necessary for final perseverance, we should simply examine ourselves (inventory, 283f) to see whether we truly love the Mother of God and Jesus' Sacred Heart. **IV. Retreat resolutions** to be effective must be concrete and must be implemented immediately. Even now one can cry out to God to accomplish in us what we desire. The smallest step may prove to be the most decisive.

Glossary (278). The English equivalents used by this translator along with the original German terms.

Theologians Today Series: Karl Rahner, SJ. Martin Redfern, ed. NY: Sheed & Ward, 1972. 128 pp.
Contents: Series Introduction (7-8).
1. "The Prospect for Christianity" (11-53). Cf., **Free Speech in the Church. FS.2.**
2. "The Sacrifice of the Mass" (57-69). Cf., *The Christian Commitment.* **CCt.5.**
3. "The Inspiration of the Bible" (73-86). Cf., **Articles in Books. AB.5.**
4. "Action in the Church" (89-128). Cf., *The Theology of Pastoral Action.* **TPA.2.**

Theology and the Future of Man. St. Louis MO: St. Louis University Press, 1968. 88 pp. A bound copy of the Ferbruary 1968 issue of *Theology Digest* commemorating St. Louis University's sesquicentennial. Its seven articles by Rahner are all abstracted in *Theological Investigations,* IX & X.

TR. *Theology for Renewal. Bishops, Priests, Laity.* NY: Sheed and Ward, 1964. 183 pp. *Sendung und Gnade.* Innsbruck: Tyrolia Verlag, 1961. Translated by Cecily Hastings and Richard Strachan. *Mission and Grace,* London: Sheed and Ward, 1964.
Contents: 1. The Episcopate and the Primacy. Cf., *Inquiries.* **Inq.4.**
2. The Parish Priest.
3. Deacons: Renewal of the Diaconate: Preliminary dogmatic Considerations.
4. Men in the Church.

5. The Scholar. Notes on devotion in the academic life.
6. The Christian Teacher: Freedom and Constraint.
7. The Student of Theology: The problems of his training today.
8. The Layman and the Religious Life. On the theology of secular institutes.

TR.1. The Episcopate and the Primacy (3-29). Cf., *Inquiries.* **Inq.4.**

TR.2. The Parish Priest. (31-44). In K. Borgmann (ed.), *Parochia.* Vienna: Kolmar (1943) 20-27.

Abstract: A parish priest, precisely because he is a priest of Christ, is necessarily both cult-man and pastor in an indissoluble perichoresis of the powers and tasks of both. He is a priest in one particular place on earth, so that the Kingdom of God may be fully present there as the home of souls.

Topics: PRIESTHOOD, nature of; PRIESTHOOD, parochial.

Subsidiary discussions: Incarnation (34f); Word, sacramental nature of (35ff); Parochial principle (42ff).

Precis: The talk begins with an invitation to prayer that God may reveal the truth of what they will be discussing. In these preliminary "points for meditation" Rahner states his simple two-part thesis: a parish priest is a *priest* tied to a *locality*. **1. A parish priest is a priest.** Unlike writer-priests or administrator-priests who can be very effective even without being very good priests, a parish priest is simply and utterly a priest and nothing else. But what is a priest? Is he a cult figure, a sacrificing priest, or is he a man on a mission, a pastoral priest? Mystic or prophet? Of course he is both because Christ, who is one, wills to live on in the priest and in what he does, and Christ is: 1) the grace of God made tangible in time and space; 2) the word; 3) in which the whole world is taken up and consecrated. Next Rahner makes explicit how these three interlocking realities (incarnation, sacramental word and consecration) place the reality of Christ at the center of Christianity (34-37). The priest is the one through whom this reality of Christ is to remain present in every place and at every time until Christ comes again in the glory of God, and human words and earthly signs will no longer be necessary. "But this means that the priest is essentially sacrificer and pastor, cult-man and apostle, mystic and prophet in one" (37). Rahner now proceeds to explain that this interior unity of sacrificer and pastor is a radical, co-conditioning unity. Neither element can be fully realized except by their mutual penetration. This is because Christ himself was both priest and prophet, sacrament and word.

2. **A priest tied to a locality.** By divine law the church of Christ is organized in territorial episcopates. The church meets people where they live and always sees the individual as a member of a local, historical community. The parish priest, by caring for a particular place, participates in this fundamental earth-bound characteristic of the church. He sees to it that in this place the faith is well-rooted, flourishes and lasts. This sets the parish priest apart from wandering apostles, driven by the Spirit over the face of the earth, intent on a particular mission. The geographical limitation imposed on a parish also provides the opportunities for success. A parish priest cannot be a specialist. He must do everything and find ways to reach out to all. He must create in the parish a heavenly home here on earth, something that has become so vitally important in these chaotic days when people are so rootless.

TR.3. Deacons: Renewal of the Diaconate: Preliminary dogmatic considerations. (45-56). *Festschrift M. Schmaus.* Munich: 1957. 135-144.

Abstract: These few theses are meant to put into proper theological focus the question of restoring the diaconate. They involve such issues as the institution of sacraments by Christ, conferral of sacramental grace, office and charism. Rahner concludes that restoring the diaconate is urgent and desirable.

Topics: DIACONATE, restoration of.

Subsidiary discussions: Holy Orders, as instituted by Christ (47f); Grace, sacramental (52f).

Precis: Avoiding great theological detail, this essay puts forward a few theses as useful preliminaries to focus the question of the restoration of the diaconate today [1957]. **1)** There exists in the church a sacrament of leadership which confers the power of office along with the claim to a corresponding grace to fulfill the office. The two poles of this sacrament present dangers: office holders suppressing those with charism; or charismatic persons having contempt for office holders. 2) Even when the church transfers only some of these powers, such a legitimate transmission of office remains a sacrament. Rahner substantiates this by arguing that by instituting the church, Christ willed everything necessary for its continuation till the end of time (e.g., Orders). Although the orders themselves are *jus divinum*, details of administering them are secondary and have been left to the church to develop over time. Various historical and dogmatic considerations support this interpretation. **a.** There is no proof Christ himself instituted various orders; **b.** Acts does recount the church's institution of the diaconate; **c.** A priori, one would expect the church to have this kind of authority; **d.** Medieval theology's endorsement of such divisions (including even minor orders) could only be justified by such a theory; **e.** Historically, it is difficult to see Christ distinguishing even between the office of bishop and priest. **f.** There are analogous cases in other sacraments (e.g., confirmation, anointing, marriage).

3) This does not mean every office in the church is a partial sharing in the hierarchical office of Christ, and hence sacramental (e.g., diocesan accountant). 4) Even when a particular office in the church does share in the hierarchical office, the conferral of this office need not be sacramental, though it may be. 5) The delimitation of the various offices, even when sacramentally transmitted, can vary over time. 6) Whenever any office forms part of the church's vital functioning it carries the promise of God's grace, even if it is not conferred by any sacramental rite. The impartation of grace is not restricted to the sacraments. However it may be imparted, what is decisive for fruitfulness is one's interior disposition. 7) Restoration of the diaconate is extremely desirable and urgent: **a.** Priests cannot do all that needs to be done; **b.** Scripture and history show diaconate is a permanent office and not merely a transitional step to priesthood. **c.** To attract competent people to serve the church in these capacities they must have the corresponding recognition and respect sacramental orders in part convey. 8) Assuming the individual who presents himself fulfills the proper conditions (list, 57f), he can be and should be ordained a deacon. For if such a sacrament exists (and in fact it does), there is no need to prove that it should exist and be administered. Rather one would have to show why, in individual cases, it should *not* be conferred.

TR.4. Men in the Church. (57-84). *Katholisches Männerwerk.* Cologne (1956) 29-45.

Abstract: Addresses the pastoral problem that so few men in the West participate in the grassroots life of the church. Rahner analyzes psychological differences between men and women in the light of theology, and makes a number of concrete pastoral suggestions to increase men's connection with the church.

Topics: CHURCH, men's participation in; SPIRITUALITY, masculine.

Subsidiary discussions: Morality, application of norms (71f); Transcendent/Categorical in religion (73); Laity, role of (78ff).

Precis: *"In relation to the ultimate question of salvation, to the total decision of life, there is no difference between the sexes.... But human beings are nevertheless seen by God as men or women"* (57f). By this Rahner means that sexuality is a constitutive dimension of one's self. It is not a factor that can be considered in isolation from the whole person. Noting the limitations and dangers inherent in any analysis of sexual identity and sexual differences (list, 59f), Rahner undertakes this analysis because even a poor answer from him will at least make this important question more prominent.

1. Masculinity in the Christian message and in the world. Rahner lists some of the many areas a serious study would have to consider, but which he cannot treat here. **2. A rough sketch of man as differentiated from woman.** After insisting that his "neutral" description of the differences between masculine and feminine traits contains no value judgment, he sets forth in some detail what he thinks constitutes the masculine. [He gives no sources.] **3. Why is religious life oriented more to women than to men?** How has it come to be that, in the West at least, women participate in religion more than men, and seem to have more intense piety and religious sensitivity? Two factors often suggested are *not* true: there is nothing specific to the nature of men or women that determines their affinity to religion; there is nothing specifically feminine about Christianity. He bases this on the theological premise that God's call is addressed to everyone, and that everyone is equally capable of responding. The history of religion also belies its being a men's affair. Nor is the loving surrender demanded by true religion particularly feminine. Whatever its cause, it remains undeniable that today in the West levels of participation in religion are much lower among men than women. This may be due in part to what Rahner calls an growing "efeminization" of Christianity: the stamping of a feminine character where it does not rightly belong. Leaving aside the causes of this development, Rahner simply appeals for a masculine Christianity. In what follows he shows what this would look like, and makes concrete, though partial pastoral recommendations.

4. **Excessive religious demands are not to be made on men.** This seemingly minimalist suggestions takes into account the increasing burdens placed on men today. Don't pastors often expect too much of men, holding out to them the example of canonized saints, against whom most men would fail to measure up? Secondly, Central-European men often do not join groups which make excessive demands for fear of joining in bad faith, knowing in advance they cannot do all that is expected. They leave it to retired men, men of means, or to the more religiously fanatic. Many clerics look on with horror as this already small group of "good Christian men" continues to shrink. 5. **Grading demands according to the degree of grace, insight, ability, milieu and age.** Must all moral demands (however objectively correct) be placed on all alike? How can the church be welcoming, gentle and tolerant, and at the same time rigid and intolerant in the moral sphere? Can no allowances be made for men of different ages, backgrounds and cultures? 6. **The categorical and transcendent elements in religion** are like body and soul, co-conditioning, inseparable, and existing for one another. No concrete (categorical) element in religion exists for itself. All exist to point beyond themselves to God (transcendent). Religion must never confuse categorical signs for the transcendent reality. One can in fact participate fully in the church and yet be far from God, and vice versa. A lack of overt religiosity can be a sign in men of deference to what they know is truly transcendent and inexpressible. It can also mask cowardice to profess publicly what they actually do believe. 7. **Men should have a share of responsibility in the church.** The piety asked of men should match their masculine character. It should engage their sense of responsibility, their talents, their joy in contributing their own actions, their ability to voice opinions (something priests tend to fear, in part because they themselves are men!). For laymen do have a Christian task in the world distinct from

the role of the hierarchy: transforming the world from the ground up beginning in their families, jobs, and public life. **8. Tasks for men in the church** include many quite small and obvious things: reasonableness, reliability, perseverance, and an ascesis that resists self-indulgence and mindless acquisition of gadgets. These seemingly natural things are also supernatural insofar as the grace to accomplish them comes from God. Even one's seemingly secular tasks in the world have a religious dimension. Here attitude is everything, since if one does not maintain perspective by focusing on God, he will either overvalue or despise his activities (summary, 82ff). There is so much to be clarified about masculinity! And Rahner fears he has not yet even made a start. Man is still in the process of discovering his true identity. But this will only be fully known when we are all made perfect in the Kingdom of God.

TR.5. The Scholar. Notes on devotion in the academic life. (85-93). *Der fahrende Scholast*, 1 (1957), Vol.2.

Abstract: This seemingly light treatment of academic life, seemingly aimed at young people, is actually quite direct and carries a punch. It raises humorously and in rapid succession various points for any kind of scholar's examination of conscience. These include, respect, hubris, skepticism, and sincerity.

Topics: EDUCATION, scholarship; EVERYDAY LIFE, scholarship.

Subsidiary discussions: Laity, role of (89f); Doubt (90f); Anonymous Christian/ity (91ff) Atheism (91ff).

Precis: A scholar's life need not automatically rule out a life of devotion. In fact, serious scholarship removes the main obstacle to belief by drawing us deeper into mystery. Though science has its uses, even the young can see its limitations. It is sad to see an older person stuck in an attitude of youthful arrogance in the realm of religion. "There are things that can only be understood by someone who loves them. The Church is one of these" (86). Christianity demands the utmost in spiritual courage and in breadth precisely because it embraces so much (list, 86). But for this very reason some see it as narrow. Though academics today have at their disposal the power to change the world, this is no excuse for them to be Cretans in the realm of religion. Whatever our technological advances, the eternal questions will remain. Those who would reform the church must always begin with themselves. And the faith of any real intellectual must acquaint itself with the great minds of history: Augustine, Aquinas, Pascal, Newman. The highest form of thought is adoration. Yet many academics are deaf to prayer. They seem not to listen for God and have nothing to say to God. Science can make great strides by specializing over a very small range of phenomenon at a very manageable level. Christians are at a disadvantage, having as their task to realize the love of God. Yet, only now, with the help of science is Christianity having its first true chance. For only now is the world becoming one. Only now do many people have sufficient leisure. And the leisure provided by science poses the question, "What now?" without being able to answer it. Christianity is the only chance the world has of surviving its good fortune.

The special role of the lay intellectual is to formulate and to voice public opinion in the church. Shyness in such matters should never mask cowardice. Hearing the nonsense many others propose as man's way forward, the Christian academic should be emboldened. True, Christian principles are general and ambiguous. But it is precisely the task of lay intellectuals to translate these into effective action within their own context. Darkness in faith is meant to stimulate thought. We are meant to puzzle over faith. And the right answer will always lead back to the mystery of God. In every other field (medicine, mechanics, etc.) we are convinced we must trust the opinion of experts. But on religious issues everyone feels omni-competent. Even atheists should have humble respect for religion, at least in its historical manifestation. For even those who explicitly reject the church may in fact share the Christian faith in essence. Hence, it is wise occasionally to ask whether we might be interpreting ourselves falsely. Living within God's creation, it is not so easy to avoid being at least a crypto-Christian. In committing oneself to a philosophy of life, one should ask whether it offers a solution to the whole human condition, or whether it just makes life better for the few. A cult of meaninglessness born of skepticism is not very deep. The Christian intellectual tradition is always marked by a return to the sources.

TR.6. The Christian Teacher: Freedom and constraint. (95-117). "The Teacher," a January 4, 1957 paper given at Frankfurt am Main to a Christian teachers' conference, published in *Der katholische Erzieher*, 10 (1957) 125-135.

Abstract: Christian teachers educate the unique individual of eternity. They do this by teaching and modeling that what seems like Christian constraint is simply refusal to be satisfied with the partial; and that freedom is the not the ability constantly to change, but to become someone of eternal validity.

Topics: EDUCATION, Christian; FREEDOM and constraint.

Subsidiary discussions: Force (100f); Faith, liberating (102ff); God, experience of (103f); Morality as liberation (106ff); Church as sacrament of freedom (109ff); Individuality, Christian (113ff); Spirits, discernment of (114ff).

Precis: This address to Christian teachers (in both Catholic and non-denominational schools) begins with two preliminary observations: 1) the teacher's task is the formation of the whole person, and the true teacher is a fully mature human being and Christian. This makes it legitimate to talk here about the human condition in general. 2) In both public and private schools, teachers are confronted with basically the same task and need the same grace of God. To speak about constraint and freedom of a human and a Christian is to talk about teachers and their task, wherever they work.

1) Constraint. Christians honestly and unashamedly profess they are subject to divine law and historical revelation. We also adhere to the church, its divine and human elements, and also to the natural moral law. The teacher must know, live and teach that we are *theonomous*, not *autonomous*. The center of our life is absolute mystery— something we often experience as constraint at the very center of our being. But Christians have to duty to interpret and to live this constraint correctly: as that which makes us free and gives life its validity. The dignity of human freedom is what it frees us *for*. It frees believers to become their eternally valid selves in the sight of God. Hence, we must not blush to champion such constraint. Furthermore, living this faith in freedom liberates the mind into the fullness of truth. Faith liberates by opening out to the absolute fullness of reality. Those who see only half of reality can never be truly free. Those who live with no experience of mystery are imprisoned within the damnation of their own finitude. This mystery is accessible within each person. Once this happens, "all the apparently bewildering multitude of mysteries in Christianity, all its articles of faith which seem merely to be imposed from the outside by formal authority, are seen to be in reality almost self-evident articulations and explicitations" (104f) of the depths of one's own being. This could never be clear without good teaching. And without good teaching one might never know where to look for the proof of this inner experience: to the person of Jesus Christ. If we keep renewing this inner experience, then faith will become one simple, whole, and self-evident mystery. This faith will liberate the believer from the bondage of half-truths. In short, the constraint imposed by faith is simply the prohibition against stopping short of the whole truth. In society, Christians are the true liberals, truly Catholic, truly integral, insofar as they embrace everything. Only such as these can be truly orthodox. Something similar can be said about the seeming constraints imposed by morality, which liberate one for the freedom to love once they have been internalized (107ff).

2) **Freedom** is the meaning and goal of constraint. The church is, in fact, "the sacrament of freedom" (109). For, "Where the Spirit of the Lord is, there is liberty" (2Cor 3:17). This is not psychological or political freedom, but the freedom of those redeemed in Christ. Thus in the heart of any teacher of true Christianity should be written: "A Christian is a free man." Teachers must live, exemplify and proclaim this truth. Though this stands out clearly compared to the desperate unfreedom of those who do not know Christ, too often we repress our awareness of the true situation of the world. But Christians should be radically honest. Only those who have tasted the depths of their imprisonment can sing the joy of being set free. Finally, is the task of the Christian teacher finished when students are inculcated in the Christian principles? No. Because Christianity is more than the application general norms to particular cases. God speaks to individuals. Teachers must assist others to develop a sensitivity to discern God's call. This cannot be taught directly, but only modeled by example, and acquired by sympathy. Teachers must do all they can to preserve this space in the individuals they teach from the encroachments of uniformity,

centralization, and a group mentality. For only the individual is worthy of eternity.

TR.7. The Student of Theology: The problems of his training today. (119-146). *Oreintierung*, 18 (1956) 87-95.

Abstract: The current way of training future priests, modeled as it is on the university system for training academics, needs a radical overhaul. The essay concludes with eight concrete suggestions.

Topics: PRIESTHOOD, formation for; THEOLOGY, teaching of.

Subsidiary discussions: Theology, kerygmatic (144f).

Precis: **1. The need for a re-examination of the question** of how candidates are prepared for priesthood is becoming more urgent, especially the matter of "academic" training. **2. The passing of the Age of Enlightenment.** The current academically-oriented system of training specialists and technicians is a response to and a product of the Enlightenment. But as academic specializations proliferate and fracture, the question arises whether this model offers the best way to train good pastors. **3. Change in aptitude amongst theological students** (not necessarily lower but different) forces us to look honestly and ask where the capacity for "scholarship" ranks among the requirements for a good pastor. **4. Lack of a theological central point** also presents a serious problem. As specializations proliferate, seminaries insist on an encyclopedic grasp of the field. The result is that the average student cannot stay abreast. He crams data he cannot appropriate in any meaningful way, and which he is not likely to need or use in pastoral care. The splintering of academic specializations also has an adverse effect on the specialist studies themselves, as they increasingly become unable even to dialogue with one another. **5. "Scholarship" and the training of theological students.** No one will disagree that seminary training should be geared toward producing priests and pastors who can "work in a scholarly way." But precisely what does this mean? If it means to think clearly and have the capacity personally to assimilate and preach the substance of faith in ever-changing circumstances, then good. But if it means being able to advance academic theology, then one must wonder. The more academic theology becomes the more neutral and impersonal it becomes. Is this really the best way to train pastors?

6. Suggestions on the direction in which to move. 1. Normal seminary training today cannot remain "academic" in the strict sense. *"The identification between the training of a pastoral priest and of a scholarly theologian must be abolished"* (134). The two goals (both good) cannot be reached by the same means. 2. A future theology curriculum should be lightened (jettison the superfluous), concentrated (focus on pastoral practice) and deepened (aim at personal appropriation so one can preach convincingly what he knows and believes). 3. Such "basic training" for priests is not just a modified academic course, but something completely new. Already this is done in almost every other field (training a high school physics teacher differs greatly from training a theoretical physicist). 4. Whether two tracks for theological preparation should be introduced (pastoral and academic) is open for discussion. 5. Theological training must be more closely connected to a candidate's spiritual life. 6. Objections: the "scholarliness" of theological training will suffer. Reply: a) the current level of real achievement is already quite inflated in relation to strict academic standards. b) the current system actually makes fewer demands on professors and encourages laziness born of isolation. They are not forced to examine the usefulness of what they know or the most appropriate way to teach it to future pastors. Ideally every pastor should be an accomplished theologian (and everyone who buys a house should be an architect!). But it is foolish to demand this *in concreto*. One need not fear that those on the pastoral track would suffer from inferiority, just as family physicians may admire surgeons and refer some of their patients to them without wishing to become a surgeon. 7. One is right to see here traces of the 1930s movement of "Kerygmatic-theology" which never really had a chance to take root. 8. There is a legislative factor in this. But since the goal of reforms is fundamentally the same as the goal of the legislation, Rahner sees no insurmountable problems.

TR.8. The Layman and the Religious Life. On the theology of secular institutes. (147-183). *Orientierung*, 20 (1956) 87-95.

Abstract: Responding to criticism from Dr. Von Balthasar, Rahner argues that secular institutes, because they embrace the evangeli-

cal counsels, are in fact a form of religious life. Hence, they do not offer a new way for being laity in the world. To insist on this actually obscures the true vocation of the laity.
Topics: LAITY; RELIGIOUS LIFE; SECULAR INSTITUTES.
Subsidiary discussions: "The World" (152 ftn 10); Perfection, states of (159ff; 170ff); Vows, public/private (162ff); Celibate chastity (172ff); Laity, vocation of (178ff).

Precis: This article responds to a complaint by Von Balthasar that Rahner fails to understand how secular institutes successfully meld the evangelical counsels with the lay state. Rahner counters that it is Von Balthasar who misrepresents the church's position [in 1956]. Rahner thinks Von Balthasar states the question poorly and that it needs clarification. Can those living the evangelical counsels pursue "worldly professions?" Yes. But according to Rahner it is less clear whether those who live the evangelical counsels in secular institutes are indeed lay people. He sets out 2 theses: Life in a secular institute is fundamentally shaped by the vows; vows essentially distinguish the professed from the laity. **1. First Step.** To achieve clarity, "the world" and "the laity" demand a clear definition, since both terms carry multiple meanings. The church does talk about "lay people living in the world." Here "the world" can mean the secular realm or the world outside the monastic enclosure. This does not automatically define everyone who pursues a profession outside a monastery as *ipso facto* a lay person. Similarly, the word "laity" arises from two sources,: it indicates non-clerics, and non-religious (those not living under vows). Hence, a non-cleric is not immediately simply a lay person. After discussing states of perfection in the church (**2. Theological investigation**) and the difference between public and private vows (**3. A digression**) Rahner moves to **4. Second step.** Having proved that members of secular institutes belong substantially to that state of perfection in the church which constitutes the life of religious orders, the question remains, are they still lay people? If one is careful and consistent in defining terms (acknowledging the inadequacy of language) Rahner concludes that members of secular institutes are not simply lay people in the world in the same way as other lay people are. After a quick summary (**5. A theological view of states in the church**). Rahner moves on to

6. Consequences of this for the secular institutes (summary, 171f). Members of secular institutes embrace the evangelical counsels (especially virginity), not merely as lifestyle choices, but in their spiritual fullness: as a renunciation of the goods of this world in an ecclesially tangible way for the sake of the Kingdom of God. This commitment makes any other "secularity" of a secular institute completely secondary. None of this in any way minimizes the fact that every Christian life must be shaped by the evangelical counsels, and that we must all somehow die to the world. **7. The apostolate of the laity and the secular institutes.** Only when this distinction is clearly maintained does the distinct vocation of the laity come into focus. There is no denying that religious can and do pursue "secular" professions in the world. Rahner wonders whether for psychological reasons many men would really be attracted to life in a secular institute without holy orders (175ff), especially since penetrating and informing the secular sphere with Christianity in a way the clergy cannot is precisely the role of the laity (178ff). For members of secular institutes, their profession will always be secondary to their public life of witness under the evangelical counsels. To hold out to others the model of the secular institute as the best way to be "laity in the world" actually has the unintended consequence of eviscerating or at least of obscuring the true role of the laity in the church and in the world. **8. Conclusions.** Recapitulation.

TPA. *Theology of Pastoral Action.* NY: Herder, 1968. Introduction; Preface; Bibliography; Index. 143 pp. "*Grundlegung der Pastoraltheologie als praktische Theologie*" in *Handbuch der Pastoraltheologie*, I/2, Freiburg: Herder, 1964. Translated by W.J. O'Hara. Adapted for English-speaking audience by Daniel Morrissey, OP. The two chapters are treated here as two distinct essays.

Contents: Chapter One: The Church: Basis of Pastoral Action. Chapter Two: Christians: Action in the Church.

General Introduction to the Series; Preface (1-25): Meant to encourage the development of a more local, North American theology, emphasizing general principles and leaving the challenge of practical application to local theologians. The first essay offers abstract principles, the second is more concrete.

TPA.1. The Church: Basis of Pastoral Action. (25-63)

Abstract: This basic ecclesiology is meant to inform the task of pastoral theology: proposing concrete act-ions within which the church fulfills her essential nature in the world. The essay proceeds from general principles to specific characteristics of the church, leaving practical applications to pastoral theologians.

Topics: CHURCH, nature of; ECCLESIOLOGY and pastoral action; THEOLOGY, pastoral.

Subsidiary discussions: Church, and inner-Trinitatiran processions (33ff, 40f); Magisterium, indefectability of (34f); Bishop/s, *Potestas ordinis et jurisdictionis* (ftn.5, 36ff); Sacraments, power to administer (ftn.5, 37ff); Petrine Office (ftn.5, 39f); Church as mystery (43f); Church as *Ur-sakrament* (44ff); Salvation, *extra ecclesia* (46ff); Church, as law and gospel (49ff); Church, permanent self-identity of (51ff); Revelation, historicity of (54ff); Church, office and charism in (59ff); Laity, charism of (59ff).

Precis: Pastoral theology is a theology of the church in action: "concrete existential ecclesiology." Because it incarnates the nature of the church in local circumstances, it presupposes familiarity with the nature of the church. What follows is a condensed dogmatic description of the fundamental nature of the church, expressing its unity and multiplicity, all tailored to support pastoral theology.

1. Fundamental nature of the church. *"The Church is the community, legitimately constituted in a social structure, in which through faith, hope and love God's eschatologically definitive revelation (his self-communication) in Christ remains present for the world as reality and truth"* (26f). Because the church is an eschatological reality (i.e., brought about and made visible by mankind's acceptance of God's prior absolute and irrevocable self-communication in the Christ-event) it is both the *gift* of salvation and the *means* of salvation. As a pastoral consequence of having been given the gift of salvation the church is apostolically active, and is continually renewed by apostolically witnessing to the world (ftn.2). Salvation itself is inescapably historical and social; God's self-communication is an historical process. All the church does in word, worship and confession of faith is made possible and supported by God's self-giving and saving grace. Revelation is essentially an event. It is no mere description. It conveys the very reality of what is revealed.

Revelation heard and accepted occurs as faith. Hence, the history of salvation, grace, divine self-communication, and revelation are all one in the same history which reaches its irrevocable culmination in Christ. Perfectly objectified in the world and in human society (empirically and historically) salvation history remains present. It subsumes all subsequent history. We call this the church.

2. The church as presence of God's truth and love. To say the church is God's eschatologically perfect self-donation to humanity in the historical and social realm means the church (like all personal, free, spiritual entities) expresses its essential nature by what it concretely does. The whole problem for pastoral theology is to discern exactly what should be manifested today to embody concretely God's saving presence. So, what really does become present in the church? Mystery (1); Truth (2); Love (3).

1) The authentic activity of the church is opening mankind to God, as God is in Himself and for us: measureless mystery that destroys the claim to finality of any finite thing. To present such a God is to oppose all idolatry, religious and secular. It is also the root of the church's necessary self-criticism. Worship in faith, hope and love is the only way the inexpressible is present.

2) Though the presence of God in the church must be experienced and accepted in its transcendental immediacy (i, e., not simply in the way we accept things) people must conceptually objectify this presence of mystery as their ground of being. This dual presence of God in the church (as mystery and ground) is God's presence as truth and love. This double mode of presence is a mode of being of God Himself expressed in the duality of the inner-Trinitarian processions, which *"forms the basis of the presence of God in the Church and is therefore the basis of the nature of the Church"* (31f). In the first Trinitarian procession, the Father (while remaining mystery) reveals and gives Himself to be possessed as the truth uttered by the Son. The church is first and foremost the presence of God as truth, the truth wherein God communicates Himself. That the church hears and proclaims the truth is the first characteristic of the church and therefore the first characteristic of its pastoral activity. The church is primarily a gift of salvation and only consequently a means of salvation. The church must always present itself as listening, hearing, and believing. It acts in faith. It teaches based on an appeal to an authority present in the church

of faith— "an active functioning of the hearing faith of the Church as a whole in contradistinction to the multitude of individuals as such" (35). After listing the characteristics of the magisterium, Rahner maintains the church fulfills its nature as the presence of God's truth when it believes, lives its act of faith, recalls its faith, and accepts with thanksgiving what is bestowed as God's truth. This free act of all believers (which makes visible in the economy of redemption the first Trinitarian procession) is the source of the church's teaching authority. From here Rahner discusses how this primary act of faith in the church relates to the classical distinction of *potestas* (powers of office and jurisdiction) and *munera*, offices (priest, prophet, king). [This discussion is found primarily in ftn. 5]. Although these standard distinctions do reflect the nature of the church as a whole even if the focus is on ministry, whatever theological basis is used to distinguish these powers and offices materially, does not invalidate the more fundamental statement about God's self-communicating presence to the church in truth and love.

3) Love is the second element of God's presence which determines the church's fundamental activity. It corresponds to the second Trinitarian procession. "The Church is the presence of God inasmuch as in it the Father reveals himself and gives himself to be possessed as a love which communicates itself in the Spirit" (40), which remains mystery. Giving to all what it has received from God belongs indefectibly to the church's nature, and the conjunction of the two (i.e., truth and love) makes the church holy. The presence of God's love in the church is realized in the objective holiness of the sacraments and in the subjective holiness of her members' love of neighbor. But are these acts of truth and love not essentially the same? Ideally, Christ's truth should appear as the innermost light of love. But truth can be proclaimed in a separate act, even though the purpose of truth in the church is to bring about the presence of love. For God, truth and love are one. But for us, due to historical contingencies, it is not always so. "Today only history and society can tell us about man and his pastoral situation, [but] only the existing, temporal Church can attain [that which is] abiding, necessary, and divine" (42f). Each of the various activities of the church may possess a different official character, but they all incarnate God's love for the world.

3. **Characteristics of the church.** Pastoral theology tries to express in existential theological propositions God's self-giving presence in truth and love. In doing so it must remain true to the following six characteristics set forth in dogmatic theology. **1. Mystery.** God is present in the church as mystery. The more the church succeeds in becoming itself, the more God and Christ and church become mysterious. The significance of this for pastoral theology is that preaching and teaching should not aim to diminish this mystery, but help the faithful to confront it. **2. Primal sacrament.** The best contemporary term to express God's self-communication to and through the church is "sacrament." Allowing that Christ Himself is the primordial sacrament, and that the church is not identical with Christ, the church is the prime sacrament insofar as it is ontologically prior to all the other sacraments. The church remains only a sign of God in the sense that it is not the exclusive area of God's presence in the world; but it is also *the* divinely-willed sign of God's grace to the whole world. Here Rahner sets out the proper sense in which the church is necessary for salvation (46ff). *"The Church is the efficacious manifest sign of the presence of God, its real symbol, containing what it signifies; by grasping the sign man experiences what it signifies"* (46). What is the significance of this for pastoral theology? The church must retain its missionary zeal because it is essentially the historical embodiment of God's promise to all mankind, and because in so doing the church actually becomes itself. **3. New Law of the Gospel.** The church is Gospel and not Law. It proclaims not that God *will* save the world, but that God *has* saved the world already, and enlists people to spread this good news and not simply to promulgate laws. God's absolute self-donation makes more profound demands than any external law. But God's love demands only what has already been given to the innermost center of human reality. What makes this gospel feel like law is the rift between the assurance of salvation of the church as a whole, and the uncertainty of an individual's salvation. But when God's life becomes the center of the individual's life this rift is healed and law is superseded. **4. Eschatological presence.** In one sense the church will cease (as a social institution), and in another sense it will endure (as union of love). It also possesses an enduring historical continuity in time. Through all its contingent changes it remains the selfsame church. Its legitimacy can be

traced back to its source though apostolic succession, sacraments, scripture and creeds. All change is validated by reference to tradition, the inner force of the old. **5. Ever new actual presence.** Revelation itself lives in history. Its history is the history of the final covenant. To say the history of revelation closed with the Apostolic Age only means that with Christ history became definitively open to God's self-communication. The history of revelation is not thereby abolished. It receives its proper final goal. We see this most clearly in development of dogma. The temporal, historical character of the church's action is of utmost importance to pastoral theology. The analysis and conclusions made by pastoral theology take history into consideration and thus can never be purely abstract deductions. Though never completely separated from dogmatic theology, pastoral theology "becomes free evaluation, decision, a part of the free historical activity of the Church, if the conclusion [of pastoral theology] is correct, [it becomes] a piece of prophecy, a charismatic summons from the future as God wills it" (57). **6. Reconciliation of the permanent and the historical.** Not even in critical self-reflection can the church ever completely distinguish its nature from its concrete embodiment. Hence, pastoral theology's attempts to offer charismatic prescriptions on how to reconcile the old and the new cannot rely solely on abstract concepts but must enlist the "instincts" of all members.

4. **Differentiation in the church: Laity and Hierarchy.** A material distinction exists among members in the church: those who hold office and those who do not. The Catholic concept of hierarchical ministry is not merely a necessary consequence of the social character of salvation. It was also willed by Christ. What follows are five principles that regulate the relation between office and office-holder, and between office-holders and the People of God. These are important to pastoral theology. *Church and hierarchy are not identical.* Christians are not the *object* of the church, they *are* the church. They are the object of "service and concern" of the whole body of Christ. *Office and function are not identical.* Every Christian has gifts from the Holy Spirit. These are to be directed to building up the church. In this sense, every Christian is commissioned and authorized at Baptism. Ecclesial office must be seen in this universal context, even if office includes rights and powers that are not shared by all. *The structure of the church is*

not merely hierarchical. There is also a free, charismatic gift of the Spirit that must be respected. Charism does not owe its ecclesial character to hierarchical blessing, and not all initiative flows down from the top. *An office-holder is also a bearer of charismatic possibilities.* The best situation is when office and personal charism merge. But there is never a human being who is exclusively either a bearer of office or of charism. Despite the fact that office and personal holiness have diverged in certain cases, official does not mean opposed to charism, since even the gift of order is itself a charism. *Not everything in the Church can be official.* "Within the Church there is always preserved a domain proper to private Christian personal life, an area which can no longer tangibly [i.e., officially] be provided by the Church" (63). Summary. Cf., TPA.2, 132f.

TPA.2. Christians: Action in the Church. (64-133)

Abstract: The principles concerning the nature of the church listed in TPA.1 are here applied to a concrete but still somewhat theoretical set of set pastoral problems: the role of the Christian faithful, office and charism in the church, 3-fold ministry, parish and diocese, cardinals, curia, the Petrine Office, etc.

Topics: CHURCH, nature of; THEOLOGY, Pastoral.

Subsidiary discussions: Church, charism in (65ff); Laity, apostolate of (68f); Church, office and charism in (70ff); Church, indefectibility of (74ff); Church, order in (78ff); Bishop/s, order of (84ff); Diocese, nature of (87ff); Priesthood, order of (95ff); Parish (100ff); Deacon, order of (106ff); Petrine Office (111ff); Magisterium, extra/ordinary (114ff); Cardinals, College of (119ff); Curia, reform of (122ff); Bishop/s, National Conferences of (129ff); Bishop/s, Synod of (131f).

Precis: Since Pastoral Theology concerns those actions that realize the nature of the church, questions arise: Who preforms the specific actions of the church? Allowing that we no longer think of the hierarchy as the only actor and we now see these tasks and functions belonging to all members, are there still essentially different roles in the church? What grounds and determines these differences?

1. The whole church. Obviously, all baptized members are able to participate in the specific activity of the church. Each member shares in the church's nature as gift and means of salvation. In addition, each member has personal gifts to be used to build up the entire body (list, 66f). Sharing one's life with Christ establishes the duty and capacity for each member to serve as a channel of salvation for all others. For what is shared is nothing less than the life of Christ. Every Christian is called to such service, *diakonia*. This approach avoids certain distortions: the nascent privatism of Protestants, the distorted clericalism of Catholicism, and the exclusive spiritualism of the Orthodox.

2. **Each member of the church** actively shares in building up the church. But this does not mean all have the same role. Each member's gift is personal and individual. But they all derive from Christ, are the gift of the one Spirit, and serve as channels of the same redemption. The efficacy of each charism depends on the existence and efficacy of all (examples, 69). The Christian apostolate remains united despite its great diversity, which is itself rooted in the diverse but connected natures of salvation (one salvation as truth and love; the gift which is God Himself and the liberated power of self-surrender, etc.) and of man (ages, sex, intelligence, etc.).

3. **Office and charism** [brief but very turgid!]. The distinction between office and charism can only be understood as a consequence of the incarnational principle, the quasi-sacramental foundation of the church itself: the unity of spirit and its historical embodiment. Just as individuals only realize even their most intimate gifts within the body of the church, all official authority is exercised *within* and not *over* the church. Despite its unique divine source, office can only be exercised within the church. For even *opus operatum* powers are efficacious only if received with proper disposition, a factor which remains a free gift of God and cannot be institutionally administered. Only if one grasps the eschatological nature of the church (the unbreakable unity between divine grace and is empirical embodiment) can one understand the fundamental unity of all divine saving activity in the church: the indivisible nature of office and charism despite their differences.

Given all these conditions and reservation, what are the differences between office and charism? (72). Rahner restates the fact that both office and free charism indisputably exist as vital parts of the church, but as different orders of gifts. The intimate connection between them cannot be clarified by starting from the legal distribution of definite powers by those who possess them. This would fail to explain the formal difference between church and synagogue, and could not explain the existence of free charism. Ultimately, the character of office derives from the fact that it is office *in the church*, and as such participates in the eschatological nature of the church. Office shares in the inseparable and unmixed incarnational unity of God and man revealed in Christ. The church manifests its essential indefectible character whenever and only insofar as it commits itself absolutely as the presence of Christ in the world. It's authority derives not from below like a democracy, but from above precisely so that it can represent the incarnational truth and grace of Christ in the world. But this is not an all-or-nothing proposition. Most particular acts of office are a mix of factors that cannot be completely sorted out, as is generally the case in the exercise of human freedom.

"The activity of the church as a whole cannot be based solely on the official ministry: it requires completion by free charism and charismatics" (76). Since not all the church's actions can be absolute (as this would contradict its historicity) both its eschatological indefectibility and its pilgrim existence must be at work in all the church does. Thus, the freest charism is specifically ecclesial, and its character is co-determined by the church's indefectible nature. Nevertheless, even the church's most indefectible sacramental acts and its most infallible magisterial acts rest on free charism. For the promise of sacramental grace is only operative when non-sacramental grace produces its acceptance, and infallible doctrinal decisions can only be grasped when heard with the grace of faith. Such grace is never subject to official organization (77). Hence, the church's entire pastoral action is based on the spiritual gifts of all members. Only after we grasp the metaphysical nature of office *a posteriori* by having experienced its concrete reality, can we draw up practical norms for it based on scripture and tradition.

4. **The church's one office.** Office in the church is one. Borne by a number of individuals in different ways, it is always in living relation with the total authority (just as individual Christians exercise their charisms validly and morally only united with the whole church). Yet how can the particular offices (bishop, priest, deacon) with their different purposes originate from a single ministry?

Through sacramental ordination the church can confer its power of office in ways that meet the needs of the time. Jurisdiction is a concrete specification of the church's single power. The 3-fold hierarchy is of divine right because church authority is of divine right, and because this irreversible articulation took place in apostolic times. Though episcopal office is personal, it demands corporate exercise. Priests do not exist just because bishops can't do everything alone. Rather, each bishop must have a council of advisors modeled on the archetype of all church authority: the apostolic college with Peter at the head.

Rahner next considers a number of historical situations (80ff): the institution of the diaconate, the commissioning of leaders, the practice of Confirmation and Penance in the East, the role of local synods, etc.). He explains these facts and their seemingly disparate doctrines in the following points: 1) "The fun-damental original and universally regulative form (structure) of the Church's one power is the apostolic college with Peter at its head, competent to act personally" (82). A bishop possesses all the power which exists in the church (except to act as president of the college) insofar as he is a member of that college. In *potestas ordinis* the bishop is equal to the pope. Although the powers of sanctification cannot be limited geographically, a bishop is assigned a territory to maintain order in the church. This jurisdiction is not, however, the source of his power. 2) The *potestas ordinis*, the bishop's single complete authority (of order and jurisdiction) is validly and irrevocably conferred by sacramental inclusion in the college of bishops. From this flow all partial powers. The power of jurisdiction is the valid exercise of these powers in union and with the consent of the pope. 3) A bishop, like the pope, should convoke a corporate body representing the plurality and variety of the flock he tends, and give it a share in his powers of order and jurisdiction in a variety of ways.

5. **The bishop and the diocese** (summary, 84). Rahner begins his consideration of particular ministries in the church with bishops because they exist by divine right, and as a college, are the subject of the highest most complete power in the church in every respect. What is a bishop? What is a diocese? Neither can be defined just in terms of the bishop's powers of order. Rahner suggests that any definition of bishops begins with the description of a diocese

which does not appeal to the known attributes of the bishop but which shows why a diocese can meaningfully be ruled only by the authority of a bishop. Rahner returns to the college of bishops and its responsibilities (87), valid inclusion within which initially does not imply territoriality. How does one become a territorial bishop (i.e., why is one exclusively assigned a particular territory, and why that territory)? Large units of the church need the guidance of immediate direction by members of the highest governing body itself. Why is the assigned person a bishop and not simply a deputy of the college? Recalling that it is the nature of the church to be wholly present in its parts (e.g., the whole church is present in each Eucharistic celebration), then each part should be headed by a member of the church's ruling body: a bishop, as was the case in the early church. Rahner suggests this norm holds true today as long as we recall this local church must carry out all the functions of the church in a way proper to it, and not just the celebration of Eucharist. Every such complete local church is a diocese. A further consideration is the fact that the only way the episcopal college (established by divine right) can actualize itself is by the supervening of juridical nomination (of human origin). All that has been said here can legitimately be applied by extension to supra-diocesan entities (metropolitanates, patriarchates, primatial sees, bishops' conferences). Rahner suggests some diocesan realignment based on these principles.

6. **The presbyterium and the individual priest.** Since not all the needs of a diocese can be met by parishes, the territorial principle cannot be the fundamental and primary principle for organizing a diocese. History shows that just as the pope cannot do without the episcopal college, so a monarchial bishop ruling a community without priests would transgress the divine law of the church. Just as the bishop's identity flows from his incorporation into the episcopal college, so the presbyterum pre-exists the individual priest. The bishop entrusts some of his functions to certain members of this council and to other servers (deacons). Their mandate, unlike the bishop's, is not territorial insofar as they can function throughout the diocese. Bishops delegate their powers based on the "function principle" further limited by persons (the personal principle) or place (the territorial principle). These three principles can explain all sorts of delegation, most especially priesthood

and diaconate. Rahner ends with some reflections on the priesthood which is most closely oriented to the bishop because priests celebrate Eucharist.

7. **The parish.** Although the parish most closely approximates the diocese, a parish is not simply a mini-diocese. Dioceses are made up of more than territorial parishes (e.g., chaplaincies, student parishes, etc.), and a diocese must be more than the sum of its parishes plus a central administration. In fact, many organizations are needed whose relation to the parish and diocese cannot simply be deduced from the nature of the church. Although history shows the territorial principle can never be the sole foundation of a diocese, it does have a positive function. It extends the opportunity for the celebration of Eucharist beyond the bishop's altar, generally into neighborhood communities of worship. The nature and function of a parish can only extend as far as can be justified from this point of view. All in all, the parish and the role of the pastor must be determined from the point of view of the altar: preparation for and celebration of liturgy, and service to the neighborhood that flows from that celebration. Other diocesan organizations and other pastoral agents should pursue other activities.

8. **The diaconate and the deacon.** Despite its having fallen into disuse in the West, the order of deacon remains part of the immutable, divinely established structure of the church. Rahner argues that the diaconal function continues to exist, even where it is not supported by the grace sacramental ordination. There are many professionally trained lay persons who work permanently in the service of the church as teachers, administrators, etc. As such, they share in the ministry of the bishop whether or not they are ordained. From this we can derive the axiom that "in the Church there should be offices and bearers of official functions separate from priesthood and priests" (107). Deacons serve the bishop side by side with the presbyterum. They have their own proper apostolate and do not simply share in the apostolate of the hierarchy. They are ministers of the bishop and not merely the assistants to parish priests. They help alleviate the priest shortage by assuming important ecclesial responsibilities that are not properly those of the priests but which now consume much of the priests' time.

9. The pope and the Roman central government. The pope and papal officials (to whom he can delegate some but not all of his functions) play an important role in the church. The pope is not the church, nor the center of its unity, nor the executor of all its spiritual gifts. His role is to insure the unity of the church in faith and love by testing charisms. This Petrine Office (along with ecumenical councils) falls under the purview of pastoral theology, since its nature and role cannot be deduced completely from dogmatic theology or canon law. What follows are a few brief reflections on some of the dogmatic principles significant for a pastoral theology of the papacy.

1. *The pope.* In terms of pastoral theology what does it mean to say the pope holds the complete, immediate, highest episcopal jurisdiction of the whole church – all dioceses and bishops? This is seen most clearly in the pope's universal juridical sway over the visible, concrete church, but not over its charismatic element. The pope, for example, is not the sole legitimate source of all initiative in the church. The positive meaning of this authority is that of representing and guaranteeing the unity of the church, established and preserved by the Spirit. He functions uniquely when he puts the fullness of authority in the church at the service of unity. This unity does not equate to maximum uniformity in administration, but to the promotion of pluralism, which is an essential a charismatic endowment of the church.

How the pope exercises primacy is a proper question for pastoral theology. Though there is no higher court competent to review the exercise of papal power, it is clear from history that popes can exceed their competence or act inopportunely. There follows a discussion of extraordinary (*ex cathedra*) and ordinary papal magisterium (114-117). Rahner concludes it is difficult fully to distinguish the two or to know what weight to give to which kinds of papal pronouncements. (He does, however, foresee a future with much less reliance on *ex cathedra* pronouncements.) These few principles indicate a regulative structure for the exercise of papal magisterium. But in addition to juridical and magisterial powers, the pope also has a *pastoral* office: "as pastor the pope has the authority to give instructions which are binding precisely because it is the pope who gives them" (117). But precisely as pastoral norms these call for a great deal of *epekeia* to implement, both on the part of the pastor and the Christian faithful. Rahner warns against a kind of creeping infallibalism which some would like to see attached to all papal initiatives. Refusal to implement pastoral norms is possible so long as one does not deny in principle the pope's right to be obeyed. Rahner reminds the reader that the practical efficacy of all doctrine depends on its acceptance by individual conscience. "The Church and its pastoral offices are entirely dependent on the good will and the conscience of the individual for its efficacy" (119).

2. *The curia.* The pope works through many Roman institutions about which pastoral theology can make a few observations. *College of Cardinals.* (119-122) has functioned historically as papal advisors and electors. Today [before the reforms of Paul VI] Rahner sees the college as a sad amalgam on both counts. Rahner proposes separating the task of administration from the role of elector. The duty to elect should fall to the universal episcopate or to a proper representation of world bishops. *Curial Offices (122-127).* Despite reforms, the curia needs further rationalization of if offices and functions. Their composition should reflect the face of an international church. These offices must not be seen nor should they act as mere legal functionaries, for they also play a charismatic role in stimulating and encouraging new initiatives, without monopolizing them. Calling on a wider circle of international advisors would keep each department in closer contact with grassroots realities. They should avoid paternalism and secrecy, allow public discussion of issues, and adopt transparent mechanisms. They should also adopt modern, efficient administrative methods and attitudes proper to contemporary governments and businesses. *Curia and the bishops (127-132).* Because most of what governs the relations between pope and bishop is "para-canonical" and what little is written down is *jus humanum,* bishops are at a disadvantage when they approach Rome. Since the curia, distinct from the pope and possessing habitual powers based in human law, is subordinate to the college of bishops, when an individual bishop approaches the curia he is not doing so as its subordinate, but as a member of the college performing his nontransferable duties. Even with regard to the pope and his officials, the principle of subsidiarity holds in reference to the episcopate. An intermediary authority such as national conferences of bishops (129ff) with proper legal standing

would be helpful in safeguarding the independence of individual bishops and in promoting the influence of the Roman offices on them. To protect the autonomy of individual bishops from national conferences, dioceses should be sufficiently large and viable to withstand pressure. In addition, fair ways must be developed for bishops' conference to exercise their own jurisdictional powers. A second intermediary institution that could help bridge the gap between Rome and individual bishops is an Episcopal Synod serving to advise the pope (131f). Summary, 132f.

T. *The Trinity.* NY: Crossroad, 1997. 120 pp. Translated by Joseph Donceel. (Treated as separate esays.). "*Der dreifaltige Gott als transzendeter Urgrung der Heilsgeschichte*" in *Die Heilsgeschicht vor Christus*, Volume 2 of *Mysterium Salutis, Grundriss heilsgeschichtelicher Dogmatik*. Einsiedeln: Beniger, 1967. Introduction, Index of Topics and Glossary by Catherine Mowry LaCugna.
Contents: Introduction. Important Terms. Author's Note.
I. The Method and Structure of the Treatise, *On the Triune God*.
II. The Main Lines of Official Trinitarian Doctrine.
III. A Systematic Outline of Trinitarian Theology.
Index.

T.Intro. Introduction. (vii-xxi)
Abstract: After explaining the essay's Neo-scholastic background and its textual origins, this excellent introduction offers a clear, concise precis of its three sections (treated below as separate essays). **I** (ix-xvi) critiques the shortcomings of the traditional treatises *On the Trinity, De Deo, On Christ* (Incarnation) and *On the Holy Spirit* (Grace). This sets the stage for Rahner's own theory. **II** (xvi-xvii) a subtle, sophisticated hermeneutic of magisterial statements and traditional Trinitarian vocabulary. **III** (xvii-xxi) Rahner's own synthesis of early Greek and later Latin theologies, advanced beyond Neo-scholasticism, and informed by modern concerns like history, personhood, subjectivity and relationality.
Topics: TRINITY.

T.1. The Method and Structure of the Treatise, *On the Triune God*. (9-48)

Abstract: The doctrine of Trinity as expounded in the West is too isolated from Christian life, leaving most Christians as tri-theists. This failure can be traced to the distinction between the two basic treatises on God, and over-reliance on faulty terminology (i.e., "persons"). Rahner's solution is to build a doctrine of the immanent Trinity on the economic, by beginning with our experience and with the divine missions.

Topics: GOD, triune; TRINITY.

Subsidiary discussions: Trinity in Augustine (18f); Trinity, pre-Christian analogies (20f; 40ff); Trinity, immanent/economic (23ff); Jesus Christ, hypostatic union of (24ff); God and "person" (42ff); Trinity as mystery (46ff).

Precis: Note (7) outlines the 3-part presentation to come, and apologizes for any unavoidable repetitions in Chapter Three which summarizes the two earlier parts. **A. The isolation of Trinitarian doctrine in piety and textbook theology.** Surprised at the general isolation of the theology of Trinity from concrete life and piety, Rahner bemoans the radical Monotheism of most Christians, and that if the doctrine of Trinity were to disappear it would have little effect. It does not help to claim the doctrine of Incarnation would uphold that of the Trinity, since most Christians tend to Monophysitism, and are content to think and say simply "God became man." After offering other illustrations (list, 12) Rahner goes on to say that the theology of grace in Christ is also basically monotheistic and not Trinitarian, in that it fails to distinguish sufficiently created from uncreated grace. "Thus the treatise on Trinity occupies a rather isolated position in the total dogmatic system" (14). Rahner asks whether this seemingly extrinsic and isolated revealed knowledge has anything to tell us about ourselves conducive to our real salvation.

B. The problem of the relation between the treatises *On the One God* and *On the Triune God* and the traditional order in which they are taught demands a reappraisal. Tradition is no legitimation, since this division itself isolates the doctrine of Trinity, and risks introducing a "divine 'essence' itself as a 'fourth' reality pre-existing in three persons" (17). Placing the treatise *On the One*

God before the treatise on Trinity also makes what follows unnecessarily philosophical, abstract, and cut off from salvation history. Not even Augustine's "psychological Trinitarianism" can rescue a Trinity that seems locked within itself and divorced from Christian life. Although these dangers do not follow necessarily from the traditional treatment of these two treatises, the point is that most theologians overlook these dangers when they take this division as necessary or obvious. Another casualty of so encapsulating the Trinity is the Patristic ability to discover outside Christianity or even in the Old Testament analogies, hints or preparations pointing toward such a doctrine (20f).

C. **The axiomatic unity of the "Economic" and "Immanent" Trinity** is the basic thesis that connects the two treatises on God and presents the Trinity as a mystery of salvation with real relevance to people today. It might be expressed: *"The 'economic' Trinity is the 'immanent' Trinity and the 'immanent' Trinity is the 'economic' Trinity"* (22). This axiom shall have been justified if Rahner can show: 1) It can account for the really binding data of the doctrine of the Trinity presented by the magisterium; 2) It can more naturally do justice to salvation history and the texts of scripture; 3) It makes clear that the Trinity is and has been present in the Christian's life and act of saving faith. This proof will demand a further clarification of Incarnation and grace. But first Rahner offers this justification for his axiom: the existence of at least one case (the Incarnation of the Logos) where the mission of at least one divine person is proper to Him and not merely appropriated. This proves three things: 1) It is *"false* to say there is nothing in salvation history, in the economy of salvation, which cannot be equally said of the Triune God as a whole and of each person in particular; 2) It is *false* to say that a doctrine of the Trinity can speak only of what occurs within the Trinity itself; 3) It is *true* to say that no adequate distinction can be made between the doctrine of the Trinity and the economy of salvation (23f).

D. **The Incarnation as an "instance" of a more comprehensive reality.** To strengthen his case, Rahner addresses three difficulties brought against it. They all center on the Incarnation of the Logos. 1) *The special nature of the "Hypostatic Union."* Galtier and others argue that one cannot simply build a notion of the Trinity by generalizing from the Hypostatic Union because it is not a particular case of a general principle. It is completely unique, revealing only one distinct divine person. Rahner counters that Galtier uses the words "person" and "hypostasis" too narrowly, and that it is possible to imagine unique hypostatic unions of distinct persons (25-28). 2. *The Incarnation of the Logos and the Immanent Trinity.* The second difficulty leans the other way. If every person of the Trinity could assume a hypostatic union (not necessarily as man), then the Incarnation of the Logos would reveal nothing distinct about the Logos Himself, and the incarnation of the Logos would actually reveal nothing about the intra-Trinitarian life itself, beyond propositions. Yet the thesis that *every* divine person might become man is false because: a) the most ancient tradition never conceived of such an idea, since if the Logos is the Word of the Unoriginated Father, then for the Father to become incarnate would be like a speaking without words. b) The possibility of multiple incarnations cannot be logically deduced from the fact of one incarnation. Finally, were this thesis true then every kind of theological chaos would follow. 3. *The Identity of the "Economic" and "Immanent" Logos.* If the human nature of the Logos has nothing more to do with the Logos than any other nature or essence, then the Logos' incarnation as man reveals nothing about the Logos proper. Then the human as such would not show us the Logos as such, but only at most His abstract formal subjectivity. Rahner maintains the relations between Logos and the assumed nature of Christ is much more essential and intimate. Human nature is no mere mask. Its openness to God's self-communication meets the Word's essence as the Father's self-expression— a topic covered elsewhere.

E. **God's threefold relation to us in the order of grace.** Rahner presupposes the following thesis: "each one of the three divine persons communicates Himself to man in gratuitous [uncreated] grace in His own personal particularity and diversity. This Trinitarian communication is the ontological ground of man's life of grace and eventually of the direct vision of the divine persons in eternity.... These three self-communications are the self-communication of the one God in the three relative ways in which God subsists" (35). Hence, what is freely communicated is the triune personal God. This is simply another way of saying the economic Trinity (God for us) is the same as the immanent Trinity

(God in Himself). Rahner ends by cautioning against *"economic Sabellianism"* and falling into either Arianism or modalism.
F. **The methodological importance of our basic thesis.** *1. The Trinity as a salvific reality and an experience of grace.* Since Trinity is an experiential and not merely a verbal reality, we can and must take our possession of Christ and His Spirit as the starting point for any doctrine. Only this approach keeps scripture from becoming a suspect quarry for abstruse doctrine. *2. On interpreting the history of Trinitarian revelation.* A doctrine of Trinity that follows the same order as the history of revelation of this mystery would allow us to understand better the opinion of the ancients that even before Christ there was already in some vague way a belief in the Trinity (especially in the Old Testament references to Word and Spirit). *3. On hidden misunderstandings and problems of terminology.* Rahner's axiom could also help to avoid the danger of the current massive tri-theism among the Christian faithful (a bigger danger than Sabellian modalism). This danger stems in large part from the traditional reliance on the term "person." The economic approach does not oblige us to begin with this term, but from the self-revelation of God (the Father) mediated by Word and Spirit. Subsequent reference to such "three-personality" adds nothing to the testimony of scripture.
G. **A new relationship between the treatises *On the One God* and *On the Triune God*** is highlighted in Rahner's approach, making it almost impossible to disconnect the two treatises as is often done today.
H. **The reality and the doctrine of the Trinity as mysteries.** The doctrine of Trinity will always have the character of mystery, not due to the logical difficulty of putting together certain concepts, but because it deals with the mystery essentially identical with God's self-communication to us in Christ and in His Spirit. Because we are the ones to whom God chooses to communicate Himself, the Trinity is also the last mystery of our reality. This is why it is wrong to deny its mysteriousness or to substitute mere verbiage for the deep truth of ourselves, something that leads to the worship of what we cannot understand. Any true statement about Trinity correctly understood points quite naturally to real life, as lived faith in grace (e.g., mission as the starting point for any doctrine of Trinity). This necessary connection between doc-

trine and life, too often missing today, is the guiding principle of Rahner's inquiry.

T.2. The Main Lines of Official Trinitarian Doctrine. (49-79)

Abstract: After affirming the perpetual mystery of Trinity (A) and distinguishing logical from ontic explanations (B), Rahner systematically lays out magisterial teaching on the Trinity in a way that underscores its harmony with his identification of the economic and immanent Trinity (C).

Topics: GOD, tiune; TRINITY, Magisterial teaching

Subsidiary discussions: Trinity as mystery (50f); Explanations, logical/ontic (52ff); Person, concept of (56; 73ff); Jesus Christ, self-consciousness of (63ff); Trinity, relations in (68ff); Appropriation, doctrine of (76f).

Precis: Though any systematic presentation of magisterial teaching on Trinity has its dangers, it is still necessary. Merely repeating magisterial doctrine cannot substitute for informed faith. What follows is not primarily a critique but an orientation deriving from the official texts. It intends to discern what is actually being said and what remains unsaid or obscure. **A. The Trinity as absolute mystery.** The church teaches that Trinity is forever an absolute mystery, even in beatitude. But it leaves undetermined the exact nature of mystery. Though this can seem like a negative value when compared to empirical statements, the theology of God's eternal incomprehensibility as it applies to the mystery of Trinity could also be seen as a positive predicate of our knowledge.

B. The meaning and limits of employed concepts. The basic concepts used to express the mystery of Trinity are "person" and "substance, essence, nature" *1. The hypothesis of the intelligibility of such basic concepts as a hermeneutic problem.* Church documents do not explain the terms "person" or "essence." They presupposes them as intelligible in themselves, insofar as they are clear from their context: that the Father who is God, the Son who is God, and the Spirit who is God come to meet us; yet in these three beings who are God, only one God is given. To express this conceptually, the words essence and person are employed. *2. The function of the basic concepts as a logical explanation of reality.* The concepts add nothing to what we already know from experience. The question arises whether these concepts offer a *logical* or an *ontic* explanation (definitions, 52). Rahner argues they offer only a logical explanation which can only point back to the reality we have experienced, i.e., the economic Trinity. 3. *Can the concept of "person" be replaced?* Yes, in principle. But it is difficult to imagine a better suited term. In large part the concept of "person" is so problematic due to its ongoing development which takes place outside the control of the church. Vigilance over such terms is part of the work of theology.

C. A systematic summary of official Trinitarian doctrine. Of the two potential starting points for a discussion of church teaching on the Father (the one God who is insofar as he is Father; or the one God whose essence subsists in three persons) Rahner prefers the former. *1. Statements about God as the Father.* **a)** The confession of the Father. This is the proper starting point and not Trinity *as such*. **b)** God known as Father. This God, the Unoriginate, and not the Trinity *as such* is the concrete God of revelation, known definitively as Father only after the Son is known. **c)** The Father of the Son. It is our experience of Son and Spirit that allows for the experience of the Unoriginate God as Father of the Son, as generating principle, as source, origin and principle of the whole godhead.

2. Statements about the Son. **a)** Basic declarations of the church doctrine. This "Father" has an only Son, eternally begotten out of nothing, consubstantial with the Father, with whom He shares everything except His "Fatherhood." Rahner prefers the term *Logos* for this reality. **b)** Differentiations in Jesus' self-interpretation as Son. Scripture shows Jesus knew His Sonship was uniquely different from the way others were related to God. But Rahner cautions against moving too quickly to conclude that Jesus thereby knew his eternal generation as Logos (dangers, 62f). **c)** The Son as the "Absolute Bringer of Salvation" and as self-communication of the Father – this is how the Son understood Himself and His mission as Messiah. **d)** "Economic" and "Immanent" self-communication to the Son. The procession of the Son as the self-communication of the divine reality of the Father is two things at once: the economic, free self-communication of the "absolute bringer of salvation," *and* the immanent self-communication of the divine reality– the Father expressing Himself as the Word. Rahner adds two clarifications: 1) The Unoriginate remains incomprehensible and distinct, even after His self-communication. 2) "this distinction 'pre-exists' the free gratuitous self-communication of God . . . as its possibility" (64). This raises the critical point: why does the possibility of the Father's self-expression to the world, even as a mere possibility, already imply an inner "differentiation" in God Himself? (64f). Christ knew himself as Son with respect to the Father and to humanity, something impossible for an incarnate Father to do, even if such an incarnation had been possible. All this is simply meant to point to the appropriate starting point for understanding the "immanent" Son of the Father, which again makes clear that our understanding of the "immanent" Trinity must come from the "economic."

3. *Statements about God as the "Spirit"* **a)** Basic statements of the magisterium. The "Spirit" of the Father and Son is the gift of the Father though the Son, in which God communicates Himself to us in immediate proximity, and through which He causes us to accept this self-communication. Spirit is freely and eternally one in being with the Father, yet distinct, not begotten, nor merely another way the Father presents Himself to us (modalism). **b)** The *Procession* of the Holy Spirit. To understand the Spirit and His procession we must return to our experience: God *really* communicates *Himself* as love and forgiveness— an experience He produces and maintains within us. "Hence the Spirit must be God Himself" (67) distinct from the Father who gives, and the Son who mediates. Christ Himself makes this very concrete distinction.

4. *The relations within the Trinity.* **a)** The concept of *relation*. Father, Son and Spirit are "relatively" distinct, i.e., what distinguishes them is nothing foundational or prior to their mutual relation. This shows that the concept of "relation" is primarily a logical and not an ontic explanation, meant to protect the doctrine from tritheistic or modalistic interpretations. To understand this concept of relation one must return once again to the economic Trinity. What follows is not so much a rational solution to the difficulty of identity and diversity within the Trinity. Rahner, "wishes only to show *negatively and defensively* that the basic difficulty —how two things which are identical with a third are not identical with each other— cannot, in the present case, be shown to be insuperable" (69). There follows a dense discussion of "virtual distinctions

between an absolute and a relative reality" and the principle of "compared identity." **b)** The identity of the essence and distinction of the Three (summary, 72). In the end we are justified to say along with Anselm: "in God everything is one except where there is relative opposition" (73). These opposed relativities are also concretely identical with both "communications" ("processions") through which the Father communicates the divine essence to the Son, through the Son to the Spirit, or through which the latter two receive this communicated essence.

5. *The basic meaning of the concepts "hypostasis" and "person" in the official doctrine of the church.* The church speaks of hypostases insofar as the divine diversity can be brought under one concept. **a)** Hypostasis. The church never explains *hypostases / subsistences* outside the context of Trinity. Hence, to understand it we must again return to our experience of the economic Trinity. Thus we might say, "these statements regarding the one same God, speak first ("economically") of three concrete ways of being given, of givenness, and then ("immanently") of three relative concrete ways of existing of the one and same God" (74). The immanent can only be understood in light of the economic. **b)** "Person" is a synonym for these three *"hypostases"* and the term adds nothing new. Modern psychological elements pertaining to consciousness do not properly apply to Trinity (cf., T.3. E).

D. Some consequences for a deeper understanding. 1. *Common activity "ad extra" and appropriation.* Even though all activity of God *ad extra* is one and is possessed in the same way by Father, Son and Spirit, nevertheless, the church rightly attributes by preference one activity to a particular person of the Trinity due to affinity, without thereby implicitly denying its possession by both other persons. But this does not exclude: a) This appropriated activity is possessed by each person in its own way; b) Non-appropriated relations of a single person are possible in reference to a quasi-formal self-communication of God. 2. *Notional and essential realities and statements* can be distinguished. "Essential" statements are all that is given with and stated with the divine essence which may be made of God and of each person (e.g., God is almighty, the Trinity is almighty, the Son is almighty). "Notional" statements are all that refer to the persons in their distinction: **a)** The two processions and the one spiration; **b)** The *three person-constitut-*

ing *relations of origin* given with the processions insofar as they imply relative opposition (e.g., unorigiated Fatherhod, begotten Sonship, etc; **c)** *The fourth, not-person constituting relation* (i.e., the active spiration of the Spirit as a common peculiarity of Father and Son). Hence, there are four "notional acts:" active and passive begetting, and active and passive spiration. **d)** There are five "notional properties:" unoriginated-ness, fatherhood, sonship, active spiration, and being spirated. **e)** All this allows us to speak of a mutual inexistence of the three persons (circumcession, circumincession, perichoresis): the Son is from all eternity in the Father, and the Father is from all eternity in the Son, and so on.

T.3. A Systematic Outline of Trinitarian Theology. (80-120)

Abstract: Rahner sets out his own doctrine of Trinity starting at the economic Trinity. He concludes the expression "distinct manner of subsisting" together with "person" could avoid many current misunderstandings. He ends with a critique of the concept "person" and of Augustine's psychological Trinity.

Topics: GOD, self-communication of; GOD, triune; TRINITY.

Subsidiary discussions: Appropriation, doctrine of (86f); Logos, relation to human nature (89); Angels (90); Person, in Trinitarian theology (103ff); Trinity, psychological (115ff).

Precis: A. The meaning and purpose of the submitted essay. Rahner now offers his "systematic" doctrine of the Trinity, saying clearly what we have already *heard*, concentrating on the issue most central to modern people and avoiding metaphysical subtleties. This interpretation involves some repetition of Parts I & II, does not say everything about the Trinity, and implicitly assumes all the church teaches.

B. Developing the starting point. 1. *The necessity of a "systematic" conception of the "economic Trinity.* More precision is needed to define "economic" Trinity. Even if one starts from scripture and salvation history, still a short systematic presentation is needed.

2. *The inner relation between the ways of God's self-communication.* **a)** The central concern are the two distinct but related ways "God" (as Father, following the Greeks) communicates himself in Word and Spirit, while remaining unoriginate. **b)** How can these two ways of the Father's self-communication be internally related to each other yet distinct, but in such a way that the distinction too may really be brought under a "concept"? **c)** Current Catholic theology is too often content to connect the Incarnation and descent of the Spirit too extrinsically. This obscures the soteriological difference between these 2 self-communications. **d)** This is why Rahner begins with the opposite assumption: when God communicates *Himself* it is and must be the Son who appears historically in the flesh as man; and it must be the Spirit who brings about the world's acceptance of this self-communication in faith, hope and love. Without this understanding it is impossible to reach an understanding of the doctrine of grace or of christology. **e)** Thus the question is, how can these two distinct moments of Incarnation and descent of the Spirit be conceptualized as the one self-communication of the Father?

3. *A formal exposition of the concept of "God's self-communication."* Assuming the very notion of "God's self-communication" is neither mythology nor theologically objectionable, Rahner turns to its 4-fold set of paired aspects (# 4-7 below).

4. *Self-communication to a personal recipient.* Although these four basic aspects do appear to us from our human point of view, they avoid modalism because first, when speaking of communication we must envision an addressee who really receives this communication and remains human. Second, creation is both a moment of God's self-communication *and* a condition for the possibility of constituting an addressee. "Christ's 'human nature' is precisely what comes into being when God 'utters' himself outwards" (89). Hence, these four aspects (structures of the world and of the person) are not extrinsic. They are the conditions for the possibility of there being an addressee of God's self-communication. "If God wishes to step freely outside himself, he must create man" (89f). The rest of this section answers an objection concerning angels as addressees of God's self-communication (90).

5. *Towards a better understanding of the single basic aspects of the self-communication.* Rahner now considers separately the four paired aspects which constitute the conditions for the possibility of God's self-communication to humans. The communication has an <u>origin and future</u>; consonant with the whole person it has a <u>history and transcendence</u>; addressed to a free being it is <u>offer and</u>

acceptance; in action it is <u>knowledge and love</u>, a duality that cannot be overcome.

6. *The inner unity of the different aspects of God's self-communication.* Either side of these 4 aspects constitutes a unity. Hence, there are two basic manners of God's self-communication which are distinct yet related. **a)** Origin-History-Offer are rather clearly related. **b)** It is difficult to see why *truth* belongs here as a moment of divine self-communication. An explanation calls for viewing truth not as a correct grasp of a sate of affairs, but as positing and accepting one's true self even in the presence of others. **c)** It is not so easy to see the unity of Future-Transcendence-Acceptance-Love, but Rahner connects the dots.

7. *The two fundamental modalities of divine self-communication.* "Hence the divine self-communication possesses two basic modalities: self-communication as truth and love" (98). This is not immediately evident. Putting the first set of modalities under the term "history," and the second under "spirit," we can say *"divine self-communication occurs in unity and distinction in history (of the truth) and in the spirit (of love)."* These modalities, though they are not the same thing, are co-conditioning, and both derive their origin from the Unoriginate Father who remains incomprehensible mystery despite these real moments of self-communication.

C. **Transition from *Economic* to *Immanent* Trinity.** Does what has been developed here about the "economic" Trinity allow us to postulate the same "immanent" Trinity acknowledged in the church's official pronouncements? If the differentiation of the self-communication of God in history (truth) and spirit (love) did not belong to God "in Himself," then we would be faced with a creaturely mediation, and there would no longer be any true divine *self*-communication. God would be the "giver," not the "gift itself." God would give Himself only insofar as He communicates a gift distinct from Himself.

D. **How the *Economic* Trinity is grounded in the *Immanent* Trinity.** [What can be said about the immanent Trinity as presented in points **a - c** is too brief and dense to be compressed any further here.]

E. **The problem of the concept of *person*** is terminological (Is this concept suited to express faithfully the doctrine of the Trinity?) and factual (What does the concept properly mean in this context?). In addition, it has special importance for this systematic treatment (Has this systematization successfully arrived at the church's doctrine?). These three points are covered in turn below.

1. *Formal terminological difficulties.* A review of a few of the difficulties in applying "person" to Trinity recalls first that since "person" is not a biblical or early Patristic term, it is not *absolutely* constitutive of our faith in Father, Son and Spirit. Its weakness lies in its tendency to generalize from something that is absolutely unique. Also, "person" as a concrete concept does not formally mean the distinction as such, but those who are distinct. Referring to God as three persons, as we would of any three individuals, also raises serious kerygmatic difficulties. This linguistic difficulty exists nowhere else. For Rahner, all this shows that in speaking of Trinity we must always return to the original experience of salvation history, the economic Trinity, before we generalize to speak of "three persons."

2. *The concept of "person" in official statements and its own independent historical development* is the main problem in applying "person" to Trinity. For modern people the term implies separate spiritual centers of activity, several subjectivites and wills. But this is precisely NOT the Trinity. This problem cannot simply be remedied by the church attempting to fix the meaning of the term, since linguistic usage is not under its sole control. But neither can individual theologians simply make up their own new terms. Any new concept must be developed in reference to the older concept and must not simply repudiate the old.

3. *The possibility of other theological ways of expression.* After summarizing the basic axiom of the relation of economic and immanent Trinity (109), Rahner suggests adopting the expression "distinct manner of subsisting" as an explanatory concept not for person, "but for the "personality" which makes God's concrete reality, as it meets us in different ways, into precisely this one who meets us thus. . . . The single 'person' in God would then be: God as existing and meeting us in this determined distinct manner of subsisting" (110). The rest of this section clarifies this expression, focusing on the word "manner," and insuring it does not permit for modalism (summary, 112f).

4. *Concrete confirmation of the new concept.* Rahner now tests the usefulness of this expression by formulating eight basic statements

about Trinity with the help of this concept, all the while avoiding the term "person" (list, 113f). Rahner concludes that employing this expression in tandem with the word "person" can help overcome false opinions regarding Trinity.

F. A comparison with the classic *psychological* doctrine. Augustine attempts by means of psychological categories to bring home to the intelligence of faith an understanding of the threefold-distinct way the one God subsists. Those who follow Augustine use a model of the spiritual self-actualization of man— a very different method than Rahner applies in this essay.

1. *The possibility of such an analogy.* Recalling that the psychological doctrine is not dogma but merely theological opinion (*theologoumena*), one is still justified to combine and connect the intra-divine procession of the Logos from the Father with God's *knowledge*, and the procession of the Spirit from the Father through the Son with God's *love*. This is justified despite the facts that scripture and the pre-Augustinian Fathers 1) only characterize Logos and Spirit in their economic-soteriological function, and 2) they do not unambiguously maintain these attributions. Nevertheless, it makes sense to connect generation of the Son with knowledge and spiration of the Spirit with love, "even though we cannot further explain *why* and *how* these two basic actions of God's essence ... constitute nonetheless the basis of the two processions and thus for the three distinct manners of subsisting" (117).

2. *Problems of theory* arise precisely here. There is no evident model from human psychology for this doctrine of Trinity. Rather it postulates a model of finite, human knowledge and love *from* the Trinity, and then reapplies it *to* the Trinity. But it fails to explain why in God knowledge and love demand a *processio ad modum operati*. Any possible usefulness of this psychological approach must be clear on the circularity of its reasoning.

3. *Methodological difficulties.* A further weakness of this method is its tendency to forget the economic Trinity. But constructing such a "psychological" theology of Trinity is only possible if one forgets this (even though what devolves from including the economic Trinity will necessarily be more modest and will give up trying to explain the *why* of the two processions). Rahner ends this section with the intriguing suggestion of building a psychological theology of Trinity, "starting from those structures of human existence

which first clearly appear in its experience of salvation history: its transcendence towards the future as lovingly opening up and accepted; in its existence in history, in which the faithful truth is present as knowledge about itself" (119f).
G. **On features peculiar to the present treatise.** Rahner is aware that his "systematic" treatment is far from encyclopedic. He omits much scholastic speculation because to him it is simply sterile, and because following his axiom, strictly speaking Christology and the theology of grace *are* the doctrine of Trinity. But he has not overlooked here anything the Bible, revelation or kerygmatic necessity invites him to say about Trinity.

W&P: *Watch and Pray with Me.* NY: Herder, 1966. 63 pp. *Heilige Stunds und Passionsandacht:* Frieburg: Herder, n.d. Translated by William V. Dych, SJ
Contents: A Holy Hour.
-The Seven Last Words.

W&P.1. A Holy Hour. (9-33)
Abstract: Using the traditional genre of meditational talks at Holy Hour, Rahner weaves together some of his favorite themes; death, surrender, etc. 1. *The Presence of Jesus and his Life.* In the presence of the Blessed Sacrament we are present to the whole Jesus, humanity and divinity, for three reasons: his sacramental presence; due to the fact that all elements of his earthly life have been taken up into eternity; and due to the fact that His solidarity with all people during His life is unbreakable. 2. *The Presence of Jesus' Agony in the Garden.* This meditation on Christ's presence overflows into a beautiful litany. 3. *The Presence of the Agony in the Garden in Us.* Our share in Christ's Holy Spirit unites our sufferings to His and transforms them. Ends with a litany for transformation.
Topics: JESUS CHRIST, agony in the garden; PRAYER, litanies; PRESENCE, of Jesus.
Subsidiary discussions: Eternal life (11ff); Holy Spirit, uniting our lives with Christ (25ff).

W&P.2. The Seven Last Words. (37-63)

Abstract: Using the traditional genre of meditations on Jesus' seven last words from the cross, Rahner weaves together some of his favorite themes. 1. Preparatory Prayer. 2. "Father forgive them, for they know not what they do." 3. "Amen I say to you, this day you will be with me in paradise." 4. "Woman behold your son; Son behold your mother." 5. "My God, my God, why have you forsaken me?" 6. "I thirst." 7. "It is finished." 8. "Father, into your hands I commend my Spirit."

Topics: JESUS CHRIST, words from the cross.

Subsidiary discussions: Forgiveness (40ff); BVM, mother of all (47ff); Cross as liturgy (52); Jesus Christ, mission of (54ff); Surrender (61ff).

APPENDIX
ARTICLES IN BOOKS ABSTRACTED ELSEWHERE

"The Apostolate of Laymen" in Robert W. Gleason, SJ (ed.), *A Theology Reader.* NY: Macmillan, 1966 (305-315). Originally *"L'apostolat des laics"* in *Nouvelle Revue Théologique* 78 (1956) 3-32. **Cf., TI 02.11** as "Notes on the Lay Apsotolate."

"The Appeal of Conscience" in Daughters of St. Paul, *Obedience, The Greatest Freedom.* USA: Daughters of St. Paul, 1966 (62-68). **Cf.,** *Nature and Grace.* **NG .2.**

"A Basic Ignatian Concept: Some Reflections on Obedience" in Raymond A. Schroth, et al. (eds.), *Jesuit Spirit in a Time of Change.* Translated by Jospeph P. Vetz, SJ and Gustav Weigel, SJ NY: Newman, 1968 (123-142). Also as "Reflections on Obedience: A Basic Ignatian Concept" in Daughters of St. Paul, *Obedience, The Greatest Freedom.* USA: Daughters of St. Paul, 1966 (200-228); Robert W. Gleason, SJ (ed.), *Contemporary Spirituality, Current Problems in Religious Life.* NY: Macmillan, 1968 (123-140). **Cf.,** *Christian in the Market Place.* **CMP.9.**

"Christ as Exemplar of Clerical Obedience" in Karl Rahner, SJ (ed.), *Obedience in the Church.* Washington, D.C: Corpus Books, 1968 (1-18). **Cf.,** *Servants of the Lord.* **SL.9.**

"Christianity and the New Earth" in Walter J. Ong, SJ (ed.), *Knowledge and the Future of Man. An International Symposium.* Translated by Francis J. Goetz, SJ, with Clyde Lee Miller, SJ NY: Holt, Reinhart, Winston, 1968 (255-268). **Cf., TI 10.14**

"Christianity and the 'New Man.' The Christian Faith and Utopian Views about the Future of the World" in Alfons Auer, et al., *The Christian and the World, Readings in Theology.* Translated by Louis Roberts, SJ Innsbruck: Canisianum. NY: P.J. Kennedy, 1965. (206-229). Also in Michael Taylor, SJ, *The Sacred and the Secular.* Engelwood Cliffs, NJ: Prentice Hall, 1968 (84-103). **Cf., TI 05.07.**

"Christianity and the Non-Christian Religions" in Hugo Rahner, SJ (ed.), *The Church: Readings in Theology.* NY: P.J. Kennedy, 1963 (112-135); John Hick and Brian Hebblewaite (eds.), *Christianity and Other Religions.* Glasgow: Collins, 1986 (32-79). **Cf., TI 05.06.**

"Christian Humanism" in Eszter Gabriella Bánffy, Hungarian Institute for the Sociology of Religion, *Marxian Ethics in Hungary.* Vienna, 1976 (139-160). **Cf., TI 09.12.**

"Christology and an Evolutionary World View" in Rosalie M. Ryan, *New Testament Themes for Contemporary Man*. Engelwood Cliffs, NJ: Prentice Hall, 1969 (217-225). Abridged from **TI 05.08.**

"The Church of Sinners" in William Birmingham, *Cross Currents: Exploring the Implications of Christianity for Our Times: an Anthology of Forty Years of Cross Currents*. Translated by William F. Gleason. NY: Crossroad, 1989 (46-62). **Cf., TI 06.17.**

"Dimensions of Martyrdom" in Brian Wicker (ed.). *Witness to Faith? Martyrdom in Christianity and Islam*. Burlington VT: Ashgate, 2006 (147-150). **Cf., C.163.**

"The Faith of the Priest Today" in Raymond A. Schroth, et al. (eds.), *Jesuit Spirit in a Time of Change*. Translated by William Dych. NY: Newman, 1968 (43-52). **Cf. *Servants of the Lord*. SL.2.**

"God in My Life" in Barry Ulanov, *Contemporary Catholic Thought* (17-22). **Cf., *Encounters with Silence*. ES.1.**

"How to Receive a Sacrament and Mean It" in *The Sacraments: Readings in Contemporary Sacramental Theology*. Michael J. Taylor, SJ (ed.). Alba House, 1981 (71-80). **Cf., TI 14.10.**

"I Believe in Jesus Christ" in *Our Christian Faith*. With K-H Wegner. NY: Crossroad, 1981 (159-179). **Cf., TI 09.10.**

"Ignatian Spirituality and Devotion to the Sacred Heart" in Raymond A. Schroth, et al. (eds.), *Jesuit Spirit in a Time of Change*. NY: Newman, 1968 (53-68). **Cf., *Christian in the Market Place*. CMP.7.**

"The Nature of a Pastoral Constitution: Theological Considerations" in Group 2000, *The Church Today. Commentaries on the Pastoral Constitution on the Church in the Modern World*. Translated by John Drury. NY: Newman, 1968 (283-300) **Cf., TI 10.16.**

"Observations on the Situation of Faith Today" in René Latourelle, *Problems and Perspectives of Fundamental Theology*. Translated by Matthew J. O'Connell. NY: Paulist, 1980 (274-291). Also in *The Word of God*. John Knox Press, 1982 (247-291). **Cf., TI 20.02.**

"Poverty" in Robert W. Gleason, SJ (ed.), *Contemporary Spirituality. Current Problems in Religious Life*. Translated by Gregory J. Roettger, OBS. NY: Macmillan, 1968 (45-78). **Cf., TI 08.10.**

"Priest and Poet" in Hugo Rahner, SJ (ed.), *The Word. Readings in Theology*. NY: P.J. Kennedy, 1964 (3-26). **Cf., TI 03.19**

"Problem of Genetic Manipulation" in Steven E. Lammers and Allen Verheny (eds.), *On Moral Medicine, Theological Perspectives in Medical Ethics*. Grand Rapids, MI: Eerdmans, 1988 (542-547). **Cf., TI 09.14.**

APPENDIX: ARTICLES IN BOOKS ABSTRACTED ELSEWHERE   529

"Religious Inclusivism" in Michael Peterson, et al. (eds.) *Philosophy of Religion: Selected Readings*. NY: Oxford, 2001 (549-559). **Cf., TI 05.06** as "Christianity and the Non-Christian Religions."

"Sins and Guilt" in Margaret Gorman (ed.), *Psychology and Religion: A Reader*. NY: Paulist, 1985 (229-231). **Cf., Opportunities for Faith. OF.4.4.**

"Some Theses on the Theology of Devotion to the Sacred Heart" in Josef Stierli (ed.), *Heart of the Saviour. A Symposium on Devotion to the Sacred Heart*. London: Herder, 1958 (131-155). **Cf., TI 03.22.**

"Theological Reflection on the Problem of Secularization" in L.K. Shook, *Theology of Renewal. Renewal of Religious Thought. Proceedings of the Congress on the Theology of the Renewal of the Church. Centenary of Canada 1867-1967. Vol. 1*. Montreal: Palm, 1968. (167-192). **Cf., TI 10.17.**

"Theology and Anthropology" in T. Patrick Burke (ed.), *The Word in History, The St. Xavier Symposium*. NY: Sheed and Ward, 1966. (1-23). Also excerpted in Ed. T. Oakes (ed.), *German Essays on Religion*. NY: Continuum, 1994 (231-243). **Cf., TI 09.02.**

"On the Theology of the Incarnation" in Leo O'Donovan (ed.), *Word and Mystery. Biblical Essays on the Person and Mission of Christ*. NY: Newman, 1968 (273-289). **Cf., TI 04.04.**

"Towards a Fundamental Theological Interpretation of Vatican II" in Lucien Richard, *Vatican II: the unfinished agenda, a look to the future*. NY: Paulist, 1987 (9-21). **Cf., TI 20.06.**

"The Unity of Spirit and Matter: a Christian Understanding" in Juan Alfaro, *Man before God. Toward a Theology of Man*. Translated by Robert Huber. NY: P.J. Kennedy, 1966 (25-51). **Cf., TI 06.12.**

"Unthematic Knowledge of God" in Margaret Gorman, *Psychology and Religion, A Reader*. NY: Paulist, 1985 (7-11). Excerpted from **Foundation of Christian Faith (21-23, 32-33).**

"On Visiting the Blessed Sacrament" in Raymond A. Tartre, *The Eucharist Today, Essays on the Theology and Worship of the Real Presence*. NY: P.J. Kennedy, 1967 (192-207). Part 2 of "Development of Eucharistic Devotion." **Cf., The Christian Commitment. CCt.5**

"World History and Salvation History" in Alfons Auer, et al., *The Christian and the World, Readings in Theology*. Innsbruck: Canisianum. NY: P.J. Kennedy, 1965 (45-67). **Cf., TI 05.05.**

ABBREVIATIONS FOR ABSTRACTED MATERIAL

AB	Articles from Books
B	Bishops, their Status and Function.
BH	Biblical Homilies.
BT	Belief Today.
CAC	Church after the Council.
CC	Christian at the Crossroads.
CCM	Can a Christian be a Marxist?
CCt	Christian Commitment.
CE	Celebration of the Eucharist.
CF	Christian of the Future.
CL	Is Christian Life Possible Today?
CMP	Christian in the Market Place.
C	*Concilium*
CP	Courage to Pray.
DBG	Do You Believe in God?
DEC	Dynamic Element in the Church.
EF	Everyday Faith.
ES	Encounters with Silence.
EP	Episcopate and Primacy.
EY	The Eternal Year.
FSC	Free Speech in the Church.
GF	Grace in Freedom.
H	Hominisation.
Inq	Inquiries.
LJLN	Love of Jesus and the Love of Neighbor.
MFS	Meditations on Freedom and the Spirit
MHL	Meditations on Hope and Love.
MM	Mary, Mother of the Lord.
MS	Meditations on the Sacraments.
NBP	The Need and the Blessing of Prayer.
NC	New Christology.
NG	Nature and Grace and Other Essays.
OF	Opportunities for Faith.
P	Priesthood.
PM	Prayers for Meditation.
RLT	Religious Life Today.
SC	Spirit in the Church.

SCC	Shape of the Church to Come.
SE	Spiritual Exercises.
SL	Servants of the Lord.
T	Trinity.
TD	On the Theology of Death.
TPA	Theology of Pastoral Action.
TR	Theology for Renewal.
WP	Watch and Pray with Me

INDEX

ADVENT: BH.15; ES.10; EF.1.1.1- .4; EY.1; MHL.1/2.
ALL SAINTS DAY: EY.16.
ALL SOULS DAY: EY.16.
ANOINTING, Sacrament of: MS.7.
ANONYMOUS CHRISTIAN/ITY: EF.1.2.4; EF.3.1; GF.3.1; MFS.1.
ANTHROPOLOGY (see: THEOLOGICAL ANTHROPOLOGY).
APOSTOLATE (see: LAITY, apostolate of): CCt.4; CMP.1.
    books: CMP.5.
    prison: CMP.4.
    railway: CMP.2.
ASCETICISM (see: RENUNCIATION).
ASH WEDNESDAY: EY.6.
ATHEISM: CL.21.

BAPTISM: MS.1.
    in the Spirit: MS.2.
    infant: MS.1.
BECOMING: H.
BEGINNINGS: EF.4.1.
BIBLE, authorship: AB.5.
    cannonicity of: Inq.1.
    inspiration of: AB.5; Inq.1.
BISHOP/s: B; Inq.4.
    College of: AB.6.
    collegiality: OF.7.2.
BODY (see: RESURRECTION OF THE BODY).
BVM (see: MARIOLOGY): MM.10; PM.8.
    and the apostolate: CCt.4.
    and the church: SE.30.
    Annunciation: MM.5; SE.15.
    as perfect Christian: MM.3.
    Assumption of: EY.15; MM.8; OF.2.6.
    doctrines: MM.1.
    Immaculate Conception of: EF.4.1; MM.4; SL.6.
    in theology: MM.2.
    Mediatrix of Grace: MM.9.
    motherhood of: MM.5.
    sinlessness of: MM.7.
    virginity of: MM.6.

CAUSALITY, divine: H.
CELIBACY (see: PRIESTHOOD; PRIESTLY LIFE): OF.6.1; SL.10.
CHARISM (see: OFFICE AND CHARISM).
CHARISMATIC RENEWAL (see: SPIRIT/s): RLT.8.
CHRISTIAN LIFE: BH.24/35/43/44.
    good intentions: BH.36.
    maturity: CL.19/23.
    temptation: BH.39.
CHRISTIANITY and absolute future: AB.1.
    and Marxism: CCM.
    and non-Christian religions: GF.3.1.
    essentials of: BH.37; CC.1.1- .3; RLT.1.
    future of: FS.2.
CHRISTOLOGY: LJLN.1; SE.12.
    ascent: MHL.5.
    descent: MHL.7.
    modern: C.153.
    searching: NC.1.
CHRISTMAS: EF.1.2.1- .5; EY.2; GF.7.3; MHL.7/8; SE.16.
    message of: MHL.5/6.
CHURCH: (see: ECCLESIOLOGY; OFFICE and CHARISM; PETRINE OFFICE) CF.4.
    and individual: NG.1.
    and the poor: CL.11.
    and the Spirit: P.23.
    and theology: GF.6.4.
    as community: CL.18.
    as founded by Christ: NC.2.
    as *Ur-Sakrament*: Inq.3.
    charism in: DEC.2.
    constitution of: SL.1.
    current status of: SCC.1.
    decision making in: GF.1.4.
    democracy in: GF.6.3.
    experimentation in: OF.7.3.
    freedom in: GF.8.3; MFS.2.
    future of: FS.2; OF.6.3; SCC.2.
    hierarchical nature of: B.
    images of: CAC.2.
    in the diaspora: CCt.1.
    individual in: CCt.3.
    leadership in: AB.6.
    men's participation in: TR.4.
    nature of: OF.6.2; RLT.4; TPA.1/2.

need for: CL.7.
of the future: CAC.2; CCt.1; GF.1.5; SCC.3.
post-conciliar: GF.1.1-.5.
pre-conciliar: OF.5.2.
prophets in: EF.3.2.
public opinion in: FS.1.
social function of: CF.3.
toleration in: MFS.3.
trust within: OF.7.1.
un/changeable elements: CF.1.
CLEMENT of Alexandria, St: EF.3.4.
COGNITION, *conversio ad phantasma*: EF.5.2.
CONFESSION (see: PENANCE, Sacrament of).
CONFIRMATION, Sacrament of: MS.2.
CONSCIENCE: NG.2.
CONVERSION: SL.8.
CORPUS CHRISTI: EF.1.5.1-.2; EY.13.
COURAGE: MFS.1.
CREATION and redemption: CCt.2.
CREED/s: OF.4.1.
brief: CC.1.1-.3; CC.1.5.
need for a brief formula of: RLT.1.
resurrection of body and life everlasting: EF.1.4.1.
CROSS: GF.5.2; SE.27.
and sin: P.21.
meaning of: MHL.9.
CULTURE and faith: GF.2.1.
transformation of: BH.10.

DEATH: CC.2.7; EF.1.5.2; MHL.6; MS.7; OF.2.2/5.4/5.5; RLT.9/10; SE.11; TD.1.2/1.3.
existential elements of: TD.1.1.
life of the dead: ES.7.
martyrdom: TD.2.
of Adam: TD.1.2.
silence of: EY.16.
DEMYTHOLOGY/ -IZING: C.33.
DESOLATION, spiritual: CL.2.
DIALOGUE (see: ECUMENISM): GF.6.4; GF.8.3; OF.7.2.
DIASPORA: CCt.1.
DIACONATE, restoration of: TR.3.
DISCERNMENT, vocational: CL.17.
DISCPILINA ARCANI: CCt.7.
DOCTRINE, development of: CF.1; Inq.1.

DUALISM, body/soul: OF.2.6.

EASTER: AB.2; EF.1.4.1 -.2; EY.10.
ECCLESIOLOGY (see: CHURCH).
    and pastoral action: TPA.1.
    post-conciliar: CAC.2.
ECOLOGY: EF.1.4.2.
ECUMENISM (see: DIALOGUE): GF.4.1-.2.
    advancing dialogue; CF.2.
EDUCATION, Christian: TR.6.
    scholarship: TR.5.
ELECTION: DEC.3.
    conflict in: SE.18.
    Ignatian: P.16/17; SE.2/3/19/21.
    predisposition for: SE.14.
EPIPHANY: EY.4.
EPISCOPATE (see: BISHOP/s).
ETHICS (see: MORALITY).
    Catholic/Protestant: CF.2.
    Medical: GF.3.3.
EUCHARIST (see: MASS): CCt.5/6; CE; EF.1.5.1; MS.3; PM.6; SE.24.
    as center of priestly life: P.19.
    real presence: BH.11.
    routine celebration of: CL.12.
    visits to: CCt.6.
EVERYDAY LIFE: BH.8/23; BT.1; CL.13/18/20; MHL.3; OF.4.6/6.4; OP.1.2.
    acceptance of: P.8.
    aging: CL.4; EY.3; RLT.9.
    depression: CL.2.
    despair: NBP.1.
    endings: CL.19; PM.9.
    gift of: BH.7.
    laughter: EY.5.
    melancholy: CL.10.
    mixed: CL.24.
    perfectionism: CL.8.
    prayer in: NBP.4.
    privacy: CCt.7.
    prudence: BH.13.
    pursuit of happiness: CL.1.
    routine: ES.6.
    scholarship: TR.5.
    self-acceptance: CL.10.

serenity: CL.8.
sickness: MS.7; OF.5.4.
trust: OF.7.1.
EVANGELICAL COUNSELS (see: RELIGIOUS LIFE).
theology of: SE.9.
EVANGELIZATION: CC.1.5.
EVOLUTION: H; C.26.
EXERCISES of St. IGNATIUS (see: ELECTION): CC.2.4.
EXPERIMENTATION: OF.7.3.

FAITH: CL.6; EY.1; FS.1; OF.1.2/3.1; SL.2.
   and culture: GF.2.1.
   and intellectual integrity: BT.3.
   and science: CL.11; DBG.5.
   as courage: MFS.1.
   dichotomous nature of: CC.2.1.
   essentials of: CC.1.1- .3.
   formal statements of: OF.4.1.
   fraternal: DBG.8.
   nature of today: BT.2.
FATE and freedom: GF.8.4.
FORGIVENESS: BH.34.
FRANCIS of Assisi, St: CL.9.
FREEDOM: CL.3/24; GF.8.2- .3.
   and constraint: MFS.2; TR.6.
   and fate: GF.8.4.
   and guilt: MS.4.
   and law: ES.5.
   and spirituality: GF.6.1.
   sphere of: GF.8.2.
   theology of: GF.8.1.
FUNDAMENTAL OPTION: BH.12/28; EF.1.3.3; NBP.6; OF.4.6.
FUTURE: CC.2.9; OF.2.1; P.22.
   Absolute: AB.1; GF.2.1.

GERMAN LANGUAGE: NBP.Trans.
GOD (see, CAUSALITY, divine): ES.1/4/6.
   and law: ES.5.
   and other things: SE.2.
   and suffering: CL.21.
   as Father: GF.7.3.
   as ground of being: CL.16.
   as mystery: EF.1.2.4; GF.7.2.
   attributes of: ES.2; SE.1.

    experience of: P.1.
    knowledge of: DEC.3.
    incomprehensibility of: CL.3/4.
    infinity of: ES.10.
    name of: EF.1.3.2.
    nature of: P.1.
    prayer to: PM.1.
    providence of: BH.31.
    remoteness of: EY.7.
    search for: EY.4.
    self-communication of: T.3.
    silence of: ES.3/7.
    triune (see: TRINITY): T.1/2/3.
GOD-TALK (see: THEOLOGICAL LANGUAGE): CMP.6; GF.7.1.
GOOD FRIDAY: EY.9.
GRACE and nature: CCt.2.
    in everyday life: BT.1.
    of everything: BH.4.
    sacramental: MS.Intro.
    uncreated: MHL.4.
GUARDINI, Romano: OF.5.2.
GUILT (see: SIN): MS.4; OF.4.4.

HEART: EY.14; NBP.2.
    human: NBP.1.
HERESY, cryptogamic: NG.3.
HELL: SE.11.
HIERARCHY, meaning of: SL.1.
HOLINESS, personal: CL.9.
HOLY SPIRIT (see: SPIRIT/s).
HOPE: CC.1.2/2.7/2.9; GF.2.1; NBP.1; RLT.2.
HUMILITY, degrees of: SE.22.
    Ignatian types: P.18.
HYPOSTATIC UNION (see: JESUS CHRIST).

IGNATIUS of Loyola, St., charism of: AB4.
IMPATIENCE, holy: GF.3.
INCARNATION: EF: 1.1.4/ 1.2.2; EY.2; GF.7.3; P.7; PM.3.
    SE.12/15/16.
INDIFFERENCE: P.3.
    Ignatian: P.18; SE.3.
INDIVIDUAL/ITY: CCt.3; NG.1.
INTELLECTUAL INTEGRITY: BT.3.

INDEX

JESUS CHRIST (see: CHRISTOLOGY; INCARNATION).
    abiding presence of: EY.13.
    Agony in the Garden: SE.25; W&P.1.
    as meaning of creation: BH.22.
    Ascension of: EY.11; SE.28.
    cross of: P.21.
    crucified: EY.9.
    death of: EF.1.4.2; MHL.6; NC.3; OF.2.2/5.5: PM.6; SE.27; TD.1.3.
    Good Shepherd: BH.41.
    hidden life of: P.8.
    Hypostatic Union of: LJLN.1; MHL.7.
    imitation of: P.6/7; PM.3: SE.13/14.
    King: BH.21.
    love for: LJLN.1.
    name of: EF.1.3.2.
    nearness of: BH.33.
    obedience of: SL.9.
    our all: PM.7.
    passion of: P.20.
    presence of: W&P.1.
    priesthood of: SE.23.
    resurrection of: AB.2; NC.1; OF.2.3- .4; P.22; SE.28.
    Sacred Heart of: CMP.6; EY.14.
    devotion to: CMP.7; SL.7.
    Second Coming of: MHL.1.
    self-awareness of: BH.17.
    temptation of: BH.2.
    way of the cross: SE.26.
    words from the cross: W&P.2.
JOHN the Baptist, St: BH.7/15; EF.1.1.2- .3; MHL.2/3.
JOSEPH, St: BH.1; EY.8.
    veneration of: EF.4.2.
JUDGMENT: PM.2; SE.11.
    final: EF.1.1.1.
    self: BH.27.
JUSTICE and peace: OF.4.5.
JUSTIFICATION: GF.4.1; OF.1.1.
    knowledge of: NBP.7.

KNOWLEDGE and love: ES.4.

LAITY: EF.3.3; TR.8.
    apostolate of: CCt.2; CMP.1.
    rights and responsibilities of: FS.1.

spirituality of: EF.3.4.
LAW: ES.5.
    divine/positive: CF.1.
LENT: EY.7.
LITURGICAL YEAR (see: specific season/feast; SERMON/S)
LITURGY and prayer: GF.6.2.
    of the world: OF.3.2.
    renewal of: CCt.5.
LONERGAN, Bernard: AB.8.
LOVE: P.24.
    and knowledge: BH.29/32; ES.4.
    degrees of: SE.22.
    dynamics of: CMP.7.
    Ignatian types: P.18.
    in St. Ignatius: SE.31.
LOVE OF GOD: CL.20; EF.2.1- .2; NBP.3.
LOVE OF GOD AND NEIGHBOR: BH.25/26; CMP.4; ES.8; RLT.6.
LOVE OF NEIGHBOR: BH.42; CL.22; EF.2.2- .3; P.13.
    and love of God: LJLN.2.
    as communion: LJLN.2.
LUMEN GENTIUM: CF.4.

MARDI GRAS: EY.5.
MAN (see: THEOLOGICAL ANTHROPOLOGY).
    as dust: EY.6.
    as sinner: PM.1.
    nature of: GF.7.1.
    substantial unity of: TD.1.1.
MARIOLOGY (see: BVM).
    fundamental idea in: MM.3.
    justification of: MM.2.
MARTYRDOM: TD.2.
    criteria for: C.163.
MARXISM: CCM.
MARY (see: BVM).
MASS (see: EUCHARIST; SACRAMENT/s): BH.6.
    broadcast of: CCt.7.
    frequent celebrations of; CE.
    nature of: CE.
    participation in: CCt.5.
    thanksgiving after: CCt.6.
MATRIMONY, Sacrament of: EF.3.5; MS.6.
MEANING, question of: CL.16.
MEDIATION: CP; MM.9.

MEDICINE, vocation of: GF.3.3.
MONO/POLYGENISM: C.26.
MORALITY, choices: DEC.1.
    Christian: BH.38.
    pre-marital sex: CL.15.
    situation ethics: NG.2.
MUSIC, liturgical: EF.5.1.
MYSTERY, patience toward: BH.14.
MYSTICISM, everyday: EF.1.3.3; EF.2.3; SC.1.

NATURE (see: THEOLOGICAL ANTHROPOLOGY)
    and supernature: CCt.2.
NEW YEAR'S DAY: EF.1.3.1 -.3; EY.3.

OBEDIENCE, clerical: SL.9.
    religious: CMP.9; P.12; RLT.7; SE.18.
OBJECTIVITY as a virtue: GF.3.3.
OFFICE/CHARISM: DEC.2; SL.1/6.
ORIGINAL SIN (see: SIN, original).
ORTHODOXY, judgment of: C.66.

PAROCHIAL PRINCIPLE: CMP.3.
PASTORAL MINISTRY, holiness in: CMP.4.
    organization of: CMP.3.
PEACE and justice: OF.4.5.
PENANCE, Sacrament of: MS.4; CC.2.5; CL.14/15.
    frequent: SL.11.
    fruits of: PM.2.
    sacramental: SE.10.
PENTECOST: EF.1.5.3; EY.12.
PERSEVERANCE: CL.6.
    grace of: SE.32.
PETRINE OFFICE: Inq.4.
    and College of Bishops: AB.6.
PRAYER: CL.5; ES.3; NBP.For; OF.3.1- .3; RLT.6.
    as dialogue: CC.2.3.
    as love: NBP.3.
    everyday: NBP.Intro; NBP.4.
    genesis of: NBP.1.
    in Jesus' name: BH.20.
    litanies: W&P.1.
    of consecration: NBP.6.
    of decision: NBP.8.
    of petition: NBP.5.

of the sinner: NBP.7.
personal: GF.6.2.
possibility of: CC.2.2.
role of the Spirit: NBP.2.
PREACHING: C.33.
PREDESTINATION: CL.3.
PRIESTHOOD: AB.7; CMP.8; ES.9; MS.5; SE.23.
    and Annunciation: SE.15.
    and asceticism: SE.9.
    and Eucharist: P.19; SE.24.
    and religious life: P.11.
    celebrations of: OF.6.2.
    celibacy in: OF.6.1.
    dangers today: P.15.
    formation for: TR.7.
    nature of: P.9; TR.2.
    nature of today: BT.2; P.14.
    office and charism: P.10; SL.6.
    parochial: TR.2.
    theological foundations: C.43.
PRIESTLY LIFE: P.13; SL.1- 5/7/8/12/13.
    and BVM: SE.30.
    celibacy: SL.10.
    frequent confession: SL.11.
    obedience: P.12; SL.9.
    temptations in: SE.20.
PRINCIPLES/PRESCRIPTIONS: DEC.1.
PROPHECY: Inq.2.
PUBLIC OPINION (see: CHURCH, public opinion in).
RAHNER, Hugo, S.J: OF.5.3.
RECONCILIATION (see: PENANCE, Sacrament of).
REDEMPTION: ES.10.
    and creation: CCt.2.
RELIGIOUS LIFE: CMP.9; RLT.2/6; TR.8.
    and priesthood: P.11.
    community: RLT.5.
    contemplative: OF.3.3.
    final vows: MS.8.
    formation: OF.3.1.
    future of: OF.6.3.
RENUNCIATION: OF.6.1/6.4; SE.2/9.
RESURRECTION: CC.2.8; EF.1.4.1- .2; OF.2.3- .4.
    of the body: EY.10/11; OF.2.6.
REVELATION: Inq.1.

close of: NC.3.
private: Inq.2.
RIGHTEOUSNESS (see: JUSTIFICATION).

SACRAMENT/s (see individual sacraments): CCt.6; Inq.3: MS.Intro; SE.10.
    nature of: OF.7.4.
SACRED HEART (see: JESUS CHRIST, Sacred Heart of).
SACRIFICE, of the cross: CE.
SAINTS (listed by first names).
    Communion of: CP.
    veneration of: CP; EF.4.3.
SALVATION (see: SIN): GF.4.1; NC.2; OF.1.3.
    God's universal will for: BH.45.
    extra ecclesia: BH.3; CF.4.
SCIENCE and faith: DBG.5.
    and God: GF.7.2.
    and theology: H.
SCRIPTURE (see: BIBLE).
SECULAR INSTITUTES: TR.8.
SECULARISM/ -IZATION: DBG.4; GF.2.2.
SERMON, Ash Wednesday: GF.5.1.
    Assumption of BVM: OF.2.6.
    Easter: OF.2.4.
    First Mass: CMP.7.
    Good Friday: GF.5.2; OF.2.2.
    Holy Thursday: GF.5.2.
    Holy Saturday: GF.5.2.
    Holy Week: GF.5.2.
    Pentecost: OF.2.5.
SERMONS: Psalm 23: BH.41.
    Matthew 1: EF.4.2.
    Matthew 1:18-24: BH.1; MHL.4.
    Matthew 4:1-4: BH.2.
    Matthew 5: SE.20.
    Matthew 5:20-24: OF.1.1.
    Matthew 8:1-13: BH.3; EF.3.1.
    Matthew 11:2-10: EF.1.1.2.
    Matthew 20:1-16: BH.4.
    Matthew 22:1-14: BH.12.
    Matthew 23:34-40: EF.2.1.
    Matthew 24:15-35: BH.5.
    Mark 6:1-6: OP.1.2.
    Mark 8:1-9: BH.6.

Mark 10:23-27: OP.1.3.
Luke 1:57-68: BH.7.
Luke 2:21: EF.1.3.2.
Luke 2:22-35: CC.2.1.
Luke 3:1-6: EF.1.1.4; MHL.2.
Luke 3:10-18: MHL.3.
Luke 5:1-11: BH.8.
Luke 8:4-14: BH.9.
Luke 11:4-18: BH.10.
Luke 14:16-24: BH.11/12.
Luke 16: 1-9: BH.13; OF.1.4.
Luke 18:31-43: BH.14.
Luke 21: 25-28 & 34-36: MHL.1.
Luke 21:25-33: EF.1.1.1.
John 1:19-28: BH.15; EF.1.1.3.
John 6:1-15: BH.16.
John 6:25-56: BH.11.
John 8:46-58: BH.17.
John 16:5-15: BH.18/19.
John 16:23-30: BH.20.
John 18:33-38: BH.21; CC.1.4.
Acts 6-7. EF.1.2.5.
Romans 8:18-23: BH.22.
Romans 12:6-16: BH.23/24.
Romans 13:8-10: BH.25/26.
1Corinthians 4:1-15: BH.27.
1Corinthians 9:24-27 & 10:1-5: BH.28.
1Corinthians 13:1-13: BH.29.
2Corinthians 6:1-10: BH.30.
Galatians 4:22-31: BH.31.
Ephesians 5:32: EF.3.5; MS.6.
Philipians 1:6-11: BH.32.
Philipians 4:4-7: BH.33.
Colossians 3:12-17: BH.34/35/36; EF.2.3.
1Thessalonians 1:2-10: BH.37.
1Thessalonians 4:1-7: BH.38.
James 1:17-21: BH.39.
James 1:22-27: BH.40.
1Peter 2:21-25: BH.41.
1Peter 3:8-15: BH.42.
1Peter 4:7-11: BH.43.
1John 3:13-18: BH.44.
Revelations 7:2-12: BH.45.
SILENCE: EF.1.2.1; EF.1.2.3.

SIN (see: SALVATION): NBP.7; OF.4.4; P.4.
    and death: TD.1.2.
    consciousness of: SE.4.
    essence of: SE.5.
    history of: SE.6.
    mystique of: NG.2.
    original: C.26.
    personal history of: SE.7.
    salvation/damnation status: P.5.
    social: CL.14.
    venial: SE.8.
SKEPTICISM: CC.1.4.
SOCIETY OF JESUS, history and charism: AB.4.
SOUL (see: DUALISM).
    eternal validity of: EY.15.
SPIRIT/s: PM.4; SE.29; SL.8.
    and prayer: NBP.2.
    as Paraclete: BH.19.
    discernment of: DEC.3; EF.3.2; PM.5; RLT.8.
    experience of: BT.1; EY.12; P.23; SC.1.
    fear of: OF.2.5.
    fruits of: PM.5.
    gifts of: DEC.2; EF.1.5.3.
    indwelling: BH.40.
    present in absence: BH.18.
SPIRITUALITY and freedom: GF.6.1.
    Ignatian: CMP.7.
    masculine: TR.4.
    modern: CC.2.6.
STEVEN, martyr: EF.1.2.5.
SUFFERING: CL.4.
    and God: CL.21.
SUNDAY OBLIGATION: CL.12; OF.7.4.
SURRENDER: OF.1.1/5.4.
SYNOD, German national: SCC.Intro.

TECHNOLOGY, lure of: BH.16.
TEMPTATION: P.16.
    and prayer: NBP.8.
THEOLOGICAL ANTHROPOLOGY (see: MAN): H; SE.12.
    anthropocentrism: P.2.
    freedom: GF.3.1.1.
    individuality: CCt.3.
THEOLOGICAL LANGUAGE (see: GOD-TALK): OF.4.3; SL.2.

THEOLOGY: EF.4.3.
   and science: H.
   Ascetical: DEC.3.
   dissent: MFS.3.
   ecclesiality of: GF.6.4.
   method: AB.8; C.66; TD.Intro.
   Moral: EF.3.3.
   Mystical: OF.5.1.
   parameters of: AB.3.
   Pastoral: TPA.1/2.
   post-conciliar: CAC.3.
   task of: C.33; SL.2.
   teaching of: C.66; TR.7.
THERESA of Avila, St: OF.5.1.
THERESA of Lisieux, St: RLT.10.
THOMAS Aquinas, St: EF.4.3.
TIME: EF.1.3.1; EY.1/2.
   and eternity: EF.1.3.3; EY.15.
   as *kairos*: BH.30.
   end of: BH.5.
TOLERATION in the church: MFS.3.
TRINITY: T.Intro; T.1/3.
   economic: MHL.7.
   magisterial teaching on: T.2.
TRANSCENDENCE in knowledge and freedom: SC.1.
TRUTH: BH.21.

UNBELIEF, sources of today: BT.2.
UTOPIA/s: OF.2.1/4.5.

VATICAN II: CF.1/4.
   ecclesiology of: CAC.2.
   implementation of: CAC.1.
   post-conciliar concerns: GF.1.1- .5.
   pre-conciliar generation: OF.5.2.
   theology of: CAC.3.
VIRGINITY, Christian: MM.6.
VISIONS: GF.9.
   criteria for: Inq.2.
VOWS (see: EVANGELICAL COUNSELS).
   perpetual: RLT.3.

WISDOM, divine: OF.1.4.
WORD of God: BH.9.

ministry of: SL.3/4.
theology of: OF.4.2; SE.15.
WORLD, (*kosmos houtos*): SE.8.
WORLD-CHURCH: C.170.

YOUTH, formation of: CCt.5.

Acts, religious: CCt.3 (86ff); CP (49ff; 54ff).
Adam, sin of: P.4 (48f); SE.6 (48f).
Altar Community (see: Church as local altar community).
Altar Devotion: CCt.6 (194f).
Analogy (see: Theological Language): AB.3 (298ff).
Angels: H (51f); T.3 (90).
    multipliability of: DEC.3 (111f).
    nature of: DEC.1 (17f); SE.15 (140f).
    relation to the cosmos: TD.1.1 (31f).
    sin of: P.4 (45ff); SE.6 (45ff); TD.1.2 (60ff).
Anointing, Sacrament of: Inq.3 (240ff; 294ff).
    and the death of Christ: TD.1.3 (85f).
Anonymous Christian/ity: AB.2 (108); AB.3 (302f); BT.2 (58ff, 85ff); CAC.2 (56ff); CC.2.8 (88); CCt.3 (104ff); CF.4 (85ff); DBG.8 (105f); DEC.2 (64ff); EF.2.2 (110, 113f); LJLN.1 (43f); MHL.8 (68f); NC.1 (15ff); P.6 (68f); RLT.2 (11f); RLT.4 (36ff); SE.12 (111f); TR.5 (91ff).
    death of: TD.2 (120ff).
Appropriation, doctrine of: T.2 (76f); T.3 (86f).
Anti-clericalism: SE.9 (76f).
Apostolic Succession: Inq.4 (340ff).
Ascension (see: Jesus Christ, Ascension of).
Ascesis (see: Renunciation): CCt.5 (164).
Atheism: DBG.5 (68f; 71f); EY.7 (67f); TR.5 (91ff).
    grounds for: AB.1 (93).
Authority and obedience: P.12 (131ff).
    in the church: SCC.2 (57ff).

Baptism: MS.4 (53f); EY.12 (107f); Inq.3 (269ff).
    and the death of Christ: TD.1.3 (82f).
    by blood: TD.2 (110f).
    character of: Inq.3 (270ff).
    in the Spirit: RLT.4 (41).
    infant: ES.4 (30f).
Beatific Vision: EY.11 (100f).
Beatitudes: SE.20 (179f).
Being, hierarchy of: CCt.2 (47f).
Bible and theology: GF.6.4 (173f).
    as a book: CMP.5 (82ff).
    authorship: Inq.1 (11ff).
canonicity of: AB.5 (13ff).
Birth Control: GF.1.5 (59f).
Bishop/s (see: Cardinals; Petrine Office).
    and priests: B (44ff).

INDEX 549

    auxiliary: B (29f).
    College of: B (17ff).
    election of: GF.6.3 (164f); SCC.3 (119ff).
    national conferences of: TPA.2 (129ff).
    of the future CF.4 (97ff).
    Order of: TPA.2 (84ff).
    personal prelature: B (57ff).
    potestas ordinis et jurisdictionis: TPA.1 (ftn.5, 36ff).
    relative/absolute ordination: B (30ff).
    synod of: B (67ff); TPA.2 (131f).
    titular: B (27ff).
Body: (see: Resurrection of; Soul/body).
BVM: P.7 (83); P.23 (263f).
    consecration to: NBP.6 (73f).
    devotion to: SE.32 (282f).
    faith of: CC.2.1 (45ff).
    hyperdulia: MM.1 (18f).
    in scripture: MM.1 (16f).
    mother of all: W&P.2 (47ff).

Canon Law, mutability of: CF.1 (12ff).
Cardinals, College of: B (23ff; ftn 15); TPA.2 (119ff).
Caritas: CMP.2 (31f).
Categorical (see: Transcendent/Categorical).
Causality, final: OF.2.2 (29f).
    sacramental: Inq.3 (216ff); SL.1 (28f).
    secondary: DEC.3 (119ff).
    supernatural: Inq.2 (126ff).
Celibacy (see: Priesthood): P.13 (144f); SE.9 (76f); SE.17(151f); SE.23 (209).
Celibate Chastity: TR.8 (172ff).
Censorship: NG.3 (78f).
Charism and office (see: Office and charism).
Christ-event (see: Jesus Christ).
Christianity and other religions: FS.2 (102ff).
    endurance of: AB.1 (78ff).
    essential: MFS.1 (25ff); MM.3 (35f).
    limits of: P.14 (154f).
Christology (see: Incarnation; Jesus Christ): BT.2 (74f).
    method in: C.153 (73ff).
    of ascent: C.153 (75).
    searching; CC.2.8 (89ff); OF.2.3 (33f).
Church (see: Magisterium; Salvation *extra ecclesia*).
    acts of: CCt.2 (41ff); SL.1 (21ff).

and inner-Trinitatiran processions: TPA.1 (33ff, 40f).
and martyrdom: TD.2 (112f).
and the poor: SCC.2 (61ff).
and the Spirit: SE.29 (256f).
apostolicity of: Inq.1 (43ff).
as "absolute": DEC.2 (48f).
as absolutely willed by God: Inq.1 (40ff).
as agent of forgiveness: MS.4 (55f).
as base community: SCC.3 (108ff).
as community of love: CAC.2 (66ff).
as law and gospel: TPA.1 (49ff).
as "little flock": AB.1 (80); SCC.1 (29ff).
as local altar community: CAC.2 (44ff); GF.1.1 (21f); Inq.3 (267f; 293f); Inq.4 (312ff); OF.6.2 (172); P.19 (212f).
as mystery: TPA.1 (43f).
as People of God: Inq.3 (193ff).
as pilgrim: GF.8.3 (258f).
as pneumatic community: CCt.3 (89f).
as present in a diocese: B (38ff; 57ff).
as sacrament of freedom: TR.6 (109ff).
as sacrament of world salvation: CAC.2 (51ff); CF.4 (81ff); MS.Intro (xv).
as Small Christian Community: CCt.3 (111f).
as *Ur-sakrament*: TPA.1 (44ff).
as willed by God: AB.5 (7f).
charism in: TPA.2 (65ff).
charismatic impulses in: SE.18 (167f).
defeatism in: CF.3 (51ff; 71).
democracy in: DEC.2 (69ff); MFS.2 (63ff); RLT.4 (32f); RLT.7 (62f).
development work of: SCC.3 (128ff).
dissent within: CF.1 (30f); GF.8.3 (251ff); RLT.4 (38ff); SL.1 (43f).
diversity in: SCC.1 (35ff).
divisions within: CC.1.2 (27f).
event of: MS.8 (103f).
ghettoization of: CCt.1 (28ff); SCC.3 (93f).
holiness of: MM.7 (76f); P.10 (110f); TD.2 (108ff).
in transition: SCC.1 (22ff).
indefectibility of: TPA.2 (74ff).
love for: AB.4 (26ff); P.23 (257ff); SE.30 (268f).
membership in: CC.1.2 (26ff); CC.1.3 (35f); SCC.2 (71f).
mission of: CF.4 (85ff).
missionary activity of: LJLN.2 (88f).
missionary nature of: CCt.1 (27ff; 33).

moral teaching of: SCC.2 (64ff).
necessity for: AB.1 (79f).
of the future: CF.4 (78ff).
office and charism in: AB.4 (26ff); NG.1 (35ff); OF.6.1 (157ff); SCC.2 (56ff); TPA.1 (59ff); TPA.2 (70ff).
order in: TPA.2 (78ff).
permanent self-identity of: TPA.1 (51ff).
planning for future of: SCC.2 (45ff).
pre-conciliar: OF.6.3 (177f).
polarization in: SCC.1 (38ff).
public opinion in: CCt.3 (110f); GF.6.3 (167f).
reconciliation with (see: Penance): SL.11 (194ff).
service to: P.23 (260f).
sinfulness of: MFS.3 (83f).
spirituality in: SCC.2 (82ff).
structure of: NC.2 (27ff).
triumphalism in: CF.3 (50ff; 71).
un/changeable elements: B (13ff).
unity in diversity: Inq.4 (370ff; 374ff).
unity of: SE.24 (215f).
Coercion (see: Force).
Cognition: H (81ff).
conversio ad phantasma: OF.7.3 (219f).
Coincidencia oppositorum: ES.6 (52).
Communicatio idiomatum: LJLN.1 (30ff).
Communication, interpersonal: LJLN.2 (79f).
Communion of Saints: EY.8 (73f; 77); MM.9 (97ff); NC.1 (14f).
Concupiscence: CCM (49); MFS.2 (44f); MFS.3 (83).
  gnoseological: BT.2 (65f); CC.1.1 (13).
Confession, Sacrament of (see: Penance).
Confirmation, Sacrament of: Inq.3 (233ff; 272ff).
Conscience: MS.4 (54); CF.2 (43ff); GF.4.2 (104f); RLT.7 (65ff); NG.1 (20); SL.1 (42f).
  dignity of: MFS.3 (85f; 112f).
  formation of: SCC.2 (68f; 77ff).
Consolation, spiritual: EY.3 (32ff).
Contemplation: EF.5.2 (203f); P.8 (97f).
Contrition, im/perfect: MS.4 (57f).
Conversion (see: *Metanoia*).
Creation: BT.3 (113f); SE.12 (106f).
  as mediating God: P.2 (28).
  meaning of: P.7 (77f).
Creed/s, brief: BT.3 (109f).

He descended into hell: EF1.4.2 (79ff); EY.10 (90f); TD.1.3 (65, 71f, 74).
Cross: (see: Jesus Christ, Cross of): P.6 (70ff); RLT.2 (14); RLT.7 (57ff; 60f); SE.6 (45); SE.14 (127ff); SE.31 (271f).
    as liturgy: W&P.2 (52).
    as source of grace: EF.3.5 (158).
    love of: P.18 (204ff).
    wisdom of: OP.1.4 (17).
Curia, reform of: TPA.2 (122ff).

Damnation (see: Salvation/damnation status): SE.6 (49f).
Deacon, Order of: TPA.2 (106ff).
Dead, indifference toward: CP (37ff).
Death: AB.2 (100ff); CC.1.2 (30); ES.3 (21; 24f); ES.4 (32); ES.6: (46f); GF.5.1 (116); Inq.3 (249f; 295f); NBP.6 (66f); OF.1.4 (17); OF.2.1 (23); OF.2.6 (49f); P.22 (241f); SE.2 (21); SE.24 (211ff).
    and Anonymous Christian/ity: P.21 (235ff).
    and asceticism: SE.9 (73f).
    and devil: TD.1.2 (59ff).
    and eternal life: AB.3 (309f).
    and freedom: TD.2 (93ff).
    and indifference: SE.3 (24).
    and sickness: RLT.2 (17f).
    and the Spirit: SC.1 (26f).
    as final renunciation: P.18 (204f).
    as separation of body and soul: TD.1.1 (24ff).
    good or bad: TD.2 (118f).
    of unbaptized infants: TD.2 (98f).
    prayer at the time of: NBP.8 (99f).
    solidarity in: CP (82ff).
    theology of: NC.3 (38ff).
    universality of: TD.1.1 (21ff).
Demythology/-izing: CCM (51); DBG.5 (73ff); SL.1 (16ff); SL.2 (57ff).
Devotio: CE (70ff).
Dialogue (see: Ecumenism): GF.1.1 (23).
    ecumenical: OF.4.3 (90f).
Diocese: Inq.4 (388ff).
    nature of: AB.6 (42f); B (34ff; 58ff); TPA.2 (87ff).
Discernment (see: Spirit/s, discernment of).
Discipleship: AB.4 (21ff).
Dissent (see: Church, dissent within).
    and orthodoxy: SCC.2 (74f).
Divorce: GF.1.5 (61f).
Docta ingnorancia: (see: Future): CC.1.1 (16f; 19).

INDEX 553

Doctrine, development of: MM.7 (78ff); MM.8 (84f).
    Marian: MM.1 (18f).
Dogma, development of: CMP.6 (107f).
Donatism: P.10 (108f); SL.6 (102f).
Doubt: OF.3.1 (56); TR.5 (90f).

Economics: CF.3 (67f).
Ecumenical Council, authority of: AB.6 (41).
    supreme power of: Inq.4 (349ff).
Ecumenism (see: Dialogue): SCC.3 (102ff).
    and episcopate: Inq.4 (381f).
Election, Ignatian: AB.4 (17f); P.24 (267f).
Epikeia: MFS.3 (113).
Episcopate (see: Bishop/s).
Error, invincible: GF.1.5 (60f).
Eschatology: ES.10 (85ff).
Eternal Life: W&P.1 (11ff).
Eternity (see: Time).
    in time: NBP.6 (68).
Eucharist: Inq.3 (264ff); MS.Intro (xvi f).
    and the death of Christ: TD.1.3 (83ff).
    as summit of church's actualization: Inq.4 (318f).
    concelebration: CE (106ff).
    real presence: CCt.6 (179ff); MS.3 (32ff).
    Spiritual Communion: CCt.6 (195ff).
Eucharistic Devotions: MS.3 (35ff).
Evangelical Counsels (see: Vows; Religious Life).
    justification for: P.12 (123ff).
    need for: P.11 (116f).
Evangelization: CMP.2 (38f); LJLN.2 (95ff).
Everyday Life: AB.7 (252).
    conflict: SE.18 (164).
    despair: SE.27 (242f).
    eating: BT.1 (32ff).
    growth, human: SE.17 (157).
    joy: OF.2.3 (35f).
    laughter: BT.1 (29ff).
    moving about: BT.1 (20ff).
    night: EF.1.2.3 (31ff).
    patience: MFS.3 (96).
    patient endurance: GF.1.1 (24ff).
    prudence: DEC.1 (23f).
    resignation: RLT.7 (57ff).
    resting: BT.1 (23ff).

routine: CMP.4 (78f).
seeing: BT.1 (26-28).
self-criticism: OF.7.1 (201ff).
self-deception: SE.9 (77f).
sleep: BT.1 (35f).
work: BT.1 (17ff).
Evil: CCt.1 (12).
reality of: SE.19 (171ff).
Exercises of St. Ignatius: AB.4 (13ff); CC.2.3 (67f).
resolutions: SE.32 (284f).
Explanations, logical/ontic: T.2 (52ff).

Faith: MHL.1 (13f); MHL.9 (79ff).
and doubt: BT.2 (64f); FS.2 (75ff).
and renunciation: OF.6.1 (148ff).
burdens of: P.14 (152f).
essence of: OF.6.3 (182f).
fides implicita: BT.2 (63f).
liberating: TR.6 (102ff).
Fideism: BT.3 (99ff).
Force: CMP.3 (57f); OF.4.5 (94ff); TR.6 (100f).
Forgiveness: NBP.7 (79); W&P.2 (40ff).
Freedom: CMP.4 (73ff); MHL.5 (39f); MS.4 (5ff; 20f, 38ff); NBP.6 (64ff); OF.4.6 (117ff); RLT.3 (25f); RLT.6 (48); RLT.7 (61f).
and coercion: MFS.3 (86f).
and death: TD.2 (93ff).
as dialogue with God: MM.5 (56ff).
dualism of: P.4 (50).
finality of: P.4 (46f).
Fundamental Option: EF.2.2 (110ff); ES.3 (20f; 24f); GF.8.1 (213f); P.5 (59ff); SE.4 (30ff); SE.6 (50).
and grace: NBP.6 (70f); TD.1.2 (51f).
Futility: P.20 (221).
Future: OF.4.5 (106f).
docta ignorantia futuri: OF.6.3 (181ff).

Germany, post war: NBP.Trans (xx); NBP.8 (97ff).
Globalization: SCC.3 (129ff).
God: BT.3 (111ff); CC.1.2 (22ff); CC.1.3 (32f); CC.2.2 (52ff); NBP.1 (7ff); OF.4.1 (81f); SC.1 (14f).
and everything else: SE.30 (266f).
and "person": T1.1 (42ff).
as absolute future: AB.1 (72ff).
as always greater: DBG.8 (106); SE.18 (163f).

as eternal future: EF.1.3.3 (64f); OF.2.1 (22f).
as goal of life: P.2 (23ff).
as grace of married love: MS.6 (70ff).
as object of theological inquiry: AB.8 (195).
as ground of freedom: GF.8.2 (226ff).
as mystery: EF.1.2.1 (24f); EF.1.2.3 (34f); LJLN1. (52f); MHL.8 (66ff); OF.1.1 (5).
as the "Wither" of transcendence: GF.8.1 (205ff).
attributes of: P.1 (13ff).
church's proclamation of: SCC.2 (86).
definition of: RLT.1 (4).
experience of: AB.4 (11ff); CMP.1 (8ff); CMP.4 (70ff); CP (46f); MHL.3 (24f); TR.6 (103f).
glorification of: CE (10ff).
honor due: SE.26 (228f).
in all things: SE.31 (273ff).
in marriage: EF.3.5 (155f).
incomprehensibility of: CC.1.1 (15ff); ES.1 (3ff).
love proper to: CCt.3 (84ff).
nature of: OF.3.2 (64ff).
oneness of: CCt.3 (78).
proofs for existence of: BT.2 (84f).
revelation of: MFS.1 (19ff).
self-communication of: AB.3 (301ff); SL.1 (16f).
silence of: EY.16 (140ff).
transcendence of: BT.2 (81ff).
un/changeableness of: SE.12 (104ff).
universal salvific will of: CMP.1 (6ff); NC.2 (24f); SC.1 (24f); TD.2 (98ff).
God-Talk (see: Theological Language): DBG.5 (70ff); DBG.8 (104f).
Governments of the future: CCt.1 (12ff).
Grace: AB.4 (15f); EF.1.2.1 (25); EF.1.3.3 (61); SC.1 (15ff).
and nature: CMP.5 (96ff).
as divine life: EF.3.5 (156f).
experience of: MS.Intro (xiii); MS.2 (23ff).
manifesting sin: SE.5 (38ff).
of election: FS.2 (91ff).
presence of: MS.7 (90ff).
sacramental: CE (62; 85ff); TR.3 (52f).
sanctifying: MM.4 (48f); MS.1 (7ff).

Heart (see: Sacred Heart): CMP.6 (111ff); ES.2 (17); SL.7 (115f).
Heaven: EY.11 (102).
Heresy: GF.6.3 (157f); MFS.3 (99).

in the church: SCC.3 (94ff).
Hierarchy, *munera* of: SL.1 (27).
    sinfulness of: SL.1 (37ff).
Hierarchy of Truths: BT.3 (108f); SL.2 (63ff).
History, meaning of: NC.3 (40f).
Holy Orders, Sacrament of (see: Priesthood): Inq.3 (230ff; 254; 277ff).
    as instituted by Christ: TR.3 (47f).
    relative ordination: SCC.3 (110; 114).
Holy Spirit (see: Spirit/s).
Hope: CC.1.1 (15ff; 21ff); EF.5.3 (207f); OF.2.3 (34); OF.4.5 (105f).
    and despair: MHL.9 (81ff).
Humani Generis: H (24ff).
Humanism: GF.8.3 (259f).
Humanity, oneness of: LJLN.2 (76f).
Humility, reverent: CMP.4 (68ff).

Imagination in St. Ignatius: SE.11 (93f).
Incarnation: BT.3 (122ff); CMP.4 (69f); CMP.5 (83f); CMP.6 (106f); EF.1.2.1 (25ff); EF.1.2.3 (33f); EF.2.2 (114ff); EY.6 (61f); GF.5.1 (114f); NC.1 (17); TR.3 (34f).
Indifference, Ignatian: SE.11 (90f); SE.12 (122ff).
    religious: CMP.7 (123ff; 131f).
Individuality, Christian: TR.6 (113ff).
Intermediate State: CE (80ff).

Jesuits (see: Society of Jesus).
Jesus Christ (see: Incarnation; Logos; Sacred Heart): BT.3 (115f); SL. (18ff).
    Agony in the Garden: EY.7 (71); NBP.2 (11f).
    and freedom: GF.8.1 (224f).
    and prayer of petition: NBP.5 (55ff).
    as absolute savior: C.153 (76).
    as God's promise: CC.1.3 (33ff).
    as Messiah: LJLN.1 (26ff).
    as savior: RLT.1 (4f).
    as sign of God's grace: Inq.3 (198ff).
    as source of all grace: C.26 (69).
    as source of hope: EF.5.3 (207f).
    as *Ur-sakrament*: MS.Intro (xiv f).
    as Word of God: ES.2 (16ff).
    Ascension of: EF.1.4.2 (81f); P.22 (244ff).
    church's proclamation of: SCC.2 (88).
    creation in: SE.6 (47, 48).
    cross of: EF.5.3 (206).

INDEX   557

    death and resurrection of: CC.1.2 (24ff).
    death of: AB.4 (20f); C.153 (76); EF.1.5.2 (92f); MS.3 (29ff); OF.5.4 (137f).
    empty tomb of: OF.2.3 (32); OF.2.4 (35).
    heart of (see: Sacred Heart): SE.27 (242).
    humanity of: LJLN.1 (54ff).
    hypostatic union of: MM.1 (11f); MM.3 (39); P.20 (217f); P.21 (233f); T.1 (24ff).
    imitation of: P.16 (179).
    immediate vision of God: SE.25 (218f; 223).
    imminent expectations of: NC.2 (21ff).
    insurpassibility of: NC.3 (34f).
    love for me: MHL.9 (83f).
    mission of: W&P.2 (54ff).
    more than a prophet: MHL.5 (47ff).
    obedience: of: P.8 (93f).
    prayer of: SE.25 (223ff).
    priesthood of: P.9 (103f).
    real presence of: MS.3 (32ff).
    resurrected body of: P.19 (214).
    resurrection of: CC.2.8 (89ff); MFS.1 (27).
    search for: AB.4 (19ff).
    Second Coming of: FS.2 (90f).
    self-consciousness of: MHL.5 (42ff); P.8 (87f); T.2 (63ff).
    surrender of: SE.25 (225f).
John of the Cross, St: OF.5.1 (126).
Judgment, final: TD.1.1 (37f).
Jus divinum/humanum: GF.6.3 (155ff; 161f); NC.2 (27ff).

Kingdom of God: MHL.5 (44ff).
Knowledge: CMP.6 (117f).
    of self: EY.14 (122).

Laity and clergy: GF.1.5 (63ff).
    apostolate of: CCt.3 (106f); GF.1.1 (20f); TPA.2 (68f).
    charism of: TPA.1 (59ff).
    consultation with: SCC.3 (121f).
    duties of: SL.1 (42f; 44f).
    faith of: BT.2 (55ff).
    formation of: GF.1.5 (55f).
    missionary task of: FS.2 (53ff).
    role of: DEC.1 (38ff); TR.4 (78ff); TR.5 (89f).
    vocation of: TR.8 (178ff); SE.17 (153).
Language (see: Theological Language): GF.7.1 (188f).

religious and secular: C.33 (20ff).
Law, culmination of: SE.25 (220).
    obedience to: SE.18 (162f).
Lent: CC.2.6 (81ff).
Liberalism: GF.8.2 (240ff).
Liturgy, cosmic: P.22 (244f).
    sacramental nature of: OF.7.4 (223f).
Logos, incarnation of: SE.12 (98f).
    relation to human nature: T.3 (89).
Love: CC.1.1 (17ff); GF.8.1 (214ff); SE.27 (238f).
    agape: CMP.4 (65ff).
    and discretion: SE.22 (200ff).
    as *imago trinitatis*: P.24 (275).
    as service: P.24 (272).
    human: LJLN.1 (16ff; 40f).
    in St. Ignatius: P.24 (275f).
    of God: ES.1 (8ff); ES.3 (22ff); LJLN.2 (69ff).
    of God and neighbor: AB.1 (75f); AB.4 (18f); CP (53ff); RLT.2 (15ff).
    of neighbor: CC.1.2 (28f); GF.8.1 (217ff); MHL.9 (84f); MS.1 (10f); RLT.4 (36ff).
    of our dead: ES.7 (56f).

Magisterium (see: Church): GF.1.5 (57f).
    competence of: H (24ff).
    concrete directives of: SCC.2 (76ff).
    extra/ordinary: TPA.2 (114ff).
    indefectability of: TPA.1 (34f).
    mandate of: MFS.3 (98f).
Man as creature: P.2 (19ff).
    historicity of: TD.1.1 (36f).
    mystery of: MS.1 (9f); MS.3 (40f).
    question of: SE.16 (148ff).
    religious propensity of: FS.2 (99ff).
Marriage (see: Divorce): Inq.3 (227ff; 289ff); SL.10 (passim).
    children as fruit of: MS.6 (73f).
    dignity of: OF.6.1 (151f; 159f).
Martyrdom (see: Baptism by blood): EF.3.4 (145).
Mass Stipends: CE (49ff; 114ff).
Meaning, global: AB.1 (67ff); LJLN.1 (49ff).
Metanoia: CC.2.4 (71ff); CC.2.5 (75f; 80); EY.12 (108ff); MS.4 (49f); OF.4.3 (88; 90).
Metaphysics: one/many: CMP.6 (105f).
Miracles as proofs of prophecy: Inq.2 (184ff).

INDEX 559

Molinism: P.18 (201).
Monasticism: EF.3.4 (148ff).
Morality (see: Theology, Moral).
    application of norms: TR.4 (71f).
    as liberation: TR.6 (106ff).
    post-conciliar: GF.1.5 (59ff).
    proclamation of: SCC.2 (64ff).
Mystery: AB.1 (64ff); CMP.6 (113ff); RLT.2 (15ff); RLT.8 (75); SE.12 (100ff; 112f).
    one and many: BT.2 (73ff); P.7 (74f).
    surrender to: LJLN.1 (41ff; 44ff).
    trust in: AB.1 (68ff).
Mystici Corporis: DEC.2 (50ff).
Mysticism (see: Theology, Mystical): BT.2 (77ff); P.1 (9f); SC.1 (7ff).
    Ignatian: DEC.3 (155f).

Neo-paganism: FS.2 (59ff).
Non-conformity: OF.2.2 (25f).

Obedience: ES.5 (43f); GF.1.5 (58f); SE.13 (119f); SE.17 (158f).
    of Jesus: SE.27 (237f).
    religious (see: Vows): AB.4 (28; 29ff); MFS.3 (110ff).
Obediential Potency: SE.12 (102f).
Office and charism: SE.23 (207f).
    unity of: CCt.4 (121f).
Original Sin (see: Sin, original).

Pantheism: EY.11 (101).
Parapsychology: Inq.2 (174ff).
Parish: TPA.2 (100ff).
    as community: LJLN.2 (93ff).
    councils: GF.6.3 (162ff).
    of the future: GF.6.3 (166f); SCC.3 (115ff).
Parochial Principle: TR.2 (42ff).
Patriarchate: B (62f).
Penance, Sacrament of: Inq.3 (275ff).
    and spiritual direction: SL.11 (190f).
    frequent: SE.10 (86f).
    services: CC.2.5 (78ff).
Perfection, states of: TR.8 (159ff; 170ff).
Person, concept of: T.2 (56; 73ff).
    in Trinitarian theology: T.3 (103ff).
Petrine Office: DEC.2 (44f; 78); TPA.1 (ftn.5, 39f); TPA.2 (111ff).
    and ecumenism: SCC.3 (105ff).

as world conscience: LJLN.2 (87f).
election to: B (18ff; 23ff; 56; ftn 11).
future of: SCC.2 (52ff).
infallibility of: AB.6 (42).
Planning: AB.1 (64; 74f); CCt.4 (133f); OF.7.3 (218).
Pluralism: AB.1 (89).
Politics, Christian participation in: LJLN.2 (89ff).
Poor, preferential option: AB.4 (33ff).
Poor Souls: CP (85f).
Poverty, religious: AB.4 (23ff); SE.17 (157f); SE.19 (176f).
Praxis: GF.2.1 (75f).
Prayer: RLT.4 (38); SE.15 (144f).
    dangers to: SE 20 (183f).
    education for: OF.3.1 (59f).
    efficacy of: MS.7 (83ff).
    of Jesus: EF.5.3 (209).
    Our Father: NBP.1 (13).
    petitionary: CC.2.2 (55ff).
    to Holy Spirit: EY.12 (110ff).
Preaching: CCt.3 (103f); CMP.5 (88ff); MS.5 (63f); OP.1.2 (9f).
    existential imagination: SCC.2 (83ff).
    weakness in: DEC.1 (32f).
Presbyterium: B (45ff).
Priesthood (see: Holy Orders): OP.1.1 (5f).
    and mediation: C.43 (82); OF.6.2 (173f).
    and sin: SE.4 (32f).
    and the Spirit: SE.29 (258ff).
    celibate: SCC.3 (110f).
    celibacy debate (passim): OF.7.2.
    courage needed today: CF.1 (37f).
    holiness of: Inq.3 (280ff).
    of the future: CCt.3 (99f); SCC.3 (110ff).
    office and charism in: CCt.4 (122f); SE.30 (264f).
    Order of: TPA.2 (95ff).
    permanent commitment to: P.8 (89f).
    spirituality of: CCt.4 (124ff).
Priests and bishop (see: Bishop/s and priests).
    and the world: SE.8 (64).
    authority of: P.13 (139ff).
    death of: SE.24 (214f).
    life and ministry of: P.8 (95f).
    of the future: CCt.1 (32f); SL.7 (111f).
    shortage: GF5 (66f).
Prophecy: CCt.1 (62f).

inspired: AB.5 (2f).
Public Opinion (see: Church, public opinion in).
Purgatory: TD.1.1 (32f; 35).

Rahner biography: NBP.Intro (vii ff); TD.Intro (9ff).
Real Symbol: Inq.3 (219ff).
Reconciliation (see: Penance, Sacrament of).
Redemption, satisfaction theory of: TD.1.3 (66ff).
Religious Life: CCt.2 (62ff); OF.3.2 (72ff).
    experimentation in: OF.6.3 (184ff).
    regularization of: DEC.2 (59ff; 78).
    vows in: OF.6.3 (188ff).
Renunciation: EF.1.3.3 (66f); MM.6 (71f); P.20 (216f); SL.10 (passim).
Resurrection (see: Jesus Christ, resurrection of): BT.3 (127f).
    of the body: AB.2 (106ff); CC.2.8 (88); MM.8 (86ff); P.22 (239); SE.28 (245); TD.1.1 (33f; 35).
Revelation: BT.2 (71ff).
    closure of: AB.5 (7); Inq.1 (71ff).
    historicity of: TPA.1 (54ff).
    theology of: C.66 (100).
    two source theory of: Inq.1 (34ff; 76ff).
Revelation History: SL.2 (58ff).
Reviviscence, sacramental: Inq.3 (215f).
Revolution: MFS.2 (53); SCC.3 (125f; 130f).
Ruysbroeck: ES.6 (50f).

Sacrament/s (see individual sacraments).
    administration of: MS.5 (64ff).
    and fundamental option: EF.1.3.3 (58ff).
    and grace: TD.2 (100f).
    and the death of Christ: TD.1.3 (80ff).
    as instituted by Christ: Inq.3 (223ff); MS.2 (21).
    as sign: CE (20f).
    as sign of redemption: SE.10 (85f).
    development of: Inq.3 (260ff).
    ex opere operatum: CE (29ff; 66ff).
    martyrdom as a: TD.2 (110f).
    number of: Inq.3 (238f; 252f).
    opus operatum: Inq.3 (206ff).
    power to administer: TPA.1 (ftn.5, 37ff).
    sacramentum/res sacramenti: OF.3.2 (67ff).
Sacred Heart, Devotion to: GF.6.2 (145); SE.32 (282f).
Sacred/secular: OF.4.6 (109ff).
Saints: (see: Communion of Saints) BT.1 (40f); CCt.3 (92).

and sinners: SE.7 (55).
and the Spirit: SC.1 (22ff).
canonization of: (87).
patronal: CP (73ff; 77ff).
unknown: NBP.Intro (xvi ff).
veneration of: EY.15 (133ff).
Salvation, as rooted in community: MM.2 (26ff).
    extra ecclesia: CAC.2 (51ff); Inq.3 (203ff); TD.2 (98ff); TPA.1 (46ff).
Salvation/damnation status: MS.4 (43ff); TD.1.2 (46).
Salvation History, official: EF.4.2 (170ff).
preaching of: C.33 (29ff).
Schismatics: MFS.3 (113f).
Science and prayer: CC.2.2 (50ff).
and theology: AB.3 (306ff).
Scripture (see: Bible).
Self-transcendence: EF.1.2.5 (45f).
and indifference: P.3 (30f).
Sensus fidelium: FS.1 (18f; 24ff).
Sin (see: Adam; Angels): CF.4 (91ff); P.20 (225f).
and prayer: NBP.5 (52ff).
ecclesial character of: SE.10 (82).
essence of: SE.27 (240f).
importance in theology: AB.3 (303f).
manifestation of: SE.26 (227f).
mortal: TD.1.2 (51f; 57f).
mortal/venial: CC.2.5 (77f); MS.4 (53ff); OF.4.6 (112f; 115f).
of the redeemed: P.4 (50f).
of the world: (218ff).
original: EF.4.1 (167f); TD.1.2 (55ff).
social aspect of: MS.4 (56ff); SCC.3 (124ff).
uncertainty principle in: NBP.7 (87ff).
venial: NBP.7 (79ff); P.5 (58ff); P.18 (194f; 199f).
Skepticism: BT.3 (95ff).
Christian: MFS.2 (49ff; 66ff).
Small Christian Community (see: Church, SCC in).
Society, current situation: CF.2 (44ff); CF.3 (58ff); CMP.2 (20ff).
Society of Jesus: RLT.5 (44).
Soul: creation of: H (93ff).
dark night of: ES.3 (25).
powers of: SE.6 (43).
Soul/body, dualism: OF.2.3 (31f); OF.2.4 (38).
unity of: CCt.2 (47f); H (19ff); SE.26 (231f).
Spirit/s and matter: H (46ff).
and the Trinity: SE.29 (251f).

as guarantor of church unity: Inq.3 (326ff).
baptism in: SC.1 (9ff).
discernment of: NG.1 (31ff); OF.6.3 (186); RLT 10 (87); SC.1 (29ff); TR.6 (114f).
experience of: CC.2.2 (60f); CC.2.3 (67f); MS.2 (23ff); SE.29 (259).
gifts of: OF.2.5 (44f).
in Ignatius: P.23 (253f).
role in obedience: SL.9 (143ff).
uniting our lives with Christ: W&P.1 (25ff).
Spiritual Direction and Confession: SL.11 (190f).
Spiritual Life, definition of: SE.9 (69ff).
Spiritual Literature: DEC.3 (85f).
Spirituality, ecclesial: SCC.2 (82ff).
need for: OF.6.3 (191f).
Supernatural Existential and prayer: NBP.Intro (ix ff).
Surrender (see: Resignation): CMP.9 (179ff); NBP.Intro (ix ff); NBP.1 (7ff); SE.21 (192); W&P.2 (61ff).
and freedom: SE.32 (279f).

Temptation: SE.11 (96).
Theologians, freedom of: FS.1 (27ff).
Theological Anthropology (see: Man; Person): CC.1.1 (11ff); CMP.5 (90ff).
transcendent/categorical: OF.3.2 (67f).
foundation for: MM.2 (23ff).
human dignity: AB.1 (76ff).
question of man: AB.1 (70ff).
task of man: CMP.2 (26ff); LJLN.2 (100ff); NG.1 (12ff).
Theological Language (see: Analogy; God-Talk; Language): AB.3 (298ff); BT.3 (117f); GF.4.1 (97); NC.1 (15f); NG.3 (76ff); SE.12 (97f; 104; 110f).
Theological Virtues: EF.2.2 (180ff); MFS.1 (12ff).
and death: TD.1.3 (79f).
Theology and faith: TD.Intro (14f).
and magisterium: TD.Intro (16f).
and science: AB.3 (306ff).
and the Spirit: SE.29 (254f).
Biblical: CAC.3 (86ff).
dangers of: GF.6.1 (132).
dissent in: GF.6.4 (176ff).
Dogmatic: CAC.3 (95ff).
Ecumenical: CAC.3 (97ff).
Historical: CAC.3 (82ff).
Jesuit: AB.4 (32).

Kerygmatic: TR.7 (144f).
  method in: C.153 (73ff).
Moral (see: Morality): CAC.3 (92f); CF.1 (26ff).
Pastoral: CAC.3 (101ff).
  pluralism in: CF.1 (34f); MFS.2 (65f).
  post-conciliar task of: GF.1.5 (54f).
  recent history of: C.66 (94f; 98f).
  relation of Fundamental to Dogmatic: C.66 (98ff).
  schools of: AB.3 (304f).
  Systematic: CAC.3 (90ff).
  task of: GF.1.3 (36).
Time (see: Eternity): OF.2.6 (47f); SE.16 (146f).
  and eternity: AB.2 (100ff); TD.1.1 (36).
Tolerance: RLT.2 (13f).
Transcendent/Categorical: NBP.1 (3ff); P.16 (177f).
  in religion: TR.4 (73).
Transcendent/ence (see: Self-transcendence): CMP.6 (116f); DEC.3 (123ff).
  horizon of: H (81ff).
  human: CC.1.1 (14f); CCt.3 (78f).
Trinity: NG.1 (13ff).
  and prayer: NBP.Intro (xi f).
  as mystery: T.1 (46ff); T.2 (50f).
  immanent/economic: T.1 (23ff).
  in Augustine (see: Trinity, psychological): T.1 (18f).
  pre-Christian analogies: T.1 (20f; 40ff).
  psychological: T.3 (115ff).
  relations in: T.2 (68ff).
  revealed in creation: P.7 (74f; 82f).
Truth (see: Hierarchy of Truths).
  and freedom: GF.8.3 (250f).
  oneness of: H (11ff).

Unbelief: CC.2.1 (46).
Universal/particular, ontology of: DEC.3 (111ff).
Utopia: AB.1 (74f); MFS.2 (50); P.22 (274f).

Vocation: CMP.7 (141ff); SE.17 (152f).
  criteria to accept: OF.3.1 (55).
Vows (see: Evangelical Counsels; Religious Life).
  monastic: MS.8 (99ff).
  public/private: TR.8 (162ff).

Women in the church: OF.5.1 (123).

ordination of: SCC.3 (114).
Word: ES.4 (31f).
  eschatological: NC.3 (36).
  ministry of: AB.7 (250f); C.43 (84); SE.23 (206).
  primordial: CMP.6 (113ff); OF.4.3 (86ff).
  sacramental: AB.7 (251); SL.3 (76); SL.4 (82f).
  sacramental nature of: TR.2 (35ff).
  Urworte: MFS.1 (9ff; 12ff).
Work: BT.1 (17ff); CMP.3 (55ff); SE.17 (158).
  and leisure: ES.6 (50f).
"World," the: TR.8 (152, ftn.10).
World, transformation of: SE.28 (246ff).
World-church: LJLN.2 (77ff; 85ff).
World View: DBG.5 (63ff).